The Paths of Heaven

The Evolution of Airpower Theory

by

The School of Advanced Airpower Studies

Edited by
Col Phillip S. Meilinger, USAF

Air University Press
Maxwell Air Force Base, Alabama

1997

Library of Congress Cataloging-in-Publication Data

The paths of heaven : the evolution of airpower theory / by the School of Advanced
    Airpower Studies ; edited by Phillip S. Meilinger.
       p.   cm.
    Includes index.
    1. Air power. 2. Air warfare—History. I. Meilinger, Phillip S., 1948–   . II. Air
University (U.S.). Air Command and Staff College. School of Advanced Airpower
Studies.

UG630.P29 1997
     358.4—dc21   97–24531
                                                     CIP

First Printing 1997
Second Printing 1998

Disclaimer

Contents

Illustrations

Foreword

For the past half century, the United States Air Force has been responsible for controlling and exploiting the air and space environment to meet the needs of the nation. We are America's Air Force—the only service that provides airpower and space power across the spectrum, from science and technology, research and development, testing and evaluation, to fielding and sustaining forces.

Although the men and women of the Air Force have recorded some outstanding accomplishments over the past 50 years, on the whole, our service has remained more concerned with operations than theory. This focus has produced many notable achievements, but it is equally important for airmen to understand the theory of airpower. Historian I. B. Holley has convincingly demonstrated the link between ideas and weapons, and in the conclusion to this book, he cautions that "a service that does not develop rigorous thinkers among its leaders and decision makers is inviting friction, folly, and failure."

In that light, *The Paths of Heaven* is a valuable means of increasing our expertise in the employment of airpower. It offers an outstanding overview of airpower theories since the dawn of flight and will no doubt serve as the basic text on this vital subject for some time to come. The contributors, all from the School of Advanced Airpower Studies (SAAS) at Maxwell AFB, Alabama, are the most qualified experts in the world to tackle this subject. As the home of the only graduate-level program devoted to airpower and as the successor to the Air Corps Tactical School, SAAS boasts students and faculty who are helping build the airpower theories of the future.

In explaining how we can employ air and space forces to fulfill national objectives, this book enriches the Air Force and the nation. Airpower may not always provide the only solution to a problem, but the advantages of speed, range, flexibility, and vantage point offered through the air and space environment make airpower a powerful instrument for

meeting the needs of the nation. Understanding these
advantages begins by knowing the ideas behind the
technology.

RONALD R. FOGLEMAN
General, USAF
Chief of Staff

About the School of Advanced Airpower Studies

Established in 1990, the School of Advanced Airpower Studies (SAAS) is a one-year graduate school for 27 specially selected officers from all the services. The mission of SAAS is to develop professional officers educated in airpower theory, doctrine, planning, and execution to become the air strategists of the future. SAAS achieves this mission through a unique educational process that blends operational expertise and scholarship in an environment that fosters the creation, evaluation, and refinement of ideas. The goal is thus twofold: to educate and to generate ideas on the employment of airpower in peace and war. SAAS is part of Air Command and Staff College, located at Maxwell Air Force Base in Montgomery, Alabama.

The SAAS curriculum consists of a series of courses that emphasize military and airpower theory, political science, economics, history, and technology. Civilian academics and high-ranking military officers are frequent visitors. All students must write a thesis and undergo an in-depth oral examination by the faculty. In addition, students participate in war games and joint exercises which hone their skills as airpower thinkers and planners. The faculty implementing this curriculum is composed of eight members—four military and four civilian—who are chosen for their academic credentials (a doctoral degree), teaching abilities, operational experience, desire to write on topics of military concern, and dedication to SAAS and its students. Strict academic and professional criteria are used to select students for SAAS, and volunteers are ultimately chosen by a special board of senior officers. The typical student is an aviator who has an outstanding military record, has been promoted ahead of his or her contemporaries, already holds a master's degree, and has a strong desire to learn and to serve his or her country. Upon graduation with a master's degree in airpower art and science, officers return to operational assignments or are placed in impact positions on higher headquarters staffs in the Pentagon and around the world.

Introduction

Col Phillip S. Meilinger

In greater skill the paths of heaven to ride.

—Gordon Alchin

Airpower is not widely understood. Even though it has come to play an increasingly important role in both peace and war, the basic concepts that define and govern airpower remain obscure to many people, even to professional military officers. This fact is largely due to fundamental differences of opinion as to whether or not the aircraft has altered the strategies of war or merely its tactics. If the former, then one can see airpower as a revolutionary leap along the continuum of war; but if the latter, then airpower is simply another weapon that joins the arsenal along with the rifle, machine gun, tank, submarine, and radio. This book implicitly assumes that airpower has brought about a revolution in war. It has altered virtually all aspects of war: how it is fought, by whom, against whom, and with what weapons. Flowing from those factors have been changes in training, organization, administration, command and control (C^2), and doctrine. War has been fundamentally transformed by the advent of the airplane.

Billy Mitchell defined airpower as "the ability to do something in the air. It consists of transporting all sorts of things by aircraft from one place to another."[1] Two British air marshals, Michael Armitage and Tony Mason, more recently wrote that airpower is "the ability to project military force by or from a platform in the third dimension above the surface of the earth."[2] In truth, both definitions, though separated in time by almost six decades, say much the same thing. Interestingly, however, most observers go on to note that airpower includes far more than air vehicles; it encompasses the personnel, organization, and infrastructure that are essential for the air vehicles to function. On a broader scale, it includes not only military forces but also the aviation industry, including airline companies and aircraft/engine manufacturers. On an even broader plane, airpower includes ideas—ideas on how it should be employed. Even before the aeroplane was invented, people speculated—theorized—on how it could be used in war. The purpose of this book is to trace the evolution of airpower theory from the earliest days of powered flight to the present, concluding with a chapter that speculates on the future of military space applications.[3]

Attempting to find the origins of airpower theory, trace it, expose it, and then examine and explain it, is no easy task. Perhaps because airpower's history is short—all of it can be contained in a single lifetime—it lacks first-rate narrative and analytical treatments in many areas. As a result, library shelves are crammed with books about the aerodynamics of flight, technical eulogies to specific aircraft, and boys' adventure stories. Less copious are good books on airpower history or biography. For example, after nearly five decades, we still do not have an adequate account of American airpower in the Southwest Pacific theater during World War II, or the role of George Kenney, perhaps the best operational-level air commander of the war. Similarly, we need a biography of one of the most brilliant thinkers and planners in US Air Force history; the only airman ever to serve as Supreme Allied Commander Europe, and the third youngest general in American history—Lauris Norstad. Nor do we have a complete, official history of airpower's employment in the war in Southeast Asia. Much needs to be done to fill such gaps.

The second roadblock to an effective concept of airpower employment in an evolving world is the lack of a serious study of airpower's theoretical foundations. For example, each of the two editions of *Makers of Modern Strategy*, the classic compendia of military theory, includes only a single chapter out of two dozen that deals with air theory—and neither is comprehensive.[4] Admittedly, however, the list of great air thinkers is not large, and in some cases the list of their writings is surprisingly thin. Nonetheless, even before the invention of the airplane, some people imagined flight as one of mankind's potentially greatest achievements. Flight would not only free people from the tyranny of gravity and its earthly chains, but it would liberate them mentally, socially, and spiritually. This linkage of the airplane and freedom was prevalent in much of the literature of the first decades of this century. This spirit dovetailed with the growing fascination with all things mechanical. The machine became synonymous with modern man, who saw the airplane as the ultimate machine. Certainly, it was capable of causing great harm—the scientific fantasies of H. G. Wells and Jules Verne anticipated this clearly—but, paradoxically, the airplane and its pilot were held up as a symbol of courage and nobility. Once in the clearness and pristine purity of the sky, the dirt and meanness of earthbound society were left behind. This was heady stuff, bespeaking the callowness of a forgotten era.

Although most military men dismissed such fantasies, arguing instead for more traditional means and methods of war, others quickly saw the airplane's potential as a weapon. Perhaps the most important air theorist was Giulio Douhet. When studying him, however, one is struck by how little has been written about the man and his ideas. No biography of Douhet has been published in English (although a useful doctoral dissertation on him appeared nearly 25 years ago), and little is known about his life. Analyses of his works are also surprising in both their superficiality and their paucity in number. Most amazing of all, although Douhet wrote prodigiously, very few of his works have been translated from his native Italian. His prewar writings, war diaries, and numerous articles and novels composed in the 1920s are unknown in English. Indeed, fully one-half of the first edition of his seminal *The Command of the Air* remains untranslated and virtually forgotten.

Nonetheless, the available writings clearly place Douhet in the top rank of air theorists. He was one of the first to think and write seriously and systematically about the air weapon and the effect it would have on warfare. Like the other early airmen, he was profoundly influenced by the carnage of World War I. Douhet was a believer in the future of airpower even before the war, and his experiences during the Great War and the horrendous casualties suffered by the Italian army on the Austrian front hardened his views even further. His basic precepts—that the air would become a violent and crucial battlefield; that the country controlling the air would also control the surface; that aircraft, by virtue of their ability to operate in the third dimension, would carry war to all peoples in all places; and that the psychological effects of air bombardment would be great—have proven accurate. Unfortunately, however, he also had a distressing tendency to exaggerate the capabilities of airpower—an endemic affliction among air theorists. He grossly overestimated the physical and psychological effectiveness that bombing would have on civilian populations. Douhet's hyperbole should not, however, allow us to ignore his very real contributions to the early development of airpower theory.

Another of the early thinkers who had a similarly great impact on the evolution of the air weapon was Hugh Trenchard. Widely recognized as the father of the Royal Air Force (RAF), Trenchard was both more practical and less inclined to exaggerate claims for the air weapon than was his Italian counterpart. As commander of the British air arm in war and peace, he was responsible not only for imparting a vision for the use and future of the air weapon, but also for carrying out the sobering task of organizing, equipping, training, and leading a combat organization on a day-to-day basis. Initially not a strong advocate of strategic airpower, Trenchard soon became a passionate proponent. Specifically, he was convinced that air bombardment of a country's industrial infrastructure would have a devastating and decisive psychological effect on the morale of the civilian population. His emphasis on morale, regrettably, was often misunderstood as a brief for population bombing. Unlike Douhet, Trenchard never advocated such an air strategy.

A major reason for this misunderstanding was an unwillingness or an inability to fully articulate his ideas on airpower. One can count the number of Trenchard's published writings, none longer than 10 or so pages, on the fingers of one hand. Added to this were his notoriously poor speaking skills; seemingly, he was not a very good communicator—although it must be said that the RAF certainly seemed to divine his drift. Thus, attempting to reconstruct his views on air warfare is not an easy task. Indeed, to write a history of RAF thought between the world wars, one must mine the fairly modest collection of essays written by serving RAF officers (mostly junior) that were published in the occasional book or in the pages of the *RAF Quarterly* and *RUSI* [Royal United Services Institute] *Journal.*

No individuals dominate this field, with the possible exception of John Slessor. But even his intellectual reputation is based largely on, first, his book *Air Power and Armies,* that contains a collection of his lectures at the British Army Staff College in the early 1930s, and, second, his later fame as a marshal of the RAF and the relatively prolific (for an airman) literary legacy that he accumulated after retirement. One should also note that there is no history of the RAF Staff College—what Trenchard called "the cradle of our brain," where airpower doctrine was formulated and promulgated between the wars. Moreover, there is not even a complete collection of Staff College lectures extant that can give us a definite picture of what was taught there.

Excavating the intellectual foundations of the US Army Air Corps can also be a challenge. We certainly have available the extensive writings of Billy Mitchell, who published five books, dozens of articles, and scores of newspaper op-ed pieces. Unquestionably, Mitchell dominated the early years of the American air arm just as Trenchard did the RAF. Like his British counterpart, this influence was due not simply to his administrative position but also to his ability to impart a vision of airpower to an eager group of subordinates. The men who would lead the Army Air Forces in World War II—Hap Arnold, George Kenney, Carl Spaatz, Frank Andrews, and others—considered him their intellectual father.

Mitchell achieved this status through the strength of his personality and through his incessant writing and speaking efforts, bringing the message of airpower to the American public. Unfortunately, Mitchell's writings become almost embarrassingly repetitious after 1925 or so. Moreover, his inordinate and near-neurotic hatred of the Navy distorted much of his writing, confused his message, and left a legacy of animosity between the two services that has never fully healed. One could certainly argue, both paradoxically and heretically, that because of his incessant attacks, the Navy was forced to adapt in ways it otherwise might not have.

Consequently, Mitchell may have been the father of both naval aviation and interservice rivalry. If this hypothesis is accurate, one could further argue that precisely because of his enormous popularity and influence within the Air Service, Billy Mitchell was both one of the best and one of the worst things that ever happened to American airpower.

Undoubtedly, many naval aviators would resent the implication that the rise of their branch was somehow due to the rabble-rousing of Billy Mitchell. Naval aircraft had participated in the Veracruz operation of 1914, and their record in World War I was sound if not glorious. After the war, farsighted naval airmen like John Towers and Ernie King pushed hard for the development of aircraft carriers and a change in naval doctrine and organization to accompany those carriers. In 1921 the Navy formed the Bureau of Aeronautics and placed Adm William Moffett in charge.

Moffett was certainly no friend of the outspoken Mitchell and people of like mind. But the former battleship captain realized that a sea change was in the offing in naval warfare and moved to alter his service's thinking to accommodate that change. In this regard, he was assisted by the Washington Naval Conference of 1921–22 that placed strict limits on the tonnage of capital ships. If battleships could not be built under the treaty, aircraft carriers certainly could, and by the end of the decade the *Langley, Lexington,* and *Saratoga* were in commission. Although surface seamen still dominated their service in the interwar years, the role of the aircraft carrier was becoming increasingly prominent. Everyone recognized that air superiority over the fleet was essential, but surface admirals saw the main decision in battle still residing with the big guns. Naval airmen quietly disagreed, thinking instead of a fleet based around aircraft carriers as the decisive arm.

The war in the Pacific, heralded by the destruction of the battleship fleet at Pearl Harbor, to a great extent fulfilled the hopes of the naval airmen. Although initially seeing their role as fleet defense and then as air support during amphibious operations, by the end of World War II their sights were set higher. In 1945 "targets ashore" increasingly became the objectives of carrier air. Thus, it was a small step in the postwar era to move from air attack of land targets to strategic bombardment, using nuclear weapons, of objectives deep inside enemy territory. Once a small and weak youngster, naval airpower became the dominant force within its service in the space of a generation. Traditional sea power had given way to airpower employed from the sea. The most interesting aspect of this transformation is that it was accompanied by surprisingly little internal bloodshed. Naval aviators saw themselves as sailors first; there was little talk of divorce. The Navy had no Billy Mitchell—and obviously has not regretted it.

Perhaps it is not surprising that Britain and the United States, traditional sea powers, embraced strategic airpower more vigorously than did other countries. Similarities exist between the type of long-term—and long-range—economic warfare characterized by a naval campaign and the aerial bombing of a country's centers of gravity. The broad, strategic thinking required of sailors was akin to that required of strategic airpower advocates. On the other hand, the four major continental powers in interwar Europe—Italy, France, the Soviet Union, and Germany—were traditional land powers. Logically, they saw airpower from a ground perspective. Giulio Douhet was an exception; most of his countrymen had different ideas on the proper use of airpower.

Amedeo Mecozzi was a decorated combat air veteran who rejected Douhet's calls for an emphasis on strategic airpower. Instead, he stressed the need for tactical aviation to cooperate with the army. His ideas were adopted by the Italian air minister, Italo Balbo, and the composition of the air arm took on a balance that Douhet would have found dismaying. It mattered little. A combination of poor leadership, political indecision, corruption, and financial constraints resulted in a weak and ineffectual air force at the outbreak of World War II—despite *il duce*'s exhortations to the contrary.

The story in France was similar. At the close of World War I, the French air force was one of the largest and most well respected in the world. The psychic paralysis that gripped the army, however, was transmitted to the entire defense establishment. With the exception of Air Minister Pierre Cot and a handful of his disciples, the French were simply not interested in a defense policy that advocated offensive operations—especially strategic air operations that might bring retaliation down on French cities. As in Italy, when World War II broke out, the French air force was hopelessly outclassed by the Luftwaffe. Moreover, French doctrine, which emphasized the primacy of defensive air operations, made the air arm almost an irrelevancy.

One finds a different story in the Soviet Union. When the Russian Empire collapsed in 1917, the country's air arm was weak and outmoded. For the next few years, this downward trend continued but began to change in the mid-1920s, when revolutionaries started rebuilding their military forces. Mikhail Tukhachevski, army chief of staff, articulated the concept of "deep battle" that was to dominate Soviet military thinking for the next several decades. Airpower played a major role in this type of warfare, mainly via interdiction of enemy troops and supplies. The predilection for tactical airpower was reinforced by the Soviets' close relationship between the wars with the German military, which also emphasized tactical over strategic airpower. Although the Soviets did not neglect bombardment doctrine or the development of bomber aircraft, by the outbreak of war, the Soviet air force had a distinctly tactical focus.

The rise of the Luftwaffe from the ashes of defeat makes for a remarkable tale. Field Marshal Hans von Seeckt was the intellectual progenitor of what would soon be called blitzkrieg. In this type of war, reminiscent of the ideas then being espoused by Tukhachevski, airpower was of great importance. More so than in any other country, the actions of the ground and air arms were closely linked—doctrinally and organizationally. The experience of the Spanish Civil War bolstered these beliefs. As a result, although the Luftwaffe flirted with the idea of strategic bombing in the 1930s, for a variety of reasons, the Germans never built a long-range air force. It is certainly debatable whether or not that was a wise decision. In any event, Germany, prostrate in 1919, had the strongest and most capable air arm in the world 20 years later.

The intellectual center of the American air arm during the 1930s was the Air Corps Tactical School (ACTS). A coterie of exceptional individuals at Maxwell Field, Alabama, devised and disseminated the doctrine of high-altitude precision bombing of an enemy's industrial centers. This was the "industrial web" concept that the Army Air Forces followed in World War II. Nonetheless, we must not forget that our knowledge of these men and their work is most unusual.

First, they published very little at the time: the Air Corps had no professional journal equivalent to the *RAF Quarterly*. The closest thing to it on this side of the ocean was *US Air Services*, an intelligent monthly magazine that dealt with aviation matters in both the military and civilian sectors. It often contained articles by American military airmen, but these were generally short and dealt with technical or tactical matters. Published herein and elsewhere were articles by George Kenney, Ken Walker, Claire Chennault, Hugh Knerr, and others. As in Britain, their names call to us from the pages of the 1930s, not really because of what their articles contained, but because of who they later became.

How then do we know in such detail the nature of American airpower thought in the 1930s? Thankfully, we have a remarkable collection of lectures, written and delivered at ACTS, carefully stored away, and often containing appendices, notes, and comments by later lecturers. Most of our knowledge and understanding of American airpower theory is based on these documents—a fact that is both comforting and dangerous. It is comforting because we have a readily accessible, discrete, limited, and authoritative cache of information that, once mastered, gives a remarkably clear view of what went on at ACTS. But does that picture reflect thinking throughout the Air Corps as a whole? Therein lies the danger.

Generally, historians base their chronicles on the written evidence at hand; if there is no written evidence, there is no history. Because of this rather simple but ironclad rule, we know precious little of what doctrinal innovation was occurring at airfields and operational units around the country. Airmen were too busy "operating" to be encumbered with writing down what they did. Their story, though crucial, is little known and thus overshadowed by that copious, clear, discrete, and "authoritative" cache referred to above. In short, do we give a disproportionate share of emphasis and credit to the thinkers and instructors at ACTS merely because they were the ones who had the time and opportunity to write all the books? Do we really know the extent of their impact on the contemporary Air Corps? Did anyone in the field actually listen to them?

There are no such doubts regarding Alexander P. de Seversky (who liked to use his reserve rank of major), a prodigious writer and speaker who had an enormous influence on the American public. De Seversky was perhaps the most effective popularizer of and propagandizer for airpower in history. He wrote three books—one of which, *Victory through Air Power*, was a Book of the Month Club selection, reportedly read by five million people and even made into an animated movie by Walt Disney. He also wrote scores of articles for magazines as diverse as *Ladies' Home Journal, Look, Reader's Digest, Mechanix Illustrated,* and *Air University Quarterly Review*. Finally, he gave hundreds of radio addresses and wrote hundreds more press releases for the news media. All were devoted to the same theme: the importance of airpower to American security.

Because he was a civilian, he did not have to worry about angering his military superiors, as did Douhet, Mitchell, Slessor, and others, and because he was a successful aircraft engineer and manufacturer, he spoke with formidable technical authority. Significantly, the target audience of de Seversky's message was the American public and its elected representatives. He decided that the civilian and military leadership of the country—including that in the Army Air Forces—was too conservative and too dominated by vested interests to be receptive to new ideas. The major, himself a simple and straightforward man, wanted his unfiltered message to reach average Americans so, collectively, they could put pressure on the country's leadership to change defense policies.

De Seversky made "victory through airpower" and "peace through airpower" household terms in America during the 1940s and 1950s. He certainly did not originate ideas about global airpower, its dominance over surface forces, or massive retaliation, but, to a very great extent, he explained and sold those ideas to the public. Despite de Seversky's many exaggerations, his repetitiveness, and his missteps, there has never been a more effective spokesman for airpower.

After de Seversky, airpower thought fell into a funk, where it lay for several decades—not that people ignored the subject, but theorists were writing little that was fresh or innovative. No major figures emerged as airpower thinkers, for a fairly apparent reason. Atomic weapons—and then nuclear weapons—appeared to throw traditional concepts of warfare and strategy out the window. This was virgin territory, and no one quite knew his way—no experience or historical models seemed relevant to this new era. As a result, a new breed of strategists invented a new field of study, related to—but not identical to—traditional airpower thought. Men like Bernard Brodie and Herman Kahn, civilian academicians rather than uniformed professionals, took the fore in thinking and writing about nuclear strategy.

These civilians had significant advantages over the airmen who preceded them. Before World War I, airpower had been largely untested, and its impact on war speculative. For many, therefore, it was easy to dismiss the ideas of the air advocates. In the decades after Hiroshima, however, the nuclear theorists had no such problem; everyone recognized the deadly seriousness and import of the new weapon. In addition, although the complexities of conventional war took a lifetime of study, the principles of nuclear theory—assured destruction, deterrence, *mutual* assured destruction, and so forth—were relatively straightforward. As one of the contributors to this book wryly puts it, any above-average graduate student can learn the rudiments of this discipline merely by watching the movie *Dr. Strangelove or: How I Learned to Stop Worrying and Love the Bomb*. Although an exaggeration, this comment has more than a little truth to it.

The product of the labors of these new thinkers was a substantial literature grounded more in the social sciences than in history. Models and case studies replaced historical narrative. Because there was virtually no experience extant on the subject of nuclear war and its effects on a population or its leaders, the new theorists wrote of models and logic. Precisely because there was no experience, there was no proof, and no one could say whether the academicians were right or wrong. These were exercises in Aristotelian logic. Thus, the new thinkers were in much the same position as Douhet, Mitchell, Trenchard, and others several decades earlier—or, for that matter, as the medieval theologians who debated how many angels could dance on the head of a pin.

During the decades of the 1950s and 1960s, this new breed dominated strategic thinking. Some people would claim that this domination was most unfortunate for the country, because thinking about conventional warfare—especially conventional air warfare—atrophied. Airmen like Douhet argued that war, though inevitable and total, would be mercifully short and decisive due to airpower. The nuclear theorists offered a more positive future: major war was now so horrible and thus "unthinkable" that it might no longer occur. Unfortunately, it did. As a result, this new breed planned and articulated, to a great extent, the strategy (or nonstrategy) of Vietnam. Military leaders, having lost their preeminence in the realm of military strategy, largely through their own intellectual lethargy, now received schemes designed by "whiz kids" and had to implement them. By necessity, airmen in the United States were forced to grapple, however tentatively, with the issue of the role of airpower in what was euphemistically referred to as low intensity conflict (LIC).

LIC is not a subject most airmen readily discuss. Indeed, most military officers prefer not to treat with the subject. LIC is a nasty and brutish affair, not conducive to the gaining of either glory or military force structure. A standard response of military leaders is to assume away the problems involved in this type of warfare, believing that preparation for general war will ensure automatic coverage of "lesser" forms of war. This was certainly the attitude in the US Air Force. Despite the hint of things to come, represented by guerrilla insurgencies in the Philippines, Malaysia, and French Indochina during the decade following World War II, airmen focused on the major nuclear threat emanating from the Soviet Union. This absorption was so pronounced that not even the Korean War, although largely conventional, could shake the belief that such conflicts were peripheral, aberrant, or both. The lack of interest generated in the subject of airpower in LIC is illustrated by the fact that during the entire decade of the

1950s, despite the four conflicts noted above, only two articles on the subject appeared in the Air Force's professional journal, the *Air University Quarterly Review.*

Quite surprisingly, this institutional reluctance to engage with the subject of airpower in LIC continued, even as the country found itself ever more deeply involved in Vietnam during the 1960s. Not until 1964 did official doctrine manuals seriously discuss the subject—and then it received a scant two pages. As the war struggled into the 1970s, this disregard increased rather than decreased. Never a popular topic, LIC became even more disdained as the Vietnam War shuddered to its unhappy conclusion. The role of airpower in LIC carried with it an odor of defeat—not a scent of victory. On the other hand, although the disaster of Vietnam had many such negative outcomes, one of the positive aspects was a resurgence of strategic thinking within the services.

Realizing that war was too important to be left to scholars, the "generals" began to reassert themselves. In the American Air Force, this trend began with John Boyd, a semilegendary cult figure in the fighter community. Boyd had flown F-86s in the Korean War and was struck by the 10-to-one kill ratio that US aircraft had enjoyed in combat with the Soviet-built MiG-15. The smaller, quicker, and more maneuverable MiG should have performed better. Although most observers attributed the Sabre's advantage to the superior quality of American pilots, Boyd thought otherwise. He theorized that the hydraulic flight controls of the F-86 were the key factor, because they allowed the pilot to move from one attitude to another more quickly than his MiG counterpart.

Upon returning to the Fighter Weapons School, Boyd continued to study what he termed "fast transient maneuvers," a concept that evolved into his famous OODA Loop. Battle was governed by the continual cycle of observing, orienting, deciding, and acting. Pilots who were able to outthink their opponents—to get inside their OODA Loop—would be successful, just as the Sabre could physically maneuver inside the MiG's decision cycle. More importantly, Boyd hypothesized that the OODA Loop concept applied at the strategic level of war as well as the tactical. Countries that could plan, decide, and carry out military operations more rapidly than their opponents would so disorient and confuse them that victory would become inevitable. At the same time, Boyd focused on the primacy of the "orient" portion of his loop, arguing that modern war demanded broad, interdisciplinary thinking that could continually extract ideas and fragments of ideas from diverse sources and then reconstruct them in new and original ways. This process of "destruction and creation" lay at the heart of "orienting" oneself in an increasingly complex world.

These theories and their implications for a rapid, paralyzing method of warfare were particularly suited to airpower. Unfortunately, Boyd has never really put his thoughts on paper, relying instead on extremely long briefings composed of scores of slides—some containing only a single word or phrase—that last for up to eight hours. As a result, his theories remain vaguely known and understood by the military and academic communities.

Another American fighter pilot who began questioning conventional wisdom emerged in 1986 at National Defense University (NDU). There, a young colonel, John A. Warden III, wrote a thesis titled "The Air Campaign: Planning for Combat," an unusual and controversial piece. Whereas most of the Air Force seemed polarized between those who saw war largely at the nuclear level and those who concentrated instead on the tactical air battle, Warden dared to consider the possibility of strategic, conventional operations. Fortunately and fortuitously, the president of NDU at the time was Maj Gen Perry McCoy Smith, who as a young officer was himself accused of being a controversial and therefore troublesome writer in matters concerning his service.[5] Smith encouraged and backed Warden in his efforts, and the thesis became a book.

Warden expanded on his theory of airpower, characterized by visualizing a society as a series of concentric rings. The most important of these rings, the center, was enemy leadership, because leaders make decisions regarding peace and war. The military, therefore, should direct its actions, both physical and psychological, towards removing, blinding, confusing, or disorienting the enemy leadership. This in turn would lead to paralyzing indecision and inaction. Although many critics have disagreed with Warden's theories, his book's importance lies in the fact that it is one of the very few works about airpower theory written by a serving American officer since World War II. More importantly, Warden would eventually end up at the Pentagon as the deputy director for war-fighting concepts development, a position he held when Saddam Hussein decided to move south. His superiors then gave him the opportunity to translate his theories into a workable air campaign plan that served as the blueprint for the air war against Iraq.

In some ways Warden was responding to a tendency he saw developing in the Air Force since the end of the Vietnam War: the increasing emphasis placed on tactical air operations. Institutionally, the US Army and the US Air Force emerged from Vietnam with much closer ties to each other than had existed before the war. As the senior leadership in the Air Force slowly changed from officers with bomber backgrounds to those with fighter backgrounds—the men who had borne the brunt of air combat in the Vietnam War—this closeness increased, especially in the sphere of doctrine. Significantly, because the Army has always taken the subjects of theory and doctrine most seriously, and because it formed a Training and Doctrine Command (TRADOC) in 1973, the Army took the lead in evolving new concepts and methods of achieving air-ground cooperation.[6] A strengthening of Warsaw Pact forces in the Central Region in Europe spurred this move. Outnumbered North Atlantic Treaty Organization (NATO) forces needed to maximize the efficiency and punch of their combat units.

The initial Army response, partly induced by the trauma still lingering from Vietnam, entailed an emphasis on defensive operations. But by the early 1980s, this posture was already moving towards a far greater concentration on the offense—specifically, deep operations employing airpower and highly mobile maneuver units that could attack second- and third-echelon forces. This concept developed into the Army's AirLand Battle doctrine, acknowledged and approved by the Air Force. In solving one set of problems, however, others arose. For decades the main area of disagreement between land and air forces has been command and control— ownership of airpower over the battlefield. In truth, the issue of the tactical battle was easily solved: the ground commander clearly had a dominant influence in matters regarding close air support of troops in contact. Similarly, the deep battle—strategic attack—was reserved for the air commander. The contentious issue became the area in between, where interdiction tended to occur. The development of new weapons—attack helicopters and surface-to-surface missiles—that allowed the Army to strike deeper than it had previously, aggravated this disagreement.

The interesting aspect of the debate was its surprisingly amiable resolution. Personalities—close personal compatibility between senior Army and Air Force leaders—were instrumental in forging a partnership between the two services. Even these close ties could not, however, completely resolve underlying tensions that emerged from the services' operating in two vastly different media. Nonetheless, the mutual trust and respect evident between Army and Air Force leaders in the period from Vietnam to the Persian Gulf War stand in marked contrast to the Air Force leadership's traditionally more stormy relationship with its naval counterparts. Personalities have been crucial in both instances.

A particular and unique strain of airpower theory evolved in Europe as a result of NATO. The mission of the alliance was to keep the peace in Europe. However, the peculiar demands of each member nation ensured that military strategy was dominated by political imperatives to an unusually high degree. For example, in order to project the image that NATO was purely defensive, military planners were not allowed to plan for offensive operations outside alliance territory. If Warsaw Pact forces attacked, they would merely be driven back. NATO had no intention of liberating even East Germany, much less Eastern Europe. In addition, the requirement that military decisions, doctrine, and policy have unanimity among all the member nations put a high premium on compromise and consensus building.

Analysts recognized early in the 1950s that NATO could never match the size of the Warsaw Pact forces opposing them. In geographic terms, this translated into a realization that West Germany—and perhaps the low countries as well—would be difficult to hold in the event of Soviet attack. To counter this deficiency, NATO relied on several factors:

technological superiority, nuclear weapons, energetic commitment to maneuver warfare, and airpower. In truth, all of these factors were directly related to airpower. This realization led to a number of doctrinal initiatives that stressed, among other things, centralized command and control of air assets. It also led to a long and spirited debate between and within member nations regarding the relative importance of strategic air attacks, air interdiction, and close air support.

The nations attained consensus, but it took many years—and it carried a price. In order to maximize the effectiveness and efficiency of NATO airpower, nations have had to specialize in those areas most useful to the overall good. In some cases, this has resulted in hopelessly unbalanced air forces: excellent interceptors, but with no ground attack capability; or perhaps a strong tactical airlift fleet, but no tankers, strategic airlifters, or ability to project power. Nonetheless, the imperative of a serious, technically sophisticated, and numerically superior foe has forced a resultant and beneficial emphasis on quality, efficiency, standardization, and professionalism.

The Soviet Union—the object of all these doctrinal evolutions both within the United States and in NATO—was undergoing its own metamorphosis. Understanding the Soviet, and then Russian, experience requires first that one recognize that doctrine and theory have a political component quite different than that operating in the West. To the Russians, military doctrine is neither a general theory nor the view of individuals. Rather, it is a system of official state views shaped and responsive to the ideological imperatives of the leadership. Although the Marxist-Leninist prism has been tarnished and discredited to a great degree, the political underpinnings of military doctrine represented by that ideology have not. The result is a relatively dogmatic approach to warfare: political objectives drive military doctrine, and that doctrine is not open for debate.

Nonetheless, change has occurred in Russia, and since 1989 that change has been dramatic. The collapse of the Soviet Union signaled both massive external and internal changes. Not only did the entire strategic situation change with the loss of ally/buffer states in Eastern Europe, but the privileged position and economic priority of the military within the state ended as well. The greatest external shock, however, occurred in 1990–91, when the Russians saw the astounding ability of the West to project power on a global basis and then employ that power in an overwhelmingly decisive way. Russian military leaders were mesmerized by the effectiveness of airpower in the Gulf War. The combination of mobility, accuracy, stealth, rapid communications, intelligence gathering and dissemination, target analysis, C^2 channels, and simple professionalism had a profound impact on Russian military leaders. In their view, airpower had become the dominant factor in modern war. The challenge, however, is not only for Russia to modernize its military forces on the Western model within the constraints of its faltering economy, but more importantly, within the parameters of an increasingly volatile political situation. Reconciling military reality with political ideology will be extremely difficult.

One should note that, until recently, most airpower theorists around the world tended to equate strategic bombing with strategic airpower. Consequently, differences between theorists have generally focused on which set of targets is most appropriate to achieve a given strategic objective. Although the Berlin airlift of 1948–49 demonstrated that one can wield strategic airpower without firing a shot, most airmen have focused on the "fire and steel" side of operations. Over the past decade, this has changed—due partly to a dramatic lowering in tensions between the superpowers, partly to increased capabilities that allow the employment of air and space assets in varied and discrete ways, and partly to heightened sensitivities over the use of force, emphasizing less loss of life and less collateral damage. This more peaceful use of strategic airpower has become a much debated and explored topic of late.

One of the main foci of that debate has been space-based assets and capabilities. In truth, it is interesting to note that for most of the past century, ideas about airpower have been far in advance of the technology needed to carry them out. Many people argue that only today are capabilities finally catching up to the predictions of the early air theorists. In the case of space, however, just the opposite is true: the technology is far in advance of the doctrine and concepts regarding its employment. Because this situation is beginning to change, it is time to examine more fully the fundamental issue of whether air and space are one and the same—or if indeed they are two separate realms. This issue is fraught with political, economic, military, and bureaucratic minefields. The Air Force, perhaps in an attempt to solidify its hold on space and keep the other services at bay, argues forcefully that space is merely a place, one that is akin to the atmosphere—which is to say it is fundamentally different from the places where land and sea forces routinely operate. The Air Force's share of the space budget, generally 90 percent, fortifies this strongly held belief by putting money where the talk is. Even airmen, however, are questioning that postulate, precisely because the cost of space is increasing dramatically, as are the capabilities it promises. In order to address this issue most dispassionately, one must examine the basic characteristics of both air and space. Once that is done, a more logical and verifiable answer will be forthcoming to the question, Whither space?

Theory and doctrine are not subjects that airmen readily take to. As Carl Builder has noted, airmen tend to be doers, not thinkers.[7] That is not a healthy trait. Unfortunately, the most recent major conflict has not helped the situation. In the Persian Gulf War, the abundance of available airpower allowed us to use it redundantly and even inefficiently in order to avoid irritating service and allied sensitivities. Doctrinal and theoretical differences were therefore papered over. But force drawdowns may not permit inefficiencies and doctrinal vagueness in future conflicts. The double bind for the future is that interservice rivalry will heighten as a result of budget cuts at precisely the time decreased forces and capabilities make any such rivalry unacceptably dangerous. Key issues such as command and control, theater air defense, the joint use of strategic tanker aircraft, the employment concepts of attack helicopters, the effectiveness of land-based versus sea-based airpower, the emerging field of information warfare, the organizational structure for employing space assets, and a host of other such issues must be addressed and resolved. Moreover, this must be done in peacetime; when a crisis erupts, it is too late to begin thinking through basic premises. It is the hope of the contributors, all associated with the School of Advanced Airpower Studies—the descendant of the Air Corps Tactical School—that this book will serve as a primer and an analytical treatment of airpower theory for fellow students of modern war.

Notes

1. William Mitchell, *Winged Defense: The Development and Possibilities of Modern Air Power—Economic and Military* (New York: G. P. Putnam's Sons, 1925), xii.

2. M. J. Armitage and R. A. Mason, *Air Power in the Nuclear Age* (Urbana, Ill.: University of Illinois Press, 1983), 2.

3. When the term *airpower* is used in this book, it refers not only to terrestrial assets, but space assets as well. The term *aerospace*, intended explicitly to include both regimes, is inelegant and has never achieved universal acceptance.

4. The first edition, *Makers of Modern Strategy: Military Thought from Machiavelli to Hitler*, was edited by Edward Mead Earle and published by Princeton University Press in 1943. The modern edition, *Makers of Modern Strategy: From Machiavelli to the Nuclear Age*, containing new essays but covering largely the same people, was edited by Peter Paret and published by Princeton in 1986.

5. Smith's controversial dissertation from Columbia University was published as *The Air Force Plans for Peace, 1943–1945* (Baltimore: Johns Hopkins Press, 1970).

6. Predictably, the Air Force responded with technology—developing the A-10 ground attack aircraft.

7. Carl H. Builder, *The Icarus Syndrome: The Role of Air Power Theory in the Evolution and Fate of the U.S. Air Force* (New Brunswick, N.J.: Transaction Publishers, 1994).

Chapter 1

Giulio Douhet and the
Origins of Airpower Theory

Col Phillip S. Meilinger

Gen Giulio Douhet of Italy was among the first people to think deeply and write cogently about airpower and its role in war, methodically and systematically elevating an idea to a level of abstraction that could be considered a theory. Many of his ideas and predictions were wrong, but echoes of his basic concepts are still heard more than 60 years after his death. Indeed, the overwhelming victory of the coalition in the Persian Gulf War in 1991 is an example of what Douhet predicted airpower could accomplish. Specifically, his formula for victory—gaining command of the air, neutralizing an enemy's strategic "vital centers," and maintaining the defensive on the ground while taking the offensive in the air—underpinned coalition strategy. Certainly, not all wars have followed or will follow this model, but unquestionably Douhet's theories of airpower employment have become more accurate as time has passed and as the air weapon has become more capable. The purpose of this chapter is to reexamine the theories of this first great air theorist, analyze them based on their own internal logic, and reassess them.

Giulio Douhet was born in Caserta, near Naples, on 30 May 1869. His father came from a long line of soldiers, and his mother was from a family of teachers and journalists. He performed well in school, graduating first in his class at the Genoa Military Academy. Giulio was then commissioned into the artillery in 1888 at the age of 19. Soon after, he attended the Polytechnic Institute in Turin and continued his studies in science and engineering. His performance continued to be excellent, and his graduate thesis, "The Calculation of Rotating Field Engines," became a standard text at the school.

Douhet's professional ability was also evident, and as a captain in 1900, he was assigned to the General Staff. There,

1

he read closely all reports regarding the Russo-Japanese War, which broke out in 1903. Early on, he predicted that Japan would emerge victorious, but few Westerners agreed with him at the time. Also while on the General Staff, he continued his technological bent and wrote several papers advocating mechanization of the Italian army. In 1901 he published a series of lectures titled "Mechanization from the Point of View of the Military," and three years later he wrote a pamphlet on the subject—"Heavy and Military Mechanization." Significantly, although Douhet saw a role for heavy trucks to move men and supplies in a theater of operations, he did not predict the development of armored vehicles for use on the battlefield. In addition, he viewed mechanization solely in terms of Italy's peculiar geographic, economic, and political limitations. Technology would compensate for Italy's inherent weaknesses in manpower and natural resources. This theme would later repeat itself in his writings on airpower.[1]

In 1905 Italy built its first dirigible, and Douhet immediately recognized its possibilities, becoming a keen observer of what he believed was a revolution in military technology. He followed aeronautical events closely, and when Italy's first airplane flew in 1908, he commented, "Soon it will be able to rise thousands of feet and to cover a distance of thousands of miles."[2] Two years later—only seven years after Kitty Hawk—Douhet predicted that "the skies are about to become a battlefield as important as the land or the sea. . . . Only by gaining the command of the air shall we be able to derive the fullest benefit from the advantage which can only be fully exploited when the enemy is compelled to be earth bound."[3] However, the superiority of the airplane over the dirigible was not yet obvious to everyone. Douhet's superior, Col Maurizio Moris of the aviation inspectorate, was a staunch supporter of the airship. He and Douhet had several clashes over the issue, most of which Douhet lost. In fact, as late as 1914, Italy was still spending 75 percent of its aviation budget on dirigibles.[4]

At the same time, Douhet realized that the aircraft could become a dominant weapon only if it were freed from the fetters of ground commanders who did not understand this new invention. He therefore advocated the creation of a separate air arm, commanded by airmen.[5] During this period, he became close friends with Gianni Caproni, a bright young aircraft engineer who held similar views on the future of aircraft. The two men teamed up to vigorously extol the virtues of airpower in the years ahead.

In 1911 Italy went to war against Turkey for control of Libya— a war that saw aircraft used for the first time. Amazingly, aircraft were used not only for reconnaissance but also for artillery spotting, transportation of supplies and personnel, and even bombing of enemy troops, supplies, and facilities— both day and night. In short, most of the traditional roles of airpower employment were identified and attempted during the very first year aircraft saw combat.[6]

The following year, Douhet, now a major, was tasked with writing a report on the meaning of the Libyan War for the future employment of aircraft. Perhaps because his superiors and colleagues were less enthusiastic about airpower than he was, Douhet's comments were muted. Most of his report dealt with the organization, training, and equipping of the Italian air arm. He did note, however, that although some people thought the primary role of aircraft was reconnaissance, "others" believed that aircraft should be used for "high altitude bombing." As for who would control airpower, Douhet suggested that aviation units be assigned to each army corps but slyly added, "This would not prevent, where necessary, grouping such flights with the Army Group, or for that matter, the formation of independent air units." Further, the major called on Italian industry to embrace the new invention and to develop its potential for both commerce and national security. The relationship between the civilian aircraft industry and the strength of a country's military defense was an important subject, one to which he would later return. Finally, when discussing the types of aircraft the air force should have, Douhet suggested that a "general purpose type of aircraft" be developed that could fulfill the roles of reconnaissance, air combat, and bombardment.[7] Significantly, this aircraft should be capable of carrying a heavy load of bombs. Overall, this report left interesting clues about the direction Douhet's ideas on airpower would soon take.

Also in 1912, Douhet assumed command of the Italian aviation battalion at Turin and soon wrote "Rules for the Use of Airplanes in War," one of the first such manuals in any air force. Interestingly, however, his superiors made him delete all passages referring to the airplane as a "weapon"; to them it was merely a "device" to support the surface forces—nothing more.[8] Douhet's incessant preaching on such matters irked his superiors, and he soon became known as a "radical." Moreover, in early 1914 he ordered, without authorization, the construction of several Caproni bombers. In truth, Douhet had tried to go through proper channels, but his superior, Colonel Moris—who was still enamored with the dirigible— dragged his feet. Characteristically, Douhet became impatient and took matters into his own hands. Such presumption, coupled with a personality variously described as dogmatic, assertive, persistent, impatient, tactless, and supremely self-confident, earned him exile to the infantry.[9] Unfortunately, Douhet's methods for advancing the cause of airpower tended to work at cross-purposes to his goals.

Douhet was serving as a division chief of staff at Edolo when Europe blundered into World War I in July 1914. He was unable to resist a prophecy. In August, barely a month after the beginning of the conflict, he wrote an article titled "Who Will Win?" In it, he stated that modern war had become total war. Moreover, because the industrial revolution of the previous century allowed the mass production of weapons, the quick wars of annihilation predicted by many people had become a thing of the past. Douhet warned instead that the new war now begun would be long and costly. Nonetheless, he concluded that in the long run, the difficulties of fighting on multiple fronts would spell defeat for the Central Powers.

Although Italy had at that point declined to enter the war on the side of the entente, Douhet called for a military buildup— especially in airpower—in case the effort to maintain neutrality failed. Even in his peripatetic position in Lombardy, Douhet, now a colonel, peppered his superiors with ideas on airpower. In December 1914 he wrote that Italy should build an air force whose purpose was "to gain command of the air" so as to render the enemy "harmless." According to Douhet, "To gain command of the air is to be able to attack with impunity any point of the enemy's body."[10] In another essay, he suggested that five hundred bombers be built to strike "the most vital, most vulnerable and least protected points of the enemy's territory."[11] He maintained that such an armada could drop 125 tons of bombs daily.

After Italy plunged into the war in 1915, Douhet was so shocked by his army's incompetence and unpreparedness that he frequently wrote his superiors, suggesting organizational reform and increased use of the airplane. He filled his diary with angry, sarcastic, and frustrated remarks regarding his superiors and their war strategy. Rejecting the offensively oriented ground strategy of the General Staff, he commented ruefully, "To cast men against concrete is to use them as a useless hammer." In another entry, he noted the existence of reports that Italian soldiers at the front did not even have rifles. Perhaps, he offered, "if an enemy attacks they could always beg a mule to kick him."[12] In yet another memo to his superiors, the colonel advocated that a bomber force drop one hundred tons of explosives on Constantinople each day until the Turkish government agreed to open the Dardanelles to Allied shipping.[13] Typically, he even wrote Gen Luigi Cadorna, the Italian commander in chief, about his concerns and was twice reprimanded for his intemperate remarks.

Beginning in 1916, Colonel Douhet started corresponding with several government officials, including Leonida Bissolati, a cabinet minister known to be an airpower advocate. His letters to the minister were especially candid, even for Douhet. In one, he roundly criticized the Italian conduct of the war, noting that "we find ourselves without a reserve, in a crisis of munitions, with all our forces engaged in an offensive already halted, with the rear threatened by old and new enemies, exposed to being attacked at any moment and overcome decisively in the shortest moment."[14] Unfortunately, a copy of Douhet's scathing missive reached General Cadorna, who labeled it "calumnious." As a result, in September 1916 Douhet was arrested and court-martialed for "issuing false news . . . divulging information differing from the official communiqués . . . diminishing the prestige and the faith in the country and of disturbing the public tranquillity."[15] He did not deny writing the letter to Bissolati but insisted he was motivated strictly by love of country and a desire to see Italy win the war. But his reputation as an agitator had preceded him, and the court found him guilty. Douhet was sentenced to a year in jail at the fortress of Fenestrelle, beginning his incarceration on 15 October. One can only speculate on whether Douhet was actually relieved to have finally brought matters to a head. In a mood that echoes of resignation, mingled with frustration, he confided in his diary, "They [the government] can no longer say that they were not warned."[16]

Colonel Douhet continued to write about airpower from his cell, finishing not only a novel on air warfare but suggesting in a letter to the war minister that a great interallied air fleet be created. He envisioned a fleet of 20,000 airplanes, mostly provided by the United States, whose role would be to gain command of the air and carry out a decisive air attack on the enemy.[17]

Meanwhile, the fortunes of the Italian army continued to plummet, culminating in the disaster of Caporetto in October 1917, when the Italians lost three hundred thousand men. Released from prison that same month, Douhet returned to duty, and, because calamity breeds change, he soon became central director of aviation at the General Air Commissariat, where he worked to strengthen Italy's air arm. He also continued his close relationship with Caproni, and it is likely the two had a role in determining the force structure and philosophy of the new American Air Service.

Shortly after entering the war in April 1917, the United States sent a mission to Europe headed by Col Raynal Bolling to decide which aircraft were most suitable for construction in America. A member of the Bolling team, Maj Edgar Gorrell, had several talks with Caproni, who persuaded him to purchase the rights for several hundred of his heavy bombers for construction in America. Soon after, Gorrell wrote Caproni, requesting information on German industrial targets for use in planning Allied bombing missions. Douhet probably helped Caproni compile this information, since Douhet also was collecting intelligence on the location of German factories. Although the Caproni bomber contract was not fulfilled, the relationship established among these men planted the seeds for American airpower.[18]

At the same time, Caproni provided Gorrell with a copy of a polemic written by Nino Salvaneschi, an Italian journalist and friend of Douhet. Titled "Let Us Kill the War, Let Us Aim at the Heart of the Enemy!" this propaganda pamphlet accused the Germans of endless atrocities, thereby justifying any and all actions taken to defeat Germany. Although Germany quite clearly had attempted to bomb Britain into submission by zeppelin attacks, the airship could not achieve decisive results. Now, however, the Allies had large aircraft (not coincidentally, Capronis) capable of carrying tons of bombs. These aircraft, termed "battle planes" by Salvaneschi, meant that "the sky is the new field of combat and death which has unbarred her blue doors to the combatants." The purpose of these battle planes was "to kill the war," not by destroying the enemy army but by destroying its "manufactories of arms." This in turn would leave the enemy with insufficient strength to carry on the war.[19]

Gorrell was quite taken with Salvaneschi's piece and distributed numerous copies of it within the American Air Service. Over the months that followed, Gorrell wrote a remarkably farsighted memo on the desirability and feasibility of strategic bombing. Perhaps not surprisingly, strong similarities existed among Gorrell's memo, Salvaneschi's piece, and the ideas then being expounded by Douhet.[20]

In June 1918 Douhet retired from the army, disgusted with the inefficiency and conservatism of his superiors, and returned to writing. Soon after the armistice, he became upset with the government for not dealing adequately with veterans of the war. He therefore started *Duty*, a newspaper that dealt largely with domestic, economic, and political issues. In this position, he learned that the government had launched an official investigation into the battle of Caporetto. The report concluded that defeat resulted from deficiencies in organization and leadership, many of which Douhet had noted. The retired colonel therefore petitioned to have his court-martial reexamined. When the judges perceived the accuracy of his criticisms and predictions, they decided that Douhet had indeed been primarily interested in the safety of his country—not in personal gain. The verdict was overturned in November 1920, and he was promoted to general.[21]

Rather than returning to active duty, Douhet continued his literary efforts. In 1921 he completed his most famous work,

The Command of the Air, published under War Department auspices—an indication of how completely his reputation had been restored. During this same period, Douhet became a supporter of the Fascist party and Benito Mussolini, even participating in the "March on Rome" in October 1922. When Mussolini assumed power soon after, he endorsed Douhet's ideas and appointed him commissioner of aviation. Douhet was unhappy as a bureaucrat, however, hoping to be appointed as chief of the air force. The offer was not forthcoming, so after only a few months, the general retired a second time to devote himself to writing.

This he did for the next eight years, publishing dozens of essays and articles on airpower, as well as several novels and plays. Unfortunately, few of his many works have been translated into English. Indeed, fully one-half of the first edition of *The Command of the Air,* comprising a lengthy appendix discussing the principles of flight and technical details of aircraft and seaplane construction, has never been translated and remains largely forgotten.[22] Giulio Douhet died of a heart attack on 15 February 1930, while tending his garden at Ceschina, near Rome.

Douhet was profoundly affected by the trench warfare of World War I. Like most of his generation, he was appalled by the carnage and feared that such a catastrophe would recur. He believed that wars were no longer fought between armies but between whole peoples. All the resources of a country—human, material, and psychological—would focus on the war effort. Whereas Napoléon sometimes gained victory with a single battle, the effort now required a series of battles and a series of armies. Indeed, the *nation* would have to be exhausted before it would admit defeat. But reaching this point became increasingly more difficult in an age of industrialization, when factories could produce the implements of war in a seemingly inexhaustible supply.

What made the attritional war of 1914–18 more horrifying was advancing technology—specifically the machine gun—that gave an overwhelming advantage to the defender. Defense behind prepared positions had always possessed inherent benefits, so an attacker required a preponderance of force to ensure success—usually at least a three-to-one advantage.

The world war proved to Douhet that new technology required greater superiority for an attack to succeed (surely a misnomer if it meant the slaughter of thousands). Although convinced that technology had granted the defense a permanent ascendancy in land warfare, he argued, paradoxically, that although technology had caused the trench stalemate, technology—in the form of the airplane—would end it. Only aircraft could overcome the fundamental problem of a prolonged war of attrition caused by mass armies equipped with modern weapons.

Douhet argued that airpower was revolutionary because it operated in the third dimension, unhampered by geography. Indeed, the weapon was not so revolutionary as the medium of the air itself, which granted flexibility and initiative. Aircraft could fly over surface forces, which then became of secondary importance. If one no longer needed to control the ground, then the forces used to control it diminished in significance. Contrary to conditions on the surface, Douhet continued, the aerial offense was stronger than the aerial defense because the vastness of the sky made defense against the airplane virtually impossible. In Douhet's formulation, the speed of aircraft relative to ground forces plus the ubiquity of aircraft—the ability to be in so many places in a short period of time—equaled offensive power.

Writing before the advent of radar, he argued that a defender's inability to know the exact time and location of an attack gave an enormous advantage to the offense, virtually assuring tactical surprise. On the other hand, defense required a huge air fleet because each protected point needed an air contingent at least the size of the attacking enemy. This situation was precisely the opposite of the one on the ground, because it meant that successful air *defense* required the preponderance of force, leading Douhet to term the airplane "the offensive weapon *par excellence*."[23]

Just as Douhet discounted the possibility of aerial interception, so too did he dismiss ground-based air defenses. Further, he deemed antiaircraft guns wasteful because they seldom hit anything. Douhet sarcastically conceded that ground fire might down some aircraft, much like muskets shot in the air might occasionally hit a swallow, but it was not a

9

serious deterrent to air attack. People who believed that artillery was an effective counter to the airplane "had confused aircraft with snails." Douhet stated flatly, "I am against air defense because it detracts means from the Air Force . . . I am against it because I am absolutely convinced that . . . it cannot achieve its aim."[24] Thus, in Douhet's eyes, the best defense—indeed, the only defense—was a good offense. For the same reason, he eschewed an air reserve. All aircraft were committed; holding forces in reserve exemplified the outdated and defensive thinking of surface commanders. The speed and range of aircraft created their own reserve because they were able to react quickly and engage in different locations long before surface forces could move there.

These beliefs regarding the nature of modern war and the inherent characteristics of the airplane led Douhet to a theory of war based on the dominance of airpower. His most fundamental precept[25] was that an air force must achieve command of the air—air supremacy in today's parlance.[26] Without it, land and sea operations—even air operations— were doomed. Moreover, a country that lost control of its airspace had to endure whatever air attacks an enemy chose to carry out. Command of the air meant victory.

Because predicting the specific time and place of an air attack was virtually impossible, Douhet saw little chance of an air battle occurring. He reasoned that a stronger air force would be foolish to seek out its weaker enemy in the air. Rather, it should carry out the more lucrative task of bombing the enemy's airfields and aircraft industry—"destroying the eggs in their nest." The weaker force also had no incentive to seek an air engagement that would likely lead to its destruction. The only hope for the weaker side lay in striking even more violently at an enemy's homeland. Douhet thus envisioned a rather peculiar scenario in which opposing air forces studiously ignored each other while flying past to destroy the other's airfields and factories—something akin to "mutual assured destruction" without nuclear weapons. He realized, however, that achieving aerial dominance was not an end in itself but an enabler that allowed airpower to conduct its primary task of reducing an enemy's will and capability to wage war.

The objective of war had always been to impose one's will on the enemy by breaking the latter's will to resist. This, in fact, happened to Germany, Austria, and Russia in the Great War—their armies were still largely intact in the fall of 1918, but the will of these nations to continue the fight had dissolved. In Douhet's view, airpower could break a people's will by destroying or neutralizing a country's "vital centers"— those elements of society, government, military, and industrial structure essential to the functioning of the state. Because of their value—as well as their immobility and vulnerability— these centers were protected by fortresses and armies. It was therefore necessary to defeat these armies and reduce these fortresses to expose the soft, inner core. Once disarmed, a country would then usually surrender rather than suffer the humiliation of an enemy occupation.

Over time, many people began to equate destruction of the army with the objective of war, rather than merely as a means to an end. The Great War demonstrated that such a goal could have catastrophic consequences. Douhet reminded his readers that the true objective in war was the enemy's will, and only aircraft could strike it directly, overflying and ignoring the surface conflict below. In short, aircraft could obviate the bloody first step of destroying the enemy army, which now became superfluous.

Douhet was perhaps the first person to realize that the key to airpower was targeting, because although aircraft could strike virtually anything, they should not attempt to strike everything. One had to identify the most important objectives and hit them most forcefully. Choosing the proper targets would not be an easy task and would require great insight; in this area, air commanders would prove their ability. Because the choice of targets would depend on a number of circumstances— economic, military, political, and psychological—it would be variable. But Douhet identified five basic target systems as the vital centers of a modern country: industry, transportation infrastructure, communication nodes, government buildings, and the will of the people.[27]

To Douhet, this last category was the most important, because the total wars of the new industrialized age were no longer a contest between armed foes: all people were combatants—women and men alike—and their collective will would have to be broken. Douhet bluntly stated that one could do this most effectively by urban bombing, which would terrorize the population. But that is precisely why it would have such great effect: "Normal life could not be carried on in this constant nightmare of imminent death and destruction."[28] In "The War of 19—," which described a fictional war between Germany and a French-Belgian alliance, Douhet had German bombers striking cities immediately after the outbreak of war to make a "moral impression" on the population.[29]

Significantly, Douhet implied that one might not need such terror bombing because gaining command of the air would be so psychologically devastating that destruction of vital centers would be unnecessary. The side that lost control of its own airspace would realize what was in store and surrender rather than face devastation. Thus, war would become so horrible it would be humanizing, a paradox which generated in Douhet a strange ambivalence about the righteousness of airpower that he never fully resolved. Also of interest is his emphasis on the importance of gaining command of the air, which implied that this effort was comparable to clashes between opposing armies, wherein a decisive battle meant victory in the war: "Once a nation has been conquered in the air it may be subjected to such moral torture that it would be obliged to cry 'Enough' *before* the war could be decided upon the surface" (emphasis in original).[30] In other words, he came close to identifying the enemy air force as the key vital center. In a sense, therefore, Douhet also stressed the need for a decisive counterforce battle, as did the land-war theorists he so decried.

Douhet did not advocate that aircraft attack or assist surface forces. The strength of airpower lay in its use as a strategic weapon, not a tactical one. He did concede, however, that the air campaign might take six days or six months, "depending on the intensity of the offensive and the staunchness of the people's hearts." This meant that although command of the air and the subsequent devastation of a country's vital centers would probably produce victory, airpower might still need to defeat the enemy's ground forces if surrender were not immediately forthcoming. If all else failed, ground troops would occupy enemy territory. To Douhet, this last option would seldom be necessary; even the need to defeat the surface forces was unlikely.[31] In reality, this prediction has yet to come true, because defeat of an army has a psychological as well as a physical effect. Now, as then, a country is generally unwilling to yield if its ground forces are still intact. The Persian Gulf War of 1991 seemed to indicate that, for psychological reasons, defeating the Iraqi army was still necessary, but in this case airpower was able to do so with incomparably greater efficiency and at lower risk than by using ground forces.

Because Douhet thought air attacks on a country's vital centers were of primary importance, he saw little use for "auxiliary aviation" (pursuit or attack aircraft). His ideas on this subject grew more radical over time. In the first edition of *The Command of the Air* (1921), he recognized the utility of auxiliary aviation. However, in the second edition (1927), Douhet went much further, stating that he had been deliberately mild in his earlier edition so as not to cause too much consternation, but now he had to be completely honest. He maintained that, in truth, auxiliary aviation was "useless, superfluous and harmful"[32] and was merely a collection of airplanes—it was not airpower. Convinced that an army or navy without control of the air above it was an army or navy about to be destroyed, he termed command of the air essential— the key strategic objective. After achieving command of the air, aircraft could assist in any tactical operations still in progress on the surface. But diverting assets from the strategic air battle to support surface operations was folly. If one lost command of the air, one lost the war, regardless of the situation on the surface.

One must remember that Douhet was formulating a theory of war applicable to Italy—a country of modest resources, powerful neighbors, and mountainous northern borders.[33] He believed it relatively easy to defend the mountain passes—as indeed Austria had done in the Great War. Certainly, auxiliary aviation would prove useful in that defense, but to what end? Victory on the surface was prohibitively expensive, if not impossible. Italy would do well to hold on the ground and attack in the air. Douhet admitted, however, that a country with great resources—such as the United States—could afford to build both a strategic and an auxiliary air force.[34]

To implement his ideas, Douhet called for an independent air force (IAF). Airpower divorced from army and navy control was essential because it could not be the "Cinderella of the family," dependent on the generosity of older sisters,[35] but must see to its own needs. Even the most conservative soldier and sailor recognized how essential aircraft had become to their operations. Although denying that airpower could be a decisive factor in war, they realized that victory was unlikely without it. To Douhet, this realization was dangerous if it meant that surface commanders could demand airpower, under their control, to support tactical operations. In this circumstance, the aviation defense budget would suffer a fatal split between independent and auxiliary airpower—a situation that would help no one.

The IAF would consist largely of "bombardment units" and "combat units," the former comprising long-range, heavy-load-carrying aircraft of moderate speed. Although Douhet considered interception of a bomber force unlikely, he admitted the possibility of such an eventuality and therefore called for "combat units" or escort aircraft. With approximately the same performance characteristics as the bombers, these escorts would carry machine guns to ward off enemy interceptors. Notably, because he did not anticipate the actual occurrence of an air battle, he claimed that one would not really require such defensive armaments, but he included them as a comfort to aircrew morale.[36]

The only other aircraft Douhet thought necessary was a fast, long-range reconnaissance plane to fly over enemy territory, photographing potential targets. One needed reconnaissance for effective targeting, not only to pinpoint objectives but also to determine the effectiveness of air attacks on those objectives. In the revised edition of *The Command of the Air,* Douhet combined the functions of bombardment and escort into one aircraft—the battle plane, which he envisioned flying en masse towards an enemy's vital centers carrying both bombs and defensive machine guns.[37]

Significantly, unlike many other writers of the period who tended to glorify air warfare—especially the role of the fighter pilot—Douhet took a decidedly nonromantic view. No passages in his writings speak of the exhilaration of flight, the conquest of nature by man and machine, or the near-mystical experiences of people who have become unfettered by the tyranny of geography. He did not compare pilots to modern knights—bold, chivalrous, and dashing—but portrayed aviators simply as determined and stoic professionals who went about their deadly business in an unremarkable way. And this business was indeed a deadly one.

Because most attacks would be on area targets, Douhet did not believe that bombing accuracy was especially important: if targets were so small as to require high accuracy, then they were probably not worthwhile targets. Aircraft conducting these area attacks would use a mixture of high-explosive, incendiary, and gas or biological (aerochemical) bombs. The explosives would produce rubble; the incendiaries would start fires in the rubble; and the aerochemical bombs would prevent firefighters from extinguishing the blaze. In *The Command of the Air*, Douhet states only that aircraft would use these bombs "in the correct proportions," but in "The War of 19—" German battle planes carry bomb loads in the ratio of one explosive to three incendiary to six aerochemical bombs.[38] Douhet thus recognized that a combination of different types of weapons can produce a greater result than can any single weapon. Of note, during World War II, Allied bombers often carried a mix of both high-explosive and incendiary bombs to achieve the results suggested by Douhet.

The general also insisted that air attacks be carried out en masse. In the air, as on the surface, piecemeal attacks were counterproductive. His emphasis on mass in the air—one remembers his call for 20,000 aircraft in 1917—was every bit as pronounced as that of surface generals of the late war. Of equal importance was the rapidity of these mass strikes. The speed and range of aircraft provided the flexibility to strike several targets simultaneously, which would cause paralysis and collapse. Air strikes would occur so rapidly and massively over a wide area that the collective will of a country would simply disintegrate. In today's parlance, Douhet was referring to "parallel operations"—the ability to operate simultaneously against several different target sets at both the strategic and tactical levels. Several decades would pass before the accuracy and effectiveness of aircraft and their weapons would allow such parallel operations, but the principle Douhet outlined in 1921 was certainly viable.

Because defense against air attack was impossible, Douhet also stressed the need for an air fleet in-being to attack immediately and relentlessly once hostilities began. Unlike surface forces that could have weeks or even months to prepare, airpower would have no time to mobilize in future wars. A country not ready for war would lose command of the air and, with it, the war itself. Indeed, an unstated conclusion of this position is that airpower would be particularly effective at "first strike" or preventive war. If mobilization were not a factor in air warfare and if air defense were impossible, then obviously the country that struck first would enjoy an enormous, almost insurmountable, advantage. Assuming Douhet's formulation, therefore, in times of crisis one would tend to use the air weapon precipitously. Thus—even more so than in the era before the Great War, when mobilization was tantamount to a declaration of war—the inexorable, almost inevitable, nature of air attack might mean that the slightest twitch in times of crisis could lead to catastrophe. The air weapon, by its nature, sported a hair trigger.

Douhet recognized that the strength of a country's air force was integrally related to the condition of its civil aviation industry; indeed, he viewed military air as even more dependent on the civil sector than either land or sea power. Douhet saw a strong and symbiotic relationship among an air force, the aviation industry, the government, and a country's commercial vitality.[39] He argued that the government must subsidize and support civil aviation in three general ways. First, it should establish air routes consisting of airports, emergency landing fields, radio and signal beacons, and weather stations. Second, it must fund research and development—aircraft and their special high-performance engines were too expensive to expect industry to assume the financial burden for their development. Third, Douhet believed that civil airliners should be capable of performing military missions. He envisioned airliners with the same specifications as battle planes—and thus able to augment the air force in war.[40]

16

This idea has some validity. Although complete commonality has not been possible, the technological relationship between civil and military aircraft has always been close because scientific advances often benefit both sectors. During the 1930s, commercial designs like the Boeing 247, Lockheed "Vega," and Douglas DC-3 led military aircraft development. Even today, it is no coincidence that Boeing and Lockheed airliners closely resemble Air Force tankers and cargo aircraft. Even so, the increasing complexity demanded of military aircraft is making this decades-old technological marriage tenuous.

Finally, Douhet expected civil aviation to establish an "airmindedness" among the population. Not only must a pool of pilots and aircraft mechanics be trained for war, but events like air shows and demonstration flights would educate people to the importance of aviation and the economic, social, and military benefits it could bestow. The people must think of themselves as an airpower nation.

In evaluating the writings of Douhet, one must note the existence of three incarnations of the theorist who wrote about airpower over a 20-year period. The first was a relatively young man, fascinated by machines and gadgets, who witnessed heavier-than-air flight in 1908 and began dreaming about its possibilities. Over the next four years, he sketched an outline of the importance of aircraft and ways for using them in war. By the time Italy had entered World War I, Douhet had already decided upon the basic thrust of this theory: war had become total and stagnated, and airpower would provide the antidote. It would do this by taking the offensive at the outset of war and by bombing the enemy country's vital centers. The world war merely provided more detail and specificity to his theories. The stalemate and horror of land warfare was even worse than he—or anyone else—had imagined. The few and fairly weak attempts at strategic bombing seemed to provide disproportionately large results. Douhet therefore expanded upon his earlier ideas, threw in a few examples from the war, and produced the first edition of *The Command of the Air* in 1921.

The response to his work was fairly muted. Perhaps because of Europe's inevitable revulsion to war in the wake of the armistice or because of the great turmoil occasioned by the rise of Mussolini and the Fascist state, Douhet's book caused little stir initially. During the six years after the publication of his book, the "second theorist" continued to think and write, out of the public eye, and in the process his radicalism grew. The result was the second edition of *The Command of the Air*, which, as we have seen, was more extreme than the first. The revised work reduced the role of the army and navy but increased the importance of strategic airpower. As a consequence, the utility of auxiliary aviation became nil. Finally, Douhet placed even greater faith in the ability of the bomber to penetrate enemy airspace and destroy targets. Escorts were unnecessary. Unlike the first edition, the 1927 version of *The Command of the Air* had a noisy reception.

The third Douhet spent the last three years of his life reacting to the firestorm created by his revised work. Because of his reputation and personality, as well as the primitive state of aviation even into the mid-1920s, ignoring Douhet had been easy. Clearly, his superiors—even those involved with aviation or sympathetic to it—had not taken him too seriously. As a consequence, his writings up to 1927 had generated little debate within his profession. After that date, however, such was not the case. Mussolini clearly approved of airpower; new airmen like Italo Balbo were becoming national heroes and gaining international reputations; and the aircraft themselves were becoming increasingly capable. The ideas of Douhet thus posed a threat to the proponents of land and sea power, whom he was constantly attacking.

Not used to defending himself from incessant and virulent attack, Douhet for the first time had to engage in an intelligent, albeit heated, debate with his military peers. Nonetheless, given the gusto with which he responded to his critics between 1927 and 1930, largely through the pages of *Rivista Aeronautica*, he certainly seemed to enjoy the controversy. What effect did this long overdue dialogue have on his theories? The impact was mixed. On the one hand, it forced him to clearly define terms like *command of the air*, and this clarification enhanced his theory.[41] On the other hand, however, it drove him to dig in his heels even more adamantly regarding the dominance of airpower over surface warfare.

The increased radicalization of Douhet's ideas, spurred by the heated debate in professional military journals, culminated in his last work, "The War of 19—," written in the last months of his life but not published until soon after his death. In many ways, this piece combined and magnified Douhet's most extreme positions. The entire war lasts less than two days, and dozens of major cities lie in ashes. The battle planes of the victorious Germans suffer enormous losses, but succeeding waves continue and are unstoppable. The morale of the civilian population quickly collapses, and the political leadership sues for peace, while the land forces of the belligerents have barely even begun their mobilization and assembly. The war of the future is therefore rapid, violent, relatively bloodless (compared to the Great War), and dominated completely by airpower. This vision—almost hopeful and utopian in some respects—would dominate airpower theory for the next decade. It is therefore imperative at this point to examine more closely Douhet's assumptions and conclusions, many of which, quite simply, were wrong.

Douhet initiated a fundamental debate, never resolved, over whether airpower is unique and revolutionary or whether it is just another arrow in a soldier's or sailor's quiver—and thus evolutionary. Debate hinges on the alleged decisiveness of airpower.

Can airpower be decisive in war? Perhaps the answer depends on the definition of that term. Some people use it to imply that airpower can (or cannot) win wars independently of other arms. But no service is likely to win a war alone in the modern age, so that definition is not useful; moreover, few airmen would make such a claim. Others define decisiveness in terms of destruction of an enemy force or the occupation of territory. Douhet argued that these results were not the objects of war and were often irrelevant. Trafalgar did not end the Napoleonic wars, and although Hannibal occupied most of Italy for a decade and destroyed several Roman armies, he still lost the war.

A more useful meaning of the term entails identifying the force predominant in achieving the desired goal. If that goal includes the quarantine of a belligerent, as in the Cuban missile crisis of 1961, then sea power will dominate. If, on the other hand, the goal is to topple a dictator and restore democracy, as in Panama, then ground forces will dominate. But in other instances, such as the Persian Gulf War, airpower is dominant. In terms of this meaning, Douhet believed passionately that airpower could be decisive in war and thus revolutionary. He did, however, stumble in several key respects.

One of Douhet's more glaring errors was his overestimation of the psychological effects of bombing. He believed that people would panic in the face of a determined air attack. To a great extent, however, one can excuse Douhet for this mistake since he had little empirical evidence to draw upon—and the available evidence was quite supportive. For example, in 1925 military theorist Basil H. Liddell Hart commented on the psychological effect of German bombing attacks on Britain in World War I:

> Witnesses of the earlier air attacks before our defence was organized, will not be disposed to underestimate the panic and disturbance that would result from a concentrated blow dealt by a superior air fleet. Who that saw it will ever forget the nightly sight of the population of a great industrial and shipping town, such as Hull, streaming out into the fields on the first sound of the alarm signals? Women, children, babies in arms, spending night after night huddled in sodden fields, shivering under a bitter winter sky.[42]

Douhet had read of such panic during the war and noted it in his diaries. Clearly, these reports made a deep impression on him. In truth, one could find many such descriptions in the literature of the time, and even Stanley Baldwin, former British prime minister, proclaimed glumly in 1932 that "the bomber would always get through."[43] People clearly believed such warnings: during the Munich crisis of 1938, fully one-third of the population of Paris evacuated the city to avoid a possible German air assault.[44] The problem with such apocalyptic predictions was that they failed to address whether morale was even a relevant issue in a tightly organized police state—as were Germany and Japan during World War II. In addition, the dire predictions of Douhet and others erred by underestimating the resiliency of human beings in the face of adversity. Civilian morale did not break in World War II with anywhere near the rapidity or finality predicted by Douhet: cities were not inhabited by mere rabble who would collapse at the first application of pressure.[45] Perhaps, as one observer noted, Douhet's theories assumed wars occurring between the democratic countries of Europe,[46] whose governments are responsive to the wishes of the population. However, such is not generally the case in a dictatorship, whose leaders may ignore the desires of the people; indeed, the state police may prevent the people from making their wishes known. In such a circumstance, the morale of the population, even if affected by aerial bombardment, may be irrelevant to the despot. Similarly, a country in the throes of civil war may not be responsive to *any* government, or a government may have little control over its population. In such situations, the moral effect of bombing would be negligible—or, at least, would not operate using the mechanism envisioned by Douhet.

Similarly, Douhet exaggerated the physical effects of aerial bombs, but in this case he should have known better. He postulated absurdly uniform and effective bombing—no duds, no misses, no overlap, no difference in the composition and construction of targets struck. In fact, he seemed to assume that all wars occurred in clear weather and that all pilots and bombardiers—and their equipment—performed flawlessly. For example, he stated that a 100-kilogram bomb (220 pounds) would destroy anything within a 50-meter diameter; that is, a target 500 meters in diameter would require 10 tons of explosives. Because aircraft of the day could carry two tons, one needed five aircraft to effect this destruction. Magnanimously, Douhet doubled that number and claimed that 10 aircraft would "destroy entirely everything that exists upon an area of 500 meters diameter."[47]

Such calculations were simplistic in the extreme. For example, a circle that size has an area of approximately .19 square kilometers. London was about one thousand times as large at that time (about 75 square miles or 196 square kilometers). Thus, even using Douhet's hopelessly optimistic figures for bomb effectiveness, one would have needed 10,000 tons of high explosives to level London—or a force of five thousand aircraft. Even had such an air fleet been available, it would not necessarily have produced the results expected by Douhet.

One historian has noted that in the first six months of Operation Barbarossa in 1941, the Soviet Union lost 40 percent of its population, 63 percent of its coal, 58 percent of its steel, 68 percent of its pig iron, 60 percent of its aluminum, 38 percent of its grain, 95 percent of its ball bearings, and 99 percent of its rolled, nonferrous metals.[48] If a strategic bombing force had attained those staggering statistics, they would have been the envy of any air commander. But of course the Soviet Union not only did not collapse, it went on to defeat Germany. Modern nations had a toughness and resiliency undreamed of by Douhet.

Douhet also proposed that aerochemical bombs be employed with the high explosives, thinking they would be especially effective against urban targets. Gen Nicholas N. Golovine noted, however, that based on wartime experience, one needed 25 grams of poison gas to "put out of action" one square meter. London, for example, would have required 5,750 tons of poison material "for an effective gassing."[49] Adding to the tonnage of high explosives noted above, including an appropriate number of escort aircraft, and assuming some attrition of the striking force, an attack on London of the destructive magnitude envisioned by Douhet would have required nearly 20,000 aircraft. Yet, "The War of 19—" lasts only 36 hours because more than two dozen of the major cities in France and Belgium have been reduced to ashes—and by only fifteen hundred aircraft using bombs of a mere 50 kilograms, a size so small as to be virtually useless.

Although repeatedly claiming that his methods were scientific and mathematically precise, it is nonetheless true that for a trained engineer, Douhet's mathematical and technical gaffes—as well as his sophomoric attempts to estimate bomb damage "scientifically"—are baffling. Where is the empirical evidence supporting his assertions regarding the effectiveness of high explosives against reinforced structures? He had none. One gains little comfort from realizing he was not alone in these errors.[50] Unfortunately, this attempt to imbue airpower with a false "scientism" has never been fully overcome. Airpower theorists seem to have a peculiar penchant for devising technological solutions for what are often very human problems.

To make matters worse, Douhet then stated breezily that in order to achieve optimal bomb dispersion, crews should be trained to "scatter their bombs" in a "uniform fashion."[51] Nothing more clearly exposes a key flaw in Douhet's theories. He was out of touch with the details and showed no understanding of the tactics needed to implement those concepts. Apparently, Douhet was not an aviator; consequently, he frequently made serious missteps, such as this bizarre comment about scattering bombs uniformly, even in the heat of combat.[52]

Moreover, Douhet had an irritating tendency to exaggerate his prophetic powers. In *The Command of the Air,* he quotes at length from a piece he published in 1910, in which he predicts the coming dominance of the airplane. However, other pieces he wrote during that same period were far more conservative. As noted above, his official report on the Libyan War was strongly muted, dealing mostly with organizational and technical matters. In addition, in 1910 he published an article titled "The Possibilities of Aerial Navigation" that was similarly unremarkable. Douhet sang the praises of the airplane, but stopped far short of calling for an independent air arm or even emphasizing the role of strategic bombing in future wars. Instead, he stressed the reconnaissance and tactical aspects of aircraft and their importance in battle.[53] Thus, Douhet's need to backdate his airpower theories to well before World War I gives us an interesting insight into his personality. Being an early air theorist was not enough—he had to be the first.

Douhet was also guilty of virtually ignoring the air battle required to attain command of the air. Because the airplane's inherent attributes of speed and range granted it tactical surprise, he believed that one could achieve command of the air without a fight. (In "The War of 19—," the air battle lasts a mere three hours.) A tension in war has always existed between the strategies of annihilation and attrition. The latter definitely characterized land warfare in World War I. Airpower has promised annihilation but generally provided attrition. Although Douhet stated that airpower would eliminate the counterforce battle, it was still necessary in World War II—but the trenches had moved to 20,000 feet. Nearly 80,000 Royal Air Force (RAF) crew members and a like number of Americans were lost in the air battle over Germany. Indeed, that battle revealed that meeting the Luftwaffe in the air was wiser than attacking the German aircraft and engine factories. In effect, Allied bombers became the bait that brought the Luftwaffe's planes—and pilots—into the air, where they could be destroyed. One reason Douhet discounted the air battle was that few had occurred on a major scale in the Italo-Austrian front during the war.

Possibly, Douhet ignored the air battle because admitting its likelihood would contradict one of his main tenets—that airpower eliminated the counterforce battle. Towards the end of his life, he began to modify these views. In "The War of 19—," the German battle planes suffer horrendous losses—100 percent of the attacking force is shot down by enemy pursuit in the initial waves—but succeeding waves press on and ultimately achieve victory.[54] In other words, Douhet conceded that defense was possible, at least tactically. Certainly, a fuller exploration of the distinction between tactical and strategic air superiority and ways of achieving such superiority would have been useful.

The Battle of Britain refuted Douhet's premise that the weaker air force must assume an ever more violent offense because defense is futile. In that battle, radar stripped away the airplane's surprise. One would do well to remember, however, that this battle of 1940 has been the only clear-cut defensive air victory in history.[55] Today, electronic warfare—the jamming of communications and radars, and especially stealth technology—has tilted the balance back in favor of the aircraft as an offensive weapon for countries that have invested in such technology. The Persian Gulf War presented a situation predicted by Douhet: attacking aircraft (F-117 stealth bombers) arrived over targets unannounced, destroyed those targets, and then departed with impunity, all because they had achieved tactical surprise.

The Italian theorist also erred in foreseeing only total war, perhaps because his view was colored by a conflict that seemingly had no rational objectives. The political scientist Bernard Brodie accused him of failing to understand that war must follow policy, but this misses the mark.[56] Rather, Douhet expected that future wars would be just as inane as the Great War. More cynic than realist, he was profoundly skeptical of human nature and rejected arguments that war could be carefully guided or finely tuned to reflect political will: "War . . . is a kind of irrepressible convulsion, during which it seems to lose or suspend every human sense; and it [humanity] appears to be invaded by a devastating and destructive fury."[57] Fortunately, he was not completely correct; World War II was not as devoid of clear objectives as was the Great War. Moreover, limited wars like those in Korea and Vietnam have become the norm in the second half of this century, and in many of these wars—as against the Vietcong for example—airpower, as he envisioned it, is largely inappropriate.

Douhet denigrated limitations imposed by law and morality and continued to advocate aerochemical attacks on cities, even after Italy had ratified the Geneva Protocol of 1925 that prohibited them. This too showed Douhet's pessimistic view of human nature. He was certain that total war would rationalize any type of activity, stating, "He is a fool if not a patricide who would acquiesce in his country's defeat rather than go against those formal agreements which do not limit the right to kill and destroy, but simply the ways of killing and destroying. The limitations applied to the so-called inhuman and atrocious means of war are nothing but international demagogic hypocrisies."[58]

Given the world war hecatomb, it is not surprising that Douhet was so pessimistic. But as horrendous as was the destruction in World War II, none of the belligerents resorted to gas warfare, although most possessed the means to do so.[59] Moreover, since 1945 several conventions have been held regarding the law of war and have proposed a variety of rulings. Most of these limitations are contained in the Geneva Protocols of 1977, and although the United States rejected them, it still follows their basic thrust.[60] This was the case in Operation Desert Storm, when coalition airmen went to great lengths to restrict the types of targets struck and weapons employed so as to minimize civilian casualties and collateral damage. Now that precision bombing has become more routine, such scrupulous targeting likely will become standard practice.

Another example of Douhet's shortsightedness was his failure to forecast advances in surface technology. Despite saying that everything in this world undergoes improvement, he foresaw no evolution in surface weapons and claimed that ground war had reached perpetual equilibrium. Thus, he ignored the development of tanks and armored doctrine, which played a major role in restoring mobility to the battlefield. Tanks, which were used by most of the major belligerents during the war and which underwent significant improvement in the decades that followed, are not even mentioned in *The Command of the Air*. Significantly, however, the French army in "The War of 19—" does possess a strong tank contingent; but France loses the war before they can ever be put to use.

Obviously, Douhet is making a point. The surface stalemate of the Great War was certainly very real and had an enormous psychological impact on the people who fought in it, but one must ask what happened to the Giulio Douhet who wrote so presciently concerning the potential of ground-force mechanization in his early career. A skeptic might ask whether such ideas would have undermined his theories regarding the primacy of airpower.[61] Also of note is the fact that Douhet took pains to single out small-caliber machine guns as contributors to the trench stalemate of World War I. He did not mention the enormous and continually growing use of large-caliber artillery, which also played a major role in the stalemate. This is a curious omission, especially from an artillery officer. One possible explanation is that Douhet was reluctant to call attention to a weapon whose explosive impact bore at least some resemblance to that of an aerial bomb. He did not want anyone to think of airpower as flying artillery.

Douhet also missed the mark on air defense. Despite the existence of a counter to air attack, he insisted that antiaircraft fire and interceptors were ineffective and would remain so. Moreover, Douhet denied to defensive airpower the same flexibility, speed, and ability to mass that he granted the offense. Even before the invention of radar, this attitude is not understandable. As early as 1917, the British had established a sophisticated system of air defense, consisting of multiple "spotting stations" connected by telephone to a central headquarters in London. Telephones tied this headquarters to various airfields housing interceptor squadrons. These airfields, in turn, maintained contact with their airborne aircraft via wireless. The system was relatively effective, as Douhet must have known.[62] In one of his more memorable and maladroit comments, Douhet mused, "Nothing man can do on the surface of the earth can interfere with a plane in flight, moving freely in the third dimension."[63] Once again, one searches for the lieutenant who began his career as an artillery officer. He must have known that Allied gunners shot down more than one thousand German aircraft during the war and that because of improvements in fusing, the number of rounds fired to achieve a hit fell by one-half between 1915 and 1918.[64] He should have expected continued improvements in air defenses, yet he ignored them.

One must note that Douhet predicated his argument regarding the inherently offensive nature of the airplane on the belief that only aircraft could stop other aircraft. Given the vastness of the sky, this position has some merit, though not as much as Douhet claimed. It has even less merit, however, if one admits that antiaircraft guns can also be effective against air attack. In such an instance, the numerical advantage gained by an attacker achieving tactical surprise and avoiding airborne interception quickly evaporates. Theoretically, if antiaircraft guns are extremely effective, interceptor aircraft are not even necessary for a successful defense.

Moreover, Douhet seemed to assume that in order for a defense to be effective, it must stop all of an attacker's aircraft. World War II proved that this was far from the case. Even in those instances in which the defense—using both interceptors and antiaircraft guns—was able to shoot down "only" 20 percent of an attacking bomber force, the effect on the attacker was nearly catastrophic. As the American strikes on Schweinfurt in the fall of 1943 showed, such loss rates were not simply unacceptable but were well within the capabilities of a defender to achieve. In truth, although Douhet—like many of his contemporaries—vilified the generals of the Great War for foolishly falling into a "cult of the offensive," the Italian air theorist followed much the same path. In this sense at least, Douhet was philosophically at one with the surface generals he so roundly criticized.

Somewhat surprisingly, Douhet did not adequately address the issue of objectives, even though he recognized their importance and saw targeting as the most important task of the air commander. In the exasperated words of Bernard Brodie, "How could one who had so little idea of what it is necessary to hit be quite so sure of the tremendous results which would inevitably follow from the hitting?"[65] Although Douhet mentions general target sets, nowhere does he undertake a systematic examination of what would be necessary to dismember a country's industrial system. This omission may partly be a result of his belief that the will of the people was a target of such overwhelming importance that elaborating on the other vital centers was unnecessary.

In addition, disassembling these centers was not nearly as simple as Douhet suggested. For one thing, aircraft cannot operate at will, anytime or anyplace. Rather, many limits may be imposed on airpower: political restraints and goals, range, national boundaries, darkness, weather, the electromagnetic spectrum—even the duration of the war itself can significantly affect target selection. Yet, Douhet believed that because aircraft operated in the third dimension, they had no limits and that they could quickly and effectively attack all targets. This interpretation is too facile. Targets are not destroyed simply because they are attacked, and merely identifying targets to strike is no substitute for a coherent air strategy.

Most surprisingly, Douhet is not alone in this shallow thinking. None of the classic airpower thinkers—Billy Mitchell, Hugh Trenchard, John Slessor, Alexander de Seversky, and so forth—ever went beyond the most fundamental stages of attempting to identify the key vital centers of a country. Moreover, they simply do not discuss the question of which specific target sets within those vital centers—industries, transportation nodes, and command and control facilities—were most important and what the order of priority was for striking them. The theorists at the Air Corps Tactical School at Maxwell Field, Alabama, in the 1930s made some initial inquiries in this area and quickly concluded that just as targeting is the key to airpower, so is intelligence the key to targeting.

Unfortunately, although military intelligence organizations had existed in some form for centuries, the information they gathered was generally of the type needed at the tactical level: the number of enemy troops, their location, the capabilities of their weapons, the location of their supply depots, and so forth. Air war now required fundamentally different types of intelligence regarding a country's industrial and economic structure and potential. Because intelligence agencies did not yet exist that could provide this type of information, Douhet and others were left with vague and simplistic platitudes. Failing to identify and seriously address the vital connection between targeting and intelligence was a serious oversight.

It took Desert Storm to furnish the third pillar of this trio: the key to intelligence in modern war is the ability to assess the results of an air campaign on a complex system. Given the interdependent and linked nature of modern societies, neutralizing a certain target does not necessarily mean that one achieves a strategic gain or that it was the one intended. In addition, the *pace* of air war has now become so rapid that near-real-time intelligence has become essential. Moreover, precision weapons demand precision intelligence: if one can now strike a specific office in a large military headquarters, then one needs to know the correct office.

Another example of Douhet's exaggeration is his attitude towards the army and navy. Although Douhet paid lip service to the other arms, he saw little use for them, and his tendency to move from the dominance of airpower to its omnipotence grew. Because he did not expect surface forces to be decisive, he gave little thought to their future development, organization, or employment. In the defense department, he envisioned that surface forces would have degenerated into impotence—merely serving to guard Italy's mountain passes and harbors. Douhet's thinking therefore became dangerously one-dimensional.

Finally, he failed to see the importance of history—of looking to the past to illuminate the present. In this regard, he was in the same position as the nuclear theorists following World War II. Because little empirical evidence existed upon which to base a model of how one could use nuclear weapons in war, their theories became intellectual exercises that relied on the force of logic. Similarly, Douhet chose to ignore what little evidence did exist from World War I: "The experience of the past is of no value at all. On the contrary, it has a negative value since it tends to mislead us."[66] He took this position not because he believed that history was useless, but because it provided the wrong lessons for airpower. Paradoxically, however, at the same time he denigrated the lessons of the Great War, he built a theory of airpower based on that war's repeating itself. The result was a curious mixture of past and future, with no apparent anchor in either dimension.

Using World War II as a test of Douhet's theories, most critics found them wanting. Detractors noted that the war proved him wrong on many counts: the land war did not stagnate; a prolonged and deadly air battle was necessary to gain command of the air; civilian morale did not collapse; no one employed aerochemical bombs; and auxiliary aviation (tactical airpower) proved enormously valuable. Defenders of Douhet see a different picture: command of the air did in fact mean the difference between victory and defeat; the German and Japanese war economies were devastated; and although not destroyed, civilian morale was severely damaged by bombardment. Moreover, advocates maintain that Douhet's theories were never given a fair test because the basic tenet of his war-fighting philosophy—hold on the ground while attacking in the air—was never carried out, resulting in a diversion of effort that detracted from the potency of the air offensive.

The arguments of these advocates are not credible. Millions of tons of bombs were dropped over a period of six years—a scale far in excess of anything imagined by Douhet—but the results did not fulfill his prophecies. (One should remember, however, that Douhet's theories presumed the use of gas bombs. It is impossible to say whether or not their use would have made a significant difference in the results of the air campaigns waged by Germany, Japan, Britain, and the United States. Nonetheless, it is useful to remember the extreme anxiety, bordering on panic, that occurred in Israel during the Persian Gulf War, when the Israelis feared that Iraqi Scud missiles had chemical warheads. Who would have thought that a country as inured to warfare and the threat of terrorist attacks as Israel would react in such a fashion?)

A seemingly more reasonable approach maintained that atomic weapons vindicated Douhet; after all, an invasion of Japan proper was unnecessary, and the only battle of the home islands was the one conducted by American B-29s. Atomic weapons seemed to grant new relevance to Douhet because a handful of bombs could now devastate a country, as he had predicted.[67] Such arguments may be even less credible than the claims that Douhet did not receive a fair test in World War II. If the only circumstance that makes Douhet relevant is nuclear holocaust, then he is totally irrelevant.

Given the limited wars of the postwar era, especially Vietnam, Douhet's ideas on airpower seemed best confined to the dustbin of history. This has now changed because the thawing of the cold war and the collapse of the Warsaw Pact, coupled with the decreased presence of forward-deployed American troops, have put a premium on the ability to project power over great distances. This requirement is a natural characteristic of airpower, and the efficacy of the air weapon was never demonstrated more clearly than in the Persian Gulf War. For decades, airmen described airpower with terms like *furious, relentless, overwhelming,* and so forth, but to a great extent those were just words, because the technology did not exist to make them true. But the air war in the Gulf finally lived up to the prophecies of the past seven decades.

One of Douhet's ideas that has become increasingly relevant is his call for a single department of defense. Douhet advocated such an organization as early as 1908, when he wrote a stinging essay titled "The Knot of Our Military Question," which criticized the lack of cooperation between the Italian army and navy. He suggested the establishment of a single ministry of defense headed by a civilian. At the same time, he called for a military chief of staff to coordinate the combat operations of the services.[68] His superiors ignored the proposal, but he would return to the idea later.

In *The Command of the Air,* he enlarged his defense ministry to include an air force, but the services were still united under a single civilian head, and military operations were coordinated by a chief of staff. Douhet's rationale was not based on economic efficiency but military necessity. One could not subdivide war by medium—air, land, and sea. It was a whole, and only people who understood the use of military forces in all three mediums could understand war: "There are experts of land, sea and air warfare. But as yet there are no experts of warfare. And warfare is a single entity, having a single purpose."[69] He therefore proposed a national war college to educate soldiers, sailors, and airmen in the overall conduct of war.

Douhet also perceptively noted the tension between separateness and joint action between the services. His call for a unified defense department on the one hand and an air force which dominated that defense department on the other was not inconsistent. Service cooperation did not mean equality. Merely dividing the defense budget into three equal parts would be dangerous if the roles played by those parts were not equal. Hard choices had to be made, and to Douhet the logic was inescapable. Since land and sea forces could not survive in the face of air attack, it was folly to pretend that those arms were the decisive forces in war and should be supported by air. The opposite was true. Airpower was now the key arm, and armies and navies must support it.

Although Douhet was the first and most noteworthy of the early airpower theorists, the extent of his influence is debatable. Largely because he wrote in a language not shared by many military thinkers—a circumstance exacerbated by the fact that he deliberately confined his writing to the professional journals of his own country—Douhet initially was not well known outside his native land. The British, for example, may have heard of his ideas, but the first article to appear in the official journal of the Royal Air Force was not published until 1933.[70] *The Command of the Air* was never required reading at the RAF Staff College between the wars, and one historian states flatly that Douhet had no influence in Britain prior to World War II.[71]

The situation in France was somewhat different. French airmen were followers of aviation developments in Italy, and in 1933 the magazine *Les Ailes* published a partial translation of *The Command of the Air*. French air leaders, specifically

Generals Tulasne and Armengaud, were receptive to his ideas.[72] In 1935, Col P. Vauthier wrote an analysis of Douhet's theories titled *La Doctrine de Guerre du General Douhet,* which further elucidated the Italian's theories and disseminated them to a wider audience. In fact, the accounts of Douhet that began appearing in British and American periodicals about this time likely were based on the French works rather than the original Italian.

German military leaders were even more receptive to new ideas than were the French. Because of their failure in the Great War, German military leaders made a point of closely monitoring foreign developments. Although *The Command of the Air* was not published in German until 1935, it appears that Hitler was initially taken with Douhet's ideas: he appreciated the terroristic aspects of his air bombardment theory, made evident at the time of the Munich crisis in 1938. Douhet's influence did not extend to the Luftwaffe as a whole, however, and the official doctrine with which it entered the war focused on army cooperation.[73]

Douhet had his earliest and greatest influence in America, but even then it was not great. In 1922 the Italian air attaché wrote about *The Command of the Air* in *Aviation* magazine, and Billy Mitchell later admitted that he had met with Douhet during a trip to Europe in 1922. About that same time—perhaps even as a result of that meeting—a translation of exerpts from *The Command of the Air* made its way into Air Service files, and in 1923 a longer translation circulated at Air Service headquarters. One historian claims that Mitchell heavily "borrowed from" this translation, and it in turn formed the basis of early Air Service Tactical School texts that dealt with strategic bombardment.[74] This claim is questionable, but by the mid-1930s, articles discussing Douhet began to appear in American military publications, and a translation of the second edition of *The Command of the Air* circulated around the Air Corps in 1933.[75]

In sum, European and American airmen apparently had become well aware of Douhet's writings in the decade prior to World War II. Because many people in many places were attempting to come to grips with the new air weapon, drawing clear lines of influence among them becomes virtually impossible. That many of the ideas percolating throughout the various air forces were quite similar to those expounded by the Italian air general does not mean those ideas were based on Douhet. What is clear, however, is that by the end of World War II—and as a result of the massive strategic bombing campaigns conducted throughout—the theories of Douhet were commonplace. This notoriety became even greater in the decade that followed, given the emergence of nuclear weapons delivered by airpower. Although equating Douhet solely with the destruction of cities and their populations is simplistic and incomplete, his name has nonetheless become synonymous with a particular version of air warfare.

Giulio Douhet has generated intense and partisan debate over the past seven decades. Undoubtedly, he had many things wrong, but he also had many things right. World War II and Desert Storm proved the accuracy of his fundamental premise—that command of the air is crucial to success in a conventional war. Despite Douhet's many theoretical deficiencies, the scope and audacity of his work point to a man of great intellect. Considering that it took over two thousand years of warfare on land and sea to produce Henri de Jomini, Carl von Clausewitz, and Alfred Thayer Mahan, we should not be overly critical of the airman who began writing a theory of air war scarcely one decade after the invention of the airplane.

Notes

1. Frank J. Cappelluti, "The Life and Thought of Giulio Douhet" (PhD diss., Rutgers University, 1967), 3–7, 10. Incidentally, Caserta is the present location of the Italian air force academy.

2. Giulio Douhet, *The Command of the Air*, trans. Sheila Fischer (Rome: Rivista Aeronautica, 1958), from the introduction by Gen Celso Ranieri, ix. The Italian air force considers this the official translation of Douhet's major works; I have therefore used it where possible. Unfortunately, this version does not contain complete translations of "Probable Aspects of Future War" or "The War of 19—," which are included in the Ferrari translation of 1942, cited in note 29 below.

3. Douhet (Fischer translation), 22.

4. Cappelluti, 66.

5. Douhet (Fischer translation), x.

6. *The Origin of Air Warfare*, 2d ed., trans. Renalto D'Orlando (Rome: Historical Office of the Italian Air Force, 1961), passim; and D. J.

Fitzsimmons, "The Origins of Air Warfare," *Air Pictorial*, December 1972, 482–85.

7. *The Origin of Air Warfare*, 214–16.

8. Douhet (Fischer translation), 123.

9. Cappelluti, 69; K. Booth, "History or Logic as Approaches to Strategy," *RUSI* [Royal United Services Institute] *Journal* 117 (September 1972): 35; and Claudio Segrè, "Douhet in Italy: Prophet without Honor?" *Aerospace Historian* 26 (June 1979): 71.

10. Cappelluti, 70, 84.

11. Douhet (Fischer translation), x.

12. Cappelluti, 90. These diaries were published in 1920 and 1922.

13. Ibid., 109.

14. Ibid., 127.

15. Ibid., 133; Thomas Mahoney, "Doctrine of Ruthlessness," *Popular Aviation*, April 1940, 36; and John Whittam, *The Politics of the Italian Army, 1861–1918* (London: Croom, Helm, 1977), 201.

16. Cappelluti, 129.

17. Douhet (Fischer translation), xi; and Cappelluti, 138. In late October 1918, a few weeks before the armistice, the Allies did indeed form an interallied air force, commanded by Gen Hugh Trenchard of the Royal Air Force; the IAF's mission was to take the war to Germany via strategic bombing of its vital centers.

18. Caproni's diary, December 1917. Translated portions of this diary plus the correspondence between Douhet and Caproni and between Caproni and Gorrell are located in the US Air Force Historical Research Agency at Maxwell AFB, Alabama, file 168.661. See also J. L. Atkinson, "Italian Influence on the Origins of the American Concept of Strategic Bombardment," *The Air Power Historian* 5 (July 1957): 141–49; and William G. Key, "Some Papers of Count Caproni de Taliedo: Controversy in the Making?" *Pegasus*, January 1956 (supplement), 1–20. Atkinson and Key argue that Caproni was the mouthpiece of Douhet.

19. Nino Salvaneschi, "Let Us Kill the War, Let Us Aim at the Heart of the Enemy!" Milan, 1917. A copy is located in the US Air Force Historical Research Agency, file 168.661-129, pages 24, 47, 62.

20. For the contents of the Gorrell memo, see Maurer Maurer, ed., *The U.S. Air Service in World War I*, vol. 2 (Washington, D.C.: Government Printing Office, 1978), 141–51.

21. Cappelluti, 155–58.

22. Translations of Douhet's works have been sporadic at best. Key items that have not been translated into English include the 93-page appendix to the first edition of *The Command of the Air* noted in the text, his war diary, "The Army of the Air" (an essay written in 1927), and his novels on air warfare. In addition, "Recapitulation"—a collection of Douhet's letters to the editor of *Rivista Aeronautica*, written between 1927 and 1930 and published in the Dino Ferrari translation of 1942—includes only Douhet's

responses, not the critical letters from Italian airmen, soldiers, and sailors to which he was responding.

23. Douhet (Fischer translation), 13.

24. Ibid., 144. Douhet recognized a distinction between air defense and protection from air attack: one cannot stop the rain, but one can carry an umbrella to avoid being soaked. Nonetheless, he believed that civil defense actions such as underground shelters and evacuation plans were of little use. The people must expect bombardment and endure its horror. Ibid., 198.

25. I use the term *precept* rather than *principle* because Douhet rejected the latter term. In his view, common sense should prevail in war. Unfortunately, when a concept was elevated to the status of a "principle," it too often became a dogmatic assertion divorced from common sense. Airpower required new thinking and the rejection of dogmatic assertions applicable only to a bygone age.

26. The Department of Defense's current definition for air superiority reads, "That degree of dominance in the air battle of one force over another which permits the conduct of operations by the former and its related land, sea and air forces at a given time and place without prohibitive interference by the opposing force." Air supremacy is defined as "that degree of air superiority wherein the opposing air force is incapable of effective interference." Joint Pub 1-02, *Department of Defense Dictionary of Military and Associated Terms*, 23 March 1994. Douhet's concept of command of the air is closer to our notion of air supremacy.

27. Douhet (Fischer translation), 47–48. In a memo written in 1916, Douhet was a bit more specific, listing the following as potential targets: "railroad junctions, arsenals, ports, warehouses, factories, industrial centers, banks, ministries, etc." Cappelluti, 107.

28. Douhet (Fischer translation), 48.

29. Giulio Douhet, *The Command of the Air*, trans. Dino Ferrari (1942; reprint, Washington, D.C.: Office of Air Force History, 1983), 367–68. Although the editors have added a brief introduction, the pagination of the essays themselves remains the same as in the original.

30. Douhet (Fischer translation), 171.

31. Ibid., 83–84.

32. Ibid., 86.

33. There is little indication Douhet attempted to spread his ideas on airpower outside Italy. He wrote virtually all of his works for Italian magazines and journals—he was not a propagandist in the mold of Billy Mitchell. Although he probably attempted to influence the Bolling Commission during World War I, he did so to enlist the United States as a useful ally and partner in the war against the Central Powers.

34. Douhet's reference to the United States is significant and is exemplified today by our Army's helicopter fleet, one of the largest air forces in the world with more than six thousand aircraft. Its sole mission is to

support ground operations. Douhet would not have dreamed of diverting so many resources to such a mission.

35. Douhet (Ferrari translation), 229.

36. Douhet envisioned "combat units" flying low over enemy defenses to draw fire so that their positions could be identified and then destroyed. This procedure is similar to that of the "Wild Weasels" in the Persian Gulf War: F-4G aircraft carrying antiradiation missiles flew ostentatiously over Iraqi territory, hoping to attract the attention of ground-defense radars. When the Iraqis turned on these radars to track the Weasels, those aircraft launched missiles that homed on the source of the radar beam.

37. During World War II, some B-17s were modified to carry extra armor and machine guns. These aircraft, YB-40s, were then mixed in with the bomber formations striking Germany. However, these modified battle escorts were too heavy to keep up with the bomber stream after the bomb-release point, so the experiment was discontinued. By contrast, the small size of the air-to-air missiles carried by today's F-15E—the modern equivalent of the battle plane—allows a potent defensive capability that does not diminish the plane's offensive punch.

38. Douhet (Fischer translation), 34; and idem (Ferrari translation), 347.

39. This concept is echoed in Secretary of the Air Force Donald B. Rice, An Aerospace Nation (Washington, D.C.: Department of the Air Force, 1990).

40. Civilian aircraft were perhaps most effectively used in the Persian Gulf War as cargo aircraft—an application not envisioned by Douhet. Activation of the Civil Reserve Air Fleet brought over three hundred commercial airliners under military control, and these aircraft moved over four hundred thousand personnel and 95,000 tons of cargo to the Middle East—representing 64 percent of the passengers and 27 percent of all cargo moved by air.

41. Douhet (Ferrari translation), 220.

42. Basil H. Liddell Hart, Paris, or the Future of War (New York: Dutton, 1925), 39. As late as 1937, Air Chief Marshal (ACM) Hugh Dowding, commander of RAF Fighter Command, stated that bombing attacks on London would cause such panic that defeat could occur "in a fortnight or less." ACM Sir Hugh Dowding, "Employment of the Fighter Command in Home Defence," Naval War College Review 45 (Spring 1992): 36 (reprint of 1937 lecture to the RAF Staff College).

43. Eugene M. Emme, ed., The Impact of Air Power (Princeton, N.J.: Van Nostrand, 1959), 51–52. See also "War in the Air and Disarmament," The American Review of Reviews, March 1925, 308–10; and H. de Watteville, "Armies of the Air," The Nineteenth Century and After, October 1934, 353–68. For an overview of popular literature on this subject, see I. F. Clarke, Voices Prophesying War, 1763–1984 (London: Oxford University Press, 1966).

44. George H. Quester, Deterrence before Hiroshima, rev. ed. (New Brunswick, N.J.: Transaction Publishers, 1986), 98.

45. The best studies on the effects of morale bombing are the US Strategic Bombing Survey, Report no. 64b, "The Effects of Strategic Bombing on German Morale" (1947); Fred C. Iklé, *The Social Impact of Bomb Destruction* (Norman, Okla.: University of Oklahoma Press, 1958); and Irving L. Janis, *Air War and Emotional Stress* (New York: McGraw-Hill, 1951).

46. "What Lessons from Air Warfare?" *U.S. Air Services,* April 1938, 7–8. This editorial argues that the civil war in Spain was simply not a condition anticipated by Douhet.

47. Douhet (Fischer translation), 17.

48. Barry H. Steiner, *Bernard Brodie and the Foundations of American Nuclear Strategy* (Lawrence, Kans.: University Press of Kansas, 1991), 94.

49. Lt Gen N. N. Golovine, "Air Strategy," *Royal Air Force Quarterly* 7 (April 1936): 169–72. Golovine was a Russian expatriate who had served in World War I. Douhet gave no estimates on the amount of incendiary bombs needed to burn a target. They had not been used extensively during the war, so there was little experience on which to base calculations. Gen Billy Mitchell, in his 1922 manual "Notes on the Multi-Motored Bombardment Group" (page 81), estimated that only 30 tons of gas were required to render an area of one square mile "uninhabitable." That's about one-third the amount suggested by Golovine.

50. For example, one US Navy officer stated in 1923 that "there is scarcely a city in America which could not be destroyed, together with every living person therein, within, say, three days of the declaration of war." "Airplanes, and General Slaughter, in the Next War," *Literary Digest,* 17 November 1923, 61. Amusingly, the first page of this article has a picture of the hapless Barling Bomber with the caption "A few of these could wipe out a city." Likewise, in 1920 the chief of the aircraft armament division in the US Army declared that a one-hundred-pound bomb would destroy a small railroad station or warehouse, and a one-thousand-pound bomb would completely demolish a large factory. William A. Borden, "Air Bombing of Industrial Plants," *Army Ordnance,* November–December 1920, 122.

51. Douhet (Fischer translation), 185.

52. Lee Kennett, *A History of Strategic Bombing* (New York: Scribner's, 1982), 55. Kennett states that Douhet's name does not appear on the lists of licensed Italian pilots through 1918. One should know, however, that when Douhet took command of the Aviation Battalion in 1913, he was already 43 years of age—too old to take on the arduous task of learning to fly the dangerous and flimsy aircraft of the day. On the other hand, Douhet worked closely with Caproni in developing an aircraft stabilization device and an aerial camera, as well as designing a special bomb that was flight-tested in 1912. Although he may not have been a pilot, Douhet understood many of the technical problems of flight. Cappelluti, 59; Caproni diary, March 1913; and Lee Kennett, *The First Air War: 1914–1918* (New York: Free Press, 1991), 37.

53. Giulio Douhet, "Le Possibilite dell' aereonavigazione," *Rivista delle Comunicazioni*, August 1910, 758–71. I am indebted to my colleague, Lt Col Peter R. Faber, for translating this article for me.

54. Besides making it clear in "The War of 19—" that one should not be in the first plane of the first wave, Douhet also tantalizes his readers by referring to 180 "explorer" aircraft in the German air force. These were high-speed pursuit planes whose mission "had not been exactly determined." They encounter French pursuits during the war but play no significant role. Why were they even mentioned? Douhet (Ferrari translation), 342, 383.

55. Douhet would no doubt have maintained that the Germans bungled the operation by shifting to urban attacks before they had achieved command of the air—a violation of his most cardinal precept.

56. Bernard Brodie, *Strategy in the Missile Age* (Princeton, N.J.: Princeton University Press, 1959), 37.

57. Cappelluti, 80.

58. Douhet (Ferrari translation), 181.

59. Although poison gas was not used in World War II, the Italians did employ it against Ethiopian civilians in 1935. In a sense, therefore, Douhet was correct in maintaining that humanitarian impulses would have little braking effect on a country; it would seem that fear of retaliation prevented the use of gas in World War II.

60. W. Hays Parks, "Air War and the Law of War," *The Air Force Law Review* 32 (1990): 1–226.

61. An exception to his technological myopia is Douhet's enthusiasm for submarines, which he saw as dominating surface fleets as aircraft would dominate armies. Indeed, there are some similarities between aircraft and submarines—including their stealth characteristics.

62. Maj Gen E. B. Ashmore, *Air Defence* (London: Longman's, Green, 1929), 93–94. Ashmore was the chief of the London Air Defence Area during the war.

63. Douhet (Ferrari translation), 9.

64. Kenneth P. Werrell, *Archie, Flak, AAA, and SAM: A Short Operational History of Ground-Based Air Defense* (Maxwell AFB, Ala.: Air University Press, December 1988), 1–2. Golovine states that the improvements in antiaircraft defenses in World War I were even more dramatic: in 1916 it took 11,000 shells to bring down a plane; in late 1918 it required only fifteen hundred. Golovine, 170.

65. Bernard Brodie, "The Heritage of Douhet," *Air University Quarterly Review* 6 (Summer 1963): 122.

66. Douhet (Fischer translation), 132.

67. This is the thesis of Brodie, *Strategy in the Missile Age* and "The Heritage of Douhet"; Cappelluti; Louis A. Sigaud, *Air Power and Unification: Douhet's Principles of Warfare and Their Application to the United States* (Harrisburg, Pa.: Military Service Publishing Co., 1949); Lt Col Joseph L. Dickman, "Douhet and the Future," *Air University Quarterly Review* 2

(Summer 1948): 3–15; and Cy Caldwell, "The Return of General Douhet," *Aero Digest*, July 1949, 36–37, 90–92.

68. Cappelluti, 18–22.

69. Douhet (Fischer translation), 187.

70. [Brigadier General Tulasne], "The Air Doctrine of General Douhet," *Royal Air Force Quarterly* 4 (April 1933): 164–67.

71. Robin Higham, *The Military Intellectuals in Britain, 1918–1939* (New Brunswick, N.J.: Rutgers University Press, 1966), 257–59. On the other hand, one historian has seen strong similarities between Douhet's work and the early writings of J. F. C. Fuller; he therefore speculates that Douhet may have had a significant, though indirect, influence on the RAF. Brereton Greenhous, "A Speculation on Giulio Douhet and the English Connection," in *La Figura E L'Opera Di Giulio Douhet*, ed. Aniello Gentile (Italy: Società di Storia Patria, 1988), 41–51.

72. De Watteville, 360–63.

73. Horst Boog, "Douhet and German Politics: Air Doctrine and Air Operations, 1933–1945," in *La Figura E L'Opera Di Giulio Douhet*, 81–107.

74. Raymond R. Flugel, "United States Air Power Doctrine: A Study of the Influence of William Mitchell and Giulio Douhet at the Air Corps Tactical School, 1921–1935" (PhD diss., University of Oklahoma, 1966). Flugel's methodology is to compare the text of *The Command of the Air* with some of Mitchell's writings and with those in the Tactical School texts. The words and phrases are quite similar. Flugel then reveals that a translation was available at Headquarters Air Service as early as 1923. This is quite a revelation. However, Flugel erred mightily: instead of using the 1923 translation, which presumably Mitchell would have used, he compared quotations from the Ferrari translation of 1942. Because the two versions have significant differences, Flugel's charges of plagiarism remain unproven.

75. This was the translation done by Dorothy Benedict with the assistance of Capt George Kenney. It is based on the French translation in *Les Ailes* of 1933 and can be found in the US Air Force Historical Research Agency, file 168.6005-18. For other writings about Douhet at the time, see Col Charles DeF Chandler, "Air Warfare Doctrine of General Douhet," *U.S. Air Services*, May 1933, 10–13; "Air Warfare Trends," *U.S. Air Services*, August 1933, 8–9; L. E. O. Charlton, *War from the Air: Past, Present, Future* (London: Thomas Nelson, 1935); and "Air Warfare," *Royal Air Force Quarterly* 7 (April 1936): 152–68.

Chapter 2

Trenchard, Slessor, and Royal Air Force Doctrine before World War II

Col Phillip S. Meilinger

British airmen believed in the efficacy of strategic airpower almost from the inception of the airplane, perhaps because Britain was a traditional sea power. Naval war is in many respects economic war; although battles occur, the primary objective is generally to apply pressure on a country's commerce and economy to force a change in policy. To an extent, airpower flows from the same basic premise. Airmen argued, however, that the new medium could apply such pressure far more comprehensively, directly, and quickly. The catastrophic experience of the Great War confirmed for Royal Air Force (RAF) leaders that traditional methods of warfare no longer served a useful purpose. If war were to be at all viable, it had to be fought in a more rational fashion and not require the destruction of an entire generation. British airmen returned to the basics.

The object of war was to force an enemy to bend to one's will, accomplished by breaking either his will or his capability to fight. Armies were generally condemned to concentrate on the latter by seeking battle. Hugh Trenchard, the first chief of the RAF and its commander from 1919 to 1930, focused instead on the "will" portion of that equation. Trenchard's influence on the RAF cannot be overestimated. The near genius he brought to the task, despite his notoriously poor communicative skills, was crucial. Trenchard believed that the airplane was an inherently strategic weapon, unmatched in its ability to shatter the will of an enemy country. Yet, he could not erase the long British tradition of economic warfare. The result was a unique blend—an airpower theory that advocated attacks designed to break the morale of factory workers by targeting enemy industry and, by extension, the population as a whole. Trenchard's instinctive beliefs on this subject found

41

form in the official doctrine manuals of the RAF. In turn, this doctrine was taught and institutionalized at the RAF Staff College, where most of the officers who would lead their service in World War II were educated.

The most intellectually gifted man in this group, John "Jack" Slessor, had worked on Trenchard's staff in the late 1920s, and he understood airpower as well as anyone in the RAF. After attending the RAF Staff College, he spent three years instructing at the British Army Staff College. Combining his knowledge of aviation with the distinctive perspective of the army, he produced a brilliant book, *Air Power and Armies*—perhaps the best treatise on airpower theory written in English before World War II. This chapter traces the evolution of RAF doctrine between the wars, highlighting the special contributions of Hugh Trenchard and John Slessor.

Britain, like all other belligerents, entered the Great War with a small number of rudimentary aircraft but little or no doctrine on how to employ them effectively. Over the course of the next few years, the RAF, which became a separate service in 1918, grew to be the largest and most effective air arm in the world. Although airpower played a peripheral role throughout the conflict, its potential captivated the imagination of the public, politicians, and military thinkers. They were particularly enthusiastic over one particular aspect of airpower's many roles and purposes—strategic bombing. The actual experiences of the bomber forces—scanty though they were—constituted a source of debate for the next two decades.

In World War I, Germany waged the first systematic strategic air campaign in history. Beginning in early 1915, rigid airships—zeppelins—began making the long nighttime journey from their sheds on the North Sea to drop bombs on military and industrial targets in Great Britain. At first, they conducted these attacks with impunity. But the British soon cobbled together fighter planes, artillery, and searchlights into a makeshift air defense system,[1] which was reasonably effective: the last great zeppelin attack of the war occurred on 19 October 1917, when five out of 11 airships went down.[2] The Germans thereafter concentrated on large, multiengined aircraft—Gothas and later Giants—that were faster and more maneuverable than the airships and thus considerably more difficult to intercept and shoot down.

It is difficult to exaggerate the fear, bordering on panic, that these bombing strikes caused among the British population and its government—for the next two decades. Because Britain had remained sheltered behind its impassable moat for centuries, this fear proved worse than it would have been for a country that had no such tradition of invulnerability. The psychological effect of losing this shield was enormous. As a consequence, the government appointed a well-known general, Jan Smuts of South Africa, to study the problem. Assisting him in this task was the commanding general of the Royal Flying Corps (RFC), Lt Gen David Henderson, a strong advocate of bombardment.

Smuts turned in two reports—one, a fairly straightforward plan for a well-organized and capable defensive network centered on London, and the other, a more theoretical treatise. In the latter, Smuts called for a separate air force that combined the units of the fleet (the Royal Naval Air Service [RNAS]) and the army (the RFC) into a single command. In words cited by airmen ever since, Smuts prophesied that "the day may not be far off when aerial operations with their devastation of enemy lands and destruction of industrial and populous centers on a vast scale may become the principal operations of war, to which the older forms of military and naval operations may become secondary and subordinate."[3]

Although officials had talked since the beginning of the war of combining the army and navy air arms into a single unit in the interests of efficiency and standardization, the German air attacks and the resultant recommendations of the Smuts report served as decisive catalysts. The RAF was established on 1 April 1918, charged with preventing further German incursions, while retaliating against Germany. Lord Rothermere assumed the new position of air minister, with Henderson his deputy. Maj Gen Hugh Trenchard, Henderson's subordinate as commanding general of RFC units in France, became chief of the Air Staff (CAS). The new arrangement proved unsatisfactory, however. By all accounts, Lord Rothermere was a difficult and erratic personality who understood little about airpower. Neither Henderson nor Trenchard could work with him effectively (although no one ever accused Trenchard of being easy to get along with). After continual and sterile strife, all three men resigned within a fortnight in April 1918. Rothermere and Henderson then disappeared from the military aviation scene. Sir William Weir became the new air minister, and Maj Gen Frederick Sykes the new CAS.

After a somewhat unseemly display of petulance, Trenchard was returned to France in May, only this time as commander of the newly created Independent Force (a rather unfortunate name).[4] Sykes, a proponent of strategic airpower, pushed this organization, which contained a contingent of bomber squadrons pulled from other units in France. It was designed to carry the war to Germany both day and night. In one sense, this move was quite a demotion for Trenchard (he now commanded barely 10 percent of the British air units in France), but in another sense, it forced him to concentrate on the mission of strategic bombing—an effort that would have significant, long-term consequences.

Early in the war, Trenchard's thoughts on airpower had begun to coalesce into the form they would take so forcefully in the interwar years. In a memo of September 1916, he wrote that the aeroplane was an inherently offensive weapon: "Owing to the unlimited space in the air, the difficulty one machine has in seeing another, the accidents of wind and cloud, it is impossible for aeroplanes, however skillful and vigilant their pilots, however powerful their engines, however mobile their machines, and however numerous their formations, to prevent hostile aircraft from crossing the line if they have the initiative and determination to do so."[5]

This basic concept would remain a recurring theme among air theorists up to the present, but Trenchard's emphasis contained a unique single-mindedness bordering on stubbornness. Because the aeroplane was an offensive weapon, one had to guide it "by a policy of relentless and incessant offensiveness":[6] the deeper that British planes flew into German territory, the better—regardless of losses incurred or physical damage caused. Trenchard believed that the *act* of the offensive was essential because it granted a "moral superiority" to the attackers. This attitude—the aerial equivalent of French Plan XVII—explains not only why Field Marshal Douglas Haig thought so highly of Trenchard, but also why he acquired the reputation as a stubborn and uncaring commander who needlessly threw away the lives of his men in a vicious battle of attrition every bit as deadly as the one conducted on the surface.[7]

Obviously, the question of precisely how one should use aircraft offensively behind German lines was crucial. Trenchard argued that, first, one had to attack enemy airfields to keep the Germans out of the sky and thus ensure air superiority for the Allies. Like his successors, Trenchard realized the essentiality of air superiority for the successful conduct of military operations.[8] Beyond that, the general insisted that air operations be conducted in conjunction with the ground effort. The situation for the British army throughout the war was precarious, and Trenchard realized the importance of the air arm's protecting the fragile forces of Haig. Consequently, he envisioned an air campaign focusing on what today we would term "interdiction" targets: railroad marshaling yards, bridges, supply depots, and road networks that provided men and material for the front. As he phrased it, "I desire to emphasize that operations conducted by bombing squadrons cannot be isolated from other work in the air, and are inseparable from the operations of the Army as a whole. . . . If an offensive is being undertaken on the ground, the work of bombing machines should be timed and co-ordinated so as to produce the maximum effect on the enemy."[9]

In addition, Trenchard foresaw possibilities of more overarching value for strategic bombing and singled out several industries as particularly important: iron and coal mines, steel mills, chemical production facilities, explosive factories, miscellaneous armament industries, aero engines and magneto works, submarine and shipbuilding works, large gun foundries, and engine repair shops. Significantly, he selected many of these targets on the basis of their large size and easy identification; blast furnaces, for example, had one-hundred-foot towers, and their fiery ovens could be seen for many miles at night.[10] The problems of navigation and target identification hinted at here would continue for the next several decades.

In his official report soon after the war, Trenchard reiterated his previous stance that the aerial needs of the British army in France had had first priority, but after his air forces met those needs, the bombing of Germany became "a necessity." Its objective was to achieve "the breakdown of the German army in Germany, its government, and the crippling of its sources of supply." Recognizing that he had insufficient forces to collapse the German industry, he nonetheless attempted to hit as many different factories as possible as often as possible, so that no one felt secure anywhere within range of his bombers. Using a subjective and unprovable statistic that earned him much (largely deserved) ridicule, Trenchard stated that the psychological effects of bombing outweighed the material effects at a ratio of 20 to one.[11] During its short life, the Independent Force flew all of its missions against targets with military significance.[12] Thus, one must understand that Trenchard did not advocate the bombing of German population centers with the intention of causing a popular revolt (the concept put forward by his contemporary in Italy, Gen Giulio Douhet). Rather, Trenchard implied that the act of bombardment in general—and the destruction of selected German factories in particular—would have a devastating effect on the morale of the workers and, by extension, the German people as a whole. He had seen such effects in Britain as a result of German air attacks and was profoundly influenced by them. He would articulate this concept more clearly in the years leading up to World War II.

Some critics later argued that Trenchard's enthusiasm for strategic bombing did not develop until after the war. Further, they maintained that during the war, he remained an implacable foe not only of strategic bombing but also of a separate RAF and the Independent Force that it spawned. These accusations are inaccurate. In October 1917 Trenchard proposed the combination of the RNAS and the RFC into a single service under an air secretary and an air chief of staff. The following month, he stated that "long distance bombing . . . ought to be vigorously developed as part and parcel of the

Royal Flying Corps." He repeated this call for a strategic air offensive in a memo of June 1918.[13]

Trenchard was aware, however, of the difficulties experienced by British aircraft manufacturers. Airplane losses in France were so high that production could not keep pace. He did not wish to deprive combat units of machines in order to establish the new strategic air force. Frederick Sykes argued that a "margin" of excess aircraft produced by the manufacturers would allow formation of the Independent Force without hurting the combat situation on the western front. Trenchard disagreed that such a margin existed. Therefore, one can better understand his reluctance to assume command of the Independent Force by recalling his devotion to Haig and the British army.

In 1918 ground forces were paramount, and Trenchard neither advocated nor approved of air operations divorced from the ground situation. In addition, as Trenchard himself later maintained, his bombers had neither the range nor the mass to carry out effective strategic strikes (barely one-third of the Independent Force missions struck targets in Germany). Consequently, he objected to dividing up limited air resources, some for army operations, some for fleet defense, and still others for long-range bombing: "I believe the air is one."[14] He perceived an evolutionary path for airpower and recognized the folly of moving too far too quickly.

Trenchard was not unusual in this regard. In America, Billy Mitchell, Ben Foulois, and Hap Arnold all made similar intellectual journeys from skepticism to advocacy. The fact that Trenchard refused to accept the exaggerated claims of men like Sykes and Smuts was more a sign of measured maturity than of fickleness.

After a victorious war effort, the military forces of democracies typically do not simply demobilize—they disintegrate. For example, by March 1919 the RAF had dropped from a force of some 22,000 aircraft and over 240,000 personnel to only 28 understrength squadrons (about two hundred planes) manned by fewer than 30,000 people. The plight of the RAF seemed especially wobbly when Prime Minister David Lloyd George decided in early 1919 to combine the Ministry of War and Ministry of Air into a single unit. Fortunately for the RAF, the man chosen to head this combined ministry—and presumably oversee the demise of the infant RAF—was Winston Churchill.

A former army officer who had headed the Admiralty during the first year of the war, Churchill nonetheless possessed an unusually flexible mind that remained open on the question of airpower. He did not, however, get on well with Frederick Sykes, who exacerbated matters by submitting a plan shortly after the armistice that called for an enormous air force—fully 154 squadrons, exclusive of training units—deployed through-out the empire. In a war-weary Britain strapped for funds, such a proposal was fanciful at best and irresponsible at worst.[15] Sykes, therefore, was nudged into retirement, and Trenchard—who had served with Churchill in India many years before—was brought back as CAS. More than any other factor, this decision saved the RAF as a separate service.

Trenchard has had many detractors, but few would deny his ability as a bureaucratic infighter. Given the weakness and unsettled nature of his service; his relatively junior rank; his lack of a strong faction in Parliament, the press, or the public; and his notoriously poor writing and public speaking skills; his ability to get his way with the government and the other services was remarkable.

When the government slashes funds, interservice rivalries tend to flare as the military arms begin to scramble for an adequate share of a severely shrinking budget—as was the case in postwar Britain. Determining who threw the first punch is difficult, but relations between Trenchard and his service counterparts—Field Marshal Henry Wilson and Adm David Beatty—were stormy, bordering on rude. Wilson and Beatty made no secret of their desire to disband the RAF and restore its airplanes (few though they were) to the army and fleet from whence they came. For his part, Trenchard fought back by noting the high cost in sterling and lives of traditional war making, costs dramatically reduced through airpower.

For example, one Air Ministry pamphlet suggested the existence of "certain responsibilities at present assigned to the Navy and Army which the Air Force is *already* technically capable of undertaking, and for which it may be found economical in the near future to substitute to a greater or lesser extent air units for military or naval units" (emphasis in

48

original).[16] When the army and navy continued to push to disband the RAF in the interests of economy, the CAS responded in a wonderfully Trenchardesque style: "The Field Marshal wishes to lay axe to the roots, as by doing so he thinks he may the easier obtain the fruit. What is wanted in order that the maximum amount of fruit may be got for our money is a severe pruning of the overhead fruitless branches of some of the neighboring trees which are at present crowding out the younger and more productive growth and thereby preventing its vigorous expansion to full maturity."[17]

Given the increasingly heated verbal and bureaucratic sparring, it is surprising that Trenchard was able to win a major concession from Beatty and Wilson in late 1921. Catching them off guard and appealing to their sense of fair play, Trenchard convinced them to cease attacking his service for one year while he attempted to organize his fledgling command and make their struggle a more equal one.[18] The two men later regretted their decision, because Trenchard used that time to solidify his power, establish the RAF on a strong organizational and administrative footing, and devise a use for the air weapon that would ensure its survival as a separate service—air control of colonial territories.

Administering the world's largest empire was an expensive and labor-intensive enterprise, each colony requiring a garrison of sufficient size to maintain peace and order. In the aftermath of the war, such an expense caused consternation in the British government. In mid-1919, therefore, Trenchard suggested to Churchill that the RAF be given the opportunity to subdue a festering uprising in Somaliland. Churchill agreed. The results were dramatic: the RAF chased the rebel ringleader, "the mad mullah," out of the area and pacified Somaliland at a cost of £77,000 rather than the £6 million it would have cost for the two army divisions originally planned.

As a consequence, the demand for air control grew quickly, and over the next decade the RAF deployed—with varying degrees of success—to Iraq, Afghanistan, India, Aden, Transjordan, Palestine, Egypt, and Sudan.[19] The strategy employed in these campaigns involved patrolling the disputed areas, flying political representatives around to the various tribes to discuss problems and devise solutions, issuing ultimatums to recalcitrants if persuasion failed, and as a last resort, bombing selected rebel targets to compel compliance. To be sure, these air operations were neither grand nor glorious, but they kept the RAF alive while it sought a more suitable foe.

This foe seemed to present itself in 1922, when continual arguments between Britain and France over occupation policy, trade, and colonial issues bubbled to the surface. For centuries, these two countries had been bitter rivals, and more recent cooperation had not yet hardened into goodwill and a meeting of the minds. Displeasure with France turned to concern when the government received an intelligence report that showed a great and growing superiority in French air strength. France allegedly had an air force of 123 squadrons comprised of 1,090 aircraft and planned to expand to 220 squadrons of over two thousand aircraft—nearly 10 times the size of the RAF. To make matters worse, 20 of the RAF's 28 squadrons were stationed overseas, leaving a mere two fighter squadrons to defend the British Isles.[20]

Studies done by the RAF speculated that if half the projected French air force struck London, it could deliver one hundred tons of bombs in the first 24 hours, 75 tons in the second 24 hours, and 50 tons each day thereafter. Using the experience of the German air attacks on London during the Great War as a guide, Britain could expect to suffer an average of 50 casualties for each ton of bombs dropped (17 killed and 33 wounded). That is, French air strikes would cause over 20,000 casualties in the first week of war. A maximum effort by the French would double those figures.[21]

Although British leaders did not seriously believe that war with France would occur, they were concerned that the capability of their own air force had fallen so far so quickly. In addition, they realized that such military weakness could have other negative effects. During the Ruhr crisis of 1922, Harold Balfour stated, "Mere fear of war in quite conceivable circumstances greatly weakens British diplomacy and may put temptation in the way of French statesmen that they would find it hard to resist."[22] As one might expect, Trenchard encouraged such thinking, but as one observer put it, "Trenchard exploited the government's fears but he did not create them."[23] As a consequence, Parliament moved to expand the RAF by adding 52 squadrons by 1928, specifically designated for the air defense of Great Britain. Fiscal realities would prevent the realization of this force, but its prospect caused the RAF to begin thinking seriously about how best to employ such a sizable air force.

Trenchard's views on the importance of strategic airpower had solidified since the war, due to several factors: Britain no longer maintained an army in Flanders dependent on airpower for its survival; aircraft capabilities had increased; and the RAF needed a separate mission if it intended to remain a separate service. The possibility of a genuine Continental menace helped to crystallize Trenchard's thoughts on that separate mission. One finds commendable his flexibility of mind in shifting so quickly and effectively from one strategic scenario to another.

Trenchard carried three main beliefs with him from the war: air superiority was an essential prerequisite to military success; airpower was an inherently offensive weapon; and although its material effects were great, airpower's psychological effects were far greater. In a speech on 13 April 1923, he fleshed out these ideas: "In the next great war with a European nation the forces engaged must first fight for aerial superiority and when that has been gained they will use their power to destroy the morale of the Nation and vitally damage the organized armaments for supplies for the Armies and Navies." He then expanded on the importance of the morale factor: war was a contest between the "moral tenacity" of two countries, and "if we could bomb the enemy more intensely and more continually than he could bomb us the result might be an early offer of peace." Significantly, Trenchard did not claim that an air campaign by itself would bring victory in war against a major European foe; rather, it would create the conditions necessary "in which our Army can advance and occupy his territory."[24]

Regarding the belief that airpower was essentially offensive, the CAS used the example of a football match: a team may not lose if it spends all its efforts defending its own goal, but it certainly will not win. In air war the offense—not the defense—was the stronger form of war. He did concede, however, that some form of defense (interceptors and antiaircraft guns) could be useful "for the morale of our own people." In a typical bit of British sangfroid, Trenchard commented, "Nothing is more annoying than to be attacked by a weapon which you have no means of hitting back at."[25] In practical terms, this meant as many bombers as possible and as few fighters as necessary.

The ratio eventually arrived at was two to one. Thus, of the 52 squadrons designated for "home defense," fully 35 were to be bombardment.[26] Interestingly, this force ratio seemingly caused little debate at the time or, indeed, throughout most of the interwar period. Unlike the situation in the American Air Corps, where fighter advocates like Claire Chennault argued vociferously for reduced emphasis on the bomber, no such open debate occurred in the RAF. Not until the late 1930s and the ascendance of Hugh Dowding at Fighter Command did anyone seriously question Trenchard's fundamental principles regarding force structure.

The real key to the concept of strategic airpower espoused by Trenchard was the selection of targets. By this time, he had changed his views on the desirability of attacking enemy airfields in an effort to gain air superiority. During the war, the Independent Force had directed fully 40 percent of its strikes against airfields, but these attacks had slight effect. As a result, he now envisioned a great air battle taking place between opposing air forces. When one side gained the upper hand, it would then concentrate on paralyzing the enemy nation and breaking its morale.

Precisely how did he expect the morale of an enemy to break? Like most airmen, he was frustratingly vague on this issue. Airpower was simply too new, and one sensed rather than understood the possibilities it offered to wage war in a fashion previously impossible. At its worst, such vagueness took the form of an address by Trenchard in October 1928: "The objectives to be attacked will be centres which are essential for the continuance of the enemy's resistance. They will vary frequently and the air forces will be directed against the one which at the moment is the best for air attack."[27] In another instance, he maintained that air attack would "induce the enemy Government, by pressure from the population, to sue for peace, in exactly the same way as starvation by blockading the country would enforce the Government to sue for peace."[28] When pushed for specificity, he referred to "centres of communication" such as roads, rail lines, telephone exchanges, and munitions factories.[29]

Because Trenchard typically proved inadequate at expressing his strongly held beliefs regarding targeting, he left it to his staff officers—his "English merchants"—to translate his rumblings into prose. In addition, he relied on two other avenues to formalize and institutionalize his beliefs on airpower: RAF doctrine manuals and the Royal Air Force Staff College.[30]

In July 1922 the RAF published its first doctrine manual, CD 22—titled simply *Operations*. To a great extent, CD 22 echoed the ideas Trenchard had expounded since 1917, noting that air forces must cooperate with surface forces because often the objective of a campaign was "the destruction of the enemy's main forces." It also stressed the importance of morale in war and the idea that victory occurred when one imposed so much pressure on the people they would "force their government to sue for peace." Regarding the importance of air superiority, it argued that other targets were subsidiary and that one should not attempt them until one had inflicted "a serious reverse" on the enemy air force.[31]

The issue of which targets would most effectively achieve the anticipated moral effects was, as usual, unstated, although it did refer to naval bases, munitions factories, and railway junctions.[32] The manual did, however, point out that bombing attacks were to be carried out in accordance with international law. Attacking "legitimate objectives" in populated areas was permissible, although one must take "all reasonable precautions" to spare hospitals and other privileged buildings.[33] This issue became the subject of much contention in the years ahead.

Although air policing remained a major RAF mission between the wars, the service did not want to hang its doctrinal hat on this mission since it garnered no glory and generated little force structure. CD 22 contained a chapter titled "Aircraft in Warfare against an Uncivilized Enemy" but clearly considered such operations of far less importance than conventional air warfare. The long-term effects of such air control operations on RAF thinking were mixed.

Operations remained official doctrine until July 1928, when it was superseded by AP 1300, *Royal Air Force War Manual,* a more sophisticated effort that discussed air strategy in a broader sense, yet reduced administrative and organizational material. Many of its arguments were the same as those in *Operations:* war was largely a psychological effort; airpower was an inherently offensive weapon; airpower would serve as part of a joint force in which all the services worked together to attain the government's objectives; at times, the most effective use of airpower was to defeat the enemy's army; and air superiority was crucial to military success.

The first major change concerned the sequence of the air superiority battle. Instead of directing that one resist all distractions until one decisively defeated the enemy air force, AP 1300 regarded the strategic bombing campaign as primary and the air superiority battle as a diversion.[34] This reversal from previous doctrine no doubt reflected a desire to avoid the counterforce battle. The Great War had degenerated into a bloody slugfest between opposing forces; airpower was supposed to eliminate—not perpetuate—that intermediate step to victory.

The most important aspect of AP 1300 was the extent to which it discussed the rationale behind strategic bombing and the selection of targets. The choice of bombing objectives depended on five factors: the nature of the war and the enemy; the general war plan of the government; diplomatic considerations; the range of the bombers; and the strength of the enemy air defenses. As a general rule, the manual opined that "objectives should be selected the bombardment of which will have the greatest effect in weakening the enemy resistance and his power to continue war."[35]

In some cases, this meant attacking the "vital centres" of an enemy country rather than assisting armies and navies directly. Vital areas included organized systems of production, supply, communications, and transportation: "If these are exposed to air attack, the continual interruption, delay and organization of the activities of these vital centres by sustained air bombardment will usually be the most effective contribution which can be made by air power towards breaking down the enemy's resistance."[36] Interestingly, the manual also noted that one needed in-depth understanding of an enemy country. Although AP 1300 did not use the term *economic intelligence*, that is precisely what it meant. Such intelligence, hitherto unnecessary in warfare, now became essential.

One should note that AP 1300 never referred to the bombing of population centers, suggesting targets of a military nature only. Yet, it repeated the decade-old adage that victory in war resulted from the collapse of civilian morale. How could one break the will of the people without bombing them? The formulation supplied by the Air Staff writers asserted that the bombing of industrial centers would destroy the factories that employed the workers. Loss of work would have a shattering effect on the work force—presumably due to dislocation and loss of salary—that would cascade throughout society.[37] Through this interesting though questionable logic, AP 1300 clearly advocated a strategy fundamentally different than that proposed by theorists such as Douhet, who deliberately targeted the population. Although both formulations sought a collapse of morale that would lead to a change in government policy, the methods of achieving that collapse differed, subtly though clearly.

Unquestionably, the RAF was sensitive about the issue of targeting morale. People outside the service did not understand the nuances of bombing theory noted above, and the RAF frequently had to defend itself against charges of making war on women and children. Because air control operations in the Middle East were especially misconstrued as bloody and remorseless attacks against defenseless natives, the RAF produced studies showing that far fewer people died, on both sides, in air operations than in traditional pacification efforts carried out by ground troops. For example, an examination of colonial campaigns between 1897 and 1923 indicates that over five thousand British soldiers lost their lives at a cost of nearly eight hundred tribesmen. Since the arrival of the RAF, however, friendly casualties numbered a mere dozen men, while native losses hovered between 30 and 40 killed. Moreover, one report illustrated the point by quoting from a 1920 British army directive to its troops in Mesopotamia: "Villages will be razed to the ground and all woodwork removed. Pressure will be brought on the inhabitants by cutting off water power and by destroying water lifts; efforts to carry out cultivation will be interfered with, and the systematic collection of supplies of all kinds beyond our actual requirements will be carried out, the area being cleared of the necessities of life."[38] This was hardly a policy of moderation.

Not content to criticize air control as immoral, some people charged that air bombardment in general was indiscriminate and in violation of international laws regarding the immunity of noncombatants. Repeatedly, RAF leaders decried any such intention. In a strongly worded and lengthy memo to the other service chiefs, Trenchard rejected claims that the RAF was intent on population bombing. Attacking legitimate objectives in populated areas was inevitable, and "writers on war of every nation have accepted it as axiomatic" that such targets can be struck. Terror bombing was "illegitimate," but it was a different matter "to terrorise munitions workers (men and women) into absenting themselves from work . . . through fear of air attack upon the factory or dock concerned." Trenchard's memo angrily concluded, "I emphatically do not advocate indiscriminate bombardment, and I think that air action will be far less indiscriminate and far less brutal and will obtain its end with far fewer casualties than either naval blockade, a naval bombardment, or sieges, or when military formations are hurled against the enemies' strongest points protected by barbed wire and covered by mass artillery and machine guns."[39]

Another senior air leader, Air Commodore Edgar Ludlow-Hewitt, stated flatly that population bombing amounted to "sheer unintelligent frightfulness based on the same kind of false doctrine which, in common with all attempts to win by terrorising civilians, has ended in failure. It is a senseless, inhuman method of warfare which I believe will never succeed against any nation of stamina and spirit."[40] Wing Commander Arthur Tedder (later Marshal of the Royal Air Force Lord Tedder) similarly argued, "Terrorising of enemy people as a whole by indiscriminate bombing does not comply with principles of concentration. It is morally indefensible, politically inexpedient and militarily ineffective."[41]

One must note that the RAF opposed bombing other than legitimate military targets not merely for humanitarian reasons. Public opinion played a significant role, as did the purely practical matter of urban bombing's inefficiency. Because gas warfare had been outlawed in 1925, the amount of high explosive necessary to cause significant damage to a major city was enormous. Given the modest size of the RAF and its bomber aircraft, pilots would do better to drop their payloads on specific targets. Moreover, Britain felt particularly vulnerable to air attack because its key center of gravity was, unquestionably, London. The concentration of political, financial, social, and industrial power in the London area made it the most valuable target in the country. Worse, its proximity to the English Channel put it within easy striking range of air bases on the Continent. The fear of a "bolt from the blue" against London preoccupied British political and military leaders from the early 1920s on.

In 1932 former prime minister Stanley Baldwin made his glum prediction that the bomber would always get through. He added his pessimistic assessment that the only way to prevent the destruction of one's cities was to bomb an enemy's even more viciously (Trenchard's maxim that the best defense is a good offense). In reality, Baldwin advocated no such thing. In fact, the week following this comment, he proposed at the Geneva Disarmament Conference the abolition of aerial bombardment. Obviously, he made this offer as much for strategic reasons as for humanitarian: because of the unusual vulnerability of Britain to air attack, it had more to gain from such a prohibition.[42] The point to note, however, is that British political and military leaders had little incentive to push for a city-busting air strategy; in fact, they advocated precisely the opposite.

The other method of articulating and then disseminating airpower concepts throughout the RAF involved the Staff College at Andover. Soon after the war, Trenchard realized that in a fundamental sense the RAF would stand or fall, based on how well it was run. As a separate service, it quickly had to develop the capability of organizing and administering its own affairs. As a consequence, he established three major schools in the first three years of peace: a technical school at Halton to train "aircraftmen" in specific mechanical skills; a cadet college at Cranwell, similar to Sandhurst, for educating young officers; and a staff college at Andover, like the army's at Camberley, to teach midcareer officers staff skills as well as give them a higher understanding of war. Trenchard referred to Andover, opened in 1922, as "the cradle of our brain."[43]

At the Staff College, a small faculty (originally five officers, all of whom later attained flag rank) presented lectures each morning, which the students (generally around 30 each year) then discussed in seminar. Reading requirements were not heavy, and students usually received a detailed outline of each lecture to help them prepare. Guest speakers from government, business, or other military services lectured frequently, usually in the evenings. Tactical air exercises were common, and each student had to write an essay on his experiences, the best of which were published each year and distributed throughout the RAF. Most of them dealt with air operations in the Great War. As time went on, more students wrote of air control activities in the Middle East. Further, the faculty and staff had at their disposal a handful of aircraft for refresher practice.[44]

In keeping with the RAF's need for competent staff officers who could work effectively in a joint environment, the curriculum—especially in the early years—emphasized administrative duties, tactics, and the missions and capabilities of the other services. For example, in the second class (1923–24) only about two weeks of the entire year's curriculum were devoted to air strategy.[45] Interestingly, however, the Staff College's first commandant, Air Commodore Robert Brooke-Popham, taught these lessons himself, thus lending considerable prestige to the subject and setting a precedent for all succeeding commandants prior to the war.[46]

Brooke-Popham had been a successful combat commander in France, so his reputation and seniority gave credibility to Andover. Although some of his ideas seem a bit bizarre today, his views on airpower were well thought out and compelling.[47] In his first lecture, the commandant argued that due to industrialization, the growth of democracy, and trade unionism, people as a whole were now more directly affected by war. Just as important, they were more able than in the past to influence or even stop a war via the vote or a strike. As a result, "it is now the will power of the enemy nation that has to be broken, and to do this is the object of any country that goes to war."[48] The first step in this process was to win air superiority. Unlike CD 22, which implied that this was an end in itself, Brooke-Popham cautioned that gaining control of the air was useful only in that it allowed an air attack on the vital centers. Because neutralization of such centers brought victory, air leaders should not lose sight of their true goal. These vital centers would vary, depending on the enemy—they might even be the armed forces—but the ultimate objective was to break the will of the enemy.

Regarding how one might best affect that will, the commandant took a slightly different view from the official line. If government policy called for bombing a town, he stated that "we must faithfully carry out any decision of our Government in the matter, even if such decisions be repugnant to our own private conceptions of morality." Such a "we must all be good soldiers" approach offered a dangerous loophole, quickly entered: "This being so, we must study how best to utilize such forms of violence."[49] Air Commodore Ludlow-Hewitt, Brooke-Popham's successor as commandant, echoed that sentiment: "War is a wild beast which when uncaged is soon out of control and running amuck. . . . Let us abolish war if we can, but so long as war is possible then we must face all that war entails."[50] Such a view can easily become a self-fulfilling prophecy—preparing for the worst because it may occur can help make it occur.

Ludlow-Hewitt's lectures on air strategy during his tenure as commandant were quite good. For example, he too realized that air superiority was essential, but one would have to fight for it. However, bringing the enemy to battle was difficult, because one could not fix the enemy in the sky as was the case on the ground. He therefore argued that one had to "find some way of drawing the enemy to some spot chosen by us." The obvious method used to coax the enemy into battle entailed "threaten[ing] something vital to his security."[51] Significantly, the Allies used this very "bait" technique in 1944 to bring the Luftwaffe to battle by attacking German aircraft factories and oil refineries.

The air commodore also went into some depth on the subject of targeting. Noting that the key areas of an enemy country would vary with circumstances, Ludlow-Hewitt nonetheless identified three major target sets in a modern, industrialized country: (1) the system of commerce, industry, and distribution—including food, munitions, ore deposits, and coal supplies; (2) communications, including not only land systems but also port facilities and harbors; and (3) industrial workers. The latter were particularly important: "If their morale can be tampered with or can be depleted—if their security can be endangered—their work will fall off in quantity and quality."[52] Paralleling the RAF doctrine manuals, Ludlow-Hewitt maintained that one could more likely achieve the collapse of morale "by crippling his industries, delaying his railways and stopping his ports than by spraying the whole population with bombs." He quickly noted, however, that the success of the air offensive resulted from selecting the proper targets, which in turn required a special intelligence that established an enemy's habits of life, mentality, political system, economic apparatus, communications systems, commodities flow, and so forth.[53] Unfortunately, although other air leaders echoed his calls for a robust intelligence network attuned to the needs of air warfare, little was done to establish it prior to the war.

Through the interwar years, other people at the Staff College addressed the issue of breaking the enemy's will. Arthur Tedder, an instructor in the early 1930s, noted the effect that one might expect from air strikes on industry: "Men driven off their tools, clerical staffs from their offices, work decelerated and finally stopped. Material ruined and operations interrupted. Consequent delay, and final complete dislocation and disorganization of systems attacked. Spread of panic. Bombardment of one area likely to stop work in others."[54] This was an air strategy of paralysis—not obliteration.

One should also note that the RAF carried out a number of major exercises during the interwar years, the first of which occurred in 1927. Others were held most years thereafter until World War II. The scenarios for these exercises were ostensibly defensive in nature—enemy countries like "Southland," "Red Colony," and "Caledonia" were set to attack, usually London. The air-defense-observer network, controllers, fighter squadrons, and searchlight units received a thorough workout, as well as the bomber units. In general terms, the purpose of the bombing strikes was "to break enemy national resistance by intensive air bombardment of the vital points in the economic and industrial systems." More specifically, the targets designated for these bombing units were military objectives that required precise application of force: the "seat of government," airfields, munitions factories, docks, arms depots, chemical industries, and power stations.[55]

One of Trenchard's bright young protégés who later attained high rank was Jack Slessor, also one of the more articulate and thoughtful airpower theorists. Unlike Douhet, Trenchard, and Billy Mitchell, who had begun their careers as army officers, Slessor started off as a flyer in 1915. One might wish to speculate on how the lack of army experience during his formative military years—and the backlash it seemed to incur in many airmen—affected his outlook on airpower. During the war, Slessor flew air defense in England, while also seeing combat in the Middle East (where he was wounded) and in France. Between 1931 and 1934, he was an instructor at the Army Staff College at Camberley. His seminal work, *Air Power and Armies,* is a collection of his lectures there, edited and compiled a few years later while he was stationed in India.

In assessing this book, one must remember, first, his audience at Camberley and, second, his admonitions—repeated throughout—that he is writing about a war in which the British army has already committed itself to a land campaign. Slessor acknowledged that a primary function of airpower is strategic bombing, but he intended to discuss how airpower could complement surface operations. Indeed, he chastened his readers that "no attitude could be more vain or irritating in its effects than to claim that the next great war—if and when it comes—will be decided in the air, and in the air alone."[56]

Readers of *Air Power and Armies* are struck by the fact that Slessor bases his arguments not only on logic—the method employed by most air theorists—but also on history. Noting that history enables commanders and staff officers "to be wise before the event," he relies heavily on the history of war, concentrating especially on the Great War and airpower's role in it. Most airmen of that era disdained history, perhaps because it seemed to teach the wrong lessons for airpower.

Responding to this tendency, Slessor wrote, "If there is one attitude more dangerous than to assume that a future war will be just like the last one, it is to imagine that it will be so utterly different that we can ignore all the lessons of the last one."[57] One of the lessons of that war, as indeed of those in the past four centuries, was that Britain had to maintain a balance of power in Europe. Specifically, the security of the country demanded that the low countries remain in safe hands—an issue worth fighting for.

Slessor believed that the character of war had changed dramatically. Unlike Douhet, he believed that trench stalemate was over. The advent of the tank and airplane meant that the static warfare of the western front was an aberration. In the future, small maneuver armies would dominate war. Clearly, his tour at Camberley had kept him abreast of the latest developments in mechanized warfare.[58] In addition—and not surprisingly—Slessor believed that airpower would play a key, perhaps dominant, role in future war. He saw it as the third revolution in warfare, behind gunpowder and machine guns. However, air was the most important development: although the first two allowed more efficient killing on the battlefield, "AIR may stop men or their supplies arriving at the battle-field at all" (emphasis in original).[59] In fact, he saw airpower as the antidote to modern weapons of surface warfare.

In keeping with the book's focus of assuming a land campaign, airpower's role was "to assist and co-operate with the army in the defeat of the enemy's army, and of such air forces as may be co-operating with it."[60] As will soon become clear, this translated into attacking the communications and supply lines of the enemy forces—interdiction—rather than conducting strategic air strikes against the enemy's vital centers. The first requirement for assisting the army, however, was obtaining air superiority, because without it, ground operations would fail. In fact, Slessor hinted that achieving air superiority may of itself cause the enemy to surrender, "but these are not the conditions which it is the object of this work to examine."[61] He realized, however, that air supremacy over an entire theater was unlikely and unnecessary due to the immensity of space. He therefore stressed the need for local air superiority, but even this was difficult and required constant maintenance. Air superiority was not a phase; it required persistence.

Slessor also emphasized that winning the air superiority campaign demanded initiative. Here he echoed the views of his mentor, Trenchard, by noting the importance of morale. One did not achieve victory by waiting for the enemy but by striking first and hard.[62] Slessor did not advocate the bombing of airfields, which he considered ineffective and at best a temporary nuisance; nor did he see much utility in air patrols. Such activities might prove useful, but the primary means of destroying the enemy air force remained air combat. One must bring the enemy air force to battle, but this could be difficult. Unlike armies that had to fight in order to achieve their objective of defeating the enemy army or preventing it from overrunning their country, air forces could avoid battle yet still bomb a country's vital centers.

Thus, one need not choose between air superiority and bombardment—one could wage both campaigns simultaneously. This ability to conduct parallel—not merely sequential—combat operations was one of the factors that differentiated airpower from surface forces. Even so, Slessor remained ambivalent about the air superiority campaign, arguing on the one hand that it was necessary but on the other that one should not see it as an end in itself. A line, fine though it might be, clearly existed between aggressively waging the battle for air superiority while also avoiding its distractions in order to conduct a more lucrative bombing

Slessor posited a war in which the British army had deployed to the Continent to secure the low countries from a hostile power. The initial stages of that joint campaign were therefore symbiotic: the army and navy secured a foothold and established air bases, and the air force then protected the surface forces from enemy attack. That done, one could carry out a strategic air campaign against the enemy's vital centers.[63] Unfortunately, Slessor declined to discuss the details of such an air campaign. Instead, he concentrated on the preliminary joint campaign, largely because he believed that airpower would not stop a major land assault by itself and that hitting strategic targets would not take effect quickly enough to prevent the British army from being overwhelmed. Therefore, air, land, and sea commanders had to cooperate to stop and perhaps drive back an enemy offensive.

Nonetheless, Slessor's general comments regarding a strategic air campaign are interesting. He had difficulty identifying the most lucrative targets; indeed, he recognized that most countries had several centers of gravity that might change over time. Unlike some theorists, he carefully avoided equating strategic bombing with a mechanistic destruction of target sets. One need not always obliterate the objective; rather, neutralization for a specific time period could be satisfactory. He used the example of a man's windpipe: it was not necessary to sever it; simply interrupting it for a few minutes would achieve the same result.

Further, Slessor lent only tepid support to morale bombing. Although he appreciated the importance of psychological pressure, he saw the reduction of industrial capacity as both more practical and more quantifiable. Also stressing the need for industrial intelligence, he called for detailed technical expertise to ensure effective targeting. In this regard, he was obviously hinting at the concept then under consideration by the American Air Corps—the analysis of industrial systems to identify weak points or "bottlenecks." In truth, these brief insights into strategic air warfare are intriguing. It is interesting to speculate on what type of book Slessor would have written had he instructed at Andover rather than Camberley.

But we must be content with the book Slessor did write. In it, he focused on the theater—what we now call the operational level of war—arguing that the neutralization of key nodes at that level would prevent effective operations. He decried people who advocated using airpower as "flying artillery." It was not a battlefield weapon; rather, he believed that one should attack the enemy repeatedly, as far from the battlefield as possible. In this regard, Slessor envisioned airpower as the key element in sealing off the enemy's forces and strangling them into submission. In short, he promoted interdiction as the primary air mission of air forces cooperating in a land campaign. In this regard he tended to favor supply interdiction (material and equipment) over force interdiction (troops and combat vehicles), maintaining that movement by rail and road was virtually impossible in daylight for the side that had lost air superiority. One probably could not cut off all supplies and communications but could severely curtail them.

Moreover, as with strategic air warfare, he argued that the goal should be paralysis—not destruction.[64] Significantly, Slessor recognized that truly effective interdiction required cooperation between air and ground units. He even opined that some occasions required the detailing of ground forces to support the air effort—a heretical belief among most ground officers at the time. Finally, he argued that airpower must be commanded and directed by an airman who was equal in authority to the ground commander. These two individuals and their staffs would collaborate in the design and implementation of the theater commander's overall plan. Notably, he speculated that the theater commander could be an airman.

Although Slessor cautioned against extensive use of airpower in a tactical role, he did offer some guidelines for occasions requiring such operations. The first requirement was air superiority—as was the case with all air missions. Second, even more than in interdiction operations, the air and ground commanders had to coordinate their efforts closely—if possible, their headquarters should be collocated. Because of the proximity of friendly troops, one could not tolerate mistakes. After careful planning, one could use airpower tactically in three different situations: in attack to facilitate a breakthrough; in pursuit to turn victory into rout; and in defense to prevent an enemy breakthrough on the ground.

Slessor's later career and writings make clear that he was an advocate of strategic airpower. (One arrives at the same conclusion after examining his attitude towards Trenchard, as revealed in *Air Power and Armies*.) Indeed, several hints dropped throughout his book suggest that he wanted to write about strategic airpower. The fact that his army audience would have none of it, however, compelled him to write a book that assumed a land campaign. *Air Power and Armies* stands as perhaps the best treatment of this subject written in English before World War II.

The book features several notable aspects: his detailed discussion of air superiority—what it is, how one gains it, and when one needs to maintain it; his emphasis on the need for specialized air intelligence; and his detailed discussion of an army's center of gravity—its supply lines. Slessor argued that one wasted airpower by using it merely as a tactical weapon when cooperating in a land campaign; rather, airpower should concentrate on the disruption, destruction, and neutralization of enemy armaments and supplies—interdiction. Given his penetrating examination—despite his fairly convoluted prose—it is most unfortunate that Slessor did not write a companion volume on strategic air war. (His many writings after World War II are concerned primarily with nuclear deterrence and the situation in Europe.)

In a sense, Slessor's masterful volume served as a transition between the RAF of the post–World War I era and the RAF of the pre–World War II era. The rise of Nazi Germany, "the ultimate potential enemy," forced air leaders to begin planning for a genuine military threat, not just an inconvenient diplomatic nuisance as in the decade previously. As a consequence, the RAF went through a period of frenzied planning and expansion that would last the remainder of the decade. Although the Air Ministry and the government tended to focus on these various expansion schemes—fertile fields for historians—the operational RAF went about its business of thinking through the matter of war fighting. This effort culminated in a new edition of AP 1300 written during peace but published soon after the outbreak of war.

The new manual again stressed national will as the key to war: "A nation is defeated when its people or Government no longer retain their will to prosecute their war aim."[65] Several factors buttressed this will: the armed forces, manpower, the economic system, and finances. The purpose of military forces was, therefore, to defeat enemy forces in battle, starve the people into submission through blockade, or instill a sense of "war weariness" in them by disrupting their normal lives—considered the true path to victory for airpower. As before, the method advanced to effect this disruption was bombing the enemy industrial and economic infrastructure, such as public utilities, food and fuel supplies, transportation networks, and communications. Hopefully, the destruction of such targets would cause "a general undermining of the whole populace, even to the extent of destroying the nation's will to continue the struggle."[66] One notes the muted hope that bombing would make a bloody land campaign unnecessary.

AP 1300 also increased its emphasis on air defense, finally acknowledging the necessity and even desirability of both active and passive measures. In truth, this trend had been in motion for some years, largely imposed on the RAF from without. The argument that the best defense was a good offense fell out of favor as the Luftwaffe grew increasingly powerful from 1935 onwards. Intelligence predictions regarding the size of the German air force—and worse, its superior production rate—forced Britain to reevaluate its air strategy. At the same time, however, the British economy remained depressed and unable to keep pace with German expansion.

In 1937 Thomas Inskip was appointed minister for the coordination of defense, with guidance to check the rising defense budget. Although often vilified for his stringent fiscal policy in the face of a looming German threat, Inskip did reorient military aircraft production. Three fighters could be built for every bomber, so—given the possibilities offered by the new communications warning net and especially the dramatic breakthroughs in the field of radar—Inskip gave priority to the production of fighter aircraft.[67] The notion that bombers could strike virtually anywhere, anytime, from any direction, and achieve tactical surprise was no longer viable: bombers could be detected, intercepted, and stopped. The new fighter planes on the horizon, the Hurricane and Spitfire—fast, maneuverable, and heavily armed—promised to tip the balance of the air battle once again against the bomber. As a consequence, strong air defenses combined with hundreds of new fighters were in place in England by 1940: Air Chief Marshal Hugh Dowding's Fighter Command was ready for the Battle of Britain. The new war manual belatedly ratified these developments.[68]

As in previous manuals, AP 1300 took pains to stress that although the civilian populace was more involved than ever in the business of war, it was not, as such, a legitimate target. Consequently, the manual rejected area bombing: "All air bombardment aims to hit a particular target," and in every case "the bombing crew must be given an exact target and it must be impressed upon them that it is their task to hit and cause material damage to that target."[69] Nonetheless, even if "the people" were not targets, "the workers" most certainly were, because they put weapons in the hands of soldiers and because they had a decisive grip on the actions of political leaders. The point in attacking certain industries was thus not only to destroy the tools with which the enemy waged war, but to instill such fear in the people making the tools that they simply refused to show up for work. Hence, one should attack factories when the maximum number of workers are present.

This scrupulous regard for precise targeting of specific military objectives was not just for public consumption. The air targets committee in the Air Ministry looked closely at potential target sets in Germany and prepared an extensive list of suitable possibilities—specific military objectives such as oil, gas, electricity, chemicals, explosives, nonferrous metals, ferro alloys, the aircraft industry, iron and steel, roller bearings, raw materials, transportation, and optical glass. Seemingly, foodstuffs constituted an exception to this list, but they were a traditional objective of naval blockade and thus well established as a legitimate target in international law.[70]

In addition, a classified study written in 1938 by the Air Staff and endorsed by Air Commodore Slessor (now director of plans), spelled out RAF bombing policy. The document noted that no internationally agreed-upon laws regarding air warfare existed—conferences convened since the turn of the century had failed to reach agreement. Consequently, air warfare tended to follow the same rules as did war at sea (which were much less restrictive than those for land warfare). The key legal tenet guiding air leaders forbade the deliberate bombing of civilian populations: "A direct attack upon an enemy civil population . . . is a course of action which no British Air Staff would recommend and which no British Cabinet would sanction."[71]

The Air Staff, however, worried that other countries did not share Britain's traditional respect for law. Specifically, one could hardly rely upon Nazi Germany, which had driven "a coach and four through half a dozen international obligations," to keep its word regarding the largely unwritten rules of air bombardment. Britain must, therefore, maintain a defensive and offensive air capability that would prove effective, regardless of laws and agreements: "Expediency too often governs military policy and actions in war."[72] This parting caveat was prophetic because expediency did in fact later shape British bombing policy. But it seems clear that the RAF leadership going into the war had drawn a clear line regarding the issue. One should also note that at the same time, lectures at Andover followed the line described above almost exactly.[73] This policy carried over into the war.

The week before Germany invaded Poland, the CAS sent a letter to Bomber Command stating RAF policy in the clearest of terms: "We should not initiate air action against other than purely military objectives in the narrowest sense of the word, i.e., Navy, Army and Air Forces and establishments, and that as far as possible we should confine it to objectives on which attack will not involve loss of civil life."[74] During the campaign in France the following year, the CAS reiterated this policy in a classified message to all RAF commanders: the intentional bombing of civilian populations as such was illegal. One must identify the objectives in advance, attack with "reasonable care" to avoid undue loss of civilian lives in the vicinity of the target, and observe the provisions of international law.[75]

The CAS then elaborated on the thorny subject of what precisely constituted a "military objective," listing military forces; works; fortifications; barracks; depots; supply dumps; shipyards and factories engaged in the manufacture, assembly, or repair of military material, equipment, or supplies. Also included were power stations, oil refineries, and storage installations, as well as lines of communications and transportation serving military purposes. Following the provisions of international law regarding land warfare, the directive concluded that "provided the principles set out above are observed [regarding the prohibition of deliberately bombing the population] other objectives, the destruction of which is an immediate military necessity, may be attacked for particular reasons."[76]

To be sure, the motives for such restraint were not completely noble. Years of fiscal stringency had left the RAF with a small and marginally capable force. Although up to the task of air control, it lacked the mass and sophistication required to mount a strategic air campaign against a major power. The bewildering variety of expansion schemes that began in the mid-1930s as a result of Luftwaffe growth only confused matters in the short term by adding the requirement for simultaneous growth and training in new equipment. As a consequence, despite 20 years of doctrine that emphasized the primacy of offensive airpower, the RAF found itself woefully unprepared to conduct such operations once war broke out. The RAF therefore was unwilling to throw the first stone when it believed that the Luftwaffe had a larger supply of bricks near at hand.[77] In addition, Britain—already acutely aware of the necessity of maintaining the friendship and moral support of the United States—knew that indiscriminate bombing would quickly sour such relations.[78] Nonetheless, RAF doctrine and policy throughout the interwar years—indeed, for the first year of the war—consistently stressed the principle of avoiding civilian noncombatants while concentrating on enemy industry. Unfortunately, the propensity of RAF thinkers to link this industrial targeting strategy with the morale of the enemy nation caused untold confusion to outside observers then and since.

There is a tendency to read the history of Bomber Command in World War II backwards from Dresden in 1945 to Hugh Trenchard in 1919. Because Air Chief Marshal Arthur Harris carried out a ruthless and single-minded strategy of urban area bombing and because he was a protégé of Trenchard, many historians have seen a direct linkage between 1929, when Trenchard retired, and the assumption of command by Harris in 1942.[79] This connection seems plausible because the common term tying them together was *morale bombing*. Actually, the similarity is apparent rather than real.

Although RAF policy in the first year of the war followed the guidelines noted above, the pressure of war soon forced changes. France, indeed most of Europe, was now part of Hitler's empire; the British army had been thrown off the Continent at Dunkirk—leaving its heavy machinery behind; Axis forces were moving rapidly across North Africa; German submarines were sinking British shipping in the Atlantic at an alarming pace; London was suffering through the blitz; and British bombers had suffered such heavy losses in daylight that they had been driven to the relative safety of the night. In short, Britain was alone, outnumbered, outgunned, and desperate.

The choice of Arthur Harris to lead Bomber Command in this dark period was pivotal. Like Trenchard, he was single-minded in his determination. Seeing no alternative, Harris initiated an urban bombing campaign against Germany's major cities, aiming to destroy German morale by targeting residential areas where the workers lived. The abysmal accuracy of Bomber Command at night would have produced such area attacks anyway—intentional or not. Like Trenchard in World War I, Harris persisted in this strategy—even when greater accuracy became possible in 1944—with a stubbornness that earned him criticism by the end of the war. Peace and the revelation of the destruction leveled on Germany only exacerbated this feeling. As a result, Trenchard and prewar RAF leaders have been tarred with the urban bombing brush, although inaccurately.

Trenchard and his successors viewed the collapse of enemy morale as the ultimate goal, but the mechanism used to achieve that goal was the destruction or disruption of enemy industry—a legitimate military target under the laws of war. This belief was consistently reflected in the RAF's doctrine manuals, in the courses at the Staff College that its most promising officers attended, in the major exercises the RAF conducted in the 1920s and 1930s, and in the prewar guidance of its senior leaders.

RAF doctrine, which expanded and codified Trenchard's beliefs, thus constituted a unique strain of airpower theory that combined key concepts of the other two major schools of strategic bombing in the interwar years—those of Douhet and the instructors at the Air Corps Tactical School (ACTS) at Maxwell Field, Alabama. Douhet also believed that the ultimate objective in war was to destroy enemy morale, but he preached that one should do this by bombing the people directly with gas and incendiaries. But the officers at ACTS chose to concentrate on breaking the *capability* of the enemy to wage war, implementing this strategy by targeting the industrial infrastructure.

Quite simply, the RAF combined these two approaches, choosing the Douhetian objective of morale and the ACTS industrial targeting scheme. None of these three airpower theories proved completely accurate in World War II. One must remember, however, that the airplane was in its infancy and that there was very little experience upon which to base a theory of airpower. Airmen thus did the best they could, examining the history of warfare and of airpower in the Great War, calling upon their own aviation experience, and—most of all—relying on their own logic and imagination, unconstrained by temporary technological limitations.

The RAF thinker who emerges from the interwar years looking most prescient is Jack Slessor. His major study, though perhaps limited by external factors rather than his own beliefs, is the most balanced and judicious of all the treatises written about the new air weapon. The hope of air advocates that land and sea forces would play but a minor role in future war was, of course, not borne out, but Slessor barely hinted at that possibility. Instead, he presumed a major land war with a Continental power. In such a scenario, airpower was, at best, primus inter pares. Given the adolescent state of British airpower, this vision of future war was quite realistic. Even so, Slessor built his ideas on the shoulders of the man he respected and admired so deeply— Hugh Trenchard, the man who sustained his service in its bleak period after the Great War, presented a theory of strategic airpower that identified enemy morale as the key target, and then institutionalized those ideas through a series of doctrinal manuals. These precepts were subsequently taught and refined at another of Trenchard's creations—the RAF Staff College. Termed "the father of the RAF," Trenchard deserved this title, not only administratively and organizationally but also philosophically.

Notes

1. Interestingly, Lt John C. Slessor flew the first nighttime interception mission on 13 October 1915. He saw the zeppelin but never maneuvered

close enough to attack it. Marshal of the RAF Sir John Slessor, *The Central Blue: Recollections and Reflections* (London: Cassell, 1956), 10–14.

2. The German navy lost 53 of 73 airships built during the war, and the army lost 26 of 52. Approximately 49 percent of all aircrews assigned to airships were lost during the war—the worst casualty rate of any branch, including infantry. Peter Fritzsche, *A Nation of Fliers: German Aviation and the Popular Imagination* (Cambridge, Mass.: Harvard University Press, 1992), 50.

3. Lt Gen Jan C. Smuts, "The Second Report of the Prime Minister's Committee on Air Organisation and Home Defence against Air Raids," 17 August 1917, as quoted in Eugene M. Emme, ed., *The Impact of Air Power* (Princeton, N.J.: Van Nostrand, 1959), 35.

4. There are many accounts of these squabbles, and none of the principals emerge looking either statesmanlike or dignified. See especially H. Montgomery Hyde, *British Air Policy between the Wars, 1918–1939* (London: Heinemann, 1976); Andrew Boyle, *Trenchard: Man of Vision* (London: Collins, 1962); and Frederick Sykes, *From Many Angles* (London: George Harrap, 1942).

5. "Future Policy in the Air," 22 September 1916, Trenchard Papers, RAF Hendon, England, file CI/14. This memo was later published as a Royal Flying Corps pamphlet titled "Offence versus Defence in the Air," October 1917; a copy is located in Brooke-Popham Papers, Liddell Hart Archives, King's College, London, file IX/5/4.

6. Ibid.

7. Brig Gen Sefton Brancker, the deputy director of military aeronautics, made an astounding comment in this regard in a letter to Trenchard in September 1916: "I rather enjoy hearing of our casualties as I am perfectly certain in my own mind that the Germans lose at least half as much again as we do." Malcolm Cooper, *The Birth of Independent Air Power* (London: Allen & Unwin, 1986), 75.

8. "A Review of the Principles Adopted by the Royal Flying Corps since the Battle of the Somme," RFC pamphlet, 23 August 1917, Brooke-Popham Papers, Liddell Hart Archives, King's College, London, file IX/3/2.

9. "Long Distance Bombing," 28 November 1917, Trenchard Papers, RAF Hendon, England, file I/9.

10. "The Scientific and Methodical Attack of Vital Industries," 26 May 1918. This document is in the same file as the "Long Distance Bombing" memo noted above but is a fragment of a larger, unspecified document and is of a later date; see also "Memorandum on the Tactics to be Adopted in Bombing the Industrial Centres of Germany," 23 June 1918, Trenchard Papers, RAF Hendon, England, file I/10/4.

11. "Bombing Germany: General Trenchard's Report of Operations of British Airmen against German Cities," *The New York Times Current History*, April 1919, 152. Although a strategy of a geographically dispersed campaign appears to violate the principle of mass, Trenchard believed that

his forces were too small to cause catastrophic damage in any event, so opting for a psychological effect seemed wiser.

12. A list of all 350 strategic bombing missions conducted by the Independent Force and its predecessors between October 1917 and the armistice, excluding aerodrome attacks, is contained in H. A. Jones, *The War in the Air: Being the Story of the Part Played in the Great War by the Royal Air Force*, vol. 7, *Appendices* (Oxford: Clarendon Press, 1937), 42–84.

13. "Memorandum on Future Air Organisation, Fighting Policy, and Requirements in Personnel and Material," 2 October 1917, Trenchard Papers, RAF Hendon, England, file CI/14; "Long Distance Bombing"; and "On the Bombing of Germany," 23 June 1918, Trenchard Papers, RAF Hendon, England, file I/9.

14. Transcript of interview between Trenchard and H. A. Jones, 11 April 1934, Public Records Office, Kew, England, file AIR 8/179. This rationale is also developed at some length in John C. Slessor, *These Remain: A Personal Anthology* (London: Michael Joseph, 1969), 80–85.

15. Sykes, 558–61; and P. R. C. Groves, *Behind the Smoke Screen* (London: Faber & Faber, 1934), 253–59. Groves was the RAF's director of flying operations under Sykes in 1919.

16. "The Future of the Air Force in National and Imperial Defence," Air Ministry pamphlet, March 1921, Brooke-Popham Papers, Liddell Hart Archives, King's College, London, file IX/5/11, 13–14. One should also note that throughout most of the interwar period, the RAF received less than 20 percent of the defense budget.

17. Hugh Trenchard, memorandum to Henry Wilson, ca. 1920, Public Records Office, Kew, London, file AIR 8/2.

18. Boyle, 348–51; B. McL Ranft, ed., *The Beatty Papers*, vol. 2, *1916–1927* (Aldershot: Scolar Press, 1993), 84; and Malcolm Smith, *British Air Strategy between the Wars* (Oxford: Clarendon Press, 1984), 23. Naval air was generally slighted while it was part of the RAF, and the Admiralty complained that its legitimate aviation needs were not being met. It therefore insisted that naval aircraft be returned to fleet control, which indeed occurred in 1937.

19. "Notes on the History of the Employment of Air Power," August 1935, Public Records Office, Kew, England, file AIR 10/1367. For accounts of these operations, see David E. Omissi, *Air Power and Colonial Control: The Royal Air Force, 1919–1939* (New York: Saint Martin's, 1990); and Philip A. Towle, *Pilots and Rebels: The Use of Aircraft in Unconventional Warfare, 1919–1988* (London: Brassey's, 1989). The surprising success of these operations possibly fueled even further the RAF belief in the psychological effects of bombing.

20. "Minutes of Meetings and Memoranda of Sub-Committee on the Continental Air Menace," December 1921–March 1922, Public Records Office, Kew, England, file AIR 8/39.

21. "Staff Notes on Enemy Air Attack on Defended Zones in Great Britain," 28 May 1924, Trenchard Papers, RAF Hendon, England, file

CII/3/177–227. On average, the German attacks had caused 65 casualties per ton of bombs dropped in "crowded areas" and four casualties in "sparse" areas. The RAF used the compromise figure of 50.

22. As quoted by Air Vice Marshal A. S. Barratt in "Air Policy and Strategy," Staff College lecture, 14 February 1938, RAF Hendon, England, "16th Staff Course" file.

23. John Ferris, "The Theory of a 'French Menace,' Anglo-French Relations and the British Home Defence Air Force," *Journal of Strategic Studies* 10 (March 1987): 66.

24. Hugh Trenchard, "Buxton Speech," 13 April 1923, Trenchard Papers, RAF Hendon, England, file II/5/1–57.

25. Hugh Trenchard, "Speech at Cambridge University," 29 April 1925, Trenchard Papers, RAF Hendon, England, file CII/3/177–227. The Air Staff reviewed the threat from antiaircraft and concluded blithely that it was insignificant. Based on experience in the war, guns expended over 11,000 shells to down a single aircraft. Not only did that rate wear out an average of two gun barrels but if one added the cost of ground crews, lights, and so forth, each downed plane cost the defender over £50,000. Moreover, the Air Staff saw no improvements in artillery since the war, and increased aircraft speed and altitude capability would compensate for any improvements in the future. "Notes on Anti-Aircraft Gunnery," November 1926, Trenchard Papers, RAF Hendon, England, file CII/3/177–227.

26. "CAS Conference Minutes," 10 July 1923, Public Records Office, Kew, England, file AIR 2/1267; and "Air Staff Memo No. 11A," March 1924, Public Records Office, Kew, England, file AIR 8/71.

27. Hugh Trenchard, "Notes for Address by CAS to the Imperial Defence College on the War Aim of an Air Force," 9 October 1928, Trenchard Papers, RAF Hendon, England, file CII/4/1–47.

28. Hugh Trenchard, memorandum for the record [1923], Trenchard Papers, RAF Hendon, England, file CII/19/1.

29. Hugh Trenchard, "The Employment of the Home Defence Air Force," 3 February 1928, Trenchard Papers, RAF Hendon, England, file CII/4/1–47.

30. Another, less formal, avenue for disseminating ideas on airpower was through professional journals such as *RUSI* [Royal United Services Institute] *Journal* and *RAF Quarterly*. However, it is difficult to determine if RAF officers, especially senior leaders, ever read such journals. For a useful overview of this secondary source, see Robin Higham, *The Military Intellectuals in Britain, 1918–1939* (New Brunswick, N.J.: Rutgers, 1966).

31. RAF Manual CD 22, *Operations*, July 1922, Public Records Office, Kew, England, file AIR 10/1197, 5.

32. Ibid., 57.

33. Ibid., 58.

34. RAF Manual AP 1300, *Royal Air Force War Manual*, July 1928, Public Records Office, Kew, England, file AIR 10/1910, chap. 7. One should also note that the manual's cover stated that no reference would be made to

the use of gas in war due to international "engagements" on the subject to which Britain had subscribed.

35. Ibid., chap. 8.

36. Ibid.

37. Ibid.

38. "The Fallacies of 'Inhumanity' and 'Rancour,' " Staff College lecture, n.d., Bottomley Papers, RAF Hendon, England, file B2244; see also "Air Control: The Other Point of View," Staff College lecture, May 1931, Bottomley Papers, RAF Hendon, England, file B2241; and "Psychological Effects of Air Bombardment on Semi-Civilized Peoples," 7 February 1924, Public Records Office, Kew, England, file AIR 8/71.

39. Hugh Trenchard, "The War Object of an Air Force," 2 May 1928, Public Records Office, Kew, England, file AIR 9/8. A slightly different version of this memo is found in the Trenchard Papers, RAF Hendon, England, file CII/4/1–47.

40. Edgar Ludlow-Hewitt, "Direct Air Action," Staff College lecture, n.d., Bottomley Papers, RAF Hendon, England, file B2274. Ludlow-Hewitt was the commander in chief of RAF Bomber Command at the outbreak of World War II.

41. Arthur Tedder, "Aim in Air Warfare," Staff College lecture, n.d., Tedder Papers, RAF Hendon, England, file B270.

42. This is the major theme of Uri Bialer's *The Shadow of the Bomber: The Fear of Air Attack and British Politics, 1932–1939* (London: Royal Historical Society, 1980).

43. One of the great surprises of RAF historiography is that the role of the Staff College in doctrine formulation and education is scarcely mentioned. The paucity of records probably explains this gap. Only scattered documents and lectures remain, and no official history exists. Allan D. English, however, has written a useful article (based on his master's thesis), "The RAF Staff College and the Evolution of British Strategic Bombing Policy, 1922–1929," *Journal of Strategic Studies* 16 (September 1993): 408–31. For a good overview, see Wing Commander R. A. Mason, "The Royal Air Force Staff College, 1922–1972," unpublished manuscript in Staff College library, RAF Bracknell, England, 1972.

44. Mason, 9–12.

45. As noted above, the records of the Staff College (most are located in the archives at RAF Hendon, England) are spotty. However, files for each year contain a syllabus covering the entire program and an assortment of lectures that were presented. In truth, the "archivist" seems to have used no discernable system in determining which lectures to preserve; rather, he evidently chucked whatever he found into the file. Nonetheless, reviewing the files for each year gives one a reasonable insight into the curriculum in general and the treatment of some individual subjects in particular.

46. Not all of the commandants' lectures remain, but based on those extant, the best are those of Air Marshals Edgar Ludlow-Hewitt (1927–30) and Robert Brooke-Popham (1922–26).

47. Brooke-Popham had a large library of military history and theory (over six hundred volumes), which he donated to the Staff College when he left. He was an old-fashioned gentleman, and in 1922 he told his students, "I hope I shall not be accused of harping too much on the question of horses. I know there are good men who don't hunt and bad men who do, but I am certain that every man is improved by hunting or even by keeping a horse and riding it." Mason, 6.

48. Robert Brooke-Popham, "The Nature of War," Staff College lecture, 6 May 1925, Public Records Office, Kew, England, file AIR 69/6.

49. Robert Brooke-Popham, "Policy and Strategy," Staff College lecture, 6 May 1925, Public Records Office, Kew, England, file AIR 69/6.

50. Edgar Ludlow-Hewitt, "The Object in Warfare," Staff College lecture, 1928, Bottomley Papers, RAF Hendon, England, file B2274.

51. Edgar Ludlow-Hewitt, "Air Warfare," Staff College lecture, 1928, Bottomley Papers, RAF Hendon, England, file B2274.

52. Edgar Ludlow-Hewitt, "Direct Air Action," Staff College lecture, 1928, Bottomley Papers, RAF Hendon, England, file B2274.

53. Ibid.

54. Arthur Tedder, "The War Aim of the Air Force," Staff College lecture, 1934, Tedder Papers, RAF Hendon, England, file B270.

55. "Report on Air Exercises, 1932," Public Records Office, Kew, England, file AIR 10/1523. For exercises from other years, see also 1929, AIR 20/157; 1931, AIR 9/64; 1932, AIR 20/172; 1934, AIR 2/1398; and 1935, AIR 9/64. For an overview of several of these exercises, see Scot Robertson, *The Development of RAF Strategic Bombing Doctrine, 1919–1939* (Westport, Conn.: Praeger, 1995).

56. Wing Commander John C. Slessor, *Air Power and Armies* (Oxford: Oxford University Press, 1936), 214.

57. Ibid., x.

58. Slessor was awarded the Royal United Services Institute gold medal for his essay "Combustion Engines in the British Army," *RUSI Journal* 82 (August 1937): 463–84.

59. Slessor, *Air Power and Armies*, 200.

60. Ibid., 1. One finds further evidence of his broad view of joint operations in his essay "The Co-Ordination of the Future Services," *RUSI Journal* 76 (November 1931): 752–55.

61. Slessor, *Air Power and Armies*, 28.

62. In today's parlance, Slessor was advocating "offensive counterair operations" versus the more passive "defensive counterair operations."

63. Slessor, *Air Power and Armies*, 3.

64. This emphasis on paralysis sounds similar to the sort of thing then being advocated by J. F. C. Fuller and B. H. Liddell Hart. More than likely, Slessor was well acquainted with their ideas, based on his tour at Camberley.

65. RAF Manual AP 1300, *Royal Air Force War Manual*, February 1940, Public Records Office, Kew, England, file 10/2311, I/10.

66. Ibid., VIII/12.

67. Sean Greenwood, "'Caligula's Horse' Revisited: Sir Thomas Inskip as Minister for the Co-Ordination of Defence, 1936–1939," *Journal of Strategic Studies* 17 (June 1994): 17–38.

68. AP 1300, February 1940, included a new chapter titled "The Strategic Air Defensive"; Smith, 188–91; and Wesley K. Wark, *The Ultimate Enemy: British Intelligence and Nazi Germany, 1933–1939* (Oxford: Oxford University Press, 1986), 35–58.

69. AP 1300, February 1940, VIII/39.

70. "Air Targets Intelligence, Germany: Vulnerability to Air Attack and Lists of Most Important Targets," September 1939, Public Records Office, Kew, England, file AIR 20/284.

71. "The Restriction of Air Warfare," 14 January 1938, Public Records Office, Kew, England, file AIR 9/84, 22.

72. Ibid., 14; see also Slessor's memo of 9 September 1938, Public Records Office, Kew, England, file AIR 2/3222.

73. H. A. Smith, "International Law," Staff College lecture, 19 June 1939, RAF Hendon, England, "17th Staff Course" file.

74. Cyril Newall to Edgar Ludlow-Hewitt, letter, 23 August 1939, Public Records Office, Kew, England, file AIR 75/8.

75. Message, CAS, to all air officers commanding, 4 June 1940, Public Records Office, Kew, England, file AIR 8/283.

76. Ibid.

77. The sorry state of Bomber Command at the beginning of World War II is well documented in Neville Jones, *The Beginnings of Strategic Air Power: A History of the British Bombing Force, 1923–39* (London: Frank Cass, 1987).

78. John Slessor, memorandum to CAS, 9 September 1938, Public Records Office, Kew, England, file AIR 2/3222.

79. For this interpretation, see Neville Jones, cited above; Anthony Verrier, *The Bomber Offensive* (New York: Macmillan, 1968); Barry Powers, *Strategy without Slide Rule* (London: Croom Helm, 1976); Max Hastings, *Bomber Command* (New York: Dial Press, 1979); Malcolm Smith, *British Air Strategy between the Wars* (Oxford: Clarendon, 1984); and Alan J. Levine, *The Strategic Bombing of Germany, 1940–1945* (Westport, Conn.: Praeger, 1992).

Chapter 3

Molding Airpower Convictions: Development and Legacy of William Mitchell's Strategic Thought

Lt Col Mark A. Clodfelter

To many of his adversaries, Brig Gen William "Billy" Mitchell was a renegade chasing a will-o'-the-wisp; to many of his admirers, he was a brilliant theorist whose notion of an independent air force guaranteed America's national security. The real Mitchell lay somewhere in between. Intensely self-centered and supremely confident, he was consumed by his beliefs, and his zeal ultimately cost him his career. Nonetheless, his message became a beacon for American airmen who endorsed service autonomy and proclaimed that airpower could achieve decisive results in war. More than any other individual, he was responsible for molding the airpower convictions that would serve as the doctrinal cornerstones of the United States Air Force.

Perhaps Mitchell's most lasting contribution to the development of American airpower was his welding the notion of air force autonomy to a progressive view of "independent" air operations, such as strategic bombing, that aimed to achieve independent results rather than simply support land or sea forces. He proclaimed that bombers could win wars by destroying an enemy nation's war-making capability and will to fight, and that doing so would yield a victory that was quicker and cheaper than one obtained by surface forces. The key to obtaining victory through airpower lay in establishing an autonomous air force, free of control by surface commanders and led by airmen possessing special expertise. Those airmen determined an enemy state's vulnerabilities and then massed bombers against those weaknesses.

For Mitchell, these ideas developed gradually, as a result of his World War I experience and the relationships he established with British air marshal Sir Hugh Trenchard and, to a lesser extent, with the Italian general Giulio Douhet. Mitchell emerged from the war with considerable experience as a pilot and a combat air commander, which greatly enhanced his stature among the coterie of air officers who adopted his beliefs and continued his fight for service independence after he left the military in early 1926. By the time he retired, he had left an indelible mark on the people who not only would lead the crusade for independence, but also would serve as the leaders of the new United States Air Force.

Mitchell was an apt choice to serve as the messiah of American airpower. Brimming with confidence in any situation, he could charm most audiences, often by relying on his fluent French or his expert polo. Yet, his overwhelming self-assurance did not stem entirely from expertise. Mitchell was a driven man, a man on a mission, a man with little time to waste. He wrote his mother in December 1919 that he was "practically the only one that can bring about a betterment of our national defense at this time" and noted with pride in his diary on Christmas eve five years later, "Supposed to be a half-holiday, but I worked hard all day in the office nevertheless."[1] People who interfered with his promotion of airpower—or his boundless ego—incurred his wrath. "Mitchell tried to convert his opponents by killing them first," observed his wartime colleague, Hugh Trenchard.[2] During the war, Mitchell's vanity produced bitter and largely unnecessary clashes with fellow airmen Benjamin "Benny" Foulois and Edgar "Nap" Gorrell, both of whom, he believed, had snubbed him after obtaining high Air Service positions.[3]

Mitchell's birth in 1879 into the cream of American society contributed to his exaggerated view of his own self-worth. (He was born in Nice, France, where his parents were vacationing.) With a US senator for a father and a grandfather who had been a banker and railroad tycoon, he possessed ties to leaders in both government and industry. Moreover, his father's service in the Civil War produced in Billy a martial spirit that manifested itself in 1898, when war with Spain erupted. Mitchell, only 18, enlisted as a private in his father's old regiment, but almost immediately the senator's connections secured him a commission in the Signal Corps. Arriving in Cuba in time to witness the surrender of the

Spanish garrison, Mitchell remained in occupation duty for seven months before transferring to the Philippines. Service in the islands, America's first major overseas possession, proved intensely interesting and exciting for the young lieutenant. Letters to his family describe with verve the exotic jungle duty, chasing rebels and pacifying the countryside. Given special attention are various hunting and fishing expeditions, firefights with "marauders," and a nasty bout of malaria.[4] Clearly, Mitchell relished the strenuous, outdoor life of an Army officer on remote duty.

After a brief visit to China during the Boxer Rebellion, as well as stops in Japan, India, and Europe, Mitchell returned to Washington. In July 1901, Brig Gen Adolphus Greely, chief of the Signal Corps, then posted the 20-year-old officer to Alaska, which was at that point largely uninhabited wilderness, but the Army sought to tie it closer to the lower states via telegraph. Mitchell's task was to string the necessary lines across this vast area. He later wrote of these experiences in an account that is both exciting and insightful.[5] Alaska was a wild, open, forbidding, and unexplored country. Billy obviously delighted in the challenge of building a signal system in the dead of winter, when the temperature often dipped to 70 degrees below zero—a challenge that others had attempted unsuccessfully. The odd characters he met and lived with during the two years spent in the north laying two thousand miles of telegraph wire make for enjoyable reading.

More importantly, Mitchell's Alaska writings give insights into his personality. Although his tours in the tropics and the arctic seem to stand in stark contrast, in actuality they present a similar portrait. The Billy Mitchell that emerges from these early years is a restless, tireless, and self-confident man who welcomed responsibility. Solitude did not bother him. On the other hand, those assignments also fostered, by necessity, a sense of independence. Isolated from his superiors for weeks at a time, Mitchell learned to follow his own counsel and be his own boss. This proclivity for independent action would become one of his most prominent and troublesome traits.

During his last few months in Alaska, Mitchell began studying a subject that was creating a stir within the Signal

Corps—aviation. He learned the fundamentals of the new field quickly, and in 1905, while an instructor at Fort Leavenworth, Kansas, Captain Mitchell wrote a field manual dealing with communications for the Army. Although most of the manual was a pedestrian description of Signal Corps organization and equipment, the author noted the growing importance of balloons in the corps. The Germans, he wrote, had a significant balloon section attached to their army that could provide valuable reconnaissance information, via photography, to ground commanders. He then offered that rigid airships—dirigibles— were under development and were far more capable than tethered balloons. Besides simple reconnaissance work over the front lines, they could drop explosives on fortifications and even scout for the Navy. He concluded with a rather remarkable prophecy: "Conflicts no doubt will be carried on in the future in the air, on the surface of the earth and water, and under the earth and water."[6] Written barely a year after the Wright brothers' first flight, this statement presaged Mitchell's views on air and submarine warfare in the decades ahead.

Mitchell's Signal Corps service both hindered and helped his future aviation career. On the one hand, signals officers—especially those like Mitchell, who had not attended West Point—seldom rose to high rank in the Army and were treated with far less deference than were officers from the combat arms of infantry, cavalry, and artillery. As a result, brother officers could dismiss Mitchell as a dilettante and refuse to take his ideas on warfare seriously. On the other hand, the close association with technology—the Signal Corps was a leader in this area within the Army—was of great importance to the new field of aviation. This technical bent manifested itself in Mitchell's later predictions regarding such exotic innovations as cruise missiles, glide bombs, jet propulsion, supersonic flight, and space travel. Although such prophecies often earned wry smiles at the time, he was proven correct in a surprisingly short period of time.[7]

Mitchell's main focus, however, did not immediately turn to visions of airpower. After assignments once again in Cuba and the Philippines, in 1912, at age 32, he became the youngest officer on the Army's General Staff. As the lone Signal Corps representative, he was responsible for appraising its fledgling aviation—which consisted of four aircraft in various states of repair. To gain insight, he called upon Lt Henry H. "Hap" Arnold, an instructor pilot at the Signal Corps's aviation school at College Park, Maryland.[8] The two established a close friendship that endured until Mitchell's death in 1936, and their ties would have significant consequences for the development of American airpower. Arnold testified on Mitchell's behalf at his 1925 court-martial and would be "banished" to Fort Riley, Kansas, for continuing to spout Mitchell's beliefs after the hearing; as the commanding general of the Army Air Forces during World War II, he would remain committed to Mitchell's notions. Initially, however, Arnold provided aviation expertise to Mitchell, who had not yet learned to fly.

Nonetheless, at this stage, Mitchell was not yet sold on the efficacy of aviation. In 1913, when Cong. James Hay proposed a bill that would have created an "air corps" equivalent in stature to the infantry, cavalry, or artillery, Mitchell balked. He reviewed the proposal and determined that aviation was essential to Signal Corps reconnaissance and communication. "The offensive value of this thing has yet to be proved," he concluded.[9]

Yet, Mitchell was intrigued by aviation, and the outbreak of war in Europe heightened his interest in the airplane's military potential. After finishing his General Staff assignment in June 1916, he became deputy head of the Signal Corps Aviation Section and was promoted to major. He then took advantage of a provision in the National Defense Act of 1916 that lifted the ban on flight training for servicemen over 30 (Mitchell was 36). From September 1916 to January 1917, he paid a dollar a minute for 1,470 minutes of off-duty flying instruction at the Curtiss Aviation School in Newport News, Virginia.[10] Mitchell's flying "expertise" likely caused the War Department to send him to Europe as an aeronautical observer,[11] and he arrived in Paris four days after America's declaration of war on the Central Powers. Two weeks later, he spent 10 days at the front lines observing the progress of French general Robert Nivelle's disastrous offensive and visiting French aviation units. He recalled his thoughts after first viewing the deadlock of trench warfare from the air:

> A very significant thing to me was that we could cross the lines of these contending armies in a few minutes in our airplane, whereas the armies had been locked in the struggle, immovable, powerless to advance, for three years. To even stick one's head over the top of a trench invited death. This whole area over which the Germans and French battled was not more than sixty miles across. It was as though they kept knocking their heads against a stone wall, until their brains were dashed out. They got nowhere, as far as ending the war was concerned.[12]

In May, Mitchell visited the headquarters of Maj Gen Hugh Trenchard, commander in the field of Britain's Royal Flying Corps (RFC). Mitchell arrived abruptly, wearing an extravagant uniform that he had designed himself, but his unbridled exuberance persuaded the general, who was "decided in manner and very direct in speech," to give him a three-day dose of RFC operations and Trenchard philosophy. Mitchell was particularly impressed by Trenchard's commitment to a single, unified air command that would allow him to "hurl a mass of aviation at any one locality needing attack." For the British air leader, a tightly controlled, continuous aerial offensive was the key to success, and assigning air units to individual ground commanders for defense was a mistake. Trenchard highlighted the RFC's General Headquarters (GHQ) Brigade, a force designed to destroy the German army's means of supply and reinforcement but which possessed too few aircraft to do so in the spring of 1917. He argued that airpower should attack as far as possible into the enemy's country, noting that the development of new airplanes with greater ranges would make Berlin a viable target. He did not, however, contend during his first encounter with Mitchell that the quickest way to defeat the German army was through an air offensive aimed at the German nation. Although some officers in the RFC called for a "radical air strategy" against the German homeland, he remained focused on using airpower to defeat the German army on the western front. Nonetheless, Mitchell emerged from his initial contact with Trenchard profoundly affected by the general's insights and convinced that an aerial offensive was a key to winning the war.[13]

As a result of observing Allied operations, Mitchell proposed dividing the air contingent of the American Expeditionary

Force (AEF) into categories of "tactical" and "strategical" aviation. He made his proposal to Gen John J. Pershing's chief of staff, Brig Gen James G. Harbord, who arrived in France with the commanding general in mid-June 1917. "Tactical" aviation would consist of squadrons attached to divisions, corps, or armies and would operate as any other combat arm. In contrast, "strategical" aviation "would be bombardment and pursuit formations and would have an independent mission very much as independent cavalry used to have. . . . They would be used to carry the war well into the enemy's country."[14] This mission, he insisted, could have "a greater influence on the ultimate decision of the war than any other arm."[15]

Soon after receiving Mitchell's plan, Pershing selected a board of officers to determine the proper composition for AEF aviation. Because Mitchell was the senior American aviator in Europe, the general made him chief of the newly created Air Service, which had replaced the Signal Corps as the Army's air organization in the AEF.[16] Mitchell's appointment did not, however, guarantee his proposal's acceptance. On 11 July, Pershing outlined a comprehensive plan for AEF organization that authorized 59 squadrons of tactical aircraft for service with the field armies. The plan made no mention of an independent force for "strategical" operations.

Pershing's failure to approve the proposal caused Mitchell to redouble his efforts. In August 1917 he asked the AEF's intelligence branch to provide information on strategic targets in Germany and later received a list of industrial targets in the Ruhr from the French.[17] His staff also explored in more detail the possibilities of bombing Germany. His officers performed this activity in relative splendor, for Mitchell chose the Château de Chamrandes, a magnificent hunting lodge built by Louis XV, as his headquarters.[18] He was always flamboyant. One of his more capable staff officers was Nap Gorrell, a 26-year-old major whom Mitchell had selected to head the Air Service Technical Section. Gorrell directed the effort that ultimately produced the first American plan for a strategic air campaign. This plan would reflect Mitchell's ideas, gleaned largely from Trenchard, about airpower's potential to destroy the German army's means to fight.[19]

By the time Gorrell completed the plan in November 1917, Mitchell's focus had changed from strategic air warfare to that designed to provide the Army with direct support. In October Mitchell, now a colonel, left Chamrandes to become Air Service commander in the Zone of the Advance. The remainder of his assignments before the war ended—chief of Air Service, First Army; chief of Air Service, I Corps; chief of Air Service, 1st Brigade; once again chief of Air Service, First Army; and finally, chief of Air Service, Army Group—would also require him to provide direct air support to Army movements on the western front. Although after the war Mitchell would berate Pershing's staff for "trying to handle aviation as an auxiliary of some of the other branches, instead of an independent fighting arm,"[20] such criticisms during the conflict were infrequent.

In February 1918, as chief of Air Service, I Corps, he argued that the first mission of offensive airpower must be the destruction of the enemy's air force. Thereafter, bombing operations

> should be essentially tactical in their nature and directed against active enemy units in the field which will have a direct bearing on operations during this Spring and Summer, rather than a piece-meal attack against large factory sites and things of that nature. The factories, if completely destroyed, would undoubtedly have a very far-reaching effect, but to completely demolish them is a tremendously difficult thing, and, furthermore, even if they were ruined, their effect would not be felt for a long period of time (possibly a year) upon the fighting of their army.[21]

"The Air Service of an army is one of its offensive arms," he stated after taking command in the Zone of the Advance: "Alone it cannot bring about a decision. It therefore helps the other arms in their appointed missions."[22] Near the end of the war, Mitchell demonstrated his ability to manage a large operation by massing fifteen hundred Allied aircraft, most supplied by the French and British, to back Pershing's drive at Saint-Mihiel. Tactically, the operation was a great success and added enormously to Mitchell's confidence and reputation within the Air Service.

Mitchell displayed strategic creativity as well. In October 1918, he proposed to Pershing that Handley Page bombers drop the 1st Infantry Division by parachute behind German lines at Metz. Simultaneously, the Allies would attack along the front, catching the Germans in a deadly vise. Mitchell stated that the British bombers could easily carry 10 to 15 soldiers each and could later parachute supplies to them. Afterwards, he claimed that Pershing tentatively approved the plan, but the war ended before it could be implemented.[23] Although Pershing was probably not as sanguine about the plan's prospects as Mitchell believed, the idea was highly original. Further, it indicated that Mitchell's airpower emphasis remained on the land battle.

Once assured of a continued American advance on the ground, however, Mitchell's focus returned to the possibilities of strategic bombing. As long as the Army's progress remained uncertain, he devoted his full energies to providing it with immediate air support. Of course, Mitchell's ego had much to do with his pragmatic approach to airpower—he craved a combat command, and the only combat air commands available were those attached to Army headquarters. Still, by the summer of 1918, he realized that America's major contribution to the Allied advance would be made by the *ground* echelons of the AEF and that air support could enhance their impact.

Had the war continued into 1919, Mitchell, assured of a continuing American advance on the ground, planned an aerial assault against the interior of Germany. "I was sure that if the war lasted, air power would decide it," he wrote after the armistice.[24] According to his memoirs, he planned to combine incendiary attacks with poison gas to destroy crops, forests, and livestock. This air offensive, he mused, "would have caused untold sufferings and forced a German surrender."[25] Yet, the likelihood of Mitchell's vision becoming reality was remote. On 4 November 1918, Secretary of War Newton D. Baker told Gen Peyton March, Army chief of staff, to notify the Air Service that the United States would not conduct any bombing that "has as its objective, promiscuous bombing upon industry, commerce, or population, in enemy countries disassociated from obvious military needs to be served by such action."[26] Moreover, in early January 1919, Mitchell revealed that his notion of strategic bombing had come to resemble Gorrell's plan for bombing key German war industries. In a treatise entitled "Tactical Application of Military Aeronautics," he argued that the main value of bombardment would come from "hitting an enemy's great nerve centers at the very beginning of the war so as to paralyze them to the greatest extent possible."[27]

That the war ended before American bombers had the chance to bomb German soil proved significant. Production deficiencies had prevented the first squadron of American night bombers from arriving at the front until 9 November 1918. Since manufacturing problems had stymied the dream of defeating Germany through American airpower, the dream endured intact. Mitchell, Gorrell, and other Air Service officers could speculate about the probable effect that a bomber offensive would have had on the outcome of the war and could blame the lack of aircraft as a reason why the offensive never materialized. Such difficulties could be overcome. Air officers now were aware of Gorrell's postwar admonition that "money and men could not make an air program over night,"[28] and they would make amends.

For Mitchell, the prospects of applying airpower independently, rather than in support of the Army, gradually merged with the notion of an air force separate from Army control. In July 1918, he insisted that the chief of the Air Service, rather than the Army's General Staff, should direct the Air Service's GHQ Reserve, the name given to the phantom force of bombers that never materialized. He based his argument on the need for unity of command, which would allow the Air Service chief to concentrate all available airpower in a critical area for maximum impact. His plea went unheeded.

In June, Pershing's chief of staff, Maj Gen James W. McAndrew, admonished air officers who stressed "independent" air operations: "It is therefore directed that these officers be warned against any idea of independence and that they be taught from the beginning that their efforts must be closely coordinated with those of the remainder of the Air Service and those of the ground army."[29] Mitchell believed that such nonflyers had little appreciation for the airplane's unique capabilities, and he bemoaned their efforts to restrict aviation to battlefield support. He stated that Army officers—with the sole exception of Maj Gen Hunter Liggett, who had commanded First Army—did not know what airpower meant.[30]

The independent streak noted in Mitchell's early career manifested itself in France in his dealings with his superior, Brig Gen Benny Foulois, one of the Army's first and most accomplished pilots—indeed, the Wright brothers themselves had taught him to fly in 1909. While Mitchell served on the General Staff in 1916, Foulois led the 1st Aero Squadron on the Mexican border in pursuit of the bandit Pancho Villa. Yet, when Foulois arrived in France in November 1917 to take charge of American air operations, Mitchell—who had been in place for six months and thus felt he should be granted seniority—was outraged and did not try to hide his feelings. In his memoirs, he referred to Foulois as a "nonflyer" and "carpetbagger" who imposed his authority without taking into consideration Mitchell's experience in the theater. Mitchell, though, had learned to fly barely two years previously and still required the services of another pilot whenever he took to the air. For his part, Foulois was dismayed by Mitchell's reaction and in June 1918 wrote Pershing of Mitchell's "hostile and insubordinate attitude," adding that his actions were "extremely childish" and "entirely unbecoming of an officer of his age, rank and experience."[31]

Pershing grew weary of such sniping and directed his old friend and West Point classmate, Maj Gen Mason Patrick, to command the Air Service. Although Patrick was an engineer and knew little of aviation matters, Pershing selected him for his leadership and managerial ability. The commanding general's guidance was succinct: there were some fine people down there in the air arm, but they were "running around in circles." He wanted Patrick to make them go straight.[32] This episode was not the last time Mitchell's strong personality would cause problems. Most unfortunately, it put him at odds with an airman, Foulois, who was as devoted to the cause of airpower as Mitchell himself.

In the aftermath of the Great War, Mitchell began to refine his ideas on airpower. His views were intimately tied to the concept of an independent air force, and they also displayed the vestiges of progressivism that remained in postwar America.[33] Far more ambitious than his muckraker predecessors, Mitchell aimed to reform the most violent of man's activities—war. Rifled artillery, the machine gun, and poison gas had made war an endless nightmare that killed millions, as typified by the unremitting fury of the western front. Technology was the demon responsible for the slaughter, but, Mitchell believed, technology was also the key to salvation. The bomber would be the instrument of change. Not only would it prevent a naval force from attacking the United States—as he attempted to demonstrate by sinking the German battleship *Ostfriesland* with Air Service bombers off the Virginia Capes in July 1921—it would obviate trench warfare, achieving a victory that was quicker, cheaper, and hence more humane than one gained by ground combat. The wartime application of airpower would, Mitchell contended, "result in a diminished loss of life and treasure and will thus be a distinct benefit to civilization."[34]

His unabashed faith that airpower had altered the nature of war caused him to demand an air force separate from Army or Navy control, to guarantee its proper use. Moreover, this separate air force had to be commanded by an airman. In 1925 he testified before the Morrow Board that "the one thing that has been definitely proved in all flying services is that a man must be an airman to handle air power. In every instance of which I have known or heard the result of placing other than air officers in charge of air power has ended in failure."[35] Mitchell's belief that air warfare was unique complemented his conviction that only a distinctive class of combatants could wage it. He often referred to a "community of airmen" and the "air-going people" who thought and acted differently than their earthbound counterparts.[36] His vision was one of aerial knights engaged in a chivalrous contest and supported by the population at large. This romantic notion was both incongruous and appealing after the horrors of trench warfare.

Much like the muckrakers who preceded him, Mitchell took his case directly to the American public: "Changes in military systems come about only through the pressure of public opinion or disaster in war."[37] In his mind, surface officers were too conservative and hidebound to make the changes necessary to wage modern war. As a consequence, Mitchell aimed for the American people to compel the country's political leadership to create an independent air force. Many of his writings appeared in the popular press—not the professional military journals—because his intended audience was *not* the officer corps. In the aftermath of the "War to End All Wars," however, he found that his message could not persuade a populace beset by isolationism. Still, his progressive notions endured among airmen and provided the foundations for the bombing doctrine they developed during the interwar years.

After the armistice, Mitchell began his airpower crusade in earnest. Although a recognized war hero—he had won the Distinguished Service Cross and the Distinguished Service Medal, as well as several foreign decorations—his quick tongue and steadfast beliefs prevented him from commanding the Air Service. He therefore had to settle for assistant chief, which, significantly, carried with it a brigadier general's rank. Most officers had risen rapidly to high rank during the war, only to sink just as quickly to their "permanent" rank after the war ended and demobilization began. Foulois, for example, reverted to major, and Major General Patrick to the rank of colonel. Mitchell was, therefore, extremely fortunate to keep his star. Nonetheless, he stubbornly refused to cater to his Air Service chief, Maj Gen Charles T. Menoher, an infantryman who had led the 42d "Rainbow" Division in World War I. Despite Menoher's warning, Mitchell illicitly published his report of the 1921 *Ostfriesland* sinking. In the resulting power struggle, Menoher resigned in protest, left the Air Service, and returned to the infantry (later he would be promoted to lieutenant general).

Menoher's successor was Mason Patrick, who was promoted back to major general and once again called to keep the rambunctious Mitchell in line. A wise choice, Patrick learned to fly at age 60 to enhance his standing with his subordinates and to display his mettle. Upon assuming command, he notified Mitchell that he would be chief in deed as well as name. When Mitchell responded with an offer of resignation, Patrick told him that the offer would be accepted. Mitchell reconsidered.[38] Patrick realized his deputy's brilliance and even came to share his views on an independent air force, but he did not appreciate Mitchell's unorthodox methods of pursuing his goal. Cleverly, Patrick sent Mitchell to inspect European air forces to prevent him from disrupting the Washington Naval Conference of 1922. During this visit, he met and exchanged ideas with leading European airmen, including Giulio Douhet in Italy. When he returned to Washington and began making noise again, Patrick dispatched him to the Pacific in early 1924 on a similar mission.

During his Pacific trip—a "honeymoon" with his new wife, Elizabeth—Mitchell visited the Philippines, Dutch East Indies, Siam, India, China, Korea, and Japan. Throughout, he was intrigued by the role airpower would no doubt play should the United States have to fight in that part of the world. Japan loomed as a possible enemy, and the American Embassy in Tokyo told him that he could not visit the country in an official capacity. He and his wife traveled extensively as "tourists," however, and his observations on the Japanese typified the American racism prevalent at the time:

> The policy of the United States and, in fact, all of the white countries having their shores washed by the waters of the Pacific Ocean, is to keep their soil, their institutions, and their manner of living free from the ownership, the dominion, and the customs of the Orientals who people the western shores of this the greatest of all oceans. . . . Eventually in their search for existence the white and yellow races will be brought into armed conflict to determine which shall prevail.[39]

Mitchell added his thoughts about airpower's role in a future Pacific war to his account of the journey. He believed that the value of aircraft carriers was practically nil "because not only can they not operate efficiently on the high seas but even if they could they cannot place sufficient aircraft in the air at one time to insure a concentrated operation."[40] He thought that land-based aircraft were the key to dominating Pacific island groups and might enable the Japanese to launch a surprise attack on American forces in the Hawaiian Islands. Mitchell contended that only an opposing air force could stop such an aerial assault. Other defensive measures, like cannon and barrage balloons, acted "only to give a false sense of security very much [like] what the ostrich must feel when he hides his head in the sand."[41]

Despite his comment regarding the limited value of aircraft carriers, Mitchell was ambivalent on the subject. The only American carrier then in commission was the converted collier *Langley*, a poor excuse for a symbol of maritime might. The idea behind the *Langley* was another matter. Initially, Mitchell was much taken by the prospect of putting aircraft aboard ships that traveled with the fleet. Indeed, he believed that their presence was essential, theorizing that vessels of all sizes were hopelessly vulnerable to air attack. Because only aircraft could defeat other aircraft, the defensive solution was self-evident. "Airplane carriers," as he called them, were the means to provide a moveable cloak of air superiority over the fleet. Once carrier aircraft won "command of the air," they could then be used to attack enemy vessels. He speculated that this climactic air battle would occur as much as two hundred miles from the floating bases, "where hostile gun fire would play no part whatsoever, and where [our] own navy would run no risk."[42] Mitchell maintained this stance for several years, even arguing at his court-martial in 1925 that the Navy should build carriers that were large enough to carry one hundred bombers or one hundred pursuit aircraft. His published articles reiterated this suggestion, even hailing the building of the carriers *Lexington* and *Saratoga* as a step forward for naval aviation.[43] This attitude soon changed.

By 1928 Mitchell had completely turned his back on airplane carriers, now seeing them as little more than expensive floating targets, "so vulnerable that even a small bomb will put them out of business." In fact, the carrier was not only helpless, it was actually harmful because it gave an illusion of progress where none actually existed: "The Naval Airplane Carrier is merely an EXPENSIVE AND USELESS LUXURY used principally as propaganda by the Naval Services to cover up the fact that they have NO adequate defense against aircraft" (emphasis in original), he argued in 1928.[44] Two years later, Mitchell derided the carriers as merely a "delusion" of the "Navyists" who were attempting to save their service with outmoded schemes.[45]

Why the change of heart? In part, Mitchell had decided that the solution to the air defense of the fleet rested with airships. With an optimism that was totally unfounded, he envisioned dirigibles as capable of traveling thousands of miles, in all kinds of weather, while also serving as airborne platforms for pursuit aircraft. Although some airships had launched and recovered pursuit planes, the idea was a technological dead end. Both the Army and Navy were out of the airship business by the mid-1930s.

Perhaps Mitchell hoped that Congress would establish a unified air force including both Army and Navy air. He had called for such an organization since 1919. The model for this scheme existed in Britain, where the Royal Air Force maintained control of naval aviation, even that deployed at sea on aircraft carriers. In an article written in 1920, Mitchell called for "floating airdromes" *under air force control*, which would protect the American coast. This development would make airpower the first line of American defense rather than naval power.[46]

As time passed, Mitchell realized that an independent air force would not appear quickly and that the creation of big carriers like the *Lexington* and *Saratoga* posed a threat to unification. The Navy was becoming self-sufficient in airpower. Hence, he felt the need to denigrate carriers, portraying them as expensive, vulnerable, and ineffective. His efforts were futile and, paradoxically, gave a healthy boost to naval aviation by alerting the admiralty to the need for air superiority over the fleet. General Menoher's comment at the time of the *Ostfriesland* sinking—"I guess maybe the navy will get its airplane carriers now"—had become an ironic prophecy.[47]

Although Mitchell's foreign visits expanded his airpower ideas, the trips failed to curb his penchant for seeking public support for his notions. He was certain that the Army leadership would never endorse his desire for air force autonomy because his beliefs clashed with the Army's traditional views on airpower's "proper" role in war; thus, he appealed to the American populace. He understood full well the Army's desire to guarantee that it received adequate air support for its ground forces—he had provided that backing in France during the war, and he did not dismiss the need for it afterwards. Indeed, in his writings immediately after the war, he stressed the importance not only of supporting the other services but also of deliberately using airpower to attack enemy forces directly.

In other words, Mitchell was arguing that even with the advent of the airplane, wars were still won the old-fashioned way—by destroying armies and navies. Only now, the airplane made that task easier and less costly. Thus, in 1921 he advocated a balanced air force, one that consisted largely of pursuit (60 percent) with the remainder evenly divided between bombardment and attack.[48] This early emphasis on the primacy of pursuit distinguished him from his contemporaries Trenchard and Douhet. Soon, however, Mitchell abandoned this position, calling instead for an air force based largely on bombardment.

One reason for Mitchell's shift towards the bomber was the realization that auxiliary airpower offered meager prospects for overcoming the murderous technology of modern land warfare—or for justifying an autonomous air force. As long as ground advance remained the primary means to achieve victory (and Army leaders had little incentive to change that emphasis), the bomber's ability to revamp war remained limited. "Should a War take place on the ground between two industrial nations in the future," Mitchell wrote in 1926, "it can only end in absolute ruin, if the same methods that the ground armies have followed before should be resorted to."[49] In contrast, independently applied airpower presented an opportunity to decide a war by avoiding stalemate and slaughter.

Mitchell maintained that airpower could defeat a nation by paralyzing its "vital centers" and thus its ability to continue hostilities. Those centers included great cities where people lived, factories, raw materials, foodstuffs, supplies, and modes of transportation.[50] All were essential to wage modern war, and all were vulnerable to air attack. Moreover, many of the targets were fragile, and wrecking them promised a rapid victory. Mitchell asserted that

> air forces will attack centers of production of all kinds, means of transportation, agricultural areas, ports and shipping; not so much the people themselves. They will destroy the means of making war, because now we cannot cut a limb out of a tree, pick a stone from a hill and make it our principal weapon. Today to make war we must have great metal and chemical factories that have to stay in one place, take months to build, and, if destroyed, cannot be replaced in the usual length of a modern war.[51]

Only an air force possessed the means to attack vital centers without first confronting enemy surface forces, and destroying those centers would eliminate the need to advance through enemy territory on the ground. "The influence of air power on the ability of one nation to impress its will on another in an armed conflict will be decisive," he insisted.[52]

Like many Army officers of his time, Mitchell could recite Clausewitz's dictum on the objective of war, but he did so with a parochial twist. Airpower would wreck an enemy's will to fight by destroying his capability to resist, and the essence of that capability was not the army or navy but the nation's industrial and agricultural underpinnings. Eliminating industrial production "would deprive armies, air forces and navies . . . of their means of maintenance."[53] Airpower also offered the chance to directly attack the will to fight. Mitchell equated the will of a nation to the will of its populace, but he vacillated about the propriety of bombing civilians. On the one hand, he called for attacks on "the places where people live and carry on their daily lives" to discourage their "desire to renew the combat at a later date," advocated burning Japanese metropolitan areas in the event of a war with Japan, and noted that poison gas could be used to contaminate water supplies and spur evacuations from cities. On the other hand, in a bombing manual that he wrote in 1922 for Air Service officers, he argued that attacking a factory was ethical only if its workers received "sufficient warning that the center will be destroyed" and that "in rare instances Bombardment aviation will be required to act as an arm of reprisal."[54]

The dominant theme emerging from these discussions was not the desire to attack civilians directly but the desire to sever the populace from the sources of production. "It may be necessary to intimidate the civilian population in a certain area to force them to discontinue something which is having a direct bearing on the outcome of the conflict," Mitchell observed in his bombing manual. Achieving that goal might cause some civilian deaths, but the number would pale compared to the deaths produced by a ground war between industrialized powers. Moreover, once bombed, civilians were unlikely to continue supporting the war effort. "In the future, the mere threat of bombing a town by an air force will cause it to be evacuated and all work in munitions and supply factories to be stopped," he asserted.[55] In Mitchell's eyes, civilian will was exceedingly fragile, and its collapse would cause a corresponding loss in war-making capability. In addition, one did not have to attack civilians directly to produce a direct impact on an enemy's will to fight.

Although adamant about the fragile nature of civilian will, Mitchell was less than explicit about how breaking it would translate into a rapid peace. His vision of such air attacks was apocalyptic in the extreme:

> Tardy ones claw and clutch and scramble, clambering on top of those who have fallen. Before long there is a yelling, fighting mass of humanity. . . . Attacking planes, leaving New York a heap of dead and smoldering ashes, had proceeded safely to other strategic points where they duplicated their bloody triumph. . . . Gases produced by a conflagration in a city such as New York, would fill the subways and all places below ground in short order.[56]

He thus thought that air raids would trigger evacuations of hundreds of thousands of people from great cities. Those refugees would not be able to obtain adequate food or shelter, and their plight would cause a war to end. "There is only one alternative and that is surrender," he wrote in 1930. "It is a quick way of deciding a war and really much more humane than the present methods of blowing people to bits by cannon projectiles or butchering them with bayonets."[57] Yet, Mitchell neglected to say whether "surrender" would occur because the government of the battered nation was sympathetic to the plight of its people, because it feared overthrow by an irate populace, or because it had in fact been displaced by a new regime demanding peace.

In many of his futuristic examples, he depicted the United States as the country undergoing air attack, so the presumption was that surrender would stem from a sympathetic government. Mitchell claimed that America's "strategical heart" consisted of the manufacturing complexes within a triangle formed by Chicago, Boston, and the Chesapeake Bay, and that destroying those centers and their transportation links would not only wreck industrial productivity but also lead to widespread starvation if the nation chose not to capitulate.[58] In such projections, war-making capability ceased once bombs destroyed vital industries and agricultural areas, or once civilians left the factories and fields. Mitchell dismissed stockpiles of materiel, especially food,[59] and he also rejected reserves of morale. He bestowed on the governments under attack a degree of rationality that ignored the war aims of the enemy and the possibility that the population would willingly suffer to avoid capitulation. His examples intimated that all industrial powers were alike—and that all resembled *his* view of the United States. He thus overlooked crucial distinctions between nations—and the types of wars they fought—that would directly affect bombing's ability to achieve a rapid victory.

For Mitchell, the key prerequisite for achieving victory through airpower was to win control of the sky. In his first book, he stated that neither navies nor armies could operate effectively "until the air forces have first obtained a decision against the opposing air force." He was convinced that the first battles of a future war would be air battles and that the nation which won them was "practically certain to win the whole war."[60] In this emphasis on the importance of the air battle, Mitchell mirrored his contemporary in Italy, Giulio Douhet. Mitchell later stated that he had "frequent conversations" with Douhet during his visit to Italy in 1922; at any rate, he was well acquainted with Douhet's confidant—the aircraft designer and manufacturer Gianni Caproni—and received a synopsis of Douhet's classic book *The Command of the Air* in late 1922.[61]

Much of Mitchell's and Douhet's writing was remarkably similar.[62] Both agreed that "nothing can stop the attack of aircraft except other aircraft" and that after achieving air supremacy, an enemy's vital centers—a term used by both men—could be wrecked at will.[63] They differed, however, about how best to achieve air control. For Douhet, the best method was to destroy the enemy air force on the ground, either at its bases or before it left factory assembly lines.[64] Mitchell argued that air combat was also a suitable means and that attacking a critical vital center would compel the hostile air force to take to the air in defense, where it could be overcome.[65] Both thought that escort fighters for bombers were essential to ward off the enemy's fighters, although

Douhet advocated an air force based on a single type of aircraft—a bomber bristling with machine guns that he dubbed the "battle plane" in his 1927 revision to *The Command of the Air.*

Like Mitchell, Douhet argued that an independent air force built around the bomber was the cheapest and most efficient means to defend his nation. Unlike his American counterpart, Douhet had to consider that his country was susceptible to air attack. The Italian asserted that a defending air force could not protect all of a nation's vital centers, because the defender could never be certain what centers the attacker would choose to strike. His answer was to attack first, with as much airpower as possible, and destroy the enemy's ability to retaliate in kind. Once enemy bombers took to the air against an unknown target, attempting to stop them was probably futile.[66]

Mitchell realized that advancing technology would ultimately overcome the limitation on range that protected the United States from air attack by a European or Asiatic power. Under his guidance, Air Service colonel Townsend F. Dodd in April 1919 prepared a study evaluating the need for a separate air force. It concluded that "the moment that [an] aircraft reaches that stage of development which will permit one ton of bombs to be carried from the nearest point of a possible enemy's territory to our commercial and industrial centers, and to return to the starting point, then national safety requires the maintenance of an efficient air force adapted for acting against the possible enemy's interior."[67] By the time that transoceanic flight had been perfected, Mitchell aimed to make Americans an "air-going people," ready to conduct "war at a distance" through a Department of Aeronautics equal in status to Army and Navy Departments in a single Department of National Defense.[68]

Mitchell tried to transform the American populace into airpower advocates by emphasizing the progressive notions of order and efficiency. Not only could an autonomous air force protect the United States and achieve an independent victory in war, he insisted that it could do so more cheaply—and more effectively—than either the Army or the Navy. Yet, the Air Service could not perform an independent mission, Mitchell argued, as long as the Army controlled it. Because the Army divided air units among its various corps and divisions to assure that they received adequate air support, air units had a meager chance of being massed together for a long-range, independent mission in which Army commanders had little interest. "To leave aviation essentially under the dominance and direction of another department is to absolutely strangle its development, because it will be looked on by them merely as an auxiliary and not as a principal thing," he protested in December 1919.[69]

At the same time, Mitchell provoked the Navy's ire with his persistent claims that the sea service provided minimum defense for a maximum price tag. In 1922 he contended that an average battleship cost roughly $45 million to build and equip, while bombers cost $20,000 each. Thus, the nation could build either one battleship or two thousand bombers— each of which could sink a battleship![70] Mitchell's argument omitted a great deal, such as the rapid rate of obsolescence of aircraft compared to capital ships and the high costs of training aircrews and building air bases, but its simplistic logic touched a receptive chord in many Americans.

Economy was not the only issue, as Mitchell noted the mood of isolationism taking root throughout the country. He titled his book *Winged Defense*, not *Winged Offense*, and tried to show that aircraft could also be instruments of peace. He wrote that one could use airplanes to spray agricultural crops, serve as sentinels along the borders to prevent unlawful entry, patrol the national forests for fires, perform geological mapping, and carry the mail.[71] Transportation was the essence of civilization, he claimed, and the future of transportation belonged to the airplane. At the same time, one should foster the symbiotic relationship between military and civilian aviation. Every pilot and every aviation mechanic in America was an important national asset; in peace or in war, they served the country. This coterie of airmen was an essential element of airpower. To Mitchell, airpower was not merely a collection of airplanes or even of airmen. It also included the aircraft and engine industries and the entire air transportation system, which consisted of airfields, airways, meteorological stations, weather forecasters, supply depots, and radio navigation aids. All were necessary to have real airpower, and Mitchell emphatically called for its development—subsidized by the government, if necessary, as was the case with the railroad system in the previous century.[72]

In many respects, Mitchell's aeronautical ideas echoed the maritime beliefs of Alfred Thayer Mahan—an ironic bit of theoretical affinity, given Mitchell's virulent antipathy towards the Navy. Sea power, to Mahan, consisted of certain fundamentals: favorable geography, a strong technological base, popular support, and government sustenance. Those ideas applied equally to Mitchell's views on airpower. America's vast size and global involvement, the creative genius of its citizens (after all, the airplane was invented by two bicycle makers from Ohio), the call for the public to become "air-minded," and financial support from the government were all underpinnings of aeronautical strength. At the same time, Mahan's emphasis on sea power's commercial aspects and the tie between economic growth and national vigor paralleled Mitchell's call for the commercial use of airplanes. Airpower was far more than simply firebombs and high explosives.

Yet, like sea power, the essence of airpower was its combat application. Both Mahan and Mitchell called for an aggressive, offensive application of force to gain control of their medium. For Mahan, a climactic struggle between battleships would produce control of the sea, which would permit the victorious navy to control commerce and obtain natural resources. For Mitchell, control of the sky would come from an air battle or the destruction of the enemy's airpower on the ground (either by bombing airfields or aircraft factories). After achieving command of the air, Mitchell's air force would then wreck an enemy nation's vital centers and destroy the enemy's capability and will to keep fighting.

Mitchell frequently flaunted his airpower notions before Congress, and those ideas ultimately led to his banishment from his post as assistant chief of the Air Service. In December 1924, Rep. Julian Lampert, chairman of the House Military Affairs Committee, began hearings in response to Rep. John F. Curry's bill for a unified aviation service. Mitchell testified extensively at the hearings, making some of his most inflammatory accusations. "All the organization that we have in this country really now is for the protection of vested interests against aviation," he told the committee. He added that some individuals testifying for the government had showed "a woeful ignorance . . . and in some cases possibly a falsification of evidence, with the evident intent to confuse Congress." When asked by Secretary of War John W. Weeks to elaborate on his testimony in writing, Mitchell declined to provide specifics and added additional charges. He berated the Navy for the conduct of its bombing tests, remarking that it "actually tried to prevent our sinking the *Ostfriesland.*"[73] Mitchell had recently angered Secretary Weeks by publishing an explosive series of aviation articles, unreviewed by the War Department, in *The Saturday Evening Post.* The confrontational testimony following on the heels of those articles caused Weeks to shun Mitchell's reappointment as assistant chief of the Air Service when it came up for renewal in March 1925.[74] At the end of the month, Mitchell reverted to his permanent grade of colonel and was transferred to Fort Sam Houston in San Antonio, Texas, as aviation officer for the Army's VIII Corps Area.

Mitchell, however, had no intention of remaining dormant in Texas. In August 1925 he published *Winged Defense,* which expanded many of the arguments that he had made in *The Saturday Evening Post* articles. Although stressing the importance of an independent air force built around the bomber, the book continued the attack on Army and Navy leaders who opposed such an organization.[75] It also contained cartoons lampooning Secretary Weeks, who at the time of publication had become seriously ill. Mitchell had been unaware that the cartoons would be published in the book, and on 4 September he received a letter from Elizabeth, who was in Detroit with their infant daughter. His wife was greatly distressed about the appearance of the cartoons and contended that no one would believe that Mitchell had not approved them. "I don't very well see how they can avoid court-martialing you now, my sweet—but I'm sorry it will have to be over something sort of cheap like those cartoons," she lamented.[76]

Mitchell's receipt of his wife's letter coincided with the crash of the Navy dirigible *Shenandoah* in an Ohio thunderstorm and perhaps influenced his decision to make the Navy disaster his personal Rubicon. On 5 September 1925 he told San Antonio newsmen in a press release dripping with anger, frustration, and sarcasm that the airship crash, as well as other deficiencies in the Army and Navy air arms, resulted from the "incompetency, criminal negligence, and almost treasonable administration of the National Defense by the Navy and War Departments."[77] Two weeks later he was court-martialed.

For Mitchell, the trial and the "Morrow Board," which preceded it, were anticlimaxes. Enraged, President Calvin Coolidge, who called Mitchell a "God-d——d disturbing liar,"[78] proffered the court-martial charges himself. In addition, Coolidge summoned friend and J. P. Morgan banker Dwight Morrow to conduct a formal investigation of American aviation that would undercut the publicity of Mitchell's trial.[79] The president directed Morrow to produce a report by the end of November, but Morrow's hearing concluded on 15 October, 13 days before the start of the court-martial. Mitchell testified before the Morrow Board but chose to read long passages of *Winged Defense* rather than engage in the verbal sparring at which he excelled. The board's concluding report, as expected, did not endorse an independent air force. But if Mitchell's appearance before Morrow was lackluster, his performance during his court-martial the following month was even worse.

The trial began on 28 October with the prosecution reading into the record the statement Mitchell had made to the press after the *Shenandoah* crash. It was lengthier and far more vitriolic than the newspaper accounts had indicated. Nonetheless, Mitchell pleaded not guilty. The heart of the trial focused on Mitchell's testimony and his cross-examination. Mitchell's attorney, Cong. Frank Reid, had been out of a courtroom for too long and was not inspiring. The prosecution, on the other hand, was most impressive. Maj Allen Gullion began his attack by taking Mitchell's statement apart, line by line. Although Mitchell had openly criticized the Navy for its handling of aviation matters, as well as its wasteful emphasis on the surface fleet, Gullion's questioning made it clear that Mitchell knew very little about naval technology, organization, doctrine, or tactics. For example, though claiming expertise in airship design—after all, his comments on the *Shenandoah* crash had precipitated the entire crisis—Mitchell admitted he had never flown on an airship and had seen them up close only on a handful of occasions. Finally, under incessant pressure, Mitchell was even forced to concede that his lengthy diatribe to the press contained "no facts at all"—only opinions. Sarcastically, Gullion commented that it was necessary to distinguish between "opinion and imagination" and led Mitchell through a series of questions regarding Air Service accident rates, flying hours, equipment costs, and training requirements, most of which the defendant was unable to answer. Yet, Mitchell had claimed that airpower was in disastrous straits. Where were the facts to substantiate the charges of treason and incompetence? Overall, it was a dismal performance.[80]

Mitchell had obtained the forum he sought, but the results were certainly not what he had intended. One historian argues that Mitchell sincerely thought he would be found not guilty. Yet, when one remembers how intemperately he savaged the Army hierarchy, calling into question its motives, competence, integrity, and patriotism—and bearing in mind that part of that hierarchy sat in judgment of him—Mitchell's hubris in thinking he would be forgiven is a bit breathtaking.[81] His persistent and provocative explosions were simply too much. The verdict shocked no one but Mitchell himself. Found guilty on 17 December—ironically, the 22d anniversary of the Wright brothers' first powered flight at Kitty Hawk—he retired from the service on 1 February 1926 to continue his crusade, sans uniform.

Although newspapers gave the court-martial proceedings extensive coverage, no outcry for an independent air force erupted following the verdict. The Morrow Board, which had received testimony from an array of civilian and military aviation specialists, had indeed diminished interest in the court-martial. *Winged Defense* sold only forty-five hundred copies between August 1925 and January 1926, during the peak of sensationalism.[82] Although Mitchell received many letters in that span echoing the support of the "great mass of the common people of America,"[83] few individuals were willing to back his cause with a demand for legislation.

Mitchell's confidant Hap Arnold, then an Air Service major, later speculated on why the American people failed to act on Mitchell's recommendations: "The public enthusiasm . . . was not for air power—it was for Billy."[84] Flamboyant, intrepid, and cocksure, Mitchell appealed to New Era America. His message, though, struck an uncertain chord. His argument that bombers could now defend the nation more efficiently than battleships seemed to make sense, as did his assertion that bombers could defeat an enemy without the need for a ground invasion. Yet, questions remained. Defend against *whom? Whom* would airpower defeat? The Morrow Board's conclusion, "We do not consider . . . that air power . . . has yet demonstrated its value—*certainly not in a country situated as ours*—for independent operations of such a character as to justify the organization of a separate department" (emphasis added), reflected the key concerns held by the bulk of the American populace regarding Mitchell's ideas.[85] In 1925 the public realized that no enemy threatened the United States and that airplanes could not yet routinely cross the Atlantic or Pacific Oceans. The mood would endure for more than a decade.

The failure of the American public to respond directly to Mitchell's outcry did not mean that the issue of air autonomy disappeared, but it did mean that the steps taken during the interwar years would be incremental. National boards and committees continued to study the issue of how best to organize Army aviation. The Air Corps Act of July 1926 changed the Air Service's name to the Air Corps and provided an assistant secretary of war for air and special representation on the War Department's General Staff. It also authorized an Air Corps of 20,000 men and eighteen hundred aircraft, but Congress failed to fund the expansion.

The Great Depression further slowed Air Corps growth. From 1927 to 1931, Air Corps annual budgets ranged from $25–30 million; in 1934 appropriations fell to $12 million for the year; in 1938 to $3.5 million.[86] Manpower, which averaged fifteen hundred officers and 15,000 enlisted men during the first three Depression years, stood at only 17,000 men and seventeen hundred officers as late as 1939.[87] Aircraft totaled 1,619 in 1933, of which 442 were obsolete or nonstandard.[88] Still, the recommendation of the 1934 aviation board chaired by former secretary of war Newton Baker led to the creation of a GHQ Air Force, containing all Air Corps combat units, in the spring of 1935. Although the airpower comprising the GHQ Air Force was never significant—in 1939 it owned just 14

105

four-engined B-17 bombers—it nonetheless was one step closer towards Mitchell's progressive vision of an autonomous air force capable of achieving an independent victory.

Establishment of the GHQ Air Force did not indicate that either the nation or the Army had accepted Mitchell's airpower ideology. The Baker Board's final report cautioned that "the ideas that aviation, acting alone, can control the sea lanes, or defend the coast, or produce decisive results in any other general mission contemplated under our policy are all visionary, as is the idea that a very large and independent air force is necessary to defend our country against air attack."[89] The primary bomber assigned to the GHQ Air Force's three air wings at the end of the decade was the Douglas B-18 "Bolo," a dual-engined aircraft designed for short-range interdiction or battlefield support. The War Department ordered 217 B-18s in 1935 over the objections of the Air Corps, which had endorsed the B-17.

To most General Staff officers, airpower meant preventing enemy aircraft from attacking friendly troops or using friendly aircraft to attack enemy troops and supplies near the battlefield. It did not mean achieving victory from the sky—a proposition that many Army leaders viewed with thinly veiled scorn. Mitchell's public outcries led many Army officers to reject future proposals for air force autonomy out of hand. Arnold remarked that "they seemed to set their mouths tighter, draw more into their shell, and, if anything, take even a narrower point of view of aviation as an offensive power in warfare."[90] Army brigadier general Charles E. Kilbourne, chief of the General Staff's War Plans Division, critiqued Mitchell's impact on Army leadership in harsher terms. In 1934 Kilbourne remarked that "for many years the General Staff of the Army has suffered a feeling of disgust amounting at times to nausea over statements publicly made by General William Mitchell and those who followed his lead."[91]

Undoubtedly, Mitchell became more radical in his theories in the decade after World War I. Postwar budget cuts drove the services towards a bitter parochialism as they fought for a dwindling share of the defense dollar. Largely as a consequence, by 1920 Mitchell was attacking the Navy, and the climactic tests that sank the battleships in 1921 and again in 1923 convinced him he was right. In his vision of the future, the surface fleet would largely disappear, and the submarine would take its place as the symbol of maritime strength. Mitchell's attacks on the Army, muted at first, accelerated after his court-martial, and he incessantly accused the top generals of conservatism and shortsightedness. In a typically nasty fashion, he commented at one point that "we must relegate armies and navies to a place in the glass case of a dusty museum, which contains examples of the dinosaur, the mammoth, and the cave bear."[92] The animosity became mutual.

Although Mitchell may have repelled many Army and Navy officers, most airmen gravitated to his message, if not his methodology.[93] The coterie of "believers" who surrounded him during his tenure as assistant chief of the Air Service—Hap Arnold, Carl "Tooey" Spaatz, William Sherman, Herbert Dargue, Robert Olds, Kenneth Walker, Harold Lee George, and Ira C. Eaker—were not only future leaders of the Air Corps but also future theorists. Together, they refined Mitchell's notions and conveyed them throughout the close-knit community of airmen, and they found their audience receptive. Strong ties bonded the small number of aviators—the dangers of flying, even in peacetime, made the Air Service responsible for almost 50 percent of the Army's active duty deaths between 1921 and 1924.[94] Airmen realized as well that advancing in rank was tenuous as long as the Army controlled promotion lists, given the fact that most Army leaders viewed the air weapon as an auxiliary feature of a ground force. After Arnold and Dargue received reprimands in 1926 for sending congressmen proautonomy literature, most airmen adopted a stoic posture that reflected Mitchell's ideas, but they hesitated to speak those thoughts too loudly outside their clan.

Air chiefs also absorbed Mitchell's notions. Mason Patrick, who initially shunned Mitchell's ideas on Air Service autonomy and regarded him as "a spoiled brat,"[95] submitted a study to the War Department in December 1924 advocating "a united air force" that would place "all of the component air units, and possibly all aeronautical development under one responsible and directing head." As for its wartime usage, Patrick asserted that "we should gather our air forces together under one air commander and strike at the strategic points of our enemy—cripple him even before our ground forces come into contact."[96] Patrick's successors as chief of the Air Corps—James E. Fechet, Benny Foulois, Oscar Westover, and Hap Arnold—were equally committed to Mitchell's goal of an independent air force and shared his faith that airpower could win wars (although Foulois had no love lost for Mitchell personally). Maj Gen Frank Andrews, who commanded the GHQ Air Force from 1935–39, was an airpower disciple who relentlessly spouted Mitchellese to both the War Department and the public and, like Mitchell, was banished to Fort Sam Houston. Aside from Andrews and the outspoken Foulois, however, air leaders chose to restrain their advocacy. Most worked to improve relations with the War Department while securing high-visibility peacetime missions that stressed airpower's ability to defend the nation. Although Mitchell the prophet remained uppermost in their minds, so too did Mitchell the martyr.

Mitchell's prophecy not only endured among air leaders but also was the fundamental underpinning of the Air Corps Tactical School—the focal point of American airpower study during the interwar years. Mitchell had been instrumental in founding the school, and his bombing manual served as a textbook.[97] Many of the school's officer-instructors were his protégés. Sherman, Dargue, George, Olds, and Walker—the latter two had served as Mitchell's aides—filled key positions on the faculty, and all promoted Mitchell's vision of independent airpower founded on the bomber.

Mitchell's progressive vision of airpower applied against an enemy's war-making capability and will to resist will likely endure among American airmen. Perhaps Mitchell, had he lived to see the modern age of limited war, would have recanted his increasingly bold assertions regarding airpower's ability to achieve a cheap, quick victory. Still, Mitchell remains America's foremost airpower prophet. His vision included the development of precision-guided munitions, remotely piloted vehicles, stealth aircraft, and drop tanks, as well as the creation of the Federal Aeronautics Administration and the Department of Defense. Yet, his most enduring legacy remains his views on the value of an independent air force, capable of waging and winning an independent air campaign against an enemy nation. For the United States Air Force, this doctrinal cornerstone may prove impossible to replace.

Notes

1. Diary of William Mitchell, 24 December 1924, Mitchell Papers, Library of Congress, Washington, D.C. Quoted in Alfred H. Hurley, *Billy Mitchell: Crusader for Air Power*, rev. ed. (Bloomington, Ind.: Indiana University Press, 1975), 50.

2. Quoted in Andrew Boyle, *Trenchard* (London: Collins, 1962), 472.

3. Mitchell had outranked Foulois, an ex-enlisted man, before the war, so when Gen John J. Pershing elevated him to chief of the Air Service in November 1917, Mitchell was furious. His dislike of Foulois endured long after the war. Gorrell had become chief of the Air Service's Technical Section because of Mitchell's recommendation, but the friendship between the two disappeared once Gorrell joined Pershing's staff and began no-notice inspections of Mitchell's squadrons. See John F. Shiner, *Foulois and the U.S. Army Air Corps, 1931–1935* (Washington, D.C.: Office of Air Force History, 1983), 9–11; and William Mitchell to Benjamin Foulois, letter, 19 July 1918, Mitchell Papers, Library of Congress, Washington, D.C.

4. Ruth Mitchell, *My Brother Bill: The Life of General "Billy" Mitchell* (New York: Harcourt, Brace, 1953), 45–59.

5. An unpublished manuscript of these events by Mitchell exists, and Ruth's book draws heavily from it (pages 60–175). A microfilm copy of the entire manuscript is located in the Air University Library, Maxwell AFB, Ala. For an overview, see Mitchell's "Building the Alaskan Telegraph System," *National Geographic* 15 (September 1904): 357–62.

6. Capt William Mitchell, "Field Signal Communications" (Fort Leavenworth, Kans.: Infantry and Cavalry School, Department of Military Art, May 1905), 21.

7. *Hearings before the President's Aircraft Board, September 1925* [hereinafter Morrow Board hearings] (Washington, D.C.: Government Printing Office, 1925), 600; William Mitchell, "Airplanes in National Defense," *The American*, May 1927, 40; idem, "Future Flying," *Liberty*, 8 June 1929, 15–27; and idem, "The Next War in the Air," *Popular Mechanics*, February 1935, 163–65.

8. Henry H. Arnold, *Global Mission* (New York: Harper & Brothers, 1949), 37–38.

9. Quoted in Hurley, 17. One should note that when he was reminded of this opinion at his court-martial, he retorted, "I never made a worse statement." *The United States v. Colonel William Mitchell*, court-martial transcript, Washington, D.C., October–December 1925, 1607. Microfilm copy in Air Force Academy Library, Colorado Springs, Colo.

10. Bill given to Maj William Mitchell from the Atlantic Coast Aeronautical Station of the Curtiss Aviation School, Newport News, Va., 1 March 1917, Mitchell Papers, General Correspondence, 1907–1917, Library

of Congress, Washington, D.C. Mitchell tried to bill the government for his training, but the Treasury comptroller ruled that individual payments made to civilian flying schools were not refundable.

11. Hurley, 21.

12. William Mitchell, *Memoirs of World War I: From Start to Finish of Our Greatest War* (New York: Random House, 1960), 59. Parts of these memoirs were serialized by *Liberty* magazine in 1928. This memoir is based on the diaries Mitchell kept during the war. Regrettably, those diaries are now lost, so one must read this work with caution.

13. Mitchell, *Memoirs*, 103–11; Isaac D. Levine, *Mitchell: Pioneer of Air Power*, rev. ed. (New York: Duell, Sloan and Pearce, 1958), 94–97; Hurley, 25–27; and John H. Morrow Jr., *The Great War in the Air: Military Aviation from 1909 to 1921* (Washington, D.C.: Smithsonian Institution Press, 1993), 271.

14. Maj W. Mitchell, memorandum to chief of staff, AEF, 13 June 1917. Quoted in I. B. Holley, *Ideas and Weapons* (New Haven, Conn.: Yale University Press, 1953), 47.

15. Maj W. Mitchell, memorandum to chief of staff, AEF, 13 June 1917. Extract in Maurer Maurer, ed., *The US Air Service in World War I*, vol. 2 (Washington, D.C.: Government Printing Office, 1979), 108.

16. In the United States, however, the Signal Corps maintained control over its Aviation Section.

17. Hurley, 32.

18. Mitchell, *Memoirs*, 153–54, 157. Mitchell used the château to inspire his staff to converse in French, which he encouraged to enhance Allied cooperation.

19. Maurer, vol. 2, 141–51.

20. Mitchell, *Memoirs*, 146.

21. Chief of Air Service, I Army Corps, memorandum to commanding general, I Army Corps, 16 February 1918, Mitchell Papers, General Correspondence, Library of Congress, Washington, D.C.

22. Hurley, 32; and Robert Frank Futrell, *Ideas, Concepts, Doctrine: Basic Thinking in the United States Air Force*, vol. 1, *1907–1960* (Maxwell AFB, Ala.: Air University Press, December 1989), 22.

23. Mitchell, *Memoirs*, 268; "Planned to Drop Americans from Sky in Hun Rear," *New York Herald*, 8 March 1919, 2; and William Mitchell, "Wiping Danger from the Sky," *Liberty*, 24 June 1933, 17–18. In *Notes on the Multi-Motored Bombardment Group, Day and Night*, a tactical manual that Mitchell wrote for his troops in 1922, he also suggested parachuting commandos behind enemy lines to blow up key installations such as ammunition dumps.

24. Quoted in Levine, 148.

25. Quoted in ibid., 147.

26. Quoted in Hurley, 37.

27. Brig Gen William Mitchell, "Tactical Application of Military Aeronautics," 5 January 1919, 3, US Air Force Historical Research Agency [hereinafter AFHRA], Maxwell AFB, Ala., file 167.4-1.

28. Edgar S. Gorrell, "Early History of the Strategical Section," in Maurer, vol. 2, 157.

29. Maj Gen J. W. McAndrew, endorsement to chief of Air Service, 18 June 1918, in Maurer, vol. 2, 192.

30. DeWitt S. Copp, *A Few Great Captains: The Men and Events That Shaped the Development of U.S. Air Power* (Garden City, N.Y.: Doubleday, 1980), 24.

31. Mitchell, *Memoirs,* 165, 177, 185, 205; and Benjamin Foulois to John J. Pershing, letter, subject: Relief of Col William Mitchell, 4 June 1918, AFHRA, file 168.68-5.

32. Maj Gen Mason M. Patrick, *The United States in the Air* (Garden City, N.Y.: Doubleday, 1928), 16.

33. On the nature of progressivism and its lingering impact in the 1920s, see Richard Hofstadter, *The Age of Reform: From Bryan to F.D.R.* (New York: Knopf, 1968), 5, 91–93, 131–72, 270–326; Robert H. Wiebe, *The Search for Order* (New York: Hill & Wang, 1967), 286–302; Arthur M. Schlesinger Jr., *The Age of Roosevelt: The Crisis of the Old Order* (Boston: Houghton Mifflin, 1957), 72–89; and Arthur S. Link, "Not So Tired," in Arthur Mann, ed., *The Progressive Era: Liberal Renaissance or Liberal Failure* (New York: Holt, Rinehart and Winston, 1963), 105–19. Mitchell, who continually voiced progressive notions, used the term directly in the foreword to his book *Winged Defense:* "The time has come when aviation must be developed for aviation's sake and not as an auxiliary to other existing branches [of the service]. Unless the progressive elements in our makeup are availed of, we will fall behind in the world's development." William Mitchell, *Winged Defense* (New York: G. P. Putnam's Sons, 1925), x.

34. William Mitchell, "Aeronautical Era," *The Saturday Evening Post,* 20 December 1924, 99. Mitchell repeats this message in *Winged Defense,* 16, and *Skyways* (Philadelphia: J. B. Lippincott Company, 1930), 262.

35. Morrow Board hearings, 599.

36. "General Mitchell's Daring Speech," *Aviation,* 29 October 1924, 1160; and William Mitchell, "It's a Thousand to One You Can't Fly," *Liberty,* 2 January 1926, 20–22.

37. William Mitchell, "Neither Armies Nor Navies Can Exist Unless the Air Is Controlled over Them," *U.S. Air Services,* May 1925, 18.

38. Patrick, 86–88.

39. William Mitchell, "Strategical Aspect of the Pacific Problem," 1924, 1, Mitchell Papers, Library of Congress, Washington, D.C.

40. Ibid., 15.

41. Ibid., 18.

42. William Mitchell, *Our Air Force: The Key to National Defense* (New York: Dutton, 1921), 168.

43. *The United States v. Colonel William Mitchell,* 1419; and William Mitchell, "Colonel Mitchell Explains His Plan," *Liberty,* 21 November 1925, 10.

44. William Mitchell, "Look Out Below!" *Collier's,* 21 April 1928, 42.

45. Mitchell, *Skyways,* 268.

46. William Mitchell, "Our Army's Air Service," *Review of Reviews,* September 1920, 288; and idem, "Aviation over the Water," *Review of Reviews,* October 1920, 394.

47. Levine, 257. For the argument that Mitchell was to some extent the father of naval aviation, see Samuel F. Wells, "William Mitchell and the *Ostfriesland:* A Study in Military Reform," *The Historian* 26 (November 1963): 538–62.

48. Mitchell, *Our Air Force,* 15, 37.

49. William Mitchell, draft of *War Memoirs,* 3, Mitchell Papers, Diaries, May 1917–February 1919, Library of Congress, Washington, D.C.

50. Mitchell, *Memoirs,* 2; idem, *Skyways,* 253; and idem, "Our Problem of National Defense," *Outlook,* 23 January 1929, 124.

51. Mitchell, "Aeronautical Era," 99–103; see also idem, *Winged Defense,* 16–17.

52. Mitchell, *Winged Defense,* 214.

53. Mitchell, "Aeronautical Era," 3.

54. Mitchell, *Winged Defense,* 126–27; Hurley, 87; and William Mitchell, *Notes on the Multi-Motored Bombardment Group, Day and Night,* 76, 81, 93–94.

55. Mitchell, "Aeronautical Era," 3.

56. William Mitchell, "When the Air Raiders Come," *Collier's,* 1 May 1926, 8.

57. Mitchell, *Skyways,* 63.

58. William Mitchell, memorandum to Major General Patrick, 10 May 1923, Mitchell Papers, General Correspondence, Library of Congress, Washington, D.C.; and Thomas H. Greer, *The Development of Air Doctrine in the Army Air Arm, 1917–1941* (Washington, D.C.: Office of Air Force History, 1955), 57. By 1925 Mitchell had substituted Bangor, Maine, for Boston as the apex of his triangle. See Mitchell, *Winged Defense,* 184.

59. Mitchell, *Notes on the Multi-Motored Bombardment Group, Day and Night,* 94.

60. Mitchell, *Our Air Force,* xix.

61. Hurley, 74–77.

62. Douhet observed that "victory smiles upon those who anticipate the changes in the character of war, not upon those who wait to adapt themselves after the changes occur," while Mitchell noted that "victory always comes to that country which has made a proper estimate of the equipment and methods that can be used in modern ways." See Giulio Douhet, *The Command of the Air,* trans. Dino Ferrari (1942; reprint, Washington, D.C.: Office of Air Force History, 1983), 30; and Mitchell, *Winged Defense,* 127.

63. Mitchell, *Winged Defense,* xiv, 9; and Douhet, 25, 54–55.

64. Douhet, 34.

65. Mitchell, *Winged Defense,* 9–10.

66. Douhet, 18, 52–55.

67. Col Townsend F. Dodd, "Recommendations Concerning the Establishment of a 'Department of Aeronautics,'" 17 April 1919, 19, Mitchell Papers, Library of Congress, Washington, D.C.

68. Mitchell, *Winged Defense*, xvii–xix, 6, 11–17.

69. William Mitchell, "Why We Need a Department of the Air," 21 December 1919, Mitchell Papers, Library of Congress, Washington, D.C.

70. Mitchell, *Notes on the Multi-Motored Bombardment Group, Day and Night*, 72.

71. Mitchell, *Our Air Force*, 153–55; and idem, *Winged Defense*, 77–96.

72. "General Mitchell on the Aero Show," *Aircraft Journal*, 13 March 1920, 14; and "General Mitchell on Aeronautical Progress," *Aviation*, 12 February 1923, 187.

73. Adjutant General, memorandum to the chief of Air Service, 7 February 1925, with attached memorandum from William Mitchell to chief of Air Service, 2 March 1925; and W. G. Kilner, memorandum to General Mitchell, 30 January 1925, with attached memorandum from Mitchell to chief of Air Service, 5 February 1925, Mitchell Papers, General Correspondence, Library of Congress, Washington, D.C.

74. Weeks did not mince his rationale to President Calvin Coolidge. The secretary remarked, "General Mitchell's course has been so lawless, so contrary to the building up of an efficient organization, so lacking in reasonable team work, so indicative of a personal desire for publicity at the expense of everyone with whom he is associated that his actions render him unfit for a high administrative position such as he now occupies." See John W. Weeks to Calvin Coolidge, letter, 4 March 1925, Mitchell Papers, General Correspondence, Library of Congress, Washington, D.C.

75. "The personnel of these permanent establishments often tend to become uniformed office holders instead of public servants entirely engaged in furthering the betterment of their nation." See Mitchell, *Winged Defense*, 136.

76. Elizabeth Mitchell to William Mitchell, letter, 2 September 1925, Mitchell Papers, General Correspondence, Library of Congress, Washington, D.C. One should also note that Mitchell took his wife's concerns to heart. In his explosive press release of 5 September, he specifically referred to the cartoons in *Winged Defense* and publicly apologized to Secretary Weeks for any disrespect they may have implied. *The United States v. Colonel William Mitchell*, 23.

77. Quoted in Hurley, 101.

78. Quoted in Eugene M. Emme, "The American Dimension," in Alfred F. Hurley and Robert C. Ehrhart, eds., *Air Power and Warfare: Proceedings of the Eighth Military History Symposium, USAF Academy, 1978* (Washington, D.C.: Government Printing Office, 1979), 67.

79. Ibid.

80. See *The United States v. Colonel William Mitchell*, 1449–61 for Mitchell's particularly ineffectual testimony regarding naval operations. His entire testimony runs from pages 1401 to 1612. Of interest, three members of the court were challenged by the defense and dismissed: Maj Gen Charles

P. Summerall, Maj Gen Fred W. Sladen, and Brig Gen Albert J. Bowley. One who remained was Brig Gen Douglas MacArthur, an old friend of Mitchell's since childhood; in fact, MacArthur had dated Mitchell's sister at one point.

81. Michael L. Grumelli, "Trial of Faith: The Dissent and Court-Martial of Billy Mitchell" (PhD diss., Rutgers University, 1991), 262.

82. Hurley, 108.

83. See, for instance, Harvey F. Trumbore to Gen William Mitchell, letter, 27 January 1926; Elverton H. Wicks to Colonel Mitchell, letter, 31 December 1925; and Horace C. Carlisle to Colonel and Mrs. Mitchell, letter, 21 December 1925, Mitchell Papers, General Correspondence, Library of Congress, Washington, D.C.

84. Arnold, 158–59.

85. Quoted in Futrell, vol. 1, 48.

86. Ira C. Eaker, "Maj. Gen. James E. Fechet: Chief of the Air Corps, 1927–1931," *Air Force Magazine*, September 1978, 96; Jeffery S. Underwood, *The Wings of Democracy: The Influence of Air Power on the Roosevelt Administration, 1933–1941* (College Station, Tex.: Texas A&M University Press, 1991), 30–31; and Emme, 72.

87. Eaker, 96; and James Parton, "The Thirty-One Year Gestation of the Independent Air Force," *Aerospace Historian* 34 (September 1987): 153.

88. Futrell, vol. 1, 67.

89. Quoted in ibid., 70–71.

90. Arnold, 122.

91. Quoted in Shiner, 51.

92. William Mitchell, "Airplanes in National Defense," *Annals of the American Academy*, May 1927, 42.

93. Jeffery Underwood maintains in *The Wings of Democracy* that the failure of Mitchell's controversial public appeals to produce an independent air force caused his successors—with the notable exception of Air Corps chief Benjamin Foulois—to work "within the system" to secure their goal. While this was certainly true of many airmen, Maj Gen Frank Andrews, the commander of GHQ Air Force, and his chief of staff Col Hugh Knerr sometimes resorted to controversial publicity when they thought it would further the cause of an independent air force.

94. Mitchell, *Winged Defense*, 220. See also Ronald Schaffer, *Wings of Judgment: American Bombing in World War II* (New York: Oxford University Press, 1985), 17–18.

95. Quoted in Parton, 152.

96. Maj Gen Mason Patrick, memorandum to the War Department adjutant general, subject: Reorganization of the Air Forces for National Defense, 19 December 1924, Mitchell Papers, Library of Congress, Washington, D.C.

97. Maj Gen Clayton Bissell, transcript of oral history interview by Brig Gen George W. Goddard, 22 February 1966, 8–10, AFHRA, file K239.0512-987; and Hurley, 128.

Chapter 4

The Influence of Aviation on the Evolution of American Naval Thought

Dr. David R. Mets

The cast of mind of the officer corps of the US Navy is sometimes deemed Neanderthal, sometimes progressive, and, less often, radical. This chapter revisits the history of recent naval theory and doctrine to evaluate this perception and the impact of the coming of aviation on the general attitudes of the naval profession in America from the beginning of flight to the end of World War II. Previous chapters have all dealt with the impact of World War I on the theory of airpower, usually in a Continental war context. They went on to study its development in the interwar period. This chapter briefly looks at naval thought at the onset of aviation, which serves as a baseline. It continues with changes brought on by World War I and interwar evolution, and thence to the impact of World War II on the Navy's outlook.[1] In large part, naval air theory was formed in the decade after the great carriers USS *Lexington* and USS *Saratoga* came on-line at the end of 1927. That is precisely the decade in which the thinking at the Air Corps Tactical School was in its most formative phase—and that is the subject of another chapter.

The examination of each era starts with the general worldview and then considers the ways in which naval officers believed that international conflicts could be settled. It then discusses the general attitude on the proper objectives of a navy in the process, the standard methods employed in naval warfare, and changing views on the ideal organization of forces for war and their employment in international conflict. The study closes with an estimate of the state of naval thinking in all those categories as the nation approached the reorganization of its national security structure in the late 1940s. Hopefully, comparing that state with the initial one will yield some additional insight into the impact of aviation on naval thinking.

Naval Attitudes at the Onset of the Age of Flight

The collective attitude of the mainstream of the Navy at the dawn of aviation was fairly well developed. The service was thoroughly convinced that the world was made up of nation-states and that conflict of one sort or another was natural among them. The premise of Clausewitz—that war was an instrument of state policy—was well understood and accepted. In the words of Commander Patrick N. L. Bellinger, who graduated from Annapolis in 1907 and the Naval War College in 1925, "War is a political action. . . . Even when armies and fleets are not employed, their existence and the possibility of their use constantly influence the action of governments. They are instruments of statecraft. The policy of countries must necessarily be controlled by their governments, and strategy from the naval and military point of view, must be subservient to policy."[2]

However much one identified the thought of Alfred Thayer Mahan with that of Henri de Jomini (if that is supposed to mean that the adherents look upon war as a science that has natural laws that always apply and that there exists an eternal validity to principles of war), plenty of officers understood fog and friction. There were repeated assertions that both doctrine and any statement of principles were no more than guides—certainly not invariable rules that one could not violate. The officer corps was thoroughly familiar with Mahan (for some, both the man and his works—Mahan had been Adm William A. Moffett's skipper when Moffett served aboard the USS *Chicago* in the 1890s).[3] Furthermore, it was convinced that, for the United States at least, command of the sea remained the primary objective and that its exploitation could come later, through blockade or invasion. For Mahan and most of his followers, the fundamental method for achieving command was offensive—seeking out the enemy main battle fleet and destroying it.[4] Significantly, they gave a great deal more attention to achieving command of the sea than to exploiting it.

The officer corps was coming out of a period of very rapid technological advance. It had witnessed the coming of torpedoes, submarines, and destroyers—all of which had been touted as revolutionary and none of which, in the collective mind, had turned out that way.[5] The necessity for decentralized command, initiative among junior and midlevel commanders, and doctrine that tended to create a common vocabulary and outlook was widely accepted.

Methods of Conflict Resolution

Little questioned was the idea that command of the sea would be won in a single great clash between the main battle lines and that all other elements would necessarily play an auxiliary role. Notwithstanding Clausewitz's assertion that, in land warfare at least, the defensive was the stronger form of war, the Navy (and Army and Marine Corps as well) probably voiced an overwhelming preference for the offensive in both strategy and tactics.[6] Doubtless, the civilian attitude in isolationist America in the wake of the mayhem of World War I made it impolitic to dwell on this stance in public.

Practically all officers were graduates of the Naval Academy, and the bulk of the seniormost officers had been through the Naval War College—and on the eve of World War I, some of the juniors were well indoctrinated through correspondence courses.[7] There was a rather strong commitment to the idea that both study and practical experience were vital to understanding naval war. On the eve of the first air war, both the United States Naval Institute and its publishing organ, *Proceedings*, were more than a generation old. Senior and middling officers took a real interest in this journal as a forum for professional discourse—Mahan and Stephen B. Luce, the founder of the Naval War College, were both well published in its pages. The Naval Academy was one of America's first and leading engineering schools; still, the historical approach to the study of war and sea power was common—even before Mahan.[8] No one questioned the idea that the Navy constituted the first line of defense.

Ideal Organization for War

The effectiveness of the bureau organization was often debated, and the notion that the planning and operations functions should remain paramount and governed by a professional naval officer was very strong. Previously divided into line and engineering categories, a division that had caused much difficulty, the officers of the Navy found themselves reunified, first in the curriculum at the Naval Academy and then on the line of the Navy—both before 1900.[9] Strong sentiment favored avoiding such divisions.[10]

At the beginning of the era of flight, then, the US Navy's officer corps tended to consider the world as being made up of nation-states—always in conflict, sometimes at war, and never recognizing any superior authority. Achieving command of the sea remained the first objective for naval forces; that done, a variety of naval measures could help in realizing the nation's goals ashore. As yet, little thought existed about radical changes in the relationship of the Navy to the rest of the US national security structure. Most thinking held that one should be a naval officer first and a deck or engineering officer second—that the officer corps should be a monolithic whole. Even Lt Commander Henry Mustin himself argued before World War I that to be competent as a naval aviator, an officer would need a comprehensive knowledge of the duties of the surface mariner. Because acquiring that knowledge took so long, he believed that trainees for aviation must come from the line of the Navy.[11] Though, in time, Mustin would argue otherwise, the organizational implication of his belief was that one should refrain from further attempts at specialized corps (notwithstanding the continued existence of the Marine Corps)—despite the fact that the fleet itself was organized along functional lines according to ship type. Some members of the officer corps felt that the bureau chiefs were too independent and that the creation of the office of Chief of Naval Operations (CNO) was a good thing. As for the employment of navies, the consensus was that decision would come through a great sea battle between battleships and that all other vessels and organizations existed to support the main battle line.

Evolution of American Naval Air Thinking before Pearl Harbor

Naval aviators had experimented with aviation in combat against Mexico even before World War I.[12] Pilots had made landings and takeoffs from ships as well, and people harbored serious questions about whether the main air effort would lie with airships (lighter-than-air), flying boats, or shipborne airplanes.[13] The Navy had substantial experience with aviation in World War I, both in overwater antisubmarine patrol and land combat on the western front. None of that was part of major fleet action in open ocean. Henry Mustin, one of the first wave of Navy flyers, was only one of many men who brought back perceptions of air war from Europe.[14] As with the Army's Air Service, however, one could draw no definitive inferences because technology was still in its infancy, and none of the exploits even approached being decisive.[15] Only the Battle of Jutland resembled the Mahanian great battle, but because of its indecisiveness, its implications remained unclear.[16] Aviation played little role in that battle, and its impact on the antisubmarine war was significant but not decisive. Aircraft forced submarines to remain submerged and, by closing the Strait of Dover, imposed the long trip around Scotland on them. The consequent reduction of the time on station lowered the number of U-boats in the German navy.[17] At the end of the war, Britain's Royal Navy did possess three aircraft carriers, but the US Navy had none. The brief American participation and the preoccupation of Europeans with the agony of the land war left little time to do much development work in naval aviation or to reach definitive conclusions.[18]

Largely because of the institutional culture, aviation affected the thinking of the Navy in an evolutionary, rather than a revolutionary, way. This statement does not suggest that the technology of naval warfare evolved on a steady, smooth curve—only that thought about the use of the Navy as a whole to help achieve national objectives changed in a gradual way, with neither long periods of stagnation nor obvious discontinuities. On the other hand, as suggested by Dr. Gary Weir, scientific and technological innovation—dependent in part on sudden inspirations by inventors and scientists—probably can be characterized more as a sawtooth process with a generally progressive trend.[19] Certainly, the general outlook was not radical; yet, it is also probably fair to say that insofar as strategic thinking was concerned, neither was it reactionary. The line officers of the Navy may have been reluctant to shed the ideas proven in the past, but they had adjusted to the coming of steam and armor and (with the British navy) had led the world in the development of modern gunnery and fire control.

In part, external pressures forced the line officers of the Navy to accept change. One factor was the Five Power Treaty of 1922, which drove the Navy to embrace aircraft carriers more rapidly than it might otherwise have done.[20] A second was the implicit threat that if the Navy itself did not move smartly into the era of flight, then the upstart Air Service and, later, the Air Corps would gather maritime aviation unto itself.[21] As yet, only a few officers, such as Adm William Sims and Adm William Fullam, questioned whether the carrier or the battleship would be the capital ship of the future—a question that remained open until after Pearl Harbor.

Methods of Conflict Resolution

One sees a sample of the cast of mind of the earliest crop of aviators in a lecture delivered by Commander Patrick Bellinger at the Naval War College in the summer of 1924. He allowed that naval aviation had other roles, such as cooperation with the Army in coast defense, but clearly his concentration remained on aviation as an adjunct to the fleet.[22]

Despite the presence of many skeptical mossbacks not disposed to change, some naval officers did not need external prods to revise their thinking—Sims and Moffett for example.[23] However, notions that one might bypass the great sea battle through a direct air attack on the enemy's economic, cultural, and moral fabric appeared infrequently among their published and unpublished writings.

Such interpretations appeared only because the writer (e.g., Capt George Westervelt in 1917 and Adm William Pratt in 1926) questioned the morality of such operations and the validity of Douhet's notion that attacks on civilian morale would be humane because they would end the war quickly and thereby eliminate the danger of another misery in the trenches. Westervelt, even in 1917, showed considerable insight in suggesting that in the short term, the German attacks may have had military value in that they diverted very considerable military potential from the fighting front for the largely futile defense of London. In the long term, however, he speculated that Germany might come to regret it. He thought the attacks might even toughen British civilian morale on the one hand and, on the other, act as a stimulus for greater and more destructive reprisals on the Germans by British and French air forces.[24]

At the end of World War I, the General Board of the Navy—made up of a group of the service's seniormost officers, necessarily nonaviators at that time—advised the secretary on fundamental issues affecting the life of the organization. In 1919, before Billy Mitchell's bombing tests, the board held formal hearings and explicitly advised the secretary that the integration of aviation into the fleet was of the highest priority.[25]

Further, one should not infer that all the logic was on the side of the aviators and that the "gun club" was irrational in its arguments.[26] Had the flying boat proven practical in timely reconnaissance and spotting support in midocean areas in the 1920s, it might have been a better solution to the air problem than either catapult-launched or carrier-launched aircraft. Indeed, flying-boat technology was much more mature than that of the other craft, and aircraft operated from catapults or platforms atop turrets probably would have reduced the fields of fire as well as the volume and rate of fire of the main armament. (Although aerial observation would radically enhance the accuracy of fire, more might be lost than gained.) Moreover, it was hard to imagine ever developing the means of recovering such catapulted aircraft without stopping the ship—clearly suicidal in the presence of enemy surface ships or submarines.[27]

On the other hand, if one accepted the assumption that the decision in war would come through use of the battleship fleet's guns, then the provision of aerial spotting through aircraft carriers, which could recover their "birds" while under way, would introduce another whole class of ships to the Navy line. This would come at a time when funding and manning were insufficient to take care of the requirements that already existed. Flying boats, featuring long range and a developed technology, could provide both scouting and spotting without that new line of ships (and one could greatly expand their areas of coverage by the use of tenders easily converted from ships already in the Navy). The flying boats, in fact, had just achieved enormous prestige by crossing the Atlantic in 1919. They did not inhibit the execution of the primary mission of the battleships and did not compete for funds and people nearly as much as carrier planes and their required ships.

Numerous aviators would support that reasoning. Bellinger, one of the most prominent, clearly was not skeptical of the value of shipboard aviation. He did not see much of a future for kite balloons or nonrigid airships, but he saw great value in shipboard aircraft supporting the battle line once air forces had achieved command of the air. Still, in 1924, he perceived enormous potential in the development of long-range flying boats.[28] Moreover, notwithstanding the great promise and glamour of the initial operations of the *Saratoga* and *Lexington*, those operations involved many difficulties, and their security with the fleet posed constraints on the offensive preferences of the commanders.[29]

Many people made similar arguments in favor of airships. Thus, the thinking of the gun club was not nearly as Neanderthal as it might appear to observers looking back from the post–Pearl Harbor period. The common flaw to that thinking was that if a force had no carrier aircraft, an enemy with carrier planes could deny the use of the air over the battle area to the former's catapult airplanes, flying boats, and lighter-than-air craft—and thus could produce an enormous advantage for his own battle fleet. Decisiveness would arise from the fact that the side with air superiority would be able to take its enemy under concentrated, accurate fire at long ranges and during impaired visibility while the other side could not.[30]

Worldview: Continuity and Change

From about 1906, we considered the Japanese a potential enemy, though continuing some war games with a Japanese-British enemy alliance until well after World War I.[31] After the demise of German admiral Alfred von Tirpitz's fleet at Scapa Flow, both the games and the thinking increasingly concentrated on a Pacific war against Japan—although we did not completely discount war against the British.[32] Capt Yates Stirling Jr. provided us with a near-classical statement in Mahanian terms. In an article published in 1925, he painted a worldview in which seafaring capitalist nations had to have overseas trade to survive; to do that, they had to protect that trade with navies; those navies would have to have battleships to command the sea or part of it; and only Japan and Great Britain were in the game. Although Stirling more clearly identified Japan as a potential enemy, he plainly asserted that competition with Great Britain was inevitable and that only the statesmanlike work of the Washington treaties promised to contain that competition.[33] In post–World War II terms, all of this constituted a "realist" worldview.

From the early 1920s, the war-college games and fleet maneuvers came to feature surprise air attacks on Pearl Harbor and the Panama Canal, but the ultimate decision would always arise from a great clash between the main surface fleets. Even the aviators, whose first task was to kill the enemy carriers, gave at least lip service to the idea that the final decision would come from the great gun battle. The bomb-carrying capability of carrier aircraft in the 1920s and early 1930s was so limited that many aviators understood that the chances of decisive attacks on armored vessels were strictly limited; not until the late 1930s could dive-bombers employ one-thousand-pound weapons at significant distances. Until late in the game, then, many aviators were persuaded that the gun battle might indeed be decisive.[34]

Organizing for War

Creation of the office of the CNO in 1915 improved naval organization. Gradually, the traditional power of the bureau chiefs declined, relative to that of the CNO. Some flyers, such

123

as Henry Mustin, called for the creation of a separate aviation corps;[35] however, other flyers and most of the nonflyers were against it, notwithstanding the Marine Corps precedent. This attitude resulted in part from lingering bad memories about the nineteenth-century dichotomy between line officers and engineering officers, as well as a feeling that such a move would play into the hands of the Air Service's Billy Mitchell and his followers. The aviators were satisfied, at least to some extent, with the foundation of the Bureau of Aeronautics in 1921. Some of the senior officers of the Navy had opposed the congressional proposal for the bureau, but in large part the heat generated by Mitchell changed their minds.[36] Its first chief, Rear Adm William Moffett, was not a pilot, but he went immediately to Pensacola, Florida, and completed the observers' course there. Popular among the flyers, he was also a successful battleship commander; had served once on a ship whose skipper was Mahan himself, as noted above; and had attended the Naval War College while Mahan was assigned there.[37]

From the outset, under Moffett's guidance, the appearance of a new bureau—in fact, a superbureau—complicated the internal organization of airpower. Moffett did not confine his activities to technical and procurement functions, as did the other bureau chiefs. He cast a wider net—including personnel issues such as assignment policy and promotions for aviators. This brought him into conflict with the other bureaus— especially with the Bureau of Navigation, which had traditionally managed personnel policy for all naval officers. This tension continued, growing all the way up through and beyond the tenure of Rear Adm John Towers at the helm of the Bureau of Aeronautics well into World War II.[38]

From the earliest days, military men in all the services began groping for a way to properly integrate aviation into the national security force structure. As it turned out, the Army flyers would choose a more or less independent path that resulted in the creation of the US Air Force in 1947. The Navy's flyers and almost all of its sailors favored integrating airpower with sea power. One such sailor, Rear Adm Nathan C. Twining, wrote to Capt Henry Mustin in 1919, stating tentatively that he felt airpower should be kept in the Army

124

and Navy. He saw some possibilities in distant air raiding but thought that should be part of the mission of the land army. He argued, however, that the most urgent task of all was developing aviation's capabilities in spotting and scouting.[39]

Six years later, Capt George Westervelt, then manager of the Naval Aircraft Factory in Philadelphia (though not an aviator himself), expressed a similar idea with no sugar coating or hedging:

> They [the aviators] are in the Navy, of the Navy, and wish to remain there. They firmly believe that the air arm is an inherent portion of the Navy; that, as a Naval air arm, it is helpless without the Navy, and that the Navy would be helpless without it. In imagination many of them, doubtless, project themselves into the future and see the time when the air arm of the Navy will be its paramount arm, and when the surface ships will get their orders from the Commander-in-Chief flying above them, but they still see these combined elements of their country's power as the Navy, and themselves as officers of the Navy.[40]

Westervelt had visited Britain during World War I, and, undoubtedly, the Royal Navy was an influence on him and the entire US Navy—as it always had been. The story about the influence of the Royal Air Force (RAF) on US Army aviators is well known. Mitchell's visits with Hugh Trenchard during World War I are well documented.[41] Perhaps less well known is the negative impact of the RAF on the US Navy. The British integrated their naval and land-based airpower into a separate air force in 1918 and kept it so organized up to 1937. From 1918 forward, it was an article of faith in the US Navy that that decision had been a mistake and proof that an independent air force would be bad for the United States. Without arguing the virtues of the Spitfire, Fighter Command, Taranto, and victory over the *Bismarck* and the U-boats, it is clear that the stout opposition to the idea in the US Navy had its origins long before the RAF could possibly have had the deadly effects attributed to it. To cite one example, in testifying to the General Board of the Navy on 23 August 1918, Commander H. C. Dinger asserted, "Personally, I don't see how there could be any argument. They [the British] must have both Naval and Army aviation. Of course these are only my personal views. The amalgamation in England seems to have had a very bad effect."[42]

In the wake of the commissioning of the *Langley* (CV-1) in the early 1920s, articles in *Proceedings,* as well as Naval War College papers and lectures, paid increasing attention to the implications of aviation.[43] This increased sharply after the great ships *Saratoga* (CV-3) and *Lexington* (CV-2) came on-line late in 1927. No doubt, Navy people endlessly fought and refought the Battle of Jutland on the game boards at Newport and in the pages of *Proceedings,* but they also wrote many articles on aviation as well.[44]

Proper Naval Objectives in War

Even in the articles on aviation, usually the climax came in a big gun duel. Analogous to the Army experience on the western front, the most strident demand for a capability to command the air came from the most committed surface gunners. It became clear to battleship captains that aerial spotting so enhanced the power of the big gun that any admiral who lost that spotting capability found himself at a huge disadvantage.[45] The corollary to that principle, as on the western front, was that one had to make every effort to protect free use of the air over the battle and to deny it to the enemy. Thus, hardly anyone in any of the services needed much persuasion that command of the air remained a paramount consideration. In 1926, Admiral Pratt himself argued that it was a primary function of naval aviation.[46]

Although in the 1930s, mainstream thought seldom wavered from the idea that the primary and final instrument of victory would be the battleship, it held that Japan would refuse battle until the combat power of the US Navy had been diminished by projecting itself all the way across the central Pacific. Most strategic thinkers felt that the Navy could minimize this weakening if the US offensive went across the central (instead of the north or south) Pacific, invading and building up island bases as it went (as opposed to making one giant leap that would force the Japanese navy to come out and fight for the sea when the Americans arrived in the vicinity of the Philippines). Carrier airpower would always be a scarce commodity. In those days, people deemed land-based airpower a formidable threat. Without air bases to protect the line of communications and naval bases to attenuate the erosion of sea power as it projected further across the Pacific, the defeat of the Japanese fleet on the other side remained improbable.[47]

In all of this, aviation had two main functions. First, it would enhance the effectiveness of the cruisers and destroyers of the scouting fleet through reconnaissance. Second, it would enhance the effectiveness of the battle fleet through conducting reconnaissance, spotting the fall of shot, and defending against the enemy's carrier airpower (usually through sinking or disabling enemy carriers.)[48] Sometimes, aircraft might attack battleships, but usually they sought to slow them down so that the plodding American battleships could catch up with the speedier Japanese dreadnoughts to administer decisive blows with their guns.[49] Not long before his death, Admiral Moffett spoke of using offensive carrier aircraft in exactly that way to facilitate the great sea battle.[50] Even up to the eve of World War II, aviators who delivered lectures at the Naval War College on the uses of airpower were clearly reluctant to claim too much for airplanes versus battleships.[51]

To a large degree, students of the intellectual history of any military force must grapple with an eternal problem: was the glass half full or half empty? Much of the final judgment necessarily resides in the eye of the beholder. Charles Melhorn and Curtis Utz have demonstrated that declared policy and doctrine do not always match the undeclared worldview of the decision makers of any organization.[52] To some extent, the articulation of official doctrine inevitably lags. Sometimes, acquisition policies indicate the difference between declared doctrine and the undeclared vision of the future. They both show that the Navy *did* make progress in aviation between the armistice and Pearl Harbor—in fact, there were almost as many carriers as battleships under construction on 7 December 1941. Those "flattops" under construction were close to double the size of the USS *Ranger*—the first American carrier designed as such from the keel up.

The task force idea developed well before the onset of war, having its genesis even before the initial "fleet problems" of the late 1920s, in which the *Saratoga* and *Lexington* participated.[53]

In the late 1930s, the deck loads of carriers had changed substantially in an offensive direction before they were thrust into battle. Thus, naval aviators of the period and their earliest biographers and historians possibly exaggerated the weight of US Navy conservatism for a number of reasons.[54] One was physical: dive-bombers in 1930 could not carry bombs big enough to penetrate battleship armor far enough to threaten the enemy battle line; by the end of the decade, they could.[55] Clark Reynolds, long a leader in the history of naval aviation, provides a recent sample of the "half empty" part of the metaphor: "The rigid conservatism of the so-called Gun Club of battleship admirals stood in his [Moffett's] way at every turn."[56] Clearly, "rigid conservatism" can be in the eye of the beholder; Moffett himself had been a first-class battleship captain.

On the eve of war, then, the worldview of the naval officer corps had not changed much from the realist perception of the international environment held at the beginning of World War I.[57] Few people in the Navy felt that the initial objective ought to be anything other than command of the sea, which would yield the capability for exploitation in a variety of ways, such as invasion or blockade. Nor did they lend much support to the idea of bypassing sea battles, blockades, or invasions in favor of a direct attack on the morale or industrial vital targets of an enemy.

Sentiment remained strongly opposed to a separate air force—and strongly in favor of the Navy's having its own air arm. Mitchell had not persuaded many people in the sea services of the desirability of a unified department of defense. As regards internal organization, war at sea involving the use of aircraft required a task organization that put ships with varying functions under a single commander and that sought to achieve a specific goal. Everyone agreed that aircraft were a major asset in sea warfare but differed on the question of their employment—whether in auxiliary or independent roles, or both. Those favoring the offensive role for aircraft argued that the aircraft carrier would be the capital ship in the future and that all other elements of sea power should train and organize to support the air arm.

As to employment in battle, aircraft would first assure air superiority—ideally by sinking enemy carriers—and then provide reconnaissance, as well as spotting and damaging battleships to slow them down for the great sea battle, to be concluded by our own battleships. This vision of surface sailors received decreasing favor from aviators as the interwar period wore on. For the most "advanced" aviators, aircraft would win command of the sea by sinking enemy carriers, and then the air arm would turn to exploitation through mining or supporting an invasion.

The Test of War: The Pacific Campaigns

How did the experience of World War II modify this cast of mind? The war did nothing to change the worldview of the line officers of the Navy—as with the leaders of all the other services, they were very much of the realist persuasion. It also did little to change the perception that command of the sea was the first goal, but the means of achieving it went through a transformation.

Pearl Harbor confirmed the Mitchell tests of 1921—that aircraft could sink unmoving, undefended dreadnoughts. The destruction by land-based airpower of the *Prince of Wales* and the *Repulse*—both capital ships and both *under way*—had a far greater psychological impact on both the Navy and the American public. This, combined with the fact that precious few battleships remained with which to test the old notions in combat, led to the rapid acceptance of the carrier task force as the principal instrument of sea power.[58]

Objectives

Notwithstanding the fact that implementation in war differed from that envisioned, the preferred strategy of the Navy remained the same. Air battles instead of battleships won command of the sea, but the central Pacific thrust with island hopping and base development remained the strategy. The Joint Chiefs of Staff did not have the power or the inclination to force the Navy into another choice—or to persuade Douglas MacArthur in the Southwest Pacific Area to join the Navy's strategy. It worked rather as planned,[59] with the remnants of the Japanese fleet coming out to fight the final battles west of the Mariana Islands in the summer of 1944, and then again during the invasion of Leyte in October.[60]

The aviators had wound up pushing for a great sea battle at the time of the Marianas, and Adm Raymond Spruance, the surface sailor, deemed his primary mission the protection of the amphibious operation and not the destruction of what remained of the Japanese fleet. Similarly, the main criticism of Adm William Halsey came from the surface sailors who thought he should have been tied to the landing forces at Leyte rather than seeking the destruction of the Japanese carriers—in a decoy role, as it turned out.[61] In a larger sense, though, one may infer that practically everyone involved remained persuaded that Mahan was right when he reasserted that he who commands the sea commands the world. In the words of Paul M. Kennedy,

> The Second World War saw the full arrival and exploitation of this revolutionary (air) weapon and the fulfillment of the prophecies of Douhet, Mitchell, Trenchard and the others that aircraft were vital to achieve dominance over land and sea theatres. As such, this did not invalidate Mahan's doctrine that command of the sea meant control of those 'broad highways,' the lines of communication between homeland and overseas ports; but it did spell the end of the navy's claim to a monopoly role in preserving such sea masteries. And the Admiralty's established belief that a fleet of battleships provided the ultimate force to control the ocean seaways was made to look more old-fashioned than ever—and very erroneous and dangerous.[62]

The naval officer corps remained committed to the idea of exploitation through blockade rather than invasion, but it was overruled, and amphibious planning was under way when nuclear weapons came along to precipitate Japanese surrender.[63]

Even earlier, on the eve of World War II, the aviators among the naval leaders were beginning to rattle the gates to high command. However, tension had existed throughout the conflict between them and the old guard. Some of the principal decision makers like Ernest King and William Halsey did have wings, even pilot wings, but most of them had gone through flying school as senior officers and had never served as crew members at the squadron level. They were deemed Johnny-come-latelies to the flying business and therefore unable to understand air war as well as the pioneers—the chief one of whom had been at the head of the Bureau of Aeronautics when war came: John Towers. He aspired to high operational command throughout the war but was kept from it, mostly by Admiral King himself. Of the early aviators, only Marc Mitscher made it to such a level as a task force commander under the Fifth Fleet. Meanwhile, Halsey the Johnny-come-lately, Adm Chester Nimitz the submariner, and Spruance the cruiser sailor, had been sent by King to implement the important decisions of the Pacific war—most of which were made by the CNO himself.

The Postwar Attitude Adjustment

It is probably fair to assert that the naval officer corps emerged from World War II with much the same worldview of international politics as it had held before 1914. Clearly, the "Wilsonian dream" had proven a mirage and many officers, if not most, were skeptical that the "one world" envisioned in the United Nations would fare any better. The substantial skepticism toward disarmament and arms control of the interwar period remained.[64]

Methods of Conflict Resolution

The line officers of the Navy came out of the war with a strong notion that the carrier battles and the island invasions had been decisive and that the Navy remained the first line of defense, despite growing doubts on the latter point among Army airmen, Congress, and the public. As a corollary, the carrier admirals believed they would have to govern the Navy. They would never completely dominate the apex of the hierarchy, but they were well on the road to becoming the most equal among equals.[65] Not until the fighting concluded did King and Nimitz send Towers to his seagoing command to take over the Fifth Fleet from Spruance, who replaced Nimitz in command at Pearl Harbor but soon moved on to the Naval War College. Towers then came to Pearl Harbor to take charge, as commander in chief of Pacific Command, the principal striking arm of the Navy.[66]

Naval aviators were coming of age in 1945, and at the Navy's moment of glory, a substantial part of it agreed that carrier aviation was and would continue to be the core strength of the service, notwithstanding the fact that no naval threat existed anywhere in the world. Further, the United States Strategic Bombing Survey concluded that the submarine in its unrestricted, independent campaign against Japanese maritime traffic, combined with strategic bombing of the home islands, had been decisive. This use of the submarine had not been formally articulated in interwar naval theory and in fact had been rejected by US diplomats at the Washington Conference of 1921–22 as a morally illegitimate use of the weapon. (As noted above, though, officers playing enemy commanders had explored the idea in war games and informally during the periodic Submarine Officers' Conference.)

Too, naval leaders came away with the impression that the B-29s had not been very cooperative in supporting either the Okinawa operations or the mining campaign.[67] They viewed the bombing of the Japanese homeland as a waste of time, even though their carrier admirals also had targeted the airframe and engine industries in Japan at the end of the war. Increasingly in the last two years of the war, Navy flyers found their targets ashore. Traditionally, in the abstract at least, the very purpose of gaining command of the sea was to influence events ashore.[68] Attention given to the possible use of airpower directly against the sources of enemy power was minimal in the Navy prior to 1941. As the war neared its end, however—especially after command of Twentieth Air Force in the Pacific was kept out of the hands of the theater commanders—naval line officers gave a great deal more thought to the idea of strategic bombing.

Organization for War

Increasingly, naval officers voiced their concerns about the morality of strategic bombing because of the harm to civilians, notwithstanding the harm done by blockade. In addition, the war made it clear that command of the air was a prerequisite in strategic as well as tactical operations—but it was difficult or impossible to achieve in the former because of the long ranges involved. Until escort aircraft could fly all the way to the target, the bomber could not get through—or so the argument went in naval circles.[69] The implications of the coming of nuclear weapons were as yet little explored, and the result of all these factors left the naval officer corps in a state of flux—without a clear vision of its future and its purpose for one of the rare times in the twentieth century. This situation led to an institutional identity crisis that remained unresolved until a decade had passed.[70]

One problem for the Navy was that it had complete command of the sea, and nobody could challenge it. What could it use that command for? The new potential adversary was the Soviet Union, but it had no surface navy. Nor did it have any significant dependency on overseas raw materials or food vulnerable to blockade.[71] The idea of an amphibious landing against the whole Eurasian world island was preposterous—and both Napoléon and Hitler had made the idea more so in any event. The United States was coming out of two decades of serious deficit spending, and Billy Mitchell's idea of getting the job done with one air force instead of a two-ocean navy—especially an air force equipped with nuclear weapons—was highly attractive to President Truman, the Congress, and the public in general. Doing this in a unified department of defense would eliminate much duplication and make available more ample funds for domestic purposes.[72]

Attempts to resolve the dilemma were made in the Unification Act of 1947 and the Key West and Newport conferences of the following year. However, they really did not achieve much. Back in the days of Billy Mitchell, most of the Navy's officer corps had been dead set against a single military department containing all the services. But during World War II, some senior officers thought that unification might have some merit. Admiral Nimitz was one of them, but toward the end of the war, he and the rest of the mariners closed ranks against it.[73] Led by James V. Forrestal, the tactics entailed avoiding a head-on attack on the issues of unification and a separate air force because support for them was too strong— indeed, the president himself favored unification. Thus, the approach was to limit the function of a secretary of defense to powers of "coordination," avoid opposing a separate air force directly, but try to constrain its functions as much as possible. Especially important as a goal was assuring the Marine Corps and the Navy of their own air arms, completely independent of any autonomous air force.

Minority opinions inside the Navy (e.g., that of Adm Dan Gallery) proposed that since all the old visions were obsolete, the Navy ought to take over the Air Force's strategic bombing role because the Navy could do it better.[74] The legislation had emerged rather as envisioned by Forrestal, but neither that nor the subsequent Key West and Newport "agreements" calmed the waters. Perhaps the subsequent B-36 debate was a manifestation of the insecurity of naval leaders, and the main outlines of a more stable Navy worldview and vision for its future started to take shape only later as a result of the Korean War and the reversal of the decline of defense spending. Also having an effect were the march of technology that resulted in the miniaturization of nuclear weapons; the Soviet acquisition of nuclear technology; the coming of the nuclear submarines; and the submarine launched ballistic missile (SLBM).[75]

The Navy's internal organizational issues had largely been laid to rest. The powers of the CNO had been further consolidated under the wartime leader, Admiral King, when he was appointed to that office and at the same time retained the title of commander in chief of the US fleet. The flyers had become firmly integrated into the upper ranks of the Navy, and little agitation remained for a separate naval air corps.[76]

Visions of Employment in War

The vision to emerge in the mid-1950s held that the United States could exploit its command of the seas with a revised naval role—one that had both a strategic and conventional dimension. The Navy could use its carriers as it had in the Korean War—for power projection ashore. They would have nuclear weapons, not to take over the strategic bombing mission, but to facilitate the maritime campaign by targeting against Soviet submarine bases and the like.

The SLBM would give new life to the underwater arm of the Navy, even in the absence of a potential enemy with a significant surface naval or merchant marine dependency. It had the beauty of being perfectly suited to the second-strike deterrent role the United States valued. That is, Polaris missile boats were invulnerable enough to ride out the first strike, yet their accuracy was not deemed sufficient to threaten a first strike themselves—thus they added to deterrent stability. Further, the great transfer of submarine technology, doctrine, and equipment from Germany to the Soviet Union at the end of World War II—combined with the contemporaneous change in antisubmarine warfare (ASW) technique—assured the future of the attack-boat portion of the submarine force.[77] Thenceforward, one of the chief antisubmarine weapons would be submarines. The line officers' preference for the offensive again received expression in the notion of attacking the Soviet underwater forces well forward: in their home waters with ASW submarines and at their bases with naval air forces, soon to be armed with nuclear weapons.[78]

By the late 1950s, the reappearance of the naval nuclear camel's nose under the Air Force's strategic tent was not as threatening as it had been in Admiral Gallery's version of the late 1940s. The new conception called for a strategic triad, two legs of which would belong to the Air Force (ICBMs and heavy bombers) and all of which were vital to deterrence and nuclear stability. The Air Force, moreover, was no longer the new kid on the block and therefore had more confidence in its own role.[79] The Navy's new vision proved remarkably durable, and recent writings from *Maritime Strategy* to *From the Sea*[80] are really little more than a change in emphasis.

Impact of Aviation on Naval Air Thought

Aviation had not really changed the worldview of most of the Navy's officers corps by 1947. In a generic way, the primary objective of navies remained command of the sea, although not much of a challenge to the hegemony of the US Navy existed at that point. Exploitation through mining and blockade came out of the war with new prestige, at least to seamen. Even though the Navy had little enthusiasm for the invasion of Japan, the success of amphibious operations across the Pacific reaffirmed that mode as another way of exploiting command of the sea. On the eve of the unification debate, such support as had existed for either a separate air force or a unified defense department was much diminished among officers who had fought the war in the Pacific and in Washington. Internally, the task method of organization had the prestige of success in recent combat behind it.

The most significant change in naval thought had come in the employment of naval forces to achieve command of the sea. Battleships and other surface vessels found themselves largely relegated to supporting roles—as antiaircraft platforms in carrier task forces and as fire-support platforms for amphibious task forces. The aircraft carrier had become the capital ship in command of sea operations—and that change was widely accepted by Navy people. They also gave more thought to the value and limitations of strategic bombing, mostly the latter. Notwithstanding the conclusions of the US Strategic Bombing Survey, the idea that one could coerce nations without first defeating their armies and navies did not receive wide support within the Navy. The survey emphasized the great value of the submarine campaign in the Pacific war, but, clearly, the prestige of the air arm overshadowed that of the submariners.

In the end, then, aviation apparently integrated itself into the Navy and its thinking, mostly in the realm of method rather than objective. The environment for military conflict remained similar in many ways, and nation-states still responded most clearly to coercion by military force. The naval vision still largely maintained that one first had to apply force to the armed forces of an adversary, and only later directly to the territory or other values after achieving command of the sea, the air, and the land approaches. At sea, the method of applying that force had changed, in that the carrier had become the capital ship, and the rest were to lend support. This implied that the postwar reorganization should not change our national security structure radically and that the Navy should certainly retain its own air arm. Even though naval aviators had risen to commanding heights of the sea service, the opposition of surface sailors was not as reactionary as sometimes pictured. Further, it seems fair to picture the intellectual style of the Navy as tending neither toward the reactionary nor the radical—but an evolutionary or progressive cast of mind.

Notes

1. I agree with Carl Builder that the personification of institutions entails serious limitations and that there can be no all-inclusive "Navy mind" any more than a "military mind." Thus, any insight emerging from this chapter can be no more than a tendency or an approximation—if that much. Acknowledgment is particularly important in this case. Although I graduated from the Naval Academy and before that, had an aviation rating in the enlisted Navy, all that was more than 40 years ago, and I have had little to do with naval history or naval aviation since then.

I have received very important assistance for this chapter from distinguished experts in the field of naval history. Dr. Gary Weir set up a discussion seminar for an early draft of this work at the Washington Navy Yard in October 1994. Among the historians in that group were Dr. Jeffrey Barlow and Curtis Utz, and the session was a most productive one for me. Barlow's book and Utz's thesis were important aids. I also received significant insights from Dr. Clark Reynolds of the College of Charleston and Dr. William Trimble of Auburn University, the biographers of Admirals Towers and Moffett, respectively. Their work went far beyond mere professional courtesy. Dr. Evelyn Cherpak, head of the Naval Historical Collection at the Naval War College, not only was expert and most cooperative in optimizing my research effort at Newport but also read an early draft of this work and rendered significant assistance. Ms. Alice S. Creighton and Ms. Mary Rose Catalfamo were also most impressive in maximizing the effect of the research time I had available at the Special Collections Division of the Nimitz Library at the US Naval Academy.

Other important readers who helped were my colleagues—Prof Dennis Drew, Dr. Hal Winton, and Col Rob Owen—Dr. Alexander Cochran and Rear Adm William T. Pendley, as well as Dr. Mark R. Shulman; Commander Joe Tarlton, USN, Retired; Frank Uhlig; and Col Barry Watts, USAF, Retired. The original idea for the chapter was largely that of my boss, Col Phillip S. Meilinger, the former dean of the School of Advanced Airpower Studies and the general editor of this book. His support was generous and essential to the project.

2. Commander P. N. L. Bellinger, USN, "Policy" (thesis, Naval War College, 1925), in Naval War College History Collection [hereinafter NWC History Collection], Newport, R.I.

3. William F. Trimble, *Admiral William A. Moffett: Architect of Naval Aviation* (Washington, D.C.: Smithsonian Institution Press, 1993), 29–30.

4. Charles M. Melhorn, *Two-Block Fox: The Rise of the Aircraft Carrier, 1911–1929* (Annapolis: US Naval Institute [hereinafter USNI] Press, 1974), 22–23; Kenneth J. Hagan, *This People's Navy: The Making of American Sea Power* (New York: Free Press, 1991), xi–xii; and Clark G. Reynolds, "The US

Fleet-in-Being Strategy of 1942," *The Journal of Military History* 58 (January 1994): 107–18. Reynolds explains that even in the fleet-in-being strategies, the British and US approaches emphasized the preference for offensive applications.

5. Capt George C. Westervelt, USN, "Statement of Captain G. C. Westervelt (CC) U.S.N. before President's Aviation Commission" (Morrow Board, 1925), copy in E. E. Wilson Papers, Special Collections, box 22, Nimitz Library, US Naval Academy, Annapolis, Md. [hereinafter USNA Special Collections].

6. One among many who held this opinion was John Towers, one of the Navy's original aviators, who later explained that the carrier was weak defensively, which made it inherently an offensive weapon. See John Towers, "The Influence of Aircraft on Naval Strategy and Tactics" (thesis, Naval War College, 7 May 1934), Record Group 13, NWC History Collection. Six years later, he was still arguing in terms that Mahan himself would not have found objectionable. In "Naval Aviation Policy and the Bureau of Aeronautics," *Aero Digest* 36 (February 1940): 34–38, he states that US well-being depends on free use of the seas, that a navy must command the essential part of the sea (achieved through offensive operations against the enemy naval fleet), and that aviation exists primarily to support those offensive operations. For an equally clear preference by another of the early flyers, see P. N. L. Bellinger, "Lecture Delivered by Commander P. N. L. Bellinger, Aviation, 1 Aug 1924," 12, in NWC History Collection.

7. William S. Sims, "Cheer Up!! There Is No Naval War College," 1916, Sims Papers, box 74, Library of Congress.

8. Robert Seager II, *Alfred Thayer Mahan: The Man and His Letters* (Annapolis, Md.: USNI Press, 1977), 347. Mahan was only one of the most prominent officer-historians; he reached the presidency of the American Historical Association in 1902, after his many historical writings on the history of sea power had achieved worldwide notice. See also Philip A. Crowl, "Alfred Thayer Mahan: The Naval Historian," in Peter Paret, ed., *Makers of Modern Strategy* (Princeton, N.J.: Princeton University Press, 1986), 444–54.

The USNI itself was established in the 1870s, as was its journal *Proceedings*, which from the earliest times contained many articles of a historical nature. See Philip A. Crowl, "Education versus Training at the Naval War College: 1884–1972," *Naval War College Review* 26 (November–December 1973): 2–10. Carl H. Builder in *The Masks of War: American Military Styles in Strategy and Analysis* (Baltimore, Md.: Johns Hopkins University Press, 1989), 18, also argues that the Navy, above the other services, values tradition; I suppose that has some affinity for a historical approach to things. See also Commodore Stephen B. Luce, USN, "War Schools," USNI *Proceedings* 9 (1883): 633–57; and Rear Adm W. V. Pratt, USN, "The Naval War College," USNI *Proceedings* 53 (September 1927): 937–47.

9. See William E. Simons, *Liberal Education in the Service Academies* (New York: Columbia University Press, 1965), 52–53, on the line-engineer controversy at the Naval Academy.

10. Trimble, 4, 7, 67; and Capt Mark Bristol, USN, Office of Naval Aeronautics, Washington, D.C., to secretary of the Navy, letter, subject: Proposed Program, 16 August 1915, Henry Mustin Papers, box 7, Library of Congress.

11. Lt Commander Henry C. Mustin, USN, "The Naval Aeroplane," ca. 1915, Mustin Papers, box 6, Library of Congress.

12. Commanding Officer [Henry Mustin], US Navy Aeronautic Station, Pensacola, Fla., to Office of Aeronautics, letter, 28 June 1914, Mustin Papers, box 7, Library of Congress. In this letter, Mustin makes technical recommendations based on naval air experience on the Vera Cruz expedition. See also director of naval aeronautics to Chief of Naval Operations, "Annual Report on Aeronautics," 19 January 1916, Mustin Papers, box 7, Library of Congress.

13. Melhorn, 8–16, 27–35. For pre–World War I explorations of these issues, see Capt (later Adm) Mark L. Bristol, director of naval aeronautics, to Chief of Naval Operations, "Annual Report on Aeronautics," 19 January 1916; and Lt Commander Kenneth Whiting, USN, aboard the USS *Seattle*, to commander, destroyer force, letter, 16 March 1917, Whiting Papers, USNA Special Collections.

14. Capt Henry C. Mustin, USN, to the secretary of the Navy, report, "Aviation Organization in Great Britain, France and Italy," 25 August 1919, in Mustin Papers, box 3, Library of Congress.

15. Rear Adm William S. Sims to Chief of Naval Operations, letter, subject: United Air Service, 1 February 1921, Sims Papers, NWC History Collection; Capt T. T. Craven, "Naval Aviation," USNI *Proceedings* 46 (January 1920): 181–91; idem, "Naval Aviation and a United Air Service," USNI *Proceedings* 47 (March 1921): 307–21; idem, "Aviation," lecture, 5 August 1919, NWC History Collection; Commander D. E. Cummings, "Use of Aircraft in Naval Warfare," USNI *Proceedings* 47 (November 1921): 1678–688; Capt Nathan C. Twining, USN, to Capt Henry C. Mustin, USN, San Pedro, Calif., letter, 24 December 1919, Mustin Papers, box 9, Library of Congress; Mustin, "Aviation Organization"; and USN General Board to the secretary of the Navy, report, "Future Policy Governing Development of Air Service for the United States Navy," 23 June 1919, Mustin Papers, box 7, Library of Congress.

16. In "Technology, Culture, and the Modern Battleship," *Naval War College Review* 45 (Autumn 1992): 83, Jon Testuro Sumida argues persuasively that weapons systems can have important results without winning great battles—as with the British fleet in World War I.

17. As Admiral Nimitz himself testified, Jutland was studied up one side and down the other in the aftermath of World War I. See Commander Chester W. Nimitz, "Thesis on Tactics" (thesis, Naval War College, 28 April 1923), NWC History Collection. For interesting contemporary views from

outside the naval establishment on the implications of Jutland, especially the bombing tests of the 1920s, see Maj William C. Sherman's chapter on the future of naval aviation in his *Air Warfare* (New York: Ronald Press, 1926), in which he argues that the war provided even less of a historical database for speculations on the future of naval aviation than was true for Army airpower. For a contemporary notion that keeping submarines submerged rather than damaging them was the most important contribution of aviation, see Capt C. Gilbert More, Royal Navy, "Aviation Abroad," testimony, in US Navy General Board, "Proceedings of the General Board," 23 May 1918, Record Group 80, reel 12, M1493, 1918, National Archives, Washington, D.C. See also Kenneth Hagan and Mark Shulman, "Putting Naval before History," *Naval History* 9 (September/October 1995): 24–29.

18. Director of naval aeronautics to Chief of Naval Operations, "Annual Report on Aeronautics," 19 January 1916, Mustin Papers, box 7, Library of Congress.

19. Gary E. Weir, Naval Historical Center, Washington Navy Yard, Washington, D.C., interviewed by author, 6 October 1994.

20. Gerald E. Wheeler, *Admiral William Veazie Pratt, US Navy* (Washington, D.C.: Department of the Navy, 1974), 193–201; Ernest Andrade Jr., "United States Naval Policy in the Disarmament Era, 1921–1937" (PhD diss., Michigan State University, 1966), 1–12; Thomas H. Buckley, "The United States and the Washington Conference, 1921–1922" (PhD diss., University of Indiana, 1961), 19–21, 130; and Stephen Roskill, *Naval Policy between the Wars*, vol. 1, *The Period of Anglo-American Antagonism, 1919–1929* (New York: Walker, 1968), 310. Writing at the time of the Vietnam War, Rear Adm Dan V. Gallery was only one of many people who looked askance at arms control but who nonetheless thought that the Five Power Treaty helped push carrier development along. See unpublished article, Gallery Papers, box 31, USNA Special Collections.

21. Capt T. T. Craven, USN, "Aviation," lecture, 5 August 1919, page 20, NWC History Collection. In this lecture, Craven reported that he understood that the Royal Navy had lost its aviation to the RAF precisely because it had not moved vigorously to develop it itself. The same idea is one of the themes of Alfred F. Hurley in *Billy Mitchell: Crusader for Air Power* (Bloomington, Ind.: Indiana University Press, 1964, 1975), viii, wherein he suggests that Mitchell was an important catalyst for progress in naval aviation. See also Gerald E. Wheeler, "Mitchell, Moffett, and Air Power," *The Airpower Historian* 8 (April 1961): 79–87; Melhorn, 56, 57; Capt N. E. Irwin, testimony, page 177, 5 March 1919, in US Navy General Board, "GB Proceedings 80," reel 13, M1493, 1919, National Archives; and William M. McBride, "Challenging a Strategic Paradigm: Aviation and the US Navy Special Policy Board of 1924," *The Journal of Strategic Studies* 14 (February 1991): 74–75.

22. Bellinger lecture, 2.

23. For information on Sims, see, among many others, Wheeler, *William Veazie Pratt*, 149; Hagan, *This People's Navy*, 255–58; David F. Trask, "William Snowden Sims: The Victory Ashore," in James C. Bradford, ed., *Admirals of the New Steel Navy: Makers of the American Naval Tradition, 1880–1930* (Annapolis: USNI Press, 1990); and Elting E. Morison, *Admiral Sims and the Modern American Navy* (Boston: Houghton Mifflin, 1942). For information on Moffett, see Trimble; Thomas C. Hone, "Navy Air Leadership: Rear Admiral William A. Moffett as Chief of the Bureau of Aeronautics," in Wayne Thompson, ed., *Air Leadership* (Washington, D.C.: Office of Air Force History, 1986), 83–113; and Clark G. Reynolds, "William A. Moffett: Steward of the Air Revolution," in Bradford, 374–87. Lesser known was Rear Adm William Freeland Fullam, whose papers are in the Library of Congress, as are those of Admiral Sims. Moffett's papers are at the Naval Academy (microfilm copy at USAF Historical Research Agency, Maxwell AFB, Ala.). For a seminal piece on the subject, see Stephen Peter Rosen, "New Ways of War: Understanding Military Innovation," *International Security* 13 (Summer 1988): 135–67; and especially his *Winning the Next War: Innovation and the Modern Military* (Ithaca, N.Y.: Cornell University Press, 1991), 58–70, 76–80, 130–47, 234–50.

24. As Melhorn shows, the US Navy observers in Britain during World War I were aware of the German zeppelin operations, both against the Royal Navy and against London, and Mitchell and others brought the idea for such operations before the Navy's General Board and the rest of the Navy right after the war. See Melhorn, 35, 40. One of the others was Maj B. L. Smith, USMC, and Commander Kenneth Whiting himself. See testimony, page 991, in US Navy General Board, "GB Proceedings 80," reel 12, M1493, 1918, National Archives; and testimony, page 1951, 10 March 1919, in US Navy General Board, "GB Proceedings 80," reel 13, M1493, 1919, National Archives, respectively.

In a report on a trip to Europe that same year, Capt Henry Mustin discussed Italian ideas on strategic bombing and British experience with a separate air force. See "Aviation Organization in Great Britain, France, and Italy," 25 August 1919; and Capt Henry Mustin, "Abstracts of Interviews Held with Authorities in Great Britain, France and Italy," report, 1 October 1919, Mustin Papers, box 3, Library of Congress, which gives the views of Hugh Trenchard and Sir David Beatty.

Two years earlier, Capt George Westervelt, USN, kept a diary of his trip to England, in which he speaks of the relative invulnerability of the Germans bombing London and their "barbarity" in doing so. See "Off to War," diary, page 27, E. E. Wilson Papers, box 22, USNA Special Collections; and Adm William V. Pratt, USN, "Some Aspects of Our Air Policy: An Argument from the Viewpoint of American Principles and of the Law," February 1926, Record Group 4, NWC History Collection.

The staff presentations at the Naval War College increasingly included allusions to the possibility of air attack against enemy industry or civilian morale—or the possibility of such attacks on the United States—as independent air missions, but the emphasis was on airpower as an integral element of naval power. See "The Employment of Aviation in Naval Warfare," staff presentation, Naval War College, September 1937, Record Group 4, NWC History Collection; and "The Employment of Aviation in Naval Warfare," staff presentation, Naval War College, September 1940, Record Group 4, NWC History Collection. One suspects that the contemporary experience with airpower in the Spanish Civil War and Ethiopia provided the stimulus for those remarks.

25. Jeffrey G. Barlow, *The Revolt of the Admirals* (Washington, D.C.: Center for Naval History, 1994), 3; see also US Navy General Board, "GB Proceedings 80," reel 13, M1493, 1919, National Archives, wherein we clearly see the impossibility of determining how much of the enthusiasm of the General Board for aviation arises from progressive analysis and how much from Mitchell's efforts, even at this early date. For the formal report of the board, see Adm Charles J. Badger, USN, senior member present, General Board of the Navy, to the secretary of the Navy, report, "Future Policy Governing Development of Air Service for the United States Navy," 23 June 1919, General Board no. 449, Mustin Papers, box 7, Library of Congress.

26. In 1909 Sims himself argued that hitting a moving ship from a considerable height was an impractical proposition; in 1921 he reversed himself to argue that bombing from a considerable height could result in devastating hits on moving ships and that "this [the lethal area about a target vessel] could not easily be missed by a well-trained pilot." William Sims to "Turner," Norfolk, Va., letter, 19 June 1909, Sims Papers, box 47, Library of Congress; and William Sims to Vice Adm Mark Kerr, Royal Navy, London, letter, 29 September 1921, Sims Papers, box 47, Library of Congress. As it turned out, his first prediction in 1909 was the more accurate, for it was most difficult to hit a moving ship in the Pacific War from altitude, and most of the damage was done by torpedoes and dive-bombers (and kamikazes), all of which had to come too close to the vessels for comfort. See also Commander Logan Cresap's testimony, 23 September 1918, page 1074, in US Navy General Board, "GB Proceedings 80," reel 13, M1493, 1918, National Archives; and William M. McBride, "Challenging a Strategic Paradigm: Aviation and the US Navy Special Policy Board of 1924," *The Journal of Strategic Studies* 14 (March 1991): 72–89; as well as an aviator's description of these things in Commander P. N. L. Bellinger, USN, "Tactics" (thesis, Naval War College, 9 May 1925), NWC History Collection; or a submariner's conception in Nimitz, "Thesis on Tactics."

27. For a good source on some of this evolution, see Adm William H. Standley, "Naval Aviation, an Evolution of Naval Gunfire," USNI *Proceedings* 78 (February 1952): 251–55.

28. Bellinger, "Aviation," 4, 6–7, 13–15; see also Standley, 251–55.

29. Francis L. Keith, "Steps toward Naval Readiness: An Examination of United States Fleet Problems" (College Park, Md.: University of Maryland,

1976), 29–30 (copy provided to author by Curtis Utz, Defense Intelligence Agency).

30. Melhorn, 9, 21–54. For a discussion of the decisiveness of air superiority in connection with spotting for the battle line and the associated techniques, see [Henry Mustin?] "The Use of Airplanes for Observation of Fire of the Battle Line" (1920?), Mustin Papers, box 8, Library of Congress. Rear Adm J. K. Taussig, USN, "The Case for the Big Capital Ship," USNI *Proceedings* 66 (July 1940): 929–40, gives an articulate argument for the orthodox view on the eve of Pearl Harbor. For an excellent shorter summary, see Norman Friedman, *US Aircraft Carriers: An Illustrated Design History* (Annapolis: USNI Press, 1983), 8–9. For early views on the subject, see George C. Westervelt, "Aviation Situation Abroad," page 240, testimony to the General Board, in US Navy General Board, "GB Proceedings 80," reel 11, M1493, 1917, National Archives.

31. George Baer, *One Hundred Years of Sea Power: The U.S. Navy, 1890–1990* (Stanford, Calif.: Stanford University Press, 1994), 90.

32. Melhorn, 24–25; and Baer, 93, 120.

33. Capt Yates Stirling Jr., USN, "Some Fundamentals of Sea Power," USNI *Proceedings* 51 (June 1925): 889–918.

34. On war gaming against the Japanese, see Commander James A. Barber Jr., USN, "The School of Naval Warfare," *Naval War College Review* 21 (April 1969): 19–96; Lt Commander Thomas B. Buell, USN, "Admiral Raymond A. Spruance and the Naval War College," part 1, "Preparing for World War II," in *Naval War College Review* 23 (March 1971): 30–51; Crowl, "Education versus Training at the Naval War College," 2–10; Edward S. Miller, *War Plan Orange: The US Strategy to Defeat Japan, 1897–1945* (Annapolis: USNI Press, 1991); and Rear Adm William S. Sims, USN, "The United States Naval War College," USNI *Proceedings* 45 (September 1919): 1485–493.

On maneuvers, see Archibald D. Turnbull and Clifford L. Lord, *History of United States Naval Aviation* (New Haven, Conn.: Yale University Press, 1949), 270–81; Keith; Rear Adm John D. Hayes, USN, Retired, "Admiral Joseph Mason Reeves, USN," *Naval War College Review* 23 (November 1970): 54–55; and Eugene E. Wilson, "The Navy's First Carrier Task Force," USNI *Proceedings* 76 (February 1950): 159–69.

For a view that submarines and aircraft would undermine the position of the battleship although command of the sea remained a paramount consideration, see Rear Adm W. F. Fullam, USN, Retired, "Statement of Rear Admiral W. F. Fullam . . . to the Aircraft Investigating Committee of Congress," draft, 1924, Fullam Papers, box 7, Library of Congress. In a 1977 interview, page 31, USNA Special Collections, Adm John Thach recollects that he had participated in mock attacks on Panama on his first cruise in the *Saratoga*, in about 1931. In "The Influence of Aircraft on Naval Strategy and Tactics" (thesis, Naval War College, 7 May 1934), page 3, Record Group 13, NWC History Collection, Capt John H. Towers, USN, remarked that "one should in the beginning of his study definitely eliminate from his mind the idea that aircraft will revolutionize naval warfare."

35. Trimble, 67; Westervelt, in "Statement of Captain G. C. Westervelt," also argued in 1925 for the creation of a separate aviation corps within the Navy—though he was resolutely opposed to any separate air force.

36. Barlow, 4.

37. Trimble, 67–86; Clark G. Reynolds, *Admiral John H. Towers: The Struggle for Naval Air Supremacy* (Annapolis: USNI Press, 1991), 176; and idem, "William A. Moffett," in Bradford, 374. Theodore Taylor, in *The Magnificent Mitscher* (New York: W. W. Norton, 1954), 88–89, shows that Mitscher shared the harsh feelings on the parts of some aviators toward their seniors who went to flight training as senior officers, seemingly to preempt the top commands in naval aviation without having paid their dues.

38. Reynolds, *Towers*, 319, 432; and Trimble, 7–8.

39. Rear Adm Nathan C. Twining, USN, USS *New Mexico*, at San Pedro, Calif., to Captain Mustin, aboard the USS *Aroostook*, letter, 24 December 1919, Mustin Papers, box 7, Library of Congress.

40. Westervelt, "Statement of Captain G. C. Westervelt."

41. Hurley, 24–25.

42. Commander H. C. Dinger, USN, "Aviation Abroad," testimony, in US Navy General Board, 23 August 1918, "GB Proceedings 80," M1493, 1918, National Archives. In "Aviation Organization in Great Britain, France, and Italy," report to the secretary of the Navy, 25 August 1919, Mustin Papers, box 3, Library of Congress, Capt Henry Mustin, USN, expressed a contrary view. He remarked on a general tendency toward centralization of the management of airpower, including naval airpower, in approving terms. He also cited that the main opposition to the Air Ministry and the RAF in Britain lay within the ranks of the Royal Navy. See also Commander J. L. Callan, USNRF, to Capt Henry Mustin, USN, "Memo for Captain Mustin," 3 July 1919, Mustin Papers, box 3, Library of Congress, which reports on their visit to the HMS *Furious* and her captain's advice urging that the United States not follow the British example.

43. Vice Adm F. W. Pennoyer Jr., USN, Retired, "Outline of US Carrier Development, 1911–1942," draft, 17 December 1968, E. E. Wilson Papers, binder 7, USNA Special Collections.

44. Lt Commander H. T. Bartlett, USN, "Mission of Aircraft with the Fleet," USNI *Proceedings* 45 (January 1919): 729–41; Craven, "Naval Aviation," 181–91; idem, "Naval Aviation and a United Air Service," USNI *Proceedings* 47 (January 1921): 307–21; Commander D. E. Cummings, "The Air Detachment," USNI *Proceedings* 46 (January 1920): 891–94; idem, "Use of Aircraft in Naval Warfare," USNI *Proceedings* 47 (November 1921): 1677–88; Lt Forrest P. Sherman, "Naval Aircraft in International Law," USNI *Proceedings* 51 (October 1925): 258–64; idem, "Air Warfare," USNI *Proceedings* 52 (January 1926): 62–71; idem, "Some Aspects of Carrier and Cruiser Design," USNI *Proceedings* 56 (November 1930): 997–1002; Lt

DeWitt C. Ramsey, USN, "The Development of Aviation in the Fleet," USNI *Proceedings* 49 (September 1923): 1395–1417; Lt Logan C. Ramsey, "Aircraft and the Naval Engagement," USNI *Proceedings* 56 (August 1930): 679–87; idem, "Bombing versus Torpedo Planes," USNI *Proceedings* 57 (November 1931): 1509–15; idem, "Air Power Is Sea Power," USNI *Proceedings* 67 (July 1941): 921–26; Commander H. M. Kieffer, USN, "Control of the Seas by an Air Department," USNI *Proceedings* 51 (October 1925): 2265–70; Rear Adm Bradley A. Fiske (another one of those people who did not need external prodding), "The Warfare of the Future," USNI *Proceedings* 47 (February 1921): 157–67; Lt Commander H. B. Grow, USN, "Bombing Tests on the 'Virginia' and 'New Jersey,'" USNI *Proceedings* 49 (January 1923): 1087–98; idem, "Tactical Employment of Naval Aircraft," USNI *Proceedings* 50 (March 1924): 341–51; Commander Jerome C. Hunsaker, USN, "The Navy's First Airships," USNI *Proceedings* 45 (January 1919): 1347–68; David S. Ingalls, "Naval Aviation Today and in Prospect," USNI *Proceedings* 56 (October 1930): 891–94; Capt A. W. Johnson, USN, "Aviation in Coast Defense," USNI *Proceedings* 51 (September 1925): 1652–66; "Admiral Moffett Claims All Sea Flying for Navy," Professional Notes, USNI *Proceedings* 50 (August 1924): 1364–74; Lt Franklin G. Percival, USN, Retired, "Elements Contributing to Aerial Superiority," USNI *Proceedings* 57 (April 1931): 437–47; Lt DeWitt C. Ramsey, USN, "The Development of Aviation in the Fleet," USNI *Proceedings* 49 (September 1923): 1395–1417; Capt Yates Stirling Jr., USN (himself a submariner), "The Place of Aviation in the Organization for War," USNI *Proceedings* 52 (June 1926): 1100–10; idem, "Some Fundamentals of Sea Power," 899–918; Lt Frank W. Wead, USN, "Naval Aviation Today," USNI *Proceedings* 50 (April 1924): 561–74; Henry Woodhouse, "The Torpedoplane: The New Weapon Which Promises to Revolutionize Naval Tactics," USNI *Proceedings* 45 (January 1919): 743–52; and Eugene E. Wilson, "The Navy's First Carrier Task Force," USNI *Proceedings* 76 (February 1950): 59–69. Although this listing is not a complete survey, it is certainly massive enough to indicate that air-mindedness was more than a whim of the editorial staff or the mere output of a particularly prolific splinter group within the Navy.

45. See Commander Kenneth Whiting, testimony to the General Board, 8 March 1919, page 195, in US Navy General Board, "GB Proceedings 80," reel 13, M1493, 1919, National Archives.

46. Melhorn, 37–38; and Bristol letter. Though then in charge of the Office of Naval Aeronautics, Bristol was not an aviator, and he made the above analogy explicit two years before the United States entered World War I. On the general acceptance of the notion of the primary need to command the air, see Pratt, "Some Aspects of Our Air Policy." For an example as early as 27 March 1919, see Commander John Towers and Adm A. G. Winterhalter, remarks, page 364, in US Navy General Board, "GB Proceedings 80," reel 14, M1493, 1919, vol. 2, National Archives.

47. Miller; Buell, 40–46; and Louis Morton, "War Plan Orange: Evolution of a Strategy," *World Politics* 11 (October 1958–July 1959): 221–50. For an

explanation by one of the primary actors, see briefing paper, William A. Moffett Collection, part 2, item J, USNA Special Collections, probably done in preparation of the US delegation to the London Naval Conference of 1930. For a contemporary discussion of how it worked in practice, see Adm John H. Towers, "Strategic Employment of Naval Forces as the Essential Element of World War II in the Pacific," draft speech, n.d., Towers Papers, box 4, Library of Congress. There was some dissent to the idea and to the generally held preference for the offensive, as in Rear Adm W. F. Fullam, USN, Retired, "The Passing of Sea Power: And the Dawn of a New Naval Era in Which Battleships Are Obsolete," *McClure's*, June 1923, Fullam Papers, box 7, Library of Congress.

48. Bellinger, "Tactics," 12.

49. Keith, 20, 31; Barlow, 8; and Robert L. O'Connell, *Sacred Vessels: The Cult of the Battleship and the Rise of the U.S. Navy* (Boulder, Colo.: Westview Press, 1991), 301.

50. See briefing paper cited in note 47, above.

51. Elmer B. Potter, *Bull Halsey* (Annapolis: USNI Press, 1985), 136. See "The Employment of Aviation in Naval Warfare," staff presentation, Naval War College, September 1937, page 44, Record Group 4, NWC History Collection, which proclaims it "unnecessary to open the controversial subject." In his Naval War College thesis of 1934, Capt John H. Towers, USN, World War II spiritual head of the entire naval aviation community, remarked that "the generally accepted object of Naval Strategy is to gain and maintain control of the sea. There may be qualifying phrases, such as 'in the vital area' or 'in the theatre of operations' etc. The purposes of gaining and maintaining control are: to stop enemy trade while your own trade has freedom of movement, to deny overseas operations to the enemy, and be able to conduct them yourselves. . . . Its [the carrier's] missions can and should be varied, dependent upon the character of the operations, but in the final battle, its primary mission should be support of the battle line" (page 13). See Record Group 13, Naval History Collection; additional copy in Towers Papers, box 4, Library of Congress.

52. See Melhorn; and Curtis Utz, "Carrier Aviation Policy and Procurement" (master's thesis, University of Maryland, 1989), 2.

53. Keith, 2, 28, 39. For a first-person account of the development of the task force idea and carrier aviation in general, see Pennoyer.

54. Melhorn; Curtis Alan Utz, "Carrier Aviation Policy and Procurement in the US Navy, 1936–1940" (master's thesis, University of Maryland, 1989); Potter, 137; and Rosen, *Winning the Next War*, 58.

55. Baer, 143.

56. Reynolds, "William A. Moffett: Steward of the Air Revolution," 379.

57. Adm Frederick J. Horne, USN, "Kiwanis Club, 27 Oct 38," draft speech, Horne Papers, box 2, Library of Congress. In this speech, Horne renders what I deem a near-classical expression of Navy officers' general worldview; it appears to have been prepared for presentation by Admiral Horne.

58. Clearly, the idea of independent carrier task forces antedated Pearl Harbor and the lost battleships, having its genesis in part in the annual fleet exercises dating from the late 1920s. See Turnbull and Lord; Hayes, 54–55; Reynolds, *Towers*, 272, 292; idem, "The U.S. Fleet-in-Being Strategy of 1942," 109–11; and Paul M. Kennedy, *The Rise and Fall of British Naval Mastery* (Atlantic Highlands, N.J.: Ashfield, 1976), 305.

59. "It is quite possible that ORANGE resistance will cease when isolation is complete and before steps to reduce military strength on ORANGE soil are necessary. In either case the operations imposed upon BLUE will require a series of bases westward from Oahu, and will require the BLUE Fleet to advance westward with an enormous train, in order to be prepared to seize and establish bases." Nimitz, "Thesis on Tactics," 35.

60. Baer, 127.

61. Thomas B. Buell, *Master of Sea Power: A Biography of Fleet Admiral Ernest J. King* (Boston: Little, Brown, 1980), 182–97, 468–73; E. B. Potter, *Nimitz* (Annapolis: USNI Press, 1970), 271; Thomas J. Cutler, "Greatest of All Sea Battles," *Naval History* 8 (September/October 1994): 10–18; Jack Sweetman, "Leyte Gulf," USNI *Proceedings* 120 (October 1994): 56–58; and Milan N. Vego, "The Sho-1 Plan," USNI *Proceedings* 120 (October 1994): 61–63.

62. Kennedy, 303.

63. Buell, "Preparing for World War II," 45; Potter, *Bull Halsey*, 346; and Towers, "Strategic Employment of Naval Forces."

64. Melhorn, 21; Capt W. D. Puleston, USN, Retired, "The Probable Effect on American National Defense of the United Nations and the Atomic Bomb," USNI *Proceedings* 72 (August 1946): 1017–29; Chester W. Nimitz, "The Future Employment of Naval Forces" (a paper expressing the views of Fleet Admiral Nimitz on the function of naval forces in maintaining the future security of the United States), 1947, Whitehead Papers, box 648, Special Collections, National Museum of Naval Aviation, Pensacola, Fla.; Adm Arthur W. Radford, USN, "Statement of Arthur W. Radford, Admiral United States Navy, Commander-in-Chief Pacific Fleet . . . before the Armed Services Committee of the House of Representatives Investigating the B-36" [1949], Halsey Papers, box 51, Library of Congress; Adm Raymond A. Spruance, "Statement by R. A. Spruance, Admiral, US Navy, Retired, Delivered before the House Armed Services Committee" [1949?], Halsey Papers, box 51, Library of Congress; and Adm John H. Towers, USN, draft speech [1951–53], Towers Papers, box 4, Library of Congress.

65. Friedman, 3.

66. Reynolds, *Towers*, 507–45; "Aircraft Carrier," staff presentation, Naval War College, 4 February 1943, Record Group 4, NWC History Collection; Taylor, 321; and "Fast Carrier Task Force," staff presentation, Naval War College, 26 July 1945, page 1, Record Group 4, NWC History Collection.

67. Thomas B. Buell, *The Quiet Warrior: A Biography of Admiral Raymond A. Spruance* (Annapolis: USNI Press, 1987), 385–86; "Statement

by R. A. Spruance," 10–11; Potter, *Nimitz*, 356; and W. D. Lanier Jr., "Victory and the B-29s," USNI *Proceedings* 72 (December 1946): 1563–567.

68. Barlow, 292.

69. Rear Adm Ralph A. Ofstie, USN, "Statement of Ralph A. Ofstie . . . to the Armed Services Committee of the House of Representatives," n.d., Halsey Papers, box 51, Library of Congress; Buell, *The Quiet Warrior*, 350, 353, 354, 367; Potter, *Nimitz*, 372 (Potter reports that Nimitz also had his reservations about city bombing); and Steven L. Rearden, *History of the Office of the Secretary of Defense*, vol. 1, *The Formative Years* (Washington, D.C.: Office of the Secretary of Defense, 1984), 415.

70. Capt Paul R. Schratz, USN, Retired, "The Admirals' Revolt," USNI *Proceedings* 112 (February 1986): 64–71; Builder, 77–80; Lawrence J. Korb, "Service Unification: Arena of Fears, Hopes, and Ironies," USNI *Proceedings* 104 (May 1978): 170–83; and Rearden, 385–422, are only drops in a sea of literature on a subject that contains a wide variety of interpretations. Dr. Jeffrey Barlow, for example, interprets the views of Admirals Nimitz and Sherman as fairly well articulated and confident in the aftermath of the Bikini atomic bomb tests. See Barlow, 80.

71. Frank Uhlig Jr., *How Navies Fight: The US Navy and Its Allies* (Annapolis: USNI Press, 1994), 286–87.

72. Donald Edward Wilson, "The History of President Truman's Air Policy Commission and Its Influence on Air Policy, 1947–1949" (PhD diss., University of Denver, 1978); George M. Watson Jr., *The Office of the Secretary of the Air Force* (Washington, D.C.: Center for Air Force History, 1993), 35–78; Ofstie; and Friedman, 19–21.

73. Potter, *Nimitz*, 402.

74. Rear Adm Daniel V. Gallery, USN, Retired, *Eight Bells, and All's Well* (New York: W. W. Norton, 1965), 228–29. The roots of Air Force–Navy/ Marine Corps rivalry far antedate Gallery and even the Mitchell bombing tests, as shown in the testimony of the pioneer USMC aviator Alfred A. Cunningham to the General Board on 5 February 1918 with his comment, "You [the USN] could have the field [an Army Air Service base in wartime Florida] for the training of these fighting pilots and you won't have to depend on the charity of the Army, which is very unpleasant." See US Navy General Board, "GB Proceedings 80," reel 12, M1493, 1918, National Archives.

75. Gallery, *Eight Bells*, 217–35; Watson, 35–78; Rearden, 385–422; George T. Hodermarsky, "Postwar Naval Force Reduction, 1945–50: Impact on the Next War" (Newport, R.I.: Center for Naval Warfare Studies, Advanced Research Department, Naval War College, 1990), 1–69 (copy in Air University Library, Maxwell AFB, Ala.); and Uhlig, 286–87.

76. Buell, *Master of Sea Power*, 364–66, 374; Reynolds, *Towers*, 257, 370–71, and chap. 17, "Shaping the New Order of Air-Sea Power after 1945," 512–59.

77. See "Statement by R. A. Spruance," 6, wherein he cites the growing Soviet submarine threat based on technology transferred from Germany as

the single most serious problem facing the Navy at that time; and Friedman, 3.

78. Hodermarsky, 1–69; and Friedman, 17.

79. David A. Rosenberg, "American Postwar Air Doctrine and Organization: The Navy Experience," in *Air Power and Warfare: Proceedings of the 8th Military History Symposium, United States Air Force Academy, 18–20 Oct, 1978*, ed. Alfred F. Hurley and Robert C. Ehrhart (Washington, D.C.: Office of Air Force History, 1979), 245–70; and idem, "Reality and Responsibility: Power and Process in Making of United States Nuclear Strategy, 1945–68," *The Journal of Strategic Studies* 9 (March 1986): 35–52.

80. Adm James D. Watkins, USN, *The Maritime Strategy* (Annapolis: USNI Press, 1986); John J. Mearsheimer, "A Strategic Misstep: The Maritime Strategy and Deterrence in Europe," *International Security* 11 (Fall 1986): 3–57; Sean O'Keefe, "Interview: Be Careful What You Ask For," USNI *Proceedings* 119 (January 1993): 73–76; Gen Carl E. Mundy, USMC, "Coping with Change: The Department of the Navy and the Future," *Strategic Review* 22 (Winter 1994): 20–24; and Geoffrey Till, "Maritime Power in the Twenty-First Century," *The Journal of Strategic Studies* 17 (March 1994): 176–99.

Chapter 5

Airpower Thought in Continental Europe between the Wars

Dr. James S. Corum

One of the most innovative and fruitful periods in the history of airpower thought was the interwar period in Continental Europe. By the end of World War I, all the major powers had acquired considerable experience in aerial warfare. Most military professionals and civilian politicians were aware that airpower would remain a vital aspect of military power. The primary role of this revolutionary new weapon, however, remained unclear. Would the air force primarily support the other services, or would it operate independently?

The Continental powers faced the challenge of absorbing and incorporating the experiences of the world war, the capabilities of emerging aviation technology, and the traditional principles of land and naval warfare, to create a fundamental theory of airpower. They also faced the challenge, as important as the development of airpower theory, of applying this theory as practical operational doctrine, ready for use in planning and directing air operations.

The four major air powers of Continental Europe in the interwar period were France, Italy, the Soviet Union, and Germany. This chapter outlines the development of airpower theory in each nation, paying particular attention to the interrelationship of theory and doctrine.

France

France in the interwar period provides an excellent example of how the lack of effective and appropriate air doctrine reduced a nation from a premier air power at the end of World War I to a second-rate force at the outbreak of World War II. Ineffective air performance in 1940 played a decisive role in the defeat of France. The weakness of *l'armée de l'air* did not

151

result from a lack of funding or a lack of technological capability, but from a senior military leadership that had little understanding of airpower and its capabilities. In the interwar period, the French produced few original airpower theorists, and the senior military leadership at first reluctantly listened to the airpower theories developed in France and later repudiated them.

At the end of World War I, the French air service was the second largest air force in the world: 90,000 men and over thirty-seven hundred aircraft in service on all fronts.[1] During the war, the French aircraft industry and aircraft engine industry led the world in production and technical efficiency. By 1918 the French had produced the world's first supercharged engine as well as the Spad VII and Spad XIII fighters and the Breguet XIV bomber—the equal of their German counterparts. By the last year of the war, the French air force had developed into a superb tactical unit.

In 1918 the primary mission of the French air service was the support of army ground troops by reconnaissance, artillery spotting, close air support, and interdiction attacks. The air service successfully provided close air support to French and US offensives from June to November 1918. At this time, the primary targets for French airmen included German troop reserves, depots, airfields, and rail yards close to the front.[2] During the last three months of the war, the French attempted a strategic air campaign by interdicting rail shipments of iron ore in the Briey Basin. This campaign had little effect, considering the effort put into it; indeed, the French high command judged it a failure.[3]

Despite the premier position of the French air force in the aftermath of World War I, the French put little effort into developing and revising airpower doctrine for the force. A committee of 16 officers wrote the postwar French army operational regulation—*Instruction provisoire sur l'emploi tactique des grandes unités* (1921). Only one of these officers—Gen Bertrand Pujo (later chief of staff of the air force)—was an airman. Postwar army operational doctrine found itself essentially frozen in the tactical methods of 1918, known as *la bataille conduite* (methodical battle), which emphasized advances in slow stages, covered by massive artillery support.[4] In contrast to German army doctrine, French operational doctrine made little mention of airpower except in its reconnaissance and observation roles. Though revised in 1936, the principles of French army doctrine remained basically unchanged throughout the interwar period.

Prior to 1925, the primary activity of the French air force was supporting the army's ground campaigns in Morocco. In the French air service journal, most discussion concerned the tactical and support aspects of aviation.[5] By the mid-1920s, however, French airmen had begun to chafe in this subordinate role. As the army's new Maginot Line devoured a massive share of appropriations, funds available for air force modernization shrank. By tradition, French officers were not encouraged to openly disagree with official operational doctrine, so airmen sought a means of encouraging the role of airpower and the independence of the air force by discussing the concepts of the Italian general Giulio Douhet. The first discussion of Douhet's thought appeared in *Revue Maritime* in 1927.[6] In the early 1930s, French officers published books and articles that commented favorably on Douhet's theories.[7] An aviation journal, *Les Ailes*, translated a large part of Douhet's *The Command of the Air* (1921) into French.[8] Douhet's stature as a military theorist provided French airmen with a legitimate means of mobilizing popular and political support for the creation of an independent air force.[9]

Part of the independence campaign of French airmen was realized in 1928 with the establishment of the Air Ministry, which for the first time assured airmen and their views of limited access to the top defense councils. Although the air service reported to the Air Ministry in peacetime, in wartime it remained subordinate to the army. Only in 1933 did the air force officially become a separate branch of the military. The service found its independence still limited, however, because the High Command of the armed forces set objectives and provided strategic direction for all the armed forces—and the army dominated the High Command. In the interwar period, only three generals—Philippe Petain, Maxime Weygand, and Maurice-Gustave Gamelin—held the Supreme Command. All were army officers, and none had more than a minimal understanding of airpower. Army and air force understanding of doctrine grew increasingly divergent in this period. By the early 1930s, Douhet's tenets had become the predominant view among air force officers. At the same time, French army commanders continued to hold the view that the air force merely supported the infantry.[10]

French airmen enhanced service independence by putting some of Douhet's theories into practice. In the early 1930s, the Air Ministry began the production of several aircraft models that fit Douhet's conception of the battle plane: well-armed, heavy aircraft that could carry out a variety of roles but whose primary mission remained bombing. Bombing, combat, and reconnaissance (BCR) aircraft would carry out reconnaissance and ground attack for the army yet could carry out strategic bombing attacks as well. Indeed, some French air force officers openly acknowledged that designating BCR units as reconnaissance units provided the only means of building up the bomber force.[11] Only France seriously put this aspect of Douhet's theory into practice. In this instance, however, the theory failed. Designed for several missions, BCRs were not particularly effective at any one of them. The BCR program resulted in a series of thoroughly mediocre aircraft, many of which were still in service in 1940, when they served as cannon fodder for German fighters.[12]

The most original of the French interwar air theorists was Pierre Cot, who served two terms as air minister—from January 1933 to February 1934 and from January 1936 to 1938. Cot was a socialist member of Parliament and a wartime pilot who was passionately devoted to airpower. During his tenure, he attempted to build a modern strategic air force to match the German Luftwaffe and to create a foundation for the rearmament of l'armée de l'air. By 1934 the moribund French air force was far behind the Luftwaffe in technical development and airpower potential. Cot, however, pushed numerous other programs in addition to his attempts to establish a strategic air force, one of the first of which involved improving the aviation infrastructure, particularly the navigation and instrumentation capabilities of the air force and civil aviation.[13] In the popular Cot, French airmen for the first time had a champion willing to speak out forcefully and advocate the need for fundamental reforms.[14]

154

Cot's primary accomplishment during his first term as air minister was the creation of Plan I—France's first program for a comprehensive aerial rearmament. Although Cot enthusiastically believed in the primacy of strategic bombing, Plan I featured almost equal numbers of new bombers (474), fighters (480), and reconnaissance planes (411).[15]

At this time, the French aviation industry comprised numerous small companies with little capital and largely unmechanized production methods. In an attempt to create a modern aviation industry to match Germany's, Cot argued for the nationalization and reorganization of the industry. In 1936 the government consolidated small companies into larger corporations, initially resulting in confusion and a drop in production but paying off in higher production levels of more modern aircraft on the eve of World War II. Political conservatives strongly criticized Cot for nationalizing the industry, but air force officers supported his action; they understood that he was motivated not by politics but a desire to modernize the air force.

During Cot's second term as air minister (1936–38), he initiated several fundamental reforms of air doctrine and organization. Cot and senior air force generals Victor Demain and Joseph Vuillemin (air force chief of staff from 1938 to 1940) argued that "the air force must be capable of independent operations, of operations in coordination with the army and navy, and of air defense of the national territory."[16] To further this vision, Cot ordered major organizational reforms in September 1936. Instead of being divided into territorial areas and subordinated to the regional army commanders, the air force comprised three tactical commands. France's bomber force was I Air Corps, composed of nine bomber wings and nine reconnaissance wings. All the fighters—eight wings—were in II Air Corps, under a single command. And 26 groups were allocated to the army support mission under army command.[17] The two corps would serve under air force—not local army—command. For the first time, France had created—albeit with obsolete aircraft—a force capable of strategic bombing operations.

During his tenure, Cot thoroughly revised the primary operational doctrine of the air force. Operational regulations of

1936 included a strategic bombing mission: "The heavy defensive aircraft [the bomber] has the mission of attacking targets on the battlefield and enemy lines of communication as well as strategic enemy centers to the limit of their range."[18] Notably, the French government and High Command remained so defensively oriented in the mid-1930s that the air force could create strategic bombing units only by using the euphemism "heavy defensive aircraft."

Operational directives of 1937 more specifically required the targeting of enemy industry: "As an offensive battle, the air battle has the goal of destroying the primary power of the enemy by bombing the enemy armed forces as well as attacking the lines of communication, the facilities that ensure the mobility of the enemy forces as well as the centers of production which provide necessary materials to the enemy."[19]

In addition to the strategic mission, Cot argued for the necessity of gaining and keeping air superiority: "The mission of the air force in war is to create conditions so that the sky can be used for all purposes and to ensure that the enemy's ability to use the air for the same purposes is limited."[20] At the same time, Cot attempted to reassure the army that tactical and support aviation remained the primary missions of the air force: "Participation in ground operations belongs to the fundamental missions of the air force. All of the operational capabilities can be utilized for this purpose."[21]

One of Cot's most interesting innovations was the creation of an experimental airborne force in 1937. The 175-man unit, called "air force infantry," participated in the Brittany maneuvers that year[22] and showed real promise before quickly disbanding when Cot was replaced as aviation minister in 1938. By their very nature, airborne forces are offensive units. But the air force had little support in the higher reaches of the dominant army leadership for a program to create an offensive force and doctrine.

Cot revised the French air force rearmament plans in 1936 to ensure the creation of a modern, effective strategic force. Unlike his Plan I, Plan II gave top priority to bomber production (1,339 aircraft) and lowest priority to fighters (756) and reconnaissance planes (645).[23]

Reforms of air force doctrine and attempts to modernize the air force made little impression upon either the thinking of the French army's senior officers or the operational doctrine of the army. In dramatic contrast to British, German, and Soviet theorists of mechanized warfare, French theorist Lt Col Charles de Gaulle showed almost no interest in the role aviation could play in the ground battle. In his controversial book *Vers l'Armée de Métier* (1934), de Gaulle argued for a radical reformation of the French army and creation of a seven-division armored force that would form the primary offensive striking power of the army in wartime. Although he argued for giving tanks a central role in army doctrine, de Gaulle's few references to airpower dealt only with reconnaissance and observation of artillery fire.[24]

The revised French army operational doctrine of 1936 showed little confidence in the air force's ability to conduct anything more than pure support operations. Bombing enemy targets received fourth priority as an airpower mission, behind reconnaissance, liaison, and air defense.[25] Although Cot argued for an aggressive air superiority strategy, the army's operational doctrine emphasized the improbability of achieving air superiority: "Air superiority can only be achieved on the front lines and then only for limited periods."[26] In 1938 Gamelin commented, "The role of aviation is apt to be exaggerated, and after the early days of war the wastage will be such that it will more and more be confined to acting as an accessory to the army."[27]

After Cot lost his position as air minister in 1938, he wrote *L'Armée de l'Air* (1939), which provided a thorough critique of French air doctrine in the interwar period. Although the French air force had become nominally independent, airpower lacked comprehensiveness. For example, the air defense of the country came under the jurisdiction of three different ministries. The army's artillery branch produced and controlled antiaircraft guns; civil defense came under the Ministry of the Interior; and fighter defense became the responsibility of the Air Ministry. Cot criticized such decentralization, arguing for the unification of all aspects of airpower under a single command. Neither Cot nor Douhet commentators P. Vauthier and Camille Rougeron denied the importance of support aviation for the army, but the development of the strategic air force remained their top priority.

The replacement of Cot with Guy LeChambre as air minister killed any hope for real reform in the air force. LeChambre disbanded the strategic air force that Cot had tried to create, and new production plans gave fighter planes top priority.[28] The paratroop force created by Cot met the same fate, and no one seemed interested in incorporating antiaircraft defense, civil defense, and fighter defense under one command. With the support of the army's High Command, LeChambre rescinded some of Cot's most significant reforms—organizing a bomber force under air force command and placing all fighters for home defense under a single command. The bomber and fighter groups reverted to the direct control of army regional commanders. General Gamelin insisted that the primary duty of airpower lay in protecting the army from enemy air attack,[29] nullifying previous attempts to instill an offensive orientation in the French air force.

At the outbreak of World War II, in many respects, French air doctrine exhibited little change from 1918. Fighter units defended specific sectors, and air units fell under the jurisdiction and direct control of army regional commanders. Although the French air force remained by doctrine an army support force, few updates of operational doctrine for support operations had occurred. For most of the interwar period, the French air force showed little interest in dive-bombers or attack aviation. The air war in Spain from 1936 to 1939, however, led to a renaissance in doctrinal thought among French air force officers. French military journals reported and commented in great detail on the air operations of both sides in Spain. Between 1937 and 1939, German and Italian use of dive-bombers and bombers in the interdiction and close air support roles received favorable coverage on numerous occasions in both *Revue de l'Armée de l'Air* and *Revue Militaire Générale*.[30] Air force general Maginel cited the successful use of attack aviation against ground troops in the Battle of Guadalajara in 1937 as a model of airpower in support operations.[31]

Unfortunately, this innovative analysis within the officer corps came too late to enable a revision of tactical support doctrine throughout the air force. Moreover, the army was reluctant to change its methods. Army liaison and command apparatus for the air force in 1940 had not improved since 1918. When the 1940 campaign began, it took the army six hours to get a request for air support to the air force.[32] In contrast, German armor divisions could have requests for air support passed to the Luftwaffe Air Corps headquarters within minutes—and could obtain the intervention of Stukas or bombers over the battlefront within an hour.

Army commanders were primarily responsible for the lack of effective air doctrine in the interwar period. Gamelin, in particular, showed minimal interest in, and little knowledge of, military aviation. Much blame, however, resided on the air force side. In many respects, the interwar French air force culture resembled a pilots' club rather than a serious military organization. The techniques of close air support and army support were neither clearly thought through nor tested, and the few attempts airmen made to reform the system were quickly stymied.

The war in Spain triggered a serious review of airpower doctrine within the French air force officer corps. Air force officers reexamined fighter and bomber tactics and the use of attack aviation. The French air force journal *Revue de l'Armée de l'Air* published some of the best analysis of the Spanish air war. Neither the events of Spain nor the desire of air force officers to reform air doctrine, however, had any considerable impact upon General Gamelin or Air Minister LeChambre. An army-dominated High Command, largely and profoundly ignorant of the capabilities of modern airpower, frustrated France's last chance to develop an effective operational air doctrine.

Italy

Although Giulio Douhet is virtually the only name generally associated with interwar Italian aviation, the Italian military produced other notable aviation theorists whose influence, in Italy at least, surpassed Douhet's. The thesis of *The Command of the Air*, which urged the development of a strategic air force that would strike decisively at the enemy's homeland, might have found popularity in Europe, but Douhet's home country by no means accepted it uncritically. For a decade and a half, from the early 1920s to the late 1930s, the Italian air force journal *Rivista Aeronautica* witnessed a lively debate between Douhet and supporters of his strategic bombing theories, and the advocates of tactical aviation, led by the eloquent general Amedeo Mecozzi (1892–1971), a decorated airman of World War I.[33]

As a captain in the 1920s, Mecozzi began a literary campaign opposing the theories of Douhet and advocating what he termed the primacy of assault aviation—namely, that aviation was inherently joint and performed at its best in close air support and interdiction campaigns. In dozens of articles written in the 1920s and 1930s, he systematically refuted the theses of Douhet. For example, in contrast to Douhet's opposition to air reserve forces, Mecozzi stressed the importance of maintaining an air reserve for employment during critical moments of the ground battle, illustrating his principles with examples from the world war.[34] In another article, Mecozzi denied Douhet's denigration of defending against aerial bombardment by proposing, in detail, a coordinated air defense plan for Italy, with fighter groups covering specific zones.[35]

The heart of Mecozzi's air theories was his proposal for the organization of the air force into three units: a strategic bomber force to attack the enemy nation, a naval air force to oppose the enemy's navy, and a third force to oppose the enemy's army. Of the three forces, the one created to oppose the enemy army and to support the Italian army would be primary and, accordingly, would receive the largest share of aircraft and personnel.[36] From the time he began his articles in the 1920s until the outbreak of World War II, Mecozzi's concepts gained ever greater popularity within the Italian air force and military High Command.[37]

Mecozzi's ideas strongly influenced Air Marshal Italo Balbo, Italian air minister from 1926 to 1933. Although Balbo often praised Douhet, unofficial prophet of Italian air doctrine, his reverence for Douhet was more for show than for real. With his strong connections to the Fascist Party, Douhet became a popular figure in Italy, so senior air force officers claimed to follow Douhet as a display of Fascist correctness. In practice, though, Balbo tended to uphold the concepts of support and assault aviation as propounded by Mecozzi. As early as 1929, under Balbo's direction, the Italian air force organized tactical ground-attack units and practiced maneuvers based upon Mecozzi's ideas.[38] In 1931 the Italian air force established its first ground-assault group under the command of Colonel Mecozzi.[39] By 1935 the Italian Air Ministry had developed and produced a heavy, single-engined assault aircraft—the Breda 65—with a 1,000 kg bombload, in accordance with Mecozzi's theories.[40]

Mecozzi opposed Douhet's concepts on moral and practical grounds. On moral grounds, he scathingly referred to Douhet's theories as "war against the unarmed." On a practical level, Mecozzi viewed Douhet's strategic bombing concepts as inappropriate to the kind of war that Italy might have to fight. Balbo seconded this view in an article on aerial warfare published in *Encyclopaedia Italiana* in 1938. He argued that one could not apply Douhet's concepts in all circumstances, providing numerous examples, such as the colonial war in Ethiopia and the war in Spain, which did not involve strategic bombing. Nevertheless, aviation had proven an important, even a decisive, weapon in the support role.[41]

By the time of the Spanish Civil War (1936–39), Mecozzi's ideas had largely won over Italian air force officers. In Spain, the Italian air force made a major contribution to the war and, in contrast to the Italian ground forces, performed very credibly. In Spain the air force primarily provided interdiction bombing, close air support, and antishipping strikes. In all of these instances, it effectively supported the Italian and Nationalist ground troops.

In addition to providing aircraft and training to the Nationalist air force, Italy sent 5,699 air force personnel to Spain and maintained an air force contingent of 250 aircraft. Between 1936 and 1939, the Italians sent over 759 aircraft to Spain.[42] The Italian air force, like the German, viewed Spain as a testing ground for doctrine and technology, trying out its newest aircraft—the Breda 65 fighter-bomber and SM 79 bomber.[43] The Breda 65 also proved successful as a dive-bomber, further reinforcing the Italian preference for ground-attack aviation.[44] The high point of Italian air operations in Spain came in 1938, when Italian air force units attacking en masse in direct support of motorized and mechanized Nationalist and Italian army units, enabled the Nationalist army to make rapid advances across the Republican Front to the Mediterranean, isolating Catalonia from the rest of the republic.[45]

The only Douhetian-style strategic bombing executed by the Italian air force in the Spanish War involved the bombing of Barcelona in March 1938. Benito Mussolini, perhaps Italy's last true believer in Douhetian theory, ordered massive bombing of Barcelona by the Italian air force, hoping to break the will of the Catalonian population and swiftly end the war. Although the bombing produced over two thousand casualties,[46] the campaign against Barcelona had precisely the opposite effect, as the Germans and many Italians had predicted. Rather than breaking the will of the civilian population, it angered them and strengthened their will to resist. After the bombing, the Republican retreat halted, and the Catalonians held the front with renewed enthusiasm. Catalonia would not collapse for another year.[47]

By the outbreak of World War II, the Italian air force boasted a balanced force of bombers and fighters, as well as assault and reconnaissance aircraft. In Spain the air force had extensively practiced its primary operational doctrine, as advocated by Mecozzi, and had found it effective. The poor performance of the Italian air force during World War II resulted not from poor doctrine but the incapacity of Italian industry to produce aircraft and engines that could match those of its opposing air forces, either in quantity or quality. Even if Italy had made the air force its top priority and had poured all available resources into aviation, its financial and technological position still would have proved too weak to have maintained a first-rate air force by World War II. Italy, whose best aircraft lacked modern radios, bombsights, and navigation equipment, provides an example of a nation whose strategic ambitions far outreached its fairly limited capabilities.

Soviet Union

In the interwar period, the Soviet Union began with the weakest air force and aviation industry of the major powers. From this disadvantageous position, the new Soviet Union built a large, relatively effective air force, almost from scratch. The Soviet military was partial to new ideas and concepts, including new ways of looking at aerial warfare.

The two leading military theorists of the new Soviet Union in the interwar period were Gen Mikhail Frunze (1885–1925) and Marshal Mikhail Tukhachevski (1893–1937). Frunze was a successful civil war commander who became a leading theorist of the Soviet military after the civil war. A prolific writer, he advocated the creation of a highly mobile, professional army equipped with the most modern weaponry. In January 1925, Frunze became commissar for national defense, but later that year Joseph Stalin, fearing Frunze's popularity and prestige, had him assassinated. Frunze argued consistently for the importance of the offense in warfare, and in his theory of the offense, airpower played a primary role. In an article in 1923, Frunze claimed that air warfare would decide the outcome of future conflicts.[48]

Marshal Mikhail Tukhachevski succeeded Frunze as chief of staff of the army in 1925. Recognized as one of the most original and influential military theorists of the twentieth century, Tukhachevski, like Frunze, believed in the offense—and airpower played a major part in his conception of modern war. Through the 1920s and 1930s, Tukhachevski elucidated his theory of the "deep battle," which dominated Soviet doctrine until World War II. From the genesis of this doctrine, airpower played a primary role by preparing the way for the breakthrough of motorized and mechanized troops and by supporting the advances of mobile forces deep into enemy territory. By the early 1930s, these concepts had reached maturity. For example, the "encounter battle" played a major role in Tukhachevski's theory of the deep battle. In 1932 he stated that the light bomber and ground-attack air units in support of the field army would prepare the battlefield and then interdict enemy reserves. Air units belonging to the army group would then isolate the breakthrough sector and interdict the enemy's strategic reserves. Finally, aircraft would drop airborne forces behind enemy lines to seize headquarters and supply bases.[49]

Tukhachevski's most original contribution to airpower theory was his development of the world's first airborne forces during the early 1930s.[50] As always, Tukhachevski thought of aviation not as a subordinate or an independent entity but as an integral part of a joint force, with the objective of driving deep into the enemy's rear with the intention of destroying his armed forces.

One finds the most complete exposition of Tukhachevski's concept of airpower and the deep battle in the Soviet army field service regulations of 1936, in which the employment of the air force plays a central role. These regulations specify in detail the roles of ground-attack aviation, fighter aviation, and light bombers.[51] The air force had as its first objective the annihilation of the enemy air force, which would then free airpower to act decisively against enemy columns and reserves in the approach and pursuit phases of the battle.[52] Another important aviation mission entailed supporting ground forces by silencing enemy artillery.[53]

Tukhachevski did not ignore strategic bombing in his theories. In 1932 he declared that, in the future, independent air operations, which he defined as strategic bombing and airborne operations, would prove decisive in war. Tukhachevski predicted that in the near future, improved aerodynamic design would enable aircraft to fly fast, at great range, and at high altitude. Thus, he foresaw that, in a decade or so, strategic bombing, coupled with airborne drops, could seize the enemy's rail systems and paralyze the mobilization of enemy forces, thus "turning previous operational concepts inside out."[54]

In the years of the civil war (1918–22), the Red Air Force functioned purely as a support and auxiliary force for the army.[55] Provisional field regulations of 1925 emphasized support of the ground forces, and in the 1920s most air units were attached to ground units.[56] However, the concept of independent strategic airpower caught the imagination of the young service's officers. The most notable early theorist of Soviet aviation, later chief of staff of the air force, was Gen A. N. Lapchinsky, who in 1920 wrote a book and series of articles outlining how strategic bombing would become a major weapon of modern warfare.[57] In the early 1920s, at a time when the Soviets still flew a motley collection of obsolete aircraft left over from World War I and the civil war, Lapchinsky laid the theoretical groundwork for the creation of what would become the world's largest strategic air force by the early 1930s.

The enthusiasm of Soviet air officers for strategic bombing in the 1920s resulted not so much from a rational analysis of the capabilities of airpower and aerial technology than from a feeling that strategic bombing was somehow more "modern." One ought to link Bolshevism, the most "modern and scientific" of all ideologies, to the most up-to-date of all military methods—specifically strategic bombing. Contemporary German reports reflect part of the spirit of the time.

In 1925 the German army, as part of a comprehensive program to develop the Soviet military, as well as build and test German weapons in the Soviet Union, provided experienced general staff officers to instruct in the Soviet staff colleges. Capt Martin Fiebig, an experienced pilot officer, served as the senior adviser and instructor at the Moscow Academy for Air Commanders in 1925 and 1926. Part of his duties included organizing war games for the Soviet air officers. Fiebig criticized the Soviet officers' conduct of the war games, specifically their preference for a strategic bombing campaign over army support. The small and technologically backwards Red Air Force of 1925 was in no way suitable for strategic air war, argued Fiebig, and could carry out only limited support operations. Fiebig advised the Soviets to postpone strategic air campaigns until they reached a higher technological level.[58]

The German air mission to the Soviet Union, which lasted from 1925 to 1933, served not only to train future senior officers at the Red Air Force's General Staff Academy but also trained regular Soviet pilots and ground crews at the German training base at Lipetsk. No one knows the exact figures, but several hundred Soviet air officers came into contact with the Germans during this period and were strongly influenced by the ideas of the German air force.[59] The Germans were not averse to strategic bombing theory but also emphasized the fundamentals of cooperation with ground troops at the operational level.

At enormous sacrifice to the nation under Stalin's first five-year plan, the Red Air Force made tremendous technological strides in the late 1920s and early 1930s. By 1932 Soviet industry was finally able to mass-produce modern aircraft and engines. At this time, largely under the influence of A. N. Lapchinsky, the Soviets began building the largest strategic bomber force—three hundred to four hundred aircraft—in the world, with the four-engined TB3 bomber as the backbone of the force.[60] In 1934–35 the Soviets formed a special heavy bomber air corps for strategic operations.[61]

Yet, even as the Soviet Union created a strategic bomber force, mainstream thought within the Red Air Force returned to the concept of joint air-ground operations, as outlined by Marshal Tukhachevski. By the mid- to late 1930s, the experience of the war in Spain came to have a great influence upon the development of Soviet air thought. Between 1936 and 1939, the Soviet Union made a major commitment to the support of the Spanish Republic. The largest component of the Soviet commitment to Loyalist Spain numbered almost one thousand pilots and ground crews[62] and 909 aircraft.[63] In Spain, although aircraft attempted some bombing missions against cities in the early stages of the war, the primary focus of air operations on both sides took the form of army support operations.

In March 1937 Soviet aircraft and pilots flying for the Republic during the offensive at Guadalajara won one of airpower's most dramatic victories. Between 9 and 21 March 1937, Soviet airpower attacked and pushed a force of 50,000 motorized Italian troops into a rout. Up to 125 Soviet-piloted, Loyalist aircraft attacked Italian columns in what we today would term a close interdiction campaign. Italian casualties included five hundred killed in action, two thousand wounded, and five hundred taken prisoner. The Soviets destroyed an estimated one thousand vehicles and 25 artillery pieces. Air attack inflicted most of the damage and casualties.[64]

The air campaign at Guadalajara in 1937 was the most decisive example of the use of airpower against ground forces in the interwar period, and the Soviets, following the Spanish experience, placed greater emphasis upon ground-attack tactics. Even General Lapchinsky, writing in 1939, came to emphasize the tactical and operational aspects of aviation over strategic air war: "In order to conduct maneuver war, to win the air-land battles, which begin in the air and end on the ground, one must concentrate all air forces at a given time on a given front."65

Between 1938 and 1941, the Soviets went through several reorganizations. The large, independent bomber command, organized in the mid-1930s, was downgraded and reorganized in 1940.66 Bomber forces split into smaller units under the army regional command, oriented more toward tactical aviation. The Soviets' emphasis upon tactical aviation at this time was not solely a response to the experience in Spain but also a pragmatic approach to understanding their own position with respect to technology. The Soviet industry of this time did not produce the radios, navigation instruments, sophisticated bombsights, and other technologically advanced matériel needed for long-distance strategic bombing campaigns. Creation of simple, rugged aircraft to serve as light bombers and fighters, however, lay within the capabilities of Soviet industry. Therefore, on the eve of war, the Soviets reoriented much of their aircraft production to the building of assault aircraft and light bombers, as well as fighter planes to escort them. It was a wise decision.

Purges of the military enacted by Stalin between 1937 and 1939 were an unmitigated disaster for the development of Soviet air thought, as well as for the military capability of the Soviet Union. In 1937 Marshal Tukhachevski was arrested and executed. Gen Ya. I. Alksnis, commander of the Red Air Force since 1931, also was arrested and executed, and his deputy disappeared. An estimated 75 percent of Red Air Force officers vanished between 1937 and 1939. General Lapchinsky, the strategic theorist, also was arrested and executed. At one stroke, several of the most original and influential airpower thinkers of the interwar period disappeared.67

Small wonder that the Soviet air force found itself ill prepared to meet the onslaught of the Wehrmacht in June 1941. Even so, the fact that a handful of men could begin with the ramshackle Russian air force of the civil war era and within a decade and a half turn it into a formidable air force, ranks as one of the great accomplishments in airpower history. Although Soviet air doctrine often overreached the capabilities of available technology, in most respects it was eminently well suited to the

167

Soviet nation and, as regards the creation of airborne forces, was far in advance of that of other countries.

Germany

One can attribute a great part of the success of the Wehrmacht from 1939 to 1941 to the effective use of airpower. Of all the Continental nations after World War I, Germany made the most thorough and comprehensive study of airpower and, by means of analysis, managed to transform airpower theory into a highly effective war doctrine by the outbreak of World War II.

Although the interwar period featured many German civilian commentators and theorists of airpower, their impact on military organization and doctrine proved relatively minor. Airpower thought in Germany remained centered in the army and, later, in the air force General Staff. After World War I, with Germany forbidden to have an air force, the army maintained a shadow Air Staff within the army General Staff.

The enormous body of experience that the Germans had acquired by 1918 proved advantageous in the creation of airpower theory in Germany. During World War I, the German air service had fought every kind of air campaign—tactical, strategic, and support. The German military contained a large body of highly experienced air commanders and Air Staff officers. As early as 1916, the German air service had acquired a centralized command. In fact, in 1916 the air service proposed that it become an independent branch of the armed forces, equal to the navy and the army.[68] The army General Staff strongly supported this proposal. Against strong navy opposition, however, the idea foundered. Certain principles, nevertheless, were established at this time. For example, all aviation matters, from aircraft deployment and production to antiaircraft artillery and civil defense, were centralized and placed under the control of the air service.[69] In late 1916, the air service acquired its own General Staff. The German air service also enjoyed special prestige after the war. By the close of the campaign in 1918, the air service found itself the only sufficiently viable fighting force in the

German military capable of mounting an effective resistance to the Allies.[70]

By the end of the war, the strong performance and relative success of the German air service in combat assured the concept of an equal and independent air force within the German military. In fact, at the beginning of the Versailles Conference, Hans von Seeckt proposed that Germany be allowed a significant, independent air force.[71] Even though the Versailles Treaty forbade a German air force, consensus held that when rearmament came—and German officers believed that it would come again some day—Germany would have an independent air force. This attitude gave the Germans an advantage in creating an airpower theory. Secure in the idea that the military accepted the idea of service independence, German airmen felt no compunctions about creating theories and doctrines solely for the purpose of justifying service independence.

A comprehensive examination of the wartime performance of the German air service served as the first step in creating a modern air theory. Beginning in 1919, approximately 130 General Staff officers, air unit commanders, and technical experts began analyzing every aspect of Germany's performance in the air during the world war. Heading this effort was Lt Col Helmut Wilberg, who served as chief of the secret Air Staff of the army from 1919 to 1927.[72]

This thorough examination of airpower in 1919–20 formed the basis for an effective critique of the way Germany had used airpower during the war and the way it ought to use it in the future. The first principle derived from the postwar critique maintained that Germany had made a major mistake in fighting with a defensive air strategy during World War I. For most of the war, the Germans had fought a defensive air war, waiting for Allied pilots to cross their lines and then engaging them. Although this approach brought relative success and a kill ratio of approximately three to one over Allied pilots, the Allies nevertheless gained the initiative and then maintained air superiority over the battle areas.[73]

By 1920 German airmen had established the principle that airpower was intrinsically offensive and that the first duty of the air force in war was to aggressively seek out and win air superiority. Air forces would attain air superiority primarily by attacking the enemy air force on the ground, in its air bases. Army Regulation 487, *Leadership and Battle with Combined Arms* (1921), expressed the new doctrine in strong terms: "From the beginning [of the war] our forces will strive for air supremacy. . . . The battle for air superiority is an offensive one. The enemy's aviation is to be sought out and attacked forward of his own troops. The opponent is to be pushed onto the defensive, and his power and aggressiveness broken by the destruction of numerous aircraft."[74]

The postwar study established other principles of airpower as well. Although it recognized army support aviation, such as reconnaissance and artillery spotting, as an important mission, the primary mission of an air force remained bombing enemy targets. The air force had to attain air superiority to carry out its primary, offensive bombing mission. The use of light and heavy bombers was central to the air force mission. The primary duty of the air force was to provide interdiction in support of the army, but postwar German airpower theory left considerable room for the development of strategic aviation for strategic-level interdiction missions.

Along with Helmut Wilberg and his staff, which included famous air commanders such as Capt Kurt Student, Maj Hugo Sperrle, and Maj Helmuth Felmy, the most significant German airpower thinker in the postwar era was Colonel General von Seeckt, chief of staff of the army from 1919 to 1920 and army commander in chief from 1920 to 1926. Von Seeckt reoriented the German army according to his own notions of future warfare, theorizing that the mass armies of World War I were obsolete and that the next war would be fought by small but highly trained and highly mobile professional armies, which would envelop and destroy their enemies by maneuver. This stance contrasted that of the Allied armies, who considered firepower more important than maneuver. Airpower played a central role in von Seeckt's theory. Air force missions would gain air superiority and then so disrupt the enemy mobilization and transport system that rapidly moving ground forces could encircle and destroy enemy forces paralyzed by airpower. Von Seeckt wrote that the war will begin with a simultaneous attack of the air fleets—the weapon which is the most prepared and the fastest means of attacking the enemy. Their target is, however, not the major cities or industrial power, but the enemy air force, and only after its suppression can the offensive arm be directed toward other targets. . . . It is stressed that all major troop mobilization centers are worthwhile and easy targets. The disruption of the personnel and materiel mobilization is a primary mission of the aerial offensive.[75]

Von Seeckt insisted that the German army become the most air-minded in the world. Although Germany was disarmed in the air, von Seeckt ordered that the army keep 180 pilot officers to provide the core of an Air Staff.[76] He initiated a program of secret testing, training, and development of airpower in the Soviet Union.[77] German operational regulations that were developed under von Seeckt between 1921 and 1923 contained extensive discussion of airpower on both the strategic and tactical levels.

The German army of the interwar period maintained a thorough study of airpower theories and technologies of other nations. Writings and speeches of such air leaders as Gen Billy Mitchell, Air Marshal Hugh Trenchard, and Gen J. F. C. Fuller were quickly translated and disseminated throughout the German military.[78] Douhet, however, received little attention from German air thinkers in the 1920s.

Wilberg, who had made his reputation in World War I as a leader in the development of close air support, also led the Air Staff in developing concepts of strategic air war as early as 1924. That year, the Reichswehr secret Air Staff conducted an air war game that included a plan for a strategic bombing campaign against France. The Germans studied French armaments industry, listing the most vital factories and installations supporting the French army and air force, and assigning target priorities. They estimated that the destruction of 20 to 30 vital factories could severely hamper French armaments production.[79]

By 1926 postwar studies and air war games conducted by the General Staff culminated in a comprehensive air doctrine, expressed as *Guidelines for the Operational Air War*,[80] which described the air force of the future as, essentially, two forces. One would provide aviation support for the army, including reconnaissance, artillery spotting, and close air support. The second, composed of bombers, would provide long-range strategic bombing missions, as envisioned in the 1924 war games. For the first time, German doctrine acknowledged the destruction of the enemy will as an important air force mission. The German Air Staff in the 1920s, however, contained few enthusiastic Douhetians.

The German strategic bombing campaign against Britain in 1917 and 1918, especially its technical problems, was still fresh in the minds of German airmen. Because losses in aircrew and aircraft far exceeded the results achieved, by May 1918 the Germans had called off the campaign.[81] In addition to recognizing the difficulties of a strategic campaign, the Germans themselves had mounted a fairly effective defense against Allied strategic bombers.[82] Unlike Douhet, they had great respect for defense. German writings of the period emphasized the necessity of fighter escort for bombers because no one expected unescorted bombers to get through.

From the mid-1920s to the mid-1930s, the best known civilian commentator on airpower was Hans Ritter, formerly an airman and captain on the General Staff; he wrote numerous books and articles on airpower, many of which were translated into English.[83] Ritter's view of airpower included strategic bombing, which he emphasized as an important mission. Ritter, however, reflected the Air Staff's view of airpower's comprehensive nature, writing about all aspects of airpower, from naval aviation to long-range bombing to close air support and including civil defense and flak as important aspects of airpower.

In the late 1920s and early 1930s, under Chiefs of the Air Staff Hugo Sperrle, Helmuth Felmy, and Wilhelm Wimmer, the importance of the strategic bombing concept reached its high point in German airpower theory. With the Nazi assumption of power in 1933 and rearmament assured, German airmen were prepared to make strategic bombing a central part of the doctrine of a reborn air force. Although he was not a pilot when he became the Luftwaffe's first chief of staff, Lt Gen Walter Wever was well informed on airpower and an outspoken supporter of strategic air war.[84] Among the first projects of the reborn air force was the creation of prototype, long-range heavy bombers, which received strong support throughout the Air Staff.

At this point, however, the Germans ran into a technological wall that affected their perception of the strategic air war. The prototype four-engined bombers produced in the mid-1930s proved disappointing. German engine technology was years away from the development of engines capable of providing the necessary range and performance. Faced with technological limitations, as well as the greater difficulty and cost of building large aircraft, the Germans gave the heavy bomber project a low priority for development.[85] Because of the availability of technology to provide a force of modern medium bombers, dive-bombers, fighter aircraft, and reconnaissance planes, the German air force in the mid- to late 1930s developed as an interdiction and tactical support force, rather than a long-range strategic force.

In 1934 General Wever directed the writing of the primary German air doctrine of World War II, with Helmut Wilberg heading the committee. Luftwaffe Regulation 16, *Conduct of the Air War* (1935), provided a more balanced view of airpower than the 1926 regulation.[86] Although the regulation still gave precedence to strategic bombing as a primary mission, it remained more cautious about the ability of strategic bombers to damage civilian morale. In fact, the doctrine of 1935 argued against bombing cities in order to attack civilian populations on the grounds that, first, it was immoral and, second, it was likely to backfire and provide the opposite effect, strengthening civilian resistance and morale rather than weakening them.[87]

Germans remember General Wever, who died in an air crash in 1936, for his advocacy of strategic bombing, but his vision of airpower was far more comprehensive. For example, he gave the development of close air support aircraft, particularly the training of liaison teams to cooperate with the army for air support, a high priority in 1936.[88] Wever also oversaw the creation of a paratroop force that would soon become the largest and most effective airborne force in the world. First used in the maneuvers of 1937 and 1938, German paratroops greatly enhanced their reputation by successfully seizing objectives behind enemy lines.[89]

Because Nazi ideology placed a very high value upon breaking the enemy's will and upon conducting propaganda campaigns, Nazi adherents had considerable affinity for the theories of Douhet. Gen Erich Ludendorff, a World War I leader and the Nazis' chief commentator on military affairs, wrote numerous articles on his vision of a future war, which included the morale bombing of civilian populations. His most explicit description of future air war came in his books *The Coming War* (1931) and *The Total War* (1935).[90] Nazi ideology, however, had little impact upon German airpower thinkers of the 1930s. First of all, Ludendorff was unpopular with the General Staff, and his prestige had fallen after his poor performance in 1918. Second, professional airmen's understanding of the technological capabilities of airpower ruled out some of the Nazis' more far-fetched notions. Nazi enthusiasm for modernity, however, and the Luftwaffe's characterization of itself as a new National Socialist branch of the military—as opposed to the tradition-bound and noble-dominated army—guaranteed the air force massive funding and support from the government. In reality, career military professionals dominated the Luftwaffe, and the Nazis had minimal ideological influence upon the Luftwaffe and its doctrine.

From 1936 to 1939, the Luftwaffe sent several hundred aircraft and 20,000 personnel to Spain to support Gen Francisco Franco's Nationalist armies.[91] Spain had considerable impact upon the perfection of techniques and tactics of the Luftwaffe. The lessons of Spain, however, did not lead to any fundamental changes in German airpower theory or doctrine. Methods of close air support were perfected during the Spanish War, in which close air support remained a primary mission of the air force. Dive-bombing, in development since the late 1920s, was effective, but morale bombing of civilians, as tried by both sides in the early days of the war and as the Germans predicted, was not.

By the eve of World War II, the German military had generally succeeded in translating airpower theory into effective doctrine and tactics for the use of airpower. The German air force of 1939 was well organized into effective tactical air fleets that could carry out both strategic and tactical missions. The Luftwaffe comprised a bomber-heavy force, envisioned since the first days after World War I and capable of carrying out a wide variety of missions, from long-range bombing to close air support to the operational use of paratroops. As the war commenced, however, some serious failings in German airpower theory and doctrine came to light.

First, enthusiasm for the technique of dive-bombing set the development of German bomber technology back several years. Gen Ernst Udet, who took over air force technical development in 1936, insisted that in the future, all bombers be designed as dive-bombers. This necessitated the redesign of excellent aircraft like the Ju-88 and resulted in production delays.[92] Second, the German air force and navy failed to create an effective naval air doctrine in the interwar period. When the war commenced, the naval air arm had no modern aircraft capable of long-range antishipping strikes or torpedo attacks, a major failing in the war against England.

One can characterize German interwar airpower theory as comprehensive, practical, and well adapted to German strategy and technology. The greatest failings in translating airpower theory into doctrine for an effective air force came from a senior leadership imposed by the Nazi system. The loss of General Wever in 1936 was a blow from which the Luftwaffe never fully recovered. Wever had enough prestige within the armed forces to successfully challenge the ideas of Hermann Göring and Udet. With the loss of Wever, however, subsequent commanders of the Luftwaffe, although knowledgeable men, did not possess the authority required to prevent mistakes such as the appointment of Udet to the Office of Technical Development. The tenure of Hans Jeschonneck, an intelligent but flawed young officer appointed as Luftwaffe chief of staff in 1939, proved disastrous for German air theory and doctrine as the war progressed. Infatuated with the concepts of dive-bombing, Jeschonneck ignored other vital missions of the air force and gave only minimal priority to important programs such as the buildup of transport aviation and the strategic bomber program.[93]

Conclusion

During the interwar period, each major Continental air power experienced a debate between two basic airpower theories: (1) that the primary role of air forces envisioned an independent force carrying out a strategic air campaign against the enemy homeland and (2) that the primary role of airpower envisioned a support arm for land and naval forces. The combination of air/land/naval forces would create a new synergy on the battlefield.

For the most part, advocates of aviation in the support role won this debate, although the German position on airpower fell halfway between the two positions. Generally, the most important participants in the debate were within the armed forces. Douhet's influence waned quickly after he left the Air Ministry in the early 1920s. Pierre Cot wrote and spoke often on airpower before and after his tenure as air minister but had little impact outside of office. Professional German airmen explicitly rejected the Nazi view of air war as expressed by Ludendorff in the 1930s. For the most part, the decision to accept the view of the air force primarily as a support force came from within the officer corps of the air forces. Italy, the Soviet Union, and Germany allowed considerable free debate on theory and doctrine within the air force. Only France discouraged debate on fundamental military theory.

Each major air power faced unique conditions and requirements in the process of translating theory into doctrine. The Germans managed the process most effectively, primarily due to the tradition of the General Staff. They based their theory and doctrine upon a thorough analysis of the use of airpower in World War I and of airpower developments in other countries. Further, they objectively tested their ideas in war games and maneuvers. The French, on the other hand, managed the process least effectively, also due to their General Staff tradition. Whereas the Germans tolerated debate among General Staff officers and regarded that body as a collective organization, the French saw the staff primarily as assistants to the commander in chief and considered the army commander's vision the foundation of theory and doctrine. The three French army commanders of the interwar period—Petain, Weygand, and Gamelin—had little interest in the air force; consequently, doctrine suffered. Germany, the Soviet Union, and Italy were able to test their respective airpower theories and doctrines as the primary air combatants in Spain from 1936 to 1939. The experience of Spain did not result in those three countries' choosing the theory of support aviation over strategic aviation, since by 1935 advocates of support aviation were becoming predominant in all three air forces. Instead, the Spanish War confirmed the air doctrine that the Germans and Italians had already adopted and provided further impetus to Soviet advocates of ground-attack aviation.

Notes

1. Charles Christienne and Pierre Lissarague, *A History of French Military Aviation* (Washington, D.C.: Smithsonian Institution Press, 1986), 130.

2. Ibid., 127–29.

3. Ibid., 174.

4. For an explanation of the doctrine of methodical battle, see Robert Doughty, *The Seeds of Disaster* (Hamden, Conn.: Archon Books, 1985).

5. *Revue de Aéronautique Militaire* covered the air support for the Moroccan campaign in great detail in 1922–1923. In this period, no articles on independent air operations appeared.

6. Col P. Vauthier, *La Doctrine de Guerre du Général Douhet* (Paris: Berger-Levrault, 1935), 166.

7. For the first significant expression of Douhet's theories in France, see Lt Col P. Vauthier, *Le Danger Aérien du Pays* (Paris: Berger-Levrault, 1930).

8. Frank Cappelluti, "The Life and Thought of Giulio Douhet" (PhD diss., Rutgers University, 1967), 230.

9. France's premier commentators on Douhet were Lieutenant Colonel Vauthier and navy engineer Camille Rougeron, who wrote numerous articles on Douhet for *Revue de l'Armée de l'Air* during the 1930s.

10. Patrick Façon, "Douhet et sa Doctrine à Travers la Litterature Militaire et Aéronautique Française de l'Entre-Deux-Guerres: une Étude de Perception," in *La Figura e l'Opera di Giulio Douhet*, ed. Caserta-Pozzuoli (Rome: Societa di Storia Patria, 1988), 109–27.

11. Christienne and Lissarague, 259.

12. Ibid., 259–60. On the role of air doctrine and the BCR aircraft, see J. Hébrand, *Vingt-Cinque Anneés d'Aviation Militaire (1920–1945)*, vol. 1 (Paris: Albin Michel, 1946), 135–48.

13. Christienne and Lissarague, 302–4.

14. Thierry Vivier, "Pierre Cot et la Naissance de *l'Armée de l'Air*: 31 janvier 1933–8 février 1934," *Revue Historique des Armées* (December 1990): 108–15.

15. Olaf Groehler, *Geschichte des Luftkriegs 1910 bis 1980* (Berlin: Militärverlag der DDR, 1981), 211.

16. Ibid., 153.

17. Ibid.

18. Ministère de l'Air, *Règlement de Manoeuvre de l'Aviation* (1936), para. 53.

19. Ministère de l'Air, *Instruction sur l'Emploi Tactique des Grandes Unités Aériennes* (31 March 1937), para. 127.

20. Ibid., para. 126.

21. Ibid., para. 169.

22. P. Buffotot, "La Perception du réarmement allemand par les organismes de reseignements français de 1936 à 1939," *Revue Historique des Armées*, no. 3 (1979): 173–84.

23. Groehler, 211.

24. Charles de Gaulle, *Vers l'Armée de Métier* (Paris: 1934), 114.

25. Ministère de la Défense, *Instruction sur l'Emploi Tactique des Grandes Unités*, 1936, para. 50.

26. Ibid., para. 298.

27. Adam Adamthwaite, *France and the Coming of the Second World War* (London: Frank Cass, 1977), 162.

28. Air rearmament Plan V of 1938 specified production of 1,490 bombers, 2,127 fighters, and 1,081 reconnaissance planes. See Groehler, 211. Guy LeChambre testified to the Aeronautical Commission in February 1938 that "in the initial phase of the war, however, what we'll need above all is to put our airspace under lock and key, as we've done for our frontiers." Martin Alexander, *The Republic in Danger: General Maurice Gamelin and the Politics of French Defense, 1933–1940* (Cambridge: Cambridge University Press, 1992), 163.

29. Ibid., 155, 165, and 170.

30. In *Revue de l'Armée de l'Air*, see "La D. C. A. aux opérations de Bilbao," January 1938, 80–82; "La Guerre d'Espagne," June 1938, 689–97; "Combats aériens en Espagne," July–August 1939, 424–27; and "L'aviation dans la battaille d'Aragon," May–June 1939, 307–12. In *Revue Militaire Générale*, see General Armengaud, "La Guerre d'Espagne: La combinaison des forces de l'air avec les forces navales et avec l'armée de terre," March 1938, 259–82; and idem, "La Guerre d'Espagne: Technique et tactique des forces de l'air," April 1938, 413–49.

31. General Maginel, "L'intervention de l'aviation dans la lutte terrestre," *Revue Militaire Générale*, October 1938, 505–29.

32. William Shirer, *The Collapse of the Third Republic* (New York: Simon & Schuster, 1969), 621.

33. See J. Mencarelli, *Amedeo Mecozzi* (Rome: Ufficio Storico Aeronautica Militare, 1979).

34. Capt Amedeo Mecozzi, "Il volo rasente e le sue possibilità tattiche," *Rivista Aeronautica*, June 1926, 53–69.

35. Capt Amedeo Mecozzi, "Il compito di contro-aviazione," *Rivista Aeronautica*, March 1926, 58–62.

36. Maj Amedeo Mecozzi, "Le grandi Unità Aviatorie," *Rivista Aeronautica*, March 1929, 533–76.

37. Mecozzi's concept of the primacy of "assault aviation" (that is, airpower in direct support of the army and navy) was best outlined in his "L'aviazione d'assalto," *Rivista Aeronautica,* August 1934, 214–85; and his "Origini e sviluppi dell'aviazione d'assalto," *Rivista Aeronautica,* February 1935, 193–201.

38. Claudio Segrè, "Balbo and Douhet: Master and Disciple," *La Figure e l'Opera di Giulio Douhet,* ed. Caserta-Pozzuoli (Rome: Società di Storia Patria, 1988), 58.

39. Lee Kennett, "Developments to 1939," in *Case Studies in the Development of Close Air Support,* ed. B. J. Cooling (Washington, D.C.: Office of Air Force History, 1990), 30.

40. Enzo Angelucci, *The Rand McNally Encyclopedia of Military Aircraft* (New York: Gallery Books, 1990), 244.

41. Segrè, 57.

42. John Coverdale, *Italian Intervention in the Spanish Civil War* (Princeton, N.J.: Princeton University Press, 1975), 393–96.

43. Gerald Howson, *Aircraft of the Spanish Civil War, 1936–39* (Washington, D.C.: Smithsonian Institution Press, 1990), 63–65 and 270–73.

44. Peter Smith, *Dive Bomber! An Illustrated History* (Annapolis: US Naval Institute Press, 1982), 95–97.

45. F. O. Miksche, *Blitzkrieg* (London: Faber & Faber, 1942), 41, 48–49, and 80.

46. Coverdale, 347–49.

47. German officers in Spain reported to Berlin that the Italian bombing of Barcelona was a "mistake," for it "strengthened [enemy] morale and unified competing factions—and has even turned some of the Nationalist-inclined population towards the Republic." German ambassador to Spain, report of 24 March 1938 [Akt 551 in *Deutschland und der Spanischen Bürgerkrieg, Akten zur Deutschen Auswärtigen Politik, 1918–1945,* series D, vol. 3], 532.

48. Neil Heyman, "NEP and Industrialization to 1928," in *Soviet Aviation and Air Power,* ed. Robin Higham and Jacob Kipp (Boulder, Colo.: Westview Press, 1977), 35–46, especially 39.

49. Richard E. Simpkin, *Deep Battle: The Brainchild of Marshal Tukhachevskii* (London: Brassey's, 1987), 43.

50. Under Tukhachevski's direction, the Red Army formed the world's first airborne brigade in 1932. See Robert Kilmarx, *A History of Soviet Air Power* (New York: Praeger, 1962), 94–95.

51. Simpkin, 200–202.

52. Ibid., 214.

53. Ibid.

54. Ibid., 139.

55. Kenneth Whiting, *Soviet Air Power* (Maxwell AFB, Ala.: Air University Press, 1985), 2–4.

56. Heyman, 41.

57. Ibid. Lapchinsky stated that "the airplane enters the field of military equipment as a new, independent factor of war—and not just as a support weapon." Groehler, 130.

58. Manfred Zeidler, "Luftkriegsdenken und Offizierausbildung an der Moskauer Zukovskij Akademie im Jahre 1926," *Militärgeschichtliche Mitteilungen* 27 (1980): 127–74, especially 153–54.

59. The best overview of the German-Russian military relationship is Manfred Zeidler's *Reichswehr und Rote Armee, 1920–1933* (Munich: Oldenbourg Verlag, 1993). On air force training, see especially 112–17 and 175–88.

60. See Kilmarx, 123.

61. Alexander Boyd, *The Soviet Air Force since 1918* (New York: Stein & Day, 1977), 56.

62. Ibid., 75.

63. Howson, 24 and 303.

64. Richard Hallion, *Strike from the Sky: The History of Battlefield Air Attack, 1911–1945* (Washington, D.C.: Smithsonian Institution Press, 1989), 97–102.

65. Ibid., 115.

66. Kilmarx, 123.

67. Kenneth Whiting, "Soviet Aviation and Air Power under Stalin, 1928–1941," in *Soviet Aviation and Air Power*, 63.

68. Dr. Klemp, ed., "Die Luftstreitkräfte des Deutschen Reiches" (Potsdam: Bundesarchiv Militärarchiv, W-10/50845, ca. 1931), 17–32.

69. John Morrow, *The Great War in the Air* (Washington, D.C.: Smithsonian Institution Press, 1993), 158–60.

70. Ibid., 309–10.

71. Matthew Cooper, *The German Air Force, 1922–1945: An Anatomy of Failure* (London: Jones, 1981), 379.

72. James Corum, "The Old Eagle as Phoenix: The Luftstreitkräfte Creates an Operational Air War Doctrine, 1919–1920," *Air Power History*, Spring 1992, 13–21.

73. From January to September 1918, when the Allies had numerical superiority in the air, the Luftstreitkräfte shot down 3,732 Allied aircraft for a loss of 1,099. From Richard Suchenwirth, *The Development of the German Air Force, 1919–1939*, USAF Historical Study 160 (New York: Arno Press, 1968), 2.

74. Heeresdienstvorschrift 487, *Führung und Gefecht der Verbundenen Waffen*, Teil 1, September 1921, pars. 77 and 314.

75. Hans von Seeckt, *Gedanken eines Soldaten* (Berlin: Verlag für Kulturpolitik, 1929), 93–95.

76. See Suchenwirth, 5.

77. The best work on the German air program in Russia is Manfred Zeidler's *Reichswehr und Rote Armee, 1920–1933* (Munich: R. Oldenbourg Verlag, 1993).

78. James Corum, *The Roots of Blitzkrieg* (Lawrence, Kans.: University Press of Kansas, 1992), 157–59.

79. Bundesarchiv/Militärarchiv Freiburg, file RH 2/2244, *Luftschutzübung 1924.*

80. Truppenamt (L), *Richtlinien für die Führung des operativen Luftkrieges,* May 1926.

81. Raymond Fredette, *The Sky on Fire: The First Battle of Britain, 1917–1918 and the Birth of the Royal Air Force* (New York: Holt, Rinehart and Winston, 1966), 196.

82. See Groehler, 81–85, for a survey of German air defense in World War I; and David Divine, *The Broken Wing: A Study in the British Exercise of Air Power* (London: Hutchinson, 1966), 142–43, on the German defense against British bombing.

83. Ritter's best known work was *Der Luftkrieg* (Berlin: F. Koehler Verlag, 1926).

84. Suchenwirth, 172–73.

85. Edward Homze, *Arming the Luftwaffe* (Lincoln, Nebr.: University of Nebraska Press, 1976), 122–24.

86. Luftwaffendienstvorschrift 16, *Luftkriegführung,* 1935.

87. Ibid., pars. 186–87.

88. Oberbefehlshaber der Luftwaffe, "Bemerkungen des Oberbefehlshaber der Luftwaffe zur Ausbildung und zu den Übungen im Jahre 1935," January 1936, US National Archives, German Records, T-177, roll 1.

89. For an account of the 1937/1939 airborne maneuvers, see "Handstreich aus der Luft: Fallschirminfanterie nimmt Brücken über X-Fluss," *Der Adler* [a Luftwaffe magazine], Heft 2 (1939): 10-1.

90. Erich von Ludendorff, *The Coming War* (London: Faber & Faber, 1931); and *Der totale Krieg* (Munich: Ludendorff's Verlag, 1935).

91. Raymond Proctor, *Hitler's Luftwaffe in the Spanish Civil War* (Westport, Conn.: Greenwood Press, 1983), 253.

92. Homze, 164–65 and 229.

93. Richard Suchenwirth, *Command and Leadership in the German Air Force,* USAF Historical Study 174 (Maxwell AFB, Ala.: USAF Historical Division, 1969), 225 and 245–46.

Chapter 6

Interwar US Army Aviation and the Air Corps Tactical School: Incubators of American Airpower

Lt Col Peter R. Faber

In his *History of the Air Corps Tactical School* (1931), Capt J. D. Barker made a now familiar claim: World War I transformed aviation from a "plaything of sportsmen" into a powerful instrument of war.[1] Each belligerent, Barker argued, ultimately realized that airpower was "a force within itself [whose] power of destruction would perhaps be the decisive factor in the outcome of future wars."[2] In the case of the United States, however, Captain Barker was wrong; instead of consensus, there was confusion and division of opinion over the utility of airpower.

To early American air leaders and thinkers like William "Billy" Mitchell, Edgar Gorrell, Thomas Milling, and William Sherman, airpower was a new and revolutionary way of war. Capt Robert Webster spoke for a generation of American airmen when he observed that

> air power is not a new weapon of warfare. It cannot be likened to the rifle, the machine gun, or the cannon. . . . It is a means by which pressure, through the medium of destruction, may be applied against vital installations on the surface of the land or the sea, without regard to the existence of defenses which are tied down to those terrestrial installations. . . . Air power is not a new weapon—it constitutes a new force, as separate from land power and sea power as each is separate from the other. It has created a trimorph or trinity of national defense which now consists of land power, sea power, and air power.[3]

The air option, in short, offered a unique alternative to the carnage and futility of attrition warfare, as epitomized by the "great sausage machine" of World War I. For the first time in history, hundreds if not thousands of invincible, long-range bombers would effortlessly leap over an opponent's intervening ground defenses and terrorize civilians into overthrowing their own governments, as Giulio Douhet suggested, or deprive an enemy army the material capacity to wage war, as advocated by Gianni Caproni and Nino Salvaneschi.[4] In either case, the bomber was an apocalyptic instrument of war qualitatively different from any weapon that had come before. It could rapidly destroy an entire nation from the inside out rather than slowly defeat it from the outside in.

In contrast to the boosterism of interwar airmen, Army and Navy traditionalists did not believe that the modern bomber was a revolutionary, war-winning weapon. Its technology, they argued, was too primitive to match the promises made on its behalf. Further, bombers could not unilaterally defeat an enemy nation without the active cooperation of ground and naval forces; nor could they defeat an opponent quickly (i.e., humanely), as also promised. As a result, Army and Navy leaders argued steadfastly that land-based airpower was merely an auxiliary tool of war. Gen John J. Pershing, spoke for the "old guard" when he observed that

> an Air Force acting independently can of its own account neither win a war at the present time, nor, so far as we can tell at any time in the future. . . . [If] success is to be expected, the military Air Force must be controlled in the same way, understand the same discipline, and act in accordance with the Army commander under precisely the same conditions as the other combat arms.[5]

Navy spokesmen, in turn, repeatedly informed their civilian counterparts (including the Howell Commission of 1934) that the primary role of the Air Corps was to operate as an arm of the Army, and only afterwards to conduct "air operations in support of or in lieu of naval forces."[6]

The disagreement over the nature and utility of American airpower confirms that Captain Barker was wrong—military traditionalists refused to see the air weapon as "a force within itself," either in the waning months of World War I or afterwards. This conclusion, however, begs another question. Was the dispute between the regular Army and its "aeromaniacs" one between equals? On Armistice Day air enthusiasts might have said "yes." On that day the Air Service contained over 190,000 men, 40 percent of whom were assigned to the American Expeditionary Force (AEF) in Europe; it controlled 48 airfields and 19 depots within the continental United States; it owned approximately 11,000 aircraft, seventy-eight hundred of which were trainers; and it had 10,000 trained pilots.[7] However, with the end of hostilities this sizable force disappeared almost overnight. AEF commanders had expected to mount one final offensive in 1919, but Germany's "premature" collapse led to a rapid and bruising demobilization instead.[8] When the US Congress promptly rescinded $485 million in uncommitted aviation funds, the Air Service had no choice other than immediately stop its ambitious expansion program. It withdrew 91.5 percent of its outstanding manufacturing orders by mid-1919. During the following year, it sold, transferred, or disposed of an additional $173.3 million worth of equipment, and it discharged all but 1,168 officers and 8,428 enlisted men from its rolls.[9] (The latter number represented 5 percent of the Air Service's peak wartime strength.)

Not surprisingly, senior American airmen like Mason Patrick and Milling complained bitterly about the Army's frantic rush to demobilize. The rapid drawdown, in their opinion, left the infant Air Service (and its technological base) in a "chaotic," "disorganized," or "tangled state." The service, Patrick and Milling claimed, was unable to conduct postwar tactical training, establish binding policies or needed direction for local commanders, or retrieve equipment scattered throughout the United States.[10] Further, the "deplorable" military aviation industry had shrunk to 15–20 aircraft plants and three engine makers who were limping through the general demobilization by modernizing obsolescent aircraft. (In 1920, for example, the Boeing Company upgraded 111 De Havilland D.H.4s into D.H.4Bs.)[11]

Demobilization, however, was not the only reason why the postwar debate over the fate of American airpower began unequally. The idea of a debate implies that the Air Service already had a well-reasoned, universal set of principles about the proper use of airpower, particularly in war. In reality, this was not true either. After the armistice, the US Army Air Service not only lacked a coherent, working set of propositions on the proper use of military aviation, but also lacked a coherent theory, strategy, and doctrine upon which airmen could base the future development of American airpower.[12] In other words, the Air Service had yet to codify itself in any meaningful way; it still awaited the types of Progressivist reforms that Elihu Root had introduced to the "Old Army" at the turn of the century.[13]

Because of the above problems, the Air Service was clearly in a difficult position. Would it survive its own demobilization—and, by extension, the growing parsimony and isolationism of postwar America? Would it shape its own intellectual destiny, ranging from basic operating principles through a working theory of airpower, or would it remain under the strict control of the Army's "old guard," who largely dismissed airpower as airborne reconnaissance or artillery? As long as these questions remained open, the Air Service was vulnerable to the depredations of Army traditionalists, who responded to free-thinking airmen like Billy Mitchell with open suspicion, if not outright hostility. (General Pershing, for example, once attributed Mitchell's zealotry to an insidious "Bolshevik bug.")[14] Additionally, a delimited and ill-defined Air Service was in danger of never realizing what the "dervishes of airpower" wanted most—coequal status with the Army and Navy and a doctrine ultimately committed to independent strategic bombardment against the vital centers of an enemy state.

To resolve the above questions favorably and to ensure that American airpower realized its full potential, early air leaders and thinkers such as Mitchell, Patrick, Gorrell, Milling, Sherman, Benjamin "Benny" Foulois, and Henry "Hap" Arnold haltingly developed an ad hoc, four-part strategy designed either to create new roles and missions for the Air Corps or to steal old responsibilities away from the Army and Navy. Specifically, the strategy sought to (1) redefine America as an airpower rather than a maritime nation; (2) demonstrate and publicize the versatility of airpower in peacetime roles; (3) create both a corporate Air Corps identity through political maneuvering and an independent air force through legislation; and (4) perhaps most importantly, develop a unique theory of air warfare—unescorted high-altitude precision daylight bombardment (HAPDB) against the key nodes of an enemy's industrial infrastructure. (The development of air theory and doctrine became the special responsibility of the Air Service Field Officer's School [ASFOS, 1920–21], which the Army later rechristened the Air Service Tactical School [ASTS, 1922–26], and then the seminal Air Corps Tactical School [ACTS, 1926–40]. The school divided its 20-year existence between Langley Field, Virginia, and Maxwell Field, Alabama, where it moved in 1931.)[15]

The airmen's four-part strategy ultimately worked. Not only did the Air Service survive as an institution but thanks to ACTS's infamous "Bomber Mafia" and their sympathizers, the Army's semiautonomous air arm entered World War II with the necessary organization, the specific bomber, and the unique theory/doctrine ultimately used to conduct the most devastating strategic air campaign in history. To explain how this happened, this chapter explores how the first three components of the Air Corps's ad hoc strategy helped it survive and then flourish as an interwar institution. In other words, the chapter broadly (and impressionistically) reviews how zealous airmen partially succeeded in promoting America as an airpower rather than a maritime nation, in demonstrating and publicizing the versatility of airpower in peacetime roles, and in advocating an increasingly independent air force through political maneuvering and legislation. Last, the chapter focuses on the seminal role of ACTS in the development of a unique theory and doctrine of American airpower. In particular, it looks at ACTS's three distinct theoretical/doctrinal phases and the way they led to Air War Plans Division, Plan 1 (AWPD-1), America's first substantive plan for strategic air warfare.[16]

America: An Airpower or a Maritime Nation?

Although the United States has historically defined itself as a maritime power, Army airmen like Hap Arnold and Ira Eaker argued otherwise throughout the interwar years. According to them, when Wilbur and Orville Wright performed history's first controlled flight, they turned Rudyard Kipling's vision into reality—"We are at the opening verse of the opening page of the chapter of endless possibilities."[17] Henceforth, America would be an airpower nation, and it behooved the general public and the military's "old guard" to embrace a new world of time and space.[18]

187

Within the Air Service and Air Corps, manifestations of air-mindedness appeared everywhere and in odd ways. Fighter advocate Earl "Pat" Partridge, for example, taught himself to type by repeatedly transcribing *Winged Warfare,* William Bishop's inspirational recollection of his experiences as a fighter ace in World War I.[19] Walter "Buck" Weaver, a "hard disciplinarian" who first commanded Maxwell Field (1927–31) and then ACTS itself (1939–40), invented "Chess Air," a three-dimensional chess game with the top board made up exclusively of aircraft pieces.[20] Further, at the Primary Flying School in San Antonio, Texas, one particularly zealous monitor required the "Dodos" (pilot trainees) at his breakfast table to wear goggles on the mornings they ate grapefruits and, when they later performed their appointed rounds, to bank all turns made while walking (obviously, by holding their arms straight out from their sides and leaning in the direction of the turn).[21]

In the public sphere, attempts to promote air-mindedness were often as silly, but they became more clearheaded with time. In one especially fertile (yet ambiguous) attempt to connect Americanism, Babe Ruth, and airpower, the "Sultan of Swat" tried to catch three baseballs dropped from an aircraft circling 250 feet overhead. The first two balls knocked Ruth flat on his back, but on the third try he did manage to catch the ball.[22] In contrast, the motive behind the 1920 "bombing" of the Alamo Plaza by Air Service D.H.4Bs was less opaque. The Air Service clearly equated Army aviation with Americanism by "bombing" the people below with recruiting literature.[23] The air arm's innumerable flying exhibits for county fairs (and even picnics) further promoted air-mindedness in the public, as did Claire Chennault's Three Men on a Flying Trapeze—the Air Corps's first aerial demonstration team—and Jimmy Doolittle's repeated victories in highly visible national air races. (Much to the annoyance of the Navy, Doolittle won the 1925 Schneider Cup, a race reserved exclusively for seaplanes!)[24]

However, media-savvy visionaries such as Hap Arnold, who headed the Air Service Information Office in 1925–26, and Ira Eaker, who coauthored three books with Arnold, systematized the spread of "aeromania" in general—and public support for the Air Corps in particular. As the acknowledged masters of public relations in the interwar Air Corps, both men spread air-mindedness with an endless stream of press releases, interviews, attention-getting flights, newsreel and radio coverage of special events, and the ability to intertwine the glamour of Hollywood with the thrill of flying.[25]

Arnold and Eaker also concentrated on spreading aeromania to the young, who they believed were "keenly alive to the wonderful future possibilities of aerial navigation."[26] From 1926 to 1928, for example, Major Arnold wrote a six-volume adventure series for the A. L. Burt Company, a publisher whose tales provided "good, healthy action that every boy loves." (Other series printed by Burt included Clair W. Hayes's *The Boy Allies with the Army*, Ensign Robert Drake's *The Boy Allies with the Navy*, and Milton Richards's *Boys of the Royal Mounted Police*.) Arnold's popular tales featured a heroic (yet modest) young aviator named Bill Bruce, whom the airman named after one of his sons.[27] By providing an unvarnished yet inspiring collection of stories about a likable pilot's adventures in the Air Service, Arnold accomplished several goals. He created "a favorable and sympathetic view of Air Service personnel"; he quietly argued for an expanded and improved air arm; and he dramatized "values, attitudes, and behaviors" that arguably defined, along with the *Ted Scott* series and dozens of other aviation-related examples, the "national character" of an entire generation of interwar youth.[28] Among its other qualities, that confident character certainly emphasized duty before self, particularly in a professional Air Corps that fulfilled America's military needs first and foremost through the air.

In the 1930s Oscar Westover, who served as chief of the Air Corps from 1935 to 1938, joined Arnold and Eaker in trying to turn even more of America's youth into "airheads," as one wag put it.[29] In particular, they focused their attention on the Junior Birdmen of America (organized in 1932), the Jimmie Allen Flying Club, and several other boys' aeronautic organizations. (In 1936 the Junior Birdmen of America alone had 17 wings and close to five hundred thousand members.)[30] From General Westover's perspective, the members of these organizations fulfilled two needs—they acted as coworkers in a common, air-centered cause and they provided a future reserve of flying strength for America. (In the last case, Westover thought it "thrilling" that Junior Birdmen would soon fly state-of-the-art four-engined aircraft.)[31] Arnold and Eaker, in turn, had an additional hope for America's young aeromaniacs, and they expressed it in the dedication of a proposed book (*Flying and Your Boy*)—"May they grasp the controls with firm hands and . . . stout hearts to the end that America may lead the world in the air."[32] In other words, the goal of America was not only to become an airpower nation but—through its youth—to dominate the sky. (The Air Corps strove to promote both goals in myriad ways. In one example, it hosted a national Junior Birdmen event in a balloon hangar at Brooks Field, Texas, and then provided the attendees tours of Randolph Field, home of the Air Corps's Primary Flying School.)

The above examples are hardly exhaustive. They do show, however, that as part of a loose four-part strategy, members of the Air Service/Air Corps strenuously promoted the idea that America was first and foremost an airpower nation. They not only adopted and applied the idea to themselves but also tried to indoctrinate the general public—especially America's youth. Because of their efforts and the parallel successes of their civilian counterparts (like Charles Lindbergh, Wiley Post, and Amelia Earhart), they made significant progress. The Air Service did inspire a sufficient number of airheads, both in the public at large and in Congress, to ensure that it survived the parsimonious budgets of the early 1920s. Then, the Air Corps slowly but inexorably cultivated public support, not only for aviation in general but also for its drive for organizational and doctrinal autonomy. (By 1938 the public's support was broad enough that the Southeastern Aviation Conference, held at the relatively isolated Jefferson Davis Hotel in Montgomery, Alabama, attracted over two hundred participants, including such luminaries as Doolittle, Eddie Rickenbacker, and C. E. Falk, president of Delta Airways.)[33] The drive for acceptance and autonomy, however, required the Air Service/Air Corps to do more than merely promote the redefinition of America as an airpower nation.

The Versatility of Airpower in Peacetime Roles

A skeptic once asked Benjamin Franklin if untethered balloons had any utility. His rhetorical answer—"What is the use of a new born babe? It may become a man"— foreshadowed the thinking of Army aviators in the 1920s and 1930s.[34] Yes, their immediate goal was to protect the infant Air Service from the negative effects of rapid demobilization and from the possible treachery of the War Department's "old guard." However, senior air leaders like Brig Gen Billy Mitchell, who served as assistant chief of the Air Service from 1919 to 1921, and Maj Gen Mason Patrick, who functioned as chief of the Air Service/Air Corps from 1921 to 1927, knew that merely promoting aeromania was not enough.[35] If Army aviation were to survive *and* become a mature, independent way of war, it needed to create new roles and missions for itself or seize existing responsibilities from the Army or Navy. Almost from the beginning, it did both.

Like their postwar counterparts in the Royal Air Force, US airmen concluded that they needed to demonstrate quickly the versatility of airpower or perhaps see it ruthlessly starved of institutional and financial support. As a result, the Air Service and Air Corps of the 1920s willingly performed a variety of peacetime roles. In California, for example, Army airmen became airborne forest rangers who detected and reported approximately four thousand forest fires from 1919 to 1923. In Oregon, the total acreage destroyed by fire decreased 62 percent during the first three years of the Army program there. (This total far exceeded the 27 percent decrease that occurred in California.)[36]

At roughly the same time, the Air Service sought additional roles and missions. It patrolled the entire Mexican border to discourage cattle smugglers, bandits, and illegal border crossings; it conducted crop-dusting experiments (with calcium arsenate) to protect cotton and fruit crops from pests; it dabbled in the aerial seeding of farmland; and it highlighted the success of Navy aviation in mapping the Mississippi Delta for a cost of less than $8,000. (The aerial mapping was a significant feat since over 50 percent of US territory remained unsurveyed at the time.)[37] Later, when a devastating flood destroyed nearly five thousand houses and 2,615 buildings in Southern Alabama, the Air Corps demonstrated its utility in yet another arena—disaster relief.[38] During 15–20 March 1929, aircraft from Maxwell Field flew 346 flights and dropped 27.5 tons of supplies "to distressed thousands in an area which otherwise would have been inaccessible for days."[39]

Finally, the Air Service inaugurated and briefly provided airmail service in 1918. Sixteen years later, the Air Corps resumed the responsibility when Postmaster General James A. Farley abruptly suspended the work of civilian contractors. (The Roosevelt administration suspected that the contractors had used fraud and collusion to secure their routes from the Republicans previously in power.) From 19 February until 1 June 1934, the Air Corps struggled mightily to deliver the mail, but unusually bad weather, limited training and experience, and inadequate equipment left a number of pilots dead and the Air Corps's reputation sullied.[40] (A potential problem, however, turned into an advantage when Secretary of War George Dern appointed the Baker Board to investigate the Air Corps's dubious performance. The board concluded that the Air Corps was ill prepared to carry the mail, but it partially blamed government parsimony for its limited success. Ironically then, the Baker Board's investigation revived official interest and support for the Air Corps, even though it had failed to perform as advertised. According to Benny Foulois, a man who Villa Tinker claimed "had never been young," the board's criticisms shamed President Franklin D. Roosevelt into releasing impounded research and development funds and $7 million in Public Works Administration funds.)[41]

Admittedly, the above demonstrations of versatility were theatrical and of limited value. They made a modest contribution to America's growing commitment to airpower, but true progress in the dispute over military roles and missions lay elsewhere. In the case of the Army, the Air Corps and ACTS concentrated primarily on developing a new role and mission—unescorted HAPDB by as autonomous an air force as possible. In the case of the Navy, Army aviators deliberately (and incrementally) intruded into a long-standing naval responsibility—offshore continental defense. To illustrate just how the Air Corps survived and expanded by appropriating the roles and missions of others, this chapter now reviews (in broad terms) its intrusion on Navy prerogatives. (In an era when the Air Corps could not officially advocate offensive air operations against "nonmilitary" targets, except within an overarching defensive framework, the issue was a natural source of friction.)

In its incremental attempt to intrude upon the offshore and hemispheric defense functions of the Navy—and thus create an offensive bomber force through the back door—the Air Corps sought to (1) define a threat, (2) repudiate the Navy's ability to answer that threat, and (3) offer a bomber-based solution. In the first case, Air Corps (i.e., ACTS) strategists defined the threat as nothing less than an anarchic, unregulated future. According to Maj Don Wilson, a core member of ACTS's infamous Bomber Mafia, worldwide differences in standards of living and the scramble for markets (to absorb production surpluses) would inevitably lead to increased nationalism. Unregulated nationalism would then compel the United States to prevent any interference with its policies and to ensure its national defense. In ensuring its home defense, however, the United States would have to concentrate on preserving the integrity of the nation as a whole, given that whole nations (and not just military forces) waged modern war.[42] Further, these nations were exploring new ways to challenge US interests.

According to 1st Lt Kenneth Walker, another seminal ACTS figure, "The importance assigned to Air Forces by major European powers, among which may be potential enemies, leaves no doubt our future enemies will unquestionably rely greatly, if not primarily, upon the actions of their Air Forces to bring about the defeat of the United States."[43] But what would an enemy air force specifically attack? Most likely, it would be the industrial triangle extending from Portland, Maine, to the Chesapeake Bay to Chicago. Within this triangle lay 75 percent of all US factories, almost all the nation's steelworks, most of its coal, and a number of major railroad centers, including New York, Washington, Pittsburgh, and Cleveland.[44] In the opinion of Capt Robert Olds, yet another victim of "*bombus fervidus*," a devastating attack on America's industrial triangle could unfold in the following way:

> A coalition of European and Asiatic powers have declared war on the United States. Superior naval forces . . . seek a decisive naval engagement in the vicinity of the Panama Canal. . . . Such actions draw the U.S. Navy to Caribbean waters, *with its naval aviation*. Land forces from the Orient, using Alaska as an advanced base, seek . . . to establish a salient in the area Washington, Oregon, California and inland to about Salt Lake City, as a land base for further offensive operations in U.S. territory. The concentration of the U.S. Army *with its aviation*, in the western theatre of operations would be mandatory to resist the land invasion.

> Simultaneously, the mass of the Allied air forces have been flown, or shipped under submarine and patrol boat convoy, from Ireland to Newfoundland and are prepared to launch air attacks, from air bases in eastern Canada, against any targets of their choice in the vital industrial heart of our country. (Emphasis in original)[45]

The targets of choice, according to Capt Harold Lee George—doyen of the ACTS Bomber Mafia—would be rail lines, refineries, electric power systems, and (as a last resort) water supply systems. By attacking and destroying these objectives, George argued, an invader would quickly and efficiently destroy the people's will to resist—the key to success in modern war.[46]

George's emphasis on attacking will was thoroughly Clausewitzian and familiar. As a pedagogical concept, it appeared in *Influence of Airplanes on Operations in War,* a text first used at the Field Officer's School in 1920–21. The text argued that war was "a conflict of human wills, bent and twisted in the heat of violent emotions"; that aircraft had a "peculiarly demoralizing influence" on any contest between moral forces; and that material factors in war (and therefore targets) only mattered to the extent that they modified an opponent's will to resist.[47] (The text's logic was obviously deductive, as was the Bomber Mafia's. Robert Webster, for example, opined the following about human will and endurance: "There must be some limit to this endurance; it is not reasonable that a nation can see every resource that it has for waging war destroyed without realizing the folly of continued opposition.")[48]

If America's industrial triangle were the ultimate, war-winning target of an invading force, regardless of how vaguely defined, what role did the Navy have in continental defense? As Olds intimated, the Navy would have an ancillary role at best. America's primary "center of gravity" was now its industrial heartland and no longer its sea lanes of communications (SLOC). The only real threat to this new vulnerability was airpower, and this belief animated the second part of the Air Corps's intrusion on Navy roles and missions—to overtly (and consistently) question the future utility of the Navy as the prime defender of the United States.

Perhaps Thomas Milling stated the early Air Corps position best when he noted that "it needs no great stretch of the imagination to foresee the time when sea supremacy will rest entirely in air power."[49] Such revisionism partially had its roots in the Preparedness Movement of World War I, which the *Washington Herald* deftly summarized in a later byline as "Training Is Good. Flying Is Better. Look at the World. It's All Mixed Up."[50] The concern, as previously noted, was that an unstable nation-state system, coupled with revolutionary advances in armaments, guaranteed that future wars would be so deadly and terrifying that only those who were most thoroughly prepared would survive.[51] Therefore, the Army League of the United States chose as its motto, Let Us Be Safe Rather Than Sorry. But safe from what? One suggestion appeared in 1916, when preparedness advocate Alexander Graham Bell worried that "we may . . . look forward with certainty to the time that is coming, and indeed is almost now at hand, when sea power and land power will be secondary to air power, and that nation which gains control of the air will practically control the world."[52] To the great inventor, the reason for airpower's newfound stature was the dirigible, which he envisioned dropping bombs on the world's great cities with impunity.

Billy Mitchell agreed with Bell but was less equivocal. He argued in one early Tactical School text, *Tactical Application of Military Aeronautics* (1919), that air forces, given their revolutionary technologies and capabilities, would not just lead to the subordination of navies but to their eventual extinction. More specifically, navies would not be necessary in wars of the future (i.e., M-day wars), in which belligerents might have enough aircraft to devastate their opponent's centers of government, production, and military strength, and thus end armed conflicts almost before they began.[53]

Charles Menoher, head of the Air Service from 1919 to 1921, also stressed the probability of air-driven, M-day warfare to the Society of Automotive Engineers on 10 March 1920. To protect against a specific type of M-day scenario—a seaborne attack against the United States—Menoher expected continental defense to involve three interrelated (and rapid) steps: long-range air reconnaissance (against approaching aircraft and ships); an air superiority battle between opposing pursuit aircraft; and a rapid, devastating aerial attack against hostile fleets, in which battleships would be as helpless as "the armored knight when the firearm was brought against him." (In the last case, Menoher pointed out that for the price of one battleship, the Air Service could field one thousand bombers to crush a seaborne attack.)[54] Building on this logic, Milling argued further that the Air Service (and Air Corps) was America's true line of defense against sea-based invasions. If Mitchell were wrong (i.e., if the Navy had any preventive role to play at all), the sea service would function merely as an advanced point or spearhead.[55]

As the interwar period evolved, the challenge to the Navy's offshore defense mission only intensified. If America's security primarily depended on long-range air defenses, as Air Corps theorists argued, the Navy would never perform the mission. The aircraft of forward-deployed aircraft carriers, for example, would not concentrate on the air defense of the nation but on meeting the strategic and tactical needs of the fleet. In other words, the Navy would relegate national air defense to a secondary role. The true focus of carrier aviation would be to defeat the enemy fleet or help preserve US forces.[56] Any focus on land targets, bomber zealot Robert Webster observed, would be "entirely a secondary consideration."[57] Such alleged parochialism, however, was not the Navy's only problem.

A second problem was that modern warships cost too much. If the Air Corps could defend and control SLOCs just as effectively as any naval action, its boosters asked, why spend huge sums of money on unneeded battleships and aircraft carriers?

Third, advocates of land-based aviation openly doubted that naval commanders would risk their carriers in raids against land objectives, especially in the name of "defensive" operations. Commanders would have to make a difficult choice between operating range and vulnerability to land-based airpower and thus limit the carriers' performance in either case.

Finally, airmen believed that naval operations would be further impaired by international agreements, the growing scope (and importance) of coalition warfare, the division of total naval forces into unreinforceable halves (the Pacific and Atlantic fleets tenuously connected by the vulnerable Panama Canal), and the inability of naval forces to patrol and reach all access points in a timely manner.[58]

The Navy fought mightily against the fear mongering of the Air Corps, and from the standpoint of War Department (i.e., Joint Board) directives, it largely succeeded. Throughout the interwar years, the board's directives remained helpfully vague when dealing with areas of overlapping responsibility. But the Navy was fighting against an eroding tide.[59] Air-minded civilian leaders often supported the Air Service's/Air Corps's intrusion on Navy prerogatives. Calvin Coolidge, for example, decided relatively early in the roles and missions debate that "our national defense must be supplemented, if not dominated, by aviation."[60] In turn, Lt Gen Robert Lee Bullard, president of the National Security League and former commander of AEF's Second Army, argued that the Navy was rapidly becoming a mere "escort" to land-based aviation, which would sweep over land and sea with impunity.[61]

Woven into such sentiments was the assumption that the US Navy would be "inadequate and impotent" in keeping our sea lanes open and in denying them to potential enemies. As a result, enemy states or coalitions could place air bases and carrier-based aviation close enough to America's borders to destroy the great industrial triangle in an M-day attack and thus indirectly wipe out the American people's will to resist. Long-range and land-based airpower, however, offered a specific solution to sea-based air attacks and invasions, as

Hap Arnold argued in *Airmen and Aircraft* (1926), as Mason
Patrick confirmed in *The United States in the Air* (1928), and
as Millard F. Harmon reiterated while at ACTS in the late
1930s. (Harmon, however, could not decide if the long-range
bomber would "assume parity with the Army and Navy . . . or
absorb them one or both.")[62] Ultimately, from the biased
perspective of Air Corps leaders and ACTS strategists, they
had defined a new American center of gravity and abraded the
public's (and government's) faith in the Navy to safeguard the
nation from long-range attack. The only step left was for the
Air Corps to cap its intrusion into Navy prerogatives by
incrementally defining (and assuming) a role in continental
and then hemispheric defense.

The Air Corps laid claim to what had been an exclusive
Navy responsibility by systematically redefining and extending
the role of "defensive" air operations—from the waterline of the
United States to hemispheric defense and eventually to the
vital economic centers of enemy states, even if they were
thousands of miles away. The intrusion process, however, was
full of fits and starts. It received a major push in 1925, when
the Air Service Tactical School proposed revisions to the War
Department's General Order (GO) 20, which determined Joint
Board policy on the relationship between Army and Navy
aircraft. The ASTS commandant, Maj Oscar Westover,
protested innocently that the intent of the school was not to
preach or even suggest who should have particular roles and
missions. But he also noted that the growth of aviation had
brought about an appreciation of what air forces could do and
thus required a "consideration of realignment of the real
agencies making for National Defense."[63] Given this
Janus-faced sentiment, it is not surprising that the suggested
ASTS changes to GO 20 deliberately sought to blur the
geographical areas of responsibility between naval and
land-based aviation.[64] Air Corps leaders subsequently
stressed this ambiguity and increasingly demanded that
land-based aviation should operate from America's shoreline
up to six hundred miles at sea, depending on the source.

The demands, regardless of how vaguely made, spurred Gen
Douglas MacArthur and Adm William V. Pratt, as heads of
their respective services, to reach a temporary agreement on

coastal defense in 1931. They seemingly agreed that naval air forces would exclusively support forces afloat and therefore enjoy complete freedom of action, while the Army Air Corps would defend the coasts of the United States and its overseas possessions. In reality, the agreement was sufficiently vague that the Navy interpreted the arrangement more broadly than the Army did. As a result, the Navy continued to expand land-based naval facilities and develop scout bombers.[65]

The upstart Air Corps's response was twofold. First, it repeated Milling's previous, topsy-turvy complaints: it was the Navy, by stealing away precious funds for itself, that was imperiling the creation of a proper air force for national defense; it was the Navy that was encroaching on the "prerogatives and proper duties" of the Air Corps; and it was the Navy that was neglecting its own role of functioning as a spearhead operating exclusively against enemy fleets.[66]

Second, the Air Corps redoubled its efforts to assume Navy responsibilities (and more), as illustrated in a 1933 memorandum by George C. Kenney to the assistant commandant of the Army War College. (Kenney was an influential ACTS instructor from 1927 to 1931.) Yes, the role of the Air Corps was to perform coastal defense and thus provide the Navy complete freedom of action, as specified by the MacArthur-Pratt Agreement. On the other hand, specific Air Corps objectives, as suggested by Kenney, were suspiciously unorthodox. The familiar objective of air superiority was present, as was the requirement to defend vital American industrial centers, naval bases, airfields, and other critical resources. But Kenney also included as an objective "the location [of] and attack upon hostile vessels, landing parties, airdromes, troop and supply concentrations at sea or on land, vital enemy lines of communication and industrial centers."[67] Obviously, the last objective attacked Navy prerogatives on two levels. First, Kenney not only extended air operations far out to sea but also defined attacking "enemy lines of communication and industrial centers" as a defensive activity. Second, both roles were implicitly strategic and involved operating aircraft independently of land and sea forces.

199

The Navy's response to these complaints was to rescind the MacArthur-Pratt Agreement in 1935.[68] As a result, the Air Corps's ultimate intrusion into the Navy's domain was not attributable to mutual cooperation or concessions to its complaints. Instead, it was attributable to the Air Corps's ability to provide a clearly stated alternative to sea-based national defense, which then attracted the support of a very powerful friend—President Franklin D. Roosevelt.

But who specifically provided the Air Corps's blueprint for national defense in the mid- to late-1930s? Not surprisingly, it was ACTS and the Air Corps Board (ACB), a group resurrected by the Baker Board in 1935.[69] From 1935 to 1940, the revitalized ACB worked side by side with ACTS at Maxwell Field. Its members usually included the ACTS commandant and assistant commandant as ex officio members; a director of the board, who was usually its senior permanent member (Col Douglas B. Netherwood, Lt Col Edgar B. Sorensen, and Col Robert Kauch, for example); and five to eight officers and civilians who had an almost incestuous working relationship with ACTS. In the last case, bomber proponent Laurence Kuter recalled that "the school thought it could get some things through the chief's office via the board that it couldn't any other way [and that] the board was quite happy to have that arrangement too."[70] As a result of this close association, for several years ACTS formally scrubbed all ACB reports that went to the Office of the Chief of the Air Corps (OCAC); the board ensured that its studies were compatible with the principles taught at the Tactical School; and the mutual cooperation between both organizations ensured that they spoke with one voice, especially when they developed the theoretical and doctrinal "language" that the Air Corps increasingly used to claim a role in offshore defense.

In developing the above "language," the ACB fulfilled a charter that was both theoretical and practical. On the theoretical level, its role was to study Air Corps problems and issues that involved considerable study and research, as assigned by the chief of the Air Corps under the provisions of AR 95-20 (9 November 1934).[71] In 1936 Lt Col R. M. Jones, General Arnold's executive officer, highlighted two of these problems and issues in particular. First, he asked whether the

Air Corps should pursue large-scale development of costly four-engined bombers or whether it should invest in medium-range and therefore cheaper bombers. Second, he asked what types of missions long-range bombers should actually perform. (The Air Corps's two-part answer, as already suggested, was the B-17 and hemispheric defense, respectively.)[72]

In the immediate, practical sphere, the ACB's charter was to serve as an antidote to the "divide and conquer" strategy the Army adopted against its aeromaniacs, particularly after the Drum Board of 1933. In other words, the board's function—since it presumably had at least the tacit support of OCAC on certain issues—was to prevent divergences of opinion between OCAC and the newly created, semiautonomous General Headquarters (GHQ) Air Force.[73] As General Arnold and his sympathizers insisted, the Air Corps had to spread the conviction that it was "*one single body* with a single *purpose* common to all its parts" (emphasis in original).[74] Consequently, between 1935–42 the Air Corps Board undertook 77 projects, 25 of which recommended common strategies and tactics.[75] Of those ACB studies that provided airmen a "language" to assault Navy prerogatives, arguably the two most important were ACB-31, *The Functions of the Army Air Forces,* and ACB-35, *Employment of Aircraft in Defense of the Continental United States.*

The purpose of ACB-31 was to "determine the manner in which Air Forces may best perform those functions for which they are, *or should be,* responsible" (emphasis added).[76] The report, although endorsed by ACTS, was sufficiently controversial that OCAC classified it Confidential and did not formally approve it until 29 October 1936. (The office copy, for example, has warnings such as "not to leave the office" and "do not forward" scrawled and underlined on the title page.)[77] Six weeks later, on 11 December 1936, General Westover recommended that the War Department adopt ACB-31 as its official air policy. Not surprisingly, his recommendation went unheeded.

The report, although circumspect, challenged the orthodoxy of the time. It conceded that the primary role of Army Air Forces (AAF) was to defend US territory, preserve internal order, and support ground and naval forces.[78] However, since airpower was inherently strategic, it also insisted that the Air Corps develop, operate, and maintain follow-on air forces for defensive and possibly offensive strategic operations.[79] (Why? Because long-range aviation constituted a new type of force; it influenced ground *and* sea action yet operated outside their domains; and it seriously complicated an opponent's ability to wage war.)[80] Second, the report identified potential target sets for air bombardment that deliberately obscured the distinction between tactical, operational, and strategic-level objectives. The suggested targets included but were not limited to troop cantonments or concentrations, choke points in lines of communications, enemy air forces and naval vessels, fuel storage plants, power grids, munitions and aircraft factories, and assorted types of refineries.[81] Last, ACB-31's definition of air-based coastal defense was also premeditatedly vague. Yes, it included protecting shipping in coastal zones, guarding military and civilian facilities, preventing invasion, and ensuring the security of vital military and commercial coastal areas. However, the most effective way that land-based aviation could accomplish these objectives was to conduct unrestricted counterair operations against distant installations or to thwart the creation and use of staging areas for a continental attack. In either case, the need for long-range aircraft became "a matter of prime importance."[82]

In the case of ACB-35, *Employment of Aircraft in Defense of the Continental United States,* the Air Corps classified it Secret and did not release it until 7 May 1939, even though ACB had finished the original version in late 1935.[83] Nevertheless, the report passed from one influential person to another, especially between those individuals interested in providing the newly minted GHQ Air Force a shadow doctrine. As a result, ACB-35 augmented the doctrinal vocabulary provided by its predecessor. Both reports popularized the concept of a strategic strike force dedicated to destroying a spectrum of targets in the name of coastal-continental defense. ACB-35, however, made an even bigger claim—that the strategic bomber was the ideal instrument of hemispheric defense and beyond. The report noted that "the possibility of applying military force against the vital structure of a nation directly and immediately upon the outbreak of hostilities, is a most important and far reaching development."[84] In other words, the role of airpower was not just supplementary—to attack hostile forces beyond the reach of the Army or Navy—but to strike directly against an enemy nation! Its ultimate responsibility was to

> exert the greatest possible influence on the outcome of the entire campaign, rather than [be] diverted for the purpose of meeting some immediate emergency of lesser ultimate importance. Aircraft should never be used against targets appropriate for and within the range of other weapons unless there are no other objectives suitable for air attack or the situation demands the concentration of all available weapons.[85]

Therefore, to support the Monroe Doctrine properly, AAF needed to perform most of its missions over areas that were potentially far beyond the operating radius of the Army and Navy. Yes, the Air Corps had an auxiliary, defensive role, but in the name of strategic defense, it was incumbent for the GHQ Air Force to operate under the most favorable circumstances possible, which meant using bombers to the fullest extent of their ability and where the opponent was most vulnerable to attack.[86] The old areas of responsibility worked out by the Joint Board and MacArthur-Pratt no longer applied. An opponent's most vital targets might now include land forces, large naval expeditions, or the structure of an enemy nation.[87] However, in order to provide long-range defense and more, ACB-35 insisted that the B-17 make up at least one-third of the Air Corps's bomber force and thus enable it to operate as far as fifteen hundred miles out at sea or from a particular base. Hap Arnold and others subsequently used this well-developed paradigm to encroach on the long-range "defense" mission traditionally dominated by the Navy. They acted upon the ACB's recommendations, but the level of success they experienced against the Navy in the mid- to late-1930s might not have occurred without a powerful new ally—Franklin D. Roosevelt.[88]

FDR's support for long-range aviation, as a defensive and offensive tool, grew out of mounting international pressures and successful Air Corps indoctrination, as promoted by ACB-31 and ACB-35. The international pressures included the expiration of the Washington Treaty, the collapse of the Geneva Disarmament Conference of 1933, growing German rearmament, Japan's incursion into Manchuria, and the Anglo-Italian imbroglio over Ethiopia. Roosevelt concluded from these developments that he needed long-range military aviation to project power, deter aggression, and defend US territory. Thus, on the eve of World War II, the Air Corps had America's first true long-range bomber—the B-17; a semiautonomous striking force—GHQ Air Force; and both new and expropriated missions.[89] In other words, the Air Corps of the late 1930s had the means, the organization, and the conceptual "language" needed for an overlapping mission with the Navy. It had survived and codified itself not only by spreading air-mindedness but also by demonstrating its versatility in selected roles and missions. However, the air arm had yet a third part to its ad hoc strategy.

The Army and Its Air Corps: Political Maneuvering and Legislative Combat

A political and legislative assault by the Air Corps against its parent service was a third way it sought to survive and then realize its full potential in the interwar years. Initially, the assault required airmen to complain loudly and often. If one is to believe the air enthusiasts of the interwar years, whether civilian or military, Army traditionalists sought to thwart them at every turn. Col Benjamin Foulois, for example, complained to the Morrow Board in 1925 that

> a fair, just, willing and sympathetic opportunity for the Air Service to produce results has never been evidenced, from my experience of the past 17 years, and I doubt whether results can be obtained in the next 20 years if the Air Service is required to continue its struggle for existence under General Staff control.[90]

What was the reason for such hostility? Maj Gen Mason Patrick, while head of the Air Service, argued politely that in the case of the Army, its leaders were hidebound Neanderthals who did not realize the full potential of airpower and therefore took three years to acknowledge they even had an Air Service.[91] In turn, Robert Bullard claimed that the directors of

204

the older services were "jealously intent upon keeping this new [aviation] arm subordinate, as an auxiliary, lest they lose power and prestige."[92] And so the explanations and complaints continued well into the 1930s, when an anonymous airman refused to share credit or take comfort in the great strides made by Army aviation: "Although the Air Corps has escaped from its role as [the] Cinderella of the Army, it has done so through its own effort alone and is still subject to the might of its none too appreciative parents."[93] These "parents" were, in Hanson Baldwin's words, "short-sighted old fogies." They included the long-suffering Maj Gen Hugh Drum, whom the "dervishes of airpower" attacked repeatedly as a thick-witted Army traditionalist who refused to abandon his early claim that the American doughboy would forever remain the decisive element in war.[94]

Were Army airmen always right to fear their parent organization? Was the interwar Army unremittingly hostile towards its own air arm? The answer to both questions is "no," but the questions themselves are moot. For every complaint about bovine Army generals robbing the Air Service/Air Corps of its full potential and for every statistic "proving" War Department and Army parsimony, there are countervailing examples of substantive financial support and bureaucratic tolerance. The Air Service/Air Corps was, after all, an *independent* branch of the Army that was *coequal* with other combat arms. Its military expenditures, as a percentage of total War Department disbursements, grew from 11.8 percent in 1925 to 28.1 percent in 1939.[95] (In fact, in only one year between 1925–39 [1933] did Air Corps outlays fall as a percentage of War Department spending.) In the bleak Depression years of 1933–36, the Air Corps still received $113.21 million in emergency funds, and its chief, as an aviator, was the highest paid officer in the Regular Army.[96] Yet, Regular Army members were not uniformly hostile or jealous. Aviator Hugh Knerr, for example, attended the Army War College in 1930–31, where the "growing appreciation" of airpower left him "with no windmills to challenge."[97] In turn, Air Force Chief of Staff Nathan Twining later admitted that "the Army took good care of us," while Gen Howell Estes did not recall the Army treating its airmen as second-class citizens.[98]

On an objective level, Air Corps complaints about Army persecution were polemical and wrongly popularized by sympathetic aviation historians.[99] (The real problem was that Congress and the War Department failed repeatedly to disburse the funds they promised and that the Army and Navy suffered the same fate as the Air Corps—but their relative rates of deprivation were worse.) To repeat, however, the point was moot. Nothing could have placated Milling, Sherman, or the ACTS Bomber Mafia. Nothing could have minimized their adversarial approach, which did periodically lapse into persecution mania. Since the air zealots were "separatists" and Army traditionalists were "indispensabilists," they could only agree to disagree.

But who or what was a "separatist"? According to aviator Jarred Crabb, it was every man in the Air Corps who "felt as though they ought to get some bombers, that were able to do something, and separate from the Army."[100] Bomber advocate Haywood Hansell agreed—the air weapon could be decisive only if it operated outside the tactical restrictions imposed by surface commanders. It was an "inherently" offensive (i.e., strategic) instrument of war that did not fit preexisting frameworks of land and sea warfare.[101] As a result, cooperation in air warfare could only mean an intimate liaison between component parts of an air division—and not with ground troops or navies.[102] Further, the air division commander needed to administer independent, strategic airpower "like an opiate [and] in sufficient quantities to paralyze an enemy's activities in sensitive areas at crucial periods."[103] This, then, was the separatist's creed, and it was the antithesis of the indispensabilist vision of airpower.

As already pointed out, Army traditionalists truly appreciated military aviation. But like the separatists, they too had a creed, and it included the principles of economy of force and unity of command. To Army traditionalists like Drum, the lesson of World War I was that an army must use all available means to work as a single unit towards a single objective in war—victory. In particular, there was only one US Army, and airpower was an indispensable part of that indissoluble whole.[104] Yes, the Air Service/Air Corps had limited autonomy, the indispensabilists admitted, but that was only right. The air arm was not a war-winning weapon in itself; it was unable to occupy territory; it was dependent on fixed bases; and it was unable to conduct continuous and sustained operations. As a result, it had to be in "full sympathy" with the Army's other arms and subsume itself to the Army's creed.[105] At the center of that creed was the infantry, which remained the "queen of the battlefield."

Because there was no room for accommodation between Army separatists and indispensabilists, the complaints of airpower zealots could go only so far. As propagandists, they could—through mind-numbing repetition—create a climate for change, but they could not engineer change itself. Thus, to create a corporate (and independent) identity for themselves, aviators like Benny Foulois, Hap Arnold, Oscar Westover, Frank Andrews, and Robert Olds not only protested loudly but also turned Congress and the War Department into roles and missions battlegrounds. In other words, they resorted to legislation or formal boards of inquiry to realize their separatist vision.

Billy Mitchell spoke for like-minded airmen when he observed in 1925, "Let the groundman run the ground, let the waterman run the water, and let the airman run the air."[106] Mitchell and his sympathizers first hoped to turn this pithy maxim into reality via legislative means. At a minimum, they were going to prevent Army and Navy traditionalists from choking off the Air Service, bulldozing it, or holding it down "like a stepchild." In Mitchell's words, "To leave aeronautics as an orphan [was to] strangle it before it reache[d] man's estate."[107] Therefore, the only way to save Army aviation, according to Cong. Charles Curry of California, was to introduce a bill on 28 July 1919, calling for an independent Department of Aeronautics. Curry's air-minded proposal failed, but it also initiated a multiyear legislative and political struggle between the Navy and the Army, and between the Army and its own Air Corps.[108] In 1919–20, for example, no fewer than eight aviation bills appeared before Congress, all of which sought to emancipate the Air Service from Army and Navy domination, either by creating a separate executive department, as Congressman Curry wanted, or by creating a Department of National Defense with three coequal parts.[109]

Not surprisingly, postwar demobilization and the implacable opposition of the War Department doomed all eight bills. Nevertheless, the failures of 1919–20 did not sour Air Service "separatists" on the political process. They believed, in the words of Charles Menoher, that "a great majority" of the members of Congress were "friendly" to the Air Service.[110] As a result, air leaders continued to proselytize before congressional committees. (Foulois alone, for example, testified 75 times *before* he became leader of the Air Corps!)

Senior airmen also thought that congressional, War Department, and Army boards or commissions could positively define the relationship between military aviation and the older services. If one believes Maj Guido Perera, however, these boards of inquiry were frequently hostile towards the idea of independent airpower. Of the 14 interwar groups that studied the proper employment of airpower prior to 1934, Perera claimed that only one—the Lampert Board of 1924–25—recommended the creation of an independent air force within a Department of National Defense.[111] But was Perera right? Was there malfeasance or obstructionism afoot? Were the boards and commissions truly hostile, or did the Air Corps fail to control the debate properly? Did it let indispensabilists becloud the issue of independence by introducing so many details about the needs of the Army and Navy for auxiliary aviation that no one realized that these needs did not represent real defense in the air?[112]

If one analyzes the findings of individual boards or commissions, they appear typically hostile to the Air Service/Air Corps. However, imbedded within a majority of these findings is a smattering of proseparatist recommendations that, when added together over time, slowly but inexorably increased the autonomy of the Air Corps.[113]

The seminal Menoher Board, established by Secretary of War Newton Baker, is a case in point. Its report, dated 27 October 1919, was the first to argue that independent airpower could not win a war by itself and that unfettered air operations violated the principle of unity of command. On the other hand, the report was also the first to stress that the Air Service was an essential Army combat branch equal in importance to the infantry, cavalry, and artillery.[114]

At roughly the same time, General Pershing convened the Dickman Board in Paris on 19 April 1919. The board, which included Benny Foulois as its president, agreed with the Army that the primary function of military aviation was observation. However, it further argued that *most* of the Air Service should serve with ground units at the army, corps, and division levels. The remaining number of aircraft, which might include up to three brigades of attack, bombardment, and pursuit aviation, should then form a GHQ reserve that would operate throughout a battle zone. (General Pershing fought successfully to prevent the Dickman Board from referring to the GHQ reserve as a "strategical" force. He did, however, hope that the concept itself would appear progressive enough to dampen future agitation by independence-minded airmen.)

In March 1923, the Lassiter Board gave the War Department its first significant interwar air plan. It advocated an expandable Air Force based on a 10-year development program and a $495 million budget. It further elaborated on the distinction between army-centered air units and GHQ Air Forces. According to the board, which included airmen Frank Lahm and Herbert Dargue, it behooved the Army to assign attack and pursuit aircraft to each of its field armies, while also providing bombardment and pursuit striking units to a GHQ reserve.[115] Although Navy opposition prevented this recommendation from becoming law, it did influence the thinking of the Lampert and Morrow Boards, both of which reviewed, yet again, the status of the Air Service in 1925.

The air-minded Lampert Board advocated the creation of a Department of National Defense, a unified and independent air force, and the introduction of an assistant secretary for air in three federal departments—War, Navy, and Commerce. Congress, however, worried that these recommendations would further complicate the command and control of the Army air arm by its parent service. As a result, it enacted into law the more conservative and yet accommodating suggestions made by the Morrow Board. Thus, in 1926 the Air Service became the Air Corps (a change in nomenclature specifically designed to convey a new level of autonomy for Army aviation); it received formal representation on the War Department General Staff; and it temporarily gained a potential new advocate in the assistant secretary of war for air affairs.[116]

Limited but incremental progress continued with the Drum Board in 1933, although frustrated airmen now defined a board of inquiry as something "long, narrow, and wooden."[117] The board's members—including the commandant of the Army War College, the chief of the coast artillery, and other Army stalwarts—rejected the idea of an independent Air Corps, but they did endorse (yet again) the creation of a semiautonomous GHQ Air Force to conduct independent operations. Conspiracy-minded airmen like Haywood Hansell rightfully worried that the proposal was part of a divide-and-conquer strategy by the Army. If the staffs of OCAC and GHQ Air Force became bureaucratic rivals, as Army traditionalists hoped, they would quickly squander their political capital by battling each other rather than their parent service. (The hope was understandable but also unfounded. Air Corps leaders successfully prevented the rivalry from becoming unmanageable.)

Last, in 1934 the Baker Board rejected the Air Corps's familiar demands for independence and a substantive role in national defense, but the rival Howell Commission decided, as Perera observed, "that the Air Service had now passed beyond its former position as a useful auxiliary and should in the future be considered an important means of exerting directly the will of the Commander-in-Chief."[118] As a result, the commission called for a highly mobile GHQ Air Force that would operate as an "independent striking unit" and not merely as a strategic reserve. The Army, in the mistaken hope that the Air Corps would divide itself into pro- and anti-GHQ factions, finally agreed to the idea.

On 1 March 1935 the semiautonomous GHQ Air Force became a reality but only after multiple aviation boards and commissions had sponsored a number of incremental reforms. This political victory, however, was merely the third component of a four-part strategy. The remaining part required the Air Corps to develop a new theory and doctrine of warfare that maximized the independent use of airpower. The responsibility to develop this theory and doctrine devolved almost immediately to the Air Corps Tactical School.

The Air Corps Tactical School:
Incubator of Bombardment Theory and Doctrine

In reality, five organizations contributed to the development of American air doctrine in the interwar years: the conservative War Department (including the Army General Staff), the moderate Office of the Chief of the Air Corps, the equable GHQ Air Force, the progressive Air Corps Board (particularly in the mid- to late-1930s), and the radical Air Corps Tactical School. However, of the five contributors to the concept of unescorted HAPDB, the most important was ACTS. It divided its 20-year existence between Langley Field, Virginia, and Maxwell Field, Alabama, but one can arrange its theoretical and doctrinal development into roughly three phases (with some overlap between phases two and three).

From 1920 to 1926 the school established the primacy of the bomber and developed its core principles of employment. From 1927 to 1934, the Bomber Mafia developed a uniquely American way of air warfare—unescorted HAPDB against the key nodes of an enemy's industrial-economic infrastructure. Last, from roughly 1935 to 1940, faculty members not only formalized their theory into doctrine but also sought to identify what particular target sets constituted the key vulnerabilities of an enemy's industrial-economic system. Before one reviews these three rough-hewn phases, however, it is appropriate to provide a brief statistical portrait of ACTS.

Between 1921–40, 1,091 officers graduated from ASFOS/ ASTS/ACTS. The average officer was 39 years old, had 17 years of service, and had consistently received nothing less than ratings of "excellent" in previous efficiency reports. Ninety percent of the students were airmen, while the remaining 10 percent came from the other services or branches of the Army. Captains comprised the majority of the attendees (55 percent), while 29 percent were majors. (Thirty-four percent of the graduates then attended Army Command and General Staff College at Fort Leavenworth, Kansas.) Ten percent came from other services or branches of the Army. Most importantly, however, only 15 percent graduated from 1921 to 1930, when the school remained relatively unsophisticated. In contrast, 65 percent of the students attended the school from 1936 to 1940, when it taught a mature, well-established version of HAPDB. Further, of the 1,091 total graduates, 261 of them became general officers in World War II. They comprised 80 percent of the senior leadership in AAF and included 11 out of 13 three-star generals and all three of the four-star generals then in service.[119] The point is obvious—an overwhelming number of wartime Air Force leaders attended ACTS in the interwar years, and a significant number of them were systematically indoctrinated in the virtues of unescorted HAPDB against the key nodes of an opponent's material infrastructure.

In terms of actual course work, ACTS offered 40 separate courses in its heyday, and 53 percent of them centered on air subjects. The five longest courses were Bombardment, Air Force, Attack Aviation, Combined Arms, and Air Logistics. The ACTS legacy, as we know it, took shape primarily in the Air Force, Bombardment, and Combined Arms courses, which comprised roughly 10 percent of the curriculum and employed roughly 15–25 percent of the faculty. Within each course, the faculty relied on a variety of teaching methods, including lectures, discussions, quizzes, and illustrative/map problems. (The latter were pen-and-pencil war games conducted every Friday for four hours.) Students aided in their own education by giving short, supplementary talks; participating in lecture discussions (actual lectures used only half of a 50-minute period); and conducting individual student research, of which Ken Walker's 1929 thesis was the most impressive. (Entitled *Is the Defense of New York City from Air Attack Possible?* the thesis was 56 single-spaced pages long.) However, before ACTS or its students could accomplish any of the above, the school needed to accomplish some foundational steps.

ACTS Phase One (1920–26)

According to air theorist William Sherman, the relative importance of the infantry in war was not permanent; the airplane (if used properly) could diminish the queen of the battlefield's stature, especially by acting decisively against ground forces.[120] Unfortunately, after World War I the United States "found itself with an Air Service which through

212

necessity had been hurriedly gotten together and consequently poorly trained and inadequately organized."[121] One solution to these problems was a formalized and progressive school system.

On 25 February 1920 the War Department authorized the creation of 11 Air Service schools, including what soon became the Air Service Field Officers' School. The air arm then ordered Maj Thomas Milling, a protégé and former chief of staff of Billy Mitchell in Europe, to Langley Field, Virginia. Milling's charter, as he understood it, was to organize ASFOS; train officers to become competent commanders and staff officers of air units, up to and including the air brigade and army 'evel; teach these same officers air tactics; *and originate sound tactical doctrine for the Air Service as a whole.*[122]

In order to accomplish these goals, Milling recruited Maj William Sherman as his assistant. Sherman had also worked for General Mitchell in AEF and in the postwar Air Service Training and Operations Group. (Like Milling, he was a disciple of the flamboyant Mitchell.) With Sherman as his assistant, Milling hoped to develop the Field Officers' School—which the Army renamed the Air Service Tactical School in 1922—into *the* clearinghouse for air tactics and doctrine in the Army. Unfortunately, only the most meager data on air doctrine was available at the time.[123] As a result, the school first had to rely on a smorgasbord of diffused and uncoordinated texts that competed, in good Darwinian fashion, for the hearts and minds of students and operators alike.

Although ASFOS/ASTS used texts developed by a variety of sources, the majority of the early materials were Army-centered and trivialized the possible impact of air bombardment. Air Service information circulars 56, 57, 73, 75, 84, and 87—all of which functioned as early texts for the attack, bombardment, observation, and pursuit portions of what soon developed into a 10-month course—certainly emphasized the importance of traditional ground forces and the auxiliary nature of airpower. So did another conciliatory ASTS text, Billy Mitchell's *Notes on the Multi-Motored Bombardment Group, Day and Night,* which became an official Air Service publication in 1922 and which primarily stressed the role of bombardment in the immediate battle zone.

Following that was Training Regulation 440-15, *Air Tactics*, which William Sherman largely wrote in 1922 and the War Department did not accept as official Army doctrine until January 1926. It argued that the general roles of airpower included observation, artillery control, and transportation. The specific role of bombardment, in contrast, remained the interdiction of hostile land forces and targets deep in the enemy's "zone of the interior."[124] Subsequently, the ASTS *Bombardment* text of 1924–25 made a similar argument. Bomber aircraft were nothing more than large-caliber guns that could outrange and outstrike other types of guns and thus harass approaching infantry columns or disrupt the concentration of troops.[125] Last, the 1926 version of the *Bombardment* text continued to accept the largely auxiliary nature of airpower by advocating air strikes against the "spouts" of an army's supplies.[126]

All of the above texts provided a foundation for the rough-hewn ASFOS/ASTS curriculum, but they did not ultimately stray from Army orthodoxy. They agreed that workable principles of strategic airpower were still few and far between and that pursuit aviation, since it was responsible for the necessary first step of air supremacy, remained *the* arm of the Air Service. Yet, during phase one of the Tactical School's existence (1922–26), two major things happened. First, and through the intercession of two forward-looking faculty members, the fighter lost pride of place to the bomber in the school's curriculum. Second, these same airmen developed a series of working propositions that served as the bedrock of future theoretical thought.

Milling and Sherman promoted the future importance of air bombardment and codified the foundational principles of American airpower. As already mentioned, they had worked for Billy Mitchell in World War I and in the postwar Air Service Training and Operations Group. In both cases, Milling and Sherman stimulated each other's thinking and began to develop the foundations of future Air Force doctrine.[127] They then took their pro-Mitchell ideas to ASFOS/ASTS, where Milling worked from 1920 to 1925 and Sherman worked twice, from 1920 to 1923 and intermittently from 1923 to 1925.

(During the same years, the school employed an average of six instructors a year.)

Although Milling, Sherman, and their colleagues did not develop a full theory of airpower, they did do one truly critical thing. They established the Combined Air Force Course (later known simply as the Air Force Course) as the most important offering at the Tactical School. The course did not kowtow to Army directives, and it was the one place where heretical airmen could present radical ideas about the future possibilities of airpower (i.e., bombardment). As a result, the first filigrees of a new doctrine appeared in the 1925–26 Combined Air Force Course and its text, *Employment of Combined Air Force.*

Whoever wrote the 1925–26 text remains a mystery, but the fingerprints of Milling and Sherman are all over it. The text provided a series of working propositions that served as the foundation for the theoretical work done by the Bomber Mafia during phase two of the Tactical School's doctrinal development (1927–34). In particular, the *Combined Air Force* text codified five crucial propositions of air warfare for Army airmen. First, the ultimate goal of any air attack is "to undermine the enemy's morale [or] his will to resist."[128] Second, airmen can best destroy morale by attacking the interior of an opponent's territory. Attacks against vital points or centers will not only terrorize populations into submission but also save lives. (In M-day warfare, there is no need for battles of attrition or annihilation.) Third, airpower is an inherently offensive weapon that is impossible, in absolute terms, to stop. Fourth, since airpower is the only military tool that can hit distant centers of concentration and sources of supply and since it is the only tool that can undermine national morale with minimum effort and materiel, combatants should use it extensively in strategic operations. Strategic targets, after all, are almost always more important than tactical targets. Last, "In any scheme of strategical operations the object is to cause complete destruction or permanent and irreparable damage to the enemy which will have a decisive effect."[129] In other words, one must completely neutralize one target set before moving on to another. Attacking in driblets against multiple targets will not yield significant results in the shortest possible time. Decisive attacks, in contrast, will spur the collapse of a society's vital centers and thus lead to the destruction of society as a whole.

That Milling supported the above assumptions depends on strong conjecture rather than direct evidence. However, in the case of Sherman, the above views are clearly documented in *Air Warfare*, which appeared in 1926 and was the culmination of Sherman's work at the Tactical School. In the book, he echoes the *Combined Air Force* text in the following ways: enemy morale is *the* center of gravity in air warfare; one should put enemy population centers, supply systems, and other rearward objectives under pressure in an effort to paralyze an entire society; a vigorous aerial assault is appropriate since no one can wholly prevent a hostile air assault; the very nature of bombardment aircraft makes them a strategic weapon; and the skillful air leader should economize his strength "at all points to the point of parsimony, in order that he may spend with a prodigal hand at the all-important time and place."[130]

The above propositions illustrate a huge point: from 1920 to 1926, ASFOS/ASTS did not develop a specific, universally accepted doctrine for the Army Air Service. What it did do, however, was elevate the importance of the bomber and formalize a series of bedrock principles or working propositions that provided a foundation for the second great contribution of ACTS—the development from roughly 1927 to 1935 of unescorted HAPDB, a specific and unique air doctrine.

ACTS Phase Two (1927–34)

ACTS's Bomber Mafia developed HAPDB. The zealous faculty members of this group (and their dates of assignment to the school) included Robert Olds (1928–31), Kenneth Walker (1929–33), Donald Wilson (1929–34, 1936–40), Harold Lee George (1932–36), Odas Moon (1933–36), Robert Webster (1934–37), Haywood Hansell (1935–38), Laurence Kuter (1935–39), and Muir Fairchild (1937–40). Except for Moon, who died prematurely, the other bomber enthusiasts subsequently became influential generals in World War II and after. Brig Gen Robert Olds, for example, became commander of Ferrying Command. Brig Gen Ken Walker headed 5th Bomber Command in the Pacific theater. On 5 January 1943, he died while leading a daylight bombing attack against Japanese shipping at Rabaul, New Britain. (For his "conspicuous leadership" during the raid, Walker posthumously received the Medal of Honor.) Lt Gen Harold Lee George guided Air Transport Command, which became Military Airlift Command during the cold war. Maj Gen Haywood Hansell commanded 21st Bomber Command in the Pacific until he ran afoul of General Arnold.[131] Laurence Kuter, who became a four-star general and commander of North American Aerospace Defense Command (NORAD) in the cold war, served as deputy chief of the Air Staff for plans.[132] Muir Fairchild, another future four-star general, was the intellectual father of the Strategic Bombing Survey and a member of the Joint Strategic Survey Committee, which was "one of the most influential planning agencies in the wartime armed services."[133] Ultimately, the ACTS Bomber Mafia was an inordinately talented "collective brain" with a unique vision and the resolve to bring it to life. As Kuter later observed, "Nothing could stop us; I mean this was a zealous crowd."[134]

The zealotry, as already pointed out, involved unescorted HAPDB against an enemy nation's vital centers. Thanks to the initial efforts of Olds, Walker, and Wilson, the concept first appeared in 1932 and went as follows:

1. Modern great powers rely on major industrial and economic systems for production of weapons and supplies for their armed forces, and for manufacture of products and provision of services to sustain life in a highly industrialized society. Disruption or paralysis of these systems undermines both the enemy's *capability* and *will* to fight.

2. Such major systems contain critical points whose destruction will break down these systems, and bombs can be delivered with adequate accuracy to do this.

3. Massed air strike forces can penetrate air defenses without unacceptable losses and destroy selected targets.

4. Proper selection of vital targets in the industrial/economic/social structure of a modern industrialized nation, and their subsequent destruction by air attack, can lead to fatal weakening of an industrialized enemy nation and to victory through air power.

5. If enemy resistance still persists after successful paralysis of selected target systems, it may be necessary as a last resort to apply direct force upon the sources of enemy national will by attacking cities. In this event, it is preferable to render the cities untenable rather than indiscriminately to destroy structures and people. (Emphasis in original)[135]

Further, why did Walker, George, Wilson, and others prefer unescorted, high-altitude attacks? Because they believed that modern bombers could operate beyond the reach of defending fighters and antiaircraft artillery (AAA) fire. Why did they emphasize precision? Among other reasons, because government parsimony demanded that they get the biggest "bang for the buck" from the few aircraft they had. And why did they prefer daylight operations? Because then-current navigation aids and bombsights were too primitive to supplant a reliance on visual, line-of-sight techniques.

While developing the above one-of-a-kind theory, the ACTS Bomber Mafia acted, in the candid words of Donald Wilson, "on no firmer basis than reasoned logical thinking bolstered by a grasp of the fundamentals of the application of military force and the reactions of human beings."[136] In other words, they relied on deductive reasoning, analogies, and metaphors to develop their working propositions into a pseudoscientific theory of strategic bombardment. As already noted, to Wilson and his sympathizers, paralyzing a modern industrial state was relatively easy since it was made up of "interrelated and entirely interdependent elements."[137] In fact, the better a society organized its industry for peacetime efficiency, the more vulnerable it was to wartime collapse. All an attacker had to do was cut one or more of a society's "essential arteries."[138] Or, given that modern states were as sensitive as a precision instrument, all one had to do was strike an opponent's key economic nodes. Damaging them was comparable to breaking a needed spring or gear in an intricate watch, which would then inevitably stop working, or to pulling a critical playing card from a house of cards, which would then tumble to the ground, or even to breaking a significant strand of a spider's web, which would then lose its structural integrity and ability to function.[139] In all cases, however, the goal was to avoid using long-range bombers against minor targets. An inviolable principle of ACTS was that airmen use the bomber only against vital material targets located deep within hostile territory and that it never serve in harassing operations for the Army.[140]

ACTS Phase Three (1935–40)

Although Donald Wilson tried to delve into strategic targeting as early as 1932–33, the work of Robert Webster and Muir Fairchild in the mid- to late-1930s identified the industrial and economic target sets that still define modern war. As far as the bomber advocates were concerned, unescorted HAPDB would destroy an opponent's will to resist only if it focused on destroying or paralyzing "national *organic systems* on which many factories and numerous people depended" (emphasis in original).[141] These systems included electrical power generation and distribution, since virtually all industrial and economic operations depended on them; transportation networks (railroads in particular); fuel refining and distribution processes; food distribution and preservation methods; steel manufacturing, which defined a state's war-making potential; and a system of highly concentrated manufacturing plants, including those that produced electrical generators, transformers, and motors.[142]

The above approach was nothing more than an economy-of-force doctrine predicated on subjective analyses of the US economy.[143] It was best suited for the denial of war materials to a highly industrialized enemy whose industries and population were concentrated together.[144] Unfortunately—and despite the genuine belief by bomber enthusiasts that the Air Corps had the minimum skills and technology needed to meet the above targeting requirements—the strategic intelligence on which proper targeting depended was still an infant art. A priori knowledge of what constituted a legitimate target set for a given nation involved considerable guesswork and remained unreliable. As a result, immediately before and during World War II, Allied targeting groups constantly revised their target lists, either elevating or demoting particular target sets based on the sketchy strategic intelligence then available. (The two wartime cases that best illustrate the problem involve ball bearings and electricity. In the first case, Allied planners overestimated the importance of ball bearings to the German war economy and thus wasted a considerable amount of resources against perhaps a second-tier target. In the second case, although ACTS identified electricity as *the* organic essential of modern industrialized states, the Allies never mounted an air campaign against German electricity. Other, more immediate, problems seemed always to take precedence.)

Was the Bomber Mafia's theory flawed? Of course! (1) It assumed, in good Progressivist fashion, that one could scientifically manage war. Like almost all the other American theories of airpower that followed, the ACTS theory of unescorted HAPDB was part of a cause-and-effect universe where one's external means directly impacted another's internal behaviors. Unescorted HAPDB, therefore, was too mechanistic and prescriptive for its own good. It wrongly assumed that one could impose precise, positive controls over complex events. (2) The theory was suspect because of its mid-Victorian faith in technology. It wrongly assumed that revolutionary bomber-related technologies would produce almost "frictionless" wars, regardless of pesky variables such as weather. The "dervishes of airpower," in other words, saw technology as a panacea. (3) The theory failed to acknowledge properly that armed conflict was, as Clausewitz rightfully pointed out, an interactive process between at least two competing wills—not the imposition of one's own will against a passive foe. As the North Vietnamese demonstrated repeatedly in the Second Indochina War, people subjected to air attacks can substitute for and work around lost capabilities. In short, they can react. (4) Unescorted HAPDB overemphasized the offensive aspects of air warfare, like all other significant airpower theories, while minimizing the mischievous potential of defensive strategies and technologies. The theory did not properly anticipate the elaborate, radar-based fighter-AAA defense networks that appeared in World War II. Therefore, in what turned out to be an egregious error, the Bomber Mafia's belief that massed bomber formations could penetrate enemy air defenses without fighter escorts and still destroy selected targets with acceptable losses was dead wrong. Eighth Air

Force had to fight its way into Germany past intervening defenses, just like virtually all other invaders had done over the last five thousand years. To reach the vital centers of Germany, Allied airpower had to attrit the Luftwaffe from the sky—and needed long-range fighters (P-51 Mustangs and P-47 Thunderbolts) to do it. (5) It overstressed the psychological impact of physical destruction and merely assumed that the terrors inherent in bombardment would eventually destroy an enemy's will to resist. Arguably, World War II proved otherwise. (6) HAPDB repeatedly (and wrongly) used metaphors to imply that modern industrial states, with their "organic essentials," were brittle and closed socioeconomic systems—not the adaptable and open systems that they typically were, for example, in World War II. (7) The theory wrongly assumed that opposing states were rational, unitary actors that based their political decisions on lucid cost-benefit analyses and not on potentially obscure organizational, bureaucratic, or emotional factors. (Is it not possible, for example, that a state might continue to struggle—at higher costs—to demonstrate its resolve in *future* contingencies?) (8) The Bomber Mafia grossly exaggerated the frailty and manipulability of popular morale. More specifically, it failed to realize that whatever angry passions strategic bombing aroused among civilians might be directed at the attacker rather than the victim's own government. Therefore, a hostile regime might actually experience less pressure from its own people to quit fighting as a result of air attacks. If it did, would not its internal resolve exceed that of its people, as has happened before? (9) Last, as already suggested, the strategic economic targeting methods formulated at ACTS ran the risk of "mirror imaging," whereby the key nodes of one's own industrial infrastructure become confused with the critical vulnerabilities of an opponent's system.[145] For example, US air planners in World War II assumed that German machinery used the same number of ball bearings as American equipment. Since they did not, Eighth Air Force bombers attacked a target set that had considerable "slack" to expend.

An Open Conclusion

At the end of the interwar period and despite all of the above problems, the Air Corps's ad hoc, four-part strategy had largely worked. The Air Corps had survived, and through its efforts with the general public, sympathetic "fellow travelers," members of Congress, and ACTS (in all its guises), it secured a semiautonomous strike force—GHQ Air Force; it had a shared (yet still ambiguous) responsibility with the Navy for hemispheric defense; and it had a strategic air doctrine that stressed independent air operations—not against enemy armies but against the core vulnerabilities of an opposing nation's economic infrastructure.

In closing, however, one must answer one final question. Did the people at ACTS and in the field completely surrender to the new orthodoxy of HAPDB? Did everyone succumb to the vision of unescorted battle planes making protracted warfare a thing of the past? In fact, archival evidence shows that even up to the last days before the outbreak of war, both students and members of the Air Corps at large exhibited either ignorance about or resistance to the soothing answers found in the theory of unescorted strategic bombardment. To cite one representative example from ACTS, Gen Orvel Cook, who was a student in 1937–38, remembered that audiences were highly skeptical of the school's bombardment doctrine: "Some of us had had more experience than some of the instructors and, consequently, we took a lot of this instruction with a large grain of salt, and we more or less made up our minds as to what [to believe], no matter how dogmatic the instructor might be."[146] Cook went on to note that the students had as many different points of view as the instructors: "We knew they were sort of talking off the top of their heads. This was largely theory anyway."[147] Thus, if we are to believe Cook, the one prevailing attitude at ACTS and the Air Corps at large may not have been support for unescorted strategic daylight bombardment, but the less precise belief "that success in any future war would be largely dependent upon the success of the air."[148]

Since ACTS's message did not necessarily enjoy universal appeal among its students, one can further ask just how influential it was outside the classroom. Did the operational Air Corps uncritically accept ACTS bombardment doctrine, or did the airmen in the field also have their doubts? To cite a final (but again representative) example, in 1936 the GHQ Air Force's position seemed supportive: "The policy of this headquarters, for the ensuing training year, will be to comply with the teachings of all texts of the Air Corps Tactical School to the greatest degree possible in all operations and training."[149] The stated goal was to apply ACTS teachings to the actual operations of GHQ Air Force units. As a result, Col Hugh Knerr, chief of staff of the GHQ Air Force, asked operational units to study the Tactical School's 1937–38 *Air Force* text and offer constructive criticisms. The subsequent reviews were mixed, with some showing an operator's distrust of theory. That was certainly the case with Brig Gen G. C. Brant, commander of the 3d Wing, GHQ Air Force, who recommended the elimination of as much theory as possible.[150] Brant's executive officer, Lt Col George E. Lovell Jr. confessed a similar empirical bent: "I am quite uneducated in the higher art of tactics, and found this subject quite deep."[151]

Lt Col M. F. Harmon and Maj Oliver P. Gothlin Jr. were less hostile than General Brant, but they too argued that "a note of caution should be sounded against the too ardent adoption of peace time [*sic*] theories and hypothesis [*sic*] when they are not supported by actually demonstrated facts nor by the experiences of the only war in which aviation was employed."[152] Neither officer believed that historical precedent or recent experience justified the doctrine of self-sufficient bombardment. Last, Lt Col A. H. Gilkeson, commander of the 8th Pursuit Group, could not help similarly agreeing: "This recent academic tendency to minimize, if not entirely dismiss, the consideration of the fighting force as a powerful and extremely necessary adjunct of the air force has led to the teaching of doctrines which have not been established as being true and might even be fatally dangerous to our aim in the event of armed conflict."[153]

The above examples (among many others) caution us not to remember the Air Corps Tactical School as an omnipresent force that totally shaped the thinking of everyday airmen in the interwar years. Yes, ACTS theory/doctrine was an important part of the Air Corps's four-part strategy for institutional survival and growth. In that regard, it performed its role very well. But when it comes to the popularity and acceptance of HAPDB prior to World War II, we can only make a more modest, but equally powerful, final claim.

In July 1941 President Roosevelt tasked the armed services to write a war plan that would provide the number of men and equipment initially needed to win a future war against the Axis powers. Although the response of General Arnold's newly created Air War Plans Division staff could have been a short and pithy statistical portrait of future Air Force needs, the division chief thought differently. He was ex–Bomber Mafia leader Lt Col Harold Lee George, and he saw in FDR's request an opportunity to sneak ACTS doctrine into a major War Department planning document via the back door. With General Arnold's approval, George set about doing just that. However, because he needed a working group to start on the project immediately, George recruited former colleagues from ACTS—bomber enthusiasts Lt Col Ken Walker, Maj Haywood Hansell, and Maj Laurence Kuter.

From 3 to 12 August 1941, these men, with the assistance of other airmen once associated with the Tactical School, wrote AWPD-1, the air annex to the requested FDR plan. However, instead of just providing statistical tables that listed the Air Corps's future wants and needs, the four members of the working group turned AWPD-1 into a blueprint for strategic air warfare in Europe. The plan grudgingly agreed to provide hemispheric defense, *if necessary;* it unhappily agreed to support a future cross-channel invasion, *if necessary;* but its true aim was to conduct a strategic air campaign against Germany, based on the concepts of employment first developed by the Bomber Mafia at ACTS in the 1930s. George, Walker, Hansell, and Kuter spent nine long days fashioning AWPD-1, but as Hansell would later point out, the plan was seven years in the making. It called for an initial consignment of 6,860 bombers to attack 154 key targets (124 of them centered on electricity, oil, and transportation).[154] With the necessary equipment, the plan's writers argued, Germany would collapse in six months.

To paraphrase Hap Arnold, here was airpower you could put your hands around; here was the foundation for a myriad of air plans that followed in its wake. Yes, subsequent plans like AWPD-42 changed targeting priorities and made other adjustments, but the basic intellectual scaffolding provided by AWPD-1 remained in place throughout the air war. That scaffolding, coupled with the interwar success of the Air Corps in a broader four-part strategy, ensured that the Army Air Forces would become what the aeromaniacs had always wanted—an independent service with an independent mission.

Notes

1. See Capt J. D. Barker, *History of the Air Corps Tactical School,* 1931, 1, Air Force Historical Research Agency (AFHRA), Maxwell AFB, Ala., file no. 245.01B. The author would like to thank AFHRA for research funding for this essay.

2. Ibid.

3. Air Corps Tactical School, "Orientation (Lecture 1) to Air Force Course," 5 September 1935, pt. 2, p. 11, AFHRA, file no. 248.2017A. Webster's view of air warfare was not uniquely American. It echoed, for example, what Giulio Douhet said in 1921: "We find ourselves now at a particular point in the curve of the evolution of war. After this point the curve drops off abruptly in a new direction, breaking off all continuity with the past." See Giulio Douhet, *The Command of the Air,* trans. Dino Ferrari (1942; reprint, Washington, D.C.: Office of Air Force History, 1983), 29.

4. See Douhet; and Gianni Caproni and Nino Salvaneschi, *Let Us Kill the War: Let Us Strike at the Heart of the Enemy,* 1917, AFHRA, file no. 168.661-129.

5. Comments by Gen John Pershing, n.d., 11, AFHRA, file no. 248.211-16F.

6. Navy Department inputs for the Howell Commission. See "I. General Organization," n.d., 9, AFHRA, file no. 145.93-97.

7. Maurer Maurer, *Aviation in the U.S. Army, 1919–1939* (Washington, D.C.: Government Printing Office, 1987), xix, xxi, xxii. In contrast, the Army Air Service began the war with 65 officers; 1,100 enlisted men; and 55 aircraft, 51 of which were obsolete and the other four obsolescent. See *Air Service Newsletter,* 10 January 1920, 9.

8. Because of the "premature" peace, the record of the AEF's Air Service was decidedly mixed. On the positive side, its 767 pilots and 481 observers won scores of decorations for bravery. The airmen also shot down 781 enemy aircraft and 82 balloons in 12,830 flights over enemy lines. Last, they dropped 275,000 pounds of ordnance in 150 deep-interdiction

bombing raids. (The deepest raid penetrated 160 miles into enemy territory.) On the negative side, America's industrial mobilization was so chaotic that its nascent aeronautical industry provided only 196 indigenously produced aircraft before the armistice. Further, wartime bombing results were so limited, due to inadequate equipment and personnel, that anything but the tactical value of airpower remained in doubt. See Mason Patrick, *The United States in the Air* (Garden City, N.Y.: Doubleday, Doran, 1928), 44, 49–50; *Air Service Newsletter,* 10 January 1920, 9; Lt Col Herbert Dargue, AEF, to director of military aeronautics, letter, 9 November 1918, 13; and William C. Sherman, *Air Warfare* (New York: Ronald Press, 1926), 4.

9. Maurer, 9, 11, 13.

10. See Patrick, 83, 89; and Maj Thomas D. Milling, "Air Power in National Defense," ca. 1928, 3, AFHRA, file no. 248.211-122.

11. See "Statement of Brigadier General H. A. Drum, Assistant Chief of Staff, Operations and Training Division, War Department General Staff, before Board of Aviation Inquiry, Part I," 21 September 1925, 55, AFHRA, file no. 248.211-16D; and James L. Crowder Jr., *Osage General: Major General Clarence L. Tinker* (Tinker AFB, Okla.: Office of History, Oklahoma City Air Logistics Center, 1987), 96.

12. Barker, 1.

13. Thomas D. Milling, *The Air Service Tactical School: Its Function and Operation,* 1924, 1, AFHRA, file no. 245.01-3. Progressivism was an amorphous social and political movement in the late nineteenth and early twentieth centuries. As a political movement, it advocated an active government defense of the weak and oppressed. Its specific achievements included the breakup of monopolies and trusts, the introduction of lower tariffs, the popular election of senators, and the introduction of child labor laws. In the spheres of business and education, Progressivism stressed technicism, standardization, professionalization, formalized education, scientific management, and timeliness and efficiency. One can argue that Secretary of War Root's reforms, which included the introduction of the general staff system and the further rationalization of military education, were Progressivist acts. See Peter Karsten, "Armed Progressives: The Military Reorganizes for the American Century," in *Building the Organizational Society,* ed. Jerry Israel (New York: Free Press, 1972), 197–232. For a discussion on the difficulties of defining Progressivism as a movement, see Peter G. Filene, "An Obituary for the Progressive Movement," *American Quarterly* 22 (Spring 1970): 20–34.

14. Benjamin Foulois, *From the Wright Brothers to the Astronauts* (New York: McGraw-Hill, 1968), 202. More than a few airmen shared Pershing's distaste for the supercilious Mitchell. In 1919, for example, Oscar Westover (a future Air Corps leader) complained to Maj Gen Charles Menoher that "Mitchell believes that his rank entitles him to special deference as a Group Chief and that all other Air Service activities ought to cow-tow to him as Chief of the Training and Operations Group." Such arrogance drove

Westover to conclude, "I think it also unfortunate that General Mitchell is not Colonel Mitchell" and to suggest that he be reassigned as the commander of air defenses in the Philippines! Chief of the Air Corps Mason Patrick further observed in 1928 that Mitchell had a highly developed ego, loved the limelight, and thirsted for public attention. Last, the legendary hostility between Mitchell and Benny Foulois was nothing less than class warfare. Mitchell, who was an Army blue blood and cerebral by nature, was the antithesis of Foulois, who was a utilitarian mechanic by temperament. It therefore comes as no surprise that Foulois later portrayed himself as a practical everyman compelled to deal with a skittish fop who was a talker rather than a doer, who merely "sounded" like an expert, and "who couldn't agree on the color of white paper." The egotistical Mitchell did have, Foulois grudgingly admitted, a "gift of gab," but it only helped obscure his lack of practical success in the field. From the standpoint of the Air Corps and its future, what mattered was that Hap Arnold was an admirer of Mitchell. (He was, as Mitchell put it, "one of my boys.") From the standpoint of ACTS, what mattered was that key members of its faculty—Thomas Milling, William Sherman, Herbert Dargue, Harold Lee George, and others—were equally devoted. At Mitchell's trial, for example, George tried vainly to testify on his mentor's behalf, but his interlocutors deliberately restricted him to answering narrow technical questions. See Oscar Westover, memorandum to Maj Gen Charles Menoher, 20 June 1919, AFHRA, file no. 168.7089-3; Foulois, 157–58, 167, 170–71, 224; Patrick, 86; and Flint O. DuPre, *Hap Arnold: Architect of American Air Power* (New York: Macmillan Co., 1972), 41, 44–45.

15. The airfields were located in the cities of Norfolk and Montgomery, respectively. In 1922 the Air Service named Maxwell Field after 2d Lt William G. Maxwell of Atmore, Alabama, who died in the Philippines while assigned to the 3d Aero Squadron.

16. See Haywood S. Hansell Jr., *The Air Plan That Defeated Hitler* (Atlanta: Higgins-McArthur/Longino and Porter, 1972).

17. Quoted in Sherman, iii.

18. For an inspired analysis of how technology and culture created new ways of experiencing time and space, see Stephen Kern, *The Culture of Time and Space, 1880–1918* (Cambridge, Mass.: Harvard University Press, 1983). For the early cultural impact of aviation on Western society, see Robert Wohl, *A Passion for Wings: Aviation and the Western Imagination, 1908–1918* (New Haven, Conn.: Yale University Press, 1994); and idem, "Republic of the Air," *Wilson Quarterly* 17 (Spring 1993): 106–17. See also Michael Paris, *Winged Warfare* (Manchester: Manchester University Press, 1992); and Peter Fritzsche, *A Nation of Fliers: German Aviation and the Popular Imagination* (Cambridge, Mass.: Harvard University Press, 1992). For a discussion on the quest for speed and distance, see Terry Gwynn-Jones, *Farther and Faster: Aviation's Adventuring Years, 1909–1939* (Washington, D.C.: Smithsonian Institution Press, 1991).

19. Gen Earl E. Partridge, transcript of oral history interview by Tom Sturm and Hugh H. Ahmann, 23–25 April 1974, 35, AFHRA, file no. K239-0512-729. As a senior US Air Force leader, General Partridge later commanded Fifth Air Force, Far Eastern Air Forces, and Air Defense Command, among other organizations.

20. See Maj Gen John W. Sessums Jr., transcript of oral history interview by Hugh H. Ahmann, 25–28 July 1977, 8, and 26–31 March 1978, AFHRA, file no. K239-0512-951; see also file no. 168.7027-5. Another name for Weaver's game was "Modern Military Chess."

21. Maj Gen Oscar Westover, chief of the Air Corps, transcript of radio address to the Junior Birdmen of America, 12 December 1936, 2, AFHRA, file no. 168.7089-10.

22. Foulois, 204. Air zealots did eventually succeed in linking Americanism, Babe Ruth, and airpower. The influential Hap Arnold, for example, later defined the strategic bomber as the Babe Ruth of the air league—it contained the explosive power of a home run that won a game in seconds. See DuPre, 71.

23. *Air Service Newsletter*, 27 January 1920, 2, AFHRA, file no. 168.7103-26.

24. See James H. "Jimmy" Doolittle, with Carroll V. Glines, *I Could Never Be So Lucky Again* (New York: Bantam Books, 1991). Doolittle was part of a larger American quest for aerial prestige. The quest was so successful that on 1 December 1925, Americans held 25 of the world's 44 aviation records. See Henry H. Arnold, *Airmen and Aircraft* (New York: Ronald Press, 1926), 55.

25. During his tenure at March Field, California, Arnold proselytized to a steady stream of aviation-struck Hollywood stars, many of whom came to his monthly air shows. For a critique of aviation-centered films and documentaries as instruments of politico-cultural indoctrination, see Michael Paris, *From the Wright Brothers to Top Gun: Aviation, Nationalism, and Popular Cinema* (Manchester: Manchester University Press, 1995). For a general discussion of Arnold's and Eaker's public relations activities, see DeWitt Copp, *A Few Great Captains* (New York: Doubleday, 1980).

26. Arnold, v.

27. The titles in the series were *Bill Bruce and the Pioneer Aviators; Bill Bruce, the Flying Cadet; Bill Bruce Becomes an Ace; Bill Bruce on Border Patrol; Bill Bruce on Forest Patrol;* and *Bill Bruce in the Transcontinental Race.* All six volumes appeared in 1928. For a discussion of Arnold's series and other youth-centered aviation sets at the time, see David K. Vaughan, "Hap Arnold's Bill Bruce Books," *Air Power History* 40 (Winter 1993): 43–49. Although Vaughan ignores the point, Arnold's tales are a window into the bigotries of the time. In *Bill Bruce on Border Patrol,* for example, the author characterizes Mexicans as "greasers" and born smugglers. Why smugglers? As one character puts it, "They could take siestas without anyone bothering them. It was the life which they would naturally select." Arnold's protagonists also describe local Chinese as "chinks," "chinos," or "heathens." Last, people who spoke Chinese, like those who spoke Spanish,

were merely "jabbering." See Henry H. Arnold, *Bill Bruce on Border Patrol* (New York: A. L. Burt, 1928), 9, 56, 88, 90, 133, 147, 149, 215.

28. Vaughan, 44–45.

29. On 21 September 1938, the peripatetic Westover died in an aircraft accident. In a fateful move for the Air Corps, Arnold succeeded him nine days later. At the time of his death, the "plain-spoken" Westover, who was also known as "Tubby" to his West Point classmates, was one of roughly 35 Air Corps officers who held all four of its flight ratings. See AFHRA, file nos. 168.7089-3 and 168.7089-10.

30. See Westover, radio address, 12 December 1936, 1.

31. Maj Gen Oscar Westover, chief of the Air Corps, transcript of radio address to the Junior Birdmen of America, 4 May 1935, 2, AFHRA, file no. 168.7089-10. The inference, of course, was that these four-engined aircraft would be bombers.

32. Ira Eaker Papers, Personal Correspondence (1935), box 3, Library of Congress, Washington, D.C. Although *Flying and Your Boy* never appeared (as conceived) in print, Arnold and Eaker's *This Flying Game* (1936) included a dedication to the Junior Birdmen of America and the Jimmie Allen Flying Club.

33. See AFHRA, file no. 168.7023-4.

34. Quoted by Oscar Westover in "Military Aviation," speech to the Aero Club of America, Buffalo, N.Y., 7 December 1932, 16, AFHRA, file no. 168.7103-26.

35. General Pershing, who appointed the "tough but fair" Patrick, expected his West Point classmate to muzzle the garrulous and therefore subversive Mitchell. Patrick was only partially successful. However, as a respected moderate who often (but carefully) sided with his subordinates against the "old guard," he provided the Air Service with something it sorely needed—credibility. Also, it probably helped that Patrick was physically unprepossessing; his false teeth whistled when he spoke and he wore a toupee, which one unfortunate captain once pulled off while helping him remove his flight helmet. See Partridge, 84–85; and Brig Gen Ross Hoyt, "A Prisoner of War," microfilm 34472, n.p., AFHRA, file no. 168.7130.

36. See Maj Gen Grandison Gardner, *Life Memories of Grandison Gardner*, bk. 1 ("Memories of My Service in the U.S. Air Force and Its Ancestral Organizations"), 4 February 1952, 15, AFHRA, file no. 168.7016-1; August Air Defense Command letter 47-6, "History of the Army Air Forces, 1907–1947," 2 July 1947, 7, AFHRA, file no. 168.01; Lt Col Frank Lahm, to Mabel Kaplan, letter, 17 February 1925, 3, AFHRA, file no. 167.401-4; and Arnold, *Airmen and Aircraft*, 146–47. To further illustrate the value of airborne fire patrols, Secretary of War John Weeks claimed that wildfires in California increased by 23 percent when the Air Service did not provide airplanes for forest protection in 1922. See John Weeks, *Peace-Time Accomplishments of the Army*, 21 May 1923, 4, AFHRA, file no. 248.211-101.

37. Gardner, 17; Patrick, 133; Weeks, 4; Lahm, 4; Alfred Goldberg, ed., *A History of the United States Air Force, 1907–1957* (Princeton, N.J.: D. Van

Nostrand, 1957), 34–35; and A. M. Jacobs, *Knights of the Wing* (New York: The Century Co., 1926), 134.

38. *Fifty Years of Aviation History at Maxwell Air Force Base, 1910–1960* (Maxwell AFB, Ala.: Office of Information [Historian], Headquarters, Air University, 1960), 31.

39. Ibid., 31–33. Some of the items delivered included sixty-four hundred loaves of bread, fifty-four hundred blankets, 4,516 pounds of canned cooked meats, 1,651 pounds of bacon, 1,010 cans of evaporated milk, and 105 boiled hams.

40. See Maurer, 299–317; and Foulois, 242. An illustration of the Air Corps's problems is that it initially flew airmail routes totaling 40,800 miles a day—not even one-third the distance flown by the suspended contractors. By mid-March, the Air Corps's total mileage was down to 30,900 a day—almost 10,000 miles less than the previous month. A considerable number of the Air Corps's problems, however, were self-generated—its pilots lacked sufficient instrument and night-flying training; only a few of its aircraft had landing, navigation, or cockpit lights; and anti-icing equipment was unavailable. Still, it didn't help that pilots flying in one particularly stormy area of the Western Department depended on a blind weatherman for their forecasts.

41. See Crowder, 188; and Foulois, 258.

42. See Maj Donald Wilson, "Testimony before the U.S. Federal Aviation Commission," 7 May 1935, 2, Air University Library, Documents Section, Maxwell AFB, Ala., file no. UGK 27 US7. The post-Napoleonic assumption that whole peoples warred against each other went unchallenged by Air Corps strategists, who believed that no military could survive without the sinews of war—a nation's people and its economy.

43. Ibid., 9 (Walker section).

44. See Brig Gen Herbert Dargue, to Maj Gen Hap Arnold, letter, 7 October 1939, 1–2, AFHRA, file no. 168.7119-19.

45. Wilson, 3 (Olds section). Wilson argued that Olds's scenario was theoretically possible because our oceans were no longer impregnable moats and because we had militarily weak neighbors who were vulnerable to foreign control. As a result, the traditional source of America's inviolability—distance—no longer existed. See Wilson section, 6.

46. Ibid., 10 (George section). See also Harold Lee George, *Principles of War*, n.d., AFHRA, file no. 248.11-9.

47. *Influence of Airplanes on Operations in War*, n.d., 2, 17, AFHRA, file no. 248.21-121.

48. Wilson, 9 (Webster section). Did World War II prove Webster right? Soldiers, critics, and historians remain divided on the issue.

49. Thomas D. Milling, in "Testimony of General M. M. Patrick [and others] before the Morrow Board," 21 September 1925, 79, AFHRA, file no. 248.211-61V.

50. See G-2 Weekly Press Review, 23 August 1923, 4 (*Washington Herald*, 20 August 1923), AFHRA, file no. 248.501-91.

51. See G-2 Weekly Press Review, 14 February 1923, 2 (*Rochester Herald*, 31 January 1923), AFHRA, file no. 248.501-91.

52. Alexander Graham Bell, "Preparedness for Aerial Defense," address to the National Convention of the Navy League of the United States, 10–13 April 1916, 8, AFHRA, file no. 167.1-2. The Navy League saw itself neither as "pro-anything or anti-anything" but as a "just plain American" group dedicated to protecting the United States from invasion.

53. William Mitchell, *Tactical Application of Military Aeronautics*, 1919, 2, AFHRA, file no. 248.211-130.

54. Ibid., 4, 6; William L. Mitchell, "General Mitchell's Startling Testimony," *Aviation* 10 (7 February 1921): 165.

55. Milling, "Testimony of General M. M. Patrick," 81. If the Navy was the spearhead, the Army was the bulwark—or so Milling further argued. In reality, this "bulwark" remained porous, at least against attacking aircraft. By 1936 the Army's Coast Artillery Corps still relied on sightless machine guns, three-inch guns, and 105 mm pieces that fired 62-pound shells. In the case of aerial defense, the normal mission was to concentrate fire on aircraft not attacking defense batteries! Even then, the batterymen had trouble properly aiming and firing their three-inch guns six hundred yards ahead of their intended targets (to establish a killing zone for oncoming aircraft). See Maj Gen A. H. Sunderland, "The Coast Artillery Corps," lecture given at the Army War College, 9 October 1936, AFHRA, file no. 168.7001-37.

56. Wilson, 8, 9 (Walker section). In his testimony, Walker cleverly used the writings and lectures of Navy officers against their own service.

57. Ibid., 7 (Webster section).

58. Ibid., 6–8.

59. The Navy's reaction is beyond the scope of this chapter, but Josephus Daniels's huffy response to the dangers posed by land-based aviation to modern fleets was highly representative. According to Daniels, no air force would get close enough "to drop salt upon the tail of the Navy." See *New York Tribune*, 8 February 1921, 1.

60. Quoted in Westover, "Military Aviation," 9. However, did Coolidge envision a robust national defense? One should not forget the frugal president's comment to Secretary of War John M. Weeks—"What's all this talk about lots of airplanes? Why not buy one airplane and let the Army pilots take turns flying it?" See Foulois, 199.

61. Lt Gen Robert L. Bullard, "Army and Navy Become Mere Escorts to Airplane in Warfare, Says Bullard," 3–4, AFHRA, file no. 248.211-21.

62. Millard F. Harmon, "Preliminary Rough Draft on 'Policy for Future Military Education of Air Corps Officers,'" n.d., 2, AFHRA, file no. 245.04B. According to Grandison Gardner, "Miff" Harmon, who acted as ACTS commandant and assistant commandant from 1938 to 1940, was one of two officers Hap Arnold probably leaned on most. The other was Carl Spaatz. See Gardner, 160.

63. Maj Oscar Westover, "Effect of Air Service on Employment of Cavalry and Coast Artillery," 23 September 1925, 1, AFHRA, file no. 168.7089-8.

Ten years later, Harold Lee George seemingly concurred: "We must so reorganize our national defense doctrine as to make possible the extension of our frontiers through the intelligent organization and employment of our air power." What he actually meant, however, was that our "frontiers" were synonymous with the economic centers of far-flung states, regardless of where they were. See Wilson, 12 (George section).

64. See Maj W. G. Kilner, "Proposed Revision of the Policy of the Army and Navy Relating to Aircraft," 12 April 1925, AFHRA, file no. 248.121-1.

65. The Navy's justification was the National Defense Act of 1920, which stated that it would control all air activities attached to a fleet, including shore stations needed to support its operations. See Milling, "Air Power in National Defense," 18.

66. Ibid., 16–17.

67. George C. Kenney, memorandum to assistant commandant of the Army War College, 1933, 1, AFHRA, file no. 248.211-65.

68. In 1938 insult followed injury, or so air zealots thought. After three B-17s intercepted the *Rex* (an Italian ocean liner) over seven hundred miles east of New York, the Navy temporarily succeeded in restricting Air Corps aircraft to a 100-mile zone off the coast. The lead navigator of the B-17s was Capt Curtis LeMay.

69. The Baker Board's recommendation was explicit: "To assist in correcting the present unsatisfactory condition of unit training, the committee recommends the early creation of the Air Corps Board and that when created this board give prompt attention to the formulation of uniform tactical doctrines for all types of aircraft units." Quoted in Lt Col W. C. McChord, chief of the Air Corps Plans Division, memorandum to acting chief of the Air Corps, 29 November 1935, 1, AFHRA, file no. 167.5 (1935–1936).

70. Gen Laurence S. Kuter, transcript of oral history interview by Tom Sturm and Hugh Ahmann, 30 September–3 October 1974, 165, AFHRA, file no. K239.0512-810.

71. In this respect, the ACB's charter paralleled those of other branch-specific boards, including the Infantry Board, the Coast Artillery Board, and the Chemical Warfare Service Board. AR 95-20 first authorized an Air Service Board on 1 August 1922. The provisions of the regulation subsequently remained in effect, but the board accomplished little until the Baker Board inspired its reconstitution in 1934. (A revised AR 95-20 was the instrument of change.)

72. Lt Col R. M. Jones, memorandum, subject: Major Aircraft Advisory Board, 8 April 1936, 2, AFHRA, file no. 167.5 (1935–1936). Jones identified three other questions that were of special concern to the Air Corps at the time: Did two-seat fighters have any utility? Should fighter development emphasize interception or escort responsibilities? What types of all-purpose aircraft were suitable for aerial observation? In the case of two-seat fighters and fighter escort, the decisions later made by the Air Corps had unhappy consequences in the early phases of World War II.

73. Maj Gen Orville A. Anderson, transcript of oral history interview by Dr. Donald Shaughnessy, 27 October 1959, 6, AFHRA, file no. K239.0512-898. Anderson served as secretary of the ACB and thus immodestly saw himself as the organization's direct link to General Arnold.

74. Maj Gen Henry H. Arnold, ACTS graduation speech, 12 May 1939, 4, AFHRA, file no. 168.7027-9.

75. Robert T. Finney, *History of the Air Corps Tactical School, 1920–1940*, USAF Historical Study 100 (1955; reprint, Washington, D.C.: Government Printing Office, 1992), 31.

76. See Air Corps Board Report 31, *The Functions of the Army Air Forces*, 29 October 1936, 2, AFHRA, file no. 167.5-31.

77. "Analytical Study of Joint Action of the Army and the Navy," pt. 2, n.d., AFHRA, file no. 167.5-31.

78. Air Corps Board Report 3A, *Revision of Air Corps Field Manual* (FM 1-5), defined the Air Corps's perceived obligations to the Army and Navy. In the case of the Army, ACB-3A insisted that support aviation was not a tactical tool of war. Instead, it was an operational-level weapon best used against the rear area of hostile forces, where it could apply its full striking power against concentrated targets with minimum losses and maximum results. Consequently, in future wars air attacks would most likely predate the contact of surface forces and operate against enemy aircraft, lines of communications, command headquarters, supply installations, and troop concentrations. If a battle did occur, support aviation would grudgingly operate in a battle zone but only if absolutely necessary. It would strike troop transports, mechanized forces, and enemy formations. Last, in a postbattle environment, support aircraft would perform counterair operations and interdict hostile routes of retreat or the arrival of enemy delaying forces. In the case of the Navy, the role of land-based aviation in fleet actions would include attacks against battle-line, fast-wing, or individual vessels; attacks against light forces threatening battle-line flanks or disrupting friendly flanking maneuvers; the interdiction of hostile air operations through offensive operations; and attacks against convoy vessels. In particular, bombers would attack armed vessels, supply ships and transports, and naval bases. See draft of Air Corps Board Report no. 3A, "Revision of Air Corps Field Manual," 20 November 1939, 24, 27–28, 39, AFHRA, file no. 167.5-3A.

79. See ibid., 3. The report's authors made the claim even though they admitted that the Air Corps could not sustain air operations against the homeland of any major foreign power from bases in US territory. However, they believed that bomber technology was changing so rapidly that the day of long-range operations was imminent.

80. Air Corps Board Report 31, annex 2, p. 1.

81. Ibid., 5 (main text).

82. Ibid., annex 2, pt. B, 6; and annex 2, pt. C, 17.

83. "Status of Studies of the Air Corps Board as of December 31, 1940," 1, AFHRA, file no. 167.5.

84. See Air Corps Board Report 35, *Employment of Aircraft in Defense of the Continental United States*, annex 2, 7 May 1939, 3, AFHRA, file no. 167.5-35.

85. Ibid., annex 4, p. 1. ACB-35 based its argument on a major principle of war—economy of force. To use aircraft against objectives that are within range of ground or naval weapons is to use them in lieu of rather than in support of those weapons. See annex 4, p. 3.

86. "Analytical Study of Joint Action of the Army and the Navy," 3.

87. Air Corps Board Report 35, 1–2.

88. For a thorough discussion of how FDR came to support airpower as a favored instrument of diplomacy and national defense, see Jeffery S. Underwood, *The Wings of Democracy: The Influence of Air Power on the Roosevelt Administration, 1933–1941* (College Station, Tex.: Texas A&M University Press, 1991).

89. The evolution of bomber technology, although outside the purview of this discussion, played a critical role in the Air Corps's success against the Navy and in transforming a mere theory of airpower into reality. In the 1920s, bombers were cumbersome and lightly armed machines that trundled along at 110 MPH. Their operating ceiling, bomb-carrying capacity, and defensive firepower were also limited. Such aircraft, like the Curtis Condor and Barling bomber, were much too vulnerable to carry out a successful bombing campaign in the face of hostile fighters. By 1932, however, bomber technology suddenly leapt past fighter capabilities. (The change was attributable to innovations in large civilian aircraft, which then positively affected bomber development.) When it appeared in 1931, the Boeing B-9 represented a significant leap in bomber technology, although it was an interim aircraft (only nine saw service). The plane contained preliminary engineering items later found in the B-17, which at this point was entering the advanced design phase. Better yet were the follow-on B-10 and B-12. The Boeing B-10, for example, was an all-metal, midwing monoplane with retractable landing gear. It could go 235 MPH (at least 10 MPH faster than contemporary fighters), climb up to 21,000 feet, and carry five machine guns. Its other novel features included an enclosed cockpit, cowling over the engines, and cantilevered wings. Such developments encouraged new experimentation, and in September 1934, Boeing introduced the XB-17. This all-metal, midwing monoplane could do the work of four B-10s. It could also travel at 250 MPH, carry an internal bomb load of twenty-five hundred pounds for twenty-six hundred miles, and operate up to 30,000 feet. Here for the first time in history, Hap Arnold observed, was airpower "you could put your hands on." When fighter technology improved in the late 1930s, it was too late from a doctrinal standpoint. The Air Corps's prewar commitment to four-engined bombers and long-range operations was irreversible. See Thomas H. Greer, *The Development of Air Doctrine in the Army Air Arm, 1917–1941*, USAF Historical Study 89 (1955; reprint, Washington, D.C.: Government Printing Office, 1985), 46–47.

90. "Testimony of General M. M. Patrick," 71.

91. Ibid., 53.

92. Bullard, 21.

93. "[Coast Defense,] the Army Viewpoint," n.d., 2, AFHRA, file no. 211.33. Internal evidence in the statement suggests that it appeared in the 1930s.

94. See Hanson Baldwin, to Haywood Hansell, letter, ca. 16 May 1939, 2, AFHRA, file no. 168.7148. Baldwin was the military and naval correspondent for the *New York Times*. He was also a Naval Academy graduate, which may partially explain the venom in his statement. See also "Statement of Brigadier General H. A. Drum," 2.

95. "Relation of Air Corps Expenditures to Total War Department (Military) Expenditures," 1, AFHRA, file no. 167.6-5.

96. 1st Lt William A. R. Robertson, "Progress in Military Aviation," n.d., 11, AFHRA, file no. 248.211-61Y (1898–1937 folder); see also "Statement of Brigadier General H. A. Drum," 7.

97. Hugh Knerr, microfilm A1878, 109, AFHRA, file no. 168.7028-1.

98. Gen Nathan Twining, transcript of oral history interview by Arthur Marmor, November 1965, 6, AFHRA, file no. K239-0512-634; and Gen Howell M. Estes Jr., transcript of oral history interview by Lt Col Robert Zimmerman and Lt Col Lyn Officer, 27–30 August 1973, 38, AFHRA, file no. K239-0512-686. General Estes entered military service in the late 1930s. His recollections, therefore, may reflect an attitude shaped more by World War II than by the interwar years.

99. See Copp as a representative example.

100. Maj Gen Jarred V. Crabb, transcript of oral history interview by Lt Col Thomas Julian and Maj Donald Goldstein, 17 and 28 April 1970, 8, AFHRA, file no. K239-0512-622.

101. Haywood S. Hansell Jr., "American Air Power in World War II," chap. 2, microfilm 34142-43, 4–5, AFHRA, file no. 168.7148. See also Capt Charles Walton, "Is an Air Force Capable of Independent Action to an Extent Sufficient to Justify the Employment of the Term 'Air Warfare' in a Sense as Comprehensive as Our Present Use of the Terms 'Land Warfare' and 'Naval Warfare?'" 1 May 1929, 16, AFHRA, file no. 248.211-16F. Of the dozens of ACTS student papers this author has read, the title of Captain Walton's paper has no peer.

102. "Notes," n.d., 1, AFHRA, file no. 248.211-32.

103. Col B. Q. Jones, "Air Forces in the Theater," lecture to Army War College, 4 March 1939, 17, AFHRA, file no. 248.211-14B.

104. See "Statement of Brigadier General H. A. Drum," 5, 61.

105. Ibid., 6; see also Wilson, 1 (George section), 18 (Webster section).

106. William Mitchell, in "Testimony of General M. M. Patrick," 74.

107. Ibid.

108. For a background to this struggle, see R. Earl McClendon, "A Checklist of Significant Documents Relating to the Position of the United States Army Air Arm in the System of National Defense, 1907–1945"

(Maxwell AFB, Ala.: Documentary Research Division, 1949); and Maj Guido Perera, "A Legislative History of Aviation in the United States and Abroad," March 1941, AFHRA, file no. 167.401-28.

109. By 1925, and with the waning influence of Billy Mitchell, senior airmen sought more immediate goals. Mason Patrick, for example, advocated to the Morrow Board that Congress create permanent aviation committees in both houses to develop definite, comprehensive, and evolving government policies on civilian and military aeronautics.

110. Maj Gen Charles Menoher, "Address Given at Society of Automotive Engineers Dinner," 10 March 1920, 8, AFHRA, file no. 248.211-130. Mason Patrick expressed similar sentiments in his "Testimony of General M. M. Patrick," 56.

111. Perera, 57, 65.

112. See Milling, "Air Power in National Defense," 4.

113. For a discussion of the following boards and commissions of inquiry, see Robert Frank Futrell, *Ideas, Concepts, Doctrine: Basic Thinking in the United States Air Force*, vol. 1, *1907–1960* (Maxwell AFB, Ala.: Air University Press, December 1989), 29–48; and Greer, 21–29, 71–73.

114. The Army Reorganization Act of 1920 codified this view into law and made the Air Service a regular combat arm. It also provided for a chief and assistant chief of staff, and it further codified a professional school system.

115. Foulois, 199–200. Dargue later served as assistant commandant of ACTS from 1934 to 1938.

116. According to Benny Foulois, the Morrow Board's accommodations may have been part of a preemptive attempt to weaken the political impact of Billy Mitchell's upcoming trial. See Foulois, 201.

117. Hoyt, 83.

118. Perera, 61. As in previous boards and commissions that were hostile to the Air Service/Air Corps, the membership of the Baker Board was an issue. Major General Foulois, for example, was the lone Air Corps representative and faced off against four generals assigned from the Army General Staff, among other opponents. In contrast, an obviously biased Foulois thought the Howell Commission was the "most objective" board of inquiry in the interwar period. In addition to the above recommendations, it also supported the creation of the Civil Aeronautics Board and the Civil Aeronautics Authority (i.e., the forerunner of the Federal Aviation Administration).

119. For the above statistics, see C. A. McMahan, John Folger, and Stephen W. Fotis, *Graduates of the Air Corps Tactical School, 1921–1940*, April 1953, 3, 5, AFHRA, file no. K243.041-2.

120. William Sherman, *Air Tactics*, sect. 2 ("Fundamental Doctrine of the Air Service"), 1922, 5, AFHRA, file no. 248.101-4A.

121. Milling, *The Air Service Tactical School*, 1.

122. Ibid.

123. Ibid.

124. See Training Regulation 440-15, *Air Tactics*, 1926, AFHRA, file no. 248.211-65A.

125. Air Service Tactical School, *Bombardment*, 1924–1925, 66, 83, AFHRA, file no. 248.101-9.

126. Air Service Tactical School, *Bombardment*, 1926, 4, AFHRA, file no. 248.101-9.

127. See Futrell, 31.

128. Air Service Tactical School, *Employment of Combined Air Force*, 1925–1926, 3, AFHRA, file no. 248.101-7A.

129. Ibid., 3–4, 12, 29.

130. Sherman, *Air Warfare*, 6, 21, 23, 32, 130, 209–10, 217.

131. Arnold was an impatient man who demanded immediate results from his commanders. Without a rapid return on investment, he worried that funding for strategic air operations would disappear and therefore threaten his dream of an independent Air Force with an autonomous mission. To Arnold, Hansell's dogged and misplaced attempt to perform HAPDB in the Pacific theater was an example of "too little, too late." As Hansell's successor, Curtis LeMay abandoned HAPDB for low-level, almost indiscriminate incendiary attacks against Japanese urban areas.

132. Kuter showed early signs of promise. Col Millard Harmon, for example, described him as "an exceptional officer who should be given a rating of 'Superior plus'. [He] possesses superior qualifications for staff assignment and for future high command." See "Official Statement of Service," 30 January 1942, 2, Laurence Kuter Papers, box 1, folder 13, Library of Congress, Washington, D.C.

133. Quoted in Kenneth Schaffel, "Muir S. Fairchild: Philosopher of Air Power," *Aerospace Historian* 33 (September 1986): 168.

134. Kuter, oral history interview, 132, 163.

135. This synopsis of ACTS bombardment theory appears in Haywood S. Hansell Jr., *The Strategic Air War against Germany and Japan: A Memoir* (Washington, D.C.: Government Printing Office, 1986), 7, 10.

136. Donald Wilson, "Long Range Airplane Development," November 1938, 6, AFHRA, file no. 248.211-17.

137. Ibid.

138. Ibid.

139. See "Address by Major General Frank Andrews before the National Aeronautic Association," 16 January 1939, 8, AFHRA, file no. 248.211-20.

140. Kenneth Walker, "Memo to Assistant Commandant, ACTS," 24 September 1932, 3, AFHRA, file no. 248.211-13.

141. Hansell, *The Strategic Air War against Germany and Japan*, 12.

142. Ibid., 12–13.

143. Col Grover Brown, "Concepts of Strategic Air Warfare, Part I," lecture to Air War College, 3 December 1951, 4, AFHRA, file no. K239.716251-28. At the time, the War Department prohibited the Air Corps from constructing target folders on other nations. The practice was not in keeping with the avowedly defensive military policy of the United States.

144. See Lt Col William O. Ryan, "Military Aviation," lecture at Army War College, 6 March 1940, 11, AFHRA, file no. 248.211-14.

145. Since Weimar Germany deliberately reconstructed its ruined physical plant and business practices along American lines, the problem of "mirror imaging" was especially troublesome in World War II. See Klaus-Juergen Mueller, ed., *The Military in Politics and Society in France and Germany in the Twentieth Century* (Oxford: Berg, 1995).

146. Gen Orvel Cook, transcript of oral history interview by Hugh N. Ahmann and Maj Richard Emmons, 4–5 June and 6–7 August 1974, 101, AFHRA, file no. K239.0512-740.

147. Ibid.

148. Ibid.

149. Col Hugh Knerr, to commanding general, 3d Wing, GHQ Air Force, letter, 14 March 1936, AFHRA, file no. 248.126-4.

150. Ibid. (first endorsement).

151. Lt Col George E. Lovell, memorandum to Brig Gen G. C. Brant, 27 March 1936, AFHRA, file no. 248.126-4.

152. Lt Col M. F. Harmon and Maj Oliver Gothlin, "Comments on Air Corps Tactical Document," attached to Knerr letter, 2.

153. Lt Col A. H. Gilkeson, "Indorsement to Commanding General, 2nd Wing, GHQ Air Force," on Knerr letter, 2.

154. For the specifics of AWPD-1 and the creation of the plan, see James C. Gaston, *Planning the American Air War—Four Men and Nine Days in 1941* (Fort Lesley J. McNair: National Defense University Press, 1982).

Chapter 7

Alexander P. de Seversky
and American Airpower

*Col Phillip S. Meilinger**

Fighter ace, war hero, aircraft designer, entrepreneur, stunt pilot, writer, and theorist, Alexander P. de Seversky was one of the best known and most popular aviation figures in America during World War II. His passion was airpower, and his mission was to convince the American people that airpower had revolutionized warfare, becoming its paramount and decisive factor. De Seversky pursued this goal relentlessly for over three decades. In truth, although generally regarded as a theorist, his ideas on airpower and its role in war were not original. Rather, he was a synthesizer and popularizer—a purveyor of secondhand ideas. His self-appointed task entailed selling those ideas to the public, who could then influence political leaders to make more enlightened defense decisions. At the same time, de Seversky wore the mantle of prophet, using his interpretation of history and logic to predict the path that air warfare would take. Events would show that he enjoyed more success as a proselytizer than as a prophet.

*I want to thank the following individuals, who have contributed their criticisms and ideas to this essay: Duane Reed of the Air Force Academy special collections branch, Ron Wyatt of the Nassau County Library, Josh Stoff of the Cradle of Aviation Museum, Steve Chun of the Air University Library, Col "Doc" Pentland, Lt Col Pete Faber, Dr. Dave Mets, Dr. Dan Kuehl, and Mr. Russell Lee.

Regarding sources, de Seversky died in 1974 without heirs. Apparently, most of his files and personal papers were then deposited in the Republic Aircraft Corporation archives on Long Island. When that company went defunct a decade later, what was left of de Seversky's papers went to the Nassau County Library, also on Long Island. The collection is incomplete; much of it is taken up with copies of the several hundred articles, press releases, speeches, and radio broadcasts de Seversky gave over the years. Although these papers are of great value, virtually nothing of a personal nature is contained therein; nor is there much in the way of official correspondence. Material of a technical nature regarding de Seversky's patents and aircraft designs has been transferred to the Cradle of Aviation Museum, located in a hangar on the old Mitchel Field, Long Island.

His ideas, like those of many air theorists, outran the technology available to implement them.

Born in Tiflis, Russia (now Tbilisi, Georgia), on 7 June 1894, Alexander grew up near Saint Petersburg. His father was a wealthy poet and actor who also had a taste for things mechanical; for example, he purchased two aeroplanes in 1909—purportedly the first privately owned aircraft in Russia. Alexander inherited not only his father's theatrical flair but also his technological inclination—he experimented with mechanical devices as a boy, even designing several aeroplane models. Not atypically for a young man of his class, Alexander went off to military school at age ten, graduating from the Imperial Russian Naval Academy in 1914, shortly before the outbreak of the Great War. After serving for several months on a destroyer flotilla, Ensign de Seversky transferred to the navy's flying service, soloing in March 1915 at Sebastapol after a total flight time of six minutes and 28 seconds.[1]

Posted to the Baltic Sea, de Seversky and his squadron sought to prevent the German navy from clearing mines that Russian ships had placed in the Gulf of Riga. On his first combat mission on the night of 2 July 1915, he met with disaster. As he attacked a German destroyer, antiaircraft fire struck his aircraft, causing it to crash into the water. The concussion detonated one of the aircraft's bombs, killing his observer and blowing off de Seversky's right leg below the knee. Miraculously, he survived; a Russian patrol boat rescued him, and after eight months in convalescence, he returned to active duty with an artificial limb.[2]

Assigned a job in aircraft production, de Seversky applied his mechanical acumen to the design of aeronautical devices that would make a pilot's job easier, designing such devices as hydraulic brakes, adjustable rudder pedals, and special bearings for flight controls. He also experimented with a sophisticated bombsight and aircraft skis for landing on icy surfaces. His inventions won him an award in 1916 for the top aeronautical ideas of the year.[3]

Although designing aircraft was important work, de Seversky wanted to return to flying duty, but superiors denied his request. Nevertheless, when in early 1916 a group of dignitaries visited his airfield to witness the test flight of a new aircraft, de Seversky surreptitiously took the place of the scheduled pilot and put the aircraft through its paces for the assembled crowd. This stunt caused an uproar, fueling talk of a court-martial for "endangering government property." Fortunately, the czar himself heard of the incident, decided Russia needed colorful heroes, and intervened to have de Seversky returned to combat flying duty.[4]

Over the next year, he flew 57 combat missions and scored 13 kills of German aircraft. On one mission, he and his wingman bombed a German airfield and then attacked seven planes in the air, shooting down three, despite receiving over 30 bullet holes in his own aircraft.[5] For this exploit, the czar presented him a gold sword. His wooden leg did not seem to bother him. In fact, he later claimed that the injury made him a better flyer because it forced him to think more deeply about what he was doing, rather than simply rely upon physical ability. Even so, the war remained a dangerous activity for him: his good leg was broken in an accident on the ground, and on one combat sortie he was shot in the right leg— although now he required the services of a carpenter rather than a doctor.[6]

By mid-1917 the Russian monarchy had fallen. Due to lack of reinforcements, de Seversky's squadrons—he was now chief of pursuit aviation for the Baltic Sea—could not prevent the German fleet from entering Russian waters. He fled when German ships shelled his headquarters but did not get far in his damaged aircraft. After stripping the plane of its guns, he set it afire and began walking towards the Russian lines. Unfortunately, he ran into a band of armed Estonian peasants, who debated turning him over to the Germans for a reward. Upon learning that their captive was the famed "legless aviator," however, they sent de Seversky on his way—with his machine guns. This escape earned him the Cross of Saint George, Imperial Russia's highest decoration.[7] Alexander E. Kerensky, head of the provisional government, then posted Lieutenant Commander de Seversky to Washington, D.C., as part of the Russian naval mission. The Bolshevik government, which took power soon after, confirmed these orders, but within a few months of his arrival

241

in America, his mission dissolved. Nevertheless, de Seversky elected to stay.[8]

After working briefly with the American Air Service as an aircraft inspector in Buffalo, New York, de Seversky found himself out of work. Young, aggressive, and ambitious, he soon opened a restaurant in Manhattan. He fell in love with America, and when fellow émigrés complained of conditions in their new home, he grew impatient and exclaimed, "If you don't like it in this country you can always go back to Brooklyn."[9] "Sascha," as friends now called him, still viewed aviation as his chief interest, and in 1921 he met Brig Gen Billy Mitchell, the controversial and outspoken assistant chief of the Air Service. Mitchell was then trying to "prove" the obsolescence of surface ships through a series of bombing tests. However, he feared that his aircraft's bombs were not powerful enough to sink heavily armored warships. De Seversky later claimed he suggested to Mitchell the idea of dropping bombs next to the ships—not on them—to cause a "water hammer" effect that would open the seams in the side of the vessel below the waterline. Although this idea did not originate with de Seversky, it had validity.[10] In July 1921 Mitchell's aircraft used the water-hammer principle to sink several capital ships, including the German battleship *Ostfriesland,* off the Virginia coast.

Over the next several years, de Seversky worked with military airmen at McCook Field, Ohio, designing a gyroscopic bombsight hailed by Gen Mason Patrick, Air Service chief. In addition, he began work on an idea he had conceived during the war. While flying in formation with another Russian plane one day, he playfully reached up and grabbed the trailing wire radio antenna of his mate, flying along "connected" to the other plane for several minutes. He suddenly realized that one could also use a wire or tube to transfer fuel from one aircraft to another in flight. Combat had taught him that bombardment aircraft were vulnerable to enemy fighter planes; thus, one needed escort fighters to provide protection to the bombers. However, the smaller fighters did not have the range to escort bombers all the way to the target and back. Air refueling offered a solution. Although his wartime superiors would not allow him to experiment with such a device at the time, de Seversky revisited the idea when he worked with the Air Service, producing an innovative air refueling device used on the "Question Mark" flight of 1929, when an Air Corps aircraft remained aloft for seven days.[11] In 1927 de Seversky became a naturalized US citizen and received his commission as a major in the Air Corps Reserve. He was always quite proud of regaining military rank and for the rest of his life preferred to be called "major."

In 1931 he founded Seversky Aircraft Corporation and over the next decade perfected a host of patents and designs, including split flaps, metal monocoque construction, a fire-control unit for aircraft guns, retractable landing gear and pontoons, and specialized aircraft flight instruments.[12] He had obvious talent for design, his innovative SEV-3 amphibian setting world speed records in 1933 and 1935. Derivations of this model became the BT-8 (the first all-metal monoplane trainer built in the United States) and the noted P-35.

The P-35 was the first all-metal monoplane fighter mass-produced in the United States, incorporating such innovations as an enclosed cockpit, retractable landing gear, and cantilever wings. The Air Corps purchased 137 P-35s, the direct ancestor of the famed P-47 Thunderbolt.[13] The P-35 featured two other unusual characteristics. First, it was extremely fast; a civilian version of it won the Bendix Air Race in 1937, 1938, and 1939.[14] Considering the fact that contemporary fighter planes could barely keep pace with new bombers such as the B-17, this was quite a feat. Second, it was specifically designed for long range (it could fly from coast to coast with only two refuelings), unlike other fighter aircraft of the day, which were suitable only for point defense. Remembering his war experiences, de Seversky recognized the need for fighter aircraft with the range to escort bombers.[15] One solution was the air refueling device he had already patented, but extensive use of this system would have to wait another two decades. During the Vietnam War, tactical fighters became strategic bombers as a result of air refueling. In the late 1930s, however, people considered such an expedient too inefficient and costly. Designers, therefore, had to devise a method to extend the range of aircraft without air refueling.

Most of them thought that building a long-range escort fighter was technically impossible, reasoning that any plane with the necessary range would have to be quite large in order to carry the requisite fuel. A large aircraft needed more than one engine and might require additional crew members, which, in turn, meant even larger size, more weight, more fuel, and so forth. In short, escorts soon looked like the bombers they were designed to protect and thus would become easy prey for enemy fighters. De Seversky, virtually alone among designers, was convinced that one could build a long-range escort by using internal fuel tanks, which would not sacrifice the attributes characteristic of a successful fighter.

At the same time, de Seversky called for increased armament on fighter planes. Whereas standard equipment generally consisted of two .30-caliber machine guns, he advocated the inclusion of six to eight .50-caliber guns.[16] However, when de Seversky suggested this, as well as increasing range by adding more wing fuel tanks, the Air Corps turned him down, deeming such innovations not "sufficiently attractive to pursue."[17] This clash of opinion was doctrinal at least as much as it was technological. American tactical airmen such as Claire Chennault eschewed the concept of fighter escort. Although acknowledging the vulnerability of bomber aircraft, they did not relish an escort mission that would put fighter aircraft in what they saw as an inherently defensive and passive position. Most Air Corps fighter pilots at the time shared this rather peculiar notion. Not until 1944 did American airmen, because of operational necessity, embrace the mission of fighter escort, reconciling need with the imperative to maintain an offensive and aggressive character.[18] In any event, this doctrinal disagreement had serious consequences for the relationship between de Seversky and the Air Corps, already strained by his emotional and flamboyant personality.

His heroic exploits in the war were well known, as was his prowess as a stunt pilot. His wife, the beautiful Evelyn Olliphant, was the daughter of a prominent New Orleans doctor, and she also became a well-known figure. After their marriage in 1925, she met many of the famous aviation figures of the day. Too often, however, she felt at a loss when the men congregated in corners to discuss flying. She therefore decided to take flying lessons and surprise her husband; after she won her wings in 1934, her first passenger was Jimmy Doolittle. Evelyn became a noted aviatrix in her own right, logging several thousand hours and appearing frequently on radio and in the newspapers to discuss her experiences and push for more women in aviation.[19] She and Sascha made a handsome and vivacious couple, noted for their gala parties. One magazine even referred to Alexander as "one of the ten most glamorous men in New York."[20]

More significantly, he had obvious technical ability as an aeronautical engineer. His aircraft designs won him the prestigious Harmon Trophy, presented by President Franklin D. Roosevelt in 1939, and the Lord and Taylor American Design Award for 1940. He was not, however, a businessman. His corporation never made a great deal of money and ran constantly behind in its production orders. De Seversky argued that his aircraft were so original that they required new manufacturing techniques, which took time.[21] The Air Corps—indeed, most of his senior colleagues in the company—disagreed.

Executives at Seversky Aircraft complained that their president was too busy designing new aircraft instead of building the ones already on order. He spent too much money and traveled too frequently on publicity tours. He was a lackadaisical manager. The Seversky Corporation was a fairly small company during the Depression years, and the major felt close to his labor force. One shop worker later recalled de Seversky walking into his Long Island factory, announcing it was too nice a day for work, and ordering everyone down to the beach for a picnic. He supplied the beer.[22] Such affability might have won affection, but it did not fulfill military contracts.

Gen Henry H. Arnold, chief of the Air Corps, had great respect for the models de Seversky produced, but as war approached in Europe, he needed aircraft companies ready and able to meet the challenges of greatly increased production. The Seversky Corporation had a part to play in Arnold's future but only if it restructured its senior management.[23] In short, Arnold wanted de Seversky out. In May 1939, while de Seversky was out of the country, his board of directors removed him as president; in

October it ousted him entirely and changed the name of the company to Republic.[24]

De Seversky was outraged; moreover, he never forgave Arnold for the role he had played in his removal.[25] For the next several years, de Seversky blamed Arnold for every deficiency—real or perceived—that he found in American airpower. In his files he kept a list of statements made by Arnold, each accompanied by unflattering comments. For example, when Arnold opined that dive-bombers might prove useful in combat, de Seversky commented, "Another demonstration of how slow his mind digests the lessons of the war." Similarly, when Arnold drew comparisons between different types of aircraft, de Seversky grumbled that "these excerpts show how his mind rambles and how reckless his statements are."[26]

In truth, de Seversky's removal from business had positive results: Republic reorganized to become one of the top aviation companies of the next three decades. The P-47 Thunderbolt, the descendant of the major's P-35, proved vital to American air success in the war. Based on de Seversky's track record up to the time of his removal, Republic probably would not have responded so effectively to the challenge of war under his guidance. In addition, sudden unemployment left him time for other pursuits. Specifically, he used his considerable charm and communication skills to write and talk about his favorite topic: airpower. From this point on, the technical aspects of the major's career faded into the background as his primary focus became the education of the American public regarding airpower. Events would prove that de Seversky was far more influential as an author than as a builder.

When de Seversky began writing about airpower, he enjoyed two advantages over the theorists who had preceded him. First, he was not a serving military officer and therefore did not fear the retaliation of irked superiors. In view of the fact that Giulio Douhet and Billy Mitchell had been court-martialed for pressing their views on airpower too strongly, this consideration was a substantial one. Second, because of de Seversky's background as a successful aeronautical engineer and designer, he was less likely to fall into hyperbole when discussing aircraft capabilities—the blight of other airpower advocates. The freedom to speak his mind, with formidable technical authority, coupled with his dynamic and energetic personality, made him enormously popular in a very short time.

De Seversky's voluminous writings shared certain characteristics. First, they demonstrated a willingness to take on military leaders and their cherished beliefs. Second, they displayed a deep-seated anti-Navy bias that grew over time. De Seversky also employed a strategy of taking his case directly to the American people, bypassing intermediate filters imposed by military officials. Finally, the major had an unshakable belief in the effectiveness and efficiency of airpower.

For example, airpower theorists typically criticized the conservative and traditional thinking of surface commanders, whom they considered relics of a bygone age. They did not understand the new air weapon, seeing it merely as an evolutionary development—a useful tool that would help them achieve their surface goals. This attitude was standard fare. But de Seversky went a step further by taking on the leadership of the Air Corps, accusing it of equally outdated thinking. Specifically, he pointedly charged Arnold with stymying innovative thought in aircraft development and being more concerned with "military politics" than with building effective airpower.[27] When in mid-1941 the War Department announced a reorganization that created the semiautonomous Army Air Forces (AAF), most airmen hailed it as a major step towards a separate service—their cherished goal. Not so de Seversky. He saw it as a dangerous half-measure—an "administrative enslavement"—to keep airmen in their place, a ploy by Arnold to gain promotion. He did not believe it would seriously advance the cause of airpower. In a letter to President Roosevelt, he argued that the move was "positively harmful" because it gave an illusion of progress where none really existed.[28] As a consequence of these gratuitous and personal attacks, Arnold kept de Seversky at a distance; thus, these two powerful voices for airpower worked at cross-purposes, precisely at a time when they should have been close allies.

Throughout his career, de Seversky consciously attached himself to the Billy Mitchell legend. He said once that Mitchell was his best friend, and he wrote several articles about the general, even dedicating his first book to his mentor's memory. This affinity was not necessarily healthy because de Seversky inherited Mitchell's inordinate distaste for the Navy. The saying that there is no greater antipathy towards ideas than that felt by the apostate was certainly true of former naval officer de Seversky. His writings consistently stressed the fleet's lack of importance, arguing that sea power was obsolete and that surface ships were doomed in the face of airpower. Like Mitchell, he often compared the cost of ships to that of aircraft, noting that one could buy hundreds of planes for the price of a single battleship. He even began one article with the blunt announcement that "our great two-ocean, multi-billion-dollar Navy, now in construction, should be completed five or six years from now—just in time to have all of its battleships scrapped."[29]

However, de Seversky not only denigrated the gunships but also questioned the utility of aircraft carriers, seeing them as little more than attractive targets. He discounted their ability to project power ashore, asserting the inferiority of carrier planes to land-based planes. Conveniently ignoring the Pearl Harbor attack, he stated that if carriers attempted to strike a land power equipped with an air force, the latter would sink them long before their planes could perform any constructive purpose.[30] Like Mitchell's attacks, de Seversky's incessant barbs needlessly antagonized the Navy, while also spurring it to greater activity. Indeed, although the claim that Mitchell—and, by extension, de Seversky—was the father of naval aviation is far too strong, it does contain a kernel of truth.

As with most people of his generation who had lived through one world war only to see another spawned in its wake, de Seversky believed that wars had become total. Distinctions between soldiers and civilians no longer existed—all people were part of the war effort. To de Seversky, this meant that all citizens might pay the ultimate price in war and thus should have a voice in determining how those wars were fought. In a dictatorship, rulers make war with little regard for the will of the populace—but not in a democracy. War strategy had become far too important to be left to military leaders. The people must have knowledge of the inner workings of war so they can have a voice in its conduct: "over-all strategy, like any other national policy that affects the entire nation, is the province of the people."[31] Air war especially was too new and too powerful, and affected people too directly for them to be ignorant of its principles. An educated public would make its opinions known to the politicians, who in turn would determine military policy. De Seversky saw educating the people as his *duty:* "I am convinced that the best contribution I can make to America is to draw attention to what seems to me the need for an effective program of national defense in the air in order to provide genuine security for our country."[32]

Over the next decade, the major would write two books and scores of articles and press releases, and would give hundreds of radio addresses. His first literary task upon leaving business in 1939 involved telling of aeronautical conditions in Europe. He visited Britain, France, Germany, and Italy and because of his international reputation, was able to talk with leading airmen and aircraft manufacturers and tour their factories. He returned to America both sobered and heartened. On the one hand, he was convinced that Hitler was bent on war, even predicting that it would break out in September 1939.[33] He did not think the French were ready for such a war; although their air force had some useful aircraft designs, political corruption prevented their mass production. On the other hand, he was pleased with British developments—he flew the Hurricane and Spitfire and came away impressed by their speed and armament. He rated these aircraft far superior to anything the Germans had and predicted that the Royal Air Force (RAF) would prevail in any test with the Luftwaffe because of this qualitative superiority.[34] Few people were as sanguine about Britain's chances, but the major's prediction proved accurate.

Exactly what form de Seversky expected the war would take during its initial stages remains unclear. Certainly, he believed airpower would play a key role, but no evidence indicates he embraced the concept of strategic bombing. Indeed, despite his connections with Billy Mitchell, his concentration as an engineer on fighter aircraft and on the technological challenges they presented suggests he had not given a great deal of thought to the issue of strategic airpower.

This perspective changed when war broke out in September 1939. Five campaigns particularly impressed him. First, Germany's quick defeat of Poland convinced him that airpower dominated ground forces—a lesson reinforced by the French campaign the following year. France's rapid collapse shocked most of the world, but de Seversky simply remarked that the Maginot Line had become the tomb for a nation that had refused to look skyward.[35] As in World War I, the French had relied on their army. This stubborn attachment to tradition proved disastrous.

Two other campaigns gave different lessons: Norway and Crete demonstrated the superiority of airpower over naval forces. In both instances the Royal Navy, reputedly the finest in the world, had been decisively repulsed—not by German or Italian sea power, which the British had quickly disposed of—but by the Luftwaffe. The British fleet lay helpless before an enemy that controlled the air.[36] At Crete, for example, the Luftwaffe sank four British cruisers and six destroyers, while severely damaging an aircraft carrier and three battleships. Because of such staggering losses—the worst defeat of the war for the Royal Navy—the fleet could not hold the island. Later, the sinking of the British dreadnoughts *Prince of Wales* and *Repulse* off the Malayan coast by Japanese land-based aircraft served to heighten de Seversky's scorn for the capital ship.

De Seversky also argued that the rescue of the British army from Dunkirk was possible only because the RAF controlled the air above the beaches. Air superiority permitted the Royal Navy to move in and evacuate over three hundred thousand troops.[37] Had the Luftwaffe owned the skies, the British would not have attempted such an operation; if they had, the results would have resembled those at Norway and Crete. Airpower had saved the remnants of the British army.

The Battle of Britain was also compelling insofar as it demonstrated how improperly structured and poorly led airpower could squander a numerical advantage. Interestingly, although de Seversky had predicted a British victory, another famous American aviator, Charles Lindbergh, argued that nothing could stand up to the Luftwaffe's might.

Moreover, he believed that because Britain was doomed, the United States should cut ties with that country and build up its own air strength.[38] De Seversky countered that airpower had shrunk the globe to such an extent that US isolation was a thing of the past. Americans could no longer sit behind their oceans and ignore the affairs of Europe; rather, they must support England because her fight, inevitably, would one day be theirs.[39] In February 1942 de Seversky collected these lessons, combined them with his ideas on airpower, and produced *Victory through Air Power*—a book designed to alert America to the challenges of a modern, total war in which it was now involved, and to offer a strategy based on airpower for fighting that new form of war.

Victory through Air Power first takes the reader through a brief, selective history of the war, much of which repeats what de Seversky had said the previous year. People who had followed his many magazine and newspaper articles would have found little new in this survey. De Seversky reaffirmed airpower as the key to victory, maintaining that the airplane had eclipsed traditional forms of land and sea warfare. He retells the stories of Poland, Norway, France, Crete, and the Battle of Britain and derides the generals and admirals who attempted to fight with the methods and tactics of previous wars: "The lessons of this war can't be shouted down by invoking the glories of the past."[40] Although other people had begun to awake to this new form of war and sense its implications, de Seversky emphasized that it was a revolution demanding equally revolutionary responses. Unfortunately, America was not prepared for this challenge.

Perhaps because he was still obsessed with what he considered unfair treatment by the AAF, de Seversky felt the need to recount the story of his unsuccessful attempts to sell advanced fighter aircraft to the government. He regales the reader with details about his ideas for increasing the range and firepower of American planes, only to have them snubbed by military officials. These sections smack of self-justification and are of limited value. In fact, because de Seversky insisted on singling out Hap Arnold for attack, military airmen did not welcome his message.[41] Once again, he alienated the very people he should have courted. On the other hand, he

251

performed a useful service by calling attention to problems that existed in America's aircraft rearmament program.

De Seversky pointed out that American fighter planes were inferior to those of the other major belligerents. They did not have the speed, range, altitude, or armament to contest with frontline enemy fighters. Yet, press releases emanating from AAF, the government, and industry pretended that American planes were the best in the world.[42] De Seversky rejected such claims with disdain: "No one in his senses would pretend that the P-40 is a match for the Messerschmitt or the Spitfire."[43] Some people accused him of lacking patriotism, of lowering the morale of American airmen, and of disclosing important information to the enemy. The major dismissed these charges by maintaining that the people had a right to know the truth; otherwise, problems would remain uncorrected.[44]

Besides presenting a bleak picture intended to alert the public to the backward state of American airpower, de Seversky also expressed his views on the nature of air warfare. His most important idea held that airpower was an inherently strategic weapon. By this he meant that airpower's ability to fly over enemy armies and navies enabled it to strike directly at a country's most vital areas: its capital, industry, government, and so forth. Surface forces, on the other hand, generally fought only at the tactical level of war—force against force—hoping through an accumulation of victories in battle to position themselves for strategic, or decisive, military operations. Surface commanders realized, however, that their operations would prove far easier and more successful if airpower supported them. De Seversky cautioned against this, declaring that supporting an army tactically would squander airpower's unique capability. One should employ airpower primarily as a strategic weapon and use it against targets that had strategic significance. Similarly, de Seversky rejected the view that the objective of war was to occupy territory—an outdated concept. Strategic airpower could destroy the facilities and structures that made an area useful to the enemy: "Having knocked the weapons out of his hands and reduced the enemy to impotence, we can starve and beat him into submission by air power."[45] This accomplished, one required occupation of only a humanitarian or political nature: the Red Cross or similar organizations would suffice.

Second in importance, de Seversky stressed the necessity of air superiority. The first two years of the war clearly demonstrated that whoever controlled the air also controlled the land and sea below. The French campaign especially illustrated the price an army had to pay when the enemy air force dominated the sky above it. To de Seversky, the most effective method of preventing this and protecting friendly soldiers involved gaining and maintaining air superiority at the outset of a campaign.

De Seversky argued that one must seek this key battle for air superiority as early as possible and conduct it with utmost vigor. Other air theorists, notably Mitchell and Douhet, had advocated achieving air superiority by attacking enemy airfields and aircraft factories—not by engaging the air force itself. Their rationale for this approach was twofold: first, before the in vention of radar, forcing an aerial battle was considered nearly impossible. In Douhet's formulation, a stronger air force could safely ignore its weaker opponent, and the weaker air force would be foolish to look for a fight it would probably lose.[46] Second, they avoided discussion of an air battle because it tended to contradict one of their basic premises of air warfare—that it eliminated the bloody and prolonged counterforce battle.

De Seversky rejected these arguments. Enjoying the hindsight provided by the first two years of the war, he saw that an air battle not only could occur but, indeed, generally would. As a consequence, de Seversky insisted that one must resolve the air battle sooner rather than later. In fact, he later maintained that the RAF should not have stopped its daylight bombing operations and retreated to the safety of night, a decision that did not eliminate the air battle but merely delayed it.[47] British Bomber Command eventually suffered greater losses in its night operations than did the American Eighth Air Force attacking in daylight. Significantly, de Seversky even implied that air superiority could become an end in itself: once a country had lost its air force and the enemy could devastate it at will, a rational government would sue for peace. In other words, although de Seversky claimed that airpower could avoid the type of prolonged battle that occurred between armies, his call for an air battle reintroduced it—only now it would take place at 20,000 feet.

De Seversky did not claim in *Victory through Air Power* that airpower alone could win the war. Rather, he maintained that the airplane had become the dominant and decisive element in modern war. The vital role of land and sea forces was to hold the enemy in place while airpower pounded him into submission. In addition, the army and navy had to seize and hold air bases from which one could launch strategic air strikes against the enemy's heartland. Indeed, this was the strategy for the Pacific: the war against Japan was essentially a struggle for air bases. Far-flung enemy islands had little strategic consequence; rather, they were useful as air bases for striking the Japanese home islands.

As a way of lessening the dependence of airpower on these overseas air bases, de Seversky pushed for the development of "interhemispheric" bombers that could strike the enemy from the United States. He stated that such global bombers would "change the whole picture of law enforcement"; the mere *threat* of American airpower would be enough to keep the peace.[48] He pointed to the massive B-19 and Martin flying boat as examples of the type of long-range aircraft he envisioned, claiming that these behemoths had a payload capacity of over 30,000 pounds while also enjoying an unrefueled range of eight thousand miles. De Seversky wanted thousands of such aircraft built. Unfortunately, his technical expertise deserted him in this instance. Both of these aircraft were underpowered and had structural shortcomings; they never came close to the performance de Seversky claimed for them and never reached production.

For the military to utilize airpower effectively, de Seversky called for a defense department with equal branches for land, sea, and air. He remained convinced that the older services would never allow airpower to reach its full potential as a strategic weapon, simply be cause they did not understand it. Similarly, airpower needed to remain separate and distinct at the theater and tactical levels. Because of its great speed, range, and flexibility, airpower should be centralized and used en masse over the entire depth and breadth of a theater.

Under the control of land or sea commanders, airpower would languish at the tactical level and would not realize maximum effectiveness.

De Seversky's last message in *Victory through Air Power* dealt with targeting. If airpower were indeed an inherently strategic weapon, then one should take great care to determine the proper objectives for an air campaign. The fact that bombers could strike *any*thing did not mean they should strike *every*thing. Most air theorists argued that all countries had vital centers which allowed the state to function effectively: government, industry, transportation networks, financial systems, power grids, and so forth. Precisely which of those objectives were most vital and which specific targets within those categories one should attack and in what priority remained unclear. Douhet, for example, merely stated that the will of the civilian population was the key objective, allowing the "genius of the commander" to determine how best to affect that will.[49]

De Seversky was similarly vague. He did, however, reject popular will as a specific target, although not for humanitarian reasons. The war had demonstrated a surprising human resiliency, and prewar predictions of urban populations quickly panicking and breaking under air attack had proven wrong. De Seversky therefore emphasized the importance of industrial targets. In truth, de Seversky was merely echoing American Air Corps doctrine that had been in place for at least a decade prior to the war. Unfortunately, like most air theorists, he did not specify which part of the enemy's industry one should target. Debates then raged among Allied air planners over the proper objectives for attack—candidates included oil, electricity, chemicals, rubber, and ball bearings. De Seversky did not contribute to this debate, opting instead for an air campaign to obliterate *all* aspects of an industrial infrastructure. Given the size and complexity of a modern state's industrial base, combined with the limited destructive capacity and accuracy of contemporary bombs, this approach was highly simplistic and unsophisticated. De Seversky, like so many air thinkers, overestimated the physical damage of bombing.

The critical response to *Victory through Air Power* was divided. Predictably, soldiers and sailors found it both inaccurate and dangerous, questioning de Seversky's claims regarding the effectiveness of airpower in the war and totally rejecting his prophecies of air dominance. One naval advocate sniffed that although the book "purports to be a serious study" it was actually "a slipshod affair" with a "Jules Verne" quality about it.[50] A Navy public relations official candidly admitted, however, that the book posed a "special threat" because it "reaches the popular mind, and the popular mind reacts on Congressmen, and the first thing you know you are going to have Congress telling you and your colleagues in the Navy that you are not abreast of modern trends of thought in the matter of how to make war."[51] Airmen also had concerns about the book, but for different reasons. Although they welcomed the call for a separate air force, de Seversky's stinging attacks on Arnold troubled them. As a result, the AAF ignored the book, although some people made behind-the-scenes attempts to discredit it.[52] One de Seversky supporter deplored such machinations, writing that "the drive to 'destroy' Seversky is the symptom of a deeper struggle, under the surface, between military diehards and military progressives."[53]

On the other hand, several informed commentators found the book both fascinating and significant. For example, one wrote that "it is the duty of every adult citizen who can lay his hands on $2.50 to buy it and ponder its message." Another commented, "While many specific statements of this book may be questioned, an open-minded reader is obliged to conclude that the author is more nearly right than wrong in his views." Finally, one said simply that "it is more important for Americans than all the other war books put together."[54]

The public was enthusiastic about *Victory through Air Power,* and its status as a Book of the Month Club selection guaranteed a wide and literate audience. The publisher even brought it out in paperback—rare for a serious work at that time. Consequently, an estimated 5 million Americans read it. Given de Seversky's many other articles and radio addresses, George Gallup estimated that over 20 million people knew of de Seversky and his message—an astounding figure in the days before television.[55] In fact, Walt Disney approached de Seversky with a plan to turn *Victory through Air Power* into a movie.

The famed cartoon filmmaker wished to contribute to the war effort by making military training films. Donald Duck went to war to fight the Nazi menace, Mickey Mouse admonished people to pay their taxes promptly, and military units sported over twelve hundred military insignia bearing Disney cartoon characters.[56] Disney himself later said that he had had a deep interest in aviation for years and "sensed that air power held the key to the outcome of this war."[57] Although millions of people had read the major's book, Disney realized that millions of others had not, and his unique ability to use visual images and cartoons would serve to educate them as well. Disney believed he would probably lose money on the movie but stated, "I'm concerned that America should see it, and now is no time to think of personal profits."[58]

The movie, which opened on 17 July 1943, begins with a cartoon introduction to the history of flight up to World War II. The picture then switches to de Seversky, shown in his office surrounded by world maps, airplane models, and blueprints. The major relates his message of airpower and its importance to modern war.[59] Superb graphics illustrate his ideas. Nazi Germany is depicted as a huge iron wheel with factories at the hub, pumping planes, tanks, ships, and other war equipment out the spokes for use along the thick rim. Allied armies chip away at this rim by attacking individual tanks and planes, but the Nazis react by simply redirecting war material from one spoke to another to counter the threat; the rim is too strong to break. Aircraft then bomb the factories of the hub directly, destroying them and causing the spokes to weaken and the rim to collapse. In another particularly memorable sequence, Disney animates the book's depiction of Japan as an octopus with its tentacles stretched across the Pacific, encircling dozens of helpless islands. Allied armies and navies futilely attempt to hack away at these thick tentacles and free the islands. American airpower, represented by a fierce and powerful eagle, then repeatedly strikes the head of the octopus with its sharp talons, forcing the beast to release the outlying possessions so it can defend itself. However, it cannot fend off the eagle and eventually expires under the attacks. The United States achieves victory through the air. Even today, the movie remains an extremely powerful piece of airpower propaganda.

Although the film was not a commercial success, it had a significant impact. Possibly because two of his old friends on the AAF staff asked him to go easy, de Seversky removed all personal bile from the movie version—the film doesn't even mention Arnold and the growing pains encountered by American aviation. As a result, the Air Force embraced the film, finding it useful for educating recruits on airpower.[60] Air Marshal Jack Slessor, himself a noted air theorist and then commander of the RAF's Coastal Command, congratulated de Seversky: "It is certainly first-class educational value to people who are capable of thinking reasonably clearly for themselves."[61] The film so impressed Winston Churchill that he insisted that President Roosevelt watch it with him during their summit meeting in Quebec in August 1943.[62] Soon after the war ended, de Seversky interviewed Emperor Hirohito, who claimed to have watched the movie and to have been deeply troubled by its predictions concerning the fate of his country at the hands of American airpower.[63] Nevertheless, the movie had serious problems.

In keeping with de Seversky's antipathy towards the Navy, the movie depicts sea power in a hopelessly weak and ineffective light—indeed, it shows most of the surface ships resting on the bottom of the ocean. The Army fares little better; its tanks become mere toys, easily pushed over by attacking aircraft. In fact, although the movie took only three months to produce, military censors took another 10 months to clear it. Apparently the Army and Navy hierarchy pressured Disney to stop the project.[64]

In addition, the film grossly exaggerates the accuracy and effectiveness of bombing attacks. Every bomb dropped in the movie hits its target—all of which are factories or railroad yards—and nothing falls in urban residential areas. In a surprising sequence, the film depicts the new interhemispheric bomber advocated by de Seversky. Hundreds of these huge aircraft, based in Alaska, relentlessly pummel Japan. But they have no escorts; instead, the bombers bristle with radar-controlled machine guns that shoot down enemy interceptors in droves. Considering de Seversky's spirited push for long-range escort and his claims that bombers would be unable to defend themselves adequately, this scene seems somewhat bizarre.[65]

For the rest of the war, de Seversky continued to call for a strategy dominated by airpower. He wanted military leaders to emphasize emerging weapons, not obsolescent ones, but they largely rejected his pleas. Like Douhet and Mitchell before him, de Seversky saw little need for historical precedents to buttress his theories. Using history would lead to employing strategies of the past. Since generals actually continued to discuss the campaigns of 1918, they might as well examine those of ancient Greece and Persia for all their relevance to World War II![66] He wanted massive air attacks against the enemy's vital centers—not peripheral pinpricks. At one point he wrote in exasperation, "We are stabbing the enemy with penknives, trying to bleed him to death, instead of wielding the axe of true air power."[67]

When the war ended, de Seversky visited both theaters and for nearly eight months wandered the defeated countries, talked to survivors, saw scores of bombed-out cities and factories, and interviewed high-ranking military and civilian leaders. Not surprisingly, he concluded that airpower had been the decisive factor in victory by destroying the will of the German and Japanese leadership.[68] He did not denigrate the efforts of the other services, which he deemed essential, but he nevertheless saw airpower as the instrument primarily responsible for bringing victory. This proved especially true in Japan, where the atomic strikes eliminated the need for a bloody invasion of the home islands by giving the emperor, as he put it, "an excuse to make peace." De Seversky conceded, however, that Japan's far smaller military and industrial capacity, as well as its qualitatively inferior airpower, made the country an easier opponent. The Japanese simply did not understand airpower, a situation exacerbated by the decision to disperse their industry into small "cottage factories" throughout the cities. This practice not only curtailed production but also made area attacks almost inevitable: the Japanese thus committed "industrial hara-kiri."[69]

Surprisingly, de Seversky was skeptical about the power and significance of the atomic bombs. Expecting to find Hiroshima and Nagasaki "vaporized," he instead found the burned-out rubble characteristic of German cities that had suffered extensive aerial or artillery bombardment. This discovery led him to conclude that the importance of the atomic bomb was greatly exaggerated; to him, it was just another weapon. In fact, in one interview he referred to it as a mere "firecracker" that created much noise and light but little else. This stance gained him much criticism from both scientists and political leaders—and even labeled him a military conservative![70]

De Seversky's argument on this subject was not mature. Although the ability to use the medium of the air had revolutionized the nature of war, dismissing atomic bombs as merely new weapons of little import was simplistic. One must exploit the air medium—and do this through the actual employment of weaponry. Thus, airmen should have appreciated the great importance of developing air weapons, but such was not the case. Little effort had gone into developing aerial bombs between the world wars. The fact that iron blockbusters of 1917 were quite similar to those of 1945—and remained so for another three decades—proved to be a major oversight. Without effective weapons, the military often wasted airpower. Thus, although the Allies had air superiority over Germany and Japan, they could not force a rapid decision because their bombs were either too weak or, more importantly, too inaccurate to do so. Initially, de Seversky also fell into the myopic snare of not recognizing the importance of radical new air weapons such as the atomic bomb. He did, however, change his views when the hydrogen bomb, hundreds of times more powerful than the atomic devices detonated over Japan, became part of the American arsenal.

Confrontation with the Soviet Union quickly turned de Seversky into a cold warrior, profoundly suspicious of the Kremlin's motives: "They would break every promise they make if it suits them."[71] (One certainly wonders whether his Russian heritage gave him special insights or peculiar biases.) Pessimistically, he thought that the Soviet worldview was irreconcilable with the West's, thus making violent confrontation inevitable. If this were true, then his arguments regarding the folly of contesting with a powerful land foe by building a large army seem appropriate. To de Seversky, common sense demanded that America face such an enemy by utilizing its unique strength—aeronautical technology.

De Seversky believed that America remained inherently an airpower nation. Young people should see their destinies in the sky—a notion of his that antedated the war. In fact, some of his earliest radio broadcasts were for young listeners and explained how airplanes worked, how he had become interested in them, and why airpower was essential to America's future.[72] His persuasion extended to adults as well: "In this aeronautical age we ought to become a nation of aviators, in order to achieve mastery of the sky—just as in the past, in the age of sea power, England was a nation of sailors." He then expanded on this analogy: Rome had been the master on land, England on sea, and now America in the air. All used this mastery of a particular medium to dominate the world and give it peace.[73]

The major was convinced that America had the advantage in this crucial area. Not only had we employed strategic airpower in the war while the Soviet Union had not, but also we were fortunate in having friendly neighbors. The Soviets, on the other hand, had to build a large army to protect their vulnerable and extensive borders. Like Douhet, Mitchell, and Alfred Thayer Mahan, de Seversky clearly saw the significance of geopolitical factors and wrote for the peculiar American situation.[74] In his view, airpower—especially if armed with nuclear weapons—seemed the only sane path to provide the world a "Pax Democratica."[75] This was a variation of a theme that de Seversky had repeated for years: airpower and technology were related in an unusually close and symbiotic fashion. To a far greater degree than surface forces, airpower depended on a strong and vibrant scientific and industrial base. America possessed such a base; the Soviet Union did not. Moreover, when de Seversky contemplated the future of space—which he considered merely an extension of terrestrial airpower—he became even more convinced of America's potential dominance.

Like most people at the time, de Seversky was surprised by the North Korean invasion in June 1950. He immediately rejected arguments for American involvement, believing it would play into Soviet hands. Fighting a peripheral war against Soviet proxies would slowly bleed the United States white and drain it of its resources.[76] Significantly, his second

261

book, *Air Power: Key to Survival*, published soon after the outbreak of the war, prophesied that Korea would be a mistake for America and would fester inconclusively for years. According to de Seversky, the Book of the Month Club wanted to publish his new work as its main selection under the title *Peace through Air Power* but was displeased with his comments regarding the Korean War. The club's contacts with military and political leaders in Washington assured it that the Korean police action was a minor distraction that would be over quickly. Club officials therefore asked de Seversky to modify his strident views on Korea to conform to conventional wisdom. When he refused, they backed out of their offer to feature the book. De Seversky noted ruefully that because he told the truth no one wanted to hear, his book sold 30,000 copies instead of six hundred thousand.[77]

Sounding almost isolationist, de Seversky argued against US involvement throughout the Korean War. President Truman's dismissal of Gen Douglas MacArthur—a man for whom he had great respect—angered him, but he thought the action justified if it led to a serious reappraisal of American policy.[78] Such a reappraisal did in fact occur, but much to de Seversky's chagrin, the climactic hearings before the Senate tended to ratify the limited war policy so abhorred by MacArthur. The major's proposed solution was far more direct.

Air Power: Key to Survival argued that "triphibious operations"—the synergistic actions of air, land, and sea forces, which he admitted were necessary in World War II—were now a thing of the past. In a favorite analogy, he likened the situation to the man who wanted to cross a river. One contractor tells him to build a tunnel under the water; another suggests a ferry to cross on the surface of the water; while the third proposes a bridge to span above the river. Perplexed and indecisive, the man elects to pursue all three ideas, at enormous cost and effort. De Seversky saw this happening with American defense policy. Instead, he maintained that as airpower increased its range to a truly global scale, one would have little need for vulnerable surface forces that would play bit parts in a major war against the Soviet Union. Why have a navy when there were no sea lanes to protect and no enemy fleet to contest them? In a vicious comment, he dismissed fleets as henceforth existing merely in "vestigial form as a transport auxiliary of air power, but even that will be temporary."[79] Indeed, he was convinced that the Air Force (an independent service since 1947) should be dominant within the defense establishment and was suspicious of calls for greater "unification" of the armed forces. De Seversky thought that unification, like the old AAF idea of 1941, was a trick to keep airpower tied to the surface: "Because their primary functions have been obsoleted by science, the older services are trying to perpetuate them by bureaucratic law." America was more than ever an airpower nation whose destiny lay in air and space. Calls for "balanced forces" were an archaic and uninspired method of defense planning that diluted the potent and decisive aspects of airpower.[80]

When "massive retaliation" became official US strategy during the Eisenhower administration, de Seversky embraced it (indeed, his writings since the end of World War II had called for much the same thing, though without the catchy title). He rejected notions of limited war, stating that they inevitably ended in stalemate. Moreover, airpower lost its special advantages in such conflicts; Korea was an aberration, and it must stay that way. Unfortunately, Korea would lead "orthodox thinkers" to believe that such conventional war was still likely. On the other hand, in an era of decreasing defense budgets but increasing commitments, he—as well as the new president and his advisors—saw airpower as the only plausible solution. Such a strategy also necessitated a technologically first-rate air force, ready to fight at a moment's notice.

Clearly, de Seversky had come a long way since the days before World War II, when he called for a balanced defense of land, sea, and air forces, while also rejecting suggestions that airpower alone could win wars. By the mid-1950s, he saw global airpower as the solution to America's security needs. In some of his more outrageous suggestions, he called for a Department of the Air Force that contained a Bureau of Ships, a Bureau of Ground Forces, and bureaus "for other auxiliary units." The Navy would be drastically reduced so that only its antisubmarine warfare activities and naval logistics functions remained. As for the Army, it should number a maximum of 250,000 troops, and its primary mission would be to "maintain order in our country during an atomic holocaust, as well as to protect our domestic air and missile bases." Obviously, he was now consigning the Army and its leaders to the same dustbin occupied by the Navy. George Marshall had "infantryitis," Omar Bradley ("the old monkey") possessed a weak intellect, and Dwight Eisenhower would "destroy and slaughter our youth" in areas like Korea if he were elected president. (As noted above, he miscalculated dramatically regarding Eisenhower's intentions and was pleasantly surprised by most of his defense policies.) The Army, however, would also serve as an occupational police force after airpower had decided the matter.[81] Accomplishing all this was an Air Force that received two-thirds of the defense budget and that contained not a "mere" three hundred B-36 bombers then in procurement plans, but three thousand such goliaths to demolish potential adversaries with nuclear weapons from bases in the United States.[82]

He had interesting beliefs on the targeting strategy behind such strikes. After achieving air superiority, global airpower (exemplified initially by manned bombers and later by long-range guided missiles) would strike the industrial center of the enemy. De Seversky did not advocate merely bombing cities or targeting the population. Such moves would prove counterproductive because "dead people don't revolt." Instead, he wanted to drive a wedge between the people and their leaders by attacking communications and transportation networks—by "disarming the government."[83] This would result in an "internal blockade" of a country, causing paralysis and inability to conduct war effectively. This emphasis clearly differed from that espoused by Douhet, who called for attacks on the population in order to foment rebellion. It also contrasted the thinking of theorists at the Air Corps Tactical School (ACTS) in the 1930s, who concentrated on enemy industry as a means of breaking the capability—not the will—of an enemy to fight. Consequently, de Seversky offered a unique theory of strategic airpower—related to, but distinct from, that of his precursors.

The Air Force was also studying the idea of "air policing" in the early 1950s. Air planners had looked at the experiences of the Royal Air Force in the Middle East between the wars. In some cases, the RAF had been quite successful at controlling large tribal areas through threatening air attack and, if necessary, discreetly using it. Significantly, the RAF could maintain order in places like Iraq and Transjordan at a fraction of the cost of using ground forces for the same mission. In 1950 the Air Staff considered resurrecting this idea, terming it Project Control, and chose de Seversky to participate as a member of the lengthy study that ensued.

The basic premise of the project was that one could use airpower to pressure the Soviet Union into following policies favorable to the West. If persuasion and threats proved unsuccessful, then selective strikes—with atomic weapons if necessary—would put teeth in the threats. The Air Staff assumed that Soviet leaders would react just as backward tribes of the 1920s had reacted.[84] This proposal—which sounded to some extent like de Seversky's "internal blockade" plan—was, of course, never implemented. However, it received serious consideration from the Truman and Eisenhower administrations.

This entire idea of persuasion or "air policing" signified an evolution in de Seversky's thought. In *Victory through Air Power,* he had discussed only two methods of applying military force: occupation—the traditional strategy of ground warfare—and destruction, now possible through airpower. Over the next decade he modified this view, seeing not only that airpower made possible the "neutralization" of an enemy, but also that peaceful applications of airpower could achieve national objectives. Viewing airpower as an enormously effective propaganda tool, he advocated the delivery of "ideas" as well as essentials such as food, clothing, and medicine via airpower to win friends and undermine enemies. Testifying before Congress in 1951, he exclaimed that too many people saw airpower as nothing more than "bombs, bombs, bombs."[85] Yet de Seversky himself was guilty of this tendency. Indeed, by advocating massive retaliation and at the same time calling for a relatively benign air policing strategy, de Seversky created a contradiction that he never resolved.

One may attribute this ambivalence, in part, to de Seversky's role as a transitional figure. He joined the military theorists and doctrine formulators of the 1920s and 1930s (represented by Douhet, Mitchell, and the ACTS instructors) and the civilian academicians of the 1950s and 1960s (characterized by Bernard Brodie and Herman Kahn). Physically and intellectually, he had a foot in both camps: as a former combat pilot and reserve officer, he could relate to the military pilots of the Air Corps. As a businessman, designer, and writer, he also was at home with civilian thinkers who devised elaborate models to describe "the balance of terror."

De Seversky continued to write at a frenetic pace until the mid-1960s, publishing one more book in 1961, *America—Too Young to Die*, and scores more articles.[86] Although he continued to move in and out of various business ventures, his heart never seemed in them; preaching the gospel of airpower remained his primary interest. In truth, his writings became increasingly repetitious and technologically dated. The major was not an expert either in jet engine technology or the airframe design it required, and his writings on guided missiles and spaceflight were embarrassingly off the mark.[87] By the late 1950s, little of what de Seversky wrote retained either originality or interest, although he did play a useful role at Maxwell AFB, Alabama, where he periodically lectured young officers on airpower theory. Over the years, he lectured to over one hundred thousand officers, reminding them of their duty to study and promote airpower. Even in his seventies, he could deliver a spellbinding speech laced with his own peculiar brand of humor and metaphor. At Maxwell, he felt at home.

The major died in 1974 at age 80. His wife, Evelyn, who took her own life due to despondency over a long illness, preceded him by seven years.

Alexander de Seversky was the most effective and prolific airpower advocate of his era. His hundreds of articles and lectures reached millions. One must remember that he did not write to influence military leaders (they were a hopeless case); rather, he wrote for the man in the street. Because of his homey, down-to-earth style, he spoke the language that average Americans could understand.

His ideas on airpower were not original. Someone else had already articulated virtually everything he proposed. Douhet, Mitchell, Hugh Trenchard, Ira Eaker, even Hap Arnold, his bête noir, had already written of the unique characteristics and capabilities of airpower, its revolutionary nature, and its role in forever changing the face of war. His calls for air superiority, global range, and an industrial-based targeting scheme were not new. De Seversky's role was to take these ideas, repackage them, cover them with a modicum of technical credibility, and then sell them to the American people.

He was enormously popular, and his publication record was staggering—over one hundred major articles and several hundred lesser ones. Scarcely a month went by during World War II and the decade after when his articles did not appear in major magazines. Because his target audience comprised average Americans, he wrote for publications such as *The American Mercury, Reader's Digest, The Atlantic, Ladies' Home Journal,* and *Look*—representing a huge and diverse readership. Tens of millions of Americans knew of de Seversky, and he enjoyed access to the media and the people that was the envy of anyone attempting to influence public policy. In fact, Gallup polls showed that the number of Americans supporting an independent air force jumped from 42 percent in August 1941 to 59 percent in August 1943, although he certainly was not the sole cause.[88]

De Seversky sold basic, uncomplicated ideas. War had become total, involving all the resources and people of a nation. In such a titanic struggle, America must maximize its unique strength—technological superiority granted by airpower. Other countries might be willing to pay a heavy price in blood and treasure to achieve their aims, but America must not. She must restructure her defense and devise strategies that relied on airpower. Because an air force differed fundamentally from armies and navies, it must remain a separate service, commanded by airmen who understood its unique qualities—especially its ability to operate routinely as a strategic weapon. Airpower thus offered the hope of avoiding the bloody land battles of the world wars. To enhance airpower's ability to avoid such battles, one must give it global range. As long as aircraft remained shackled to airfields near the enemy, surface forces would need to seize and defend those airfields; such action could precipitate the prolonged land campaign that de Seversky hoped to avoid.

The United States must build interhemispheric bombers, whose primary aim was to gain control of the air—that achieved, an enemy became helpless. Perhaps most importantly, the American public—not just military and political leaders—must understand all these ideas. In order to ensure that this was the case, America must see itself as an airpower nation and look skyward for its destiny.

Like many other air theorists, de Seversky exaggerated the effectiveness of airpower. He overestimated the physical and psychological effects of strategic bombing. In this sense, he shared the shortcomings of his predecessors. Like Douhet and Mitchell, de Seversky understood the importance of morale and will, realizing that, somehow, one must modify or bend the enemy's will. Unlike them, however, he rejected the notion that urban area bombing best produced this effect. Instead, he opted for airpower's use against enemy industry or infrastructure.

All of these men had the same goal—to break, or at least shape, enemy will—but chose different mechanisms to reach that goal. In short, they identified different key centers against which airpower should concentrate. Again, like Douhet and Mitchell, de Seversky combined this emphasis on psychological goals with a penchant for selecting highly mechanistic methods. The major was convinced that a finite number of planes and bombs, delivered on specific targets, would equal victory. Air strategy consisted of destroying target sets, resulting in a curious blend of psychology and science.

In the parlance of more classical military theory, he melded Carl von Clausewitz and Henri de Jomini. But the product was not altogether satisfactory. For example, he never seemed to appreciate the fact that nuclear weapons had an even greater impact on the human mind than on physical structures. They represented a threshold, and discussions about their use far transcended considerations of military effectiveness.

De Seversky clearly misjudged the technical obstacles to building large aircraft. His trumpeting of the Douglas B-19 and Martin flying boat proved premature. He designed a "superclipper" in the late 1930s, but it never got off the drawing board due to technical difficulties. Although the B-29 constituted a significant advance over the B-17 and B-24, it did not approach the capabilities de Seversky called for in an interhemispheric bomber. Even the massive B-36—not a viable weapon until 1950—fell short of his predictions. In sum, building large aircraft differed significantly from designing fighter planes.

He did not foresee that precisely because total war—especially in the nuclear age—was "unprofitable," warfare would be limited or driven down to the unconventional level; such wars dissipated airpower's advantages. De Seversky argued passionately against America's involvement in limited wars such as those in Korea and Vietnam. He assumed this stance partly for cogent strategic reasons: if the Soviet threat to Europe represented the major concern, then one should not become distracted by relatively minor conflicts in Asia. On the other hand, his admission of strategic airpower's effectiveness against modern industrialized nations amounted to a tacit admission of its ineffectiveness against poor agrarian societies. And admitting the limited, "low intensity" nature of future wars amounted to admitting that airpower had clear limitations. That was unacceptable.

Finally, to an illogical and unreasonable degree, he denigrated the importance of armies and navies. Even in the total wars he predicted, surface forces would have played a greater role than merely serving as airfield gate guards and bomb transporters. One of the distressing traits of airpower theorists is their tendency to claim too much for their chosen weapon. Airpower does not have to win wars *alone* in order to be decisive, any more than does an army. True unification—what today we would call "jointness"—recognizes that all weapons and services have unique strengths and weaknesses. Wise commanders choose those weapons and capabilities that will most effectively and efficiently accomplish their objectives. In the type of war envisioned by de Seversky, the unique capabilities of airpower were at a premium. But airpower alone could not do everything.

Nevertheless, Alexander P. de Seversky captured the essence of a new weapon of war—and peace—and then conveyed an understanding of that essence to millions of Americans in a way unduplicated by anyone else, before him or since. He made terms like *victory through airpower* and *peace through airpower* familiar to an entire generation. As a prophet, he was mediocre. As a propagandizer, he was exceptional.

Notes

1. "Alexander P. de Seversky," *U.S. Air Services*, August 1937, 18–19.

2. Samuel Taylor Moore, "Amazing Adventures of Legless Aviator," *Every Week Magazine*, 1929, clipping in de Seversky Papers, Cradle of Aviation Museum archives, Long Island, N.Y. [hereinafter Cradle archives]; and Chloe Arnold, "An Ace with One Leg and Nine Crosses," *New York Sun*, 20 October 1918, 9.

3. Alexander P. de Seversky [hereinafter APS], "I Owe My Career to Losing My Leg," *Ladies' Home Journal*, May 1944, 107.

4. James Farber, "Major de Seversky—Engineer," *Popular Aviation*, August 1935, 88; and Paul Harvey, "One Bootstrap," *Flying*, September 1957, 26.

5. *Aeronautics*, 23 August 1916, 16. For more information about de Seversky's wartime exploits, see Rear Adm B. Doudoroff (his former commander), to United States Embassy, letter, 30 March 1918, Cradle archives.

6. APS, transcript of radio broadcast, 7 October 1938, Nassau County Library archives, Long Island, N.Y. [hereinafter Nassau archives]. Interestingly, de Seversky's father and brother were also military pilots; in fact, the former was a member of Alexander's squadron and thus a subordinate!

7. APS, transcript of radio broadcast, 1932, Nassau archives. De Seversky also received the Orders of Saint Ann, Saint Stanislaus, and Saint Vladimir.

8. Officially, his name was Alexander Procofieff-Seversky. However, when he was passing through Paris in 1918, French authorities inadvertently replaced the hyphen with a "de." Seversky liked the change and from then on relegated Procofieff to a middle name and used the "de." "Mr Procofieff from the North," *The New Yorker*, 5 October 1940, 14. His trip out of Russia was actually an escape. Since he was an aristocrat, local Bolshevik officials viewed him with distrust, despite his war record.

9. Ibid.

10. APS, "I Remember Billy Mitchell," *Air Power Historian*, October 1956, 179; "Alexander P. de Seversky," 19; and APS, "Sky Blazers," transcript of radio address, 24 August 1940, Nassau archives.

11. APS, transcript of radio broadcast, 9 January 1940, Nassau archives; and "Military Men Favor Air Refueling Flights," *New York Times*, 17 August 1930, 17. For the bombsight, see Major General Patrick to adjutant general, letter, 18 September 1924, Cradle archives; and C. L. Paulus, Materiel Division, memorandum, subject: Seversky's Employment at McCook Field, Ohio, n.d. [ca. October 1941], Air Force Museum archives,

de Seversky file, Wright-Patterson AFB, Ohio. The Air Service became the Air Corps in 1926 and the Army Air Forces in 1941.

12. A. D. McFadyn, "Major Alexander de Seversky," *Journal of the Patent Office Society,* April 1937, 273–76.

13. For a good description of the P-35 and its lineage, see Joshua Stoff, *The Thunder Factory: An Illustrated History of the Republic Aviation Corporation* (Osceola, Wisc.: Motorbooks, 1990), 11–35; and Edward T. Maloney, *Sever the Sky: Evolution of Seversky Aircraft* (Corona del Mar, Calif.: World War II Publications, 1979).

14. The Bendix Race was flown between Burbank, California, and Cleveland, Ohio—a distance of 2,045 miles. Interestingly, when told by the Air Corps that the P-35 was too advanced for Army pilots, de Seversky asked aviatrix Jackie Cochran to fly the plane and demonstrate its simplicity and reliability. Cochran flew the P-35 to victory in the 1938 Bendix. Dan Dwiggens, *They Flew the Bendix Race* (Philadelphia: J. B. Lippincott, 1965), 94–110.

15. De Seversky to Air Vice Marshal Sholto Douglas, letter, 8 April 1939, Cradle archives.

16. In 1967 de Seversky recalled experimenting with 37 mm and 82 mm cannon mounted on flying boats in 1917. Speech to the Naval War College, 28 April 1967, de Seversky Papers, Nassau archives. De Seversky argued for greatly increased armament, including rockets, on fighter aircraft as early as 1934. APS, "How Can Pursuit Aviation Regain Its Tactical Freedom?" *U.S. Air Services,* March 1934, 16–17. He reiterated this idea in "Lest We Forget," *U.S. Air Services,* January 1937, 16–17.

17. De Seversky wrote letters to several high-ranking Air Corps officers, including at least four to the chief of the Materiel Division, in May and June 1938, making such suggestions, but evidently the only response was from a Lieutenant Colonel Volandt at Wright Field, Ohio, who stated that the Air Corps simply was not interested. Copies of all letters are in the Cradle archives.

18. Capt Claire L. Chennault, "Special Support for Bombardment," *U.S. Air Services,* January 1934, 18–24; and Stephen L. McFarland and Wesley Newton, *To Command the Sky: The Battle for Air Superiority over Germany, 1942–44* (Washington, D.C.: Smithsonian Institution Press, 1991).

19. Evelyn de Seversky, transcript of radio broadcast, 22 June 1933, Nassau archives. In addition, both the de Severskys generally took their cocker spaniel, "Vodka," along on their flights; she logged over one thousand flying hours.

20. "Presenting Alexander P. de Seversky," *Pathfinder,* 13 February 1942, 16; *New York Daily News,* 1 August 1967, 12; APS, "Scoring the Stunt Contest," *The Sportsman Pilot,* May–June 1933, 10–12, 45–48; and John F. Whiteley, "Alexander de Seversky, A Personal Portrait," *Aerospace Historian,* Fall 1977, 155–57.

21. Alexander de Seversky, interviewed by Murray Green, New York, N.Y., 16 April 1970, Green Papers, USAF Academy archives, Colorado

Springs, Colorado. The difficulties and bickering between de Seversky and the Air Corps over the BT-8 contract's fulfillment is illustrative. See pertinent letters and reports, October 1935–March 1936, Cradle archives. De Seversky also received the Harmon Trophy in 1947 when President Truman lauded his tireless efforts during the war to alert the American public to the importance of airpower.

22. H. H. Arnold Jr., interviewed by Murray Green, Sheridan, Wyo., 29 August 1972, Green Papers, USAF Academy archives; and Landers to de Seversky, letter, 6 April 1942, Cradle archives. This letter contains a number of affidavit attachments regarding de Seversky's lawsuit against Republic. The various charges and countercharges are spelled out here, including the record of a phone conversation between de Seversky's lawyer and General Arnold, in which the latter gives credit to de Seversky as an engineer but notes that "someone else should handle other parts of the business." Another letter tells de Seversky he is spending too much money on his business trips. Wattes to de Seversky, letter, 26 November 1938, Cradle archives.

23. Arnold's motives are confirmed by his wartime chief of staff. See Lt Gen Barney Giles, interviewed by Murray Green, San Antonio, Tex., 12 May 1970, Green Papers, USAF Academy archives. One should note, however, that in an effort to boost company profits, de Seversky sold 20 aircraft to Japan in 1938, a move not welcomed by the Air Corps. Stoff, 23.

24. "The Founder Complains," *Time*, 2 September 1940, 56–57; and press release from H. A. Bruno and Associates (de Seversky's lawyers), 22 August 1940, Cradle archives.

25. Even 30 years after these events, de Seversky's 1970 interview is laced with anger and bitterness towards Arnold for taking his company away from him. On the other hand, Arnold asked his Materiel Division to search its records, talk to personnel who had worked with de Seversky, and get all available information on his employment at McCook Field, Ohio, in the 1920s. Unsigned memorandum, 8 October 1941, de Seversky file, Air Force Museum archives, Wright-Patterson AFB, Ohio.

26. APS, "Analysis of Statements Made by General H. H. Arnold," 24 May 1943, Nassau archives.

27. APS, "The Ordeal of American Air Power," *American Mercury*, July 1941, 7–14; and idem, "Victory through Air Power!" *American Mercury*, February 1942, 149.

28. De Seversky to FDR, letter, 11 July 1941, copy in Green Papers, USAF Academy archives; and "Seversky Calls Army Air Set-Up No 'Unification,' but Misnomer," *New York Herald Tribune*, 3 July 1941.

29. APS, "The Twilight of Sea Power," *American Mercury*, June 1941, 647.

30. APS, "Navies Are Finished," *American Mercury*, February 1946, 137; idem, "Ten Air Power Lessons for America," *Flying and Popular Aviation*, July 1941, 62; and idem, "When Will America Be Bombed?" *American Mercury*, April 1942, 415.

31. APS, "Air Power and Space Supremacy," speech to Virginia Military Institute, 7 March 1958, Nassau archives; and Evelyn de Seversky, transcript of radio broadcast, 2 June 1942, Nassau archives.

32. APS, "I Am an American," transcript of radio broadcast, 27 July 1941, Nassau archives.

33. "Seversky Fears September War," *New York Post*, 13 July 1939.

34. APS, "My Thoughts on the War," *Popular Aviation*, April 1940, 19; "Seversky Feels British Could Balk Invasion," *New York Herald Tribune*, 1 June 1940, 5; and APS, transcript of radio broadcast, 20 June 1940, Nassau archives.

35. "Ten Air Power Lessons," 14; and APS, "America Repeats Europe's Aviation Mistakes," *American Mercury*, October 1941, 401–4.

36. APS, "Hard Facts on Air Power," *American Mercury*, August 1940, 406–14; "'Umbrella' of Air Held Vital to Navy," *New York World Telegram*, 4 June 1940; and APS, transcript of radio broadcast, 26 May 1941, Nassau archives.

37. APS, "The Twilight of Sea Power," 648–49.

38. APS, "Why Lindbergh Is Wrong," *American Mercury*, May 1941, 519–32; and idem, "Why the Luftwaffe Failed," *The Atlantic*, March 1942, 293–302.

39. APS, "Aviation vs. Isolation," *Vital Speeches of the Day*, 1 July 1941, 557–58.

40. APS, transcript of radio broadcast, 26 May 1941, Nassau archives.

41. The previous month de Seversky had written Congress, once again recounting his plans for a long-range, heavily armed escort fighter in 1938 and complaining that Arnold had rejected his offers. De Seversky to Truman Committee Investigating National Defense, letter, 18 January 1942, Nassau archives.

42. APS, *Victory through Air Power* (New York: Simon & Schuster, 1942), 213–53; see also idem, "Aviation Ballyhoo vs. Aviation Facts," *American Mercury*, September 1942, 263–74.

43. "Seversky's Reply to Critics," *New York Herald Tribune*, 25 August 1942. This is apparently a response to a statement made by Arnold in a book he coauthored the previous year: "Comparative tests indicate there is little difference and no great disparity between them [the P-40 and Spitfire] in speed, climb and maneuverability." Maj Gen H. H. Arnold and Col Ira C. Eaker, *Winged Warfare* (New York: Harper, 1941), 22.

44. "Wing Tips," *Steel*, 14 September 1942, 100; and David Brown, "Victory through Hot Air Power," *Pic*, 15 January 1943, 7.

45. APS, *Victory through Air Power*, 307.

46. Giulio Douhet, *The Command of the Air*, trans. Dino Ferrari (1942; reprint, Washington, D. C.: Office of Air Force History, 1983), 244–50.

47. APS, "World War III and How to Win It," *Coronet*, January 1955, 118.

48. APS, "Memo on Enforcement of Peace through Air Power," 6 January 1943, Nassau archives.

49. Douhet, 50.

50. Hanson Baldwin, "Victory through Air Power? No!" *Sea Power*, June 1942, 6–8; and Hoffman Nickerson, "Seversky, Air Power! Nickerson, Not Enough!" *Field Artillery Journal*, July 1942, 543–49. For the most vicious response, see Maj Gen Paul B. Malone, "Victory through Air Prophets?" *Skyways*, November 1942, 6–9, 74–75.

51. Quoted in Russell Lee, "*Victory through Air Power:* American Army Air Forces, Navy and Public Reactions to the Book and Film during World War II" (master's thesis, George Mason University, 1992), 87.

52. Ibid., 54–62. After the war, Arnold wrote to Gen Carl Spaatz, his successor as commanding general of AAF, that de Seversky was "dangerous" because of his incessant carping on the alleged failures of American airpower during the war. Arnold to Spaatz, letter, 9 March 1946, copy in Green Papers, USAF Academy archives. Interestingly, de Seversky had great respect for Gen Frank Andrews, Arnold's contemporary, who was then commander of the Caribbean theater. Andrews died in a plane crash in May 1943.

53. William Bradford Huie, "What's behind the Attacks on Seversky?" *American Mercury*, February 1943, 156.

54. Clifton Fadiman, review of *Victory through Air Power*, *The New Yorker*, 25 April 1942, 74–76; Donald W. Mitchell, "The Dominance of Air Power," review of *Victory through Air Power*, *The Nation*, 23 May 1942, 604; and Huie, 155.

55. Cited in Lee, 34; see also Richard Shale, *Donald Duck Joins Up* (Ann Arbor, Mich.: University Microfilms International, 1982), 69. That was approximately one of every six Americans at the time.

56. Walton H. Rawls, *Disney Dons Dog Tags* (New York: Abbeville, 1992), 6. Perhaps the most well known Disney military insignia was that used by the Flying Tigers, the famed air unit based in China.

57. Transcript of BBC radio broadcast, 17 September 1943, Nassau archives.

58. APS, transcripts of radio broadcasts, 13 August 1943 and 30 January 1944, Nassau archives; and idem, "Walt Disney, an Airman in His Heart," *Aerospace Historian*, Spring 1967, 7.

59. De Seversky had taken a Dale Carnegie course in 1933 to improve his public speaking skills. Nevertheless, when rehearsing the script for the movie, he stated that German troops landed on Norway's beaches—pronouncing that word as if it were the term for female dogs. Disney then decided that Sascha needed elocution lessons. APS, "In the Lyons Den," 14 August 1943, Nassau archives.

60. Kuter, memorandum to Arnold, 23 June 1943, copy in Green Papers, USAF Academy archives. The two friends were Gen Larry Kuter and Gen Hal George. Gen Laurence Kuter, interviewed by Murray Green, New York City, 17 April 1970, Green Papers, USAF Academy archives; and Lee, 78–83.

61. Slessor to de Seversky, letter, 29 September 1943, Nassau archives. Between the wars, Slessor wrote a volume on airpower theory that is still considered a classic: *Air Power and Armies* (London: Oxford, 1936).

62. Kuter interview; and John Gunther, *Taken at the Flood: The Story of Albert D. Lasker* (New York: Harper & Row, 1960), 281–86.

63. De Seversky interviewed Hirohito on 2 November 1945. APS, transcript of radio broadcast, 1 November 1945, Nassau archives; and idem, "Report to Secretary Patterson on the Pacific War," 11 February 1946, 6, Nassau archives. The emperor reputedly added that he was convinced early on that airpower would eventually determine the outcome of the war.

64. Lee, 43–50.

65. The "superplane" is mentioned in the book but does not play as prominent a role as it does in the movie. *Victory through Air Power*, 316. When asked later about this seeming contradiction in his stance on the need for escort at that point in the war, de Seversky maintained that they had attempted several ways to explain this problem in the film, but all such solutions were too complex. They therefore decided to go with the easy— admittedly fanciful—depiction in the movie. APS, "Air Power and the Future," lecture at Royal Canadian Air Force Staff College, 25 August 1947, Nassau archives.

66. APS, "Outlines, Quotations, Lessons, etc.," ca. 1945, Nassau archives.

67. APS, "Bomb the Axis from America," *American Mercury*, December 1943, 680. De Seversky's advocacy of "precision bombing" at the same time he spoke of obliteration and destruction from the sky is an interesting paradox. To a far greater degree than his contemporaries in AAF, he saw airpower as a blunt instrument rather than a rapier. Given the technology of the time, de Seversky's perspective on this issue was the more realistic one.

68. APS, "Report to Secretary of War Patterson," 10 September 1945, 3–4, Nassau archives.

69. APS, "Report to Secretary Patterson on the Pacific War," 11 February 1946, 2–7.

70. Patterson Pacific Report, Supplement on Atomic Bombings, Nassau archives; APS, "Atomic Bomb Hysteria," *Reader's Digest*, February 1946, 121–26; and idem, transcript of radio broadcast, 15 February 1946, Nassau archives. Of note, a long-time naval adversary accused de Seversky of conservatism. See Fletcher Pratt, "Seversky and the Bomb," *New Republic*, 11 March 1946, 41. At this point, de Seversky did not understand the danger posed by nuclear radiation.

71. APS, "The Only Way to Rearm Europe," *American Mercury*, March 1949, 269.

72. APS, transcripts of radio broadcasts, 17 August 1940, 27 July 1941, 10 August 1941, and 7 February 1942, all in Nassau archives.

73. APS, transcript of radio broadcast, 27 July 1941, Nassau archives; and idem, speech to the Conference Board, New York City, 19 March 1942, Nassau archives.

74. APS, King Features Syndicate article, 12 September 1952, Nassau archives. De Seversky wrote several dozen essays for King Features, most of which were published as newspaper editorials.

75. This philosophy is fully developed in de Seversky's second book, *Air Power, Key to Survival* (New York: Simon & Schuster, 1950). See also idem, "The US Air Force in Power Politics," *Air Affairs,* Winter 1949, 477–90.

76. APS, "Wonder Weapons Can't Win a War," *This Week,* 10 September 1950, 4–8; and idem, "Korea *Proves* Our Need for a Dominant Air Force," *Reader's Digest,* October 1950, 6–10.

77. APS, "Evaluation of the Air Weapon," lecture to Air War College, Maxwell AFB, Ala., 19 November 1953, 4–5, US Air Force Historical Research Agency, Maxwell AFB, Alabama [hereinafter AFHRA], file K239.716253-63.

78. APS, King Features Syndicate article, 16 April 1951, Nassau archives; and idem, "Build an Invincible Air Force Now," *Vital Speeches of the Day,* 1 January 1951, 176.

79. APS, *Air Power, Key to Survival,* 68–79; and idem, "Navies Are Finished," 143. Not surprisingly, de Seversky later strongly opposed American involvement in Vietnam, for much the same reasons. "Dealing with a Major Subject," *New York News,* 20 June 1971, 7–9; and APS, speech to Squadron Officer School, Maxwell AFB, Ala., 18 March 1971, Nassau archives.

80. APS, "Our Current Inferiority Is Not Scientific," *Vital Speeches of the Day,* February 1958, 238–42; and idem, "Our Antiquated Defense Policy," *American Mercury,* April 1949, 389–99.

81. APS, interviewed by Mike Wallace, 20 September 1957; idem, memorandum for record, 15 April 1951; and record of telephone conversation with Gen Elbert Wedemeyer, 11 April 1951, all in Nassau archives. De Seversky's choice for the Republican nomination in 1952 was Robert A. Taft.

82. APS, "Build an Invincible Air Force Now," 175.

83. APS, "New Concepts of Air Power," lecture to Army War College, Carlisle Barracks, Pa., 18 March 1952, 10–16, AFHRA, file K239.716252-63; idem, "Evaluation of the Air Weapon," 11–12; and idem, *Air Power, Key to Survival,* 183–90.

84. For a good discussion of the British Air Control experiences of the 1920s and 1930s, see David E. Omissi, *Air Power and Colonial Control: The Royal Air Force, 1919–1939* (New York: Saint Martin's, 1990). For the best discussion of Project Control, see Maj George R. Gagnon, "Air Control: Strategy for a Smaller Air Force" (master's thesis, School of Advanced Airpower Studies, Maxwell AFB, Ala., 1993).

85. APS, transcript of testimony before Senate Armed Services and Foreign Relations Committees, 21 February 1951, 734, Nassau archives.

86. APS, *America—Too Young to Die* (New York: McGraw-Hill, 1961). This book is a highly polemical piece, as the name suggests, containing few new

ideas. It did, however, call attention to the growing importance of electronic warfare in airpower employment.

87. See, for example, APS, "Artificial Gravity for Spaceships," *Science Digest,* October 1946, 5–8; and idem, "Your Trip to Mars," *Pageant,* August 1952, 5–15.

88. George H. Gallup, *The Gallup Poll: Public Opinion, 1935–1971,* vol. 1 (New York: Random House, 1972), 293, 399.

Chapter 8

Strategic Airpower and Nuclear Strategy: New Theory for a Not-Quite-So-New Apocalypse

*Dr. Karl P. Mueller**

Many of the other chapters in this book plow surprisingly untilled ground. As Phillip Meilinger notes in his introduction to this volume, the amount that has not yet been written (or in the case of Giulio Douhet, simply translated) about strategic- and operational-level airpower is often startling. The subject of nuclear strategy is quite different: its theoretical soil has been cultivated nearly to the point of exhaustion, and in many places it has been virtually paved over by 50 years of intense study.

During its first two decades, nuclear strategic thought reached a plateau of maturity, where it essentially remains today. Although it is not quite the case that nothing new has been said about this subject since Thomas Schelling's *Arms and Influence* and Bernard Brodie's *Escalation and the Nuclear Option* appeared in 1966, subsequent work in the field generally has been limited to offering marginal (though often extremely significant) insights, challenges, and illumination of the work that went before.[1] Both new nuclear technological developments and new nuclear policy debates, some of them important, have engaged scholars and other participants during the last 30 years, but, with few exceptions, these matters represent the reemergence of much older precursors.[2]

The relative stasis of strategic nuclear thought during the last generation has led some people to characterize it as a theoretical dead end, ultimately rendered obsolete by the end of the US-Soviet cold war, if not before. In reality, however, the field reached an early theoretical plateau due to its rapid initial development, along with the intrinsic simplicity of the

*The author thanks Mark Bovankovich, Mark Conversino, Thomas Ehrhard, Charles Glaser, Jonathan Kirshner, John Mueller, Robert Pape, Dan Reiter, and Jeffrey Renehan for their generous advice and comments on this essay.

subject. Although a lifetime of scholarship is insufficient for most students of conventional warfare to master their subject, any reasonably intelligent undergraduate can learn the essentials of nuclear strategy in mere hours of instruction and study—or can become reasonably expert in the subject in a semester. Indeed, 93 minutes spent watching Stanley Kubrick's consummate film *Dr. Strangelove or: How I Learned to Stop Worrying and Love the Bomb* (1964) will teach attentive viewers much of what they need to know in order to understand the principal nuclear debates.[3]

These factors made nuclear strategy an unpromising subject for most writers of dissertations during the second half of the cold war, but they did not make it unimportant. Rather, the theories and insights developed by theorists of the "golden age" of deterrence theory—and subsequently refined by their successors—remain relevant, and one can see their growing influence on (or at least their congruence with) conventional airpower theory today.

Because other writers have already ably documented and recounted the historical development of nuclear weapons[4] and nuclear strategic theory[5] in far more substantial works, this essay does not seek to retell this story. Nor does it attempt to summarize the evolution of US or other nuclear strategies and war plans[6]—the development of which occurred parallel to but often almost completely disconnected from the work of nuclear strategic theorists—or of nuclear arms control.[7] Instead, the following sections offer a brief sketch of the technological aspects of the nuclear revolution, as well as a primer on the enduring principles of nuclear strategic thought, focusing on the similarities and differences between this discipline and the other major strands of airpower theory. Finally, the essay concludes with a discussion of both the contemporary relevance (and irrelevance) of nuclear strategy and its relationship with contemporary theories of nonnuclear airpower.

The Nuclear Revolution

Most technological revolutions happen gradually, resulting not from a single event but from the cumulative effect of a number of related innovations. This was certainly the case with the aviation revolution—and with the nuclear revolution as well. In both instances, technological developments paralleled the development of theories about their implications and application, with theorists sometimes leading the way and sometimes trying to keep pace with advances driven by technological imperatives. However, there probably has never been another revolution quite so dominated by technological forces as this one, or one in which theory and doctrine were so deductively derived from characteristics of the weapons whose use they were intended to guide. Therefore, one may reasonably begin with an overview of the key technological elements that accumulated to form the mature nuclear strategic world that we have known since the late 1960s, before turning to the theories that seek to explain it.

Nuclear Warheads

During the Second World War, the Anglo-American Manhattan Project produced the first atomic bombs—tested in New Mexico and then dropped at Hiroshima and Nagasaki in the summer of 1945. The Soviet Union tested its first atomic bomb in 1949, followed by Great Britain in 1952. This first generation of nuclear weapons derived its revolutionary explosive power from nuclear fission—the splitting of heavy, unstable elements (uranium 235 and plutonium 239) into smaller atoms, releasing vast amounts of energy as blast, light, heat, and other forms of radiation.[8] Early atomic bombs were on the order of one thousand times more powerful than conventional explosive bombs of similar size; fission weapons subsequently became smaller and more efficient, evolving into today's tactical nuclear weapons.[9]

The destruction that a single atomic bomb could wreak on a city or other target was comparable to that inflicted by a massive conventional air raid involving hundreds of heavy bombers. (One should recall that the deadliest bombing raid of the Second World War occurred not at Hiroshima or Nagasaki but Tokyo, on the first night of the US firebombing of that city, 9–10 March 1945.) One may fairly say that with this technology, airpower had finally caught up with Douhet's imagination. A state equipped with heavy bombers carrying

281

atomic bombs could destroy many of its enemy's cities in rapid succession, even in the face of substantial defenses.[10]

The next (and the last, to date) fundamental advance in nuclear explosive technology came in the 1950s, as all three of the nuclear powers developed thermonuclear (or hydrogen) weapons. Using atomic explosives as triggers, hydrogen bombs employ nuclear fusion—the combining of heavy isotopes of hydrogen into heavier helium atoms—to produce explosions one thousand times more powerful than those from similar-sized atomic bombs, or a million times more powerful than conventional explosives. Although a postwar atomic bomb could devastate the center of a medium-sized city, a reasonably large thermonuclear weapon could obliterate a large metropolitan area—even if delivered with considerable inaccuracy. Nuclear attack now threatened major powers not only with massive urban casualties and devastation but also with effective national destruction.[11]

Subsequent developments in nuclear warhead technology have occurred around the margins, as weapons have become smaller with specialized characteristics—such as reduced or enhanced radiation effects or penetration ability.[12] With the arrival of thermonuclear warheads, the locus of nuclear development shifted to the systems used to deliver weapons to their targets.

Delivery Systems

Heavy strategic bombers designed to carry conventional bombs dropped the first nuclear weapons on their targets, and bombers remained the only major nuclear-delivery system for the following decade. Subsequent generations of bombers offered advancements in payload, range, and speed, especially with the arrival of jet engines and aerial refueling. Designers increasingly optimized aircraft to carry nuclear weapons, although most also retained some capability to deliver conventional ordnance. The problem of penetrating enemy air defenses became more difficult with the development and evolution of surface-to-air missiles (SAM), necessitating the development of higher- and faster-flying bombers. In the

1960s, emphasis shifted to penetrating enemy territory at very low altitudes in order to evade detection and interception.

The 1950s saw the development of missiles as nuclear-delivery systems, beginning with short-, medium-, and intermediate-range ballistic missiles (S-, M-, and IRBM), and culminating in intercontinental ballistic missiles (ICBM), capable of striking the United States from bases in the Soviet Union or vice versa. The first public demonstration of an ICBM occurred when the USSR used such a rocket to launch *Sputnik I* into orbit as the first artificial satellite in 1957, producing unprecedented alarm in a United States accustomed both to virtual invulnerability to direct attack and to a comfortable lead on the Soviets in all things technological.

ICBMs and other ballistic missiles differed in several important respects from the bombers they first supplemented and soon began to supplant. They were far faster and able to travel from one superpower's territory to the other's in something on the order of 30 minutes. They could not be intercepted (until antiballistic missiles [ABM] were developed), whereas only some of the bombers would successfully penetrate enemy air defenses. Land-based missiles also proved more economical to maintain than bombers and their crews and proved more suitable to tight centralized control. Both of these characteristics appealed to the Soviet Union, which would end up investing a far higher proportion of its strategic nuclear resources in ICBMs than would the United States. On the other hand, one could not recall missiles after launch,[13] which meant they had to wait at their bases, perhaps vulnerable to attack, until the proper authorities decided to launch them. Further, they were inferior to bombers in payload, accuracy (until the 1980s), and—above all—versatility. Early ballistic missiles also required fueling with highly volatile liquid propellants prior to launching— which required warning time—and they could remain fueled and ready to launch only for a matter of hours before they would have to stand down for a considerable period. But the development of more advanced rocket fuels later removed these limitations.

Similar weapons took to the sea in the form of sea-launched ballistic missiles (SLBM), beginning in the early 1960s.

Generally smaller and shorter ranged than their land-based counterparts, as well as solid-fueled, SLBMs offered the tremendous advantage of being based on platforms difficult or impossible to detect and attack prior to missile launch.[14] Their principal disadvantage was a significant reduction in accuracy compared to ICBMs, which persisted until the United States deployed the Trident D-5 SLBM in the late 1980s.[15] SLBMs were also less easily controlled by central authorities than were land-based systems since their submarines had to be able to operate with a considerable degree of autonomy. This is probably why they played a relatively small role in the Soviet arsenal compared to those of the United States, Britain, and France.

As improvements in radar, missiles, and interceptor aircraft increased the difficulty of slipping through hostile air defenses, another response was to equip bombers with standoff weapons—nuclear-armed missiles that one could fire at a target from some hundreds of miles away. One could use these weapons as the aircraft's primary armament instead of free-fall bombs, to reduce the bomber's exposure to enemy fire, or could fire them at early warning radars and SAM sites in order to suppress the enemy's defenses and make penetration easier.[16]

A new technology with profound strategic implications appeared in the late 1960s with the development of multiple independently targeted reentry vehicles (MIRV). By replacing the single warhead on a missile with a postboost vehicle or "bus" carrying multiple—and now very accurate—warheads (or reentry vehicles [RV]),[17] each of which could strike a different target, a single missile conceivably could destroy a larger number of the enemy's nuclear weapons (providing incentives to strike first in a crisis, as discussed in more detail below) or other dispersed targets. Multiple warheads were also potentially useful for penetrating antimissile defenses since they would increase the number of objects the defender had to intercept. By the late 1970s, more than half of the US ICBM force and all of its SLBMs were MIRVed.

The latest development in strategic nuclear-delivery systems actually to have become operational is stealth technology, which makes aircraft difficult to detect by radar. Although stealth has achieved its greatest prominence by enabling US aircraft to penetrate enemy air defenses in order to launch conventional bombing attacks, Northrop developed the B-2 "Spirit" stealth bomber as a penetrating nuclear bomber to attack targets, including mobile Soviet ICBMs, discussed further below.

In addition to the major strategic systems—bombers, ICBMs, and SLBMs—a variety of other, shorter-range delivery systems were developed for tactical nuclear weapons—smaller warheads intended for use against enemy military forces on or near the battlefield. These included fighters and attack aircraft, short-range missiles and rockets, howitzers and other artillery pieces, atomic demolition munitions, cruise missiles, torpedoes, and depth charges. Cruise missiles eventually became important strategic nuclear weapons, as their ranges and accuracies increased and their ability to fly low-altitude, terrain-following flight paths reduced their vulnerability to interception to a very low order. Strategic nuclear cruise missiles were deployed on ground launchers, aircraft, surface ships, and submarines. Most tactical nuclear-delivery systems were dual-capable—that is, suitable for carrying either conventional or nuclear warheads.

Still other nuclear-delivery systems have been planned or developed without being deployed.[18] Most notably, the Outer Space Treaty of 1967 outlawed the placement of nuclear weapons in orbit (or on the Moon), and an international agreement in 1971 proscribed the placement of nuclear weapons on the oceanic floor. Space-based weapons were especially threatening because they could attack with little warning; similar concerns led to a ban on testing SLBMs in depressed-trajectory mode, in which a submarine fires the missile at a shallower angle than normal in order to shorten the length of its flight and minimize the defender's warning. The most recent nuclear-delivery system not quite to appear was the so-called supergun, under construction in Iraq prior to the Gulf War.[19]

Basing

The evolution of nuclear warheads and their delivery systems has principally focused on features familiar in almost all airpower theory—firepower, accuracy, speed, range, penetration ability, and flexibility. An additional area of concern (to nuclear strategists, perhaps the most important one of all) relates to the basing mode of nuclear weapons, especially as this affects their survivability in the event of an enemy first strike.

Protecting bombers from preemptive attack remained a relatively straightforward problem, particularly before the development of nuclear-armed missiles. When air bases were vulnerable only to attack by manned aircraft, one could develop and maintain sufficient early warning capabilities and alert levels to enable the bombers to take off before the enemy could destroy them on the ground. Another obvious response, but one the United States did not quickly adopt, was the basing of bombers far from the enemy's bases in order to maximize warning times in the event of an enemy attack.

Perhaps the greatest direct impact that civilian strategists ever had on American nuclear policy came in the 1950s, when Albert Wohlstetter and others at RAND explained to the Air Force that the US bomber force could be vulnerable to a surprise nuclear attack at its forward bases around the Soviet periphery.[20] The appearance of ballistic missiles complicated this problem considerably, further encouraging the dispersal of bomber forces to secondary airfields in the event of a crisis and the maintenance of some US bombers on constant airborne alert. The deployment of SLBMs, with their shorter flight times, made the problem worse, but one could still reasonably expect successful launch of at least a portion of an alert bomber force before its bases came under attack. Advances in surveillance satellites' ability to detect enemy missile launches reinforced this expectation.

The problem of ICBM survivability proved more challenging, since the missiles had to stay on the ground until authorities made a final decision to launch. One could not launch early ICBMs on short notice, due to the need to fuel them, and an enemy could easily destroy their above-ground launch sites. During the 1960s, the advent of storable liquid (later solid) rocket propellants, the deployment of ICBMs in hardened underground silos, and the development of SLBMs carried by nuclear-powered submarines addressed these problems.[21] Because one could reliably destroy hardened silos—relatively resistant to blast effects—only by the explosion of a warhead in close proximity, an enemy would have to attack each silo separately and would need to use only fairly accurate weapons against them. Thus, SLBMs would not prove useful for attacking ICBMs. Further, if two states had similar numbers of single-warhead ICBMs (assuming they were less than 100 percent effective) and if one attacked the other's missiles, the attacker's entire arsenal would not destroy all of the defender's ICBMs, leaving the attacker disarmed and the defender able to retaliate with its surviving weapons. SLBMs, effectively immune from preemptive attack except when their submarines were in port, reinforced this pattern.[22]

ICBM survivability came under much greater threat as ICBM accuracies increased and as MIRVs appeared. Consequently, these technologies quickly became the bêtes noires of arms control advocates (along with ballistic missile defenses, discussed below). If each side in a confrontation possessed one thousand ICBMs with four warheads apiece, half of either force could attack each of the enemy's ICBMs with two warheads and possibly eliminate his force in a first strike.[23] The chance that land-based missile forces might be vulnerable to preemptive attack led to a variety of responses, the primary one being deployment of missiles on mobile launchers instead of in fixed silos in order to keep an enemy from knowing the locations of the missiles. Although the United States canceled its plans for mobile ICBMs with the demise of the cold war, the Soviet Union deployed two mobile ICBM systems—one carried on railroads and the other road-mobile. In response, the United States planned to use the B-2 stealth bomber to hunt and attack these weapons. A variety of other basing schemes also addressed the ICBM vulnerability problem, especially during repeated deliberations about how to deploy the American MX (Peacekeeper) missile in the 1970s and 1980s.[24]

However, the presence of a variety of types of strategic nuclear weapons systems complicated the problem of launching a disarming first strike. Much as the rock-scissors-paper interactions of infantry, cavalry, and artillery dominated Napoleonic land warfare, the triad of bombers, ICBMs, and SLBMs proved quite robust during most of the cold war. Once the target state detected a first-strike

ICBM launch, it would have perhaps 25 minutes to launch a large number of alert bombers. On the other hand, if the attack began with a rapid SLBM strike to catch the bombers on the ground, the target might have time to launch its intact ICBM force in retaliation before the enemy could attack it. And no matter how one planned an attack, it could not destroy the enemy's patrolling missile submarines, which would therefore provide a robust second-strike capability against area targets such as cities.[25]

Strategic Defenses

All of these calculations assumed that, as Douhet and Stanley Baldwin had once predicted about conventional airpower, the bombers (and the missiles) would always get through—or at least that enough of them would to inflict catastrophic losses on the target nation. One had considerable incentive to intercept attacking missiles and aircraft—a familiar problem during the bomber age. As had happened before, the capabilities of fighter aircraft to intercept bombers and of bombers to avoid interception raced against each other as speeds, ceilings, rates of climb, ranges, firepower, and sensor capabilities improved. SAMs, first developed by Germany at the end of the Second World War, joined the combination of early warning radars, interceptors, and antiaircraft artillery (AAA). The United States deployed SAMs, air-to-air missiles, and rockets armed with small nuclear warheads to increase the effectiveness of its air defenses. The improving capabilities of air defense systems prompted rapid developments in electronic warfare and standoff weapons, a shift to low-level flight profiles to take advantage of difficulties that ground clutter imposed on radar detection, and research into stealth technologies to reduce the visibility of aircraft to radar and other sensors. Although never easy for the bomber, getting through modern air defenses was not impossible—and nuclear weapons meant that one could not disregard even a low percentage of successful penetrations.

Ballistic missiles presented an even more difficult defensive problem. In order for a SAM to be an effective ABM, it needed to be able to shoot down an extremely small, sturdy projectile reentering the atmosphere at perhaps 20 times the speed of sound, with relatively little time to detect and track the target. During the 1960s, the United States developed several such systems to the testing stage, involving large exoatmospheric interceptor missiles with thermonuclear warheads as a first line of defense, backed up by shorter-range missiles with small nuclear warheads to attack RVs that had penetrated the first layer.[26]

The arms race between ballistic missiles and ABMs had several highly unattractive features. First, as one side developed its ABM system, the other could simply increase the number of warheads it could launch in order to ensure that some of them would penetrate the defenses. This meant that one state could render itself immune to a nuclear first strike only if the other allowed it to do so (or ran out of money). However, a less-than-perfect ABM system might allow the owning state to launch a successful first strike, since defenses capable of stopping only part of the enemy's total nuclear arsenal might prove quite effective against the weaker retaliatory strike of a state just subjected to massive nuclear attack. Therefore, ABM opponents argued, investing in extremely expensive defenses made sense only for an aggressive nation—to protect second-strike countervalue forces otherwise vulnerable to preemptive attack or to limit damage from a strike by a minor nuclear power undeterred by retaliatory threats.[27] The combination of high prospective costs and limited strategic benefits led the United States and the Soviet Union to sign a treaty as part of the Strategic Arms Limitation Treaty (SALT) I agreement in 1972, effectively banning ABMs.[28] With the country vulnerable to nuclear missile attack, US investment in defenses against bombers became of limited value and gradually tapered off.

From the earliest days of the nuclear era, the desire to limit damage in the event of an enemy nuclear attack also led to civil defense efforts to protect populations and industry. In the United States, civil defense lost some of its viability and most of its popularity once the Soviet Union had achieved the ability to deliver large numbers of thermonuclear weapons against the United States. Soviet enthusiasm for civil defense persisted to a greater extent, and the United States often interpreted it as a sign of willingness to fight a nuclear war. Eventually, however, it became clear that Soviet civil defense preparedness was considerably lower in reality than in rhetoric.[29]

Ballistic missile defense (BMD) returned to prominence in the 1980s after President Ronald Reagan's announcement in 1983 of a Strategic Defense Initiative (SDI) program to build a space-based ABM system, which quickly became known as "Star Wars" to almost all but its most intense advocates.[30] Although SDI involved research into a new generation of sensors and weapons—particularly a wide range of lasers and other directed-energy weapons—the strategic and budgetary debates surrounding it were virtually indistinguishable from those about ABMs 20 years earlier. Again, the prospects for developing the complete missile shield that Reagan envisioned (generally referred to as the "astrodome" concept) appeared weak, even within the SDI organization; a variety of less comprehensive defenses remained attractive to many people but drew criticism as being unreasonably expensive, technologically infeasible, or of limited value except as a supplement to a US first strike against the USSR. The apparent decline of Soviet hostility in the late 1980s (attributed in part to Moscow's recognition that it could not afford to engage in expensive BMD and other arms races with the United States) resulted in reduced spending on SDI, but the program continued, shifting its emphasis to theater BMD against shorter-range missiles launched by regional powers such as Iraq.

Principles of Strategic Nuclear Theory

Many of the rudiments of nuclear theory have already appeared in the preceding sections, for they are inextricably tied to—and largely derived from—the infrastructure of nuclear technology. Although nuclear strategic theory may be the single most deductive body of thought in the social sciences, its development proved something less—but perhaps not far less—than a logical inevitability.

Again, one should consider the parallels between analyses of strategic airpower during the interwar years and strategic nuclear airpower after the Second World War. In both cases, theorists based their works on relatively limited empirical evidence. Douhet and his counterparts could look back at the limited applications of airpower during the Great War and extrapolate what the next war might look like. They could refer to the ways in which states and populations reacted to the privations inflicted upon them by bombing and blockade during the war, and to the ways in which armies responded to bombardment and exsanguination on the front lines. Similarly, nuclear theorists could examine the physical, psychological, and political evidence provided by atomic and conventional strategic bombing during the Second World War and seek to integrate this and other historical knowledge with more recent technological developments.[31] In both cases, the next war looked like something one should assiduously avoid, although anticipating its details involved considerable—if educated—speculation. According to Harold Macmillan, "We thought of air warfare in 1938 rather as people think of nuclear warfare today."[32]

Important differences existed between the two cases, however. First, for all the postwar theorists' hypothesizing about the future, in general they did not face great uncertainties about the physical effects of the weapons under discussion (though some of the nuclear scientists who developed the atomic bomb deduced many of the essentials of postwar nuclear deterrence theory before the advent of any real information regarding actual weapons effects).[33] Second, a far smaller number of theorists, few of them with academic training, dominated airpower thought during the interwar period. Most of them were serving military officers with operational rather than strategic experience, facing many nonintellectual challenges, including the preservation or advancement of their beleaguered service arms. The closest interwar equivalent to the community of (mostly American) postwar nuclear theorists was the US Air Corps Tactical School (ACTS) of the late 1930s. A comparison of the two is striking.

Despite the intellectual fertility of ACTS, the theories it generated were dominated by the work of a gifted few who had to be concerned not only with predicting the future but also with ensuring that independent strategic airpower would have a prominent role in it. On the other hand, strategic nuclear airpower was the subject of intense study by a large community, including many highly trained and intelligent people who could focus the bulk of their energies on the subject. Finally, one should note that after 1945 the US military almost completely abdicated its traditional responsibility for strategic airpower thought, passing it to the civilian experts they employed and whose guidance they occasionally followed. Strategic Air Command (SAC) planners remained occupied with compiling theoretical target lists and operational-level war plans and continued in general to approach strategic airpower much as their wartime predecessors had during the Combined Bomber Offensive.[34]

This is not to hold up RAND as the intellectual heir of Plato's academy; indeed, it inherited the legacy of Douhet and Alexander de Seversky. However, the nuclear theorists enjoyed the advantage of being, if not powerful themselves, at least consultants to the makers of military policy rather than prophets in the wilderness. They did not have to persuade their audience that nuclear strategy or nuclear weapons were important or cost-effective. Perhaps more significantly, for the most part their policy-making audience accepted their status as strategic experts, although this did not mean that their opinions necessarily carried weight. In fact, the opposite was more often true: the evolution of US nuclear strategy and weapons development would have differed radically at a number of points if nuclear strategists had been more influential and military and political leaders less so. But it did make their enterprise one of Big Science—in some ways not unlike the Manhattan Project itself.

In spite of the similarities between Douhet's vision of the nature of the next war and that of the nuclear strategists, they developed very different theories. Douhet's postwar intellectual successors did not share his belief in the inevitability of another great (total) war. Douhet did not envision mutual assured destruction (MAD), although he could have done so. Instead, he argued that strategic bombing would make wars inexpensive by ending them quickly and efficiently, providing an escape from the prolonged carnage of another Great War. If the next war were going to be cheap, states had little reason not to fight it. The nuclear theorists, having seen in the Second World War (like the Great War) that one cannot easily terrorize modern nations into surrendering, could not pretend that another total war would be less than horrific. They recognized that states fearing catastrophe would try to avoid it.

The body of theory that emerged from their efforts emphasizes a relatively small number of central concepts, most of which are relevant to—and many of which are borrowed from—arenas of the military and other social sciences not directly connected to nuclear strategy.

Deterrence

The most fundamental concept in nuclear strategy is *deterrence*, the idea that states will not attack each other when the expected costs and benefits of attacking appear less attractive than the expected value of not attacking. Thus, by shifting the balance in favor of the latter option, one can avert war.[35] Strategic airpower seemed to add to this calculus the ability to make war unpleasant for a prospective attacker by means independent of fighting the foe on the battlefield; nuclear weapons radically increased the amount of such damage one could inflict in a relatively short time.[36] Because of their ability to punish a state massively for launching an attack, successful or not, atomic—especially thermonuclear—weapons permitted their owners to adopt security strategies based on deterrence rather than defense.

The distinction between deterrence and defense is important and widely misunderstood.[37] On the one hand, deterrence has to do with changing the enemy's beliefs about how good or bad war will be, relative to the alternatives. A punitive threat of nuclear retaliation may deter, and so may a threat to defeat an invader's army, making war look unappealing by making defeat appear likely.[38] The latter approach to deterrence is commonly known as *deterrence by denial*, although some theorists prefer to reserve the "deterrence" label for punishment alone.[39] By the same token, one could well speak of deterring through rewards or other positive incentives—by increasing the attractiveness of not attacking rather than (or in addition to) making attacking look worse.[40]

Defense, on the other hand, has to do with making war less unpleasant for oneself. Of course, many policies contribute to both defense and deterrence, especially deterrence by denial. Building up conventional military strength, for example, largely accounts for policy makers' tendency to conflate the two concepts. However, some defensive measures, such as secret defenses unknown to the enemy, may not deter. More importantly, some measures that contribute to deterrence by making war bad for the enemy provide little in the way of defense; of these, threats of nuclear retaliation against an attacker's homeland are probably the most conspicuous.

In fact, security policies based on deterrence rather than defense existed before the nuclear age.[41] Although the nuclear revolution increased states' abilities to inflict injury upon an enemy without first winning a war, conventionally armed airpower had already made this possible to a limited degree. Many interwar airpower theorists and advocates believed that nonnuclear strategic bombing offered the opportunity to inflict truly decisive levels of punishment upon an enemy, regardless of how things transpired on the front lines. (Of course, many of their estimates of the destructive power of conventional bombing were incorrect, but because deterrence takes place in the mind of the adversary, such facts matter only when they have an impact on beliefs.) Moreover, the same was often true even before the earliest rumblings of the airpower revolution, most obviously through naval blockades against trade-dependent states.

Nuclear weapons and associated technologies brought to the table the ability to inflict catastrophic damage against an enemy, rapidly and relatively inexpensively. In one of Thomas Schelling's typically vivid expressions, they vastly increased their owners' power to hurt.[42] Because nuclear weapons systems generally didn't have to fight the enemy's nuclear weapons, the balance of nuclear forces was irrelevant; the relationship between weapons and targets determined the ability to punish, and thus to deter—and one did not need many nuclear weapons to destroy even a large target. Similarly, if each side could inflict unacceptable levels of damage on the other, it did not matter which one could cause the greater amount. Thus, a powerful state could develop more nuclear striking power than it had any use for. Although sound strategic reasons existed for the superpowers to build what critics derided as overkill capability during the cold war, both the United States and the Soviet Union could have built much larger nuclear arsenals than they actually chose to do.[43]

Assured Destruction and Mutual Assured Destruction

If deterrence is the foundation of most strategic nuclear theory, the conceptual cornerstone of the edifice is *assured destruction*—the ability of a state to destroy its enemy with a retaliatory nuclear strike even after it is attacked. A state capable of assured destruction ought never worry about attack from a state without such capability, since by choosing war, the latter would commit national suicide. Two states having such a capability exist in a relationship of *mutual assured destruction* and never should attack each other. The United States had developed an assured destruction capability against the Soviet Union by the mid-1950s, if not before. Nuclear experts often believed that the Soviets did not attain this capability towards the United States until they deployed substantial numbers of ICBMs in the mid-1960s. As Richard Betts notes, however, Washington had begun acting as if the Soviet bomber force had produced a state of MAD a decade earlier.[44]

Beneath the elementary simplicity of this concept lies a host of debates about precisely what constitutes assured destruction, but the essentials are straightforward. Having assured destruction capability requires maintaining a nuclear force that can ride out a hostile first strike and still retaliate against the enemy, inflicting so much damage that the fear of such retaliation deters the enemy from ever launching the first strike. Targets for such a retaliation ought to be whatever the enemy values—and the enemy should know this or suspect it. Such *countervalue* targets typically include cities, and discussions of the amounts of expected damage required to assure deterrence usually refer to civilian deaths and the destruction of industrial capacity. If the enemy valued something else, such as conventional military forces or the lives of its leaders, one could target these instead.[45] Most such targets (with the exception of leaders in effective shelters) are relatively easy to attack and do not require a high degree of accuracy or speed in nuclear-delivery systems—unlike targets such as hardened missile silos and underground command bunkers. Attacking the latter requires more accurate warhead delivery and usually involves greater urgency if the goal is to destroy a silo before missile launch; thus, accurate ICBMs, which possess these characteristics, have *counterforce* capability.

The survivability of second-strike nuclear forces is critical, since a nuclear state vulnerable to destruction by an enemy first strike not only lacks assured destruction capability but actually creates incentives for the enemy to strike first, in the event of a crisis likely to escalate to nuclear war. As a result of all of these factors, SLBMs are generally considered ideal second-strike countervalue weapons, since they are nearly invulnerable while on station and their limitations with respect to accuracy and command and control (C^2) do not create serious obstacles to performing this mission. However, even more vulnerable land-based systems can pose effective threats of assured destruction, since a first strike would have to destroy a very high percentage of a large force in order to reduce its retaliatory potential to a level that would not be tremendously destructive. Since even a massive countervalue strike against a superpower would require only a relatively small number of thermonuclear weapons, many believers in the deterrent efficacy of MAD argued that the superpowers' cold war nuclear arsenals were much larger than necessary.

Fears about the vulnerability of land-based nuclear weapons to an enemy first strike have prompted a number of major changes in nuclear force postures. On the American side, fears of a first strike by the strategic rocket forces of the Soviet Union encouraged a shift away from forward-based medium bombers and the ultimately abortive search for a survivable basing mode for the MX ICBM. As for the Soviets, cumulative threats posed by the highly accurate MX, the counterforce-capable Trident D-5 SLBM, and other new and accurate US weapons such as the air launched cruise missile (ALCM) spurred the Soviet adoption of mobile ICBMs in the 1980s. Improvements in missile accuracy did not threaten either country's strategic submarine forces, but the prospect of relying on only one leg of the triad appealed to neither side, and (as discussed below) the Soviets had reason to worry about the security of their fleet ballistic missile submarines (SSBN) as well. Concerns about vulnerability also prompted development of options to launch under attack (LUA) instead of riding out an enemy first strike.[46]

Assured destruction capability also requires that a state's nuclear command, control, and communications (C^3) capabilities have a reasonable chance of surviving an enemy first strike in order to avoid strategic decapitation.[47] This became the subject of extensive study by nuclear scholars during the 1980s, when concerns about the robustness of US nuclear C^2 arrangements led to a major increase in investment in this area. Such programs would replace aging airborne command-post aircraft and would harden communications systems against the effects of electromagnetic pulse (EMP).[48]

Although assured destruction and MAD underpinned American declaratory nuclear strategy, at least from the early 1960s, lesser nuclear powers such as France have based theirs on a variation on the same theme. When Sweden considered developing nuclear weapons, the Swedish military aptly described this principle as "marginal cost deterrence": the strategy of threatening to retaliate against an invader with enough force not necessarily to destroy it but to significantly negate any benefits the invader might anticipate from conquering the small nuclear power.[49] At heart, this is similar to a superpower's assured destruction threat, except that the prospective attacker's national survival may not be at stake; for the United States and the Soviet Union as well as lesser nuclear powers, nuclear deterrence simply amounted to making war look much less attractive than the alternative.[50]

This model of the adversary as a rational actor that one can rely upon not to launch a self-destructive war is central to MAD, but it is often misunderstood. For assured destruction to work as advertised, the deterred state need not *be* a rational, unitary actor (for no state actually is)— only that it behave approximately *as if* it were rational.[51] The approximation of rationality is significant. MAD has room for states to suffer from substantial misperceptions; to make poor decisions; and to be driven by domestic political, bureaucratic, and other factors beyond those of idealized international statecraft. As long as one can rely upon the state not to destroy itself deliberately, assured destruction should prevent the failure of deterrence;[52] one might say that deterrence theory assumes that states are characterized by no worse than *bounded irrationality*. The elegance of MAD lies in its total lack of subtlety.

For all its paradigmatic status, few concepts in international relations have produced as much debate as has mutual assured destruction. MAD enthusiasts, if one may call them such, emphasize the stability of such a relationship and tend to praise it with the same superficially lukewarm intensity with which Winston Churchill lauded democracy as the worst system of its sort yet devised—except for all the alternatives. Critics of MAD have attacked it on many grounds.[53] Some offer arguments about its strategic logic and assumptions, addressed below. Others base their opposition on moral objections to the targeting of civilian populations[54]—or on the grounds that dangers posed by the existence of nuclear weapons remain intolerably high, making their abolition imperative.[55]

The basic argument about whether MAD acts as a stabilizing force in international affairs also lies at the heart of the central debate regarding nuclear proliferation—the development or acquisition of nuclear weapons by previously nonnuclear states. The conventional wisdom about proliferation traditionally was, and to a considerable extent still is, that the spread of nuclear weapons is destabilizing because (1) new nuclear states are likely to be less responsible than their predecessors and (2) arsenals of so-called threshold nuclear states tend to be vulnerable to preemption—and therefore will encourage it.[56] However, a number of strategic theorists have argued that if MAD stabilizes superpower relations, one should expect it to do the same for regional rivalries among smaller powers. This school of thought rejects as ethnocentric the argument that Third World states will be more reckless in their handling of nuclear weapons than Western states have been, and proposes that the nuclear powers ought to help threshold nuclear states pass through the transition period to survivable second-strike capability as smoothly as possible.[57]

Credibility

The preceding discussion of assured destruction focused on issues of capability, but almost as important to nuclear deterrence is the credibility of threats. Actually carrying out a threat to use nuclear weapons would inevitably involve significant costs for the state concerned,[58] and these might well exceed the benefits, if any, expected from previous promises. Of course, although one need not automatically believe an adversary's threat, even a dubiously credible threat of annihilation may concentrate the mind and carry deterrent weight. Credibility is an especially significant and potentially problematic issue in two types of scenarios. One involves *extended deterrence*—threats to retaliate in response to an attack against a third party or other peripheral interest.[59] The other involves situations in which an enemy launches a limited attack, presenting the victim with a choice between backing down and avoiding additional destruction or responding to the attack and risking escalation to an all-out nuclear exchange, which would prove catastrophic for both sides.[60]

Making the response automatic would solve credibility problems posed by the possibility of a leader's unwillingness in the breach to launch a threatened retaliatory strike. This possibility found its apotheosis in Herman Kahn's hypothetical invention of the "doomsday machine," an automated system that would trigger nuclear retaliation in the event of attack without (or in spite of) human involvement— later immortalized in *Dr. Strangelove*.[61] The United States never opted to remove the human element from its deterrent threats, although some evidence exists that the Soviets did adopt a system to launch some of their missiles autonomously if the national leadership were incapacitated by an attack.[62] However, the "dead hand" was also at work in the West. For example, the fact that SSBN crews might choose to launch their weapons on their own initiative if their leaders and country were destroyed served to bolster the American threat of assured destruction against the possibility of decapitation.[63] An additional variation on the doomsday machine theme appeared in the 1980s, when scientists discovered that a massive nuclear strike might produce substantial global climatic change, raising the possibility that even a fully successful first strike could significantly injure the country that launched it.[64]

An opposite approach to the credibility problem entailed providing leaders with limited nuclear options (LNO) that might prove relatively credible, whereas an all-out attack would not. Much attention focused on LNOs in the United States during the early 1970s, but they always existed to some extent, even in the purest moments of the doctrine of massive retaliation of the late 1950s.[65] Although its opponents often accused MAD of presenting leaders with a choice between surrender and suicide in the event of limited attack, this never amounted to a fair accusation, since most of the people who lauded MAD believed in the possibility of limited countervalue attacks, at least for demonstration purposes.[66]

However, counterforce LNO enthusiasts parted company from MAD theorists in their beliefs about the controllability of nuclear war. The former tended to envision a relatively prolonged process of brinkmanship and escalation in which one could recognize limited counterforce strikes as such; the latter did not think that escalation would automatically occur, but they had little confidence that the fog of nuclear war would permit such subtle bargaining. MAD enthusiasts also refused to be alarmed by the problem of limited threat credibility, emphasizing that even a small possibility of catastrophe is very frightening.

This debate reached its zenith with arguments for and against the need for *escalation dominance*—a concept promoted by theorists who offered an alternative approach to nuclear strategy commonly referred to as nuclear war fighting.[67] War fighters who supported a "countervailing" strategy conceived of a ladder of escalation ranging from limited and major conventional war up through levels of nuclear conflict with progressively fewer limitations, before arriving at full-blown countervalue apocalypse. They argued for the necessity of maintaining escalation dominance—the ability to fight and win on whatever rung of the ladder the enemy chose—to avoid having to choose between losing, surrendering, or escalating to a more extreme level of violence. In short, if the enemy could find—or invent—a rung on the ladder from which it could prevail, it would have an incentive to strike.

Skeptics of the countervailing approach rejected the premise that such a ladder existed for several reasons. First, they maintained that limitations of sensors and intelligence prevented one from distinguishing among subtly different levels of nuclear warfare.[68] Second, they argued that even if one could make such distinctions, the scheme would work only if both sides conceived of the escalatory steps in the same way. Since one might define levels of violence by the weapons used, the types or numbers of targets attacked, the location of the targets or of the launchers, the scale of civilian damage, or other criteria (evidence indicates that Soviet and American doctrine did indeed differ in these matters), they suggested that the war fighters were trying to impose a degree of precision upon nuclear warfare that it intrinsically lacked. Third, as discussed below, they warned that war-fighting doctrines and the weapons systems associated with them would create instability and encourage preemptive attacks. Finally, they insisted that MAD had no serious credibility problems in the first place.[69]

The war-fighting school challenged other premises and arguments of the MAD theorists in addition to their views on escalation and the potential controllability of nuclear war. One of these was their attitude towards nuclear superiority. The logic of MAD implied that a state could achieve a meaningful degree of nuclear superiority only if it gained the ability to genuinely disarm the enemy by launching a first strike. Short of this, having a larger or more sophisticated nuclear arsenal than a rival didn't matter, since the enemy retained its assured destruction capability. Some war fighters responded that while such might be the case in the corridors of RAND or even the Pentagon, the appearance of nuclear inferiority—the appearance of national weakness—was significant and potentially costly in the international political arena.[70]

Another war-fighting response to this question was that smaller increments of nuclear superiority might indeed matter to deterrence, since an enemy who did not believe in MAD (especially one obsessed with correlations of forces) could well consider them significant. War fighters based this suggestion in large part on a conception of the Soviet Union as a state

301

less like the United States than MAD theorists believed it to be. As the title of one such article described it, the Soviets might think they could fight and win a nuclear war, with their leaders bunkered out of harm's way and remembering that the USSR had got along reasonably well in spite of the killing of tens of millions of its citizens by Joseph Stalin and then by the Great Patriotic War.[71] More generally, states might well behave in ways that American nuclear theorists would consider irrational, so one needed to make potential enemies realize not only that they would suffer if they started a war, but also that they would lose. In short, since punitive deterrence might not suffice, one might require deterrence by denial.

The response to this argument essentially amounted to a reiteration of the fundamentals of MAD. As Robert Jervis, the standard bearer of opposition to the nuclear war fighters in the 1980s, put it, "MAD Is a Fact, Not a Policy."[72] Whatever the differences among states' nuclear doctrines and worldviews, the basic logic of MAD is an inevitable consequence of the effects of nuclear weapons and states' pursuit of national survival. A state would have to behave with an unprecedented degree of irrationality in order to deliberately run a considerable risk of its own annihilation. Moreover, Jervis notes that irrationality may be more likely to reduce a state's willingness to take risks than it is to increase it.[73]

The various arguments of the war-fighting school were mutually supporting but not entirely interdependent. One could accept some and reject others. Their most significant interconnection lay in the policy prescriptions that followed from them: all implied that the United States ought to invest heavily in the development of tools required for nuclear war fighting. These included, among other things, highly robust C^2 systems and weapons optimized for counterforce attacks against hard targets. Perhaps most important of all, nuclear war fighting called for strategic defenses—the bête noir of MAD enthusiasts.

Nuclear Offense, Defense, and Stability

Long before the nuclear revolution, theorists and statesmen concerned themselves with the stability implications of different types of weapons.[74] In arms control efforts both before and after the First World War, negotiators sought to reduce the chances of war by banning or restricting the possession of offensive weapons without preventing states from defending themselves against aggression. People widely accepted the basic premise that offensive weapons facilitate aggression while defensive ones deter it; unfortunately, differentiating between the two categories proved extremely difficult. Even heavy artillery and long-range bombers might have defensive utility, while one might use even the most purely defensive weapons—such as fixed fortifications—for offensive purposes.

In a strategic relationship dominated by assured destruction, the difference between stabilizing and destabilizing weapons depends not on whether they are better for seizing or defending territory, but on whether they are better for starting and winning (or limiting damage in) a war or for retaliating against an attacker. Thus, accurate, MIRVed ICBMs—ideal for destroying the enemy's nuclear weapons—are relatively destabilizing because of their value in a first strike and their comparative vulnerability. On the other hand, less accurate SLBMs optimized for killing civilians are stabilizing, since their invulnerability makes them useful in a second strike, while their lack of counterforce capability prevents them from contributing much to an attempt to disarm the enemy.[75] At the risk of oversimplifying the situation, one might say that being able to kill weapons is bad, while being able to kill people is good. States whose populations are held hostage by the adversary will have to be nonaggressive. US-Soviet arms control talks particularly emphasized restricting the numbers of MIRVed ICBMs, although progress was slow until the late 1980s.[76]

This produces some counterintuitive results with respect to strategic defenses. Since the vulnerability of weapons is destabilizing, measures that increase their survivability—such as mobility, hardening, and point-defense ABMs—contribute to deterrence and to strategic stability. On the other hand, measures such as civil defense preparations and area-defense ABMs, which reduce the vulnerability of cities and other countervalue targets, are destabilizing because they threaten the adversary's second-strike assured destruction capability. For the latter reason, among others, ABMs were an early target of nuclear arms control efforts and were one of the first categories of strategic weapons virtually banned by agreement between the superpowers.[77]

Sometimes explanations of the relationship between offense and defense in the nuclear world state that nuclear weapons reverse the traditional order of things—that defenses become offensive. This statement is partially correct: strategic defenses do facilitate a nuclear first strike if they reduce—or if the enemy believes they reduce—his assured destruction capability. This is especially true of imperfect defenses that would be more useful for intercepting a retaliatory attack by a crippled foe than for stopping a coordinated first strike. However, one cannot say that BMD, air defenses, and civil defense are not defensive; by limiting expected damage in the event of war, they do provide defense. Rather, they tend to be antideterrent by encouraging an enemy to attack preventively before one can deploy or improve them—or preemptively before the state which possesses them can strike first and use them as a shield against retaliation. On a more general level, strategic defenses have the potential to weaken deterrence by making war less costly and therefore more attractive.

MAD enthusiasts see strategic defenses as extremely dangerous, but war fighters find them very appealing, in part because they could contribute to escalation dominance, although they might still encourage preemptive or preventive attacks. They also might persuade an enemy who fears defeat rather than punishment that he would lose a war on the top rung of the escalation ladder—a full-scale countervalue nuclear exchange. More fundamentally, however, war fighters tend to see damage limitation as important because their analysis of MAD indicates that nuclear war is a significant possibility. In contrast, MAD enthusiasts generally consider deterrence failure under MAD quite unlikely unless one follows extremely bad policies. Consequently, they see the stability benefits to be derived from eschewing defenses as far more valuable than a damage limitation capability that one should never need.

In considering stability, one must distinguish between the capability to launch an effective first strike and the existence of incentives to strike first. The former is very difficult to achieve against an uncooperative state with substantial resources.

However, circumstances exist under which a state might launch a preemptive or preventive attack even if it anticipated that doing so would result in severe nuclear retaliation. If nuclear war (or a comparable cataclysm, such as conquest) appeared inevitable—especially if it also appeared imminent—states would have great incentives to attack first if doing so would significantly reduce the amount of damage they would eventually suffer (or perhaps dramatically increase the damage they could inflict without increasing their own losses). In terms of deterrence theory, when the value of not starting a war begins to look extremely bad, war becomes relatively attractive; stability becomes endangered when states have reason to expect the status quo to lead to catastrophe. It becomes especially endangered when a state perceives a *window of opportunity*—a temporary chance to avert or mitigate the disaster.

In nuclear strategy, one can expect windows of opportunity for preventive war when an adversary state appears likely to acquire and use nuclear weapons in the near future—or to acquire a first-strike capability that it does not yet possess.[78] Similarly, a state might perceive such a window if its second-strike capability were threatened by an adversary's anticipated development of strategic defenses, and if it expected the adversary would then attack or otherwise exploit this escape from MAD. In the early 1980s, Barry Posen brought to light a particularly noteworthy preemption scenario by observing that the Reagan administration's new maritime strategy for offensive naval operations in the Barents Sea during a conventional war in Europe would gradually destroy much of the Soviet SLBM force, endangering Moscow's second-strike capability. At the same time, one could expect a conventional air war in Europe to incapacitate Soviet early warning radar capability in the region, giving the Soviet Union reason to fear being decapitated or disarmed by a surprise Western nuclear first strike.[79]

The Enduring Importance of
Strategic Nuclear Airpower Theory

In the post-cold-war era, nuclear theory remains important to strategic airpower, as well as to other aspects of international politics, in spite of the views of skeptics who see the subject as an obsolescent and distasteful relic of the past. Nuclear war is not likely today, but neither was it likely during the cold war, notwithstanding the shaking hands of the "doomsday clock" on the cover of *The Bulletin of the Atomic Scientists*. Today, nuclear strategy and the theories it spawned and inspired remain significant on several different levels.

First and most obviously, neither nuclear weapons nor mutual assured destruction has disappeared, and they are unlikely to do so anytime soon. Dramatic reductions in the nuclear arsenals of the superpowers are under way, as the result of both negotiated agreements and unilateral decisions, guided by the theories of deterrence and stability outlined above. US and Russian weapons are no longer aimed at their cold war targets, garnering widespread acclaim in spite of the strategic (if not political) superficiality of this measure. Yet, nuclear weapons continue to lurk in the background as the ultimate guarantors of American and Russian security, as well as British, French, Chinese, Israeli, Indian, and Pakistani security. For each of these states, essentially the same nuclear issues matter—survivability, first- and second-strike capabilities, and potential adversaries' expectations about the values of war and peace.[80] Nuclear weapons continue to figure into extended deterrence as well, most visibly in the 1990s during the Gulf War, when Britain and the United States as well as Israel made veiled and unveiled threats to Iraq of nuclear retaliation against chemical weapons attacks.

The spread of nuclear weapons continues to proceed very gradually, incessantly defying the expectations of proliferation alarmists. Prospective nuclear powers, like their predecessors, have weighed the costs and benefits of joining the nuclear club, and only a few see profit in it.[81] Even the far less expensive spread of biological and chemical weapons has been slower than many people have expected, but sound reasons remain for serious concern about this less celebrated threat.[82] In deciding how to deal with each of these developments, scholars and statesmen again turn for guidance to deterrence and other theory originally developed for the nuclear world but relevant to other weapons of mass destruction (or individual or small group destruction, for that matter). Interestingly, one can see the roots of MAD not only in the early nuclear world but also a decade earlier, when both Germany and the Allies opted not to employ nerve gas and other chemical or biological weapons during the Second World War, largely due to fear of reprisals by their enemies.[83]

In some respects, conventional airpower, too, resembles its nuclear cousin more and more as advances occur in the guidance of precision munitions, stealth, and other technologies. Contemporary arguments about the coercive impact of targeting leaders, C^2 systems, economic infrastructure, military forces, or civilian populations essentially recapitulate debates about strategic nuclear targeting from the 1980s and before, save that conventional weapons would produce far less collateral damage.[84] Schelling's coercive principle of targeting what the enemy values applies similarly in both the nuclear and conventional worlds, underpinning both yesterday's and today's debates about the relative merits of punishment and denial. Similarly, "parallel attack" and the quest for strategic paralysis achieved with conventional airpower share a distinct kinship with the pursuit of "splendid" first strikes and nuclear decapitation.

The nuclear revolution in airpower meant that the bomb (if not always the bomber) would in general get through and that nuclear powers could do all sorts of damage that they could not do before to an enemy without needing to conquer him first. To a considerable degree, the more recent conventional airpower revolution of smart weapons and stealth does something similar, except far less expensively, for both the attacker and the target. Even the concept of MAD may be relevant to sophisticated conventional strategic attack. If, as strategic airpower advocates of several generations have argued, one can effectively cripple or destroy states from the air with nonnuclear attacks against key economic, communications, and other assets, and if states value their own survival, it may not matter decisively for deterrence that this threat involves the deaths of thousands or hundreds instead of millions.

In other respects, however, conventional airpower becomes less and less like nuclear force as its ability to destroy targets inexpensively and comparatively cleanly improves, and as its employers (at least in the West) increasingly eschew the option of attacking civilian targets. In short, the deaths of millions do matter, and although conventional airpower possesses impressive speed and firepower, thermonuclear weapons, for good or ill, provide the ability in extremis to annihilate—more importantly, *to threaten* to annihilate—an enemy state. Just as warfare is the ultima ratio of international politics, so is nuclear attack the final argument in warfare. Its very extremity has always made nuclear war improbable, but the vast destructive potential of the absolute weapon still makes both the possibility of its use and the theories created to understand it important to both statesmen and strategists.

Notes

1. The most prominent works in the "golden age" nuclear deterrence pantheon include Bernard Brodie, ed., *The Absolute Weapon: Atomic Power and World Order* (New York: Harcourt, Brace, 1946); William W. Kaufmann, ed., *Military Policy and National Security* (Princeton, N.J.: Princeton University Press, 1956); Henry A. Kissinger, *Nuclear Weapons and Foreign Policy* (New York: Harper & Row, 1957); Morton Kaplan, "The Calculus of Deterrence," *World Politics* 11 (October 1958): 20–43; Albert Wohlstetter, "The Delicate Balance of Terror," *Foreign Affairs* 37 (January 1959): 209–34; Bernard Brodie, *Strategy in the Missile Age* (Princeton, N.J.: Princeton University Press, 1959); Daniel Ellsberg, *The Theory and Practice of Blackmail*, RAND Report P-3883 (Santa Monica, Calif.: RAND, 1959); Thomas C. Schelling, *Strategy of Conflict* (New York: Oxford University Press, 1960); Herman Kahn, *On Thermonuclear War* (Princeton, N.J.: Princeton University Press, 1960); Glenn H. Snyder, *Deterrence and Defense* (Princeton, N.J.: Princeton University Press, 1961); Pierre Gallois, *The Balance of Terror: Strategy for the Nuclear Age*, trans. Richard Howard (Boston: Houghton Mifflin, 1961); Herman Kahn, *Thinking about the Unthinkable* (New York: Horizon, 1962); André Beaufre, *Deterrence and Strategy*, trans. R. H. Barry (New York: Praeger, 1965); Herman Kahn, *On Escalation: Metaphors and Scenarios* (New York: Praeger, 1965); Bernard Brodie, *Escalation and the Nuclear Option* (Princeton, N.J.: Princeton University Press, 1966); and Thomas C. Schelling, *Arms and Influence* (New Haven, Conn.: Yale University Press, 1966), which probably remains the single most important treatment of the subject.

2. One should note that "nuclear theory" and "deterrence theory" are related but not synonymous. Deterrence theory applies to much more than nuclear deterrence, and long after nuclear theory had matured, deterrence theory was (and is) the scene and subject of lively debate. For reviews of deterrence theory per se and some of the debates about it, see, among many

others, Robert Jervis, "Deterrence Theory Revisited," *World Politics* 31 (January 1979): 289–324; George Downs, "The Rational Deterrence Debate," *World Politics* 41 (January 1989): 225–37; Paul C. Stern et al., eds., *Perspectives on Deterrence* (New York: Oxford University Press, 1989), especially the editors' introduction and Jack Levy's essay "Quantitative Studies of Deterrence Success and Failure"; and Karl Mueller, "Strategy, Asymmetric Deterrence, and Accommodation" (PhD diss., Princeton University, 1991).

3. Kubrick enlisted Thomas Schelling's assistance as he set out to update the 1950s novel *Red Alert* to the missile age and use it as the basis for the screenplay for *Dr. Strangelove*. During this process, Kubrick concluded that the movie would have to become a comedy. Author's conversation with Schelling, 12 October 1989. See also Fred Kaplan, *The Wizards of Armageddon* (New York: Simon & Schuster, 1983), 231; and Alexander Walker, *Stanley Kubrick Directs* (New York: Harcourt Brace Jovanovich, 1972), 156–221. *Red Alert* was also the basis for the dramatic movie *Fail-Safe* (1964).

4. See especially Richard Rhodes, *The Making of the Atomic Bomb* (New York: Simon & Schuster, 1986); idem, *Dark Sun: The Making of the Hydrogen Bomb* (New York: Simon & Schuster, 1995); and Thomas B. Cochran, William M. Arkin, and Milton M. Hoenig, *Nuclear Weapons Databook*, vol. 1, *U.S. Nuclear Forces and Capabilities* (Cambridge, Mass.: Ballinger, 1984). On the Soviet and other nuclear weapons programs, see also David Holloway, *Stalin and the Bomb: The Soviet Union and Atomic Energy, 1939–1956* (New Haven, Conn.: Yale University Press, 1994); Steven J. Zaloga, *Target America: The Soviet Union and the Strategic Arms Race, 1945–1964* (Novato, Calif.: Presidio, 1993); Thomas B. Cochran, William M. Arkin, and Milton M. Hoenig, *Nuclear Weapons Databook*, vol. 4, *Soviet Nuclear Weapons* (Cambridge, Mass.: Ballinger, 1989); Andrew Pierre, *Nuclear Politics* (London: Oxford University Press, 1972); Lawrence Freedman, *Britain and Nuclear Weapons* (London: Macmillan, 1980); Brian Cathcart, *Test of Greatness: Britain's Struggle for the Atomic Bomb* (London: John Murray, 1994); Wilfrid Kohl, *French Nuclear Diplomacy* (Princeton, N.J.: Princeton University Press, 1971); *L'Aventure de la Bombe: De Gaulle et la Dissuasion Nucléaire* (Paris: Librarie Plon, 1985); John Wilson Lewis and Xue Litai, *China Builds the Bomb* (Stanford, Calif.: Stanford University Press, 1988); Robert S. Norris, Andrew S. Burrows, and Richard W. Fieldhouse, *Nuclear Weapons Databook*, vol. 5, *British, French, and Chinese Nuclear Weapons* (Cambridge, Mass.: Ballinger, 1994); and Peter Pry, *Israel's Nuclear Arsenal* (Boulder, Colo.: Westview, 1984).

5. In addition to Kaplan's *The Wizards of Armageddon* and Richard Rhodes's works cited above, see also Bernard Brodie, "The Development of Nuclear Strategy," *International Security* 2 (Spring 1978): 65–83; Jervis; John Baylis and John Garnett, eds., *Makers of Nuclear Strategy* (New York: Saint Martin's, 1991); Barry H. Steiner, *Bernard Brodie and the Foundations of American Nuclear Strategy* (Lawrence, Kans.: University of Kansas Press,

1991); and Alastair Ian Johnston, "China's New 'Old Thinking': The Concept of Limited Deterrence," *International Security* 20 (Winter 1995/1996): 5–42.

6. Aaron L. Friedberg, "A History of the US Strategic 'Doctrine'—1945 to 1980," *Journal of Strategic Studies* (December 1980): 37–71; David Alan Rosenberg, "The Origins of Overkill," *International Security* 7 (Spring 1983): 3–67; Marc Trachtenberg, *History and Strategy* (Princeton, N.J.: Princeton University Press, 1991); Lawrence Freedman, *The Evolution of Nuclear Strategy*, 2d ed. (New York: Saint Martin's, 1989); Desmond Ball, *Targeting for Strategic Deterrence*, Adelphi Papers, no. 185 (London: International Institute for Strategic Studies [IISS], 1983); Peter Pringle and William Arkin, *SIOP: The Secret U.S. Plan for Nuclear War* (New York: Norton, 1983); McGeorge Bundy, *Danger and Survival* (New York: Random House, 1988); Steven T. Ross and David Alan Rosenberg, eds., *America's Plans for War against the Soviet Union, 1945–1950,* 15 vols. (New York: Garland, 1989); and Anthony Cave Brown, ed., *Drop Shot* (New York: Dial/James Wade, 1978).

7. The literature on nuclear arms control is truly immense. Among the best of literally thousands of publications on the subject are Bernard Brodie, "On the Objectives of Arms Control," *International Security* 1 (Summer 1976): 17–36; McGeorge Bundy, "To Cap the Volcano," *Foreign Affairs* 48 (October 1969): 1–20; Thomas C. Schelling and Morton H. Halperin, *Strategy and Arms Control* (Washington, D.C.: Pergamon-Brassey's, 1961/1985); and Thomas C. Schelling, "What Went Wrong with Arms Control?" *Foreign Affairs* 64 (Winter 1985/1986): 219–33.

8. On the effects of nuclear weapons, see Samuel Glasstone and Philip J. Dolan, eds., *The Effects of Nuclear Weapons*, 3d ed. (Washington, D.C.: US Department of Defense and Department of Energy, 1977); US Congress, Office of Technology Assessment, *The Effects of Nuclear War*, augmented ed. (Detroit: Gale Research Co., 1984); Irving L. Janis, *Air War and Emotional Stress* (Westport, Conn.: Greenwood, 1951/1976); and Jeannie Peterson and Don Hinrichsen, eds., *Nuclear War: The Aftermath* (Oxford: Pergamon, 1983).

9. For an overview of nuclear warhead technology, see Cochran, Arkin, and Hoenig, *Nuclear Weapons Databook,* vol. 1, chaps. 1–2.

10. Writers often observe that Curtis LeMay's bombing campaign against Japan in 1945 had a pronounced Douhetian flavor to it, as the armadas of B-29s inexorably razed one Japanese city after another. However, one should recall that the target country was effectively defenseless against the onslaught in this case. Not until a single penetrating bomber could destroy a city were the civilian populations of evenly matched countries vulnerable to rapid destruction from the air, as Douhet had envisioned in "The War of 19—." See Giulio Douhet, *The Command of the Air,* trans. Dino Ferrari (1942; reprint, Washington, D.C.: Office of Air Force History, 1983), 293–394.

11. The development of H-bombs also removed the constraint that limited plutonium supplies had previously placed on the expansion of the

superpowers' nuclear arsenals, since thermonuclear weapons required far less fissile material than atomic bombs, relative to their destructive power.

12. It is theoretically possible to build as large an H-bomb as one wishes, so the incentives to develop a still more powerful generation of weapons have been limited. The "neutron bomb" was a tactical thermonuclear weapon designed to have enhanced radiation and reduced blast (ERRB) effects in order to inflict destruction on enemy military forces while minimizing the operational problems posed for friendly forces as a result of tree and building blowdown and the destruction of territory. See Sam Cohen, *The Truth about the Neutron Bomb* (New York: Morrow, 1983). Earth-penetrating warheads were developed in order to attack deeply buried bunkers and other targets. During the 1980s, scientists devoted much effort to developing "third generation" nuclear weapons in the form of H-bomb-pumped X-ray lasers as part of the US Strategic Defense Initiative, but this technology failed to live up to its advocates' promises. See William J. Broad, *Teller's War* (New York: Simon & Schuster, 1992).

13. Test missiles carry range safety packages to permit their self-destruction in flight, but this has never been a popular feature for operational missiles due to their owners' fears that an enemy might be able to trigger the devices.

14. The United States also planned at one time to base Polaris SLBMs on surface vessels, included in the abortive multinational NATO Multilateral Force (MLF), but surface ships obviously lacked much of the submarine's invulnerability to preemptive attack, especially after the advent of satellite reconnaissance.

15. Although the Trident D-5 is also less accurate than its land-based contemporaries, it is accurate enough for use against hardened targets previously reserved for ICBMs and bombers, as discussed below.

16. Examples of the former included the British Blue Steel and the much longer-range US Skybolt air launched ballistic missile (ALBM), canceled in 1962; the most prominent defense-suppression missile was the American short range attack missile (SRAM), carried by B-52s and other Strategic Air Command (SAC) bombers.

17. In the US arsenal, the number of warheads per MIRVed missile ranged from three on the Minuteman III ICBM to 14 relatively small ones on the Poseidon SLBM.

18. In addition, in recent years, ballistic missiles and other strategic nuclear-delivery systems have also been adapted to carry nonnuclear warheads, including fuel-air explosives (FAE) and solid kinetic-energy projectiles.

19. Designed by Canadian artillery innovator Gerald Bull and intended for the bombardment of Israel or Teheran, one supergun was under construction in Iraq in 1990; British authorities intercepted parts for a larger version with a one-meter bore prior to shipment to Iraq.

20. See Kaplan, *The Wizards of Armageddon*, chaps. 6–8. Although SAC gradually shifted to a bomber force posture exclusively employing long-

range bombers based in the continental United States, similar concerns would arise again in the 1980s, when NATO faced the prospect of Soviet SS-20 IRBM attacks using nuclear, chemical, or FAE warheads against its major European bases for dual-capable strike aircraft.

21. The latter are known alternatively as SSBNs or (occasionally) fleet ballistic missile (FBM) submarines or, colloquially in the United States Navy, "boomers."

22. The conventional wisdom during most of the cold war held that the Soviets were generally unable to detect and track US and British ballistic missile submarines prior to launch, while the Western navies' superior acoustic-detection technology and the Soviets' noisier submarines gave the West a considerably greater but still significantly imperfect ability to track hostile SSBNs.

23. The number of warheads one can fire effectively against a single point target is limited by the problem of fratricide—the tendency of a detonating warhead to destroy those following behind it.

24. Among the more or less exotic basing schemes for the MX was a very expensive "racetrack" (or "shell game") system of multiple silos per missile connected by underground rail lines, proposed by the Carter administration; air launching from transport aircraft; road or rail mobility; launching from small coastal submarines or from superhardened, deep underground bases; and the Densepack scheme initially favored by the Reagan administration, which clustered missile silos so close together that warhead fratricide would make it impossible to attack more than a portion of them in a single strike. Passive defenses for missile silos were also discussed, including surrounding the silos with fields of closely spaced metal stakes, upon which a warhead would impale and destroy itself before it could detonate. For detailed discussion and analysis, see US Congress, Office of Technology Assessment, *MX Missile Basing* (Washington, D.C.: Government Printing Office, September 1981). In the end, the 50 MXs were placed in existing Minuteman ICBM silos, which did nothing at all to address the survivability problem. ICBM survivability concerns also led to the Small ICBM ("Midgetman") program (later canceled) to produce a single-warhead missile to be carried by hardened, off-road mobile launch vehicles.

25. This pattern changed somewhat in the late 1980s with the arrival of the Trident D-5, the first SLBM with sufficient accuracy to attack hardened point targets such as missile silos, along with the deployment of ultra-accurate Pershing II IRBMs and ground launched cruise missiles (GLCM) in western Europe, which promised to increase the ability of the United States to destroy the USSR's land-based nuclear systems in a first strike. (The deployment of the highly accurate, 10-MIRV-per-missile MX in vulnerable silos probably did little to reassure the Soviet leadership about American intentions.) The relatively small Soviet SLBM force remained unaffected, but this too would come under threat in the 1980s, as discussed below.

26. One problem with this scheme was that the electromagnetic pulse (EMP) produced by the detonation of the multimegaton, enhanced X-ray radiation, exoatmospheric ABM warheads would have done considerable damage to electronic systems on the ground, including the ABM tracking radars themselves.

27. Subsequent proposals to build a less capable US ABM system to provide protection against an isolated, accidental Soviet missile launch or a small Chinese nuclear attack were deemed unworthy of the necessary investment. Exactly the same arguments would emerge in the late 1980s for constructing Global Protection against Limited Strikes (GPALS)—a smaller version of the missile defense envisioned in the Strategic Defense Initiative—using a constellation of "brilliant pebbles" orbital interceptor missiles.

28. The ABM Treaty actually allowed each party to construct two ABM sites (later amended to one site) to protect the national capital, as well as an ICBM base, each with no more than one hundred interceptor missiles. The Soviets deployed (and continue to maintain and update) one hundred GALOSH ABMs around Moscow, but Congress ordered the single US Safeguard ABM site, constructed near Grand Forks, N.D., to be deactivated one day after declaring it operational in 1975, on the grounds of being cost-ineffective. On the US ABM programs, see B. Bruce-Riggs, *The Shield of Faith* (New York: Simon & Schuster, 1988); and Ernest J. Yanarella, *The Missile Defense Controversy* (Lexington, Ky.: University of Kentucky Press, 1977).

29. In the end, the world's most advanced civil defense program was probably that of Switzerland, perhaps due in part to the Swiss's having so little control over whether a superpower nuclear exchange might occur.

30. Among many works about SDI, see Steven E. Miller and Stephen Van Evera, eds., *The Star Wars Controversy* (Princeton, N.J.: Princeton University Press, 1986); US Congress, Office of Technology Assessment, *Strategic Defenses* (Princeton, N.J.: Princeton University Press, 1986); Kenneth N. Luongo and W. Thomas Wander, eds., *The Search for Security in Space* (Ithaca, N.Y.: Cornell University Press, 1989); William J. Broad, *Star Warriors* (New York: Simon & Schuster, 1985); and idem, *Teller's War.*

31. For example, Janis.

32. "Expert advice had indicated that bombing of London and the great cities would lead to casualties of the order of hundreds of thousands, or even millions, within a few weeks." Harold Macmillan, *Winds of Change, 1914–1939* (New York: Harper and Row, 1966), 522. On fears of air attack prior to the Second World War, see Uri Bialer, *In the Shadow of the Bomber* (London: Royal Historical Society, 1980).

33. See, for example, Rhodes, *The Making of the Atomic Bomb*, 312, 324–25.

34. See, for example, Kaplan, *The Wizards of Armageddon*, 45–47. On this subject, see also Bernard Brodie, "Strategy as a Science," *World Politics* 1 (July 1949): 467–88.

35. The seemingly obvious point that one must weigh the value of going to war against the value of not doing so is absolutely essential to deterrence theory; however, it is often ignored by deterrence theorists who find it convenient to treat states' satisfaction with the status quo as a constant instead of an important variable.

36. See, among others, Brodie, *Strategy in the Missile Age.*

37. For the classic explanation of the relationship between these concepts, see Snyder, chap. 1.

38. See, for example, ibid., 14–16; and J. David Singer, *Deterrence, Arms Control, and Disarmament* (Columbus, Ohio: Ohio State University Press, 1962), 22–24.

39. See, for example, Patrick Morgan, *Deterrence: A Conceptual Analysis* (Beverly Hills, Calif.: Sage, 1977), 20–22; Robert Art and Kenneth Waltz, "Technology, Strategy, and the Uses of Force," in Art and Waltz, eds., *The Use of Force,* 2d ed. (Lanham, Md.: University Press of America, 1983), 10.

40. The seminal presentation of such a broad perspective on deterrence can be found in Thomas W. Milburn, "What Constitutes Effective Deterrence?" *Journal of Conflict Resolution* 3 (1959): 138–45. Among the few works to have seriously addressed the use of positive incentives for deterrence are David Baldwin, "The Power of Positive Sanctions," *World Politics* 24 (October 1971): 19–38; and Peter Karsten, "Response to Threat Perception: Accommodation as a Special Case," in Klaus Knorr, ed., *Historical Dimensions of National Security Problems* (Lawrence, Kans.: University Press of Kansas, 1976), 120–63. For further discussion of deterrence definitions, see Mueller, chaps. 1–2.

41. See George H. Quester, *Deterrence before Hiroshima,* rev. ed. (New Brunswick, N.J.: Transaction Publishers, 1986); John J. Mearsheimer, *Conventional Deterrence* (Ithaca, N.Y.: Cornell University Press, 1983); and Barry R. Posen, *The Sources of Military Doctrine* (Ithaca, N.Y.: Cornell University Press, 1984).

42. Schelling, *Arms and Influence,* v.

43. It does not follow, of course, that these strategic reasons actually determined the size of the Soviet and American arsenals. Perhaps the best known of many illustrations of this notion is Secretary of Defense Robert McNamara's decision to buy one thousand Minuteman ICBMs not because he and President Kennedy thought they needed that many, but because it seemed to be the smallest number acceptable to the Air Force and Congress. See Desmond Ball, *Politics and Force Levels* (Berkeley, Calif.: University of California Press, 1980), 232–52.

44. Richard K. Betts, *Nuclear Blackmail and Nuclear Balance* (Washington, D.C.: Brookings Institution, 1987), 144–79.

45. Exactly how much damage one must inflict in order to destroy an enemy became the subject of considerable debate over the years. The best known standard for assured destruction capability was that adopted by McNamara during the Kennedy administration—that US retaliatory forces should be able to destroy 50 percent of the Soviet industrial base and kill

30 percent of the Soviet population after absorbing a Soviet first strike. For discussions of the merits of different types of targets, see Desmond Ball and Jeffrey Richelson, eds., *Strategic Nuclear Targeting* (Ithaca, N.Y.: Cornell University Press, 1986); Scott D. Sagan, *Moving Targets: Nuclear Strategy and National Security* (Princeton, N.J.: Princeton University Press, 1989); George Quester, "Ethnic Targeting: A Bad Idea Whose Time Has Come," *Journal of Strategic Studies* 5 (June 1982); and Michael J. Mazarr, "Military Targets for a Minimum Deterrent: After the Cold War How Much Is Enough?" *Journal of Strategic Studies* 15 (June 1992): 147–71.

46. On LUA, see US Congress, Office of Technology Assessment, *MX Missile Basing*, chap. 4.

47. Desmond Ball, *Can Nuclear War Be Controlled?* Adelphi Papers, no. 169 (London: IISS, 1981); Paul Bracken, *The Command and Control of Nuclear Forces* (New Haven, Conn.: Yale University Press, 1983); Bruce G. Blair, *Strategic Command and Control* (Washington, D.C.: Brookings Institution, 1985); and Ashton B. Carter, "The Command and Control of Nuclear War," *Scientific American* 252 (January 1985): 32–39. Bruce G. Blair, in *The Logic of Accidental War* (Washington, D.C.: Brookings Institution, 1993), also describes Soviet C^2 systems. See also Ashton B. Carter, John D. Steinbruner, and Charles A. Zraket, eds., *Managing Nuclear Operations* (Washington, D.C.: Brookings Institution, 1987); and on C^3 in less developed countries, see Peter D. Feaver, "Command and Control in Emerging Nuclear Nations," *International Security* 17 (Winter 1992/1993): 160–87.

48. In addition to short-warning SLBM strikes against leadership and C^2 targets, some decapitation scenarios involved the possibility of detonating large nuclear weapons at exoatmospheric altitudes in order to maximize their EMP effects, which would damage or destroy unhardened electronic systems over an enormous area. See Ball, *Can Nuclear War Be Controlled?* 10–12. Today small, nonnuclear, microwave-generating electronic countermeasures (ECM) warheads are being developed for tactical weapons to produce localized EMP-like effects against enemy C^2 targets and other electronic systems.

49. French strategists refer to essentially the same concept as "proportional deterrence." See Beaufre. Charles de Gaulle characterized it less abstractly as the ability "to tear off an arm" of the attacker. This principle clearly lay behind the British Chevaline SLBM warhead program in the 1970s, which was directed at enabling the single British SSBN on patrol during a crisis to destroy Moscow, in spite of the ballistic missile defenses deployed around that city, by firing all of its missiles at the Soviet capital. See Norris, Burrows, and Fieldhouse, *Nuclear Weapons Databook*, vol. 5, 110–12. On the Swedish nuclear program and its eventual abandonment, see Mitchell Reiss, *Without the Bomb: The Politics of Nuclear Nonproliferation* (New York: Columbia University Press, 1988), chap. 2.

50. However, assured destruction is more robust than marginal cost deterrence because a threat to annihilate an enemy's country is far less

sensitive to marginal changes in the amount of damage that one can inflict than is a threat to destroy only one or a handful of highly valued targets. Therefore, although nuclear deterrence by smaller powers is similar to that of the United States or Russia, a potentially important difference exists between the two classes of states with respect to considerations of crisis stability.

51. For further debate regarding the validity of the rationality assumptions in deterrence theory, see, among many others, Philip Green, *Deadly Logic* (Columbus, Ohio: Ohio State University Press, 1966); Robert Jervis, Richard Ned Lebow, and Janice Gross Stein, eds., *Psychology and Deterrence* (Baltimore: Johns Hopkins University Press, 1985); Edward Rhodes, *Power and MADness* (New York: Columbia University Press, 1989); Richard Ned Lebow, "Rational Deterrence Theory: I Think, Therefore I Deter," *World Politics* 41 (January 1989): 208–24; Downs; Christopher Achen and Duncan Snidal, "Rational Deterrence Theory and Comparative Case Studies," *World Politics* 41 (January 1989): 143–69; and Paul Huth and Bruce Russett, "Testing Deterrence Theory: Rigor Makes a Difference," *World Politics* 42 (July 1990): 466–501.

52. See, for example, George Quester, "Some Thoughts on 'Deterrence Failures,'" in Stern et al., 59–60.

53. An additional school of criticism challenges not the nature of MAD but the significance that many analysts attribute to it, maintaining that other factors so overdetermined the postwar peace among the nuclear powers that their nuclear strategies, doctrines, and force postures have been inconsequential. See John E. Mueller, "The Essential Irrelevance of Nuclear Weapons: Stability in the Postwar World," *International Security* 13 (Fall 1988): 55–79; idem, *Retreat from Doomsday: The Obsolescence of Major War* (New York: Basic Books, 1989); and, in reply, Robert Jervis, "The Political Effects of Nuclear Weapons: A Comment," *International Security* 13 (Fall 1988): 80–90.

54. See Russell Hardin et al., eds., *Nuclear Deterrence: Ethics and Strategy* (Chicago: University of Chicago Press, 1985); Charles J. Reid Jr., ed., *Peace in a Nuclear Age* (Washington, D.C.: Catholic University of America Press, 1986); Geoffrey Goodwin, ed., *Ethics and Nuclear Deterrence* (New York: Saint Martin's, 1982); and Charles W. Kegley Jr. and Kenneth L. Schwab, eds., *After the Cold War: Questioning the Morality of Nuclear Deterrence* (Boulder, Colo.: Westview, 1991).

55. For example, Jonathan Schell, *The Fate of the Earth* (New York: Knopf, 1982); and idem, *The Abolition* (New York: Knopf, 1984). For an argument that nuclear accidents are inevitable (along with much evidence that they are extremely unlikely), see Scott D. Sagan, *The Limits of Safety: Organizations, Accidents, and Nuclear Weapons* (Princeton, N.J.: Princeton University Press, 1993).

56. For one example among a plethora, see Lewis A. Dunn, "Nuclear Proliferation: What Difference Will It Make?" in Fred Holroyd, ed., *Thinking about Nuclear Weapons* (London: Croom Helm, 1985), 118–36.

57. Kenneth N. Waltz, *The Spread of Nuclear Weapons: More May Be Better*, Adelphi Papers, no. 171 (London: IISS, 1981); John J. Mearsheimer, "Back to the Future: Instability in Europe after the Cold War," *International Security* 15 (Summer 1990): 5–56; idem, "The Case for a Ukrainian Nuclear Deterrent," *Foreign Affairs* 72 (Summer 1993): 50–66; and Scott D. Sagan and Kenneth N. Waltz, *The Spread of Nuclear Weapons: A Debate* (New York: Norton, 1995). For counterarguments, see Sagan's chapters in Holroyd; and Steven E. Miller, "The Case against a Ukrainian Nuclear Deterrent," *Foreign Affairs* 72 (Summer 1993): 67–80. For an overview of the debate, see Peter R. Lavoy, "The Strategic Consequences of Nuclear Proliferation" and the subsequent symposium on the Waltz-Sagan dialogue, both in *Security Studies* 4 (Summer 1995): 695–810; and Devin T. Hagerty, "Nuclear Deterrence in South Asia: The 1990 Indo-Pakistani Crisis," *International Security* 20 (Winter 1995/1996): 79–114. On nuclear proliferation more generally, see, among a host of others, Leonard Beaton and John Maddox, *The Spread of Nuclear Weapons* (New York: Praeger, 1962); Stephen M. Meyer, *The Dynamics of Nuclear Proliferation* (Chicago: University of Chicago Press, 1984); Rodney W. Jones, ed., *Small Nuclear Forces and U.S. Security Policy* (Lexington, Mass.: D. C. Heath, 1984); Leonard S. Spector with Jacqueline R. Smith, *Nuclear Ambitions* (Boulder, Colo.: Westview, 1990); Benjamin Frankel, ed., *Opaque Nuclear Proliferation*, special issue of *Journal of Strategic Studies* 13 (September 1990); Zachary S. Davis and Benjamin Frankel, eds., *The Proliferation Puzzle* (London: Frank Cass, 1993); and Mitchell Reiss and Robert S. Litwak, eds., *Nuclear Proliferation after the Cold War* (Washington, D.C.: Woodrow Wilson Center Press, 1994).

58. Even a state entirely immune from military retaliation could expect under most circumstances to suffer nontrivial political and environmental costs as a result of launching a major nuclear attack.

59. Inevitably, threats to go to nuclear war over interests less than vital to a state will have reduced credibility, as dramatized in the alliterative question of whether the United States would really trade Boston for Bonn or Pittsburgh for Paris. For discussion of the subject of extended (sometimes called "type 2") nuclear deterrence, see, among many others, Schelling, *Arms and Influence*; Brodie, *Escalation and the Nuclear Option*; Snyder; Alexander L. George and Richard Smoke, *Deterrence in American Foreign Policy* (New York: Columbia University Press, 1974); John J. Mearsheimer, "Nuclear Weapons and Deterrence in Europe," *International Security* 9 (Winter 1984–1985): 19–46; and Paul K. Huth, *Extended Deterrence and the Prevention of War* (New Haven, Conn.: Yale University Press, 1988).

60. Conversely, coercive threats to use nuclear weapons for purposes other than deterrence (what Thomas Schelling labeled "compellence") have substantial credibility problems of their own and have caused much debate regarding the question of whether nuclear weapons have utility for purposes other than self-defense. Regarding nuclear compellence, see Schelling, *Arms and Influence*; Betts; Sean M. Lynn-Jones, Steven E. Miller, and Stephen Van Evera, eds., *Nuclear Diplomacy and Crisis Management*

(Cambridge, Mass.: MIT Press, 1990); Rosemary Foot, "Nuclear Threats and the Ending of the Korean Conflict," *International Security* 13 (Winter 1988–1989): 92–112; and Alexander L. George and William E. Simons, eds., *The Limits of Coercive Diplomacy*, 2d ed. (Boulder, Colo.: Westview, 1994).

61. Kahn, *On Thermonuclear War*, 144–53.

62. Bruce G. Blair, "Russia's Doomsday Machine," *New York Times*, 8 October 1993, A35; and William J. Broad, "Russia Has 'Doomsday' Machine, US Expert Says," *New York Times*, 8 October 1993, A6.

63. See Edward Rhodes, *Power and MADness*, chap. 6. Similarly, the possibility of unauthorized nuclear launches by dual-capable artillery units facing imminent destruction, as well as the existence of the British and French independent nuclear forces, bolstered the credibility of NATO's threat to escalate to nuclear warfare in the event of a successful Warsaw Pact invasion of West Germany.

64. This argument first appeared in R. P. Turco et al., "Nuclear Winter: Global Consequences of Multiple Nuclear Explosions," *Science* 222 (23 December 1983): 1283–92; and Carl Sagan, "Nuclear War and Climatic Catastrophe: Some Policy Implications," *Foreign Affairs* 62 (Winter 1983/1984): 257–92. Further study caused estimates of the probable severity of nuclear winter to diminish rapidly. See Starley L. Thompson and Stephen H. Schneider, "Nuclear Winter Reappraised," *Foreign Affairs* 64 (Summer 1986): 981–1005. For a critical overview of the debate and indictment of the wild exaggeration of the initial research results, see Russell Seitz, "In from the Cold: 'Nuclear Winter' Melts Down," *The National Interest* 5 (Fall 1986): 3–17.

65. However, early LNOs were much less limited than many of those later developed following National Security Decision Memorandum (NSDM) 242. See Lynn E. Davis, *Limited Nuclear Options*, Adelphi Papers, no. 121 (London: IISS, 1976); and Friedberg.

66. See Robert Jervis, *The Meaning of the Nuclear Revolution* (Ithaca, N.Y.: Cornell University Press, 1989), chap. 3.

67. Among the archetypal statements of the war-fighting school are Colin S. Gray, "Nuclear Strategy: The Case for a Theory of Victory," *International Security* 4 (Summer 1979): 54–87; idem and Keith Payne, "Victory Is Possible," *Foreign Policy* 39 (Summer 1980): 14–27; Paul Nitze, "Deterring Our Deterrent," *Foreign Policy* 25 (Winter 1976–1977): 195–210; Walter Slocombe, "The Countervailing Strategy," *International Security* 5 (Spring 1981): 18–27; Victor Utgoff, "In Defense of Counterforce," *International Security* 6 (Spring 1982): 44–61; and Robert Jastrow, "Why Strategic Superiority Matters," *Commentary*, March 1983, 27–32. See also Kahn, *On Escalation*. One should note that some prominent war-fighting theorists such as Colin Gray were relatively skeptical of escalation dominance and countervailing. For detailed analysis of the war-fighting school(s), see Charles L. Glaser's excellent essay "Why Do Strategists Disagree about the Requirements of Strategic Nuclear Deterrence?" in Lynn Eden and Steven E. Miller, eds., *Nuclear Arguments* (Ithaca, N.Y.: Cornell

University Press, 1989), 109–71; and Glaser's *Analyzing Strategic Nuclear Policy* (Princeton, N.J.: Princeton University Press, 1990).

68. Indeed, in the 1980s, fears arose that even the most significant intrawar escalation threshold of all—that between conventional and nuclear war—might not be recognizable because attacks with powerful conventional weapons such as IRBMs with FAE warheads might be mistaken for nuclear detonations.

69. Among the defenders of MAD against the war-fighting critiques, see especially Robert Jervis, *The Illogic of American Nuclear Strategy* (Ithaca, N.Y.: Cornell University Press, 1984); idem, *The Meaning of the Nuclear Revolution;* Glaser, *Analyzing Strategic Nuclear Policy;* and idem, "Why Do Strategists Disagree about the Requirements of Strategic Nuclear Deterrence?"

70. Many people offer this argument; perhaps the most prominent instance is in Nitze. See also Benjamin S. Lambeth, "The Political Potential of Soviet Equivalence," *International Security* 4 (Fall 1979): 22–39; Barry Blechman and Robert Powell, "What in the Name of God Is Strategic Superiority?" *Political Science Quarterly* 97 (Winter 1982–1983): 589–602; and Glaser, *Analyzing Strategic Nuclear Policy,* chap. 3.

71. Richard Pipes, "Why the Soviet Union Thinks It Could Fight and Win a Nuclear War," *Commentary,* July 1977, 21–34. One key but rarely addressed problem with the argument that the Soviets might be inclined to start a war, provided they could expect to fare better in it than would the United States, was that with both superpowers crippled, all leading powers in the postwar world would be anti-Soviet, anti-Communist, or both. On the larger issue of the problems of understanding an adversary's goals and intentions, see Robert Jervis, *Perception and Misperception in International Politics* (Princeton, N.J.: Princeton University Press, 1976), especially chap. 3.

72. Jervis, *The Meaning of the Nuclear Revolution,* see title of chap. 3.

73. Jervis, "Deterrence Theory Revisited," 299–300.

74. On offense-defense theory and its relationship to nuclear weapons, see Robert Jervis, "Cooperation under the Security Dilemma," *World Politics* 30 (January 1978): 167–214; George H. Quester, *Offense and Defense in the International System* (New York: Wiley, 1977); David Goldfischer, *The Best Defense* (Ithaca, N.Y.: Cornell University Press, 1993); and Sean M. Lynn-Jones, "Offense-Defense Theory and Its Critics," *Security Studies* 4 (Summer 1995): 660–91.

75. In practice, one can use weapons interactively to complicate matters. For example, one could use less accurate SLBMs to suppress enemy air defenses, thereby assisting bombers to attack hardened counterforce targets.

76. Finally, under the recent Strategic Arms Reduction Talks (START) II Treaty, Russia and the United States agreed to ban MIRVs on ICBMs and to reduce the maximum number of warheads per SLBM to four.

77. Other incentives for the ABM Treaty included the desire to avoid the expense of an intense arms race between offensive and defensive

capabilities and the political damage that such a competition might do to relations between the superpowers, even if effective strategic defenses proved to be a pipe dream.

78. Windows of opportunity are central to debates about the strategic implications of nuclear proliferation as well. For discussion of the concept, see Richard Ned Lebow, "Windows of Opportunity: Do States Jump through Them?" *International Security* 9 (Summer 1984): 147–86; and Dan Reiter, "Exploding the Powder Keg Myth: Preemptive Wars Almost Never Happen," *International Security* 20 (Fall 1995): 5–34.

79. Barry Posen, "Inadvertent Nuclear War? Escalation and NATO's Northern Flank," *International Security* 7 (Fall 1982); and idem, *Inadvertent Escalation: Conventional War and Nuclear Risks* (Ithaca, N.Y.: Cornell University Press, 1991). See also Desmond Ball, "Nuclear War at Sea," *International Security* 10 (Winter 1985–1986): 3–31.

80. See, for example, Charles L. Glaser, "Nuclear Policy without an Adversary: US Planning for the Post-Soviet Era," *International Security* 16 (Spring 1992): 34–78.

81. See Mitchell Reiss, *Without the Bomb*; and idem, *Bridled Ambition: Why Countries Constrain Their Nuclear Capabilities* (Washington, D.C.: Woodrow Wilson Center Press, 1995).

82. In general, biological weapons represent a far more serious threat than do chemical weapons. See Thomas L. McNaugher, "Ballistic Missiles and Chemical Weapons: The Legacy of the Iran-Iraq War," *International Security* 15 (Fall 1990): 5–34; and Steve Fetter, "Ballistic Missiles and Weapons of Mass Destruction," *International Security* 16 (Summer 1991): 5–42. One should also note that nuclear materials such as plutonium, highly toxic if inhaled or ingested, can also be used as poisons. As with so many facets of the nuclear revolution, Manhattan Project scientists had already foreseen such radiological weapons as early as 1941. See, for example, Richard Rhodes, *The Making of the Atomic Bomb*, 510.

83. In *Cooperation under Fire: Anglo-German Restraint in World War II* (Ithaca, N.Y.: Cornell University Press, 1995), Jeffrey Legro argues that important organizational factors also discouraged the use of chemical warfare by both sides.

84. See, for example, Col John A. Warden III, "Employing Air Power in the Twenty-first Century," in Richard H. Shultz Jr. and Robert L. Pfaltzgraff Jr., eds., *The Future of Air Power in the Aftermath of the Gulf War* (Maxwell AFB, Ala.: Air University Press, July 1992), 57–82. For a discussion of Warden's theories, see David Fadok's essay in this volume; for critiques of those theories, see Robert A. Pape Jr., *Bombing to Win* (Ithaca, N.Y.: Cornell University Press, 1996).

Chapter 9

Air Theory, Air Force, and Low Intensity Conflict: A Short Journey to Confusion

Prof. Dennis M. Drew

As the end of the twentieth century approaches, American airmen are confronted with two different but not mutually exclusive visions of future warfare. The first, stemming from the Gulf War, perceives airpower dominating modern mechanized warfare. The second discerns modern mechanized warfare—especially as demonstrated in the Gulf War—as a thing of the past. In the latter view, the future of warfare increasingly lies in the ill-defined realm of low intensity conflict (LIC).

Both visions may be accurate; if so, the truth of the first vision has a great deal to do with the truth of the second. After all, if airpower dominates "conventional" warfare, then countries that cannot field superior air forces must employ "unconventional" means to gain military success.

This essay does not seek to bolster or challenge either of these two visions. Rather, it explores the relationship between LIC since World War II and the theory of airpower as perceived by the US Air Force. The thesis is straightforward; specifically, the US Air Force has not effectively accounted for the realities of LIC in its theory of airpower.

As this essay demonstrates, to a large extent, the Air Force has ignored LIC as much as possible, preferring to think of it as little more than a small version of conventional war. But LIC is not just conventional war waged on a small scale. Rather, LIC differs fundamentally from conventional war. The reluctance of the world's most powerful air force to address the peculiarities of LIC, combined with the predictions of many people that such a conflict will be more common in the future, creates an important void in US airpower theory.[1]

To support these propositions, we must provide definitional clarity to the LIC muddle and examine how US airmen have reacted to the increasing challenge of LIC, both officially and unofficially. Unofficially, the essay examines the literature on the subject as it has evolved since World War II. Officially, it examines the Air Force theory of airpower as expressed in its doctrine over the same period.[2] Although this analysis concentrates on the era since the end of World War II, LIC has a much more storied history—as does airpower theory. But after World War II, limited wars began to absorb inordinate amounts of US blood and treasure. Further, after World War II the US Air Force gained its independence as a fighting arm, with the responsibility to develop appropriate airpower theory and doctrine.

Low Intensity Conflict Defined

The term *low intensity conflict* may be the most confusing misnomer ever adopted by the US military. In the first place, the term is ethnocentric because the intensity of any conflict depends on where one stands. The struggle against the Hukbalahap (Huk) insurgents in the Philippines may have been a LIC from the US point of view, but it was certainly not low in its intensity for the Filipinos. In the second place, LIC is so nondescriptive that it has become little more than the rubric for an incredible mélange of activities. At one time or another, one could find in the low intensity stewpot a distinctive type of warfare (insurgency and counterinsurgency), tactics (guerrilla methods and terrorism), short-duration conventional military operations (referred to euphemistically as "peacetime contingency operations"), diplomatic activities (peacemaking), and police activities (peacekeeping).[3]

To bring some order and sense to a chaotic situation, the Joint Chiefs of Staff published Joint Pub 3-07, *Doctrine for Joint Operations in Low Intensity Conflict.*[4] This document limited the LIC playing field to (1) insurgency and counterinsurgency, (2) combating terrorism, (3) peacekeeping, and (4) contingency operations. Although helpful in narrowing the field, the four categories remain too broad for the purposes of this analysis.

Within the four categories of LIC, one subcategory—counterinsurgency—has remained particularly troublesome and relevant for airmen. The nature of insurgency challenges nearly every facet of US airpower theory and makes the application of traditional airpower theory problematic. Thus, this analysis limits LIC to the insurgency/counterinsurgency problem. Although clearly an artificial limitation, it is most useful for the purposes sought here.

I have argued that insurgencies—particularly those whose strategies derive from the classic teachings of Mao Tse-tung and his many disciples—are fundamentally different from conventional wars.[5] Called variously "people's revolutionary wars" and somewhat later "protracted revolutionary wars," insurgencies are revolutionary civil wars that differ fundamentally from conventional warfare in at least five ways.

The first difference is time. Classically based insurgencies are designed to be protracted affairs. In the hands of an insurgent battling an entrenched government, time becomes a weapon. The longer the insurgency remains in being, the more it discredits the government trying to stamp it out. The longer the insurgency remains active, the less the government appears to be in control of its own destiny: "Time is the condition to be won to defeat the enemy. In military affairs time is of prime importance. Time ranks first among the three factors necessary for victory, coming before terrain and support of the people. Only with time can we defeat the enemy."[6]

In contrast, for at least the past two hundred years, the desire to make wars shorter and victory more decisive has driven the development of conventional warfare in the Western world. Much of the technology and virtually all of the innovations in strategy and tactics had as their aim more decisiveness on the battlefield and thus wars of much shorter duration and less cost. The development of strategic bombardment theory is a case in point.

The second fundamental difference has to do with the remarkable "duality" of classical insurgent strategy. Maoist-based insurgencies have a dual focus—one military and one civilian. On the civilian side, the object is to infiltrate the entire population with insurgent sympathizers who can undermine the government and spread disaffection. Further, they can aid the military side of the insurgency by gathering intelligence, recruiting guerrilla fighters, obtaining needed supplies, and providing funds.

On the military side, the insurgent objective is to harass government forces; demonstrate the government's inability to cope with insurgent forces; and after gaining the upper hand, take on government forces in conventional battles to administer the coup de grace. As Douglas Pike has pointed out, this remarkable duality provides the insurgency with a built-in advantage. The government under siege must win both the civilian and military struggles. The insurgent must win only one. Further, the government faces a dilemma in resource allocation. Concentrating on the civilian struggle risks defeat on the battlefield. Concentrating on the military struggle allows the civilian part of the insurgency time to infiltrate deeper and more widely into the population and governmental structures, perhaps risking a bloodless coup.[7] Conventional warfare, of course, is a web of military and nonmilitary aspects—a basic Clausewitzian notion. Rarely in conventional warfare do we find such a seamless web or such an interdependence between the two aspects.

The third fundamental difference concerns the tactics used by insurgent military forces. Guerrilla tactics are certainly not unique to insurgencies. They have been used by regular forces in large "conventional" wars (Orde Wingate's Chindits in the China-Burma-India theater in World War II) and by partisan irregulars during the same sorts of conflicts (the Soviet partisans and the French Maquis operating behind German lines). These operations, however, remained ancillary to the main military effort.

Insurgents use guerrilla tactics as their principal method of military operation—and do so out of necessity. Insurgents are the weak fighting the strong—those out of power fighting those in power. Insurgents are often outmanned and nearly always outgunned. Guerrillas negate superior government firepower by operating in small, dispersed groups that do not provide lucrative targets. Guerrilla tactics also allow the insurgents to "melt away" into the population from which they came. Thus, insurgents generally fight only when they wish to fight.[8]

The fourth peculiarity of insurgent guerrilla operations has to do with logistics. Looking at conventional logistic flows schematically, one finds that the flow of logistic support is in the same direction as the advance of the troops in the field. Lines of supply stretch out behind fielded armies to the sources of supply, in turn creating classic interdiction and strategic targets for airpower. Insurgent guerrillas, however, draw their sustenance from the very people they are trying to influence through both their military and nonmilitary operations.[9] Again thinking in schematic terms, insurgent logistical flows run opposite from the direction of insurgent military operations. As a result, airpower's classical interdiction and strategic attack missions may be of little value.

Of course, a "less than theoretically pure" insurgency may receive some support and logistical assistance from sources of supply outside the country under siege (much more the case for partisans than insurgents). To the extent that insurgents use outside sources, the more vulnerable they become to interdiction and to strategic attacks.

The fifth and most important difference between conventional warfare and protracted revolutionary warfare concerns centers of gravity for both the government and insurgent forces. In conventional warfare, although the identification of an enemy's center(s) of gravity may prove difficult, they remain clearly defined for each antagonist. That is, each side will have deployed its forces to protect its center of gravity. The enemy's center of gravity will always be "over there" behind enemy lines. The central tenet of Western military thought for at least the past two hundred years has been to attack or put one's forces in a position to attack an enemy's center of gravity, thus either destroying the enemy's ability to resist or coercing capitulation.

By contrast, in an insurgency, *both antagonists have the same center of gravity*—the people. Neither the government in power nor the insurgency can long exist without support from the people. Without some support from the people, or at least their neutrality in the struggle, the insurgent underground infrastructure would find itself quickly exposed and eliminated. With the destruction of the infrastructure, the insurgency has no political arm, no intelligence apparatus, no source of military manpower, and no logistical support. At the same time, no government can survive without the acquiescence of the people—least of all a government actively opposed by an attractive and aggressive insurgent movement.[10] All of this, of course, brings into question the applicability of Western military and US airpower theory advocating the attack of an enemy's center of gravity by putting fire and steel on target.

The Rise of Protracted Revolutionary Warfare, 1945–64

Not long after World War II, Western democracies faced the very different challenge of protracted revolutionary warfare. Many of the difficulties arose in Southeast Asia when the collapse of Japanese forces created a power vacuum prior to the return of the colonial powers.

In the Philippines, the Communist-led People's Anti-Japanese Army quickly changed its name to the People's Liberation Army and changed its mission to establishing a "People's Democratic Republic by overthrowing American imperialism."[11] The Huk insurgency was on.

By 1950 the insurgents had 15,000 men under arms, another 80,000 active supporters, and an estimated support base of at least half a million. At one point during that crucial year, insurgents threatened Manila itself with a force of 10,000. The government did not get the insurgency under control until 1954—and only after a shift in strategy that made civilian pacification programs (land reform and other social welfare reforms) an equal partner with military action.[12]

One finds a similar story in Malaya. After the Japanese surrender, the Communist-dominated Malayan People's Anti-Japanese Army disbanded but reappeared in a new guise, bent on throwing out the British. The situation in Malaya, however, differed significantly from problems faced by the government of the Philippines and by the French in Indochina. In the Malayan case, the insurgent movement resided almost exclusively in the Chinese population—ethnically and culturally distinct from the native Malays.[13]

The combined military-civilian campaign waged against the Malayan insurgents was a strategic masterpiece, and, in retrospect, the insurgents never came close to winning.

However, the protracted affair sputtered on through 1958 (the so-called Year of Mass Surrender)—not formally declared finished until July 1960.

Meanwhile, the French faced very similar problems in Vietnam. The Vietminh, who had fought the Japanese occupation forces, resisted the return of the French and finally took to the hills to wage a bloody protracted revolutionary war. Unable to cope with the Vietminh, the French gave up the attempt after a major defeat at Dien Bien Phu in 1954. Left in the wake of the French disaster was a divided Vietnam—the northern half controlled by the victorious Vietminh and the southern half a rump state created from those areas of less pervasive Vietminh influence. The Vietminh would soon turn their attention to uniting all of Vietnam.

The Unofficial Response

With a significant portion of Asia embroiled in Communist-backed protracted revolutionary wars during the late 1940s and much of the 1950s, one would have expected a significant intellectual response from US airmen. However, the interests of the US military largely emphasized other areas and other concerns. US airmen focused on organizational independence from the US Army and on missions that best justified independence (i.e., strategic bombing and, to a lesser extent, deep interdiction). Further, airmen were particularly enamored with nuclear weapons that promised to bring the concepts of strategic bombing to fruition.

The United States soon became involved in the Korean conflict, which, although fought with frustrating limitations, was a conventional war. Korea, however, became a sideshow for the US military. The "real" threat remained in Europe, where the Soviets faced the North Atlantic Treaty Organization (NATO) with powerful forces and a threatening attitude.

Nor was there much room for thinking about protracted revolutionary warfare in the years following the Korean conflict. Europe remained the focal point. Military budget cutting by the Eisenhower administration played directly into the hands of people who believed that "atomic airpower" could deter all forms of warfare and, if deterrence failed, could quickly defeat any enemy.[14] Nuclear strategists, nuclear deterrence theorists, and Strategic Air Command (SAC) dominated US thinking and military forces. In all of this, one assumed that preparation for global war meant preparation for wars of lesser magnitude. As demonstrated in the Philippines, Malaya, and Indochina, the problem was not wars of a lesser kind but wars of a fundamentally different kind.

The struggles in Southeast Asia did spark some interest in the professional military literature, although far less than the major themes of "lessons" from World War II and Korea, the Soviet confrontation in Europe, and nuclear subjects.

French general G. J. M. Chassin, air officer commanding, Far East, published an important article in an English language journal in late 1952 that dealt exclusively with the ongoing use of French airpower in Indochina. Although he failed to address the fundamental differences between conventional and insurgent warfare, he did offer insights (prophetically for US airmen a decade hence) into appropriate command structures, close support and interdiction missions, and the extreme difficulty of finding guerrilla targets:

> In the tactical field the chief characteristic of the war in Indochina is the invisibility of the enemy. . . . Here there are no columns on the march . . . no convoys of vehicles. . . . Once outside the controlled zone, there is not a soul to be seen in the fields. When an aircraft flies over a village, the latter empties itself completely, even the domestic animals taking cover. It needs an unusual degree of skill and experience to detect the presence of Vietminh troops in the mountains and forests, where they live under perfect camouflage.[15]

The professional journal of the US Air Force published only two significant articles concerning airpower and the ongoing insurgencies in Southeast Asia during the entire decade of the 1950s. One concerned the Huk rebellion in the Philippines;[16] the other addressed the broader concerns of tactical airpower in limited war but included a scathing indictment of the French use of airpower in Indochina.[17] The Philippine article addressed broader civil-military issues at the level of overall strategy but also discussed tactical lessons learned from hard experience. The article attacking the French airpower effort in Indochina concentrated on command and control (C^2) issues and failed to give even passing mention to the very different kind of war the French faced.

Perhaps the most important document published during the 1950s was a three-volume analysis of the French effort compiled by the French high command.[18] These remarkable volumes contain captured Vietminh documents describing ways by which their tactics could obviate superior enemy airpower[19] and the difficulty of interdicting an enemy who required few supplies and relied on a very primitive and easily repairable logistic transportation system.[20] Finally, these volumes directly called into question the applicability of the central tenets of American airpower theory, which the French referred to in these volumes as "the extremist thesis of Douhetism."[21]

The continuing problems in Southeast Asia during the latter part of the decade and the election of John F. Kennedy to the presidency in 1960 spurred more interest in insurgencies in the professional literature.[22] This was particularly true at Air University, Maxwell AFB, Alabama, where a number of student research papers directly addressed issues related to airpower and the wars in Southeast Asia.

One of the earliest of these research efforts showed the influence of the Air Force fascination with nuclear weapons, the author calling for their use to seal off the borders of Laos and Vietnam. He went on to address the problem of finding enemy forces who used guerrilla tactics by suggesting the use of "napalm blankets" to burn off the jungle cover, and the application of chemical defoliants to kill vegetation too wet to burn.[23] Although the report was extreme in its recommendation of nuclear weapons, the suggestion for defoliation proved prescient, given the Operation Ranchhand defoliation program that began in January 1962.[24]

During 1962 and 1963, Air University students produced a number of insightful research papers concerning US involvement in Southeast Asia. In general, they all addressed counterguerrilla uses of airpower, but, in fact, most put the problem in the broader context of counterinsurgency. They reflected a general appreciation of the civil-military duality in protracted revolutionary warfare and an awareness of the inappropriateness of airpower's traditional focus.[25] One of the studies called into question all firepower missions and maintained that the supporting roles of airpower (airlift, psychological operations, etc.) would likely prove most important.[26] Others, however, remained sanguine about the use of aerial firepower against insurgents, even in the difficult jungle terrain of Southeast Asia: "To moan the lack of strategic targets or the ability to see tactical targets and therefore conclude that air power is limited is to overlook the inherent flexibility of the air vehicle. There is no such thing as limitations or impossible conditions, only incorrect tactics or poor employment."[27]

Articles concerning insurgency in the professional journals from 1960 through 1964 also increased significantly as US involvement in Southeast Asia deepened. Remarkably few, however, dealt with the use of airpower. Noted academics Peter Paret and John W. Shy published perhaps the most important article that provided insights into the philosophy and strategy of protracted revolutionary warfare. Appearing in the *Marine Corps Gazette* in January 1962, it provided an authoritative tour de force on insurgencies and the problems one faced when combating them.[28] Unfortunately, the authors paid scant attention to airpower, and the article apparently received very little attention from Air Force airmen. The *Gazette* and the corps continued their interest in the subject with an article on how President Sukarno crushed an insurgency in Indonesia during 1958[29] and with a four-part series on the struggle to put down the Huk insurgency.[30]

Although the Marine Corps showed great interest in protracted revolutionary warfare, Air Force airmen published very little on the subject in their own professional journals. In 1962 a member of the History Department faculty at the Air Force Academy published an article about the use of airpower against the Huks,[31] and in late 1963 the *Air University Review* carried a short article on using airpower to escort ground convoy movements in Vietnam.[32] Beyond this meager showing, the Air Force seemed either supremely uninterested in the subject or assumed that, in terms of airpower, protracted revolutionary warfare was just conventional warfare writ small.

The Official Response

In spite of protracted revolutionary wars raging throughout Southeast Asia from the end of World War II through the decade of the 1950s, in spite of deepening involvement after the election of John F. Kennedy to the presidency, and in spite of a growing body of literature on the subject, the official response of the Air Force was both slow and distinctly muted.

Air Force basic doctrine first appeared in 1953 and changed in 1954, 1955, and 1959. Each version seemed to assume that the struggles in Southeast Asia did not exist and, for the most part, that the Korean War had not happened.[33] None of them mentioned terms and concepts such as LIC, protracted revolutionary warfare, and guerrilla tactics. Not until the 1955 edition was the broader concept of limited war even mentioned in basic doctrine.

At lower levels of Air Force doctrine, the story remained much the same. For example, the *Theater Air Operations* doctrine manual published in 1953 did mention "special operations" but only in terms of inserting agents behind enemy lines, supplying partisans, and delivering propaganda. The version reissued in 1954 made no further elaboration.[34]

Although the "official" Air Force seemed almost mesmerized by strategic nuclear airpower throughout the 1950s, some people seemed to recognize that the kinds of struggles seen in Southeast Asia might require different responses. For example, as early as March 1954, the Air Force vice chief of staff sent a message to Air University, Tactical Air Command (TAC), and Far East Air Forces (FEAF) questioning whether or not the Air Force could adequately respond to the challenge presented by Ho Chi Minh, implying that the Air Force could fight only a major war.[35]

The first concrete actions taken in response to the threat of protracted revolutionary warfare included the establishment of the 4400th Combat Crew Training Squadron (CCTS) at Eglin AFB, Florida, in April 1961, followed by its absorption into the newer and larger Special Air Warfare Center at the same location in April 1962. Both actions came only after direct prodding by the Kennedy administration, which considered the threat of insurgent warfare very real.

The 4400th CCTS, nicknamed Jungle Jim, trained foreign airmen and at the same time developed appropriate counterinsurgency tactics and techniques. In late 1961, Jungle Jim elements deployed to Vietnam in Operation Farmgate. The Special Air Warfare Center had essentially the same mission as Jungle Jim but was considerably larger and better organized to develop specialized tactics, techniques, and procedures.[36]

At the same time (April 1962), Gen Curtis E. LeMay, Air Force chief of staff, took official notice of the budding insurgency/guerrilla warfare problem in the publication *Air Force Information Policy Letter for Commanders*. Here, he discussed not only the ability of airpower to concentrate firepower quickly but also other advantages that airpower could bring to such struggles:

> Air forces also are essential in the fast transport and resupply of counterinsurgent forces, as well as in providing reconnaissance, leaflet delivery and defense against insurgent air activities. To the central government of the nation under insurgent attack, airpower provides quick access to all parts of the country so it can maintain civic morale and stability through personal contact.

> I would like to see you familiarize yourself with the literature on this form of warfare. . . . And also remember these two facts: (1) general war poses the primary military threat to the security of the Free World and (2) it is under the umbrella of strategic superiority that the United States has freedom of maneuver in the lesser forms of conflict.[37]

Two things are striking about this policy letter. First, the broad approach taken to the value of airpower in other than firepower roles is unusual, especially coming from the airman most closely associated with strategic bombing doctrine, nuclear weapons, and SAC. The second notable point is the continuing reference to strategic superiority and freedom of maneuver in "lesser" wars rather than "different" wars. Even at this late date, with personnel already deployed to Vietnam in the Farmgate program, the Air Force still regarded insurgent warfare as a lesser, rather than fundamentally different, form of warfare.

On 21 September 1962, Brig Gen Gilbert L. Pritchard, commandant of the new Special Air Warfare Center, spoke at a symposium on limited war and counterinsurgency held as part of the Air Force Association national convention. Later published by the Air Force, Pritchard's speech provided an accurate primer on the classic concepts of insurgent warfare and called for the close coordination and cooperation of airpower with other forms of military power and with nonmilitary government agencies in a comprehensive and integrated campaign—including civic actions and "nation-building."[38] Personnel at the Special Air Warfare Center were doing their homework.

Just as clearly, interest by US airmen in insurgency and counterinsurgency began to grow. The establishment of the Special Air Warfare Center, the publication of information policy letters, the symposium held by the Air Force Association, and the ever-deepening involvement of the United States in the struggle for Vietnam culminated in a new Air Force basic doctrine manual in August 1964.

Given the fact that previous basic doctrine manuals had failed even to broach the subject of insurgency, this document was remarkable. In one short chapter, the new manual provided a very accurate description of insurgent warfare and the objectives of counterinsurgency. In terms of airpower, it described both firepower and nonfirepower missions, as well as some of the difficulties in interdicting guerrilla lines of supply.[39]

However, in terms of the war that the Air Force was about to enter, the scant two pages devoted to counterinsurgency had the flavor of "too little, too late." The manual devoted a full 11 pages to air operations in general and tactical nuclear warfare; another two pages addressed conventional air operations. Although the Air Force recognized insurgency and counterinsurgency, the emphasis in its doctrine (and by inference, its thinking and theory) remained where it had been since the advent of nuclear weapons and the creation of the independent Air Force.

The Vietnam War and Its Aftermath, 1965–80

The war in Vietnam was a watershed event that tore at the social fabric of the nation and bred distrust of the government. It proved no less traumatic for the US Air Force.

Even though some American airmen had given serious thought to the unique problems of protracted revolutionary warfare, it quickly became clear that they remained firmly wedded to the theory of strategic attack on an enemy's vital centers to produce victory.

When planning for full-scale intervention by US airpower began, it focused on North Vietnam rather than the struggle in the South. The original Air Force plan called for a classic strategic bombing campaign against the so-called 94-target list, designed, among other things, to destroy "North Vietnam's capacity to continue as an industrially viable state."[40] Such was not to be, at least not to the degree that US airmen envisioned an aerial "blitzkrieg" against North Vietnam. Fears of escalation, Chinese intervention, and even nuclear confrontation with the Soviet Union convinced the political leadership that a "slow squeeze" was more appropriate than aerial blitzkrieg.[41]

This produced the "Rolling Thunder" bombing campaign, which would last from early 1965 until the fall of 1968. During that time, US aircraft would attack all of the original 94 targets in a campaign controlled directly from the White House and conducted more to send signals of strength and resolve to the North Vietnamese than to destroy North Vietnam as "an industrially viable state." Airmen chafed under the tight political controls, restrictions, and lengthy bombing pauses designed to entice the enemy to the negotiating table.

Airmen argued that because of all the political restrictions and bombing pauses, the bombing of the North did not constitute a test of traditional airpower theory. Critics argued that a traditional strategic bombing campaign was not appropriate. In their view, the situation lacked the major assumptions behind strategic bombing theory. The struggle was not a war to overthrow and destroy the North Vietnamese, and North Vietnam was not a modern industrialized state.[42]

Ironically, strategic bombing advocates believed that their vindication lay in the two Linebacker air campaigns waged in 1972. In the first campaign, both strategic and tactical uses of airpower played a significant, perhaps even decisive, role in defeating the North Vietnamese "Easter offensive." In December of that year, President Richard Nixon turned airmen loose to bomb previously restricted targets—including targets in Hanoi and Haiphong—in Linebacker 2. Shortly after this concentrated 11-day bombing campaign, the North Vietnamese agreed to a cease-fire and the return of US prisoners of war—a clear sign to many airmen that, had the politicians turned airmen loose earlier, they could have completed the struggle in Vietnam quickly and successfully.

The Unofficial Response

One of the earliest responses by an American airman came with the publication of an important book by Maj John Pustay, a member of the US Air Force Academy faculty. Pustay devoted an entire chapter to air operations in such conflicts, drawing heavily on the experiences of the British in Malaya, the French in Vietnam, and reports from US advisors in Vietnam. Pustay paid particular attention to the nonfirepower missions. As to firepower missions, he explained why aircraft should be able to fly low and slow and why they would be well served to have a second crew member for spotting fleeting guerrilla targets in difficult terrain.[43]

At about the same time that Pustay published his book, the Aerospace Studies Institute at Air University completed a study on the French use of airpower against guerrilla forces in Algeria between 1954 and 1964. Although far from exhaustive and relying on mostly secondary sources, the study did provide at least one prophetic insight when the authors noted, "If the cause of an insurgency is not, or cannot be, erased, then the best military effort will probably be defeated in the long run."[44]

Perhaps the most important article published in the professional military literature in 1965 was a lecture delivered by Bernard Fall at the Naval War College. It provided extremely lucid insights into the nature of protracted revolutionary warfare that should have caused all US military leaders to reflect on the "American way of war" in the Vietnamese context.[45]

In retrospect, it seems amazing that a survey of the American military literature reveals an almost total absence of articles and books that dealt directly with the use of airpower in counterinsurgencies between the spring of 1965 and the spring of 1967. Nor did the situation improve significantly for the remainder of the decade.

However, in April 1967 Maj Gen Rollen H. Anthis wrote an article for *Air Force Magazine* that displayed both considerable insight and considerable weakness of military thought. Anthis, the former commander of 2d Air Division (later redesignated Seventh Air Force) in South Vietnam from 1961 to 1964, defended the use of airpower in Vietnam against its critics. He cited the ability of airpower to find the enemy, transport troops and supplies to vital points, provide firepower to outposts under siege, maintain government lines of communications (LOC) and supply, and harass enemy guerrilla forces. However, he failed to mention the importance of the nonmilitary side of insurgent operations and the importance of integrating military and nonmilitary counterinsurgent operations.[46]

An Air War College student research paper of 1967 provided a more balanced view of airpower in counterinsurgent operations. Col Robert L. Hardie's study emphasized the dual nature of insurgent warfare and the requirement to integrate military and nonmilitary counterinsurgent operations. Drawing on the writings of insurgent war theorists as well as the experience of the British in Malaya and the French in Algeria, Hardie provided considerable evidence that the proper use of airpower would depend upon the phase of insurgent operations.[47] Hardie's paper is significant, for it represents the first example of a serious attempt to link insurgency theory and experience directly to air operations. However, it was the only such example found in the US professional literature until the decade of the 1980s.

As to the remainder of the 1960s, two other items in the professional periodical literature are worth noting. The first article, written by a civilian historian working at Headquarters SAC, touted the effectiveness of the B-52 bomber in countering guerrilla forces.[48] The second, from Great Britain, provided the first indication in the literature that aircraft on the ground were particularly lucrative targets for guerrilla operations and that this vulnerability would be a difficult problem to solve.[49]

Although the professional journals contained few articles on airpower and protracted revolutionary warfare and although

Air University published little in the way of serious research on the subject, civilian publishing houses provided a number of books during the 1960s that should have made it clear to airmen that the kind of warfare waged in Vietnam was very different from the nuclear or conventional war paradigms reflected in US Air Force doctrine. Unfortunately, these books dealt with airpower only tangentially.[50]

If the response by American airmen in professional military journals was sparse in the mid- and late 1960s, it was almost nonexistent during the 1970s. The seriously mixed feelings about the denouement of US combat involvement in Vietnam, the unfortunate final outcome of the struggle in 1975, the desire to put the entire experience to rest, the perceived need to refocus on the Soviet threat, and a variety of other factors combined to limit debate and research about airpower in protracted revolutionary warfare.[51]

The professional military journals in Great Britain had better luck in publication during the 1970s, but few of the articles dealt with the basics of airpower theory and doctrine in protracted revolutionary war. Rather, they recounted historical episodes or dealt with airpower very much at the tactical level.[52]

The publication in Great Britain in 1970 of the Royal Air Force (RAF) official history of the Malayan Emergency should have been far more important. It laid out in detail—and remarkable objectivity—RAF contributions to the successful counterinsurgent operations.[53] No evidence indicates that this volume had a significant impact in the United States.

The commercial press boasted a wealth of book-length literature during the 1970s.[54] These offerings included the first memoirs of senior military leaders involved in the Vietnamese struggle.[55] Unfortunately, they shed little real light on the use of airpower in counterinsurgency or protracted revolutionary warfare. This was particularly disappointing in the cases of Gen Edward Lansdale and Gen William Momyer. Lansdale served as an advisor in both the Philippines and Vietnam, but his book says little about the use of airpower in those conflicts.

Momyer, who commanded Seventh Air Force in Vietnam until 1968, produced an excellent operational history of the air war in Vietnam but stayed away from in-depth analysis of the peculiarities of airpower in that struggle. In his final chapter, however, he did draw some "lessons" about C² (the continuing validity of centralized control of airpower under a single theater air component commander), counterair operations ("the contest for air superiority is the most important contest of all"), interdiction ("we must focus . . . upon the most vital supply targets: factories, power plants, refineries, marshaling yards, and the transportation lines that carry bulk goods"), and close air support ("the tactical air control system must be very responsive").[56] In fact, all of these "lessons" were reaffirmations of traditional views and could have come from the history of a conventional war.

The Official Response

The first doctrinal response appeared in March 1967 with the publication of an Air Force manual exclusively devoted to "special air warfare."[57] A remarkably perceptive document, AFM 2-5, *Tactical Air Operations Special Air Warfare*, defined special air warfare as a rubric for the air aspects of psychological operations (PSYOP), counterinsurgency, and unconventional warfare.[58] The manual clearly indicated that military and nonmilitary counterinsurgency actions must be totally intertwined and mutually supporting, and called for the establishment of a "country team" (including representatives of the diplomatic mission, other civilian aid and information agencies in-country, the military assistance advisory group, the unified military command, and the military component commands) to establish and direct a unified strategy.[59]

The manual went on to indicate that the military portion of the strategy must vary by the phases of the insurgency (an obvious but unstated reference to classic protracted revolutionary war theory) and that within these phases, special air warfare actions would range from nation-building efforts to open combat.[60] It stressed the difficulty of target identification during combat—separating friend from foe. This was a crucial point because "military actions by friendly units which kill or injure innocent civilians can lose the loyalty of an otherwise friendly village."[61] Again, this reference pertains to classic insurgent theory and the fact that both sides in an

338

insurgency have the same center of gravity (the people) and that their objective is to capture the support of the population.

Unfortunately, the publication of AFM 2-5 did not establish a trend. By September 1971, when a new edition of Air Force basic doctrine appeared, the so-called Vietnamization of the war in Southeast Asia was well under way; most US combat forces had withdrawn; and the war itself had begun to take on the character of a conventional conflict. Interest began shifting back to the pressing problems of confronting potential Communist aggression in the more familiar climes of Europe and Korea.

The new basic doctrinal manual now devoted its final chapter not to the use of airpower in counterinsurgency, but to the broader subject of Air Force special operations. This new rubric, intended to replace "special air warfare" used in the 1967 version of AFM 2-5, introduced yet another new term, *foreign internal defense,* by which the manual writers meant *counterinsurgency.*[62]

In the scant one-and-one-half page chapter devoted to special operations, foreign internal defense rated only one paragraph. It did, however, reinforce the notion introduced in 1967 that one must closely coordinate air operations with civil actions as well as surface operations in a coordinated military-civilian campaign to eliminate the causes of popular disaffection and build a sense of national unity.

During the remainder of this period, doctrinal interest in protracted revolutionary conflicts declined, at least in terms of basic doctrine. The Air Force republished the basic doctrine manual in January 1975, retaining only two generalized subparagraphs (one pertaining to special operations and the other to subtheater and localized conflicts).[63] The same sort of very brief, very generalized treatment of insurgency-related topics carried forward to the 1979 edition.[64]

Intellectual Fervor and Official Disdain, 1980–94

The period beginning in 1980 and extending to the present writing has been a study in contrasts. On the one hand, enough time had passed since the trauma of the Vietnam experience that more balanced and objective analyses of the war began to appear from the pens of both civilian and military analysts. Ongoing events further spurred interest in limited warfare, LICs, and protracted revolutionary warfare. The mujahideen's protracted guerrilla struggle against Soviet occupation of Afghanistan became of great interest. Closer to home, insurgent movements in El Salvador and Nicaragua and continuing guerrilla struggles in Guatemala and Peru captured one's attention. Other protracted struggles in the Philippines and Sub-Saharan Africa helped prompt the outpouring of research literature in the civilian and military press. During much of this period, LIC and, more specifically, protracted revolutionary warfare remained "hot" topics, thought by many people to presage the future.[65]

On the other hand, the official response of the Air Force reflected confusion and disdain. At one level, the Air Force made significant progress toward an airpower theory that included protracted revolutionary warfare. At another level, the service ignored and contradicted that theory. The result, as of this writing, is confusion.

The Unofficial Response

Compared to that of previous periods, the literature on protracted revolutionary warfare was extensive. Importantly, analysts reached consensus about (1) the nature of LIC, (2) the general outlines of counterinsurgency strategy, (3) the airpower technology required, and (4) the role of airpower in the military portion of a counterinsurgency strategy.

Deryck Eller, Rod Paschall, Thomas Hammes, William Olson, Larry Cable, and I all came to the conclusion that LIC really means protracted revolutionary warfare (insurgency) or, at least within the low intensity field, that insurgency should remain the central consideration of policy makers and the military.[66] This conclusion is in line with the notions of Sam C. Sarkesian, who noted that the "substantive dimensions of such conflicts evolve primarily from revolutionary and counterrevolutionary strategy and causes. . . . Limited conventional wars and acts of terrorism are outside the boundaries of low-intensity conflicts. Revolution and counterrevolution are the major categories."[67]

Prescriptively, these authors also demonstrated large areas of consensus. First, virtually all agreed that increasing the legitimacy of the government under siege was the key to successful counterinsurgency. Accordingly, the government must secure the population from rebel threats and address the sources of insurgent dissatisfaction.[68] To reach these goals, the government must cut across traditional lines of authority and responsibility to produce a mutually reinforcing interagency effort. Further, almost all the authors agreed that the military portion of the struggle must minimize lethality in order to minimize collateral damage. The objective of military operations is not so much to kill insurgents as it is to coerce them and destroy their political will.

However, both Grant Hammond and Cable emphasized that counterinsurgency is not some sort of sociopolitical experiment. Hammond declared that we must see it for what it is—war, albeit very different from traditional notions of warfare.[69] Cable reminded his readers of the "simple fact that once armed insurgency has commenced, it becomes the functional equivalent of a total war of national survival in which only one of the two contenders for power will be extant at war's end."[70]

Airmen voiced considerable interest and consensus in the airpower technology required in such conflicts.[71] They nearly universally agreed that very sophisticated aircraft with attributes suitable for employment in high-speed conventional warfare are inappropriate and often ineffective in operations against enemy forces using guerrilla tactics, particularly in complex surface environments such as jungles. Jerome Klingaman summed up the problem by saying that "visual, aerial reconnaissance and surveillance of the guerrilla operating area is most effective when conducted at low altitude (below 1500 feet) and at low speed (under 125 knots). The effectiveness of visual surveillance deteriorates rapidly above these limits. Very few jet pilots actually saw a human target during the war in Southeast Asia."[72]

Further, the authors nearly universally agreed about the utility of the helicopter, including the armed helicopter, for many important roles. However, several of them expressed concern about slow, low-flying aircraft (whether fixed or rotary wing) in light of the development of effective shoulder-fired surface-to-air missiles (SAM). The Soviet experience in Afghanistan proved particularly enlightening insofar as these missiles seemed to change the entire character of the air war against the mujahideen rebels. As Aaron Karp noted, "The Stinger has quickly become the most celebrated rebel weapon of the West. Soviet Mi-24 Hind gunships, once the scourge of the battlefield, have now become the quarry."[73]

The right technology was only part of the problem for airmen. Best use of that equipment in a comprehensive strategy presented a problem that had not previously received extensive attention. During this period, much of the literature attempted, at least in part, to examine the theoretical side of airpower employment in counterinsurgent operations.[74] David Dean, for example, noted that "low-intensity conflict needs to be considered in terms of assistance, integration of forces, and intervention."[75] Writing in the mid-1980s, Dean focused on using special operations forces rather than the whole Air Force.

Olson took a broader view, extending well beyond special operations. He noted, for example, that traditional tactical airpower doctrine is inappropriate for counterinsurgencies: "Tactical air doctrine and the attending force structure are designed for conventional wars against conventional enemies. In most low-intensity conflict situations, control of the air is established by default, while isolation of the battlefield, where there are few and fleeting fixed battles, is a non sequitur."[76]

Olson went on to claim that airpower is most useful in supporting roles such as reconnaissance, troop transport, resupply, and presence.[77] John Green agrees that these noncombat roles are central to the contribution of airpower but maintains that close air support and possibly close interdiction can prove crucial if enemy guerrilla forces either attack isolated friendly forces or if one can fix them and force them to stand and fight.[78]

Drawing on the extensive literature of the RAF role in the Malayan Emergency, I agreed that the supporting roles of airpower are important—so important that to call them supporting is difficult. The utility of the traditional role of delivering firepower was controversial in Malaya and has remained so. However, technological advances in delivering aerial firepower may make it much more useful than the RAF found it to be. The key to the effective use of airpower in a counterinsurgent role, however, remains the total integration of the airpower role in the overall military campaign—and the total integration of the military campaign in the overall politico-military struggle. In many ways, the military portion of the struggle is the least important element of the effort.[79]

David Parsons produced the most innovative and comprehensive theoretical approach but came to many of the same conclusions as the authors previously cited. Using a relatively obscure essay published in 1970 by Nathan Leites and Charles Wolf Jr. as a framework,[80] Parsons produced both a general philosophical approach to counterinsurgency and the role of airpower in such efforts. According to Parsons, Leites and Wolf characterized an insurgency as a system of inputs, conversions, and outputs—all three of which form centers of gravity for an insurgent movement. A comprehensive counterinsurgent campaign must perform four functions: interdict inputs, disrupt the conversion process, reduce outputs, and build a government's capability to resist.[81]

Although military forces can prove useful in performing all four functions, their primary role lies in reducing outputs in the form of insurgent military forces, particularly their leadership cadre. In this role, conducting reconnaissance, maintaining air LOC, and flying close air support are most effective. However, airpower, in the form of PSYOP, can also be an effective tool in disrupting the conversion process—and the maintenance of air LOC can be crucial to building a government's legitimacy and capacity to resist the insurgent movement.[82]

Airmen concerned with protracted revolutionary warfare and other forms of LIC also experienced one severe disappointment during this period. Critics hailed *The Air Campaign: Planning for Combat* (1988) by Col John M. Warden III as the most significant theoretical work on airpower since the days of Billy Mitchell. Unfortunately, Warden addressed only conventional warfare and failed even to acknowledge the fundamental differences between conventional warfare and protracted revolutionary warfare.[83] The fact that Warden's subsequent writings have also ignored the subject is particularly unfortunate because his influence has become so pronounced within the Air Force. As one of the architects of the air campaign against Iraq in the Gulf War and subsequently as the commandant of Air Command and Staff College at Maxwell AFB, his stature as an authority on airpower theory has grown significantly, and his influence over an entire generation of Air Force officers is enormous.[84]

The Official Response

With the introduction of a new basic doctrine manual dated 16 March 1984, LIC had all but disappeared, save for two generalized paragraphs on special operations. But much more positive actions that held the promise of developing a theory of airpower applicable to protracted revolutionary warfare quickly overwhelmed this "slow start."

In 1985 the Air War College's annual Airpower Symposium at Maxwell AFB focused on LIC. Also in the mid-1980s, the Air Force established a Center for Low Intensity Conflict (which quickly became an Army–Air Force venture) and took part in a Joint Low Intensity Conflict Project sponsored by the Army's Training and Doctrine Command. Each of these developments represented growing interest in the subject, although the latter two developments produced nothing useful in terms of airpower theory.[85]

A major step forward was the publication in December 1990 of an Army–Air Force pamphlet devoted to LIC.[86] It introduced the internal defense and development (IDAD) strategy as the basis for all actions (military and civilian) within the LIC arena and brought together most of the concepts generally agreed upon in the professional literature over the previous 30 years. The pamphlet, however, presents its subject at a level of abstraction that precludes specifics about the use of airpower. For example, appendix E, "A Guide to Counterinsurgency Operations," includes only one sentence about airpower.[87]

The IDAD strategy, which blends interdependent civil-military functions, was the most comprehensive plan yet seen in official literature for preventing or defeating insurgencies. Its four functions—balanced development, mobilization of resources, population security, and neutralization of insurgents—provided the framework for a comprehensive doctrinal statement about airpower in counterinsurgency operations that appeared two years later.

On 3 November 1992, the US Air Force published its operational-level doctrine for foreign internal defense (by now the accepted terminology for counterinsurgency) within the IDAD strategy framework.[88] In chapter three of the manual appeared two paragraphs that represented the culmination of more than 30 years of field experience, unofficial professional literature as well as official publications, symposia, and the like.

The first of these two paragraphs discussed priority operations for airpower during the development and mobilization functions of the IDAD strategy: "Where ground lines of communication cannot be established and maintained because of terrain or enemy presence, aerial logistic and communication networks carrying information, supplies, and services to civilian elements establish a critical link between the government and the population."[89]

The second paragraph addressed priority of operations for airpower during the security and neutralization functions: "Insurgents generally possess no air capabilities . . . have no heartland, no fixed industrial facilities, and few interdictable LOC. . . . Their irregular forces are deployed in small units that . . . usually present poor targets for air attack. In such cases, air support for security and neutralization should be used primarily to inform, deploy, sustain, and reinforce surface elements of the internal security force."[90]

These paragraphs constituted more than a statement of operational doctrine. They embodied airpower theory stated in the best traditions of the early airpower theorists. Like the kind of warfare with which they deal, these paragraphs stand conventional airpower theory on its ear.

Thus by 1992 airmen had made considerable progress in modifying traditional airpower theory to the special case of insurgency or protracted revolutionary warfare. However, during the 1980s and early 1990s, while these events were taking place, a very different chain of events that would stifle and confuse the progress was also under way.

The perceived importance of protracted revolutionary warfare was far from universal. A significant number of military officers—many of them very senior—believed for one reason or another that special attention to such "unconventional" strategies was ill advised and perhaps counterproductive. For example, in the mid-1980s a very senior Air Force general officer told me that the Air Force should not be distracted by "those kind of wars" (insurgencies) since we can always just "muddle through." Rather, we should concentrate on wars "that can eat our bacon."

Eventually, the belief by some senior officers that protracted revolutionary warfare was ordinary, unimportant, or counterproductive from the standpoint of airpower, eliminated discussion of the subject from the highest level of Air Force doctrine—AFM 1-1, *Basic Aerospace Doctrine of the United States Air Force* (1992). The theory so painstakingly developed thus languished at lower levels in an obscure manual of operational doctrine—namely, the aforementioned AFM 2-11.[91] In fact, at one point the basic doctrine of 1992 appears to contradict directly the theory promulgated in AFM 2-11. Specifically, AFM 2-11 notes that insurgents "have no heartland, no fixed industrial facilities, and few interdictable LOC,"[92] whereas AFM 1-1 declares that "any enemy with the capacity to be a threat is likely to have strategic vulnerabilities susceptible to air attack."[93]

Conclusion

US airmen have long been known for their fascination with technology and the mental toughness required to press home a bombing attack against fierce resistance or to outduel an enemy fighter. But they have never been known for their academic inquisitiveness, their devotion to the study of the art of war, or their contributions to the theory of airpower. Instead, American airmen have remained "doers" rather than introspective "thinkers."

Nowhere was that more evident than in the US Air Force approach to the problem of protracted revolutionary warfare. Wedded to the concept of "atomic airpower" (and its power to justify an independent Air Force) during the 1950s and early 1960s, American airmen virtually ignored the problem of insurgent warfare until they entered the Vietnam War.

After the United States withdrew from Vietnam, bitter memories, confusion about the impact of strategic bombing on the war's end, disagreement over the very nature of the conflict, and the continuing Soviet threat made it all too easy for US airmen to push the unsettled enigma of protracted warfare into the background. Retreating to the familiar problems of strategic nuclear warfare and conventional warfare in Europe seemed much more comfortable.

But the problem would not go away. Afghanistan, El Salvador, Guatemala, Peru, and other trouble spots forced the subject to the surface in the 1980s, and some airmen began to seriously investigate the peculiarities of airpower application in insurgent warfare. They succeeded in producing a concise, well-reasoned modification of traditional airpower theory based on the consensus developed over nearly 40 years of experience, research, and publication.

Unfortunately, the doctrine they developed has not had the impact it deserves. It remains buried in an obscure operational-level doctrinal manual that few people know exists and even fewer have ever read. Basic Air Force doctrine, the capstone of Air Force airpower theory, remains virtually unaffected at best and contradictory at worst. Most importantly, however, the theory so painstakingly developed—the one that airmen may need to deal with the post-cold-war world—remains largely unknown.

In the grand scheme of things, the four-decade journey from the grandiose theory of strategic bombardment and atomic airpower to the subtle complexities of protracted revolutionary warfare has been quite short. Unfortunately for American airmen, the journey has ended in contradiction and confusion.

Notes

1. For example, see Richard E. Simpkin, *Race to the Swift* (London: Brassey's Defence Publishers, 1985), chap. 18; and Martin van Creveld, *The Transformation of War* (New York: Free Press, 1991), particularly his short chapter entitled "Postscript: The Shape of Things to Come."

2. Doctrine has many functions, but one can adequately define it as a "framework for understanding how to apply military power. It is what history has taught us works in war, as well as what does not." US Air Force basic doctrine is officially described as "what we have learned about

aerospace power and its application since the dawn of powered flight" and a "broad conceptual basis for our understanding of war, human nature, and aerospace power." Finally, it is officially described as "the starting point for solving contemporary problems." Air Force Manual (AFM) 1-1, *Basic Aerospace Doctrine of the United States Air Force*, vol. 1, March 1992, v, vii. Although doctrine may not fulfill all of the requirements of a formal academic definition of theory, it fulfills most of the same functions and in that sense forms a "poor man's" theory of airpower.

3. The Joint Chiefs of Staff (JCS) define low intensity conflict as "political-military confrontation between contending states or groups *below conventional war and above the routine, peaceful competition among states.* It frequently involves protracted struggles of competing principles and ideologies. Low intensity conflict ranges from subversion to the use of armed force. It is waged by a combination of means employing political, economic, informational, and military instruments. Low intensity conflicts are often localized, generally in the Third World, but contain regional and global security implications" (emphasis added). Such a broad definition lends itself to the inclusion of a wide variety of activities, especially since the upper boundary (conventional war) is not defined by the JCS. Joint Pub 1-02, *Department of Defense Dictionary of Military and Associated Terms*, 23 March 1994, 222.

4. Joint Pub 3-07, *Doctrine for Joint Operations in Low Intensity Conflict*, October 1990.

5. Col Dennis M. Drew, "Insurgency and Counterinsurgency: American Military Dilemmas and Doctrinal Proposals," CADRE Papers, no. AU-ARI-CP-88-1 (Maxwell AFB, Ala.: Air University Press, March 1988).

6. Ho Chi Minh, quoted in Douglas Pike, *PAVN: People's Army of Vietnam* (Novato, Calif.: Presidio Press, 1986), 219.

7. Ibid., 222–30. The Vietnamese called their version of this dual strategy "dau tranh." Pike also notes that "the basic objective in dau tranh strategy is to put armed conflict into the context of political dissidence. . . . Conceptually they cannot be separated. Dau tranh is a seamless web." Ibid., 233.

8. Between 1965 and 1968 in the Vietnam conflict, 75 percent of all the battles occurred at the insurgents' choice of time, place, and duration. Further, fewer than 1 percent of the nearly 2 million allied small-unit offensive operations resulted in any contact with the enemy. See W. Scott Thompson and Donaldson D. Frizzell, *The Lessons of Vietnam* (New York: Crane, Russak, 1977), 92, which quotes a national security study memorandum of 1968 to this effect.

9. To my knowledge, the first person to point out this logistics phenomenon was Sir Robert Thompson, the British expert on counterinsurgent warfare. See his book *No Exit from Vietnam* (New York: David McKay, 1970), 32–34.

10. Drew, 18–19.

11. Communist Party of the Philippines Secretariat, memorandum to the Central Committee, quoted in Lt Col Tomas C. Tirona, "The Philippine Anti-Communist Campaign," *Air University Quarterly Review*, Summer 1954, 42–55.

12. Ibid., 46–52.

13. Daniel S. Challis, "Counterinsurgency Success in Malaya," *Military Review*, February 1987, 57.

14. In 1957 Secretary of Defense Charles Wilson testified before Congress that the "capability to deter large wars also serves to deter small wars." The following year, Wilson told the Congress, "There is very little money in the budget . . . for the procurement of so-called conventional weapons. . . . We are depending on atomic weapons for the defense of the Nation." Robert Frank Futrell, *Ideas, Concepts, Doctrine: Basic Thinking in the United States Air Force*, vol. 1, *1907–1960* (Maxwell AFB, Ala.: Air University Press, December 1989), 454, 459.

15. G. J. M. Chassin, "Lessons of the War in Indochina," *Interavia* 7 (1952): 670–75.

16. Tirona.

17. William M. Reid, "Tactical Air in Limited War," *Air University Quarterly Review*, Spring 1956, 40–48.

18. The first volume, written by the Instruction Bureau of Commander in Chief Indochina, was entitled *Notes on Combat in Indo-China* (1954). The second volume, written by the Supreme Command Far East, was entitled *Lessons from the Indo-China War*, vol. 2 (1955). The third volume, apparently also written by the Supreme Command Far East, was entitled *Lessons from the Indo-China War*, vol. 3 (ca. 1955–1956). It is unclear when the English translations of these documents became available to the US military. The Defense Documentation Center did not receive copies until 3 January 1967. Not requesting and/or receiving copies prior to 1967 would represent a major failure of the US military to tap into the knowledge and experience of a major NATO ally.

19. *Notes on Combat*, 34. This Vietminh document accurately described what later became known as "clinging to the enemy's belt"—that is, remaining so close to the enemy that both airpower and distant, heavy artillery fires become unusable.

20. *Lessons from the Indo-China War*, vol. 2, 297–98; and vol. 3, 32–37.

21. *Lessons from the Indo-China War*, vol. 3, 38.

22. Many people viewed Kennedy's inaugural address, which promised to "fight any fight, bear any burden," as a sign that the United States would become much more heavily involved in wars such as those ongoing in Southeast Asia.

23. Richard E. Stanley, "A Concept of Anti-Guerrilla Operations in Indo-China" (Maxwell AFB, Ala.: Air Command and Staff College, April 1961), 44–54.

24. Guenter Lewy, *America in Vietnam* (New York: Oxford University Press, 1978), 257. However, Lewy also notes that the British had made use

of defoliants in Malaya and that the United States began testing defoliants as early as 1958.

25. See the following unpublished research papers: William R. Becker, "Air Power in the Fight against Guerrillas" (Maxwell AFB, Ala.: Air Command and Staff College, 7 May 1962); John L. Phipps, "Basic Problems in Counter-Guerrilla Air Operations" (Maxwell AFB, Ala.: Air Command and Staff College, 7 May 1962); William C. Lockett Jr., "COIN in the Air: A Study of the Role of Airpower in Counterinsurgency" (Maxwell AFB, Ala.: Air Command and Staff College, 22 April 1963); and Rupert L. Selman, "What Operational Concepts Should Govern the Use of Tactical Air Forces in Guerrilla War?" (Maxwell AFB, Ala.: Air War College, April 1963).

26. Lockett states that "normally, there are no strategic targets, no opposition to air superiority, and very few tactical targets. Therefore, air operations are primarily involved with indirect support of ground forces" (page 54).

27. Becker, 91.

28. Peter Paret and John W. Shy, "Guerrilla War and U.S. Military Policy: A Study," *Marine Corps Gazette*, January 1962, 24–32.

29. D. G. Loomis, "Counter-Insurgent Operations in Indonesia-1958," *Marine Corps Gazette*, October 1962, 34–41.

30. N. D. Valeriano and C. T. R. Bohannon, "The Philippine Experience," *Marine Corps Gazette*, September 1963, 19–24; October 1963, 42–45; November 1963, 46–51; and December 1963, 41–43.

31. William J. Thorpe, "HUK Hunting in the Philippines, 1946–1953," *The Airpower Historian*, April 1962, 95–100.

32. James F. Sunderman, "Air Escort—A COIN Technique," *Air University Review*, November–December 1963, 68–73.

33. AFM 1-2, *United States Air Force Basic Doctrine*, 1953, 1954, April 1955, and December 1959. The next issue of the basic doctrine manual (AFM 1-1) did not appear until fall 1964.

34. AFM 1-3, *Theater Air Operations*, September 1953 and April 1954. The next edition of this manual (AFM 2-1) did not appear until June 1965.

35. Message, DTG 302128Z, vice chief of staff, Headquarters USAF, March 1954, as quoted in David J. Dean, *The Air Force Role in Low-Intensity Conflict* (Maxwell AFB, Ala.: Air University Press, October 1986), 87.

36. Dean, 87–94; and Robert Frank Futrell, *Ideas, Concepts, Doctrine: Basic Thinking in the United States Air Force*, vol. 2, *1961–1984* (Maxwell AFB, Ala.: Air University Press, December 1989), 257–58.

37. Curtis E. LeMay, "Airpower in Guerrilla Warfare," *Air Force Information Policy Letter for Commanders* 16, no. 80 (15 April 1962).

38. Gilbert L. Pritchard, "Communism and Counterinsurgency: Air Force Role in Combined Support Action," *Air Force Information Policy Letter Supplement for Commanders*, no.113 (3 November 1962).

39. AFM 1-1, *United States Air Force Basic Doctrine*, 14 August 1964. See in particular chap. 6, "Employment of Aerospace Forces in Counterinsurgency," 6-1 through 6-2.

40. United States Department of State, *United States-Vietnam Relations, 1945–1967* (Washington, D.C.: Government Printing Office, 1971). This is the official, multivolume "Pentagon Papers," also published in two other unofficial forms. See in particular, McGeorge Bundy, "A Policy of Sustained Reprisal," in vol. 4, C. 3:35, annex A, 7 February 1965. Also refer to the narrative found in vol. 4, C. 3:4.

41. *United States-Viet Nam Relations*, vol. 4, C. 3:4 and 3:35–38; William Bundy, "Draft Position Paper on Southeast Asia" (29 November 1964), as found in Gerald Gold, Allan M. Siegal, and Samuel Abt, eds., *The Pentagon Papers, New York Times Edition* (New York: Bantam Books, 1971), 373–78; John T. McNaughton, "Annex—Plan for Action for South Vietnam" (24 March 1965), as found in Gold, Siegal, and Abt, *The Pentagon Papers*, 434; and Doris Kearns, *Lyndon Johnson and the American Dream* (New York: Harper & Row, 1976), 264–65.

42. Raphael Littauer and Norman Uphoff, eds., *The Air War in Indochina* (Boston: Beacon Press, 1972), 37.

43. John S. Pustay, *Counterinsurgency Warfare* (New York: Free Press, 1965), 116–35. Pustay retired as a lieutenant general.

44. Concepts Division, Aerospace Studies Institute, "Guerrilla Warfare and Airpower in Algeria, 1954–1960" (Maxwell AFB, Ala.: Air University, March 1965), 88.

45. Bernard B. Fall, "The Theory and Practice of Insurgency and Counterinsurgency," *Naval War College Review*, April 1965, 21–37.

46. Rollen H. Anthis, "Airpower: The Paradox in Vietnam," *Air Force Magazine*, April 1967, 34–38. Anthis maintained that field commanders recognized airpower as "dominant in combat" (page 34). He also stated that US airpower and nuclear superiority forced the Communists to resort to insurgency and guerrilla tactics in their quest for world domination. This, of course, raises the question of why the same insurgent/guerrilla tactics were used against the British in Malaya and the French in Vietnam, neither of whom had overwhelming airpower—let alone nuclear superiority.

47. Col Robert L. Hardie, "Airpower in Counterinsurgency Warfare," Report no. 3373 (Maxwell AFB, Ala.: Air War College, April 1967).

48. Robert M. Kipp, "Counterinsurgency from 30,000 Feet," *Air University Review*, January–February 1968, 10–18.

49. P. Brighton, "The War in South Vietnam," *Royal Air Forces Quarterly*, Winter 1968, 289–93. One sees the truth of this observation in the fact that sapper attacks on US air bases in South Vietnam destroyed 96 aircraft (about one and one-third fighter-wing equivalents)—nearly 33 percent more than those destroyed in air-to-air combat and nearly as many as destroyed by the vaunted North Vietnamese surface-to-air missile systems. Nor does the figure of 96 destroyed include aircraft damaged and other destruction accomplished by sapper attacks, which adversely affected air operations. Walter Kross, *Military Reform: The High-Tech Debate in Tactical Air Forces* (Washington, D.C.: National Defense University Press, 1985), 98.

50. Among the well-read books concentrating on the military struggle that should have caught the serious attention of American airmen were Bernard B. Fall's four books—*Street without Joy* (Harrisburg, Pa.: Stackpole, 1961); *The Two Viet-Nams: A Political and Military Analysis* (New York: Praeger, 1963); *Viet-Nam Witness, 1953–66* (New York: Praeger, 1966); and *Hell in a Very Small Place: The Siege of Dien Bien Phu* (Philadelphia: Lippincott, 1967)—Jules Roy's *The Battle of Dienbienphu* (New York: Harper & Row, 1965); Ho Chi Minh's *On Revolution* (New York: Praeger, 1967); Vo Nguyen Giap's *The People's War, People's Army* (New York: Praeger, 1962); Douglas Pike's *War, Peace, and the Viet Cong* (Cambridge, Mass.: MIT Press, 1969); and Sir Robert Thompson's *No Exit from Vietnam* (New York: David McKay, 1969).

51. During the 1970s, Air University attempted to produce monographs about important subjects/events in the Vietnam conflict, resulting in the *Southeast Asia Monograph Series* published through the US Government Printing Office between 1976 and 1979. Evidently, this effort was neither well organized nor supported because some of the nine monographs produced appear to have been "sponsored" either by Air War College or Air Command and Staff College. Some appear to have been student projects while others were written by general officers. The final two monographs were produced under the auspices of the Airpower Research Institute. Additionally, the subject matter varies widely, ranging from in-depth analyses of individual air operations to broad views of entire air campaigns. The final monograph in the series is a "puff piece" about Air Force heroes of the war in Southeast Asia. The lack of monograph titles (only nine covering nearly a decade of US involvement in Vietnam), the lack of consistent sponsorship, and the occasionally slipshod editing and publishing of the series may be a further indication of the lack of serious interest in the Vietnam War following the US withdrawal. In a sense, US airmen may have been suffering from collective intellectual "battle fatigue."

52. See, for example, the following: S. W. B. Menaul, "The Use of Air Power in Vietnam," *RUSI Journal of the Royal United Services Institute for Defence Studies*, June 1971, 5–15; Thomas H. Henriksen, "Lessons from Portugal's Counter-insurgency Operations in Africa," *RUSI Journal of the Royal United Services Institute for Defence Studies*, June 1978, 31–35; and Thomas Arbuckle, "Rhodesian Bush War Strategies and Tactics: An Assessment," *RUSI Journal of the Royal United Services Institute for Defence Studies*, December 1979, 27–33.

53. Royal Air Force, *The Malayan Emergency, 1948–1960* (London: Ministry of Defence, 1970).

54. Among the most important of these were three different editions of the so-called Pentagon Papers, all published in 1971 by Beacon Press, Bantam Books (via the *New York Times*), and the US Government Printing Office; Don Oberdorfer's *TET!* (Garden City, N.Y.: Doubleday, 1971); Sir Robert Thompson's *Peace Is Not at Hand* (New York: David McKay, 1974); Robert Asprey's *War in the Shadows*, 2 vols. (New York: Doubleday, 1975);

W. Scott Thompson and Donaldson D. Frizzell's *The Lessons of Vietnam* (New York: Crane, Russak, 1977); Lewy's *America in Vietnam;* and Peter Braestrup's *Big Story* (Boulder, Colo.: Westview Press, 1977).

55. Included among these were Edward Geary Lansdale's *In the Midst of Wars* (New York: Harper & Row, 1972); William C. Westmoreland's *A Soldier Reports* (New York: Doubleday, 1976); U. S. Grant Sharp's *Strategy for Defeat* (San Rafael, Calif.: Presidio Press, 1978); and William W. Momyer's *Airpower in Three Wars* (Washington, D. C.: Government Printing Office, 1978).

56. Momyer, 337–38.

57. AFM 2-5, *Tactical Air Operations Special Air Warfare,* 10 March 1967.

58. Ibid., 18. The manual defined "unconventional warfare" as efforts to "strengthen or create resistance to enemy authority among the people within enemy territory." Put another way, unconventional warfare was insurgency rather than counterinsurgency.

59. Ibid., 13.

60. Ibid., 14.

61. Ibid., 16.

62. AFM 1-1, *United States Air Force Basic Doctrine,* 28 September 1971, 6-1.

63. AFM 1-1, *United States Air Force Basic Doctrine,* 15 January 1975, 3-4, 3-6.

64. AFM 1-1, *Functions and Basic Doctrine of the United States Air Force,* 14 February 1979, 1-9, 1-10.

65. During this period, both Simpkin and van Creveld published their widely read analyses, both of which predicted that such conflicts would be the future of warfare. See note 1.

66. Deryck J. Eller, "Doctrine for Low Intensity Conflict" (paper presented to the Ninth Air University Airpower Symposium, Air War College, Maxwell AFB, Ala., March 1985); Rod Paschall, "Low-Intensity Conflict Doctrine—Who Needs It?" *Parameters* 15 (1985): 33–45; Thomas X. Hammes, "Insurgency—The Forgotten Threat," *Marine Corps Gazette,* March 1988, 40–44; William Olson, "The Concept of Small Wars," *Small Wars and Insurgencies,* April 1990, 39–46 (although he did not directly so state, Olson agreed by implication); Larry Cable, "Reinventing the Round Wheel—Insurgency, Counter-Insurgency, and Peacekeeping Post Cold War," *Small Wars and Insurgencies,* April 1993, 228–62; and Drew.

67. Sam C. Sarkesian, "Low-Intensity Conflict—Concepts, Principles, and Policy Guidelines," in David J. Dean, ed., *Low-Intensity Conflict and Modern Technology* (Maxwell AFB, Ala.: Air University Press, 1986), 12.

68. Drew, 35–36, refers to the co-option of the insurgent cause, while Cable, 235, refers to preemptive reforms.

69. Grant T. Hammond, "Low Intensity Conflict: War by Another Name," *Small Wars and Insurgencies,* December 1993, 231.

70. Cable, 252.

71. See, for example (listed in order of publication), Mark Lambert, "Counter-Revolutionary Air Power," *Interavia,* May 1981, 475–77; Jerome W.

Klingaman, "Low-Intensity Conflict and Modern Technology: Light Aircraft Technology for Small Wars," in Dean, *Low-Intensity Conflict and Modern Technology;* Anthony A. Cardoza, "Soviet Aviation in Afghanistan," US Naval Institute *Proceedings,* February 1987, 85–88; David A. Reinholz, "A Way to Improve Our Marginal Counterinsurgency Airlift Capability," *Armed Forces Journal International,* July 1987, 40–46; Victor J. Croizat, "Helicopter Warfare in Algeria," *Marine Corps Gazette,* August 1987, 23–25; Aaron Karp, "Blowpipes and Stingers in Afghanistan—One Year Later," *Armed Forces Journal International,* September 1987, 36–40; Raymond Knox, "High Speed Jets in a Low Speed War—The Utility of Tactical Airpower in Low-Intensity Conflict" (Fort Leavenworth, Kans.: School of Advanced Military Studies, US Army Command and General Staff College, 20 April 1989); Vance C. Bateman, "The Role of Tactical Air Power in Low-Intensity Conflict," *Airpower Journal* 5, no. 1 (Spring 1991): 72–81; and George C. Morris, "The Other Side of the COIN—Low-Technology Aircraft and Little Wars," *Airpower Journal* 5, no. 1 (Spring 1991): 56–70.

72. Klingaman, 9.

73. Karp, 40.

74. See, for example (listed in order of publication), John D. Green, "Reflections on Counter Guerrilla Tactical Air Operations" (paper presented to the Ninth Air University Airpower Symposium, Air War College, Maxwell AFB, Ala., March 1985); William J. Olson, "Airpower in Low Intensity Conflict in the Middle East" (paper presented to the Ninth Air University Airpower Symposium, Air War College, Maxwell AFB, Ala., March 1985), subsequently published in *Air University Review,* March–April 1986, 2–21; Dean, *The Air Force Role;* David Willard Parsons, "Toward the Proper Application of Air Power in Low Intensity Conflict" (thesis, Naval Postgraduate School, December 1993); and Dennis M. Drew, "Air Power in Peripheral Conflict," in Alan Stephens, ed., *The War in the Air, 1914–1994* (Royal Australian Air Force [RAAF] Base Fairbairn, Australia: Air Power Studies Centre, 1994), 235–70.

75. Dean, *The Air Force Role,* 110.

76. Olson, "Air Power in Low-Intensity Conflict" (*AU Review* version), 17.

77. Ibid., 18.

78. Green, 7–11.

79. Drew, "Air Power in Peripheral Conflict," 241–48, 263–64.

80. Nathan Leites and Charles Wolf Jr., *Rebellion and Authority: An Analytic Essay on Insurgent Conflicts* (Chicago: Markham Publishing, 1970).

81. Parsons, 60–63.

82. Ibid., 71–75.

83. John A. Warden III, *The Air Campaign: Planning for Combat* (Fort Lesley J. McNair, Washington, D.C.: National Defense University Press, 1988). The index of this book includes no listing for low intensity conflict, insurgency, counterinsurgency, protracted revolutionary warfare, or partisan warfare; it includes only one reference to guerrilla warfare—in connection with the futility of aerial interdiction against self-sufficient forces.

84. Actually, Warden has published very little. Other than his book, his only other publications are "Planning to Win," *Air University Review* 34, no. 3 (March–April 1983): 94–97; "Employing Air Power in the Twenty-first Century," in Richard H. Shultz Jr. and Robert L. Pfaltzgraff Jr., eds., *The Future of Air Power in the Aftermath of the Gulf War* (Maxwell AFB, Ala.: Air University Press, 1992), 57–82; and "The Enemy as a System," *Airpower Journal* 9, no. 1 (Spring 1995): 40–55. When he served as commandant of Air Command and Staff College, he produced several unpublished essays, one of the most well known of which is "Air Theory for the Twenty-first Century." For an insightful critique of Warden, see David S. Fadok's chapter in this volume.

85. The Army–Air Force Center for Low Intensity Conflict produced 51 major studies between 1987 and the present writing. Only three pertained directly to airpower: *Logistic Support for Low Intensity Conflict—An Air Force Perspective; Planning Considerations for the Combat Employment of Air Power in Peacetime Contingency Operations;* and *A Security Assistance Example—The US Air Force and the African Coastal Security Program* (Langley AFB, Va.: Center for Low Intensity Conflict, 1988, 1988, and 1989, respectively). Nonairmen dominated the Joint Low Intensity Conflict Project (only 13 percent of the participants were from the Air Force). Its final report addressed only three airpower issues—all concerning specialized aircraft. *Joint Low Intensity Conflict Project Final Report* (Fort Monroe, Va.: Joint Low Intensity Conflict Project, United States Army Training and Doctrine Command, 1 August 1986).

86. Field Manual (FM) 100-2 and Air Force Pamphlet (AFP) 3-20, *Military Operations in Low Intensity Conflict,* 5 December 1990.

87. Ibid., E-4.

88. AFM 2-11, *Foreign Internal Defense Operations,* 3 November 1992.

89. Ibid., 9, par. 3-3a.

90. Ibid., 9–10, par. 3-3b.

91. I was the team leader and one of the principal authors of the Air Force basic doctrine manual published in March 1992. Early drafts of the manual contained extensive information about the peculiar nature of protracted revolutionary warfare and extensive comment about the employment of airpower in such conflicts. All of this was essentially eliminated at the general-officer level after lengthy arguments between me and the general officers concerned. What remains are vague references rather than explicit theory.

92. AFM 2-11, 9–10, par. 3-3b.

93. AFM 1-1, *Basic Aerospace Doctrine of the United States Air Force,* vol. 1, March 1992, 12, par. 3-5a(5). This particular assertion was inserted at the general-officer level over my objections. Interestingly, vol. 2 of the manual, which contains evidence for every doctrinal statement made in vol. 1, contains no evidence of any kind to support this particular assertion.

Chapter 10

John Boyd and John Warden:
Airpower's Quest for Strategic Paralysis

Lt Col David S. Fadok

A strategist should think in terms of paralysing, not of killing.

—B. H. Liddell Hart

Since the advent of heavier-than-air flight in 1903, theorists have posited numerous schemes to exploit the inherent ability of aircraft to rise above the fray of the battlefield and go straight to the heart of an enemy nation. From seeds sown by the Italian pioneer Giulio Douhet, strategic airpower theory has steadily evolved throughout the twentieth century. Along the way, it has been fashioned by harsh lessons of war, advances in technology, and the visionary concepts of a few, select airmen.

Two modern-day theorists, Col John Boyd, now deceased, and Col John Warden, now retired from the US Air Force, have significantly contributed to this evolutionary process. Although Boyd does not offer an airpower theory per se, his thoughts on conflict have significant implications for the employment of airpower at all levels of war. In contrast, Warden has developed an airpower theory but focuses primarily on the strategic application of the air weapon. This chapter summarizes and critiques each man's thoughts as they pertain to strategic conventional airpower.[1] Further, it identifies and explains the theoretical linkages and disconnects between the two and highlights their contributions to the evolution of airpower theory.

Specifically, I contend that (1) Boyd's theory of conflict and Warden's theory of strategic attack share a theme common to most, if not all, theories of strategic airpower—the goal of defeating one's adversary by strategic paralysis; (2) their divergent thoughts on strategic paralysis represent two

357

distinct traditions regarding the nature and purpose of theory; and (3) together, the paralysis theories of Boyd and Warden represent a fundamental shift in the evolution of strategic airpower thought from an emphasis on economic warfare to an emphasis on control warfare.[2] To demonstrate these assertions, one must first define the concept of strategic paralysis.

Seven years after the "war to end all wars," Basil H. Liddell Hart published the first of his many books on military strategy and modern-day war. Its clever title, *Paris; Or the Future of War*, recalls the mythical defeat of Achilles by his opponent Paris, via the surgical strike of a well-aimed arrow. As the title further suggests, attacking enemy vulnerabilities (instead of strengths) could and should serve as the role model for the conduct of war in the years ahead. The killing fields of World War I had certainly made Paris's strategy preferable; the technologies of flight and mechanization seemed to make it possible as well. Thus, the search began for those key vulnerabilities of an enemy nation that were crucial to its survival and protected by the sword and shield of its armed forces. Along the way, airpower theorists reintroduced the notion of paralysis into the lexicon of military strategy.

These early air enthusiasts extolled the "third dimension" that the aerial weapon added to the battlefield. The airplane's unique ability to rise above the fray of surface battle led many people to speculate that airpower could defeat an enemy nation and its armed forces by incapacitating—or paralyzing—the vulnerable war-making potential in the rear. Inflicting paralysis through aerial attack upon the Achilles' heel of the enemy nation seemingly promised decisive victory at significantly lower cost in terms of lives and treasure.

To more clearly define the concept of strategic paralysis, one should examine the idea in light of the theoretical constructs developed by two preeminent military writers—the British strategist J. F. C. Fuller and the German historian Hans Delbruck. Fuller's typology helps distinguish what strategic paralysis is, while Delbruck's demonstrates what it is not.

In *The Foundations of the Science of War*, Fuller sets out to examine the nature of war as a science, beginning his study by introducing the concept of the threefold order. He insists that this order is "a foundation so universal that it may be considered axiomatic to knowledge in all its forms."[3] Since humans consist of body, mind, and soul, wars as human activities must be subject to a similar constitution. Adopting the threefold order as the framework for his military study, Fuller posits three spheres of war—physical, mental, and moral.[4] Respectively, these spheres deal with destruction of the enemy's physical strength (fighting power), disorganization of his mental processes (thinking power), and disintegration of his moral will to resist (staying power). Fuller adds that forces operating within these spheres do so in synergistic, not isolated, ways: "Mental force does not win a war; moral force does not win a war; physical force does not win a war; but what *does* win a war is the highest combination of these three forces acting as *one* force" (emphasis in original).[5] This threefold order proves useful in beginning to understand the essence of strategic paralysis.

Paralysis of an adversary consists of physical, mental, and moral dimensions. As a strategy, it entails the nonlethal intent to physically disable and mentally disorient an enemy so as to induce his moral collapse. Although nonlethal intent does not necessarily preclude destructive action or prevent fatal results, it does seek to minimize these negative outcomes as much as possible.[6] These physical, mental, and moral effects may be short or long term, as required by one's grand strategy. Put another way, strategic paralysis aims at the enemy's physical and mental capabilities to indirectly engage and defeat his moral will.[7]

In addition to his threefold order, Fuller offers another theoretical proposition in *Foundations* that helps define strategic paralysis. Appropriate for any scientist of war, Fuller establishes a variety of battle principles to assist his students of military strategy. The overriding principle that governs the conduct of war—the "law" from which he derives nine subordinate principles—is economy of force. What this law contributes to the definition of strategic paralysis is the concept of expending minimum effort to produce maximum effect—something Paris did quite well against his nemesis Achilles.

Having constructed a partial definition of paralysis (a three-dimensional strategy characterized by nonlethal intent and force economization), we can now examine this notion in light of Delbruck's typology, to further refine our concept by demonstrating what strategic paralysis is not. In a truly seminal work with a distinct Clausewitzian flavor, Delbruck presents a comprehensive *History of the Art of War within the Framework of Political History.* In it, he addresses two traditional strategies of combat—annihilation and attrition. The strategy of annihilation aims to destroy enemy armed forces, whereas the strategy of attrition seeks to exhaust them. Unfortunately, as Delbruck himself feared, the majority of his readers misconstrued these as the strategy of the strong (i.e., quantitatively superior) and of the weak, respectively.

Delbruck coins the term *Ermattungs-Strategie* (strategy of attrition) as an opposite to Carl von Clausewitz's *Niederwerfungs-Strategie* (strategy of annihilation) but confesses that "the expression has the weakness of coming close to the misconception of a pure maneuver strategy."[8] Since by definition, annihilation strategy always seeks destruction of enemy armed forces through decisive battle, he worries that people will misinterpret his notion of attrition strategy as the constant avoidance of battle through maneuver. To clarify, Delbruck further defines the strategy of attrition as "double-poled strategy," one pole being battle and the other maneuver. A military commander employing an attrition strategy would continually shift between battle and maneuver, favoring one pole over the other as circumstances dictate.[9] Thus, while strategies of annihilation produce rapid decisions through overwhelming defeat of enemy armed forces, strategies of attrition produce more drawn-out affairs capped by the slow but steady softening of the enemy's will.[10]

In contrast, strategic paralysis is a strategy neither of annihilation nor attrition but a third type of warfare. It does not seek rapid decision via destruction of enemy armed forces in battle. Likewise, it does not seek drawn-out decision via exhaustion of the enemy by continual shifting between the poles of battle and maneuver. In contrast to both, it seeks rapid decision via enemy incapacitation by fusing battle and maneuver. It bypasses battle with enemy armed forces in favor of attack upon the sustainment and control of those armed forces. Strategic paralysis is neither pure battle nor pure maneuver but a unique melding of the two—"maneuver battle" against war-making potential.

To summarize, we note that strategic paralysis is a military option with physical, mental, and moral dimensions that intends to disable rather than destroy the enemy. It seeks maximum possible political effect or benefit with minimum necessary military effort or cost. Further, it aims at rapid decision through a maneuver battle directed against an adversary's physical and mental capability to sustain and control his war effort in order to diminish his moral will to resist. With this working definition in place, the chapter now traces how the thread of strategic paralysis became woven into the fabric of airpower thought.

In the wake of World War I, two British veterans of that tragic carnage—Fuller and Liddell Hart—weighed in on the side of strategic paralysis. Fuller, the designer of what is perhaps the first modern-day operational plan aimed at enemy paralysis (Plan 1919), later wrote that "the physical strength of an army lies in its organization, controlled by its brain. Paralyse this brain and the body ceases to operate."[11] Fuller insisted that such "brain warfare" remained the most effective and efficient way to destroy the enemy's military organization and hence its military strength. To economize the application of military force, one needed to produce the instantaneous effects of a "shot through the head" rather than the slow bleed of successive, slight body wounds.[12]

Liddell Hart was Fuller's kindred spirit in the field of military strategy. Like his fellow countryman, Liddell Hart was a vigorous advocate of strategic paralysis. Arguing that "the most decisive victory is of no value if a nation be bled white gaining it," he insisted that the more potent and economical form of warfare was disarmament through paralysis—not destruction through annihilation.[13]

Fuller and Liddell Hart witnessed the introduction of the aerial weapon in war, and both envisioned a decisive role for airpower in inducing strategic paralysis. Fuller predicted "an army holding at bay another, whilst its aircraft are destroying the hostile communications and bases *and so paralysing*

361

enemy action" (emphasis added).[14] Likewise, in 1925 Liddell Hart reasoned, "Provided that the blow be sufficiently swift and powerful, there is no reason why within a few hours, or at most days from the commencement of hostilities, the nerve system of the country inferior in airpower should not be paralysed."[15] They were not alone in their grand visions of airpower. Many veteran airmen of World War I supported the cause. Two men—Hugh Trenchard and William Mitchell—stand out because of their influence upon the initial development of strategic air doctrine.

Marshal of the Royal Air Force (RAF) Lord Trenchard, the "father of the RAF," believed in strategic paralysis. In a memorandum of 1928 to the chiefs of staff on the war object of an air force, Trenchard explicitly states that the goal of air action is "to paralyse from the very outset the enemy's production centres of munitions of war of every sort and to stop all communications and transportation."[16] He argues that paralyzing attacks upon an enemy's "vital centres" offer "the best object by which to reach victory" because they obtain "infinitely more effect" and "generally exact a smaller toll from the attacker" than strikes against the surface and air forces that defend them. Coincidentally, across the Atlantic, a man whom Trenchard met and influenced on the western front was airing similar views in a distinctly American manner.

An outspoken advocate of airpower, Brig Gen Billy Mitchell also believed in strategic paralysis. In 1919 he asserted that aerial bombardment's greatest value lay in "hitting an enemy's great nerve centers at the very beginning of the war so as to paralyze them to the greatest extent possible."[17] Six years later, during his well-publicized court-martial, Mitchell spoke fondly of airpower's unique ability to incapacitate one's foes. Finally, in his last book, *Skyways*, Mitchell concludes that "the advent of airpower which can go straight to the vital centers and entirely neutralize and destroy them has put a completely new complexion on the old system of war. It is now realized that the hostile main army in the field is a false objective and the real objectives are the vital centers. The old theory that victory meant the destruction of the hostile main army is untenable."[18]

Clearly, both Trenchard and Mitchell were early proponents of strategic paralysis. Their hauntingly similar writings proclaim the revolutionary nature of aerial warfare. The airplane possessed a unique ability to avoid the bloody stalemate on the ground and to combine shock and firepower into a single weapon able to strike deeply into the enemy heartland. Given the substantial influence of Trenchard and Mitchell on their respective air services, the notion of paralysis became imbedded in the theoretical foundation of British and American strategic air doctrine, resurfacing most recently in the ideas of John Boyd and John Warden.

The tactical seeds of John Boyd's theory of conflict were sown during the Korean War, when Boyd, a fighter pilot who flew the F-86 Sabre in "MiG Alley," developed his first intuitive appreciation for the efficacy of what he would later refer to as "fast transient maneuvers." Although the Soviet-built MiG-15 proved technologically superior to the F-86 in many respects, the latter's hydraulic flight controls provided Sabre pilots a decisive advantage over their opponents—the ability to shift more rapidly from one maneuver to another during aerial dogfights. Just when the MiG pilot began reacting to the initial Sabre movement, a rapid change in direction would render the enemy response inappropriate to the new tactical situation. This agility contributed to the Sabre pilots' establishment of an impressive 10-to-one kill ratio against the formidable MiG-15. A few years later at Eglin AFB, Florida, Boyd quantified these air-to-air combat lessons in the form of his energy maneuverability theory—a collection of tactical principles that still guides the training of Ameican fighter pilots.

Yet, not until his retirement did Boyd set out to expand his tactical concepts of aerial maneuver warfare into a more generalized theory of conflict.[19] Beginning in 1976 with a concise, 16-page essay entitled "Destruction and Creation," Boyd's strategic ideas evolved over the next decade into an unpublished, five-part series of briefings—"A Discourse on Winning and Losing." Ironically, the "Discourse" itself is a product of the very process of analysis and synthesis described in "Destruction and Creation," a cognitive process that Boyd insists is crucial to prevailing in a highly unpredictable and competitive world. It is a form of mental agility, "a process of reaching across many perspectives; pulling each and every one apart (analysis), all the while intuitively looking for those parts of the disassembled perspectives which naturally interconnect with one another to form a higher order, more general elaboration (synthesis) of what is taking place."[20] Using the dialectic process of "Destruction and Creation," Boyd embarked upon an in-depth review of military history to unravel the mysteries of success and failure in conflict. Boyd's firm belief in fast transient maneuvers instilled during his fighter days undoubtedly influenced this scholarly exercise. The end product is an eclectic and esoteric discourse on how to survive and win in a competitive world.

Boyd's theory of conflict advocates a form of maneuver warfare that is more psychological and temporal in its orientation than physical and spatial. Its military object is "to break the spirit and will of the enemy command by creating surprising and dangerous operational or strategic situations."[21] To achieve this end, one must operate at a faster tempo or rhythm than one's adversaries. Put differently, Boyd's maneuver warfare aims to render the enemy powerless by denying him the time to cope mentally with the rapidly unfolding—and naturally uncertain—circumstances of war.[22] One's military operations aim to (1) create and perpetuate a highly fluid and menacing state of affairs for the enemy and (2) disrupt or incapacitate his ability to adapt to such an environment.

Based upon an analysis of ancient and modern military history, Boyd identifies four key qualities of successful operations— initiative, harmony, variety, and rapidity.[23] Collectively, these characteristics allow one to adapt to and to shape the uncertain, friction-filled environment of war. Boyd credits Clausewitz for recognizing the need to improve one's adaptability in war by minimizing one's own frictions. In addition, borrowing from Sun-tzu, Boyd insists that one can use friction to shape the conflict in one's favor by creating and exploiting the frictions faced by the opponent. He then relates this idea of minimizing friendly friction and maximizing enemy friction to his key qualities of initiative, harmony, variety, and rapidity.

To minimize friendly friction, one must act and react more quickly than the opponent—specifically, by exercising initiative at the lower levels within a chain of command. However, a centralized command of what and why things are done must guide this decentralized control of how things are done. This shared vision of a single commander's intent ensures strategic and operational harmony among the various tactical actions and reactions. Without a common aim and similar outlook on how best to satisfy the commander's intent, subordinate freedom of action risks disunity of effort and an attendant increase in friction.[24]

To maximize enemy friction, one should plan to attack with a *variety* of actions that one can execute with the greatest possible *rapidity*. Similar to the contemporary notion of parallel warfare, this lethal combination of varied, rapid actions serves to overload the adversary's capacity to properly identify and address those events that appear most threatening. By steadily reducing an opponent's physical and mental capability to resist, one ultimately crushes his moral will to resist as well.

Boyd argues that severe disruption occurs by rapidly and repeatedly presenting the enemy with a combination of ambiguous (but threatening) events and deceptive (but nonthreatening) ones. These multiple events, compressed in time, quickly generate mismatches—or anomalies—between those actions the opponent believes to threaten his survival and those that actually do. The enemy must eliminate these mismatches between perception and reality if his reactions are to remain relevant—that is, if he is to survive.

We should hamper the opponent's ability to process information, make decisions, and take appropriate action, thus ensuring that he cannot rid himself of these menacing anomalies. In consequence, he can no longer determine what is being done to him and how he should respond. Ultimately, the adversary's initial confusion degenerates into paralyzing panic, and his ability and/or willingness to resist ceases.

Boyd views the adversary as a three-dimensional being, consisting of "moral-mental-physical bastions, connections, or activities that he depends upon."[25] To defeat this being, Boyd advocates standing Clausewitz on his head. Instead of destroying "hubs of all power and movement," one should create noncooperative centers of gravity (COG) by attacking the moral-mental-physical linkages that bind the hubs together. This destroys the enemy's internal harmony and external connection to the real world, producing paralysis and collapsing resistance.

In perhaps the most well known feature of Boyd's theory, he contends that one can depict all rational human behavior—individual or organizational—as a continual cycling through four distinct tasks: observation, orientation, decision, and action. Boyd refers to this decision-making cycle as the "OODA loop" (fig. 1).

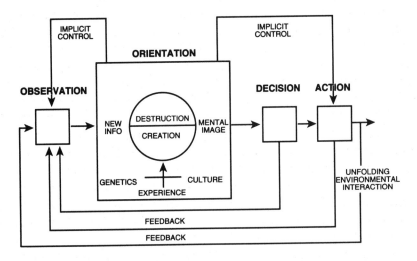

Figure 1. Boyd's OODA Loop

Using this construct, the crux of winning becomes the relational movement of opponents through their respective OODA loops.[26] Whoever repeatedly observes, orients, decides, and acts more rapidly (and accurately) than his enemy will win.[27] By doing so, he "folds his opponent back inside himself" and eventually makes enemy reaction inappropriate to the situation at hand.[28] The key to attaining a favorable edge in OODA loop speed and accuracy (hence, to winning) is efficient and effective orientation.

To survive and grow within a complex, ever-changing world of conflict, we must effectively and efficiently orient ourselves;

that is, we must quickly and accurately develop mental images—or schemata—to help comprehend and cope with the vast array of threatening and nonthreatening events we face. This image construction—or orientation—is nothing more than the process of destruction (analysis) and creation (synthesis) described earlier. In Boyd's words, it involves the process of "examining the world from a number of perspectives so that we can generate mental images or impressions that correspond to that world."[29] Done well, it becomes the key to winning instead of losing. Done exceedingly well, it becomes the mark of genius.[30]

The mental images we construct are shaped by our personal experience, genetic heritage, and cultural traditions. They determine our decisions, actions, and observations.[31] Observations that match up with certain mental schemata call for certain decisions and actions. The timeliness and accuracy of those decisions and actions are directly related to our ability to orient and reorient correctly to the rapidly unfolding, perpetually uncertain events of war. Mismatches between the real world and our mental images of that world generate inaccurate responses. These, in turn, produce confusion and disorientation, which then diminish both the accuracy and the speed of subsequent decision making. Left uncorrected, disorientation steadily expands one's OODA loop until it eventually becomes a death trap.

Tying the preceding comments together, Boyd proposes that success in conflict stems from getting inside an adversary's OODA loop and staying there. The military commander can do so in two supplementary ways. First, he must minimize his own friction through initiative and harmony of response. This decrease in friendly friction acts to "tighten" his own loop (i.e., to speed up his own decision-action cycle time). Second, he must maximize his opponent's friction through variety and rapidity of response. This increase in enemy friction acts to "loosen" the adversary's loop (i.e., to slow down his decision-action cycle time). Together, these "friction manipulations" assure one's continual operation within the enemy's OODA loop in menacing and unpredictable ways. Initially, this produces confusion and disorder within the enemy camp. Ultimately, it produces panic and fear that manifest themselves in a simultaneous paralysis of ability to cope and of willingness to resist.

Using an analytical model developed by political scientist Robert Pape,[32] one can graphically depict Boyd's theory of strategic paralysis (fig. 2). As Boyd himself would admit, his theory of conflict is quite esoteric. He speaks of dismembering the "moral-mental-physical being" of the enemy and of getting inside his "mind-time-space," yet he offers few, if any, operational details about accomplishing these abstract aims. The absence of detail is particularly frustrating for the practically minded war fighter whose profession centers on translating relatively obscure political ends into concrete military ways and means. Although Boyd's purpose is not to frustrate, neither is it to dictate.

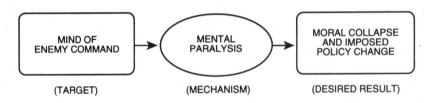

| MIND OF ENEMY COMMAND | → | MENTAL PARALYSIS | → | MORAL COLLAPSE AND IMPOSED POLICY CHANGE |
| (TARGET) | | (MECHANISM) | | (DESIRED RESULT) |

Figure 2. Boyd's Theory of Conflict

As he tells it, John Boyd is a believer in theories, not theory—in doctrines, not doctrine.[33] He refuses to advocate any one approach, any one formula; following a single path to victory makes one predictable and vulnerable. Moreover, through the study of all theories and doctrines, the warrior accumulates a full bag of strategic tricks. Then, as a particular conflict unfolds, he can pick and choose from this bag as the situation demands. So, although Boyd's work is void of practical recipes for success, it is so by design.[34] A more appropriate critique of his discourse on winning and losing lies elsewhere.

Ironically, one of the greatest strengths of Boyd's theory is, at the same time, a potential weakness—his emphasis on the temporal dimension of conflict. Reflecting an American bias for fast-paced operations and the related preference for short wars, Boyd *presumes* that operating at a faster tempo than one's opponent matters—or, more to the point, that it matters to the enemy. He may not care that we are "OODA looping" more quickly. Indeed, it may be in his interest to refuse to play by our rules. To illustrate this point, I turn to the game of basketball.

If our opponent is not particularly suited to a "fast break" style of play, it is in his interest to slow things down if we are a "run and gun" team. If he refuses to play at our faster pace and intentionally tries to slow things down, he may succeed in taking us out of our game just enough to win—even if we retain a relative advantage in speed throughout. Boyd would no doubt argue that the fast-breaking side will paralyze its opponent because of its quicker tempo, a point that may be true in some instances. It is certainly true if the naturally slower opponent agrees to speed things up. If, however, he slows the pace down, knowing full well that our fans will tolerate nothing other than fast-break ball, he may sufficiently frustrate our game plan so that, in the end, he wins. This basketball analogy seems to apply even better when, as in war, we remove the time clock.

In fact, Mao Tse-tung advocated precisely this approach as the strategy for liberating China from the scorch of the Rising Sun in the War of Resistance against Japan. In contrast to both the subjugationists within the Kuomintang government and the theorists of quick victory within his own Communist Party, Mao proposed the notion of "protracted war" as the way for defeating the militarily superior Japanese aggressors.

In a series of lectures from 26 May to 3 June 1938, Mao explained and justified his plans for protracted war against Japan, couching his descriptions and arguments in the traditional Eastern dialectic of yin and yang. For Mao, this Taoist "duality of opposites" informed not only the object of war but also the strategy for war. He argued that in war, one seeks to destroy the enemy and preserve oneself.[35] This twofold object "is the essence of war and the basis of all war activities, an essence that pervades all war activities, from the technical to the strategic." As such, "no technical, tactical, or strategic concepts or principles can in any way depart from it."[36]

In consequence, he preached that one should not characterize the War of Resistance against Japan by either the "desperate recklessness" of perpetual attack or the "flightism" of perpetual retreat.[37] Instead, the current military advantage enjoyed by Imperial Japan demanded a blend of attack and retreat—of operational/tactical swiftness and strategic protraction. In this way alone could the Chinese resistance simultaneously preserve itself and defeat the enemy through gradual erosion of his relative superiority.

Mao insisted that calls for quick victory within the Chinese Communist camp had no basis in an objective appraisal of current capabilities and therefore played into the hands of the Japanese army. Similarly, calls for national subjugation within the Kuomintang government had no basis in an objective appraisal of future possibilities. In other words, Mao claimed that the Chinese could defeat Japan tomorrow if they could survive today. Brandishing time as a weapon to achieve the dual object of enemy destruction and self-preservation, Mao's strategy of protracted war proved successful in the Chinese resistance of Japan and, later, in the Vietnamese resistance to both France and the United States.

Boyd readily acknowledges the influence of Maoism and other Eastern philosophies of war on his own thoughts, an impact most evident in his emphasis on the temporal dimension of war—specifically, in his incorporation of the notion of time as a weapon. Yet, Boyd fails to fully appreciate this weapon in the context of Taoism's yin and yang. The "duality of opposites" suggests—and twentieth-century revolutionary warfare supports—the conclusion that time can be a most potent force in either its contracted or its protracted forms.

Throughout his retirement, Boyd has briefed his "Discourse on Winning and Losing" to hundreds of audiences in both civilian and military circles, leaving copies behind to assure a degree of permanence for his ideas. Interestingly, one of the agencies he talked to several times in the early 1980s was the newly formed Checkmate Division within the Air Staff at the Pentagon. This division's responsibilities include short- and long-range contingency planning for the employment of the United States Air Force. Eventually, this division would have as its chief our second modern-day theorist of strategic paralysis.[38]

John Warden has emerged as a leading advocate of force application in the third dimension. Credited as the originator of the air campaign that guided allied efforts during Operation Desert Storm, Warden has a vision of twenty-first-century warfare that unabashedly asserts the dominance of aerospace power over surface force. Furthermore, in concert with the "Long Blue Line" of American air theorists, he contends that the most effective and efficient application of airpower lies in the strategic realm. However, unlike the strategic air warfare of his predecessors, particularly those at the Air Corps Tactical School (ACTS), Warden's is more political than economic in nature. Targeting enemy leadership to produce desired policy changes is the overarching aim that should guide the employment of air forces. In this respect, Warden acknowledges an intellectual debt to the British military theorist J. F. C. Fuller. One of Fuller's classic works, *The Generalship of Alexander the Great*, convinced him of the efficacy of attacking the command element as a means of defeating armed forces—a strategy of incapacitation through "decapitation."

While a student at the National War College, Warden began to construct his theory of airpower. An academic thesis, originally planned as an examination of Alexander's genius, evolved instead into *The Air Campaign: Planning for Combat*. An influential text on the use of airpower in war, this book focuses on translating national political objectives and strategic military goals into theater campaign plans, with primary focus on planning airpower's contribution to the overall effort. The book reflects the unique heritage of American air theory and practice. Warden's belief in the predominant role of air superiority flows directly from the pages of the Army's Field Manual (FM) 100-20, *Command and Employment of Airpower* (1943). Likewise, his emphasis on air strikes against enemy centers of gravity recalls the writings of Billy Mitchell and his kindred spirits at ACTS with regard to attacks against "vital centers" deep within the enemy heartland.[39]

The main theme of *The Air Campaign* is that airpower possesses a unique capacity to achieve the strategic ends of war with maximum effectiveness and minimum cost. Airpower's inherent speed, range, and flexibility allow it to strike the full spectrum of enemy capabilities in a swift and decisive manner. Central to this theme is the Clausewitzian concept of an enemy's COG, defined by Warden as "that point where the enemy is most vulnerable and the point where an attack will have the best chance of being decisive."[40] Properly identifying these COGs is the critical first step in planning and conducting military operations.

As suggested earlier, the incorporation of this notion of COGs into airpower theory is by no means novel. However, Warden's description above suggests that such centers are both strengths and vulnerabilities.[41] This dual nature of COGs has implications for campaign planning, particularly in terms of identifying which force—ground, sea, or air—is key. As Warden noted, "Air must be the key force when ground or sea forces are incapable of doing the job because of insufficient numbers or inability to reach the enemy center of gravity."[42] Airpower's ubiquity theoretically makes many more strategic COGs vulnerable to attack relative to surface forces, providing air forces with a higher degree of strategic decisiveness.[43]

Although it stresses the importance of correctly identifying and appropriately striking COGs, *The Air Campaign* does not elaborate on how to go about doing so. Warden's process of identifying COGs materialized some years after publication of his first work. While working at the Pentagon, Warden recognized the need for a coherent theory of airpower. Having searched for some organizing scheme appropriate to the concept of COGs as related to airpower, in the late fall of 1988, he developed such a model in the form of five concentric rings—an air force targeting bull's-eye of sorts (fig.3).

Analyzing the enemy as a system, Warden contends that one can break down all strategic entities into five component parts.[44] The most crucial element of the system—the innermost ring—is leadership. Extending outward from the center, in descending importance to the overall functioning of the system, are the rings of organic essentials, infrastructure, population, and fielded forces.[45]

Within each ring exists a COG or collection of COGs that represents "the hub of all power and movement" for that particular ring. If the COG is destroyed or neutralized, the effective functioning of the ring ceases, which affects the

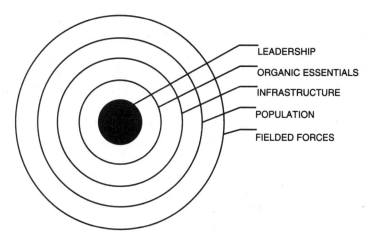

LEADERSHIP

ORGANIC ESSENTIALS

INFRASTRUCTURE

POPULATION

FIELDED FORCES

Figure 3. Warden's Five Strategic Rings

entire system in more or less significant ways (depending upon whether it is an inner or outer ring). To facilitate the accurate identification of these key hubs within each ring, Warden proposes the further breakdown of any given ring into five subrings (of leadership, organic essentials, etc.) and these into five more, if necessary, until the true COG surfaces.

The central theme of the five-rings model is that the most effective strategic plan always focuses on leadership, first and foremost. Even if leadership is unavailable as a target set, the air strategist must still focus on the mind of the commander when selecting COGs among the other rings.[46] Within these rings lie COGs that, when hit, impose some level of physical paralysis, thereby raising the costs of further resistance in the mind of the enemy command.[47] The implicit message is that destruction or neutralization of the leadership COG(s) produces total *physical* paralysis of the system, whereas successful attack upon COGs within the other rings produces partial physical paralysis but unbearable *psychological* pressure upon the leadership.

When Iraq invaded Kuwait in August 1990 and US military planners considered possible responses, Warden's Checkmate Division developed an air option. Firmly believing in the efficacy of striking enemy COGs, he resurrected the five-rings model to guide the creation of a strategic air campaign. As Warden observed, "This was a case where the theory existed before the fact and the facts validated the theory."[48]

Further refinement of his strategic air theory occurred in the afterglow of Desert Storm. Warden drew several lessons from the Gulf War that would influence his thinking. Among the most prominent were (1) the importance of strategic attack and the fragility of states at the strategic level; (2) the fatal consequences of losing strategic and operational air superiority; (3) the overwhelming effects of parallel warfare (that is, the near-simultaneous attack upon strategic COGs throughout the entire theater of war); (4) the value of stealth and precision weaponry in redefining the principles of mass and surprise; and (5) the dominance of airpower as the key force in most, but not all, operational- and strategic-level conflicts within the next quarter to half century.[49]

Coupling his early thoughts on airpower with his experiences in the Gulf War, Warden established a theoretical foundation for employing airpower in the twenty-first century. Fundamentally, this groundwork relates ends, ways, and means. First, air strategists must appreciate the political objectives sought by military action (ends). Second, they must determine the best military strategy to induce the enemy to comply, as defined by those political objectives (ways). Third, they must use the five-rings systems analysis to identify which COGs to subject to parallel attack (means).

In terms of ends, Warden accepts Clausewitz's maxim that all wars are fought for political purpose. Although wars may have their own distinct capabilities and limitations relative to other tools available to the statesman, they are by nature political instruments.[50] Seen as such, wars are essentially discourses between policy makers on each side. The aim of all military action, then, is not the destruction of enemy armed forces but the manipulation of the enemy leadership's will. Warden elaborates:

> Wars are fought to convince the enemy leadership to do what one wants it to do—that is, concede something political. . . . The enemy leadership agrees that it needs to make these political concessions when it suffers the threat or the actuality of intolerable pressure against both its operational and strategic centers of gravity. . . .

> Thus, one does not conduct an attack against industry or
> infrastructure because of the effect it might or might not have on
> fielded forces. Rather, one undertakes such an attack for its direct
> effect on national leaders and commanders.[51]

Warden proposes three main ways to make the enemy do
what one wants him to do—the military strategies of imposed
cost (coercion), paralysis (incapacitation), and destruction
(annihilation).[52] Collectively, these strategies represent a
continuum of force application. The point chosen along that
strategy continuum should coincide with the level of objective
intent.

An *imposed cost strategy* seeks to make continued
resistance too expensive for the enemy command. It attempts
to do so by estimating the opponent's pain threshold, based
on his value system, and then exceeding this threshold as
violently and instantaneously as possible through
simultaneous or parallel attacks upon the designated target
set. Theoretically, such attacks coerce the enemy leadership to
accept one's terms and change its policy through the actual
imposition of partial system paralysis, as well as the potential
or threatened imposition of total system paralysis.

A *paralysis strategy* seeks to make continued resistance
impossible for the enemy command. It does so by thoroughly
and simultaneously incapacitating the entire enemy system
from the inside out. This total system paralysis, in turn,
provides one the freedom of movement to change policy for the
enemy leadership without interference.

Finally, a *destruction strategy* seeks to annihilate the entire
system, making policy change by the enemy leadership
irrelevant. However, as Warden cautions, "the last of these
options is rare in history, difficult to execute, fraught with
moral concerns, and normally not very useful because of all
the unintended consequences it engenders."[53] In light of these
observations, he dismisses this military strategy as politically
unviable for twenty-first-century warfare.[54]

Regarding means, Warden advocates the continual
breakdown of each strategic and operational ring until one
uncovers the key to partial or total paralysis. Such successive
differentiation exposes the interdependent nature or
"connectedness" of the enemy as a system.[55] Consequently, a

thorough systems analysis may reveal COGs acting as linkages between rings, as well as components within them.

Summarizing the salient points of Warden's theory of strategic paralysis, one first notes that the air strategist must fully appreciate the general nature and specific content of the objectives set by his political masters; these objectives prescribe the behavioral change(s) expected of the enemy leadership and suggest the level of paralysis needed to effect the change(s). Second, the air strategist must focus all energies in war on changing the mind of the enemy leadership, directly or indirectly, through the imposition of the necessary level of paralysis upon him and/or his system. Third, the air strategist must analyze the enemy as an interdependent system of five rings to determine those COGs within and between rings whose destruction or neutralization will impose the necessary level of paralysis. Fourth, the air strategist must plan to attack all defined targets in parallel in order to produce the most rapid and favorable decision.

At first glance, Warden's theory of strategic paralysis (fig. 4) is marked by a type of reductionism inherent in any systems-analysis approach. It attempts to simplify complex, dynamic sociocultural phenomena (the constitution, operation, and interaction of strategic entities) by reducing them to their basic parts or functions. In so doing, his theory risks losing explanatory power and practical relevance.

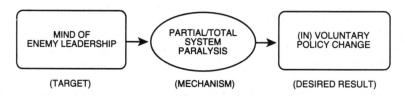

Figure 4. Warden's Theory of Strategic Attack

Arguing that "social scientists make bad generals," Eliot Cohen cautions against such an analytical approach to military strategy since it regards the enemy as "a passive collection of targets," assumes that the enemy resembles us, and considers technology rather than human nature the controlling element in war. He goes on to argue that these assumptions "discourage the detailed study of one's opponent, his language, politics, culture, tactics, and leadership."[56] Col Pat Pentland contends that such comprehensive study is crucial to effective strategy development since sociocultural factors determine both the *form* or structure of an enemy and the *process* or dynamics by which it operates.[57]

To be fair, one must note that Warden does not deny the need for thorough examination of the enemy as a political, economic, military, and sociocultural system. In addition, he would argue that, while the basic five-rings model may be an oversimplified, "first order" analysis, successive differentiation of the rings reveals dynamic interrelationships within and between rings that are unique and important to the particular society or culture in question. The standard five-rings model simply serves as a starting point for further "higher order" analysis, a theoretical framework to guide air strategists in their critical task of identifying enemy COGs.[58] Thus, Warden's model reflects a subtle holism which undercuts the normal criticism that it is reductionist and oversimplistic.

Clausewitz may have penned a more accurate criticism over 150 years before Warden published his ideas:

> It is only analytically that these attempts at theory [i.e., those of H. D. von Bülow, Antoine Henri Jomini, etc.] can be called advances in the realm of truth; *synthetically, in the rules and regulations they offer, they are absolutely useless.* They aim at fixed values; but in war everything is uncertain, and calculations have to be made with variable quantities. *They direct the inquiry exclusively toward physical quantities*, whereas all military action is intertwined with psychological forces and effects. *They consider only unilateral action*, whereas war consists of a continuous interaction of opposites. (Emphasis added)[59]

As applied to Warden's theory of strategic paralysis, this Clausewitzian critique is threefold, as suggested by the italicized passages in the above quotation.

First, even if Warden's analysis of the enemy system is correct, his "synthesized" rule of targeting leadership does not necessarily follow. Although his analogy with the human brain is seductive, the center ring of leadership is not always the most important target. Other rings (or linkages between rings) may, and often do, offer more lucrative COGs. Warden would not disagree with this assessment but would insist that one must select outer-ring targets so as to influence the leadership's cost-benefit calculus. But doing so assumes that this calculus remains relevant to the defeat of the enemy, which may or may not be true. The leadership may decide one thing—the population or armed forces another. What matters most—the true COG—may be what matters to the society as a whole, not just to its leadership.

Second, despite Napoléon's observation that the moral is to the physical as three is to one, Warden focuses exclusively on the physical aspects of war. He justifies this by contending that one can mathematically represent enemy combat effectiveness by the equation "combat effectiveness = physical strength x moral strength."[60] Using this formula, one can theoretically eliminate the fighting power of an opponent through exclusive attack upon the physical component of that power. If one drives the physical variable to zero, the moral variable can remain at 100 percent, yet combat effectiveness remains zero. Additionally, Warden notes that destroying physical targets is easier than destroying the enemy's moral will to resist. He explains that "the physical is conceptually knowable. So theoretically, if I knew everything about the enemy, I could drive the physical side of the equation to zero. Morale, I know almost nothing about."[61] Practically, however, driving the physical side to zero (i.e., annihilating the enemy system) is, to borrow Warden's own words cited earlier, "rare in history, difficult to execute, fraught with moral concerns, and normally not very useful because of all the unintended consequences it engenders."[62] Consequently, one must still consider the issue of moral strength.

Third, Warden's theory deals with unilateral action taken against an unresponsive enemy and thus disregards action-reaction cycles and their attendant frictions that mark the actual conduct of war. Again, Warden feels justified in doing so because he claims that the parallel hyperwars of the twenty-first century will eliminate the possibility of enemy reaction at the strategic and operational levels. In fact, Warden goes so far as to proclaim that the revolution in warfare ushered in by Desert Storm has made most Clausewitzian notions irrelevant: "The whole business of action and reaction, culminating points, friction, et cetera, was a function of serial war and the imprecision of weapons. . . . [These nineteenth century concepts are] an accurate description of the way things were, but not a description of how they ought to be or can be."[63] Although theoretically possible, one has difficulty imagining real war that is reactionless and friction free, even if conducted in parallel fashion at hyperspeed. If human nature rather than technology is indeed the controlling element in war, then war will remain an unpredictable, nonlinear phenomenon, even in the presence of technological revolution.

The previous sections revealed notable overlap between the theories of John Boyd and John Warden. Both men contend that the target for all military action should be the enemy command and that the most effective and efficient mechanism for translating military expenditure into political gain is paralysis of that command. Although they may share certain fundamental beliefs about the proper conduct of war, Boyd and Warden diverge sharply in theoretical approach. Their distinct approaches represent two traditions regarding the nature and purpose of theory, best personified by two nineteenth-century theorists of war—Antoine Henri Jomini and Carl von Clausewitz.

The Jominian tradition believes that one can reduce the practice of war (i.e., its strategy) to a set of general principles or rules for scientific derivation and universal application. It recognizes that the nature of war may change due to political and/or moral variables but that the conduct of war is constant and governed by principles. For Jominians, theory uncovers these immutable truths and advocates their adoption and use. In the words of Jomini himself, "Convinced that I had seized the true point of view under which *it was necessary to regard the theory of war in order to discover its veritable rules* . . . I set myself to the work with the ardor of a neophyte" (emphasis added).[64]

The Jominian school acknowledges that the nature of war is complex and dramatic and that, consequently, its complete mastery is truly an art form. However, the strategy of war is scientific, knowable, constant, and governed by principles of eternal validity. Borrowing a concept from the emerging science of chaos and complexity, one notes that Jominians are predominantly "linear" thinkers regarding the conduct of war.

They believe in a certain causality or predictability of actions taken in war. That is, they believe that similar inputs produce similar outputs. Translated into the language of strategy, if a given plan of attack is devised and executed in accordance with veritable principles of war, it will produce victory time and again.

Believing, as they do, that one can reduce strategy to a science, Jominians tend to be more prescriptive than heuristic in their presentation of military theory. In other words, Jominian theories tend toward teaching soldiers how to act rather than how to think. Theory should provide answers to the warrior facing the daunting prospect of battle.[65]

In contrast, the Clausewitzian tradition views the practice of war from a more nonlinear perspective.[66] Similar inputs or strategies often do not produce similar outputs or desired end states. War's natural uncertainty makes it impossible to guarantee that what worked yesterday will work tomorrow. This unpredictability demands that any theory of war be more heuristic than prescriptive since "no prescriptive formulation universal enough to deserve the name of law can be applied to the constant change and diversity of the phenomena of war."[67] As Clausewitz continued, "Theory should be study not doctrine. . . . It is meant to educate the mind of the future commander, or, more accurately, to guide him in his self-education, not to accompany him to the battlefield."[68]

Thus, the Clausewitzian school insists that the primary function of military theory is to provide the intellectual methods by which to unveil the answers to war's perplexing questions rather than to provide the answers themselves. It should develop a mind-set or way of thinking rather than prescribe rules of war; in the former lies the key to victory in the midst of war's fog and friction.

The Clausewitzian school seeks to permanently arm the military commander with genius, which the Prussian himself defined as "a very highly developed mental aptitude for a particular occupation." In the profession of war, this mental aptitude represents a psychological strength that entails a harmonious balance of intellect and temperament and allows one to function in the presence of uncertainty. Furthermore, one can develop this aptitude: "That practice and a trained mind have much to do with it is undeniable."[69] Thus, Clausewitzians share the belief that one can define and should teach the genius of war—a cherished conviction similar to the Jominian belief in the principles of war.

Evaluating our theorists of strategic paralysis in this light, we note that Warden's thoughts are predominantly Jominian in their character, content, and intent, while Boyd's are predominantly Clausewitzian. Warden's theory of swift, simultaneous attack against the enemy's physical form, as depicted by the five-rings model, is practical, concrete, and linear. He prescribes direct and/or indirect attack upon the enemy leadership as the way to impose one's will in a world of conflict. Though one may want to vary one's tactical approach, if a "bullet through the brain" has worked once, it will always work; therefore, it should remain the strategic aim of military operations.[70]

In addition, Warden's representation of combat effectiveness as the multiplicative product of physical and moral strength allows him to focus on the tangible variable in the equation to the exclusion of the intangible one. Decimating the enemy's physical capability renders his moral strength irrelevant. Thus, in both the practice and the theory of war, emphasis on the physical sphere is understandable, acceptable, and—indeed—preferable.

In contrast, Boyd's theory of maneuvering inside the enemy's mental process, as depicted by the OODA loop model, is more philosophical, abstract, and nonlinear. He recognizes the uncertainty of war and the subsequent need for mental agility and creativity—in short, genius. He believes that one can teach genius and sets out to do just that for his audience by means of the mental process of "destruction and creation." He preaches familiarity with many different theories, doctrines, and models so that, through the genius of "destruction and creation," the military strategist can build from the gems in each of them a plan of attack most appropriate to the situation at hand. Furthermore, through extensive training and practice, the strategist can build such a plan at a faster tempo than his adversary so as to fold him back inside himself and ultimately defeat his will to resist.

Warden asserts that success in twenty-first-century war will result from adherence to the principles of parallel, inside-out attack. Boyd asserts that success in future war, as in all past wars, will result from genius in the face of menacing uncertainty. As Grant Hammond observes, "Boyd knows certainty doesn't exist; Warden wants it to."[71]

Having explored the respective ideas of Boyd and Warden and highlighted areas of convergence and divergence, we can now examine the contribution of both theories to the evolution of airpower thought in the twentieth century. As we shall see, the works of these two airmen represent a fundamental shift in strategic air theory—one from paralysis via economic warfare to paralysis via control warfare.

As the twentieth century passed its midpoint, the modern world began a slow metamorphosis from an industrial society to an informational society. Fueled by steady advances in computer and communications technologies, this transfiguration continues today. Interestingly, methods of aerial warfare appear to be changing in parallel. Boyd and Warden stand as transitional figures in this evolution of strategic airpower theory. Although paralysis remains the common underpinning for all twentieth-century thought on the subject, the theoretical transformation represented by Boyd and Warden is one from economic warfare based on industrial targeting to control warfare based on informational targeting.

In the first half of airpower's inaugural century, strategic air doctrines that evolved in both Great Britain and the United States were fashioned by the theory of strategic paralysis and a belief that one best induced incapacitation of a hostile nation and its armed forces by striking directly at the enemy's economic, war-making potential. RAF strategic bombardment doctrine reflected the man in charge from 1919 until 1928—Air Marshal Sir Hugh Trenchard, whose air policy aimed to bring about the disintegration and collapse of the enemy's war economy. In the last of his 10 years as air chief, he produced perhaps the clearest statement of his beliefs on air warfare in the form of a memorandum to his fellow service chiefs. In it, Trenchard proposed the following war object for the RAF: "The aim of the Air Force is to break down the enemy's means of resistance by attacks on objectives selected as most likely to achieve this end." He went on to specify these military objectives as the enemy's "vital centres" of production, transportation, and communication from which the enemy sustains his war effort.[72]

Trenchard highlighted the moral effect of such attacks, claiming they would "terrorise munition workers (men and women) into absenting themselves from work or stevedores into abandoning the loading of a ship with munitions from fear of air attack upon the factory or dock concerned."[73] Thus, British air policy had a dual nature in that it focused on destroying enemy capability and will to resist. It sought to produce strategic paralysis by means of the psychological dislocation and terror that ensued from economic disruption and collapse.

Meanwhile, in the United States, the Air Corps Tactical School took the lead in developing American doctrine for strategic bombardment. As mentioned, the preachings of Billy Mitchell did influence this doctrinal development but so did the ideas of a fellow World War I veteran, Col Edgar Gorrell. As chief of the Air Service Technical Section in France, Gorrell was responsible for the Air Service's strategic air program for the war. Writing after the war, Gorrell noted that "the object of strategic bombing is to drop aerial bombs upon the *commercial centers and the lines of communications* in such quantities as will wreck the points aimed at and cut off the necessary supplies without which the armies in the field cannot exist" (emphasis added).[74] He went on to compare the enemy's armed forces to a drill bit. The "point" of the army would remain effective only so long as the "shank" of supporting infrastructure remained intact. Break the shank and the entire drill becomes useless.

The ACTS instructors fine-tuned Gorrell's ideas of economic warfare, transforming the "shank of the drill" into a closely knit industrial web requiring precision bombardment to unweave it.[75] They did not discount the potentially incapacitating effects on morale that such precise bombing might provide as the natural consequence of economic deprivation. However, the instructors primarily focused (publicly, at least) on the physical paralysis induced by precise industrial targeting, as opposed to the British emphasis on the physical and psychological paralysis of economic area bombing.

Both the British and the American versions of economic warfare through strategic air attack would be severely tested after Germany's lightning strikes into Poland and France ignited World War II. The end of that war coincided with the dawn of the Information Age. Alvin and Heidi Toffler contend that this information revolution will transplant the industrial revolution of the nineteenth and early twentieth centuries and transform both wealth creation and war making accordingly.[76] Although theorists did not completely dismiss the notion of strategic paralysis through economic warfare, a new form of incapacitation warfare held great promise—control warfare against an enemy's systems of governance and information processing.[77]

John Boyd is one contemporary theorist who focuses on paralysis through control warfare.[78] More specifically, he concentrates on disorienting the mind of the enemy command by disrupting the process for exercising command and control (C^2). Boyd represents this process in the form of the OODA loop.[79] As we have seen, one ensures victory in conflict by securing a temporal advantage over one's opponent in transiting the OODA loop, which in turn produces a psychological paralysis of his decision-making and action-taking processes.

In addition to being a governance loop, the OODA model represents the process of information collection, analysis, and dissemination. In this sense, Boyd clearly reflects the influence of the Chinese warrior-philosopher Sun Tzu on his thinking by highlighting the importance of information to successful combat operations. He does so by tying it to speed and accuracy in the decision cycles of strategic, operational, and tactical commanders. He who has better control of the information flow can observe, orient, decide, and act in a more timely and appropriate manner and can thereby operate within his adversary's OODA loop. This control provides the opportunity to deny and/or exploit the information channels of one's adversary while simultaneously protecting access to one's own channels.

Likewise, John Warden advocates paralysis through control warfare based on command targeting. However, in contrast to

Boyd's *process*-oriented theory, Warden focuses on the *form* by which one exercises C^2, euphemistically describing the leadership bull's-eye of his five-rings model as the brain and all its sensory inputs. If, for political or practical reasons, one cannot attain a direct "shot through the head," indirect attack through the destruction, disruption, and/or exploitation of the brain's informational and control channels can be equally effective.

Warden also recognizes the importance of information management to the effective operation of the enemy as a system,[80] speculating that the five strategic rings are connected by an "information bolt" that holds all the rings in place. If the bolt is destroyed, components within the rings may spin wildly out of control,[81] suggesting that information linkages between rings may present the key to taking down the entire enemy system.

Together, Boyd and Warden have transformed paralysis theory as it pertains to strategic conventional airpower. They have shifted the focus from war-supporting industry to war-supporting command—from economic warfare to control warfare. Yet, Boyd and Warden do not represent the end of the road. As many futurists predict, the information revolution will continue to affect how governments and their militaries wage war.

Former RAF Marshal Sir John Slessor once wrote, "If there is one attitude more dangerous than to assume that a future war will be just like the last one, it is to imagine that it will be so utterly different that we can afford to ignore all the lessons of the last one."[82] One of the foremost lessons of applying strategic airpower in the Persian Gulf War of 1991 was the efficacy of information dominance.[83] By destroying Iraq's eyes, ears, and mouth and by exploiting their own surface- and aerospace-based data platforms, coalition forces quickly established a form of information superiority that may have been as decisive as the more traditional control of the air. The increasing dependence of modern war-fighting machines upon efficient information-processing systems will continue to create opportunities to deny, disrupt, and manipulate the collection, analysis, and dissemination of battlefield information.[84] Therefore, one may reasonably suggest that future wars will resemble Desert Storm in at least one important respect—the strategic and operational pursuit of information dominance via control of the war-fighting "datasphere."[85]

RAND's John Arquilla and David Ronfeldt have termed these future battles for information dominance "cyberwar." As they define it,

> cyberwar refers to conducting, and preparing to conduct, military operations according to information-related principles. It means disrupting if not destroying the information and communications systems, broadly defined to include even military culture, on which an adversary relies in order to "know" itself. . . . It means trying to know all about an adversary while keeping it from knowing much about oneself. It means turning the "balance of information and knowledge" in one's favor, especially if the balance of forces is not.[86]

In a sense, Arquilla and Ronfeldt are speaking of inducing strategic paralysis by attacking (physically and/or electronically) key information-related centers of gravity, be they nodes or connections.

Future advances in command, control, communications, computers, and intelligence (C⁴I) technologies and their integration with weapons-delivery platforms promise to increase the tempo of twenty-first-century warfare.[87] Friendly and enemy OODA loops will "tighten" enormously as one collects, analyzes, disseminates, and acts upon battlefield information within a matter of minutes—not days. As a result, controlling the datasphere will become a top priority in most, if not all, future conflicts since "defeating the collection or dissemination of the information [upon which "shooters" so depend for effective strikes] will be tantamount to destroying the attacking platform itself."[88] Achieving information dominance will become key to military victory, since it will provide both the means to remain oriented and the opportunity to disorient the enemy. In this way, one can obtain relative advantages in the speed and accuracy of the OODA process.

Although the information revolution may not affect the *process* of decision making as described by Boyd, it threatens to fundamentally alter the *form* of the enemy system as depicted by Warden's five-rings model. As Arquilla and

Ronfeldt astutely observe, there are both technological and organizational dimensions to this new revolution.[89]

In his 1982 best-seller, *Megatrends,* John Naisbitt accurately forecasts organizational trends that accompany the shift from an industrial society to an information society. Centralization gives way to decentralization, and networks replace hierarchies.[90] As they are currently unfolding in the business community, these trends produce what Naisbitt calls "a vertical to horizontal power shift."[91] As strategic decision making and control become decentralized, lateral cooperation between semiautonomous agents and agencies becomes more vital to effective system operation than top-down command.

However, as Alvin Toffler speculates, of the "big three" organizations—economic, political, and military—the military will likely be the last to undergo a vertical-to-horizontal power shift due to its particular affinity for hierarchical institutions. Still, recent organizational adjustments within the US military ushered in by "total quality management" do mirror changes in the business world and suggest that, even if the military is the last to change, change will indeed occur.

If a worldwide military power shift does occur, it will make the leadership bull's-eye of John Warden's five rings increasingly less relevant to system operation. On the other hand, a vertical-to-horizontal power shift, with its emphasis on "distributed problem-solving,"[92] will add a great deal of credence to John Boyd's notion of noncooperative COGs. Control warfare based on lateral cooperation targeting may indeed replace control warfare based on top-down command targeting as the paralysis "strategy of choice" in the twenty-first century. Yet, as the Tofflers point out, all future warfare will not be exclusively "third wave," or information, warfare. That is to say, "first wave" (agrarian) and "second wave" (industrial) war forms will not disappear with the emergence of the Information Age. Instead, we will observe that "every large-scale conflict will be distinguished by a characteristic combination of these war-forms. Put differently, each war or battle will have its own 'wave formation' according to how the three types of conflict are combined."[93]

Thus, although the future of strategic paralysis *theory* may lie in the concept of control warfare ushered in by Boyd and

Warden, actual *plans* to incapacitate an adversary may themselves remain "characteristic combinations" of the three war forms of paralysis discussed above—economic warfare based on industrial targeting, control warfare based on vertical command targeting, and control warfare based on lateral information targeting.

Though experiencing a renaissance in the wake of Desert Storm, the notion of strategic paralysis has been around for quite some time. The nonlethal intent of incapacitating (instead of annihilating or attriting) the enemy sprang quite forcefully from the carnivorous trenches of World War I. Airpower's first major war was one of mankind's bloodiest and most senseless. Unsurprisingly, then, air veterans of that war heeded the strategic call to "think in terms of paralysing, not of killing."[94] Two modern-day airmen, John Boyd and John Warden, have done just that.

As I have explained, Boyd's thoughts are *process* oriented and aim at *psychological* paralysis. He speaks of folding an opponent back inside himself by operating inside his OODA loop, an action that severs the adversary's external bonds with his environment and thereby forces an inward orientation upon him. This inward focus necessarily creates mismatches between the real world and his perceptions of that world. Under the menacing environment of war, the initial confusion and disorder degenerate into a state of internal dissolution that collapses his will to resist. To counter this dissolution, Boyd offers the orientation process of destruction and creation—a form of mental gymnastics designed to permit more rapid construction of more accurate strategies in the heat of battle. His theory of conflict is Clausewitzian in the sense that it remains philosophical, emphasizes the mental and moral spheres of conflict, and upholds the importance of teaching warriors how to think—that is, teaching the genius of war.

Warden's theory of strategic attack is *form* oriented and aims at *physical* paralysis. It advocates parallel, inside-out strikes against an enemy's five strategic rings, with unwavering emphasis on the leadership bull's-eye. Continual differentiation of these rings by air strategists reveals those COGs within and between rings that, when struck, incapacitate the enemy system through the rapid imposition of either total or partial paralysis. Warden's theory is Jominian in the sense that it remains practical, emphasizes the physical sphere of conflict, and upholds the importance of teaching warriors how to act—that is, teaching the principles of war.

The ideas of Boyd and Warden complement each other and, together, have helped usher in the era of inflicting strategic paralysis by means of control warfare. Although this general war form may become predominant in the Information Age, specific targeting schemes may need to vary somewhat. Thus, as always, the practical application of airpower theory must remain flexible and responsive. Tomorrow's airmen should remain forever mindful of the Tofflers' warning that first- and second-wave war forms do not disappear in the era of third-wave conflict. Caveats aside, if twenty-first-century technologies ever enable nonlethal capability to match nonlethal intent, then the strategic paralysis theories of John Boyd and John Warden may offer the guidance necessary for effective and efficient operations inside the loops and rings of first-, second-, and third-wave adversaries who threaten us.

Notes

1. In this respect, the works of Boyd and Warden represent a resurgence in strategic *conventional* airpower theory. As Col Phillip Meilinger argues, the three decades of airpower prior to Operation Desert Storm witnessed the diminished doctrinal significance of strategic conventional airpower. He cites two primary reasons for this phenomenon: (1) the organizational rise of tactical airpower in the era of limited war and (2) the identification of strategic airpower with nuclear weapons in the age of the atom. Lt Col Phillip S. Meilinger, "The Problem with Our Airpower Doctrine," *Airpower Journal* 6, no. 1 (Spring 1992): 24–31.

2. RAND's John Arquilla and David Ronfeldt have coined the term *cyberwar* to describe the nature of future conflict. The prefix *cyber* comes from the Greek root *kybernan*, meaning to steer or govern. They contend that *cyberwar* is a more encompassing term than *information warfare* since "it bridges the fields of information and governance better than does any other available prefix or term." A RAND colleague, Denise Quigley, offers the German term *Leitenkrieg*, which roughly means control warfare. I prefer the latter term to describe the content of Boyd's and Warden's theories of strategic paralysis.

3. J. F. C. Fuller, *The Foundations of the Science of War* (London: Hutchinson, 1925), 47.

4. Interestingly, Fuller's three spheres bear notable resemblance to Clausewitz's famed trinity of armed forces (physical), government (mental), and population (moral).

5. Fuller, 146.

6. Nonlethal intent distinguishes paralysis from more traditional strategies of annihilation. For a differing opinion, see Maj Jason B. Barlow, "Strategic Paralysis: An Airpower Strategy for the Present," *Airpower Journal* 7, no. 4 (Winter 1993): 4–15. He contends that the difference between paralysis and annihilation is one of technological capability rather than politico-strategic intent.

7. David Shlapak writes of "indirect engagement" as a mode of attack whereby "the effect is meant to be felt primarily elsewhere than at the point of attack." However, he defines paralysis as a "reduction in a combat force element's *capability* resulting from indirect engagement of that element" (emphasis added). In contrast, I view paralysis as a direct engagement of physical and mental capabilities so as to indirectly engage will. See David Shlapak, *Exploring Paralysis: An Introduction to the Study*, RAND Report PM-107-AF (Santa Monica, Calif.: RAND, December 1992), 5.

8. Hans Delbruck, *History of the Art of War within the Framework of Political History*, trans. W. J. Renfroe Jr., vol. 4 (Lincoln: University of Nebraska Press, 1986), 279.

9. Generally, though not exclusively, relative numbers and/or material considerations dictated the decision for battle or maneuver. However, they could also include such political factors as the aim of the war, possible repercussions within one's own government or nation, and the individuality of the enemy government and people.

10. Delbruck, vol. 1, 136.

11. Fuller, 314.

12. Ibid., 292.

13. Liddell Hart wrote that "a strategist should think in terms of paralysing, not of killing. Even on the lower plane of warfare, a man killed is merely one man less, whereas a man unnerved is a highly infectious carrier of fear, capable of spreading an epidemic of panic. On a higher plane of warfare, the impression made on the mind of the opposing commander can nullify the whole fighting power his troops possess. And on a still higher plane, psychological pressure on the government of a country may suffice to cancel all the resources at its command—so that the sword drops from a paralysed hand." Basil H. Liddell Hart, *Strategy* (London: Faber & Faber, 1954), 212.

14. Fuller, 181.

15. Basil H. Liddell Hart, *Paris; Or the Future of War* (New York: Dutton, 1925), 40–41.

16. Quoted in Charles Webster and Noble Frankland, *The Strategic Air Offensive against Germany, 1939–1945*, vol. 4 (London: Her Majesty's Stationery Office, 1961), 72.

17. Quoted in Thomas H. Greer, *The Development of Air Doctrine in the Air Arm, 1917–1941* (Washington, D.C.: Government Printing Office, 1985), 9.

18. William Mitchell, *Skyways* (Philadelphia: J. B. Lippincott, 1930), 255.

19. Boyd's theories have significantly affected the operational doctrines of both the United States Army, as reflected in Field Manual (FM) 100-5, *Operations*, May 1986, and of the Marine Corps, as reflected in Fleet Marine Force Manual (FMFM) 1, *Warfighting*, 6 March 1989. His ideas have had lesser influence upon Air Force and Navy operational doctrines.

20. John R. Boyd, "A Discourse on Winning and Losing," August 1987, 2, document no. M-U 30352-16, no. 7791, Air University Library, Maxwell AFB, Ala.

21. William S. Lind, "Military Doctrine, Force Structure, and the Defense Decision-Making Process," *Air University Review* 30, no. 4 (May–June 1979): 22.

22. This psychological paralysis often entails physical destruction, but such destruction is never an end in itself.

23. For Boyd's analysis, see his "Patterns of Conflict" briefing within "A Discourse on Winning and Losing."

24. Boyd's coupling of initiative and harmony stems from his study and acceptance of the German concepts of *Auftragstaktik* (mission order tactics) and *Schwerpunkt* (focus of main effort).

25. Boyd, "Patterns of Conflict" in "A Discourse on Winning and Losing," 141.

26. William S. Lind, "Defining Maneuver Warfare for the Marine Corps," *Marine Corps Gazette* 64 (March 1980): 56.

27. Boyd treats decision making and action taking as the process and product of a unitary rational actor. However, as Graham Allison argues, other models of nation-state behavior account for the bureaucratic nature of governments and the complications this introduces into the behavioral equation. See Graham T. Allison, *Essence of Decision: Explaining the Cuban Missile Crisis* (Boston: Little, Brown, 1971). Boyd would maintain, however, that minimizing the impact of such bureaucratic factors by streamlining organizational form and process is just another way to enhance one's own OODA loop.

28. By "folding an opponent back inside himself," Boyd simply means restricting an opponent's ability to reorient to a rapidly changing environment.

29. Boyd, "The Strategic Game of ? and ?" in "A Discourse on Winning and Losing," 10.

30. Boyd's dialectic process of destruction and creation corresponds fairly well to the modern scientific literature on genius. In "The Puzzle of Genius," *Newsweek*, 28 June 1993, 121, Sharon Begley suggests that genius rests in the ability to combine in novel ways elements from seemingly unrelated fields. Interestingly, Boyd's analysis/synthesis also correlates with the bihemispheric organization of the human mind as indicated by modern split-brain research. Pioneered by the California Institute of Technology's R. W. Perry, psychologist and cowinner of the 1981

Nobel Prize, this research suggests a division of labor between the left and right cerebral hemispheres of the brain. As Jan Ehrenwald explains in *Anatomy of Genius* (New York: Human Sciences Press, 1984), the left side is analytic and rational in its thinking, focusing on the trees. In contrast, the right side is holistic and artistic, focusing on the forest. He then states that concerted evidence supports a combined left- and right-hemispheric approach to the mental process we call genius (pages 14–19). R. Ochse offers a similar definition of creative genius in *Before the Gates of Excellence* (Cambridge: Cambridge University Press, 1990). It involves bringing something into being that is original (new, unusual, novel, and unexpected) and valuable (useful, good, adaptive, and appropriate).

31. This is precisely why Boyd claims that orientation remains the most important portion of the OODA loop.

32. Pape has introduced a methodology for analyzing strategic theories, particularly those dealing with the application of coercive airpower. Very simply, his approach links military means to political ends by way of "mechanisms," which address *why* theorists expect their proposed means or target sets to achieve the ends or desired results. In other words, if one attacks a given target (means), something will happen (mechanism) to produce the desired results (ends). Depicted graphically, TARGET → MECHANISM → RESULT.

33. John R. Boyd, Maxwell AFB, Ala., interviewed by author, 30 March 1994.

34. For those disappointed readers still looking for an operational example of Boyd's ideas, I offer the following, both of which were acceptable to Boyd as possible applications. The first is the Russian concept of the operational maneuver group (OMG), a combined-arms team of raiders, paratroopers, and diversionary units designed to operate *within* enemy formations. As Dr. Harold Orenstein describes it, "Such activity changes the classical concept of crushing a formation from without (by penetration, encirclement and blockade) into one of splitting it from within (by raids, airborne landings and diversions)." See Harold Orenstein, "Warsaw Pact Views on Trends in Ground Forces Tactics," *International Defense Review* 9 (September 1989): 1149–52.

35. Clausewitz defines the "ultimate object" of war in identical terms. See Carl von Clausewitz, *On War*, ed. and trans. Michael Howard and Peter Paret (Princeton, N.J.: Princeton University Press, 1976), 484.

36. Mao Tse-tung, *Six Essays on Military Affairs* (Peking: Foreign Languages Press, 1972), 273.

37. Ibid., 299.

38. Regarding his briefings to the USAF Checkmate Division, Boyd implies that he implanted this idea of strategic paralysis in the Air Staff (see Boyd, interview). However, the historical review presented earlier suggests that this notion has underpinned US strategic air theory from its earliest days. Boyd does not recall briefing John Warden directly, and Warden claims to have only a superficial appreciation of Boyd's ideas. He is,

however, most familiar with those concerning air combat and energy maneuverability, owing to his fighter background. Col John A. Warden III, commandant, Air Command and Staff College, Maxwell AFB, Ala., interviewed by author, 27 January 1994.

39. One detects a distinct "strategic" flavor to Warden's discussions of air superiority and interdiction in *The Air Campaign: Planning for Combat* (Washington, D.C.: National Defense University Press, 1988). Emphasizing that "command is the *sine qua non* of military operations," he advocates attacking the three elements of command (information gathering, decision, and communication) as part of the effort to win air superiority (pages 51–58). Likewise, he clearly prefers "distant interdiction" against the source of men and materiel as the "most decisive" form of interdiction (pages 94–95).

40. Ibid., 9.

41. In defining a center of gravity as "the hub of all power and movement," Clausewitz viewed COGs as strengths alone. Also, in his quest to reduce the enemy's COGs to a single, omnipotent hub, Clausewitz diminished the strategic significance of interrelationships between COGs. He did acknowledge that one could not always reduce several COGs to one (though these cases were "very few" in number). He also recognized a certain "connectedness" between COGs when he wrote of their "spheres of effectiveness" to describe the influence of one hub upon the rest. However, Clausewitz still advocated attacks upon the COGs themselves, overlooking the possibility of targeting the vulnerable linkages between COGs. These linkages and interactions are addressed by Boyd, Warden, and, most recently, Maj Jason Barlow through his creative concept of national elements of value (NEV). For more on NEVs, see Barlow.

42. Warden, *The Air Campaign*, 149.

43. This assertion contains two presumptions: (1) an enemy's COGs are material in nature and (2) an enemy possesses COGs that are vulnerable to attack. Regarding the first presumption, certain nonmaterial COGs may actually be more vulnerable to attack by surface forces than by air forces. For example, if popular support is the strategic COG for a guerrilla insurgency, then surface forces may have the advantage over air forces due to their ability to occupy territory and, if necessary, separate the population from the insurgents. In terms of the second presumption, an enemy may have no vulnerable COGs at all due to the inherent redundancy and/or resiliency of his system.

44. Warden defines a strategic entity as "any organization that can operate autonomously; that is, it is self-directing and self-sustaining." As he goes on to explain, this definition implies that his theory of strategic attack against the enemy as a system is "as applicable to a guerrilla organization as to a modern industrial state." See Col John A. Warden III, "The Enemy as a System," *Airpower Journal* 9, no. 1 (Spring 1995): 55, note 1. Although one can certainly argue with Warden's contention that his theory applies to all forms of warfare, one cannot insist (as many do) that he assumes the enemy is a modernized nation-state. He does presume that one can analyze

the enemy, whether a nation-state or a guerrilla organization, as a system of five strategic rings with leadership at the center.

45. Warden uses a biological analogy to draw parallels with the human body. The brain, receiving inputs from the eyes and central nervous system, represents the body's leadership. Food and oxygen are two organic essentials, while blood vessels, bones, and muscles provide the infrastructure. Cells constitute the body's population, while specific lymphocytes and leukocytes, along with other white blood cells, provide protection from attack. A cessation in functioning of any part of the body will have a more or less important effect on the rest of the body. Although this analogy is attractive in its simplicity and familiarity, Neustadt and May caution that one must temper reasoning from analogies by considering differences as well as likenesses. See Richard E. Neustadt and Ernest R. May, *Thinking in Time: The Uses of History for Decision-Makers* (New York: Free Press, 1986), 41.

46. The terminology often used by Warden to discuss the leadership ring suggests that, like Boyd, he treats governmental decision making as the process and product of a unitary rational actor—Allison's model 1 (see Allison). However, he argues that one can describe and target the leadership bull's-eye in terms of model 1 (rational actor), model 2 (organizational process), or model 3 (governmental politics). In fact, the analysis or breakdown of the center ring into its subsystems will reveal the model 1, 2, and/or 3 dynamics at play. The job of the air strategist is to determine how best to influence leadership decision making, given its particular system dynamics. Col John A. Warden III, commandant, Air Command and Staff College, Maxwell AFB, Ala., interviewed by author, 17 February 1994.

47. Warden, interview, 17 February 1994.

48. Ibid.

49. Col John A. Warden III, "Air Theory for the Twenty-first Century" (Maxwell AFB, Ala.: Air Command and Staff College, January 1994), 14–19. Interestingly, both Billy Mitchell and the Air Corps Tactical School drew similar lessons from their examination of World War I; these lessons subsequently affected their visions of future war and airpower.

50. Although the depiction of war as an extension of politics is widely accepted in both civilian and military circles, two prominent military historians have recently cast doubt on this proposition in their latest publications. See Martin van Creveld, *The Transformation of War* (New York: Free Press, 1991); and John Keegan, *A History of Warfare* (New York: Alfred A. Knopf, 1993). If, as they claim, war is a sociocultural phenomenon rather than a political one, this has significant implications for Warden's emphasis on enemy leadership as *the* critical center of gravity.

51. Col John A. Warden III, "Employing Air Power in the Twenty-first Century," in *The Future of Air Power in the Aftermath of the Gulf War*, ed. Richard H. Shultz Jr. and Robert L. Pfaltzgraff Jr. (Maxwell AFB, Ala.: Air University Press, July 1992), 62, 67.

52. For additional detail, see Warden, "Air Theory for the Twenty-first Century," 8–14.

53. Ibid., 3.

54. In certain respects, Warden's dismissal of destruction strategies resembles Clausewitz's idea that absolute war (involving pure violence and the total annihilation of the enemy state) was virtually impossible to conduct due to real-world constraints.

55. As mentioned in footnote 41, Major Barlow provides an excellent discussion of the dynamic interactions between what he calls national elements of value. He explains that these NEVs are both interdependent and self-compensating—both critical attributes to consider when one is trying to dismantle the enemy as a system.

56. Eliot Cohen, "Strategic Paralysis: Social Scientists Make Bad Generals," *The American Spectator*, November 1980, 27.

57. Col Pat Pentland, class notes, Course 633, Center of Gravity Analysis, School of Advanced Airpower Studies. See also idem, "Center of Gravity Analysis and Chaos Theory: Or How Societies Form, Function, and Fail" (Maxwell AFB, Ala.: Air War College, 1993–1994).

58. Warden, interview, 17 February 1994.

59. Clausewitz, 136.

60. Warden, "The Enemy as a System," 43. Again, notable parallels exist between Warden's formula and the following one developed by ACTS: NATION'S WAR-MAKING POTENTIAL = WAR-MAKING CAPABILITY x WILL TO RESIST.

61. Warden, interview, 17 February 1994.

62. Warden, "Air Theory for the Twenty-first Century," 3.

63. Warden, interview, 17 February 1994.

64. Antoine Henri Jomini, *The Art of War*, in *Roots of Strategy*, bk. 2 (Harrisburg, Pa.: Stackpole Books, 1987), 436.

65. Interestingly, many prominent historians note that the Jominian tradition has dominated American military thinking over the past century and a half. For example, Michael Howard argues that "it is in Jominian rather than in Clausewitzian terms that soldiers are trained to think" since the complicated craft of war is most easily taught by focusing on the mechanics of military operations rather than on the more nebulous features of morale, genius, and so forth. Peter Paret traces this Jominian dominance back to the "intensely empirical atmosphere" of the late nineteenth century. Michael Howard, "Jomini and the Classical Tradition in Military Thought," and Peter Paret, "Clausewitz and the Nineteenth Century," in *The Theory and Practice of War*, ed. Michael Howard (Bloomington, Ind.: Indiana University Press, 1975), 13–14, 31.

66. In an extremely thought-provoking article, Alan Beyerchen argues that Clausewitz himself was a "nonlinear" thinker and that *On War* is a classic exposé of the essential nonlinearity or unpredictability of battle. See Alan Beyerchen, "Clausewitz, Nonlinearity, and the Unpredictability of War," *International Security* 17 (Winter 1992–1993): 59–90.

67. Clausewitz, 152.

68. Ibid., 141.

69. Ibid., 100, 110.

70. Col John A. Warden III, commandant, Air Command and Staff College, Maxwell AFB, Ala., interviewed by author, 23 February 1994.

71. Grant T. Hammond, chair of national security strategy/professor of international relations, Air War College, Maxwell AFB, Ala., interviewed by author, 3 February 1994.

72. Quoted in Webster and Frankland, vol. 4, 72.

73. Ibid., 73. Trenchard deplored "the indiscriminate bombing of a city for the sole purpose of terrorising the civilian population." That said, he did focus heavily on the moral effects of strategic bombardment. The minutes of a meeting he chaired in July 1923 quote him as advocating "the policy of hitting the French nation and making them squeal before we did. . . . [This is] more vital than anything else" (page 67). Similarly, Air Staff memorandum 11A of March 1924 succinctly states that the proper employment of the RAF is "to bomb military objectives in populated areas from the beginning of the war, with the object of obtaining a decision by the moral effect which such attacks will produce and by the serious dislocation of the normal life of the country." Col Phillip S. Meilinger, "Trenchard and 'Morale Bombing': The Evolution of Royal Air Force Doctrine before World War II," *Journal of Military History* 60 (April 1996): 256.

74. Col Edgar S. Gorrell, "Gorrell: Strategical Bombardment," in *The U.S. Air Service in World War I,* ed. Maurer Maurer, vol. 2 (Washington, D.C.: Government Printing Office, 1978), 143.

75. One should note that ACTS's strategic bombardment doctrine was not the War Department's official doctrine as laid out in TR 440-15, *Employment of the Air Forces of the Army.* Despite only lukewarm endorsement by the Army General Staff, the school's "high altitude, daylight, precision bombing" of the enemy's industrial web did form a basis for US air plans in World War II and is widely recognized as the definitive American strategic air doctrine in the interwar period.

76. The Tofflers contend that "the way humans make wealth and the way they make war are inextricably connected. . . . It is still not fully appreciated that the great age of industrialism is behind us. The basic system for wealth creation is being revolutionized—and war, as usual, is mutating in parallel." Alvin Toffler and Heidi Toffler, "War, Wealth, and a New Era in History," *World Monitor* 4 (May 1991): 52.

77. This notion of control warfare assumes that the enemy possesses a developed, identifiable, and vulnerable system of governance and information processing upon which he depends to conduct his affairs.

78. As Alan Campen points out, "Actually, the Soviet Union moved to formalize targeting of command and control almost two decades ago when it adopted Radio-Electronic Combat (REC) as a formal doctrine and created forces to execute the concept of physical and electronic attacks on enemy command and control systems." See Alan D. Campen, *The First Information*

War (Fairfax, Va.: Armed Forces Communications and Electronics Association [AFCEA] International Press, 1992), xxi, note 6.

79. In his briefing "Organic Design for Command and Control," Boyd specifically states that the OODA loop is, by its very nature, a C^2 loop (page 26). See "A Discourse on Winning and Losing."

80. Warden states that precision, speed, stealth, and information management are the essential ingredients of parallel warfare. Col John A. Warden III, "War in 2020," Spacecast 2020 lecture, Air War College, Maxwell AFB, Ala., 29 September 1993.

81. Warden, interview, 23 February 1994.

82. J. C. Slessor, *Airpower and Armies* (London: Oxford University Press, 1936), x.

83. Andrew Krepinevich of the Office of the Secretary of Defense (OSD) defines "information dominance" as a *relatively* superior understanding of an enemy's political, economic, military, and social structures. He contends that establishing such information dominance may be the decisive operation in future wars. See Andrew Krepinevich, "The Military-Technical Revolution" (paper for the OSD Office of Net Assessment, Washington, D.C., Fall 1992), 22.

84. Clearly, our potential adversaries differ significantly in terms of their reliance upon advanced information technologies; consequently, the viability of paralysis by control warfare based on information targeting must vary likewise.

85. In fact, the most recent Joint Publication 1, *Joint Warfare of the US Armed Forces*, 11 November 1991, codifies the use of advanced technologies to establish a favorable "information differential." It states that "the joint campaign should fully exploit the information differential, that is, the superior access to and ability to effectively employ information on the strategic, operational and tactical situation which advanced U.S. technologies provide our forces" (page 57). In addition, the National Defense University at Fort Lesley J. McNair, Washington, D.C., opened a School of Information Warfare and Strategy in August 1994. Its 10-month-long curriculum focuses on advances in information technology and the ways these affect the definition of national security needs and the development of military strategy.

86. John Arquilla and David Ronfeldt, *Cyberwar Is Coming*, RAND Report P-7791 (Santa Monica, Calif.: RAND, 1992), 6.

87. This assertion does not imply that all future wars will be high-tech, hyperspeed infowars. I agree with Alvin and Heidi Toffler's view that the advent of information warfare does not eliminate other forms of conflict. Generally speaking, however, advances in information technology will increase the pace of twenty-first-century warfare, albeit to varying degrees based on the technological capabilities of the opposing sides.

88. Maj James L. Rodgers, "Future Warfare and the Space Campaign," Air Campaign Course Research Projects (Maxwell AFB, Ala.: Air Command and Staff College, 1993–1994), 116.

89. "The Information Revolution reflects the advance of computerized information and communications technologies and related innovations in organization and management theory. Sea-changes are occurring in how information is collected, stored, processed, communicated and presented, and in how organizations are designed to take advantage of increased information." Arquilla and Ronfeldt, 2.

90. John Naisbitt, *Megatrends: Ten New Directions Transforming Our Lives* (New York: Warner Books, 1982), 1–2.

91. Ibid., 204.

92. "Distributed problem solving is the solution to problems through the use of multiple cooperative (usually physically separated) problem solvers. Truly distributed problem solving must be contrasted with centralized problem solving with remote execution. In true distributed problem solving, no one element has access to all the information which will be used in the eventual solution. The essential issues involve the decomposition of problems, insuring cooperation among problem-solving elements, managing communications, and dynamically adjusting the system problem statements in response to changes in the situation." Maj George E. Orr, *Combat Operations C3I: Fundamentals and Interactions* (Maxwell AFB, Ala.: Air University Press, 1983), 41–42.

93. Toffler and Toffler, 52.

94. Liddell Hart, *Strategy*, 212.

Chapter 11

An Ambivalent Partnership:
US Army and Air Force Perspectives
on Air-Ground Operations, 1973–90

*Dr. Harold R. Winton**

*It is my conviction that the characteristics commonly
associated with chamber music can be achieved in
symphonic orchestras far more readily than is customarily
imagined. It is a matter, first, of the excellence of the
players themselves, and second of the manner in which
they are trained to listen to what others are doing and to
make their individual part contribute to the ensemble
synthesis.*

—George Szell

The era between the Vietnam War and Operation Desert
Shield proved highly significant for all of America's armed
forces but particularly for the Army and the Air Force, both of
which came out of Vietnam with a mixed legacy. On the one
hand, proponents could point to battlefield successes. On the
other, both internal and external critics contended that the
Army and the Air Force had failed to develop strategic and
operational concepts that contributed to preservation of an
independent, non-Communist Republic of Vietnam. These
analysts argued that although part of the failure to achieve
American political objectives lay at the doorstep of misguided
political direction and at times overly restrictive constraints
and restraints, the services themselves suffered from
intellectual deficiencies that detracted significantly from their
overall effectiveness. Debates over these issues led to internal
turmoil in both services, though more so in the Army than the

*The author wishes to thank Andrew Bacevich, Dennis Drew, Douglas Johnson,
Thomas Keaney, Phillip Meilinger, David Mets, and John Romjue for their substantive
and useful comments on an early draft of this essay. All matters of fact and interpretation herein remain, however, the author's responsibility.

THE PATHS OF HEAVEN

Air Force. Two other conditions affected both services: (1) the emergence of technological capabilities that accentuated the speed, lethality, and precision of weapons systems for both land and air warfare and (2) the identification of a possible Warsaw Pact invasion of western Europe as the single most significant threat for which the United States had to prepare conventional forces.

This essay provides a critical, comparative analysis of Army and Air Force doctrine regarding air-ground operations in the period 1973–90. For purposes of the analysis, the essay defines air-ground operations as attacks from the air against enemy ground targets that have either tactical or operational consequence for friendly ground formations. One usually classifies such attacks under the rubrics of close air support (CAS) and air interdiction (AI). The essay excludes explicit consideration of tactical air reconnaissance and tactical airlift. The analysis seeks to determine the degrees of commonality and divergence that marked the two services' approaches to air-ground operations and the underlying reasons for either the compatibility or tension between the emerging doctrinal positions. Initial factors examined here include the services' reactions to the external influences mentioned above as well as the following internal factors: their visions of the nature of war, their doctrine-development processes, and the roles of key Army and Air Force personalities in shaping doctrine.

The first part of the essay focuses on the period from 1973 to 1979, when the Army and the Air Force began a partnership based primarily on the Army's realization of its need for Air Force support in executing its Active Defense doctrine. The second examines the period from 1980 to 1986, when the Army's move from a doctrine of Active Defense to AirLand Battle and its grappling with the concept of the operational level of war served to strengthen that partnership. The final section assesses the era from 1987 to 1990 in light of the Army's efforts to develop capabilities to execute deep battle and of the emergence of unofficial thought within the Air Force concerning the operational level of war.

This essay fits within the general field of peacetime preparation for war and institutional responses to challenges imposed by such preparation. As Michael Howard noted in

"Military Science in an Age of Peace," a lecture he gave in 1973, one may find the fog of peace even more difficult to penetrate than the fog of war.[1] This situation requires military institutions in peacetime to navigate by dead reckoning, never quite sure of what they will encounter when the fog partially lifts and the bullets, missiles, and electrons begin flying with malice. Military leaders sailing through this fog of peace not only must articulate a reasonably accurate vision of the nature of future war and define new operational concepts for fighting it successfully, but also—through fiat, consensus building, or some combination thereof—must convince their service that the course upon which they are embarked is correct. Further, they must implement a coherent policy that will mold the service to meet its anticipated challenges.[2] None of this is easy, but these peacetime challenges become significantly more difficult when the issues require the active participation of two services with significantly different institutional histories, self-images, and battlefield perspectives.

Unsurprisingly, the Army and the Air Force look at war from two sharply contrasting points of view. To most Army officers, it is axiomatic that ground soldiers with weapons decide the ultimate outcome of any war. The consideration of terrain is part and parcel of everything they do. Although weather influences their operations, it does not preclude them. Furthermore, soldiers live where they fight: on the ground, with almost constant exposure to privation and danger. The primary force they must reckon with is the enemy ground formation. But—and this is a very important *but*—virtually all thinking soldiers also remain painfully aware of their need for air support: to keep the enemy air force off their backs and to reduce the effectiveness of the enemy's ground formations.

Airmen live in an entirely different mental and physical universe. They do not accept the axiom that the ultimate result comes from soldiers on the ground. Many airmen believe passionately that airpower is a liberating force that can produce tactical, operational, and strategic results quite independently of land formations. Features of terrain are at most minor nuisances that one must take into account when planning flight routes and final approaches. Weather, on the other hand, is a very significant consideration that can severely degrade and, under certain conditions, prevent air operations. Although airmen's exposure to danger is intermittent, they rely absolutely on the proper functioning of their equipment for survival in the hostile and unforgiving environment in which they fight. Furthermore, most airmen remain completely convinced that the sine qua non of effective operations is the neutralization or destruction of the enemy's air force and air defenses. This accomplished, all else can follow. Although airmen largely depend upon soldiers to keep enemy ground forces at bay, this dependence is nowhere nearly as strong as soldiers' dependence upon them. The asymmetry of this dependence lies at the root of many of the tensions that exist between the Army and the Air Force regarding air-ground operations.

Forming the Partnership, 1973–79

The Vietnam experience significantly affected both the Army and the Air Force, but in noticeably different ways. The Army was virtually shattered. The proud, confident days when troops had helicoptered into the Ia Drang Valley and put to flight multiple North Vietnamese Army (NVA) regiments were a faded and distant memory by 1973. Instead, at the forefront of the Army's consciousness one found (1) a series of battles that were, at best, tactical stalemates and (2) a deep malaise brought about by an unpopular war, an inequitable draft system, a progressive unraveling of small-unit discipline, and a severe questioning of the competence and integrity of its senior leaders. Although some voices placed the onus for the Vietnam debacle on misguided policy and faulty military strategy directed from the E ring of the Pentagon, others realized that if the Army were to provide effectively for the common defense, it must reform itself both morally and intellectually. The intellectual component of that transformation would center first in doctrine.

The Air Force experience in Vietnam was not as searing as the Army's, but it did possess some doctrinal implications. First, the evidence on AI remained mixed. Although it had not appreciably altered support to guerrilla warfare, it had substantially disrupted the logistical flow to conventional offensive operations. Second, seven long years of operating under a badly fragmented command system significantly reinforced the Air Force's institutional preference for a single air commander in each theater of operations, working under the direct purview of the theater commander. More ambivalent were the implications of the Vietnam experience for the theory of strategic attack in negating an opponent's military capability and undermining his political will. On the one hand, many Air Force analysts insisted that Linebacker 2 demonstrated what airpower could do when politicians took the gloves off.[3] More thoughtful analysts, however, pointed out that no panacea target set neutralized the military capability of the Democratic Republic of Vietnam (DRVN) and that President Richard Nixon purchased the political objective of disengaging America from Vietnam with the carrot of concessions as much as he imposed it with the stick of airpower.[4] In sum, Vietnam provided rather uncertain grist for the Air Force doctrinal mill.

Before examining the development of Army and Air Force doctrine in the period following the Vietnam War, one should note that the two institutions have divergent perspectives about the nature and purpose of doctrine itself. In its military guise, doctrine forms the essential link between theory and practice. It remains, in essence, a medium of transmission in which general ideas about the nature, purpose, and employment of violence in service of the state (theoretical propositions) receive sanctioned, practical expression peculiar to the time and setting of the military institution promulgating the doctrine of a particular era. As such, doctrine always involves both thought and action.[5] But the Air Force emphasizes the cerebral component of doctrine, while the Army concentrates upon the musculature. The Air Force's propensity to emphasize the conceptual component of doctrine is clearly evident in the statement attributed to Gen Curtis E. LeMay, which appeared inside the front cover of the 1984 edition of Air Force Manual (AFM) 1-1, *Basic Aerospace Doctrine of the United States Air Force:* "At the very heart of warfare lies doctrine. It represents the central beliefs for waging war in order to achieve victory. Doctrine is of the mind, a network of faith and knowledge reinforced by experience, which lays the pattern for the utilization of men, equipment, and tactics."[6]

The Army view of doctrine seems much more practical. Chapter 3, "How to Fight," of the 1976 edition of Field Manual (FM) 100-5, *Operations,* meant exactly what it said. This does not imply that the Air Force's doctrine has no active component or that the Army's has no theoretical content. Each is clearly a mix of both. Two distinct institutional preferences exist, however, and the divergence of these emphases was, in and of itself, a factor that complicated cross-service communication.

Differing command echelons that developed each service's most significant doctrine also influenced Army–Air Force communications on doctrinal matters. The Air Force doctrinal structure envisioned three levels: basic or fundamental doctrine, normally written at the Air Staff; operational doctrine, the responsibility of the major subordinate commands; and tactical doctrine, developed by a variety of schools and agencies.[7] Army doctrine has a similar structure but remains more closely tied to its level of organization. At the top is capstone doctrine, the rough equivalent of Air Force basic doctrine but, as we have seen, a much more explicit guide to practice than its Air Force counterpart. Subordinate doctrine addresses war-fighting and support concepts appropriate to corps, divisions, brigades, battalions, and ultimately even minor tactical units.

The major difference between the Army and the Air Force after 1973 was that the Army formed in that year a single organization—Training and Doctrine Command (TRADOC)—responsible for the development of virtually *all* its doctrine, from the capstone manual to the lowest tactical publication. Thus, the Army had a powerful integrating agency that could, and did, make doctrine the engine that drove the Army. This development directly reflected the personal philosophy of TRADOC's first, and arguably most dynamic, commander—Gen William E. DePuy. The more diffuse locus of doctrinal development in the Air Force reflected the anomaly that, LeMay's assertion to the contrary, doctrine was a much more tangential concern in Air Force than in Army life. This diffusion also created problems in institutional communication.

Both the Air Force and the Army recognized that the former's Tactical Air Command (TAC), which owned all US-based aircraft that flew CAS and interdiction missions, was the logical point of contact for interaction with TRADOC on doctrinal matters. Although the TAC-TRADOC dialogue proved extraordinarily productive, it had two drawbacks. The most significant was that TAC *did not* speak for the Air Force—the Air Staff closely guarded its prerogatives in doctrinal matters and reserved the right to review all TAC-TRADOC agreements.[8] From the Army perspective, this seemed to imply that when TAC and TRADOC worked out a doctrinal solution to a common problem, someone on the Air Staff was standing in the corner with his fingers crossed behind his back.[9] The other, less significant, problem was that on doctrinal matters, TRADOC *did* speak for the Army. This at times created frustration in the minds of Air Staff action officers, who, when approaching their Army counterparts for coordination of doctrinal matters, received perplexed reactions that said, in effect, "Don't bother me; that's TRADOC's business."[10]

Despite the perceptional differences on the nature of doctrine itself and distinctly divergent institutional arrangements for the formulation thereof, one actually finds a significant amount of cooperation between the two services during the era between Vietnam and Desert Shield. That story begins with the development of the Army's Active Defense doctrine, published in 1976.

Three dynamics drove the 1976 edition of FM 100-5: the reorientation of the American national security focus from Indochina to Europe; the increased range, accuracy, and lethality of direct-fire weapons evident in the Middle East War of 1973; and General DePuy's personal energy and determination. The situation in Europe appeared grim. There, the insatiable manpower appetite of the war in Vietnam had bled Army forces white, and the continuously modernized Warsaw Pact forces appeared capable of launching a successful offensive into North Atlantic Treaty Organization (NATO) territory. Further, the Middle East War of 1973 served as a wake-up call for the US Army. Both sides lost more tanks and artillery pieces than existed in the complete US inventory of those systems in Europe, and Egyptian antitank gunners had successfully engaged Israeli tanks at distances of up to two thousand meters.[11] Last, General DePuy supplied the energy to apply the lessons that he derived from the Arab-Israeli War to the fashioning of an American Army tactically capable of repelling a Warsaw Pact invasion in Europe.[12]

The centerpiece of this transformation was the 1976 edition of FM 100-5. Clothed in a camouflage cover; replete with numerous charts, graphs, and diagrams; written in a simple, direct style; and printed with the liberal use of eye-catching bold-and-italic, black-and-brown type; this manual was clearly designed to grab and hold the reader's attention. The second paragraph of the opening chapter contained the clear imperative that "today the US Army must, above all else, *prepare to win the first battle of the next war*" (emphasis in original).[13] The entire second chapter provided a discourse on the effects of modern weapons that graphically depicted their increased range and lethality from World War II to the Middle East War of 1973. The chapter's most arresting statement took the form of a stern injunction to its readers about the capabilities of the modern tanker: "What he can see, he can hit. What he can hit, he can kill."[14] The manual's conceptual heart lay in chapter 3, "How to Fight." Here, soldiers learned that "the most demanding mission that could be assigned the US Army remains *battle in Central Europe against the forces of the Warsaw Pact*" (emphasis in original) and that generals concentrate the forces, colonels direct the battle, and captains fight the battle.[15] The manual also informed them of the many advantages of firepower: **"MASSIVE AND VIOLENT FIREPOWER IS A CHIEF INGREDIENT OF COMBAT POWER. . . . FIREPOWER SAVES MANPOWER AND THUS SAVES LIVES"** (emphasis in original).[16]

Contrary to many popular conceptions, the manual gave almost equal coverage to offensive and defensive operations, providing 12 pages to the former and 14 to the latter. It also stated explicitly in the defensive chapter that **"attack is a vital part of all defensive operations"** (emphasis in original).[17] Nevertheless, in the face of the overwhelming numbers of Warsaw Pact tanks envisioned on a breakthrough frontage, the manual stipulated that active defense (the phrase from which the doctrine drew its appellation) in the main battle area would have to be elastic and that "counterattacks should be conducted only when the gains to be achieved are worth the risks involved in surrendering the innate advantages of the defender."[18]

Of particular interest to this essay is chapter 8, "Air-Land Battle," the second paragraph of which explicitly addressed the Army's dependence upon the Air Force: "Both the Army and the Air Force deliver firepower against the enemy. Both can kill a tank. Both can collect intelligence, conduct reconnaissance, provide air defense, move troops and supplies, and jam radios and radar. But neither the Army nor the Air Force can fulfill any one of those functions completely by itself. Thus, *the Army cannot win the land battle without the Air Force*" (emphasis in original).[19]

This analysis paid particular attention to the suppression of Warsaw Pact air defenses, asserting that "whenever and wherever the heavy use of airpower is needed to win the air-land battle, *the enemy air defenses must be suppressed*" (emphasis in original).[20] The manual depicted this suppression as a joint effort that required the integration of the intelligence and strike capabilities of both services. It cautioned, however, that even with the best of air defense suppression, the Air Force, in a future European battle against the Warsaw Pact, would not be able to provide the unopposed CAS to which the Army had become accustomed in its three previous wars. In short, the Army's 1976 doctrinal prescription for a future war in Europe clearly recognized cooperation with the Air Force as a tactical and institutional imperative.

Air Force basic doctrine in the period 1973–79 does not reflect a similar sense of commonality. The 1975 edition of AFM 1-1 was a bland document that reflected the desire of Air Force leadership for a manual that "more accurately and fully restates the role and purpose of USAF aerospace power, relating [it] more directly to national policy and national security strategy."[21] In other words, the manual sought to demonstrate the Air Force's relevance in the post-Vietnam era. It listed eight combat operational missions: strategic attack, counterair, AI, CAS, aerospace defense of the United States, aerospace surveillance and reconnaissance, airlift, and special operations. It also provided the stock definitions of and commentary on AI and CAS operations, the former defined as those "conducted to destroy, neutralize or delay enemy ground or naval forces before they can be brought to bear against friendly forces." Aerospace forces engaging in interdiction had to be capable of timely response to fleeting point and area targets. CAS operations were "intended to provide responsive, sustained and concentrated firepower of great lethality and precision . . . in close integration with the fire and maneuver of surface forces." However, nothing in this edition of AFM 1-1 indicated that the conditions for executing AI and CAS had recently undergone radical transformation or that close cooperation with the Army, particularly in the area of the suppression of enemy air defenses (SEAD), had become a key element in the Air Force's ability to conduct these operations without suffering unacceptable losses.[22]

The 1979 edition of AFM 1-1 did little, if anything, to improve this situation. Now widely derided by airpower analysts, the manual prompted one informed critic to refer to it as "the nadir of Air Force doctrine."[23] Despite this criticism, it contained some useful elements. The closing chapter offered a concise summary of the evolution of Air Force doctrine and a selected bibliography of publications dealing with military history and strategy, NATO and joint doctrine, and international relations. In perusing this list, however, one is struck by the fact that it does not include a *single* work dealing with the strategic, operational, or tactical employment of airpower! One is even more struck by the presence of numerous penned sketches of people, ranging from President Jimmy Carter and former president Dwight Eisenhower to the chief master sergeant of the Air Force and the ranking female officer on active duty at the time, each accompanied by a seemingly relevant quotation. The manual appears to meet the objective stated by its original drafters three years earlier to "provide a document that is interesting, relevant, and useful at all Air Force organizational levels."[24] However, in attempting to be all things to all people, the manual also appears to lose its focus.

The fuzziness of Air Force basic doctrine, however, presents a somewhat misleading picture. Considerable evidence indicates that the Air Force was closely scrutinizing the realities of a possible war in Europe and was actively cooperating with the Army to reach mutually acceptable solutions to those problems. The concern with possible war is reflected in the decision to develop a single-mission CAS aircraft, and in a series of RAND studies commissioned by the Defense Advanced Research Projects Agency (DARPA) and the Air Force to examine the details of a possible Warsaw Pact invasion of western Europe. The numerous joint ventures between TAC and TRADOC speak to the Air Force's cooperation with the Army at this time.

Development of the A-10 ground-attack aircraft represented the most tangible and, in many ways, most significant indicator of the Air Force's commitment to air-ground operations between Vietnam and Desert Shield. The origin of the A-10 goes back to the late 1960s, when Air Force planners, based on requirements evident in the Vietnam War, developed preliminary specifications for an ideal CAS platform. Criteria included the ability to operate from short, unimproved airstrips; high reliability and ease of maintenance; capacity to carry large amounts of tank-killing ordnance; long loiter time; 350-knot speed with high maneuverability; survivability for both pilot and plane in the face of heavy air defenses; and low cost.[25] But how could one kill tanks with air-delivered munitions? The A-10 answered that question with its 20-feet-long, four-thousand-pound, seven-barrel Gatling gun that fired three to four thousand rounds of 30 mm armor-piercing ammunition per minute.[26] Two quiet, reliable General Electric turbofan engines canted upwards near the rear of the fuselage enhanced the plane's survivability. A titanium "bathtub" that shrouded the cockpit enhanced the pilot's survivability. Although slightly underpowered and ungainly, the "Warthog" was a ground-attack pilot's dream. From the Army's point of view, fielding the A-10 not only underscored the Air Force's commitment to the CAS mission, it also created a corpus of pilots whose whole professional being centered around providing that support.

The Air Force's analytical focus began to shift toward the problems of a European war in the mid-1970s. In late 1974, RAND produced a study that examined the implications of air-and ground-delivered precision-guided munitions (PGM) for the defense of NATO.[27] The report concluded that PGMs might "add to the 'glue' of NATO and create problems for Pact strategists."[28] In late 1975, RAND completed a study that examined the relative merits of additional manned aircraft, remotely piloted vehicles, and standoff munitions for improving air-ground capability in NATO.[29] The study concluded that for an investment of $1 billion over 10 years, CAS standoff munitions launched by A-10s would kill the most armor and that terminally guided standoff munitions would kill the most enemy aircraft on the ground.[30]

In May 1976, the Air Force sponsored a two-day conference at RAND's offices in Santa Monica, California, to explore in some detail exactly how the Warsaw Pact ground forces might attack NATO.[31] Presenters included analysts from the Central Intelligence Agency, the Army's Combined Arms Combat Development Activity (a TRADOC agency), and RAND. Representatives from the Air Staff's Directorate of Plans and Operations and the USAF Fighter Weapons Center (a TAC agency) at Nellis AFB, Nevada, also attended. Issues addressed included how the war might start, principal attack axes, the primacy of the offensive in Soviet doctrine, Soviet concepts and tactics, logistical support, air defenses, and chemical warfare capabilities. One presenter opined that Soviet forces arrayed in East Germany consisted of 31–32 divisions organized into five armies, possibly augmented by 26 additional Warsaw Pact divisions.[32]

Other RAND studies requested by the Air Force included a 1978 analysis of the effects of weather on battlefield air support in NATO and a 1979 assessment of the potential vulnerabilities of Warsaw Pact forces to attacks against their tactical rear areas.[33] The main conclusion one draws from these analyses is that in the early post-Vietnam years, the Air Force took its mission to support the Army in a European war very seriously indeed and engaged in a comprehensive effort to determine how best to accomplish this mission.

The most obvious institutional arrangement that reflected Army–Air Force cooperation was the connection between TRADOC and TAC. One finds the genesis of this dialogue, which emerged into a full-blown partnership, in the desire of Gen Creighton W. Abrams, Army chief of staff, for close relations with the Air Force, and in a concern that during a period of fiscal austerity, the two services not engage in dysfunctional quarreling that could harm them both.[34] Abrams directed DePuy to establish a close working relationship with his counterpart at TAC, Gen Robert J. Dixon; to ensure that both remained fully engaged in the effort, he enlisted the support of Gen George S. Brown, Air Force chief of staff, who had served as his deputy for air operations and commander of Seventh Air Force in Vietnam.[35]

The commands held initial meetings in October 1973, and on 1 July 1975 they established a joint office known as the Directorate of Air-Land Forces Application (ALFA).[36] ALFA's location at Langley AFB, Virginia, TAC's headquarters and a mere 15-minute drive from TRADOC's headquarters at Fort Monroe, Virginia, facilitated communication. Officers from both services manned ALFA, whose actions were guided by a joint steering committee headed by TAC's deputy chief of staff for plans and TRADOC's deputy chief of staff for combat developments. A colonel, whose branch of service alternated annually, directed ALFA on a day-to-day basis.[37] On 15 July 1976, TAC and TRADOC each established an Air-Land Forces Program Office (ALPO) to convert ALFA's recommendations into service-specific programs.[38]

During the period 1975–79, ALFA successfully resolved many of the tactical and procedural issues regarding air-ground interface on a highly lethal battlefield. A TRADOC-US Army Forces Command (FORSCOM)-TAC publication addressed airspace management—successfully tested in the Return of Forces to Germany (REFORGER) exercise of 1976.[39] The agency also produced a comprehensive volume on the Soviet air defense threat and a study of this system's vulnerabilities.[40] In September 1977, tests under ALFA's aegis conducted at Fort Benning, Georgia, evaluated techniques for the combined use of attack helicopters and A-10 aircraft against enemy ground formations. ALFA also produced a

411

study examining ways to counter the emerging threat of the Soviet Hind helicopter and prepared plans for the Fighter Weapons Center at Nellis AFB and the Combined Arms Center (CAC) at Fort Leavenworth, Kansas, to develop and evaluate specific antihelicopter tactics.[41]

At higher levels, however, ALFA could not bridge the gap between Army and Air Force views on air-ground cooperation. The genesis of the problem was Abrams's decision in 1973 to eliminate the field army as an echelon of army organization. The demobilization of the Army and the elimination of the peacetime draft at the end of the Vietnam War led to a precipitous reduction in Army manpower. In order to satisfy Congress with an acceptable "tooth-to-tail" ratio and stabilize the Army's force structure, Abrams struck an agreement with Secretary of Defense James Schlesinger to retain 16 divisions on active duty in return for a guaranteed force of roughly 785,000. To hold up his end of the bargain, Abrams had to do two things: (1) put a major portion of the support structure into the reserves (which also acted as a prophylactic against the Army being called to war in the future without a reserve call-up) and (2) cut manpower at command levels above the division. Ergo, the field army as an organizational echelon disappeared.[42]

The field army headquarters, however, had served as the nexus of air-ground cooperation in both World War II and Korea. The most famous example of this cooperation was the virtual marriage between Lt Gen George Patton's Third Army and Brig Gen O. P. Weyland's XIX Tactical Air Command.[43] The fundamental precept that emerged from this relationship held that each field army would receive support from a colocated tactical air command that worked for the theater air commander but whose raison d'être was assisting the supported ground commander in the accomplishment of his mission. In January 1974, the Air Staff surfaced the problem to the Army Staff, from which a proposal emerged for the establishment of an Army tactical air support liaison element located at the air force component commander's tactical air control center (TACC).[44] This arrangement proved insufficient, however, to provide detailed tactical coordination between ground and air formations; and in January 1976 Dixon notified DePuy that the situation required more work, particularly when multiple corps deployed in a single theater.[45] The proposal that emerged from these discussions entailed retaining an Army element at the TACC, now redesignated the battle coordination element (BCE) but supplementing this with a robust Air Force liaison element at each corps headquarters, tentatively designated a tactical air coordination element (TACE). The Blue Flag exercise of December 1977 tested this arrangement.[46]

In January 1978, TRADOC published its analysis of this exercise in an air-land forces interface study, which concluded that the TACE provided adequate representation to the corps and that the BCE provided adequate Army representation to the TACC.[47] Two anomalies, however, surfaced in this report. The first was that it envisioned individual corps commanders communicating directly with the air component commander regarding the redistribution of sorties among the corps—clearly not a position the Air Force relished.[48] The second was that it did not represent the opinion of corps commanders in NATO, who felt that mere liaison at the corps level was not enough—that the corps battle required much more detailed interface with the Air Force than a liaison party could provide.[49] Both of these issues derived from the demise of the field army, and both continued to bedevil Army and Air Force planners in the years ahead.

In surveying the formation of the Army–Air Force partnership during the early post-Vietnam years, one must also consider the development of Army attack helicopters. During the Vietnam War, the Army had developed the AH-1 Cobra, an attack variant of the ubiquitous "Huey." Clearly, however, the Cobra had neither the lethality nor the survivability to fight successfully in central Europe. Hence, the Army embarked on an ambitious program to design a new generation of attack helicopter from the ground up, resulting in the AH-64 Apache.[50] The Apache's lethality derived from eight laser-guided Hellfire missiles, a 30 mm chain gun, and two pods of 2.75-inch rockets. Its design allowed it to withstand single hits from 12.7 mm armor-piercing rounds and 23 mm high-explosive cannon and continue to fly for 30 minutes. Equipped with a sophisticated target-acquisition and night-sensor system, the Apache was, indeed, a formidable weapons system.

But its very effectiveness raised the question of whether the Army had developed this helicopter because it did not trust the Air Force to provide needed CAS. One cannot entirely rule out this hypothesis. However, in the context of the Apache's development, several other explanations appear at least as operative as lack of interservice trust. First, the Apache represented a logical continuation of attack helicopter development during the Vietnam War. Second, it reflected a belief shared by the Army and the Air Force that a Warsaw Pact invasion of central Europe demanded the development of a wide variety of antiarmor systems in large numbers. Third, one can view the Apache as a response to aggressive Soviet development of attack aviation.[51]

In summary, one sees in the early post-Vietnam years a deliberate effort on the part of the Army and the Air Force to prepare themselves to defend western Europe. The creation of TRADOC and the conscious use of doctrine as the device to refashion the Army in the wake of the Vietnam trauma drove that service's effort. In contrast, Air Force basic doctrine appeared to lack a unifying vision. Nevertheless, the Air Force developed an aircraft tailor-made for killing enemy tanks in Europe, and it carefully assayed both the Warsaw Pact ground forces and the physical environment in which it would have to operate to help the Army defeat them. Finally, the TAC-TRADOC partnership embodied a promising start at forging cooperation between the two services. Remaining, however, was the troubling issue of restoring the higher-level ground-air interface in the wake of the Army's decision to eliminate the field army as an organizational echelon.

Strengthening the Partnership, 1980–86

Over the next six years, the Army significantly revised its capstone doctrine from Active Defense to *AirLand Battle,* the latter term generating a great deal of misunderstanding, particularly during the Gulf War. One must remember that AirLand Battle was *Army* doctrine (i.e., it was *not* Air Force doctrine, and it was *not* joint doctrine). The Air Force rearticulated its basic doctrine in 1984, providing a somewhat more coherent view of the theory and application of airpower than had its predecessors. Air Force cooperation remained absolutely essential to the execution of the Army's AirLand Battle doctrine. That cooperation was evident in the development of the "31 initiatives," which focused mainly on programmatic activities between the Army Staff and Air Staff, and in ALFA's publication of several practical biservice manuals. However, the inherent tension between Army and Air Force perspectives regarding air-ground integration again surfaced, this time with regard to incorporating NATO doctrinal prescriptions for the control of AI into US Air Force practice.

General DePuy had clearly intended the 1976 edition of FM 100-5 to be widely read—it was. It also was widely debated. As the debate matured, criticism of Active Defense focused on several key issues. First, it was too oriented toward weapons systems—soldiers became mere operators, not warriors. Second, the defensive method of moving from blocking position to blocking position seemed to cede the initiative to the adversary. Third, the emphasis placed on winning the *first* battle left open the more important question of winning the *last* battle. Additionally, the doctrine's focus at division level and below omitted the important contribution made by the corps, particularly in disrupting Soviet second-echelon forces. Last, almost as insult added to injury, the manual contained no consideration of the "principles of war." Although outside analysts, in part, prompted and abetted this debate, it largely remained an internal affair.[52] Army officers read DePuy's manual closely, and the more they read it, the less they liked it.[53]

This dissatisfaction in the ranks corresponded to two developments at the top. On 1 July 1977, Gen Donn A. Starry replaced General DePuy as TRADOC commander; and in June 1979, Lt Gen Edward C. Meyer, Army deputy chief of staff for operations and chief of staff designate, suggested to Starry that the Army should begin work on a new FM 100-5.[54] Starry was already so inclined.[55] Although as commander of the Armor Center and as a DePuy protégé, he had served as one of the key participants in developing the 1976 edition of FM 100-5, his perspective began to change when he took command of V Corps in Europe.[56] Here, he realized the vital

415

importance of engaging Soviet second-echelon forces and not simply blunting the initial attack.[57] When Starry assumed command of TRADOC, he began thinking and talking about the *extended battlefield,* a term that entered the TRADOC lexicon in the form of an emerging concept briefed to and approved by General Meyer in October 1980.[58] Several months later, after continuing to cast around for a term that would adequately convey the sense of the doctrinal shift he envisioned and after consulting with Lt Gen William R. Richardson, commander of the CAC, Starry announced his decision to refer to the Army's approach to warfare as AirLand Battle.[59]

Two aspects of this decision are noteworthy. First, although the doctrine espoused in the 1976 edition of FM 100-5 came to be known as Active Defense, it was a derived name—not a given one. In contrast, Starry deliberately hung a label on his emerging doctrine. Second, although he may have partially intended the "Air" part of AirLand Battle to make Army officers more air-minded, one may conclude that he also intended to signal the Air Force that the Army envisioned a strong partnership between the two services on any future battlefield.[60]

The 1982 edition of FM 100-5 reflected both Starry's guidance and the input of a number of midgrade officers who had found the previous edition badly wanting.[61] The new manual addressed virtually all of the concerns raised by the latter. Although it acknowledged the importance of "armaments sufficient for the task at hand," the manual stated categorically that "first and foremost, [combat power] depends on good people—soldiers with character and resolve who will win because they simply will not accept losing."[62] This statement marked a return to the Army's traditional view of war as a struggle waged between people who use weapons, consciously rejecting DePuy's notion of war as a contest of machines operated by people.

Analysis of the defense stated that it "consisted of reactive and offensive elements working together to rob the enemy of the initiative"; approvingly cited Carl von Clausewitz's description of the defense as a "shield of [well-directed] blows"; and explicitly warned against the Active Defense's technique of laterally shifting committed forces.[63] Gone was the single focus on the first battle. Instead, the manual introduced the concept of an operational level of war that involved the planning and conduct of campaigns, defined as "sustained operations designed to defeat an enemy force in a specified space and time with *simultaneous and sequential battles*" (emphasis added).[64] Throughout the manual, one found allusions to corps, divisions, brigades, and battalions working together to accomplish the mission.

Finally, the principles of war reappeared, albeit in an appendix and apparently subordinated to AirLand Battle's four "basic tenets of *initiative, depth, agility, and synchronization*" (emphasis in original).[65] The tenet of depth led to the concept of "deep battle," particularly significant for air-ground operations, for it clearly signaled the Army's realization of the need to delay or disrupt (i.e., interdict) Soviet second-echelon formations before they made contact with friendly troops.

In one sense, however, AirLand Battle remained an anomaly. Whereas the 1976 edition of FM 100-5 had contained a specific chapter focused on the dynamics of air-ground operations, the 1982 manual limited its treatment of "joint operations" to a series of wiring diagrams and an explanation of the various responsibilities of unified and specified commands, joint task forces, and service component headquarters. In short, the Active Defense embodied a much greater elaboration of AirLand Battle than did the original version of AirLand Battle.

This changed in 1986, when the Army published a new edition of FM 100-5, which reaffirmed the doctrinal thrust of AirLand Battle but updated and expanded it, based on the lessons learned in classrooms, war games, and field exercises.[66] This edition paid much more explicit attention to the conduct of campaigns and major operations. Of particular note for the conduct of air-ground operations was the statement that

> operational level commanders try to set favorable terms for battle by synchronized ground, air, and sea maneuver and by striking the enemy throughout the theater of operations. Large scale ground maneuver will always require protection from enemy air forces and

417

> sometimes from naval forces. Commanders will therefore conduct reconnaissance, interdiction, air defense, and special operations almost continuously. Air interdiction, air and ground reconnaissance . . . must all be synchronized to support the overall campaign and its supporting operations on the ground, especially at critical junctures.[67]

This was a much different statement than that contained in chapter 8 of the 1976 edition, for it moved the locus of concern from the winning of a single battle to the winning of a *campaign*. It also reflected a growing maturity on the part of Army doctrinal writers, for it specifically referred to *supporting* operations on the ground. Further, it established the ground forces' need for air protection and for the synchronization of interdiction with those forces, especially at critical junctures. However, this doctrinal statement implicitly accepted the proposition that one would make critical decisions on how the synchronization would take place in the context of *campaign* objectives, not merely the tactical dictates of individual *battles*. This realization brought it much more in tune with the Air Force perspective on the employment of airpower.

The 1984 edition of AFM 1-1, now titled *Basic Aerospace Doctrine of the United States Air Force*, formally updated that perspective. Apparently aware of the deficiencies of the previous edition, Air Staff doctrine writers set out to give the new manual "a new face and thrust."[68] They fully achieved the former objective—the latter, partially. Packaged in a slim blue binder, printed in understated blue type, and limited to 43 pages of text, the manual appeared to be a "statement of officially sanctioned beliefs and warfighting principles which describe and guide the proper use of aerospace forces in military action."[69] Its four chapters dealt with the military instrument of power; the employment of aerospace forces; missions and specialized tasks; and issues of organization, training, equipment, and sustainment. The second chapter contained the key doctrinal imperatives, reviewing the oft-repeated characteristics of speed, range, and flexibility and informing the reader of the importance of the "three essential factors in warfare: man, machine, and environment."[70] It enjoined aerospace commanders to employ their forces as an indivisible entity, conduct simultaneous strategic and tactical actions, gain control of the environment, attack the enemy's war-fighting potential, consider both offensive and defensive action, and exploit the psychological impact of aerospace power.[71] Discussion of the coordination of interdiction activities with surface forces was particularly apt:

> The effect of these attacks is profound when the enemy is engaged in a highly mobile maneuver scheme of operation dependent on urgent resupply of combat reserves and consumables. Air and surface commanders should take actions to force the enemy into this intense form of combat with a systematic and persistent plan of attack. The purpose is . . . to generate situations where friendly surface forces can then take advantage of forecast enemy reactions.[72]

Although the manual did not go as far as some critics might have liked in discussing the inherent fog and friction of war, it did at least caution readers to respect the flexibility of enemy forces.[73] Perhaps the most serious charge that one could level against it was its failure to explicitly consider the emergence of the operational level of war as the connecting link between military strategy and tactics. But the Army, which had first articulated the strategic-operational-tactical paradigm in American doctrine in 1982, was still working its way toward a mature statement of the implications of that model during the drafting of the 1984 edition of AFM 1-1. In sum, this statement of Air Force basic doctrine represented a more coherent explication of airpower principles than did its predecessor and recognized some of the potential for the cooperation of air and ground forces at the operational level. However, it stopped short of a fully developed typology of how one could best achieve this synergism.

At the tactical level, however, the TAC-TRADOC partnership was producing great dividends. Gen Wilbur L. Creech—Dixon's replacement at TAC—and Starry continued the well-developed institutional dialogue and met quarterly for face-to-face consultations.[74] The most obvious result of this cooperation was a series of joint manuals dealing with key issues of air-ground operations. These manuals emerged primarily from Army–Air Force participation in the Blue Flag command-post exercises at Hurlburt Field, Florida, and the Red Flag force-on-force exercises at Nellis AFB but also reflected an expansion of the TAC-TRADOC partnership to involve the Marine Corps and the Navy. Further, they laid out procedures for joint SEAD, joint attack of the second echelon, joint air-attack team operations (employment of A-10s and attack helicopters), and joint application of firepower.[75] These manuals represented a great deal of trial and error on the part of Army and Air Force officers working hard to figure out what would probably work best. Their very existence and the signatures of the multiple commanders who promulgated them constitute vivid evidence of how strong the Army–Air Force partnership had become by the mid-1980s.

A formal understanding at the departmental level "for enhancement of joint employment of the AirLand Battle Doctrine"[76] also strengthened the partnership. This April 1983 document, signed by General Meyer and Gen Charles A. Gabriel, Air Force chief of staff, committed the two services to use the 1982 edition of FM 100-5 as the basis for seeking increased integration of Army and Air Force tactical forces, enhancing interservice planning and programming, continuing the dialogue on doctrinal matters, working together on deep-attack systems, coordinating airlift requirements, and resolving issues concerning the integration of AirLand Battle into theater operations. A memorandum of understanding signed by Gabriel and Gen John A. Wickham, the new Army chief of staff and Gabriel's West Point classmate, followed it in November 1983. This paper emphasized the planning and programmatic aspects of the previous memo and pledged the services to "initiate herewith a joint process to develop in a deliberate manner the most combat effective, affordable joint forces necessary for airland combat operations."[77]

Apparently fearful of resistance from within their own services over "too much cooperation," Gabriel and Wickham instructed their operations deputies, Lt Gen John T. Chain and Lt Gen Fred K. Mahaffey, to establish a small interservice working group, reporting directly to these officers, that would develop specific proposals to implement their agreement and would *not* release information on the deliberations of this group to other members of the service staffs.[78] Based on the work of this group, Gabriel and Wickham, after some minor internal coordination in each service, proclaimed their intention to move forward together in a publicly released memorandum of 22 May 1984.[79] This agreement committed the services to exploring 31 specific initiatives regarding air-ground operations that dealt with issues of air defense, rear-area operations, SEAD, special operations forces, munitions development, combat techniques and procedures, and the fusion of combat information.[80]

The 31 initiatives achieved mixed success. Within 15 months, action on 18 of them had been completed, including the Air Force's decision to cancel the development of a "mobile weapons system" (an ersatz tank) for air base defense and a ground-based radar jamming system; concomitant cancellation of an Army program for an airborne radar jammer; development of a joint tactical missile system (JTACMS) and a joint surveillance, target attack radar system (JSTARS); and agreement between TAC and TRADOC regarding procedures for CAS in the rear areas.[81] The services were not, however, able to implement the initiative that called for the transfer of HH 53-H PAVE LOW III search and rescue helicopters from the Air Force to the Army.[82] And they continued to have difficulty settling the issue of air-ground interface at the operational level of war.

The focal point for this obstacle was the divergence of perspectives over battlefield air interdiction (BAI), addressed as initiative 21. BAI had a long and checkered past that arose from three issues: (1) the divergence between the Army and the Air Force concerning the relative authority of various command echelons in directing aircraft to provide ground support, (2) the elimination of the field army as a ground echelon of command, and (3) the influence of NATO tactical air doctrine on US Air Force doctrine. The Air Force command philosophy, expressed most recently in the 1984 edition of AFM 1-1, was one of "centralize control—decentralize execution."[83] Although the doctrine did not spell out the *level* of centralization, the Air Force preferred control at the theater of operations. Here, the air component commander would recommend to the theater commander an *apportionment* of assets among the functions of offensive and defensive counterair, AI, and CAS.[84] Based on the theater commander's decision, the air component commander would *allocate* specific numbers of sorties by aircraft type to subordinate air formations to perform the various functions.[85] The theater air commander, however, retained responsibility for control and direction of the AI effort, and ground commanders supported by various air formations had a voice only in the suballocation of CAS sorties to their subordinate units. As we have seen, however, the structure of the air-ground interface process was now in a state of disarray brought about by the disappearance of the field army.

The military command structure in Allied Forces Central Europe (AFCENT) and divergences between British and American philosophies of air-ground operations further complicated the problem. AFCENT's organization included a theater headquarters; a supporting air headquarters known as Allied Air Forces Central Europe (AAFCE), which contained the 2d and 4th Allied Tactical Air Forces (2ATAF and 4ATAF); and two subordinate land headquarters—Northern Army Group (NORTHAG) and Central Army Group (CENTAG). Although 2ATAF and 4ATAF remained subordinate to AAFCE, they had responsibility for providing air support to NORTHAG and CENTAG, respectively. Although both ATAFs and both Army groups were truly allied formations, the British dominated 2ATAF and NORTHAG, while the Americans dominated 4ATAF and CENTAG.

The British and Americans had distinctly different perspectives on air-ground operations. Based on philosophy, economics, and technology, the Royal Air Force (RAF) preferred to generate a large number of sorties in small, two-plane formations with relatively little centralized control. It also preferred relatively shallow interdiction to deep interdiction. The USAF, on the other hand, preferred a slightly more "above the fray" approach that emphasized a fewer number of large formations under relatively tight centralized control. In light of its possession of platforms that could conduct deep interdiction and its concern for the high density of air-defense weapons arrayed at and immediately behind the front lines of Soviet forces, it preferred deep rather than shallow interdiction.[86]

In the development of NATO doctrine, however, one could not ignore the British position. Therefore, a compromise in NATO tactical air doctrine provided for both relatively deep AI and relatively shallow BAI.[87] This doctrine also provided for joint BAI and CAS in a category known as offensive air support (OAS).[88] Reflecting the British preference for the nexus of air-ground operations at the army group/ATAF level rather than at the AFCENT/AAFCE level, once the *apportionment* decision was made, OAS sorties were *allocated* to the ATAF commanders. Furthermore, because the ATAF had responsibility for supporting an army group, the latter's commanders had significant influence in determining how the OAS sorties were suballocated among the corps under their command. On the whole, the US Army was quite satisfied with this arrangement. The CENTAG commander had to trade off proximity to his fighting corps for proximity to his supporting air commander in choosing his command location. But the OAS = BAI + CAS formulation gave him sufficient influence over air operations to prosecute the major land operations he had to execute under the rubric of the theater campaign plan. Although this arrangement did not provide subordinate corps commanders the amount of influence over air operations they felt they required to deal with Soviet second-echelon formations, it did give them access to an Army commander in the person of COMCENTAG, to whom they could make their case for priority of *both* BAI and CAS sorties. The USAF, however, remained much more ambivalent about BAI. Although the constraints of allied diplomacy had obliged senior American airmen to accept it as NATO doctrine, they were reluctant to incorporate into US doctrine any provisions for ground commanders to influence air interdiction.

An unprecedented "20-star" conference held at TRADOC in October 1979 reviewed a number of air-ground issues, including the BAI question. Attendees at this meeting included Generals Meyer, Lew Allen, Starry, and Creech, as well as Gen John W. Vessey Jr., the Army vice chief of staff, who had served with the Air Force at Udorn AFB, Thailand, during the Vietnam War. At this meeting, the TAC briefer on OAS stated that although use of the A-10 to attack Soviet second-echelon forces was not desirable, it would be feasible if both the Army and the Air Force were willing to "pay the price" in SEAD resources.[89] The meeting produced a consensus that AI, counterair/air defense, and SEAD were the priority study issues for ALFA.[90] It failed, however, to resolve the essential procedural issues of BAI, for on 22 December 1979, the Air Staff issued a new position paper that proposed retaining control and direction of BAI at the air component level—like AI.[91] This position represented a "doctrinal step backward" for TRADOC planners, who quickly rolled into high gear in their coordination with their TAC counterparts to reverse the Air Staff position. Agreements signed at the deputy chief of staff level in April 1980 and at the command level in September 1980 marked preliminary success in this regard.[92]

A long period of negotiation at the departmental level followed, culminating in a position paper on the apportionment and allocation of OAS, signed off by the operations deputies on 23 May 1981.[93] In essence, this document constituted formal biservice cognizance of the NATO doctrine on OAS spelled out in Allied Tactical Publication 27(B), *Offensive Air Operations*, previously ratified by the NATO Tactical Air Working Group. It stipulated that in the NATO Central Region, apportionment would take place at the AFCENT/AAFCE level and that OAS allocation, including CAS and BAI, would take place at the army group/ATAF level. It also codified the previously agreed arrangement for assigning an air support operations center (ASOC) to each corps, explicitly recognizing that "generally, only at Corps level will sufficient information be available to determine whether it is possible to engage and counter a threat with conventional organic firepower or whether it is necessary to have this organic firepower supplemented by OAS."[94]

In other words, the Army not only persuaded the Air Force to subscribe to the NATO doctrine on BAI but also extracted an admission of the reality that the ATAF commander's critical decision on the allocation of OAS sorties between BAI and CAS would depend upon intelligence developed at the corps level and passed through the army group to the ATAF. However, two problems arose. First, the position paper was just that—a statement of position, *not* doctrine. Second, the signature of the Air Force deputy chief of staff for plans and operations did not remove underlying Air Force reservations about giving the Army influence over any form of interdiction.[95]

In sum, between 1980 and 1986, the Army and the Air Force institutionalized the partnership formed from 1973 to

1979. This regularization, centered around the Army's development and refinement of its AirLand Battle doctrine, manifested itself in the series of "J" manuals produced by the TAC/TRADOC relationship and in the 31 initiatives at the departmental level. The Air Force also developed a more coherent statement of its basic doctrine. Although this doctrine did not take explicit cognizance of the operational level of war articulated in the 1982 and 1988 editions of FM 100-5, it at least demonstrated a preliminary vision for how air and ground forces might cooperate at this level. However, divergences of perspective remained about air-ground interface: although the interdepartmental position paper on OAS apparently resolved these differences, they continued to boil beneath the surface.

Crosscurrents, 1987–90

From 1987 to 1990, the Army–Air Force partnership continued to mature. Two developments, however, one in each service, influenced the partnership in ways not immediately apparent. The first was the Army's effort to develop a detailed doctrine for the corps's conduct of deep battle; the second was the publication of a National Defense University thesis entitled "The Air Campaign: Planning for Combat," written by a relatively obscure Air Force colonel named John Warden.

The continuation of a number of biservice projects reflected the strength of the Army–Air Force partnership. By December 1987, TRADOC and TAC, operating under the aegis of the 31 initiatives, developed a draft summary of requirements for a follow-on to the A-10 as a CAS aircraft.[96] By 1988 the services estimated that their joint force-development initiatives had resulted in a savings of $1 billion dollars in cost avoidance.[97] Additionally, they had reached agreement on concepts for joint attack of Soviet helicopters, the alignment of air liaison officers and forward air controllers with Army maneuver units, and a follow-on to the JSEAD manual of 1982. An article entitled "The Air Force, the Army, and the Battlefield of the 1990s" by Gen Robert D. Russ, Creech's successor at TAC, provided further indication of institutional solidarity. Here

425

Russ stated categorically that "everything that tactical air does directly supports Army operations."[98]

Meanwhile, the Army was hard at work developing guidelines to help the corps commander fight the deep battle. This effort had begun in 1984 with formation of the Deep Attack Program Office at Fort Leavenworth, operating under the CAC aegis.[99] By 1985 CAC had produced a field circular on corps deep operations. This publication contained an integrating concept for fusing Army intelligence, fire support, air defense, and maneuver assets with tactical air support to attack a Soviet second-echelon force, as well as the ground and air infrastructure of Soviet CAS formations.[100]

In 1987 the Army took another step forward in the maturity of its deep battle concept with the publication of a handbook describing the capabilities of existing and developmental deep battle systems. The handbook outlined an integrated group of Army and Air Force systems to sense enemy targets, process information about these targets, communicate the information to appropriate agencies, and control the Army and Air Force weapons used to strike them. The Air Force's precision location strike system (PLSS) and JSTARS and the Army tactical missile system (ATACMS) were particularly important components of the future architecture for deep battle.[101] This piece de résistance of deep battle publications, *Corps Deep Operations (ATACMS, Aviation and Intelligence Support): Tactics, Techniques and Procedures Handbook* (1990), outlined the imperative for the corps commander simultaneously to control significant engagements in close operations, deny the enemy the ability to concentrate combat power, attack enemy forces in depth, and retain freedom of action in his own rear area.[102] The key to performing these functions lay in the corps commander's ability, as part of a theaterwide concept, to influence enemy ground and heliborne operations three to four days in the future.[103] This called for very close integration of the corps maneuver and fire support assets with Air Force BAI and electronic countermeasures.[104] In sum, the work was exactly what its title implied—a handy how-to book for use by corps commanders and their principal planners in sorting out the difficult coordination issues involved in attacking second-echelon divisions of a Soviet-style combined-arms army. It reflected six years of hard thinking that conceptually represented the practical link between technology developed to fight the deep battle and the overarching doctrine of AirLand Battle.

One had to examine the other side of the coin, however. By developing extended-range systems that allowed the corps commander to fight the deep battle, the Army raised the question of coordinating the effects of these systems with air operations. The immediate focus of this issue became the placement of and procedures surrounding the fire support coordination line (FSCL)—originally known as the "no-bomb line" and developed in World War II as a coordination measure to mitigate against the chances of aircraft dropping ordnance on friendly troops. It was defined as a line *short of which* the release of air weapons required the prior clearance of a ground commander, and it applied primarily to aircrews returning from interdiction and armed reconnaissance missions with unexpended ordnance, who wanted to be able to take advantage of targets of opportunity without endangering friendly ground forces. The rule of thumb for the FSCL was to place it at the limit of the range of friendly artillery. As long as this range remained in the neighborhood of 10–15 kilometers beyond the friendly front lines, this placement did not present much of a problem because one would coordinate air strikes within that range with ground forces. However, with the advent of the multiple launch rocket system (MLRS) and, later, ATACMS, the Army had systems that could range out to roughly 30 and one hundred kilometers, respectively. Additionally, the corps deep-attack manual envisioned Apache helicopter attacks to a depth of 70 to one hundred kilometers beyond the front lines.

These newly developed capabilities placed the Army and the Air Force at loggerheads. If, on the one hand, the FSCL were pushed out to the depths of new Army weapons, it would significantly interfere with Air Force interdiction efforts and could allow enemy forces to escape attack by friendly air formations. If, on the other hand, the FSCL were kept relatively close to friendly front lines, the corps commander would lose freedom of action in the employment of fire support assets if he had to coordinate these fires with the Air Force prior to execution. This conundrum defied mutually satisfactory resolution.[105]

Another indicator of the potential fraying of the Army–Air Force partnership was the publication in 1988 of Warden's *The Air Campaign: Planning for Combat*.[106] One could interpret this book on two levels. At the most obvious level, it was an intelligent and imaginative tract that took the basic logic of operational art—the linkage of strategic objectives and tactical goals—and applied it to air warfare. As such, it addressed classic military questions such as the relationship between offense and defense, the trade-offs between concentration and economy of force, the employment of operational reserves, and the use of deception in war—all from an air perspective. In this sense, it was hardly revolutionary. Many people interpreted the book as simply the work of a thoughtful airman who wished to encourage his colleagues in the Air Force to consider the implications of operational art for the practice of their profession. In another sense, however, it constituted an airpower manifesto in the tradition of the works of Giulio Douhet, Billy Mitchell, and Alexander de Seversky. Although carefully qualified, a theme of airpower dominance ran through the book like a brightly colored thread. Chapter subheads such as "Single Arms Can Prevail," "War Can Be Won from the Air," and "Command Is True Center of Gravity" suggested an airpower-centered approach to warfare that had perhaps not fully matured at the time of publication.

That soon changed. The pivotal question that *The Air Campaign* had not addressed was, If airpower *can* be a war-winning instrument, *how* does it become one? In the summer of 1988, Warden conceived of an answer to that question.[107] Picturing an enemy society as a system, he reasoned that its ability to generate power depended on five subsystems: leadership, organic essentials, infrastructure, population, and fielded forces (in decreasing order of significance).[108] Warden represented these subsystems as five concentric rings, with leadership in the center and fielded forces on the circumference. This formulation directly confronted a central concern of almost all airpower thinkers—what to target. To Warden the answer was clear: one should start at the inside and work out.

In ordinary times, Warden's book and his subsequent musings on targeting philosophies would have held not much more than academic interest.[109] Regardless of the strengths or weaknesses of his approach to warfare, one thing remained certain: it was *not* Air Force doctrine. It did, however, represent a view in the Air Force that one could—perhaps even should—think of the application of airpower as independent of ground operations. To this extent, it constituted another crosscurrent in the story of Army–Air Force partnership

Conclusions

This study has endeavored to answer questions about the areas of convergence and divergence between Army and Air Force perspectives on air-ground operations between the end of the Vietnam War and the eve of Operation Desert Shield, and the underlying causes for them. Clearly, the services agreed about a great deal—that CAS was important, that it was an Air Force mission, and that they needed a dedicated CAS platform (and, therewith, a dedicated group of pilots whose sole training focus would address execution of the CAS mission). They agreed on the importance of SEAD, the fact that it was a shared responsibility, and the detailed procedures required to effect it. They agreed on the importance of attacking enemy second-echelon forces, the use of Army helicopters and Air Force platforms working in close cooperation to accomplish this mission, and the detailed tactical procedures required to do it. They disagreed over two issues: (1) the amount of influence that senior ground commanders should have over Air Force interdiction operations and (2) the mechanisms for coordinating the effects of fixed-wing air and extended-range Army systems. At the risk of being somewhat simplistic, one can conclude that although very significant agreement existed at the tactical level, noticeable divergence characterized the operational level.

One can gain insight into the dynamics behind these similarities and differences of perspective by surveying the centripetal forces that tended to pull the Army and the Air Force together and the centrifugal forces that tended to pull them apart.

One can attribute the relative cohesion and strength of the Army–Air Force partnership from 1973 to 1990 in rough priority to (1) the unifying effect of the NATO defense mission, (2) the close cooperation of personalities at or near the top of each service, (3) a leadership shift in the Air Force that put fighter rather than bomber pilots in the majority of influential positions, and (4) the clarity of the Army's vision of how it intended to fight a future war that tended to pull the Air Force in its wake. The NATO defense mission gave each service a clear and *unifying* mission. The ability to defeat a Warsaw Pact invasion of western Europe below the nuclear threshold remained, for the period under analysis, the single most significant criterion of operational effectiveness for both services. When the Army and the Air Force looked at this challenge, each realized it needed the other. Despite the fact that the Army had greater dependence on the Air Force than vice versa, one could not deny that in the SEAD mission, the Air Force distinctly needed Army help. Furthermore, in order to make manifest its contribution to the national defense, the Air Force had to demonstrate its ability to destroy Soviet tanks as well as Soviet MiGs.

The close personal relations established between senior Army and Air Force leaders proved vital to the strength of the partnership. The positive personal chemistry apparent in, among others, the Abrams/Brown, DePuy/Dixon, Wickham/ Gabriel, and Starry/Creech relationships helped forge a partnership in peace that would hopefully withstand the rigors of war.[110] A gradual but distinct change in Air Force leadership abetted these relationships.

In 1960 bomber pilots held 77 percent of the top Air Force leadership positions—fighter pilots, 11 percent.[111] By 1975 the figures were 43 percent for bomber pilots and 41 percent for fighter pilots; by 1990 they had largely reversed themselves to 18 percent for bomber pilots and 53 percent for fighter pilots. The more prominent role of fighter pilots in the Vietnam War and the declining numbers of bombers in the inventory seem to have driven this shift, at least in part. Although the analysis has complications (e.g., General Brown had flown as a bomber, fighter, and airlift pilot), the trend remains clear; further, one can legitimately suspect that the Air Force fighter community proved slightly more favorably disposed to welcome the Army's doctrinal advances than did the bomber community.

The final factor pulling the Army and the Air Force together was the Army's clear vision of how it wanted to fight a future war and its distinct realization that Air Force support was absolutely essential for winning one. Air Force centrality to the Army's view of tactics was integral to both doctrines of Active Defense and AirLand Battle; and the Army's articulation of the operational level of war in the latter also contained an explicit acknowledgment of the importance of coordinated air support. In something of a doctrinal muddle for several years after Vietnam, the Air Force appeared to follow the Army's lead.

Some forces, however, tended to pull the services in opposite directions. These included the operational differences between the media in which they fought, the cultural implications these differences engendered, varying approaches to the meaning of doctrine and the institutional structure for developing it, and the capabilities of emerging technology. Air and land forces fight in two distinctly dissimilar environments. The former enjoy the flexibility to focus their effects at different loci, depending on the strategic, operational, and tactical dictates of the moment; but their presence is relatively transitory. The latter offer the offsetting advantage of much more permanent effects, but gravity limits their flexibility. These diverging operating characteristics produce cultural approaches to war that maximize the inherent strengths of each force (i.e., flexibility and permanence). Beyond these endemic difficulties of developing common doctrine, the Army decided in 1973 to create a major subordinate command dedicated to the formulation and promulgation of doctrine and the integration of that doctrine into its training, organization, and equipment-development systems. That decision, together with the Air Force's choice *not* to create such a command, made it difficult for the two services to develop a common doctrinal framework. Finally, the technological evolution that extended the ranges of land-based indirect fire systems and armed helicopters blurred the line between what had served as the relatively exclusive operational domains of the two services, thus creating new doctrinal challenges that defied easy solution.

Interestingly, the partnership between the two services appeared to be independent of two factors that frequently play a role in interservice relationships: the size of the defense budget and external pressure for cooperation. The partnership began in the mid-1970s, when the defense budget fell steadily in the aftermath of Vietnam, and it continued to prosper throughout the 1980s, when the defense budget proved relatively robust. Further, outside pressure for greater joint cooperation evidently did not foist the partnership on the services. Congress passed the Goldwater-Nichols Department of Defense Reorganization Act of 1986 well after the TAC-TRADOC dialogue had matured into a partnership and after the Wickham/Gabriel regime had officially formulated its 31 initiatives. Also, *Doctrine for Joint Operations*, the key joint publication resulting from the Goldwater-Nichols Act's specific recognition of the chairman of the Joint Chiefs of Staff as the promulgator of joint doctrine, was still in draft form in 1990.[112] The drive for jointness, therefore, had virtually no effect on the cooperation established between the two services during the period addressed in this essay. Although one could argue that an earlier start on joint doctrine might have settled unresolved issues between the Army and the Air Force prior to 1990, the extent to which joint doctrine can compensate for a lack of internally generated interservice cooperation remains to be demonstrated.

If one takes George Szell's criteria for the production of high-quality symphonic music as the basis for judging the Army and the Air Force from 1973 to 1990, one finds that they fall just short of the maestro's high standards.[113] They were magnificent individual performers. Each had equipped and trained itself to play its part as a virtuoso. Each had also listened to the other enough to recognize how they could most harmoniously blend their effects in a number of specific passages. But underlying philosophical differences about the nature of their activity and certain matters of interpretation had the potential to produce discordance. The quality of the performance, therefore, would depend somewhat upon the venue in which it took place. The acoustical properties of some theaters would tend to magnify the harmony, while those of others could just as easily emphasize the discordance.

From 1973 to 1990, the Army and the Air Force formed a solid partnership centered around the Army's ability to execute its AirLand Battle doctrine with Air Force support. Extensive biservice training, doctrinal publications, and programmatic cooperation reflected the strength of this partnership. There existed, however, an underlying ambivalence that one can attribute primarily to the services' diverging perspectives about the modalities of air-ground cooperation at the operational level of war. Had war broken out in western Europe, one might argue that the strengths of the partnership would have proved much more apparent than its weaknesses. However, the ambivalent aspects of the partnership became rather more apparent in the weeks and months after 2 August 1990, when Saddam Hussein's tanks rolled into Kuwait, triggering the American-led coalition's responses of Operations Desert Shield and Desert Storm. This theater subjected the Army–Air Force partnership to severe strain. Indeed, the performance resembled neither a delicately balanced chamber session nor a finely tuned symphony but a concerto in which all performers believed they were playing the featured instrument. Here, mutual listening skills proved exiguous, and the interaction between the two services at times resembled a dialogue of the deaf.[114] But that is another story.

Notes

1. Michael Howard, "Military Science in an Age of Peace," *Journal of the Royal United Service Institute for Defence Studies* 119 (March 1974): 2.

2. Stephen Peter Rosen, *Winning the Next War: Innovation and the Modern Military* (Ithaca, N.Y.: Cornell University Press, 1991), 8–22. Rosen highlights the need for senior military leaders to identify junior officers who share their vision of the new operational concept and to accelerate the career advancement of those officers.

3. Gen William Momyer, who commanded Seventh Air Force in Vietnam, is explicit here: "It was apparent that airpower was the decisive factor leading to the peace agreement of 15 January 1973." William M. Momyer, *Airpower in Three Wars (WWII, Korea, Vietnam)* (Washington, D.C.: Office of Air Force History, 1978), 243.

4. Mark Clodfelter, "Nixon and the Air Weapon," in Dennis E. Showalter and John G. Albert, eds., *An American Dilemma: Vietnam, 1964–1973* (Chicago: Imprint Publications, 1993),182–83.

5. On this point, see James J. Tritten, "Naval Perspectives on Military Doctrine," *Naval War College Review* 48 (Spring 1995): 23.

6. Air Force Manual (AFM) 1-1, *Basic Aerospace Doctrine of the United States Air Force*, 1984.

7. Ibid., v–vi.

8. The TAC problem was exacerbated by the fact that it did not even speak for the entire tactical air community in the Air Force. United States Air Forces in Europe (USAFE) and Pacific Air Forces (PACAF), like TAC, were four-star commands with their own perspectives on air-ground operations issues.

9. See, for example, discussion below of the Air Staff's reversal of TAC-TRADOC agreements on battlefield air interdiction.

10. Brig Gen Huba Wass de Czege, US Army, Retired, interviewed by author, Fort Leavenworth, Kans., 16 February 1995.

11. Paul H. Herbert, *Deciding What Has to Be Done: General William E. DePuy and the 1976 Edition of FM 100-5, "Operations"* (Fort Leavenworth, Kans.: Combat Studies Institute, 1988), 30, 33.

12. Additional details on DePuy's personal role and TRADOC's institutional role in driving the lessons of the 1973 Middle East War into the Army's psyche are found in the "TRADOC Report of Major Activities, FY 1974," 1 August 1975, 14–19; "TRADOC Report of Major Activities, FY 1975," 20 September 1976, 1–10; and William E. DePuy, "Implications of the Middle East War on U.S. Army Tactics, Doctrine, and Systems," in Richard M. Swain, comp., *Selected Papers of General William E. DePuy* (Fort Leavenworth, Kans.: Combat Studies Institute, 1994), 75–111.

13. Field Manual (FM) 100-5, *Operations*, 1976, 1-1.

14. Ibid., 2-6.

15. Ibid., 3-1, 4.

16. Ibid., 3-5.

17. Ibid., 5-2.

18. Ibid., 5-13, 14.

19. Ibid., 8-1.

20. Ibid., 8-4.

21. History, AF/XO Directorate of Doctrine, Concepts, and Objectives, 1 July–31 December 1993, 35, USAF Historical Research Agency, Maxwell AFB, Ala. (hereinafter AFHRA), file no. K143.01.

22. AFM 1-1, *United States Air Force Basic Doctrine*, 1975, 3-2.

23. Dennis M. Drew, "Two Decades in the Air Power Wilderness: Do We Know Where We Are?" *Air University Review* 37 (September–October 1986): 12.

24. History, AF/XO Directorate of Concepts, 1 July–31 December 1976, 62, AFHRA, file no. K143.01

25. William L. Smallwood, *Warthog: Flying the A-10 in the Gulf War* (Washington, D.C.: Brassey's [US], 1993), 10–11.

26. Details on the A-10's design from ibid., 11–17.

27. James F. Digby, *Modern Precision Weapons: Assessing Their Implications for NATO* (U) (Santa Monica, Calif.: RAND, 1975). (Secret) Information extracted is unclassified.

28. Ibid., 76. The author of this report was forced to admit, however, that while the state of analysis for single weapons versus point targets was fairly well advanced, one could not find detailed studies that "treat ground forces and air forces working together in a two-sided campaign." Ibid., 77. Information extracted is unclassified.

29. Donald E. Lewis et al., *An Analysis of Alternatives for Improving U.S. Air-to-Ground Capability in NATO (1980): Final Report* (U) (Santa Monica, Calif.: RAND, 1975). (Secret) Information extracted is unclassified.

30. Ibid., vi. The report also examined the potential effectiveness of remotely piloted vehicles (RPV), although its conclusions about them were ambivalent. It did note, however, that "as enemy ground defenses become more effective, RPVs (and standoff systems) become more attractive." Ibid., viii. Information extracted is unclassified.

31. J. H. Hayes, H. A. Einstein, and M. Weiner, *How the Soviet Ground Forces Would Fight a European War: Proceedings of a Workshop Held at the RAND Corporation, 19–20 May 1976* (U) (Santa Monica, Calif.: RAND, 1977). (Secret) Information extracted is unclassified.

32. Ibid., 11–18, 204–5. Information extracted is unclassified.

33. See R. E. Huschke, *Effect of Weather on Near-Term Battlefield Air Support in NATO: Weather and Warplanes VII* (U) (Santa Monica, Calif.: RAND, 1978). (Confidential) Information extracted is unclassified; and D. E. Lewis et al., *Potential Vulnerabilities of the Warsaw Pact Tactical Rear: Analysis and Results* (U) (Santa Monica, Calif.: RAND, 1979). (Secret) Information extracted is unclassified.

34. Herbert, 68. An address prepared by a member of the Air Staff for Maj Gen James R. Brickel, director of concepts, for presentation to the Royal Air Force Air Power Seminar on 26 January 1978, explicitly acknowledged the maturity of this relationship into a partnership. It stated categorically that "the TAC/TRADOC relationship has matured from a dialogue to a way of life—a partnership." The RAF made a special request for this presentation in order to study how it might work out a similar partnership with the British army. History, AF/XO, "TAC/TRADOC Partnership," 1 January–30 June 1978, AFHRA, file no. K143.01.

35. Herbert, 68.

36. Annual Historical Review (AHR), TRADOC, FY 1976/7T, 22 September 1977, 55, TRADOC History Office, Fort Monroe, Va. (hereinafter THO). ALFA was subsequently redesignated the Air-Land Forces Application Agency.

37. "TAC/TRADOC Partnership." When the colonel came from the Air Force, he worked for the Army general, and vice versa.

38. Ibid.; and AHR, TRADOC, 57.

39. AHR, TRADOC, 56.

40. AHR, TRADOC, 1 October 1976–30 September 1977, 29 August 1978, 34, THO.

41. Ibid., 38.

42. Lewis Sorley, *Thunderbolt: General Creighton Abrams and the Army of His Times* (New York: Simon and Schuster, 1992), 322–25.

43. The definitive work on this subject is a manuscript by David N. Spires, "Air Power for Patton's Army: The XIX Tactical Air Command in the Second World War," forthcoming from the Air Force History Support Office.

44. History, AF/XO Directorate of Doctrine, Concepts, and Objectives, 1 July–31 December 1974, 35, AFHRA, file no. K143.01.

45. AHR, TRADOC, 1 October 1976–30 September 1977, 35.

46. Ibid., 36.

47. AHR, TRADOC, 1 October 1977–30 September 1978, 1 November 1979, 177, THO.

48. Ibid.

49. This issue is discussed in depth, below.

50. For background on the Apache's development and technical details, see Doug Richardson, *AH-64: Modern Flying Aircraft* (New York: Prentice Hall, 1986), 4–5, 16–21, and 26–41.

51. Gen Bernard W. Rogers, supreme allied commander, Europe, to various US senators and representatives, letter, subject: Fielding of the Apache, 22 July 1982. This letter stated in part, "Since the early 1970s I have been involved personally in the Army effort to field an AAH [advanced attack helicopter], and have seen previous attempts fail. During the same period, the Soviets have made steady and dramatic advances in this field where we wrote the book." Cited in ibid., 13.

52. One of the earliest external critiques was William S. Lind, "FM 100-5, *Operations:* Some Doctrinal Questions for the United States Army," *Military Review* 57 (March 1977): 54–65.

53. For a hard-hitting critique of Active Defense, see Gregory Fontenot and Matthew D. Roberts, "Plugging Holes and Mending Fences," *Infantry* 68 (May–June 1978): 32–36. Robert S. Doughty and L. D. Holder, "Images of the Future Battlefield," *Military Review* 58 (January 1978): 56–69, contains a more scholarly and muted criticism that saw the "new tactics" as an intermediate step in a longer process. See also John M. Oseth, "FM 100-5 (Operations) Revisited: A Need for Better Foundation Concepts?" *Military Review* 60 (March 1980): 13–19. For additional details, see John L. Romjue, *From Active Defense to AirLand Battle: The Development of Army Doctrine, 1973–1982* (Fort Monroe, Va.: US Army Training and Doctrine Command, 1984), 13–21. For a perceptive assessment of the criticism of Active Defense doctrine, see Richard M. Swain, "Filling the Void: The Operational Art and the U.S. Army" (paper presented at the Kingston Royal Military College Military History Symposium, Kingston, Ontario, 23–24 March 1995), 15–22.

54. Romjue, 30.

55. In an address to the Tactics/InterUniversity Seminar Symposium at Fort Leavenworth on 30 March 1978, Starry defended the rationale behind

Active Defense but admitted that improvements could be made in the doctrine and that emerging dialogue on the subject was useful. Donn A. Starry, "A Tactical Evolution—FM 100-5," *Military Review* 58 (August 1978): 2–11.

56. For the subtleties of the DePuy-Starry relationship during development of Active Defense doctrine, see Herbert, 81–83.

57. Starry recollected this experience, noting, "The fact that we needed to fight the deep battle, not just with firepower, but by going deep with maneuver forces as well, starting with attack helicopters, followed by ground maneuver forces, much on the order that the Israelis did on the Golan Heights in October 1973, highlighted the deep surveillance-deep fires and command and control needs." Gen Donn A. Starry, interviewed by John L. Romjue, Fairfax Station, Va., 19 March 1993, THO. One of the interesting aspects of this revelation concerns the way in which Starry's perception of the lessons of the Middle East War differed from DePuy's. To Starry the war demonstrated the need to maneuver deeply; to DePuy it indicated the need to blunt the breakthrough attack.

58. Romjue, *From Active Defense*, 43.

59. Message, TRADOC commander, subject: Air Land Battle, 29 January 1981, THO. The Army experienced some initial debate about whether the proper rendition of the term was *Air Land Battle*, *Air-Land Battle*, or *AirLand Battle*. This discussion mirrored the as yet unresolved debate within the Air Force concerning the propriety of *air power* versus *airpower*. Starry's consultation with Richardson was significant, for Richardson had drafted the Meyer letter to Starry suggesting that it was time for a new version of FM 100-5. Swain, "Filling the Void," 21.

60. Starry confirmed that the term *AirLand Battle* had its roots in the extensive discussions that had taken place between TAC and TRADOC since 1973. Gen Donn A. Starry, US Army, Retired, Gettysburg, Pa., interviewed by author, 13 May 1995. Starry also told his doctrine writers that getting the Air Force on board was absolutely necessary to make the doctrine work. See de Czege, interview.

61. One of the interpretive issues here is the extent to which AirLand Battle represented a logical extension of Active Defense and the extent to which it represented an overthrow thereof. Starry took the former position (i.e., AirLand Battle = Active Defense + Deep Battle). Starry, interview, 13 May 1995. One of the two principal authors of the 1982 edition of FM 100-5 saw the AirLand Battle and Active Defense doctrines as almost antithetical. De Czege, interview. Swain points out Richardson's key role as the intermediary between Starry and the doctrine writers and his role in keeping these opposing views in balance during the drafting of the 1982 edition of FM 100-5. Swain, "Filling the Void," 24–28.

62. FM 100-5, *Operations*, 1982, 1-5.

63. Ibid., 10-1; 11-1, 9.

64. Ibid., 2-3.

65. Ibid., appendix B and 2-1.

66. FM 100-5, *Operations*, 1986, i. Wass de Czege, who also worked the second draft of this edition, maintained that the first several years of teaching in the School of Advanced Military Studies at Fort Leavenworth, for which he served as the first director, were essential to expanding the treatment of the operational level of war. De Czege, interview.

67. FM 100-5, 1986, 28.

68. History, AF/XO, Director of Plans, 1 July–31 December 1981, 84, AFHRA, file no. K143.01.

69. AFM 1-1, 1984, v.

70. Ibid., 2-2, 4.

71. Ibid., 2-10-17.

72. Ibid., 2-14.

73. Ibid., 2-17. In December 1984, Lt Col Barry Watts, USAF, published a trenchant critique of mainstream Air Force doctrine for its approach to war as an engineering problem and its consistent disregard for the Clausewitzian realities of uncertainty in war. Lt Col Barry D. Watts, *The Foundations of Air Force Doctrine: The Problem of Friction in War* (Maxwell AFB, Ala.: Air University Press, 1984). No one knows the extent to which the Air Staff writers of the 1984 manual were aware of Watts's work in its draft form. Drew's judgment is that although the 1984 edition of AFM 1-1 had "many serious flaws, it is a quantum improvement over the 1979 version." Drew, 12.

74. AHR, TRADOC, 1 October 1977–30 September 1978, 176.

75. TAC Pamphlet 50-24/TRADOC Pamphlet 525-9, *TAC/TRADOC Concept: Joint Suppression of Enemy Air Defenses*, 1981; TAC Pamphlet 50-26/TRADOC Pamphlet 525-16/US Readiness Command (USREDCOM) Pamphlet 525-4, *Joint Operational Concept: Joint Attack of the Second Echelon (J-SAK)*, 1982; TRADOC TT 17-50-3/TACP 50-20/USREDCOM PAM 525-5, *Joint Air Attack Team Operations*, 1983; and TACP 50-28/TRADOC PAM 34-2/US Atlantic Fleet (LANTFLT) TIP-2/ Marine Corps Development and Education Command (MCDEC) OH 6-2C/USREDCOM PAM 525-9, *Joint Application of Firepower (J-FIRE) Reference Guide*, 1984.

76. US Army, memorandum of understanding with US Air Force, subject: Joint USA/USAF Efforts for Enhancement of Joint Employment of the AirLand Battle Doctrine, 21 April 1983, reprinted in Richard G. Davis, *The 31 Initiatives* (Washington, D.C.: Office of Air Force History, 1987), 91–92.

77. US Army, memorandum of understanding with US Air Force, subject: Initiation of a Joint US Army–USAF Force Development Process, 2 November 1983, reprinted in Davis, 93.

78. Davis, 40–47.

79. US Army, memorandum of agreement with US Air Force, subject: US Army–US Air Force Joint Force Development Process, 22 May 1984, reprinted in ibid., 105–6. It is perhaps significant to note that this was a memorandum of *agreement*, as opposed to the previous two memoranda of

understanding, suggesting a greater institutional commitment to the terms thereof.

80. Davis established these categories of initiatives for purposes of historical analysis; the memorandum of agreement merely listed the initiatives themselves. See Davis, 47–64.

81. Ibid., 71–79.

82. Ibid., 75.

83. AFM 1-1, 1984, 2-20.

84. According to Joint Pub 1-02, *apportionment* is "the determination and assignment of the total expected effort by percentage and/or by priority that should be devoted to the various air operations and/or geographic areas for a given period of time." Joint Pub 1-02, *Department of Defense Dictionary of Military and Associated Terms,* 22 March 1994, 31.

85. Joint Pub 1-02 defines *allocation* as "the translation of the apportionment into total numbers of sorties by aircraft type available for each operation/task." Ibid., 23.

86. See Steven L. Canby, "Tactical Air Power in Armored Warfare: The Divergence within NATO," *Air University Review* 30 (May–June 1979): 2–20.

87. This doctrine was codified in the NATO Allied Tactical Publication 27(B), *Offensive Air Support,* May 1980.

88. Stephen T. Rippe, "An Army and Air Force Issue: Principles and Procedures for AirLand Warfare," *Air University Review* 37 (May–June 1986): 63. For a more extended analysis of the OAS/BAI issue from the ground perspective, see idem, "An Army and Air Force Issue: Principles and Procedures for AirLand Warfare: A Perspective of Operational Effectiveness on the Modern Battlefield" (thesis, School of Advanced Military Studies, Fort Leavenworth, Kans., 1985).

89. ALFA, memorandum for record, subject: "20-Star Meeting, Headquarters TRADOC, 11 October 1979," 12 October 1979, THO.

90. TAC deputy chief of staff, plans memorandum, subject: Update of ALFA Activities, 17 October 1979, in History, TAC, 1 January–31 December 1979, AFHRA, file no. K417.01.

91. Romjue, *From Active Defense,* 62.

92. The phrase "doctrinal step backward" comes from ibid.

93. Army deputy chief of staff for operations and plans/Air Force deputy chief of staff for plans and operations, information memorandum, subject: USA and USAF Agreement on Apportionment and Allocation of Offensive Air Support (OAS), 23 May 1981, THO.

94. "USA and USAF Position on Apportionment/Allocation of OAS," attachment 2 to ibid., par. 6d.

95. The AF/XO history of the period reflects these reservations: "Following the Field Review, AF/XOXID forwarded much of the background data on the OAS Agreement to TAC and USAFE in an effort to defend the issue. However, it is obvious that opinions continue to differ and that discussions on this subject will continue in the coming months." History,

AF/XO Director of Plans, 1 July–31 December 1981, 90, AFHRA, file no. K143.01.

96. AHR, TRADOC, 1 January–31 December 1987, August 1988, 93, THO.

97. AHR, TRADOC, 1 January–31 December 1988, June 1989, 36–37, THO.

98. Gen Robert D. Russ, "The Air Force, the Army, and the Battlefield of the 1990s," *Defense 88,* August 1988, 13. Russ's statement proved quite controversial within some circles of the Air Staff because it seemed to preclude the use of tactical air assets for strategic attack.

99. Army deputy chief of staff for operations and plans, memorandum, subject: Combined Arms Center Annual Historical Review, 11 December 1984, attachment, "Deep Attack Program Office," draft charter, CAC historical files.

100. Field Circular 100-15-1, *Corps Deep Operations* (U), 1985, ii, B1-29, CAC historical files. (Secret) Information extracted is unclassified.

101. *Deep Operations Capabilities Handbook: Present and Future* (U) (Fort Leavenworth, Kans.: US Army Combined Arms Center, 1987), iii, 1–21, CAC historical files. (Secret) Information extracted is unclassified.

102. *Corps Deep Operations (ATACMS, Aviation and Intelligence Support): Tactics, Techniques and Procedures Handbook* (Fort Leavenworth, Kans.: US Army Combined Arms Center, 1990), 1–5, CAC historical files.

103. Ibid., 4–8.

104. Ibid., 4–16.

105. The TRADOC history of 1988 mentions an agreement signed that year by the service chiefs that established notification and coordination procedures for Army fires beyond the FSCL. AHR, TRADOC, 1 January–31 December 1988, 35. However, as in the case of the BAI agreement signed by the service operations deputies, the provisions of this agreement were not incorporated into doctrine.

106. John A. Warden III, *The Air Campaign: Planning for Combat* (Washington, D.C.: National Defense University Press, 1988).

107. Col John A. Warden III, USAF, Maxwell AFB, Ala., interviewed by author, 6 June 1995. In this interview, Warden explicitly stated that his purpose was to create a new vision of airpower that would supplant the Creech/Russ view that airpower's primary function was to support the Army.

108. One can find the fully developed concept in Col John A. Warden, "The Enemy as a System," *Airpower Journal* 9, no. 1 (Spring 1995): 40–55.

109. The role that Warden's ideas played in shaping the American military response to Iraq's invasion of Kuwait in August 1990 is beyond the scope of this study. One version of that story is dramatically outlined in Col Richard T. Reynolds, *Heart of the Storm: The Genesis of the Air Campaign against Iraq* (Maxwell AFB, Ala.: Air University Press, January 1995).

110. Starry was emphatic on this point. He stated categorically that "we would not have had AirLand Battle had it not been for him [Bill Creech]. I could not have carried it off by myself." Starry, interview, 13 May 1995.

111. These figures and those that follow are taken from James M. Ford, "Air Force Culture and Conventional Strategic Airpower" (thesis, School of Advanced Airpower Studies, Maxwell AFB, Ala., 1992), 60.

112. The Joint Chiefs of Staff issued Joint Pub 3-0, *Doctrine for Joint Operations*, as a test publication on 10 January 1990. AHR, TRADOC, 1 January–31 December 1990, June 1991, 55, THO. The manual was not published in final form until 1994.

113. Robert C. Marsh, "The Cleveland Orchestra: One Hundred Men and a Perfectionist," *High Fidelity* 11 (February 1961): 38.

114. The literature of the Gulf War is replete with instances of ineffective communication between the Army and the Air Force. See, inter alia, Rick Atkinson, *Crusade: The Untold Story of the Persian Gulf War* (New York: Houghton Mifflin, 1993), 151–52, 218–23, 338–40; Robert H. Scales, *Certain Victory: The United States Army in the Gulf War* (Washington, D.C.: Office of the Chief of Staff, United States Army, 1993), 174–81, 315–16; Richard M. Swain, *"Lucky War": Third Army in Desert Storm* (Fort Leavenworth, Kans.: US Army Command and General Staff College Press, 1994), 181–90; Michael R. Gordon and Bernard E. Trainor, *The Generals' War: The Inside Story of the Conflict in the Gulf* (Boston: Little, Brown, 1995), 203–4, 324–48, 447–54, 494; and Barry D. Watts's perceptive review essay of Gordon and Trainor's work, "Friction in the Gulf War," *Naval War College Review* 48 (Autumn 1995): 105. For a dissenting view, see Edward Mann, who contends that "the air campaign plan would eventually meld perfectly with schemes of surface maneuver to be developed later." Col Edward C. Mann III, *Thunder and Lightning: Desert Storm and the Airpower Debates* (Maxwell AFB, Ala.: Air University Press, April 1995), 175.

Chapter 12

The Evolution of NATO Air Doctrine

Col Maris "Buster" McCrabb

The Atlantic Alliance played a central role in maintaining peace in Europe—at least the absence of major war—since its founding in 1949. It did not accomplish this by remaining stagnant in its military strategies or doctrines; instead, it underwent significant changes. This chapter assesses how its air strategies and employment doctrines reflected those changes.

The evolution of North Atlantic Treaty Organization (NATO) air doctrine highlights the intertwined nature of political imperatives and military strategy.[1] This essay assumes that one cannot understand air doctrine outside the larger military strategy it supports and that, especially in the case of NATO, one must place the wider strategy within its political context.[2] In NATO, Carl von Clausewitz's dictum that war is an extension of politics is a day-to-day reality.[3]

This chapter seeks to identify the sources and characteristics of NATO air doctrine and trace its evolution from the beginnings of the alliance to the post-cold-war era. As NATO expands and becomes engaged in out-of-area missions—such as those conducted in the former Yugoslavia—in the 1990s, its air doctrines must change to conform to new realities.[4] An understanding of the origins and evolution of the current air doctrine illuminates the "opportunity set" for this inevitable evolution. Further, the chapter highlights points of divergence and convergence between NATO and US air doctrines.

Briefly stated, NATO air doctrine reflects the alliance's three political realities. First, the need to maintain alliance cohesion requires that the alliance look and act defensively, drive for consensus, and consider the United States as only the first among equals. Second, the alliance must take full cognizance of unique national requirements—for example, British and French autonomy, especially in nuclear weaponry, and the issue of West Germany's reintegration into Europe in the

1950s and the reunification with East Germany in the 1990s. Third, the alliance must recognize fiscal restraints that arise from US global commitments and the competition for resources arising from European social welfare commitments.[5] In other words, as Richard L. Kugler so aptly remarked, one must remember that "strategy comes with a dollar sign."[6]

NATO's air doctrine also reflects the alliance's military realities. For most of its history, the alliance confronted a numerically superior foe and geopolitical realities that prevented a military strategy which traded space for time; the alliance also relied on both the US strategic nuclear umbrella and conventional reinforcements from North America. Further, NATO air doctrine is very much negotiated doctrine, especially cross-nationally—mainly between the United States and the United Kingdom—and intranationally, among the US services. The efforts of NATO's Tactical Air Working Party (TAWP) to write NATO's air doctrines best exemplify this situation.[7] Negotiated doctrine is neither necessarily bad nor bland; however, it is time-consuming because one must obtain consensus from a group of sovereign countries that belong to a voluntary association.

NATO's influence on US Air Force doctrine has been cyclical: closely associated in the 1950s and largely built around massive retaliation, the two doctrines began diverging in the 1980s, as USAF doctrine began emphasizing offensive operations. They may, however, be reconverging in the 1990s, due to the influence of the Persian Gulf War. Further, the Goldwater-Nichols Department of Defense Reorganization Act of 1986 mandated the development of joint US military doctrine, thereby enhancing and constraining the US negotiation position. That is, the US position is now consolidated, but USAF doctrine must more closely conform to the larger set of US doctrine. Moreover, the US positions at TAWP, for example, reflect the consensus views of all the US services—not just the USAF.

This chapter outlines and explains the political and military context of NATO's air doctrine because, as mentioned above, one cannot explain air strategy without understanding the military strategy it supports, and one cannot understand the military strategy without understanding its political context.

The essay's major divisions mark changes in NATO military strategy, focusing on the 1970s and 1980s—the "Golden Age" of the development of NATO air doctrine. This assessment does not imply a retrenchment in doctrinal development within the alliance since that time. Rather, it suggests that those two decades represent the process of doctrinal creation and refinement. Indeed, the 1990s may yet become the true Golden Age.

NATO's Central Region receives most of the emphasis here because therein lay the threat from massed Warsaw Pact and Soviet forces. However, significant differences in doctrinal development existed between the Central Region and the other two major areas—the Southern Region and the Northern Region. Also highlighted is the Supreme Allied Commander, Europe (SACEUR) area of operations (which includes the three major NATO regions); however, discussion of Supreme Allied Commander, Atlantic (SACLANT)[8] is limited to air doctrine for tactical air support of maritime operations. Additionally, this chapter addresses the way in which NATO produces its doctrine.[9]

Origins to 1967

Although this chapter does not intend to cover the political origins of NATO,[10] four key events greatly affected the military strategy adopted by the alliance in the early 1950s. First, NATO came into existence after the World War II alliance among the great powers of the West (the United States and the United Kingdom) and the Soviet Union had irrevocably dissolved. Failure to achieve a peace treaty, the Soviet blockade of Berlin, and the continued presence of massive Soviet forces outside the USSR's borders all pointed to an increased, not decreased, security threat.[11] The coup in February 1948 that overthrew the democratically elected government in Czechoslovakia prompted the eventual formation of NATO in 1949.[12] Second, after the Federal Republic of Germany formed in 1949, certain states sought to secure West Germany's fortunes to those of its erstwhile enemies in the West. France in particular wished to tie West Germany politically, economically, and militarily to the

Western states.[13] Third, although countries recognized the need for a security arrangement in Europe, an attack from Soviet forces did not appear imminent. This perception changed with the outbreak of war in Korea. Fourth, and most importantly, the United States overturned 150 years of its history of avoiding formal overseas commitments with the announcement of the Truman Doctrine and the Marshall Plan, both designed to tie the United States to the security and prosperity of western Europe.

The first political hurdle the alliance overcame was the issue of West Germany.[14] Treaties providing for the rearmament of that country and its incorporation into NATO specified that the new West German military become part of an international command (NATO) and retain only limited capabilities for independent national command. Consequently, no German command structure exists for air operations above the wing level, and all German air defense aircraft remain under NATO command, even in peacetime—thus there is no uniquely "German" air doctrine.[15]

The second major political event occurred in 1966, when France withdrew from the NATO military command structure. Explanations of this event generally emphasize the personality of French president Charles de Gaulle and his alleged anti-Americanism, but the roots of the split lie much deeper.[16] For NATO, beyond having to move its headquarters from Paris to Brussels, the French withdrawal posed problems related to its military strategy: in times of crisis, what role would French forces play, and to what extent would they be reintegrated into the NATO command structure? And how would France employ the nuclear forces it was developing? According to French defense planners, the answer to that question depended upon the military situation in Europe in relation to France.[17]

One of the fundamental issues NATO planners dealt with in the formative years of the alliance was the kind of attack they could expect from the Warsaw Pact.[18] Options included a full-scale conventional attack following a buildup of forces; a more limited attack against key NATO installations (particularly nuclear ones), utilizing a high degree of surprise; or a full-scale conventional attack with minimum warning time. Compounding this problem was the need for US

446

reinforcements to arrive in time to shore up NATO forces—believed insufficient to thwart the Warsaw Pact's advances. NATO military planning assumed the worst case—an all-out attack with limited warning. Furthermore, in a comparison of NATO weaknesses to the opposition's perceived strengths, planners tended to assume that any such war would be of short duration. The key question was how soon US reinforcements could close on the continent.

The first formal statement of strategy, Military Committee (MC) Report 14/1, adopted at the Lisbon summit in 1952,[19] dealt with the counteroffensive. That is, if Soviet forces invaded, a light force of 20–30 NATO divisions would screen the attack until US strategic air forces could arrive to deliver an atomic interdiction blow against the invaders. NATO would then launch a ground offensive to recover lost territory and even free eastern Europe. MC 14/2 (1957) dropped the latter requirement, assuming that a nuclear attack would leave nothing worth liberating.[20]

The strategy of 1957 also paved the way for stationing in Europe what later became known as theater nuclear forces.[21] Although planners still accepted NATO's inferiority in conventional power, they recognized that the bulk of Soviet forces were in fact stationed in the USSR and would take some time to move forward. This fact, plus the economic imperatives of providing for defense at minimum cost,[22] led to an acceptance of a "sword and shield" strategy whereby permanently stationed troops would guard against a surprise or rogue attack (the shield) while in-theater nuclear forces would threaten follow-on Soviet forces (the sword).[23]

One can hardly overestimate the impact of nuclear weapons on NATO's military strategy.[24] On the one hand, they made up for NATO's numerical inferiority in conventional forces. On the other, they permitted NATO to accept that gap in the capability of its conventional forces in relation to the Warsaw Pact. Furthermore, they presented a deterrent posture that appealed to the European public. Finally, they promised defense at lower cost, which appealed to every NATO member.[25]

This military strategy channeled NATO's air strategy to achieve three tasks in the early days of war: (1) secure the initial deployment within the alliance from air attack, (2) protect ports for the follow-up deployment of US and Canadian forces, and (3) preserve subsequent NATO ground forces' freedom of maneuver. At the same time, however, NATO recognized a need to attack Warsaw Pact second-echelon forces and even airfields. How NATO expected to balance these requirements requires further investigation.

First, NATO planners did not see air forces as mere "flying artillery" that supported the ground force's close battle—the traditional use of close air support (CAS). They did recognize, though, that the alliance would need airpower if Warsaw Pact forces achieved a breakthrough or if the initial NATO deployment was incomplete. The primary air-to-ground mission of NATO air forces entailed interdicting rear areas and follow-on forces—the traditional mission of air interdiction (AI). Furthermore, the primary targets for these missions were Warsaw Pact forces themselves, especially armored forces, rather than their means of transportation (e.g., trucks or trains) to the front. Bridges were the only nonmobile targets generally mentioned in this context.

Second, these missions were to be flown largely within the confines of East Germany, mainly to an operational depth of about two hundred kilometers from the political borders—a stipulation reflected in NATO force structure. Most of the alliance's aircraft were of relatively short range, typifying their defensive nature. These missions sought to disrupt the intentions of Warsaw Pact commanders by forcing them to disperse as they moved towards the battle and to force a deployment of air defense assets to protect second-echelon forces and hence minimize NATO air losses at the front.

Forward defense, as both a strategic and an operational plan, stated that NATO should defend its Central Region (West Germany) as far forward as possible, with defense beginning immediately behind the border, and that its forces should not surrender territory without a fight. Again, planners always kept nuclear weapons in mind because political realities dictated that NATO could give little ground before having to employ these weapons against invaders.

In this early period, USAF and NATO doctrine starts to diverge over the use of air forces to secure command of the air. Although USAF doctrine emphasized air superiority as a prerequisite for further air operations, NATO softened this to emphasize air defense that provided only a favorable air situation, because NATO believed it had insufficient aircraft to dedicate to the air superiority role. Further, NATO emphasized the "defense" aspect of air defense and did not foresee a large, offensive counterair (OCA) mission for fighter sweeps, escort, or a major commitment to attacking Warsaw Pact airfields. This thinking was in line with NATO's strategy of integrated air defenses, whereby ground-based air defense systems enhanced fighter aircraft.

Another area of apparent divergence involved the efficacy of aerial attack against vital targets—economic as well as military—deep within enemy territory. Within a decade after the close of World War II, whose lessons taught many airmen that the strategic bombing of Germany was at least *a*—if not *the*—decisive element in Germany's defeat, NATO abandoned plans to attack the sorts of targets hit by British and US bomber fleets during the war. NATO's reasoning was that it did not wish to present even the *appearance* of being a threat to the USSR, fearing that long-range conventional bombers would suggest as much. Further, the advent of nuclear weapons had changed air doctrines since World War II, altering the air bombardment equation in two ways: (1) the immense destructive power of atomic weapons rendered them ill suited for a precision bombing role and (2) most people thought that a nuclear war would be over quickly. In such a scenario, attacks against economic or industrial targets, because they seemed to offer mostly long-term benefits, became militarily insignificant. In reality, however, NATO never really abandoned strategic bombardment but deferred to the largely US-based bomber force to accomplish this mission.[26] Thus, the one area of convergence between US and NATO air doctrine—the one deemed most critical by both—remained nuclear doctrine.

Although NATO political and military strategies served well during an era of unmatched US political and military dominance, external and internal changes to the alliance in the mid-1960s caused the questioning and revising of both strategies. This stimulated a quest for modernization of conventional forces and a determination to confine any war to the nonnuclear level.

Modernization, 1967–89

Starting in the late 1970s and continuing into the mid-1980s, NATO substantially upgraded its conventional and nuclear forces.[27] The USAF removed most of its older weapon systems and introduced newer aircraft such as the A-10, F-111F, F-15, and F-16. European countries introduced new platforms such as the Tornado and F-16 into their inventories, although at a slower pace than did the United States. NATO also acquired precision-guided munitions such as laser-guided bombs, electro-optical guided bombs, precision television-guided and infrared-guided antitank missiles, and runway attack munitions. NATO's decision in 1979 to deploy nuclear-armed ground launched cruise missiles (GLCM) and Pershing II missiles—to enhance deterrence by countering Soviet SS-20s—proved both a major milestone in alliance military history and a highly political act. Upgrades to the command and control (C^2) arena included a NATO airborne early warning (NAEW) aircraft, based upon the US E-3 airborne warning and control system (AWACS) aircraft, and the allied C^2 system.

The late 1960s witnessed numerous changes that would ultimately lead to a major reexamination of NATO's military strategy. Following years of modernization prompted by the Soviet humiliation during the Cuban missile crisis of 1962, the Soviets appeared to gain parity with US forces in the strategic nuclear arena. Further, appraisals of Warsaw Pact capabilities led some people to conclude that NATO's conventional forces were in a much better position than they were in the 1950s.[28] And in the political arena, a spirit of détente[29] and movement towards arms reduction agreements[30] between the superpowers led to a further lessening of tensions.

In 1967 NATO adopted MC 14/3, the strategy of flexible response, marking a significant change in both the political outlook and the military strategy of the alliance.[31] Although it retained the option of a strategic nuclear response from the United States[32] to counter any Warsaw Pact breakthrough in

Europe, the strategy placed new emphasis on conventional forces' ability to deter—even defeat—an all-out attack from the East.[33] This emphasis, however, did not imply either an offensive strategy or a belief that the opposition had altered its objectives. Conventional wisdom still maintained that the Warsaw Pact was organized, trained, and equipped to conduct a short-notice attack against Allied Forces Central Europe (AFCENT) in order to achieve the Rhine crossings and capture ports on the North Sea within a few days.[34] Perhaps the most significant change in MC 14/3 was that nuclear employment became part of a "deliberate escalation" rather than an inevitable response to an invasion.[35]

USAF and NATO air defense doctrine continued to diverge during this time period, as NATO continued to emphasize defensive counterair (DCA). For example, it increased its use of hardened aircraft shelters and modernized ground-based air defenses (such as Patriot missiles) as a counter to the newer Warsaw Pact air forces. Notably, no other NATO air force sought the longer-range, more capable air-to-air fighters such as the F-15 or F-14, which the United States brought on-line in the 1970s. Furthermore, no countries other than Great Britain planned to use the multinational Tornado, developed in an air defense variant, primarily for interdiction. Nevertheless, this period remains the high point of convergence between USAF and NATO air strategy, for planners framed USAF doctrine and force structure in almost an exclusively European context. Furthermore, this period saw the convergence of opinion between the US Army and the USAF over the role of airpower on the NATO battlefield.[36]

In July 1970 Gen Andrew Goodpaster, SACEUR, requested that the Military Agency for Standardization (MAS)[37] form a working party "to develop a tactical air doctrine that would provide a common understanding of the role of air power in allied operations, and a set of common procedures for successfully implementing air operations."[38] The primary driving force at work here was the strategy of flexible response. As NATO began exploring a more robust conventional deterrent and war-fighting strategy, the requirement for NATO's ground, air, and naval forces to work together effectively in a joint and combined environment became more insistent, rendering essentially national doctrines untenable.[39] The Air Board of the MAS took two actions over the next several years. First, it established working parties (e.g., the TAWP) to draft the doctrine and procedures, which initially involved identifying agencies within each member nation to represent national positions during the negotiations. For the United States, this responsibility fell to the Doctrine Division of the USAF's Air Staff.[40] Second, the MAS Air Board requested SACLANT's input following the latter's objections that drafts coming out of the working party failed to include practices of the naval air arm.

The document that would become Allied Tactical Pamphlet 33 (ATP-33), *Tactical Air Doctrine,* took form through a series of working party meetings and drafts from November 1970 until its release on 11 March 1976. One should note three points about the development of this seminal document of NATO air doctrine. First, the initial US working party included only USAF members, which prompted the US Navy to get the development process out of USAF hands and into those of the Joint Chiefs of Staff. Although the effort proved unsuccessful, the US Navy, Army, and Marine Corps soon joined the development and coordination process. Second, the development of ATP-33 brought to the fore the differences of opinion on C^2 of air assets, both among NATO member nations and within the US military. As David Stein points out, the USAF and Supreme Headquarters Allied Powers Europe (SHAPE) wanted centralization of control *functions* at the highest practicable level of command, while the US Navy, US Marine Corps, and the United Kingdom's Royal Air Force (RAF) wanted decentralized control of air operations at the lowest possible *level* of command.[41] This disagreement permeates discussions over NATO air doctrine to this very day. Finally, the process of developing, coordinating, and finally ratifying this keystone document[42] reveals the slowness of doctrine development—almost six years from SACEUR's original tasking to an approved document.

The last point becomes especially important in understanding the role played by the United States in developing NATO's initial air doctrines. US officers working this process tended to have much shorter tours of duty than other NATO members (especially the RAF). Thus, some negotiations once thought final would reoccur as new US action officers came on-line with less than complete knowledge of the preceding negotiations. Further, these negotiations occurred during the infancy of US joint doctrine. The lack of a "US" position versus "USAF" or "US Navy" positions complicated and slowed negotiations within the working parties.[43]

Basic Tactical Air Doctrine

The purpose of ATP-33 is to ensure the effective employment of NATO air resources in tactical air operations to attain and maintain air superiority, interdict enemy combat forces and their supporting installations, and assist—through combined/joint operations—ground or naval forces in achieving their objectives.[44] This doctrine, like basic USAF doctrine, recognizes the priority of air superiority—a perspective based on NATO's recognition that air superiority provides freedom of movement to friendly forces and, by denying it to enemy forces, facilitates other NATO air missions. Furthermore, contrary to the beliefs of most airpower advocates, it foresees airpower as essentially playing a supporting role to naval and ground forces. As shown later, efforts that allow a more independent role for airpower constitute one of the great doctrinal changes that NATO is contemplating in the 1990s.

Basic NATO air operations include counterair, interdiction, reconnaissance and surveillance, offensive air support (OAS), tactical transport, support of maritime operations, and other supporting operations such as electronic warfare, suppression of enemy air defenses (SEAD), air-to-air refueling, search and rescue, and special operations. Each of these operations warrants a specific chapter in ATP-33, and most have a more detailed ATP of their own. (The doctrinal pamphlets on air superiority [ATP-42] and OAS [ATP-27] receive more detailed treatment below.) First, however, one should examine the doctrinal guidance on C^2 of overall air operations provided in ATP-33.

NATO defines *command* as the authority to direct, coordinate, or control one's own forces; *control* is the authority to do those same tasks over forces not under the individual's command. Furthermore, C^2 is divided between operational and tactical, the latter applying only to the accomplishment of *specific and generally local* missions or tasks.[45] The pamphlet calls for the planning and direction of tactical air operations at an air command operations center (ACOC), with control delegated to subordinate allied tactical operations centers (ATOC). The pamphlet stresses the principles of centralized control (to promote an integrated effort in execution of plans) and decentralized execution (to provide flexibility in the detailed planning and execution of those plans).[46] However, as Stein observed above, the disagreement over the dividing line between these two defines the essential differences between the United States and the United Kingdom and between services in the US military.

Centralized control of air resources provides allotment, apportionment, allocation, and tasking of resources. Allotment, exercised by the commander having operational command, assigns forces among subordinate commands. Apportionment determines and assigns the total expected air effort by percentage and/or priority, while allocation translates that determination into total numbers of sorties by aircraft type for each operation or task. Tasking, then, takes the allocation and turns it into an order to an individual unit.[47]

Counterair Doctrine

One finds NATO's doctrine for counterair in ATP-42.[48] Closely tied to it is ATP-40, *Doctrine and Procedures for Airspace Control in the Combat Zone.*[49] NATO has always recognized a need for air superiority. The two major areas of disagreement lie in the role of attacks against the enemy's integrated air defense system (IADS)—commonly referred to as SEAD—and C^2 of counterair resources.

The pamphlet defines counterair operations as "those operations conducted to attain and maintain a desired degree of air superiority" to produce a "favourable air situation essential for the successful conduct of combat operations."[50] Although doctrine separates these into "offensive" and "defensive" operations, it recognizes that, particularly since they often use the same resources, one cannot view them in isolation from each other. ATP-42 considers SEAD part of the offensive operations and defines it as activity which "neutralizes, destroys or temporarily degrades enemy air defense systems in a specific area by physical attack and/or electronic warfare."[51]

SEAD became an important area of dispute between the USAF and NATO. USAF doctrine considers SEAD coequal with OCA and DCA, while NATO, as shown above, views SEAD only as part of OCA. Specifically, at the most basic level, USAF doctrine assumes a global perspective whereas, obviously, NATO doctrine covers a more narrowly focused region. In the 1970s, the USAF had an opportunity to test its doctrines in the skies over Vietnam. One important lesson it learned there was that SEAD deserved to be elevated to a position coequal with OCA and DCA. Further, few NATO air forces other than US forces have resources (such as the US F-4G Wild Weasel aircraft) for the SEAD mission.[52] These countries feared that a separate SEAD mission would require them to buy SEAD-dedicated aircraft. Also, within NATO itself, a difference exists between separate allied tactical air forces (ATAF). As Stein, Kimberly Nolan, and Robert Perry write, 2ATAF (dominated by the RAF) and 4ATAF (largely a USAF operation) "tend to operate as 'national' tactical air forces rather than as a 'combined' force."[53] For example, although 2ATAF does not have specific doctrine for SEAD, 4ATAF does.

The C^2 of counterair operations flows from the major NATO commanders (e.g., SHAPE) through major subordinate commanders (MSC—e.g., AFCENT) to principal subordinate commanders (PSC—e.g., of Air Forces Central Europe [COMAIRCENT]), who generally exercise operational control[54] for counterair operations (and other air missions) though, in practice, tactical control is further delegated to ATOCs and their subordinate sector operations centers (SOC). Furthermore, the operational commander designates an airspace control authority (ACA), who has responsibility for planning, coordinating, and operating an airspace control plan. Key elements of this plan include airspace control measures and means such as control zones, restricted operations areas, and transit routes. Finally, these measures consist of positive and procedural controls plus established rules of engagement.[55]

Some distinctions exist among NATO's Central, Northern, and Southern Regions as they relate to counterair operations and airspace control concepts. In the Northern Region, Norway and Denmark view their defense needs as largely self-defense measures focused on maintaining territorial integrity. However, they have not insisted on any reservations to either ATP-40 or ATP-42.[56] In the Southern Region, ongoing disputes over national domain of the Aegean Sea complicate airspace control systems in the eastern Mediterranean.[57]

Air-to-Surface Doctrine

Although NATO countries generally agreed on the proper air-to-air role of airpower, the air-to-surface role proved considerably more contentious.[58] The primary doctrinal pamphlet that covers these missions is ATP-27, *Offensive Air Support Operations.*[59] The four areas of disagreement included battlefield air interdiction (BAI), follow-on forces attack (FOFA), AirLand Battle, and C^2 of these air resources, including request procedures, approval authority, planning locations, and control functions.

OAS operations involve those that support land forces. The first rendition of this doctrine, ATP-27(A), included three functions under the OAS umbrella: CAS, AI, and tactical air reconnaissance (TAR).[60] During discussions about revisions to ATP-27(A) at the 1977 TAWP,[61] the USAF objected to the inclusion of AI as an OAS mission because it is not a support mission; its objectives derive from the overall goals of the *combined* force—not those specifically derived from the *land* force commander. Furthermore, since these missions occur outside the direct scope of land operations, they do not require the detailed integration with the fire-and-maneuver scheme of ground forces—a requirement inherent in CAS.[62] TAWP accepted this, and ATP-27(B) removed AI from OAS but replaced it with BAI: "air action against hostile surface targets which are in a position to *directly* affect friendly forces and which requires joint planning and coordination" (emphasis added).[63]

Some understanding of the evolution from AI to BAI rests on the different approaches the RAF and the USAF took to the management of airpower and air-to-ground coordination.[64] The Americans viewed airpower as a theaterwide asset with inherent flexibility. As such, this required a C^2 structure over the entire Central Region—the role of Allied Air Forces Central Europe (AAFCE). Although the British recognized the flexibility of airpower, they preferred a national chain of command (such as existed between the British-dominated 2ATAF and Northern Army Group [NORTHAG]) that would provide a more direct and immediate means of coordination. The RAF feared that losing "control" over AI would limit the ability of its airpower to relieve pressure on NORTHAG forces.[65] Therefore, it proposed BAI as a way to provide additional air support (beyond CAS) to NORTHAG. (BAI is essentially a mission between the closely coordinated and integrated CAS and AI, which, under ATP-27[B], required no coordination of integration between ground and air forces.) In order to solve the disagreement between the RAF and USAF, the TAWP set up a "drafting committee" to iron out a compromise. Notably, the committee included representatives of both the air and ground services of only three countries: the United States, the United Kingdom, and West Germany.

The USAF voiced three objections to BAI. First, it imposed air-ground coordination where none had previously existed under the prevailing AI concept. Second, it required coordination at a level—proposed to be the army corps—that seemed inconsistent with a theaterwide view of airpower management. Third, the USAF viewed BAI as an intrusion on airpower prerogatives in determining the best employment of scarce airpower resources. The final document, ATP-27(B), reflected a compromise between the USAF and RAF positions. BAI, unlike CAS, would not be conducted under ground-force direction, thus maintaining the principle of centralized control. Furthermore, one could execute BAI to fulfill ground *or* air commanders' requests and thus could fly BAI on *either* side of the fire support coordination line (FSCL)—the traditional dividing line between CAS and AI. Finally, BAI was maintained at the ATAF/army group level and not allocated down to corps/air support operations centers (ASOC), as with CAS.

AirLand Battle and Follow-on Forces Attack

Several key initiatives converged in the late 1970s that would result in a strategic and operational split within NATO. The US Army, reacting to lessons learned in the Vietnam War and the 1973 Yom Kippur War as well as an analysis of emerging Warsaw Pact capabilities and doctrinal changes,[66] started to focus its doctrinal development on attacking enemy forces well before they entered the close-combat arena. Furthermore, it examined the utility of counteroffensive operations to defeat a numerically superior foe. All this resulted in AirLand Battle doctrine—not necessarily well received by NATO. Specifically, many NATO members mistook the doctrine—an *operational* concept—for a *strategic* initiative, believing that, as a defensive alliance, NATO should not advocate offensive operations into Warsaw Pact territory. Further, the doctrine relied on emerging—primarily US—technologies that many NATO countries believed they could ill afford, especially at a time when NATO was attempting to upgrade its main defensive forces.[67] Also, many NATO air force members saw AirLand Battle as an attempt to gain control over air resources. The doctrine stressed shaping enemy forces through deep attack, thereby implying ground-commander control over deep-attack assets that were primarily air assets.[68] Further, AirLand Battle focused on the corps as the operational maneuver force, an emphasis that went against an air perspective—particularly that of the USAF—that stressed theaterwide air employment.

Since 1979, however, NATO had entertained an initiative involving the attack of Warsaw Pact second-echelon forces before they entered the main defensive belt. This initiative, formally announced by Gen Bernard Rogers, SACEUR, in 1983 and incorporated into ATP-35(A), *Land Force Doctrine*, in 1985,[69] was known as FOFA. Like others, it met a contentious reception within NATO. In one sense, FOFA was merely an extension of the long-standing NATO doctrine of AI.[70] However, two of its implications disturbed many NATO members. First, FOFA implied early border-crossing authority (something it held in common with OCA operations)—a highly sensitive issue within NATO, especially for the West Germans.

Second, some nations voiced concern that FOFA would draw
air resources away from operations such as counterair or
CAS/BAI—essential missions in the early days of a massive
Warsaw Pact attack.[71] Finally, many NATO members
remained skeptical over whether these "smart" technologies
would work or, even if they did, thought that the Soviets
would quickly (and inexpensively) find countermeasures to
them.

NATO OAS doctrine deals extensively with BAI and CAS
procedures for requests, approval, planning (especially
targeting), controlling, and execution. ATP-27 provides the
clearest example of the different levels of detail found in
NATO, as opposed to US, doctrine. From one perspective,
NATO doctrine is written for "generals to captains" or from the
"operational to the tactical level." For example, ATP-27
includes organizational diagrams and flowcharts outlining
how OAS requests (both preplanned and immediate)[72] are
processed, planned, and decided—an essentially operational-
level process. It also provides detailed tactical procedures and
techniques, including holding patterns for forward air
controllers, tactics for attack aircraft, and standardized
terminology.

Aside from its level of detail, ATP-27 specifies that one can
initiate OAS requests from "any *land force* level of command"
(emphasis added),[73] which emphasizes the *support* part of
OAS. However, it also calls for the planning of OAS as a *joint*
air and ground responsibility accomplished at the
ACOC—envisioned as part of the joint command operations
center found at the ATAF/army group level. Further, the
pamphlet provides for the tasking of OAS missions from the
ATOC (which has tactical control over the flying units) via an
air tasking order/message (ATO/ATM). One may further
delegate this tasking authority to an ASOC normally colocated
with a field army/corps—important because ATOC/ASOC
normally has diversion authority, which allows the
accomplishment of higher priority missions by diverting lower
priority missions. In most cases, this would entail diverting
BAI to CAS, although the opposite is possible—but improbable.
The pamphlet does not address whether a BAI mission,
requested by the air commander, is subject to diversion to a

459

CAS mission requested by the ground commander. Since ATP-27 implies that CAS and BAI provide support to the land force commander, the diversion request would apparently take priority.

In sum, one can call the period following the adoption of flexible response the Golden Age of NATO air doctrine. Before the Goodpaster initiative in 1970, the doctrine that existed was largely national. The doctrine that emerged was a negotiated doctrine. No one member dominated the ideas concerning airpower employment that NATO eventually adopted. The arguments and final outcomes of the BAI and SEAD issues clearly point this out. Despite national preferences, airmen from every member country held similar beliefs on the proper role of airpower. The near unanimity over counterair operations (besides SEAD) and CAS attests to this fact.

During this period, NATO took the first steps towards rationalizing its air structure, primarily through the creation in 1974 of AAFCE, located at Ramstein Air Base, West Germany, to command 2ATAF and 4ATAF. Although this did not provide a true centralized control apparatus (for example, BAI was still allocated, tasked, and executed at the ATAF level), it began the process of integrating air assets into a theaterwide view versus a more narrowly defined (by land-force boundaries) view of airpower. This move was essential if airpower intended to play a more decisive role in blunting massive Warsaw Pact attacks through interdiction against second-echelon (and deeper) forces. Furthermore, planning of air defense and offensive air operations became combined in the ATOC, which eliminated the false distinction between these air operations. It also recognized the importance of both missions to the counterair struggle and acknowledged that one would likely use the same assets in both roles. Again, this action highlighted a theaterwide view of airpower employment.

NATO in the Post-Cold-War Era

Undoubtedly, the dissolution of the Warsaw Pact and the Soviet Union represented the most monumental change that took place in NATO's history. Although the collapse of

Communism in Europe was significant, to say the least, other events rank high in NATO's recent past. For example, despite NATO's peripheral involvement in the Persian Gulf War of 1991, many European NATO countries (and air forces) played a significant role in that conflict. Further, throughout its history, NATO avoided out-of-area operations; however, by the mid-1990s, it found itself actively involved in combat operations in the former Yugoslavia.[74] Lessons learned from the Gulf War and the Balkans affected the development of NATO air doctrine in fundamental ways; further, NATO and US air doctrines are once again merging in significant ways, mirroring the earliest days of the alliance.

Four major geopolitical changes occurred in the late 1980s and early 1990s: the dissolution of the Warsaw Pact and the breakup of the Soviet Union; the breakup of Yugoslavia and the subsequent civil war; the Persian Gulf War; and the denuclearization of NATO. The first event seemingly eliminated NATO's raison d'être, while the second and third reinforced the fact that Europe—as well as areas critical to Europe—remains less than peaceful; further, turmoil in these areas, even if it does not directly (or immediately) appear to threaten NATO, still poses problems for the alliance. The final event eliminated a core part of NATO's long-standing military strategy. Even during the heyday of conventional war fighting, nuclear weapons provided a reassuring backstop to NATO war plans.

The demise of the Warsaw Pact generated both external and internal military changes in Europe. Most importantly, Soviet forces, which constituted the backbone of Warsaw Pact capability, withdrew from eastern and central Europe, thus no longer occupying territory adjacent to NATO. To military planners, this move seemed to offer substantially increased warning time, even if Russian forces attempted to invade western Europe. Likewise, the fact that former Warsaw Pact members were politically distancing themselves from Moscow offered the potential scenario that a resurgent Russia might have to fight its way west, even to reach NATO lands. Further, political instability in Russia and the rapid downsizing of the military forces of former Warsaw Pact countries led the latter to seek closer ties to NATO for purposes of security.

Internal changes in NATO often mirrored those in the now-defunct Warsaw Pact. Foremost was the withdrawal of substantial US forces from Europe. By the mid-1990s, the United States maintained one army corps and fewer than 10 fighter squadrons in Europe—down from two corps and almost 25 fighter squadrons. Furthermore, most of these combat units disbanded, thus reducing the number of available units in the event of increased tensions in Europe. This downsizing also is taking place in the European states. For example, the German *Bundeswehr* (federal armed forces) will be cut from 515,000 to 370,000 personnel. Also, operational readiness postures will be reduced and many aircraft, tanks, and warships will be retired.[75] Additionally, for both the United States and other NATO countries, domestic fiscal pressures drastically reduced modernization initiatives. Finally, within western Europe, the Western European Union (WEU) and Eurocorps both present Europe-only alternatives to NATO, while the Partnership for Peace (PFP) program may result in a further extension of NATO's area of operations right to the eastern limit of the European continent.[76]

Otto von Bismarck, the great nineteenth-century German geopolitician, allegedly said that "some damn thing in the Balkans" would mark the end of stability in Europe. Some people argue that his prediction came too bloody true in the fields of France from 1914 to 1918. Some also believe that it might again prove true in the 1990s, as civil strife runs rampant in the former republics of Yugoslavia. In this cauldron in 1994, NATO found itself conducting its first combat operations. The ironies are rampant. For 40 years, NATO girded for an onslaught of conventional forces from the east; what it got was insurgency and terrorism in a civil war fueled by ethnic and religious forces. For 40 years, NATO prepared on the central front, only to find its first operation in its largely ignored Southern Region. For 40 years, European NATO forces that planned to fight from their fixed areas and air bases now found themselves deploying to fight. Finally, after 40 years of preparing to fight as NATO, it found itself as only the military appendage of the United Nations, taking orders from and requiring permission from a completely separate political organization.

Although space precludes a full rendering of the role that NATO, both as individual member countries and as an alliance, played in the Gulf War, one should note three important events. First, and most importantly, NATO *did* respond as an alliance—for the first time in its history—to an area (southeastern Turkey) few people would have imagined and against a threat (Iraq) even fewer would have foreseen.[77] The statement by the North Atlantic Council was unequivocal on this point: "We note that the crisis in the Gulf poses a potential threat to one of our Allies having common borders with Iraq, and we affirm our determination to fulfill the commitments stipulated in Article 5 of the Washington Treaty."[78] This posture reaffirmed the commitment made by NATO secretary-general Manfred Wörner on 10 August 1990. Second, NATO responded with more than statements, sending the NAEW aircraft[79] to Turkey within a week of Iraq's invasion of Kuwait; activating the Naval On-Call Force Mediterranean on 14 September 1990; and deploying the Allied Command Europe, Mobile Force (AMF)-Air[80] to bases in eastern Turkey in early January 1991. Most notably, these actions demonstrated the alliance's political will (something many commentators had questioned) and its basic defensive posture. The third key aspect of the Gulf crisis is that 14 of the 16 NATO members sent forces to support the anti-Iraq coalition.[81] (Iceland has no military forces but did contribute funds; Luxembourg has only minimal forces.)

In late 1991, NATO substantially changed the role of nuclear weapons in its military strategy, reducing by 80 percent the substrategic stockpile—everything from GLCMs and surface-to-surface missiles to atomic artillery shells and free-fall nuclear weapons carried by tactical fighter aircraft. Most importantly, it changed the mission of these weapons. Traditionally, nuclear weapons played a backstop role to preclude a Warsaw Pact victory, either through conventional means alone or through the Warsaw Pact's own use of nuclear weapons. However, the new strategic concept (see below) calls for the retention of NATO's nuclear weapons as a deterrent to the use of nuclear weapons or other weapons of mass destruction, such as chemical or biological weapons.[82]

Despite the rapid changes that occurred from 1989 through 1991 and despite an image of lethargy, NATO's political and military planning arms responded quickly and comprehensively to redirect the alliance's strategy to cope with the changes.[83] From the London declaration in July 1990 to the new strategic concept issued at the Rome summit in early November 1991, NATO undertook the most comprehensive review of its strategy since its founding.[84] Perhaps reflecting the changed times, the new concept that replaced MC 14/3 was the first to be made public.[85]

The document did not change the purely defensive nature of the alliance but reaffirmed it, as was the case with the indivisibility of NATO's security, the collective nature of its defense, and the critical linkage between Europe and North America. It recognized the absence of the monolithic threat and its replacement by "a situation in which many of the countries on the periphery of the Alliance were faced with economic, social and political difficulties which might result in crises and in turn could lead to a range of unpredictable, multi-faceted and multi-dimensional risks to Allied security."[86] The military forces needed to fulfill this new role—including deterrence and support for crisis management, peacekeeping, humanitarian assistance, and the defense of Alliance territory—were flexibly organized into three tiers.[87] The first tier consists of immediate-reaction forces and more capable rapid-reaction forces, made up of multinational,[88] rapidly deployable air, land, and sea forces.[89] The second tier, comprising the bulk of the forces, includes regionally oriented, in-place, main defensive forces consisting of both active and mobilization units. The third tier includes augmentation forces primarily from Canada and the United States—also made up of active and reserve forces.[90]

In light of these changes, NATO's doctrines—even the process—could not help being affected. At the 18th TAWP, the Air Board charged the meeting to consider including PFP countries at future TAWPs and determining which ATPs could be released to those countries, under the general NATO guidance that any unclassified NATO document can be released to a PFP country. This mandate placed the working party in a somewhat uncomfortable position of determining whether a previously unclassified document should now be classified or whether parts of the document (such as the detailed tactics, techniques, and procedures) should be stripped out of the parent document and be made separate documents. Some members expressed concern that certain information, such as procedures for aborting a CAS attack, is somewhat sensitive and that releasing that information could come back to haunt NATO sometime in the future. In the end, however, the TAWP decided to release all of these publications, at least partly because ongoing and future joint exercises between NATO countries and PFP countries required the sharing of these procedures to accomplish the exercises successfully.[91]

Despite ongoing changes, some key trends are emerging within NATO's air doctrine. The most fundamental changes sprang from a seminal paper on joint air operations written by Maj Luigi Meyer of the USAF's Doctrine Center, located at Langley AFB, Virginia. This paper outlined US views (not just those of the USAF) on such issues as strategic attack, command relationships, and battlefield control measures. Many of these concepts are making their way into NATO doctrine. For example, Allied Joint Pub (AJP)-1(A), *Allied Joint Operations Doctrine*,[92] states that its primary objective is "to provide a 'keystone' doctrine for the planning, execution, and support of allied joint operations."[93] The publication includes strategic attack as an air operation, recommends the designation of a joint force air component commander (JFACC) to ensure unity of the air effort, and further recommends that the JFACC assume additional responsibilities as air defense commander (ADC) and airspace control authority (ACA).[94] This "trihatted" approach precisely mirrors US joint doctrine and USAF doctrine. AJP-1(A) also includes a chapter on command and control warfare (C^2W)—a rapidly developing area of US doctrine.

One must still resolve the issue of whether these concepts will continue to filter down to other NATO doctrinal publications. For example, the proposed change three to ATP-33(B) does not list strategic attack as an air operation against enemy surface assets, retaining instead the classic missions of AI and OAS, the latter still including CAS and BAI.

However, the proposed section on C² of tactical air forces, while not specifically mentioning a JFACC, does include a discussion of centralized C² and decentralized tactical execution not in conflict with US doctrine. Specifically, it states that "unity of effort is best achieved when authority for command and control of the air effort is established at the highest practicable levels under a designated commander while ensuring tactical control is passed down to the level necessary to provide timely, flexible response to battlefield initiative." It further argues that "centralized control is achieved through a designated air commander who directs the total air effort by exercising operational control of tactical air forces assigned or attached."[95] Finally, the pamphlet does not preclude strategic attack as an air operation. It specifically defines interdiction, for example, as air operations "conducted to destroy, neutralize, or delay the enemy's military potential before it can be brought to bear effectively against friendly forces" but delimits "the enemy's military potential" to "those *forces* not engaged in close combat, his supplies . . . and the means by which these unengaged forces and supplies are moved" (emphasis added).[96] In contrast, Meyer defines strategic attack as an action against enemy centers of gravity, which include "characteristics, capabilities, or locations from which alliances, nations and military forces derive their will to fight, their physical strength, or their freedom of action."[97] By implication, this includes attacks against command, control, communications, and intelligence (C³I) targets, basic industrial targets, and fundamental infrastructure targets not solely devoted to military forces.

The latest versions of the counterair and airspace control pamphlets, however, continue to reflect NATO's long-standing commitment to the primacy of the air superiority mission,[98] especially DCA,[99] and the imperatives of an integrated airspace control scheme. While not defining a JFACC/ACA relationship specifically, ATP-40(A) stresses that the ACA must have the authority to plan, coordinate, and organize the airspace control system (ACS), including all weapons (both aerial and surface-to-surface) that operate within the ACS. The planning process, therefore, must include all users.[100]

Finally, ATP-27(C) on OAS still firmly holds to the concept of BAI but specifies that OAS missions include only those flown between the forward line of own troops (FLOT) and the corps area of responsibility. This places OAS firmly in a battlefield context and not as deep as either AI or strategic attack. Again, although not specifying the JFACC concept, ATP-27(C) does emphasize the requirement for unity of command under a single air commander—specifically (in the Central Region), COMAIRCENT, a PSC under commander in chief Central Europe (CINCENT).[101] Notably, COMAIRCENT would have operational control of the forces assigned to that region. In this case, the pamphlet specifies that CINCENT makes the apportionment decision (again, the determination, by percentage or priority, of how much of the total air effort goes to a specific air operation), based upon COMAIRCENT's recommendation and after consultation with the other component commanders (e.g., the land and/or naval commander). NATO organizational charts anticipate these decisions, and the consequent planning functions will be colocated at the joint command operations center while the tasking of OAS (and all other air missions) will originate with the combined air operations center.

In summary, NATO has undergone substantial political, military, and doctrinal changes in a relatively short period of time. Certainly, NATO air forces have learned substantial lessons from the experience of both the United States and other countries in the Gulf War. Despite significant merging between US and NATO doctrine, vestiges of older doctrines remain entrenched, the most notable example of which is BAI. In assessing the future direction of NATO air doctrine, Col Robert D. Coffman, commander of the USAF's Doctrine Center, believes that NATO will ultimately accept the JFACC and strategic attack, and that BAI will probably remain. He also believes that, despite the drawdown of US forces in Europe, the United States retains significant influence in NATO's doctrinal discussions. Finally, in assessing the impact of the Goldwater-Nichols Act, which reinvigorated US joint doctrine, he maintains that the act served as a strengthening step for the United States because it forced other NATO countries to face a unified doctrinal front from America.[102]

Conclusions

NATO's first priority has always been alliance cohesion; its second, a deferral to national preferences—witness the initial decision to sacrifice operational depth of maneuver in favor of forward defense along the inter-German border (IGB) and the preponderance of European air forces still deployed in their home countries. One also sees these priorities in the deployment of NATO's ground forces (and the subsequent strain that placed on NATO's air forces), which is more a reflection of postwar occupation areas than militarily viable defensive positions.

The third priority of the alliance remains the strict maintenance of the image and reality of a defensive organization, which enhances alliance cohesion in several ways. For instance, every nation can agree on the defense. Offensive operations imply an out-of-area objective, specifically rejected by NATO from its inception. From the mid-1950s on, liberating eastern Europe or even East Germany was never an overt objective. Further, presuming that defensive forces are less expensive than offensive ones, this strategy eases the fiscal burdens of European members—an especially critical point in the 1950s, when Europe was rebuilding from the ashes of World War II. Also, a defensive posture remains critical to maintaining stability in Europe because it denies anyone an excuse to launch an attack against the alliance.

NATO's force structure, deployment posture, and air doctrines reflect these priorities. From its founding, the alliance has employed a threefold air strategy. The first priority, air defense, did not imply air superiority as the USAF defines it. Air planners never foresaw gaining command of the air but focused more narrowly on achieving security against a Warsaw Pact air attack on NATO's ports and major lines of communications. Furthermore, air defense remained largely a passive campaign, featuring DCA patrols integrated with ground-based systems, albeit paying some attention to attacking Warsaw Pact airfields.

The second priority for NATO's air forces was attacking Warsaw Pact second-echelon forces. The early years saw these attacks as heavily orchestrated with NATO's ground forces, but later years saw an evolution to FOFA, which gave air forces freedom to attack lucrative targets in order to shape the close battle. However, in all cases the strategy first called for attacks against Warsaw Pact forces, mainly armor, and second, for strikes against countermobility targets, usually bridges.

The third priority called for support of engaged ground forces. From the beginning, NATO air strategists recognized the expense of this mission. But they also recognized that it might prove the most critical, especially in a short-warning attack scenario in which airpower might represent the only significant combat power available to NATO commanders. Particularly after the adoption of flexible response in 1967, the need to prevent a Warsaw Pact breakthrough took on greater significance because of the ever-lurking presence of nuclear weapons. NATO strategists truly wanted to take any measures necessary to avoid employing these weapons of mass destruction. Beyond purely moral reasons, they eventually realized that nuclear weapons did not favor the side with smaller conventional forces. Had Warsaw Pact forces accomplished a breakthrough, forcing NATO to employ nuclear weapons, presumably the Warsaw Pact would retaliate in kind. The result perhaps would have been an even quicker Warsaw Pact victory but at a considerably higher cost to both sides—especially in civilian casualties.

Over the three periods examined here, a few themes emerge regarding the influences of NATO air doctrine on USAF doctrine and vice versa. Specifically, during the early years of the alliance, NATO's strategy for the use of nuclear weapons—the doctrine of massive retaliation—fitted well with USAF doctrine and force structure.[103] However, by the time NATO shifted focus in the late 1950s, the two doctrines started to diverge. Whereas NATO contemplated a DCA battle, a reflection of its political imperatives, the USAF stressed the need for an OCA campaign in order to destroy Soviet and Warsaw Pact air forces that might deliver nuclear weapons against the allies. In large part, this divergence reflected the overwhelmingly strategic orientation of the USAF as opposed to the more tactical focus of NATO. Another theme was that

NATO planners did not envision total air superiority over all of western Europe, seeking instead only local or battlefield air superiority, while USAF doctrine emphasized the critical requirement for theaterwide air superiority as the first priority of an air force.

By the 1970s and 1980s, NATO and USAF doctrines were back in sync, not because NATO changed but because USAF doctrine dramatically shifted from an offensive, global, nuclear orientation to a conventional, European one. Perhaps the most dramatic example of this shift lay in the changing perception of the role of airpower in the opening days of a conflict. Under the NATO scenario—assuming the numerical superiority of Warsaw Pact forces, a Warsaw Pact initiative, and a requirement for US air and ground support—USAF and NATO commanders recognized that a specific battle for air superiority, especially through offensive airfield attacks, would have to wait. The immediate priority would be air defense of ports, nuclear facilities, command centers, and movements of NATO ground forces, along with battlefield support to prevent a Warsaw Pact breakthrough.[104]

The latest version of USAF basic doctrine, published in 1992, had no link to NATO air doctrine[105] and came at a time when NATO underwent massive changes. Unsurprisingly, the two doctrines diverged somewhat. However, in the mid-1990s, both USAF/US joint doctrine and NATO doctrine are undergoing substantial changes that promise a new era of convergence. One should note that the USAF doctrine preceded both the joint and NATO doctrinal development. Of course, one should expect this, insofar as doctrinal innovations should come from the air service first, because of its expertise and familiarity. It then diffuses through the other doctrinal outlets, such as joint doctrine or NATO pamphlets.

The role played by operating commands in doctrinal development reveals another important aspect of the differences between the US and NATO experiences. The Goldwater-Nichols Act specifically defined a role for US war-fighting commands (e.g., US European Command, Pacific Command, Atlantic Command, and others), whereas in NATO, the war-fighting commands (e.g., Allied Forces Central, Allied Forces South, and their subordinate allied air commands) play a more limited role. For example, although the MSC/PSCs can propose doctrinal changes, they have no vote in the ratification process. Furthermore, although US joint doctrine is authoritative and directive, US commanders can deviate for cause. NATO's military commanders, however, are much more closely tied to the doctrinal prescriptions found in NATO publications. Finally, for most NATO countries, NATO doctrine is "national" doctrine, in that no other doctrine exists—as it does in the United States. Thus, these NATO countries might take a much more interested posture in NATO doctrinal development. This is particularly true for countries such as the United States, United Kingdom, and France, that have more global interests and thus tend to write doctrine from that perspective, unlike other NATO countries with a more "European" view.

Three examples of convergence between US doctrine (both USAF and joint)[106] and emerging NATO doctrine[107] lie in C^2 arrangements, synergy from an integrated AI and ground maneuver scheme, and the role of strategic attack against enemy centers of gravity. All three doctrinal manuals recognize unity of effort as a key requirement for successful integration of air resources, and all recognize the JFACC as the proper mechanism for achieving this integration.[108] Each relates how meshing AI with ground maneuver presents the enemy with an "agonizing dilemma": if the enemy disperses to avoid air attack, he becomes more susceptible to piecemeal destruction by friendly maneuver forces; but if the enemy force concentrates, it leaves itself open for devastating air attack.[109] Finally, all three documents recognize that direct attack against key enemy centers of gravity—most effectively accomplished by airpower—offers potential payoffs much greater than those produced by air resources used in more traditional OAS roles.[110]

Undoubtedly, NATO air doctrine has undergone tremendous changes over the past several years, matching the rapidly changing geostrategic environment. Former foes are now friends; former off-limits operations—out-of-area missions—now occupy NATO's day-to-day concerns; we have witnessed an explosion in the technology of war; and we have learned much from the lessons of the Gulf War. What other challenges may lay on the horizon, and how will they become part of NATO's air doctrine?

In their study of the process and problems in the development of NATO's doctrine, Stein, Nolan, and Perry emphasize two critical aspects. First, although national doctrines often reflect unique national service traditions and capabilities, gaining NATO-wide acceptance for those views can prove difficult. This is especially true of US doctrine if other countries believe it may harbor hidden agendas or may result in expensive modernization schemes. Second, they argue that NATO has experienced difficulty keeping its doctrine in tune with rapidly changing developments—both technological and political.[111] NATO finds itself in such a situation now. The unanswered question is, How will its air doctrine evolve in light of these unprecedented changes?

One may gain some insight from the 18th TAWP held at NATO headquarters in April 1995. At that meeting, some familiar processes still existed: the degree of participation by the various countries related mainly to the issue at hand. For example, Spain did not send a delegate at all, while Turkey's delegate attended sessions that dealt only with specific ATPs (such as the one dealing with airspace) in which it had a particular interest. On the other hand, in order to facilitate progress, delegates acting as individuals often attempted to clarify issues or offer proposed solutions (especially when two countries differed). Likewise, the TAWP, recognizing the slow and cumbersome process of making changes to existing doctrine, acknowledged the need to speed up the process in light of changing circumstances—witness the requirement to update procedures used in CAS missions, found in two annexes of ATP-27.

AIRCENT had submitted extensive changes for new procedures (e.g., on night CAS, laser operations, etc.), based upon the experience of Operation Deny Flight (then being conducted by NATO over the former Yugoslav Republic of Bosnia-Herzegovina). The TAWP, recognizing both the existence of a short-term problem on updating guidance on OAS procedures to get to the field and a long-term philosophical debate on OAS, decided to hold the doctrinal debate in abeyance and proceed with updating the applicable

ATP-27 annexes. It then continued the philosophical debate with the goal of producing a "way ahead" framework for the subsequent development of NATO air doctrine. Rapidly finding common ground on the procedures, the TAWP recommended that the Air Board quickly seek ratification of the procedures and publish them as an interim supplement to ATP-27 while the more laborious work on the basic document's philosophy took place.

Thus, it appears that NATO air doctrine may be entering another Golden Age of development as air-minded people, sharing a common foundation of bedrock beliefs on the proper way to employ airpower, struggle with the massive political and military changes under way within and outside NATO, and seek to produce air doctrines to cope with those changes.

Notes

1. The difference between doctrine and strategy often lends itself to debate. As used in this chapter, *strategy* refers to a plan of action for the allocation of resources—based upon an anticipated contingency and specifying the simultaneous and sequential orchestration of military objectives—to achieve a political objective. *Doctrine* is "what we [the USAF] hold true about aerospace power and the best way to do the job in the Air Force." Air Force Manual (AFM) 1-1, *Basic Aerospace Doctrine of the United States Air Force*, vol. 1, March 1992, vii. Thus, since both terms deal with action and "doing the job," they are used interchangeably throughout this chapter, except when they allude to a specific concept or document (e.g., the strategy of flexible response or NATO tactical air doctrine).

2. This is not to overlook economic, cultural, or even historical explanations of NATO's choice of strategy. However, this chapter argues that, ultimately, one expresses those reasons in political terms. Furthermore, since this chapter focuses on military strategies, political reasons are of overriding importance.

3. This is especially true in the case of Germany. Largely due to its experiences with a powerful General Staff, the strategy of the postwar German air force lies in civilian hands. Furthermore, the German military embraces that concept and stresses that any NATO military plan must be "directly and significantly shaped by policy considerations." More importantly, the German constitution prohibits planning for, or conducting, offensive war. Michael E. Thompson, "Political and Military Components of Air Force Doctrine in the Federal Republic of Germany and Their Implications for NATO Defense Policy Analysis" (Santa Monica, Calif.: RAND Graduate School, 1987), 2.

4. Additionally, some people have argued that NATO organizations must undergo far-reaching changes. For one view, see Willard E. Naslund, *NATO Airpower: Organizing for Uncertainty* (Santa Monica, Calif.: RAND, 1993).

5. It is easy to overlook the economic dimension of NATO or to simply dismiss it as penny-pinching. Yet, as Andrew J. Goodpaster (former supreme allied commander in Europe) points out, from the earliest days, the United States and western European countries recognized that "strengthened economies were an essential underpinning to sustained and stable security efforts and to the military budgets and programs on which such efforts depended." Article 2 of the NATO Treaty specifically recognized this link. See Goodpaster's "The Foundations of NATO: A Personal Memoir," in James R. Golden et al., eds., *NATO at Forty: Change, Continuity & Prospects* (Boulder, Colo.: Westview Press, 1989), especially 25–26.

6. Richard L. Kugler, *Commitment to Purpose* (Santa Monica, Calif.: RAND, 1993).

7. TAWP delegates, who represent 14 of the 16 countries currently in NATO (Iceland has no military forces, and Belgium represents Luxembourg's interests), share a common heritage of airpower. Most are pilots—though the percentage of delegates from other services (army, marine forces, and navy) has increased over the years—and their countries ostensibly choose them as representatives because of their expertise in the areas under discussion. Each country realizes that, because of the iterative nature of the doctrine-development process, compromise is better than confrontation, over the long run. In other words, except for rare instances, each country knows that it has more to lose than to gain from a rigid insistence on national stances.

8. For most of its history, NATO has included three major commands: SACEUR, SACLANT, and Channel Command, the latter absorbed by SACLANT in 1994.

9. Countries assume responsibility for certain documents. For example, Great Britain is the custodian of Allied Tactical Pamphlet 33 (ATP-33); Germany maintains ATP-27; and the United States is the custodian of ATPs 40 and 42. These publications are reviewed on a periodic basis, and proposals for change are submitted from the countries or the affected NATO commands, collated by the custodian, and then reviewed at the working parties (e.g., the TAWP). The recommended changes are then proposed to the working parties' sponsoring board, which acts as the coordinating agent to gain ratification from the individual countries (the NATO commands do not have a vote). Once a sufficient number of countries ratifies the changes (each board decides the appropriate number), the board promulgates them. Group Capt Alan E. Hotchkiss, Royal Air Force (RAF), Retired, chairman, 18th TAWP, Brussels, Belgium, interviewed by author, 26 April 1995. One can find the detailed process in Allied Administrative Publication 3, *Development, Preparation, and Production of NATO Publications*, 1 July 1995. Much of the discussion in this chapter comes from this TAWP, which the author attended as an observer. According to Group Captain Hotchkiss,

who has successively attended nine of the 18 TAWPs, this one was representative of most TAWPs.

10. For information about the founding of NATO, see Don Cook, *Forging the Alliance: NATO, 1945–1950* (London: Martin Secker & Warburg, 1989); William Park, *Defending the West: A History of NATO* (Brighton, England: Wheatsheaf, 1986); or Escott Reid, *Time of Fear and Hope: The Making of the North Atlantic Treaty, 1947–1949* (Toronto: McClelland & Stewart, 1977).

11. The rapid and extensive demobilization undertaken by the West after World War II had the effect of worsening this situation.

12. Josef M. A. H. Luns, former secretary-general of NATO, in Golden et al., x.

13. The Schuman Plan (named after the French foreign minister), announced in May 1950 and eventually becoming the European Coal and Steel Community (the antecedent organization to the European Economic Community formalized in the 1957 Treaty of Rome), is another example of a measure undertaken to tie Germany and its former adversaries together.

14. West Germany also presented NATO with a significant military problem in that it forced the alliance into a strategy that became known as "forward defense," which in 1963 tasked NATO ground forces with defending the inner German border and precluded them from trading space for time.

15. Thompson, 2–3. See also Werner Kaltefleiter, "NATO and Germany," in Lawrence S. Kaplan et al., eds., *NATO after Forty Years* (Wilmington, Del.: Scholarly Resources, 1990); and Ian Smart, "The Political and Economic Evolution of NATO's Central Region," in Golden et al.

16. Pierre Melandri, "France and the United States," in Golden et al. Melandri argues that events such as the Marshall Plan, German rearmament, colonial policies (especially in Algeria and Indochina), the 1956 Suez crisis, and even the formation of NATO itself, bespoke increasing French dependency on the United States, which sparked a nationalistic backlash. Kugler points out that France, under the conditions of the 1946 McMahon Act, which prohibited the United States from sharing information about atomic weapons even to its allies, was not included in a 1958 amendment that allowed Britain to receive nuclear help (page 86).

17. Melandri, 66.

18. This is not to imply that NATO waited until the Warsaw Pact's founding in 1955 before assessing the attack options from the east. Rather, this constitutes a more general statement on the threat assessment NATO planners undertook in these early years. Furthermore, while other Warsaw Pact countries did retain significant military forces, planners always considered Soviet forces the major threat, particularly those in eastern Europe.

19. MC 14/1 dates from the beginning of the alliance in 1949. However, NATO did not formally accept the force goals needed to implement the strategy until the Lisbon summit in 1952. NATO intended to attain these goals by 1954 but never did so, abandoning them in December 1953,

following the easing of tensions in Europe that arose from the signing of the armistice in Korea and the death of Stalin. See William H. Park, "Defense, Deterrence, and the Central Front: Around the Nuclear Threshold," in Kaplan et al., 222.

20. Philip A. Karber, "NATO Doctrine and National Operational Priorities: The Central Front and the Flanks: Part I," in Robert O'Neill, ed., *Doctrine, The Alliance and Arms Control* (Hamden, Conn.: Archon, 1987).

21. This chapter principally addresses NATO's conventional strategy. However, no analysis of NATO military strategy gets very far before the issue of nuclear weapons, both their deterrent effects and their employment options, comes to the fore. Without going into a detailed recap of nuclear deterrent strategy, suffice it to say that two concepts—central deterrence and extended deterrence—are key. The first refers to the US strategic nuclear forces and their deterrent effect of precluding general nuclear war, which presumably would have included the NATO countries. The second refers to the deterrent effect of US strategic forces precluding general war, either conventional or nuclear, within Europe, which presumably could have spread to general nuclear war between the United States and the USSR.

22. One must recall that western Europe was still rebuilding from the devastation of World War II; despite the aid arriving under the Marshall Plan, the European "economic miracle" was just beginning to unfold in the mid-1950s.

23. Philip A. Karber and A. Grant Whitley, "The Operational Realm," in Golden et al.

24. Besides Park in Kaplan et al., see also Richard K. Betts, "Alliance Nuclear Doctrine and Conventional Deterrence: Predictive Uncertainty and Policy Confidence," in Golden et al.

25. Park in Kaplan et al., 224.

26. The US Joint Chiefs of Staff made the same assumption in approving the Mutual Defense Assistance Act of 1949. See Robert Frank Futrell, *Ideas, Concepts, Doctrine: Basic Thinking in the United States Air Force*, vol. 1, *1907–1960* (Maxwell AFB, Ala.: Air University Press, December 1989), 249.

27. The heart of this upgrade program is the Long Term Defense Program, consisting of 10 separate yet integrated initiatives formally adopted by NATO in 1978. However, the genesis of the modernization goes back to the early 1970s.

28. See Barry R. Posen, "Measuring the European Conventional Balance," *International Security* 9 (Winter 1984/1985); and John J. Mearsheimer, "Why the Soviets Can't Win Quickly in Central Europe," *International Security* 7 (Summer 1982).

29. At the same time NATO adopted MC 14/3, it also adopted the Harmel Report, which called for arms-reduction negotiations between the Warsaw Pact and NATO.

30. Two examples were the NATO/Warsaw Pact Mutual and Balanced Force Reductions (MBFR) talks started in Vienna in 1968 and the 35-nation

Conference on Disarmament in Europe (CDE) held in Stockholm. The latter evolved into the Conference on Security and Cooperation in Europe (CSCE) and, as such, formally declared the end of the cold war with the signing of the Charter of Paris on 20 November 1990.

31. One can trace the origins of this strategy to speeches made by Secretary of Defense Robert McNamara in Athens at the NATO ministerial meeting in the spring of 1962 and a commencement address he gave at the University of Michigan at Ann Arbor a few weeks later. See Kugler, 140–42. He formalized the strategy in a draft presidential memorandum in 1965. In that document, McNamara challenged the underlying assumptions of NATO's nuclear policy—specifically the notions that these weapons could somehow compensate for NATO's inferiority in conventional forces and that the Europeans would really permit nuclear war on their territory. See Park in Kaplan et al., 225.

32. By the mid-1960s, the United States had removed B-47 strategic bombers and shorter-ranged ballistic missiles such as Jupiter and Thor from Europe, largely due to its fielding of the longer-ranged B-52s, Minutemen ICBMs, and the advent of sea-launched ballistic missiles. A proposal to establish a nuclear multilateral force under NATO control, floated briefly in the early 1960s, never gained acceptance and became a dead issue by 1964. See Kugler, 154–63.

33. Gen Bernard Rogers, former supreme allied commander, characterized this strategy as "delayed tripwire." See his "Greater Flexibility for NATO's Flexible Response," *Strategic Review* 11 (Spring 1983): 16.

34. Peter Stratman, "NATO Doctrine and National Operational Priorities: The Central Front and the Flanks: Part II," in O'Neill.

35. Besides the cost issue, NATO policy makers were unwilling to separate themselves completely from nuclear weapons. Even if a conventional defense were completely successful, it would leave much of western Europe devastated but the Soviet homeland untouched.

36. In 1973, under the guidance of senior Air Force and Army leaders, the Air Land Forces Application (ALFA) directorate was set up to work out common tactics and procedures. A similar organization was established in Europe between United States Air Forces in Europe (USAFE) and United States Army Forces, United States European Command (USAREUR).

37. The MAS, dating from 1951, produces standardization agreements (STANAG) and consists of three service boards (Navy, Army, and Air Force) and a joint board (to resolve differences between service boards) plus a terminology and thesaurus section and the Office of Chairman. See Giovanni Ferrari, "Unglamorous Force Multiplier—The Military Agency for Standardization," *NATO's Sixteen Nations*, nos. 3/4 (1994): 19–22.

38. Quoted in David J. Stein, *The Development of NATO Tactical Air Doctrine, 1970–1985* (Santa Monica, Calif.: RAND, 1987), 14.

39. David J. Stein, Kimberly Nolan, and Robert Perry, *Process and Problems in Developing NATO Tactical Air Doctrine* (Santa Monica, Calif.: RAND, 1988), 4. Willard Naslund believes that the United States hoped to

use NATO doctrine as a means of transferring US war-fighting concepts (which tend to a more offensive bent) to the overly defensive-minded NATO. Interviewed by author, Langley AFB, Va., 17 March 1995.

40. With the establishment of the USAF's Doctrine Center in 1994, that responsibility now lies with that organization.

41. Stein, 17.

42. NATO ATPs have never been hierarchical, unlike US doctrinal publications; nor is there any logic behind their numbering. For example, although ATP-33 is the keystone document on tactical airpower doctrine, laying out the larger picture of air missions, ATP-27 elaborates on one set of those missions—OAS—while ATP-42 limits itself to another set—counterair. At the 18th TAWP, the United Kingdom proposed a more rational structure, whereby ATP-33 truly became a keystone document (e.g., reducing some of the detail and overlapping information contained in other ATPs), with the other ATPs (e.g., ATP-27, -40, and -42) subordinate to it.

43. Stein, Nolan, and Perry, 7–10.

44. ATP-33(B), *Tactical Air Doctrine,* 1 November 1986, 1-1.

45. Further, *coordination* authority allows one to require consultation but not to compel agreement. Ibid., 3-2.

46. Ibid., chap. 3. The "B" designation refers to the second complete revision of the document; minor revisions are made via changes. ATP-33(B) incorporating change one is the subject of this section. Change two (January 1992) and the proposed change three (December 1994) are the subject of the section on post-cold-war/post–Gulf War revisions to NATO air doctrine.

47. Ibid., 3-4 through 3-5.

48. ATP-42, *Counter Air Operations,* March 1981; with change one, 28 January 1982.

49. ATP-40, *Doctrine and Procedures for Airspace Control in the Combat Zone,* January 1977. A new pamphlet, discussed in the following section, was published in December 1994.

50. ATP-42, pars. 201–2.

51. Ibid., annex A.

52. Stein argues that other NATO members feared that "statements of operational requirements would follow on the heels of any TAWP upgrading of SEAD's doctrinal status." He further points out that the primary objections came from the RAF, Belgium, and the Netherlands, although they, along with other member air forces, "exhibited no reluctance in accepting US SEAD support" (page 48 and notes 42–43).

53. Stein, Nolan, and Perry, 11.

54. In the Central Region, 2ATAF and 4ATAF commanders were PSCs whose command centers were ACOCs. Commander, Allied Air Forces Central Europe was an MSC who operated out of a regional air operations center. The following section examines the evolution of these C^2 systems.

55. ATP-40, chap. 2.

56. Reservations occur when a member nation refuses to abide by a particular section of the document. For example, the Netherlands registered a reservation to three paragraphs of ATP-42 that deal with SEAD.

57. Stein, Nolan, and Perry, 5–6.

58. Naslund believes that this attitude arises from a systems orientation towards doctrine which holds that if a service (or country) *owns* a system, it must *control* it. On the other hand, he believes that the British take an opposite approach: since they do not own enough resources themselves, they wish to control those of other countries—hence their support of BAI, which, in essence, gives them fire support to their ground forces from other countries' air forces. Naslund.

59. This section focuses on ATP-27(A), *Offensive Air Support Operations*, February 1975, and the (B) revision, published in May 1980 (as well as the changes between the two). The following section on the post-cold-war/post–Gulf War era examines proposed changes in the (C) revision.

60. ATP-27(A), par. 102b.

61. One should recall that the TAWP is the detailed working group organized by the MAS Air Board. It includes members from each country, except Luxembourg and Iceland, as well as every NATO regional command.

62. Stein, 27.

63. ATP-27(B), par. 106.

64. This paragraph and the following one are based upon Stein, 26–35. One should note that the BAI/AI discussion extended beyond an RAF-USAF disagreement. The US Army and its AirLand Battle doctrine also played an important role in the emergence of BAI as a separate category of air-to-surface airpower employment. See Robert Frank Futrell, *Ideas, Concepts, Doctrine: Basic Thinking in the United States Air Force*, vol. 2, *1961–1984* (Maxwell AFB, Ala.: Air University Press, December 1989), 546–55.

65. NORTHAG covered the relatively flat, open spaces of the North German plain and was defended by 17 divisions from five countries (Denmark, Holland, United Kingdom, Belgium, and West Germany) whose land forces generally had less firepower than US forces further south (who also had more favorable defensive terrain). This situation was exacerbated by NATO's forward defense posture, which required these forces to be spread thin along the inter-German border (IGB), and the Warsaw Pact's blitzkrieg strategy, which sought a breakthrough along a narrow front followed by exploitation into NATO's vital rear areas. This attack would destroy logistics networks, envelope NATO forces, and defeat them in detail. See Kugler, 433–37.

66. Of particular concern were Warsaw Pact (mainly Soviet) operational maneuver groups (OMG), which were highly mobile, second-echelon forces designed to exploit any breakthrough by first-echelon Warsaw Pact forces and then wreak havoc in NATO rear areas—particularly nuclear systems

(storage and launch facilities), command centers, airfields, and logistics dumps.

67. Critical technologies required for AirLand Battle included (1) intelligence technologies that could detect and identify Warsaw Pact echelons and relay that data in a timely manner in order to strike at these (presumably) fleeting targets; (2) precision, all-weather attack resources (both platforms and weapons); and (3) the support assets needed to get them through the dense Warsaw Pact IADS.

68. Naslund stressed this point, specifically relating his belief that the US Army used the threat posed by Warsaw Pact OMGs to gain control over NATO's deep-strike air assets.

69. The initiative was also proposed for inclusion into US joint doctrine. Joint Test Pub 3-03.1, *Joint Interdiction of Follow-on Forces Attack*, 16 June 1988, essentially followed the same logic as the NATO concept. Notably, FOFA never became part of either NATO *air* doctrine manuals or USAF doctrine.

70. The primary difference between classic AI and FOFA was the former's emphasis on fixed targets such as bridges, while the latter focused on forces most likely on the move. Identifying moving targets in a timely fashion required more sophisticated technologies. See Wing Commander A. V. B. Hawken, RAF, *Follow-on Force Attack—Now and in the Future*, Research Report (Maxwell AFB, Ala.: Air War College, 1990). The joint surveillance, target attack radar system (JSTARS), which played such a role in the 1991 Gulf War, was developed precisely for this mission, as was the tactical missile system (TACMS) family of surface-to-surface missiles with "smart" antiarmor submunitions.

71. General Rogers refuted each of these concerns. Arguing that the purpose of FOFA was to "restore flexibility to Flexible Response," he claimed that FOFA was complementary to defensive operations because "defense . . . protects our [NATO's] means to attack Soviet follow-on forces, and attacking in depth . . . will help to keep the force ratios at the GDP [General Defensive Position] manageable." Finally, he strenuously disputed the idea that FOFA was a new strategy. See his "Follow-on Forces Attack (FOFA): Myths and Realities," *NATO Review* 32 (December 1984): 1–9 (quotes on pages 1 and 5). For an opposing view—one that claims FOFA was an "idea whose time may well have passed" because OMGs were so close to the first-echelon forces that attack against targets any deeper than, say, one hundred kilometers would be a waste of resources—see David Greenwood, "Strengthening Conventional Deterrence," *NATO Review* 32 (August 1984): 8–12 (quote on page 9).

72. Preplanned requests include those passed up through the land-force chain of command; one includes them in the daily tasking after accomplishing the joint coordination and planning. Immediate requests are just that: immediate calls for air support beyond that provided in the daily allocation of air resources. See ATP-27(B), par. 602. Often confused in this regard are airborne versus ground alert missions—both are allocated air

resources, differing in the degree of responsiveness. Obviously, airborne assets are the most responsive. ATP-27(B), par. 410.

73. Ibid., par. 506.

74. NATO's 1949 charter specifically forbids involvement in operations outside its members' territories. Ironically, the United States, fearing that the alliance would become entangled in Europe's colonial wars, insisted on the inclusion of this provision. Now, of course, the United States, with its global commitments, is seeking a change in this posture and more support from the allies. See David C. Morrison, "Beyond NATO," *National Journal,* 23 February 1991, 452–54. An interesting question undergoing debate within NATO is, Precisely what is "out-of-area"? Is not Europe (hence the Balkans) within NATO's "area"? What of the southern rim of the Mediterranean, which is arguably contiguous with NATO's area? Finally, what of the Middle East, with its rich oil reserves upon which most European countries depend (much more so than the United States)?

75. Thomas-Durell Young, *The "Normalization" of the Federal Republic of Germany's Defense Structures* (Carlisle, Pa.: US Army War College Strategic Studies Institute, 1992).

76. In reformulating their strategy (discussed below), NATO politicians and planners recognized that NATO must forge closer links with the WEU and the Organization for Cooperation and Security in Europe (OCSE). Thomas-Durell Young argues that such cooperation will provide a means for NATO members to coordinate on out-of-area operations without appearing to establish a situation in which member states might feel "trapped" in other members' "adventures" outside of NATO's traditional areas of concern. See his "Preparing the Western Alliance for the Next Out-of-Area Campaign," *Naval War College Review* 45 (Summer 1992): 28–44.

77. For a full discussion, see Jonathan T. Howe, "NATO and the Gulf Crisis," *Survival* 33 (May/June 1991): 246–59. At the time, Admiral Howe was commander in chief of allied forces in NATO's Southern Region (which includes Turkey and the Mediterranean); thus, he had operational command over Southern Guard (NATO's response to the crisis) and its two military measures—Dawn Set (in southeastern Turkey) and MedNet (in the Mediterranean). Dawn Set included Operation Ace Guard, which involved the deployment of the Allied Command Europe, Mobile Force (AMF)-Air and Patriot missiles to Turkey (see below).

78. North Atlantic Council, Statement on the Gulf, 18 December 1990, par. 5. Article 5 of the treaty states that an armed attack against one member is considered an attack against them all.

79. The NAEW aircraft maintained 24-hour coverage of eastern Turkey. As an aside, during the Gulf War, since Joint Task Force Proven Force, conducting US offensive air missions out of Incirlik, Turkey, did not have sufficient US E-3 AWACS aircraft to cover all its missions, it "borrowed" NAEW threat warning (*not* positive control) for some attack packages.

80. AMF-Air's major forces included 18 Belgian Mirage Vs, 18 German Alpha Jets, and six Italian RF-104G reconnaissance aircraft, plus a Dutch Patriot surface-to-air missile battery. Additionally, six US F-15C aircraft at Incirlik, as part of Proven Force, were placed on air defense alert under NATO control. Notably, NATO offensive aircraft were stationed at Erhac, Turkey—out of range of the Iraqi border, further testimony to their purely defensive role.

81. "NATO Countries' Gulf Role," *National Journal*, 23 February 1991, 454. Britain and France played the largest role, contributing both air and ground forces to the coalition. However, both Italian and Canadian fighter aircraft flew combat missions from the Arabian peninsula. The majority of the other countries contributed naval forces plus essential basing and overflight rights (especially Portugal and Spain).

82. See the Nuclear Planning Group communiqué of December 1991; Michael Legge, "The Making of NATO's New Strategy," *NATO Review* 39 (December 1991): 13; and Gen John R. Galvin, "From Immediate Defence towards Long-Term Stability," *NATO Review* 39 (December 1991): 17–18. At the time, Legge was the assistant secretary-general for NATO's defense planning and policy and chairman of the Strategy Review Group; Galvin was SACEUR.

83. Manfred Wörner, "NATO Transformed: The Significance of the Rome Summit," *NATO Review* 39 (December 1991): 3. He was secretary-general of NATO at the time.

84. For a summary of the London declaration, see the US Department of State *Dispatch*, 8 October 1990, 163. Significant changes included calling for a move away from forward defense, reducing readiness, reducing the number and size of units and exercises, relying more on multinational forces and reconstitution, and modifying flexible response to make nuclear weapons truly weapons of last resort. For the text of the London declaration, see *NATO Review*, August 1990, 32.

85. Legge, 9. For the texts of the new strategic concept and the accompanying Rome declaration, see *NATO Review*, December 1991, 19–22, 25–33.

86. Legge, 12.

87. Galvin, 15.

88. The theme of multinational forces runs throughout NATO's discussions. This concept replaces NATO's "layer cake" approach, whereby essentially autonomous national corps fought side-by-side under a (loosely) multinational command headquarters. It proved politically important because it spread German ground forces along the IGB, interspersed with other national corps. Doing so precluded a Warsaw Pact attack against German forces only, which, some people believed, might have reduced other countries' commitment to fight. It also tied the smaller NATO countries, such as Belgium and the Netherlands, to IGB defense. See Kugler, 214–20. As to multinationalism, three key issues are yet to be answered. The first concerns which countries will provide what types of forces to these units.

The second issue involves logistics. Historically, NATO has relied on the doctrine of national logistics, which requires each country to supply its own forces. Lacking complete standardization and interoperability, this doctrine would create a nightmare of logistics in a multinational force. The third issue entails command arrangements. Traditionally, NATO senior commands have either been allocated to a particular country (e.g., SACEUR has always been a US general) or rotated on a rigid schedule. No one knows whether this practice will suffice in multinational forces. See David Greenwood, "Refashioning NATO's Defences," *NATO Review* 38 (December 1990): 2–8.

89. The immediate reaction force (IRF) is an augmented AMF of about five thousand troops able to deploy anywhere within Europe within 72 hours. The Allied Command Europe Rapid Reaction Corps (ARRC) consists of upwards of one hundred thousand multinational troops deployable within six to 10 days. See David M. Abshire, Richard R. Burt, and R. James Woolsey, *The Atlantic Alliance Transformed* (Washington, D.C.: Center for Strategic and International Studies, 1992), 22.

90. Galvin, 15–17.

91. A somewhat related issue that arose in the 18th TAWP dealt with former Warsaw Pact material now in NATO. For example, Germany retained a squadron of MiG-29 Fulcrum aircraft from the former East German air force. Delegates expressed concerns about identification-friend-or-foe issues that directly affect NATO airspace control doctrine.

92. A preliminary draft is just a working document. After all the issues are ironed out, a final draft is sent to the countries for ratification. As outlined earlier, after ratification, the document (whether a change, major revision, or new document) is promulgated.

93. AJP-1(A), *Allied Joint Operations Doctrine*, 22 November 1996, par. 0001.

94. AJP-1(A), chap. 18, "Joint Air Operations and Airspace Control."

95. ATP-33(B), proposed change three, December 1994, par. 306. At the 18th TAWP, the United Kingdom proposed suspending further work on ATP-33 and -27 pending a complete review of NATO air doctrine. Much like the earlier TAWP that established a separate forum to work out the differences between the United States and United Kingdom over BAI (see above), this TAWP established a working group—which met in Germany in 1995—to study these issues (e.g., the Meyer paper and a contending United Kingdom proposal).

96. Ibid., par. 505–6.

97. Maj Luigi Meyer, memorandum to Tactical Air Working Party agencies, subject: US Paper on Joint Air Operations, Department of the Air Force, 27 July 1994, 5.

98. ATP-42(B), *Counter Air Operations*, December 1994. Paragraph 503 states that "Offensive Counter Air should be the prime consideration in the effective employment of friendly tactical air resources."

99. Ibid., par. 802c: "Indeed, the first positive indication of an impending conflict may be the need to conduct air defence operations."

100. ATP-40(A), *Doctrine for Airspace Control in Times of Crisis and War,* December 1994, chap. 3.

101. In the early 1990s, NATO renamed some of its MSCs and PSCs. Hence, AAFCE became AIRCENT.

102. Col Robert D. Coffman, USAF Doctrine Center, Langley AFB, Va., interviewed by author, 17 March 1995.

103. Gen Thomas D. White, Air Force vice chief of staff, said that the strategy allows recognition of the Air Force as an instrument of national power. Furthermore, he noted that the strategy was in line with the ideas of Giulio Douhet, Billy Mitchell, Hap Arnold, and other early airpower theorists and leaders. See Futrell, vol. 1, 432.

104. Futrell, vol. 2, 494–95. Futrell extensively quotes Gen David C. Jones, USAF chief of staff, who came to the chief's position from commanding all USAF and allied air units in Europe. General Jones explicitly outlined NATO's air requirements of blunting the Warsaw Pact armor attack, providing some battlefield air superiority, and attacking Warsaw Pact second-echelon forces.

105. Col Dennis Drew, USAF, Retired, team chief and principal author of the 1992 edition of AFM 1-1, interviewed by author, Maxwell AFB, Ala., 10 March 1995.

106. For USAF doctrine, the primary publication is AFM 1-1. For joint doctrine, the key publication for operations is Joint Pub (JP) 3-0, *Doctrine for Joint Operations,* 9 September 1993.

107. For NATO, the keystone doctrine for the planning, execution, and support of allied joint operations is AJP-1(A).

108. See AFM 1-1, vol. 1, par. 3-1; JP 3-0, chap. 2; and AJP-1(A), chap. 18, sec. 3.

109. See AFM 1-1, vol. 1, par. 3-5b(1); JP 3-0, chap. 4, 3f. AJP-1 does not address this level of specificity; however, ATP-33(B), proposed change three, par. 506–7, discusses the need for close coordination between AI and ground maneuver.

110. See AFM 1-1, vol. 1, par. 3-5a; JP 3-0, chap. 4, 2c; and AJP-1(A), chap. 18, par. 1805.

111. Stein, Nolan, and Perry, 12–13.

Chapter 13

Soviet Military Doctrine and Air Theory: Change through the Light of a Storm

Lt Col Edward J. Felker

Often, advances in technology have caused revolutions in military affairs as they transformed the nature of war. Tanks, motor transport, mobile communications, and airpower altered the battlefield of the early twentieth century. In midcentury, nuclear weapons and missiles altered the strategy of the battlefield. Today, we see high-tech conventional alternatives replacing battlefield nuclear weapons. These new weapons reduce the likelihood of escalation yet create little or no collateral damage.[1]

These were the changes to the future battlefield the Russians analyzed in the Gulf War of 1991. The collapse of the Soviet Union, the waning of the cold war, and the end of the confrontation between communism and capitalism created a new political-military situation. As a result, the Soviets/Russians altered their military doctrine and view of the nature of future war, based on their perceptions of airpower in the Gulf War.

To the Soviets, military doctrine represented neither a general theory nor the view of individuals. Instead, it was a system of official state views, encompassing the leading, fundamental, official principles of military theory for mandatory practice. In its simplest form, military doctrine carried politically approved sanctions of law for military structure and function. Doctrine codified the country's political goals and economic potentials into legislative acts, government decrees and resolutions, military regulations and manuals, and basic military orders.[2]

485

Russian View of Military Doctrine

To understand how the Gulf War affected the evolution of Russian airpower doctrine, one must understand the broader context of military doctrine from which it came. The Voroshilov Lectures define military doctrine as a system of theories accepted by the state and the armed forces regarding the character, form, and conduct of war.[3] They characterize military doctrine as the body of thought that prepares a nation and its armed forces for war. Political leadership develops the theories according to domestic and foreign policy, ideology, and military-scientific achievements. Thus, military doctrine reflects the economic, political, military, and historic character of the people and their international commitments.[4] Benjamin Lambeth, a RAND analyst, defines this view of military doctrine as "the sum total of scientifically based views accepted by the country and its armed forces on the nature of contemporary wars that might be unleashed by the imperialists against the USSR, and the goals and missions of the armed forces in such a war, on the methods of waging it, and also on the demands which flow from such views for the preparation of the country and the armed forces."[5]

Charles Dick notes a dual social-political and military-technical aspect of Soviet military doctrine. Political and military leadership decides the tenets of military doctrine according to "socio-political order, the level of economic, scientific, and technological development of the armed forces' combat material, with due regard to the conclusions of military science and the views of the possible enemy."[6] The political aspect is dominant and directive, while military doctrine forms the bedrock for force structure and military plans. The General Staff uses the social-political aspect of doctrine to develop military strategy and operational art.[7]

Relationship between Military Doctrine and Strategy

Military strategy decided the nature and role of the armed forces in war. It resolved the form, type, organization, and theoretical principles to plan the strategic actions of the armed forces and provided an analytical foundation for studying strategy, characteristics, and capabilities.[8] Military strategy provided the theoretical framework that united domestic politics, economics, history, morale, science, international politics, and military forces. It also unified military doctrine and operational art—its ultimate application. Military strategy linked political leadership and the Soviet High Command in preparing the nation for war. The Soviet High Command organized strategy, planned force deployments, prepared the armed forces for war, and controlled them during war. Military strategy's political basis directly influenced the military-technical fundamentals of doctrine. Because of this circular relationship between military strategy and doctrine, any change in the theoretical base of one produced changes in the other. Doctrine's views about future war guided strategy. Simultaneously, strategy affected the formulation and perfection of doctrine's military-technical component.

This military-technical aspect of doctrine remained a dynamic idea, constantly adjusted to reflect changes in force posture, political requirements, economic factors, scientific achievement, and changes introduced by potential enemies. Timothy Thomas notes six considerations embraced by the military-technical dimension of military doctrine: (1) the character (nature) of the military threat; (2) the type and struggle that may result (future war); (3) the requirements for defense (historical paradigm about war's beginning, initial period, timing, and interaction of technology); (4) the required armed forces (strategic posture, mobilization, and deployment); (5) the means to conduct armed struggle and the use of the armed forces (force generation, manning, and equipping); and (6) preparation of the armed forces to accomplish these tasks (training, etc.).[9]

Soviet military doctrine guided the development of military art, but military art was not its subset. Doctrine consisted of general principles regarding the nature of war, whereas military art concerned the practical issues of war fighting.[10] Given military doctrine's view of the future battlefield, military art described the nature of warfare in general terms. It articulated the likely enemy, types of action to expect and prepare for, and measures to equip and train forces. Further, it provided the synthesis of the national economy and population in supporting future war. Military art and its doctrinal underpinnings, therefore, were closely coordinated. In the initial period of war, this coordination became critical.[11] According to army general M. V. Gareyev, the response in the initial period most directly reflected the Soviets' political intent. He observed that "while politics usually prevails throughout a war, the political aspects are most prevalent on the eve or at the beginning of a war."[12]

Evolution of Soviet/Russian Military Doctrine

Soviet military doctrine changed in response to the complex interrelationships that formed it—international political and military environments, foreign military doctrines, history, technology, and ideology, as well as internal political, social, moral, and economic constraints. Perceived strategic imbalance has remained the prime motivator in the Soviets' doctrinal evolution. Michael MccGwire notes that "Soviet military doctrine has evolved in response to what have been seen as a series of direct threats to the state's existence. . . . Nuclear testing aside, Soviet actions and the doctrines behind them must be seen as responses to the perceived threat posed by American decisions."[13]

Russian military doctrine, therefore, represents an amalgam of factors. The international political environment and an assessment of the probability of war formed its political component. The evolution of Soviet military doctrine reflected the influence of foreign doctrines. Soviet history forged the Soviet perspective of war. World War II, with its more than 20 million Soviet deaths, had a profound effect.[14] Internal political, economic, and social constraints, as well as the nature of Soviet decision making, greatly affected the nature of doctrine. Technological innovation also played a key role. Thus, Soviet military doctrine arose from the interaction of a multitude of often conflicting factors.

Post World War II: Stalin's Era (1945–53). The formative impact of World War II led military doctrine to cast future war in the mold of that experience—protracted land war, with ground troops directly supported by tanks, artillery, and aircraft. Soviet leaders believed that surprise attack characterized this period.[15] Although the war laid the foundation of military doctrine, the Soviets conducted little critical examination of their failures in 1941 and 1942. Furthermore, Joseph Stalin placed great importance on atomic weapons and rocketry for international prestige. US superiority in strategic nuclear weapons and airpower prompted a Soviet emphasis on strong conventional forces and offensive counterattack into Europe from Soviet bases in Eastern Europe. The international political environment and Marxist-Leninist ideology also shaped military doctrine. Marxist idealism included the inevitable clash between capitalism and socialism, which reinforced the Soviets' view of the world.

Most influential was the role played by the nature of the internal Soviet political system. Under Stalin, the Soviet Union became more authoritarian. Elevating to doctrinal status those factors he believed were responsible for winning the war, he ignored developments in conventional weapons, the role of surprise on the battlefield, and any failures the Soviets may have had during the German push to Moscow, Leningrad, and Stalingrad. Stalin considered these deficiencies irrelevant to victory.

Both defense and offense played major roles in conventional warfare. Victory resulted from accumulating successful battles along slowly moving, continuous *fronts*. Frontal breakthroughs occurred by massing forces on a main axis of attack. The military concentrated its forces in strike sectors for speed, firepower, and shock to penetrate, envelop, and thrust into the enemy's rear areas. Combined arms, with preeminent ground forces in a European environment, became the primary vision of future war.[16]

Khrushchev's Era (1954–64). Freed from the stupefying control of Stalin, military doctrine changed significantly under Nikita Khrushchev. The major doctrinal trend became adapting nuclear weapons and missiles to the old concepts of future war.[17] Khrushchev dropped the idea of the inevitability of a protracted ground war in Europe. Instead, war would result from the presumed escalation of a small conventional war into a nuclear one. Short, intense, and massive exchanges of nuclear weapons dominated this view of war.[18] Because of this outlook, Khrushchev downgraded and partially demobilized ground forces and tactical air forces. Conventional options became obsolete, and the strategic rocket forces received the lion's share of the Soviet defense budget. Nuclear weapons provided the means of establishing favorable conditions for rapid ground advances. With the defense weakened, ground forces would break through and carry out decisive maneuvers to the enemy's flanks and rear.[19] This view led to the offense's becoming the dominant form of battle, accordingly emphasizing the role of surprise. Since war likely would not last long, the initial period became most important, motivating both sides to achieve the initiative immediately.

This doctrine created a different set of contributions for airpower. No longer viewed as long-range artillery directly supporting ground forces, it became a prime instrument for delivering nuclear blows. Additionally, it became the force of choice to counter an enemy nuclear response to the Soviet offense.[20] US strategic nuclear superiority and the cold war challenge led to the Soviet policy of preemption. Now that the Soviets no longer considered idealistic war inevitable, Marxist-Leninist dialectic had less impact on doctrine than it did under Stalin. Replacing the dialectic became a concentrated analytical process for determining historical lessons.

Brezhnev's Era (1964–82). Only minor changes in thought occurred under Leonid Brezhnev. Given the massive nuclear capabilities on both sides, military doctrine reflected a belief that conflict would eventually involve large-scale exchanges of nuclear weapons.[21] Conventional strategic operations within the Western theater of military operations (TVD) opposite NATO became dominant.[22] The Soviets believed that a Warsaw Pact strategic conventional offensive could preemptively deny NATO any incentive to initiate a nuclear war. Success depended on (1) early air superiority, (2) timely cooperation among the Warsaw Pact allies, and (3) strategic surprise.[23] Thus, the reemergence of conventional operations became the primary doctrinal change. In 1961 the United States began moving away from massive retaliation to flexible response, making conventional operations more interesting to Soviet planners—especially if the enemy might not strike with nuclear weapons first. As a result, the initial conventional phase took on very specific characteristics. Time was the "coin of the realm." Friendly forces needed to destroy both the enemy's defensive lines and tactical nuclear weapons quickly.[24] Since the most likely scenario involved a surprise attack by the enemy, doctrine logically insisted on the primacy of the offense.

Other internal and external factors drove doctrine. After achieving nuclear parity with the United States, the Soviet Union for the first time possessed a credible nuclear offensive capability to deter nuclear escalation. In the international political arena, tensions eased with other countries. As their economy began to expand domestically, the Soviets could field the forces necessary to carry out the military doctrine they espoused. The historical significance of two major world wars on the continent continued to influence military doctrine's reliance on large conventional forces. The internal political apparatus under Brezhnev became more conservative, pluralist, and bureaucratic in decision making. The military, KGB, and heavy and light industry all received representation on the Politburo. As a result, real appropriations to each of these sectors increased significantly. In this context, military doctrine emphasizing a conventional option enhanced the role of the ground forces, again making them "a more integral and legitimate actor in the decision making process."[25]

Gorbachev's Era (1983–89). The era of Mikhail Gorbachev saw perhaps the most sweeping changes in Soviet military doctrine. In the mid-1980s, perestroika (restructuring) markedly accelerated changes in military doctrine, and emphasis on strategic defense, rather than preemptive conventional offense, marked the doctrine emerging from this period. Many factors drove changes to this "defensive" doctrine. The inevitability of this change appears in the comments of Eduard Shevardnadze, then the Soviet foreign minister:

> The achievements of our foreign policy would be much more impressive if we could assure greater internal stability. The numerous misfortunes that have befallen our country recently, the critical situation in the economy, the state of ethnic relations and natural calamities are reducing the chances of success in our foreign policy. The policy of reform thanks to which our country has restored its good

name is undoubtedly giving rise in the world to a feeling of compassion and a desire and readiness to help us. But it should be frankly said that if our domestic troubles are multiplied by conservatism and ill will, intolerance and selfishness and clinging to dogmatic principles of the past, it will be more and more difficult for us to uphold the cause of peace, reduce tensions, fight for broader and irreversible disarmament, and integrate our country into the world system. That is why our diplomats are not living with their heads in the clouds. Their thoughts are turned to the harsh realities of our domestic life.[26]

Military planners and politicians firmly believed that nuclear escalation would destroy the Soviet state. They saw that their previous preemptive doctrine created a deadly paradox. Rapid conventional success against NATO on any axis might accelerate NATO's nuclear first use—exactly what preemption was trying to preclude. Thus, the previous Soviet strategic concept contained the seeds of its own destruction. Further, in the 1970s and early 1980s, NATO leaders perceived the Soviet buildup as threatening and destabilizing. As such, NATO responded with deliberate political and military measures. The resultant NATO buildup in technologically superior forces and the political will for rapid reinforcement decreased the Soviets' likelihood of winning a conventional war in the initial period.[27] This produced an economically and technologically draining competition with the Soviet civilian economy. The military capability to carry out preemptive doctrine became a burden the Soviet economy could not endure. Direct costs imposed by military demands on the workforce, material, and technology exacerbated the Soviets' decline on the world's stage. Finally, the Soviet Union's internal political turmoil resulted in the virtual disappearance of Marxist-Leninist ideology from the formation of military doctrine. The Soviets put their view of others on a "back burner" in order to concentrate on their view of themselves.

In 1985 the Soviet political leadership redefined military doctrine to support pressing political, economic, and societal concerns. Under the new doctrine, the defensive operation acted as a precursor to strong conventional counterstrikes, followed by a concentrated counteroffensive. Doctrine designed the defensive phase as a temporary measure to buy time in the initial period of a conflict. The Soviets would use this time to mobilize, reinforce, and move rear echelons forward for the counteroffensive. The new doctrine focused almost exclusively on the initial period of the defense, saying little about the counterstrike and counteroffensive periods.[28] It shifted away from the aggressive nature of the Brezhnev years, becoming a so-called defensive doctrine with weapons of "reasonable sufficiency."[29] The new doctrine led the Soviet military to develop plans to conduct a more prolonged initial defense.

The new military doctrine, however, included a provision to switch, perhaps suddenly, from the general strategic defensive to a counteroffensive, marking the end of the initial period of war. To achieve a sufficient correlation of force for the counteroffensive to succeed, the Soviets needed more forces than the new defensive doctrine prescribed. This put a premium on mobilization of strategic reserves and forward movement of follow-on echelons. After forces from the strategic reserve moved forward, they would exploit the success achieved by early counterstrikes at the front. Without fire superiority, the counterstrike's surprise, maneuver, and decisiveness were impossible. Soviet forces had to destroy enemy deep-fire systems and reconnaissance, mostly by air, so that maneuver forces had freedom of action.

This scenario mandated answering a NATO attack with a "devastating rebuff," although the doctrine did not clarify whether one limited this rebuff to a counteroffensive only or expanded it to a full-scale, strategic offensive operation. In 1987 Defense Minister Dimitriy Yazov called for a decisive offensive to follow a counteroffensive. By late 1989, however, when the new military doctrine emerged, he said, "Until recently, we planned to repel aggressions with defensive and offensive operations. Now, however, we are planning defensive operations as the basic form of our combat action."[30]

Central to the defensive doctrine was the prevalent concept that victory came only by defeating the enemy through the offensive mode. Yet, the Soviet military said little publicly on issues related to the debate over the counteroffensive. John Hines and Donald Mahoney feel that the military's reticence stemmed from the atmosphere of uncertainty characterizing Soviet military affairs after the announcement in December 1988 of unilateral force reductions.[31] Michael M. Boll asserts that the Warsaw Pact continued to exercise with simulated nuclear weapons, in sharp contrast to the doctrine's reorientation, which emphasized defensive preparation. He argues that the Soviets' announced defensive position remained more "in the realm of intent . . . than . . . immediate reform."[32] Officially, the General Staff embraced the defensive but continued an offensive spirit.

Immediate Pre–Gulf War Era (1990–91). This period marked the end of communism, the breakup of the Warsaw Pact, the dissolution of the Soviet Republic, the rise of Boris Yeltsin, and the formation of the Russian Federation. In 1989 Gorbachev announced unilateral force reductions in Europe, a move toward professionalism versus conscription, and force development began to focus on qualitative factors. Political factions reassessed the military threat from the West and declared it less daunting. The central theme of doctrine evolution during this period addressed ways of making defensive doctrine and reasonable sufficiency work after military restructuring. According to Lester Grau of the Foreign Military Studies Office, many indicators show that the declaration of a defensive doctrine was "a purely political decision made for economic and political purposes and imposed on the military with little regard for the military logic of that doctrine."[33] He points out that, after the new doctrine declaration, professional books and journal articles published in the USSR continued to reflect the Soviet military's conservative approach to operational art. The Soviets found themselves on a trip down a poorly lit and twisting path, where perceptions and reality would come into sharp conflict.

New US and NATO systems were clearly a generation ahead of those of the Soviets. The role of precision-guided munitions (PGM) and electronic warfare (EW) had added a great combat additive to NATO forces. Although the Soviets clearly lagged behind, they did not intend simply to mirror NATO's reliance on technology as a force multiplier.[34] Soviet military professionals asserted that they would "not follow in the wake of the probable enemy and copy his weapons and employment concepts [but would] seek asymmetrical solutions, combining high combat effectiveness with economic efficiency."[35] The Soviet forces "are to become equipped with the latest in science and technology and become increasingly more flexible, cohesive, and mobile."[36] The revamped force structure would become compact, ready, and easily expandable by an enhanced mobilization base. Finally, the restructured force relied on fully automated command, control, and communications (C³) infrastructure to facilitate mission execution.[37] The Soviets hoped that the synergy produced by these factors would amount to an order-of-magnitude increase in combat effectiveness.

The Soviets envisioned the future battlefield as a high-intensity, dynamic, high-tempo, air-land operation extending over vast land areas and space. The operation orchestrated elements and preplanned fires, maneuver, counterattack forces, and counterstrike forces. Maneuver and countermaneuver ensured the viability of the defense and created conditions favorable to a counteroffensive. Tempo allowed the Soviets to counterattack into the operational depth of the enemy during operational/strategic counteroffensives.

One finds an interesting characteristic of this doctrine common to all Soviet military doctrine. That is, the defense creates a favorable condition to culminate in an offensive. Forces allotted to the defense remained secondary to the counteroffensive, while operational reserves exploited the counteroffensive. More than blunting an attack, the defense became the means to seize the initiative from the aggressor, creating conditions leading to the enemy's defeat. Counterstrike and preemption become keys to seizing the initiative. Although a defensive doctrine highlighted this era, *maintaining offensive capability remained the essence of this defensive doctrine.* Therefore, one can view the ideas of the "strategic defensive" and counteroffensive as the same doctrinal concept.

Soviet Military Doctrine Stereotype

Throughout its evolution, Soviet military doctrine took on certain primary characteristics, albeit in many forms. But in looking at the doctrine closely, we see a persistent and recurrent theme involving offensive action—the doctrinal template the Soviets applied when the air phase of the Gulf

495

War began in January 1991 and the comparative paradigm they used to measure Western military performance against their 40-year-old ideas about the nature of future war.

In the strategic-operational plan, the high command of forces organized on one or more strategic axes in a TVD.[38] Operational commanders within this TVD aimed to destroy the enemy and weaken his political alliances. The weakest points of the enemy received the major blows, and in areas likely to receive counterattacks, friendly forces built defenses. Envelopment would destroy the enemy. The key to the strategic-operational plan lay in achieving significant tactical superiority in a strike sector where the main blow fell, while accepting local inferiority in passive or secondary sectors not coming under attack. Soviet military planners stressed that only the offensive could achieve victory. Seizing the initiative at the outset of hostilities, before the enemy could fully deploy, offered the Soviets the best opportunity to mass forces to break through the enemy's prepared defenses.

The Offensive. Successful deep operations required simultaneous fire suppression of the enemy throughout the depth of the defense, rapid penetration, and high-speed, deep attacks to achieve the objective as quickly as possible.[39] Motorized rifle, tank, and air-assault forces characterized these high-speed strikes. Echeloning forces built pressure on the weakest sector. Generally, combined-arms armies made up the first echelon of a front, containing the bulk of its forces, with tank armies normally in the second echelon. The mission of this first echelon was to overcome the enemy's defenses and attack through to the immediate operational depths.

The front's second echelon, normally one army, exploited the success of the first echelon and continued the main thrusts to the subsequent objective. Thus, a significant force remained out of contact with the enemy until the first forces in contact either reached their objective or achieved a breakthrough. Echeloning served to ensure the availability of freshly committed forces for exploitation.[40] Given the importance that Soviet planners placed upon the attack, the Soviets regarded the breakthrough as their center of gravity upon which operational—and, by inference, strategic—

objectives rested.[41] The second operational echelon contained up to one-half of the entire front's committed force to exploit the breakthrough and advance into the enemy's rear.[42]

Air support of ground forces during the offensive consisted of four stages. First, support of the movement forward called for giving priority to deep targets, especially nuclear weapons, enemy aircraft on airfields, and combat helicopters—forces that might strike friendly forces far removed from the forward edge of enemy defenses. The second stage occurred before the onset of a ground offensive across a specified frontage. This stage increased the mass of fires by combining artillery and air strikes in the attack's preparatory stage. An extension of the second stage, the third stage provided direct support of ground forces after the offensive started, concentrating on targets beyond the range of frontal artillery. The Soviets called the final stage the "air accompaniment." It occurred during the advanced stage of the offensive, when progress of the ground forces had outstripped the prepared fire-support plan. This stage ensured support of ground forces as they penetrated the enemy's defensive positions.[43]

The Air Operation. Generally, strategic operations began with an air offensive. As part of a strategic offensive operation, an air operation functioned as a joint operation of all aviation resources coordinated on an operational-strategic scale.[44] Air operations entailed the aggregate of mass strikes, air engagements, and successive actions coordinated and conducted simultaneously—or successively—by air force operational formations. They aimed to destroy enemy air as well as operational and strategic reserves in the TVD. Additionally, the air operation prevented enemy strategic movement within the TVD and destroyed the enemy's military and economic potential.[45]

Thus, the air operation attempted to destroy the enemy's main aviation groupings and create a favorable air situation. This required air forces to seize the initiative, retain strike power, provide freedom of movement to frontal forces, and guarantee operational success. As the air operation concluded, aviation units reverted to direct support of ground units.[46] The air operation—the principal component of the total Soviet effort to negate enemy nuclear capability in the initial periods of a conflict—sought to establish air superiority. It differed from support of the general offensive because it did not occur coincidentally with the advance of ground-maneuver forces.

Russian Impression of the Gulf War

Studying the Gulf War proved important for the Soviets as they redefined their military doctrine. Unfortunately, however, as Ben Lambeth says, "Operations Desert Shield and Desert Storm occurred at a time when the Soviet political system was hopelessly unsuited to profit from any teachings of the war because of more pressing distractions, notably an economy in ruin and the rapidly accelerating disintegration of the Soviet Union."[47] Despite the unpropitious political climate, the military's receptivity remained keen. After all, military history and experience are key factors in the formulation of Soviet doctrine. Unsurprisingly, then, lessons from the Gulf War influenced the form that the new Russian military doctrine eventually took. The Russians also used the Gulf War in defining the nature of future war.[48]

When the war began, the Soviet High Command set up a special operations group "to gather, generalize, and assess information received, and to evaluate the nature of the new arms and equipment being used, forms and methods of preparing and waging contemporary air-ground and amphibious assault operations, the control and communications systems, and questions of overall support." General of the Army Mikhail Moiseyev believed that the Gulf War served as a testing ground for the military actions and state-of-the-art hardware of the United States and NATO, and that the results would affect NATO structure and equipment in the near future.[49]

These forums combined internal and external analysis with recommendations for doctrinal changes. David M. Glantz of the Foreign Military Studies Office notes that the Soviet General Staff's assessment of the Gulf War followed six key elements: (1) the initial period of war, (2) the likely intensity and scale of combat, (3) the means (weaponry) employed, (4) the consequences for the Soviet economy and population, (5) the duration of the war, and (6) the influence of US and NATO doctrine on the Soviet doctrine of reasonable sufficiency. Glantz notes that the Soviets found the Gulf War significant because it "posed a new model of future combat in which the new military-technical dynamics of conventional combat not only have an impact upon the course and outcome of the initial period of war in the theater of military operations, but also have become synonymous with the very outcome of the war itself."[50]

Strategy

To the Soviets, strategy linked political aims with the posture of the military forces; it defined war's conditions and characteristics. Through strategy, the Soviets identified and adapted experiences related to the preparation and conduct of past wars with the study of future wars. Thus, the Gulf War was not just an exercise in weapons evaluation but a necessary and basic requirement of the Soviets' strategy-formulation process. The Gulf War altered their strategic concept about the characteristics of the danger or threat, the nature of future war, and the importance of the initial period of war.

For four decades, the Soviets' military doctrine concerned itself with opposing NATO. In evaluating the causes of the Gulf War, the High Command drew several conclusions concerning the West. It believed that the United States showed weakness in signaling a warning to Saddam Hussein of its probable response in late June 1990, when Iraq massed forces at the Kuwaiti border. The High Command also believed that the failure of the United Nations to act against aggression in South Lebanon and Panama gave Saddam a false sense of security. Further, it believed that the Western powers thought they could achieve strategic goals through local conflicts, so that now they actually encouraged war. In all these beliefs, the Soviets reinforced their old mistrust of Western hegemony.[51]

Maj Gen V. Zhurbenko, deputy head of the main department of the Soviet General Staff, said in an interview with *Tass* that the Gulf War was "without analog since World War II."[52] Mary C. FitzGerald points out that since Soviets structured the armed forces according to their view of the nature of future war, their military doctrine is "riveted to future military capabilities and environments" even in the era of "new thinking" and perestroika. Under the influence of Marshal N. V. Ogarkov in the early 1980s, the Soviets began to focus on developing advanced conventional munitions (ACM), directed-energy weapons, and space-based systems. The Soviets became convinced of the inevitability of wide-scale deployment of these weapons by their opponents. Before the Gulf War, Soviet military theorists envisioned a future war whose political-military objectives were not driven by seizing territory but by destroying the opponent's military capability and infrastructure. To FitzGerald, the Gulf War represented a confirmation of how the Soviets envisioned future war. She notes three significant effects on Soviet military thought. First, the Soviets saw a new arms race coming that emphasized implementation of strategic mobilization and deployments to theaters far from the homeland. Second, they placed new emphasis on the role of surprise as the key to victory, with airpower as the main means of achieving it. Finally, the Soviets stressed that the Gulf War served as the prototype of technological operations. They responded to the war as a confirmation of Marshal Ogarkov's ideas about technology, an invalidation of the defensive doctrine of 1987, a redefinition of deterrence in terms of nonnuclear parity, and a cause for serious concerns about the future of US-Soviet arms negotiations.[53]

Soviet concepts of future war focused on keeping war conventional. To achieve parity, the Soviets assumed that having the same number of weapons as their adversary created stability. For 40 years, they had emphasized quantity, but in the 1980s Marshal Ogarkov emphasized quality and high technology. He redefined the type of war the Soviets might realistically envision and the adjustments they might have to make to their military art.[54] The Gulf War heightened and clarified the implication of future war and the development of Soviet weapons.

Because the old idea of a military doctrine with little flexibility to respond to a variety of threats was no longer viable, the Soviets required a more varied force structure and strategic posture. Rapid reaction rather than defensive parity had to become the hallmark of Soviet strategy. Preparation for future war would require greater flexibility and diversity in forces. Military scientists would have to rely on their creativity and adaptability to new circumstances, despite economic and political problems.[55]

Local war rather than conflict between blocs of power in a TVD replaced the Soviet view of the operational-strategic scenario. Maj Gen Vladimir Slipchenko of the General Staff noted that advanced-technology weapons created a military-technical revolution in military affairs. He noted that future wars would have "no front lines or flanks," that enemy territory would consist of "targets and nontargets," and that new technology would end wars quickly: "the political structure will destroy itself, and there will be no need to occupy enemy territory."[56]

The General Staff determined that local conflicts could lead to strategic victories. Rather than an incremental tactical-operational/strategic progression, strategic goals may become the first ones attained in future war. The staff saw a serious danger, since local conflicts generate a different set of military-political objectives than do bloc struggles; thus, the old concepts of struggles for national survival and unconditional surrender were no longer operative. In many ways, the Soviets saw this situation as a cause of direct US involvement and of their own indirect involvement in a dispute among Iraq, Kuwait, and Saudi Arabia.

The General Staff argued that preemption offered the only way to avoid defeat in progressively threatening situations against a powerful opponent because the military would have no time to develop a defensive phase while preparing for a viable counteroffensive.[57] This course of action became particularly important if the opponent waged an air operation similar in size and scope to that in the Gulf War. The war vividly displayed the new strategic importance of the initial period. If the fighting involved high-tech precision munitions, the Soviets realized that the initial period might decide the war rather than simply influence its outcome and length. Future weapons capitalized on the qualities of speed, mobility, lethality, and accuracy, thereby significantly increasing the value of two of the Soviets' prized principles of war—surprise and initiative. One General Staff officer observed that the "war's outcome was decided by gaining the initiative and winning air superiority; Hussein did not preempt and so he lost!"[58] Security and support advanced from secondary to strategic importance. General of the Army N. Klokotov noted that "Iraq made a strategic error. Its forces were prepared for a battle in which the means of 'strike' were preeminent. To civilized states this is a thing of the past. Now not only means of strike but also means of security such as reconnaissance, radio-electronic warfare, means of guidance, and effective defense are of prime importance. Therefore Iraq's strike means were unprotected."[59]

The Soviets said that the conduct of the air operation represented the most important factor in changing the relevance of the initial period. Lt Gen A. E. Maliukov, then chief of staff of the Soviet air force, said that the Gulf War confirmed the impact of aviation on tactical surprise and its execution. Future war required an air capability to repel initial attacks and then mount its own air offensive. The key, as the Soviets defined the Gulf War, lay in protecting the control of air forces and training air commanders to act independently.[60]

Of all the Soviet statements made about the Gulf War, Lt Gen A. I. Yevseyev's proclamation for Soviet doctrine had no precedent. In contrast to past wars, he noted that "the main content of the initial period can be the delivery by the belligerents of nuclear strikes or strikes with conventional means of destruction . . . for achieving the war's main objectives."[61] In the past, Soviet military theorists believed that only nuclear weapons achieved a war's main objective in the initial period. To Soviet military theorists, the coalition had achieved nuclear effects in the initial period by using air-delivered, high-tech conventional weapons.

Operational Art

Operational art describes how Soviet forces are formed, organized, and employed to achieve military strategy. Soviet operational art, which encompasses the operational-level commander's sphere of actions, had become focused on speed, mass, shock, and firepower of preeminent ground forces, with other services in a supporting role. The success of the coalition air operation in the Gulf War caused Soviet military theorists to reassess their old concept of operational art.

Airpower's Role. One of the first assessments appearing in the Soviet press addressed airpower's ascendancy. The Soviets noted that the priority of actions of the United States (and possibly theirs, by inference) had changed. *Tass* military analyst Vladimir Chernyshev commented, "The 'classic' form of combat gave the main role to land forces in military actions, and the air force supports them. Here [the Gulf War] everything has been different: I would say the basic blows of strategic, decisive significance were struck by the Air Forces."[62]

The Soviets saw the Gulf War as a repudiation of Giulio Douhet's ideas about airpower.[63] They did not feel that the Gulf War justified building a force structure that emphasized strategic bombardment; however, they felt they needed parity in ground-air-space weapons to present a credible deterrent to a potential threat.[64] Although the Soviets saw success in war as a joint effort of all the services, General Maliukov found Douhet's ideas of attacks against industrial and population centers relevant to the Gulf War's outcome.[65] He viewed these strikes as part of the psychological warfare to wear down the Iraqi people. In the May 1991 issue of *Voennaia mysl (Military Thought)*, he said that the initial period of war confirmed the increased role of aviation to combat power. The Gulf War confirmed the impact of aviation on tactical surprise and its execution. More importantly, he said that the defensive cast of Soviet military doctrine implied an air capability able to repel initial attacks and mount its own air operation. He went on to state that this would occur only by protecting the control of the air and giving air commanders the ability to operate independently.[66]

General Maliukov also said that the Gulf War "constituted a textbook example of what air supremacy means—both for the country that gained it and for the country ceding it to the opponent." When asked whether he felt the war reflected a practical application of the American doctrine of AirLand Battle, he answered,

> I do not think so. There was no classical "air-land battle." Why? The point is that this war—and here General [Michael] Dugan comes to mind—was obviously conceived from the outset as an air war to wear out the opponent by means of air strikes, disorganize his command

503

systems, destroy his air defenses, and weaken the ground forces' striking power. In terms of the choice of objectives, it was more a case of a classic air offense. And these objectives were achieved. Broadly speaking, this is the first time we have seen a war which aviation took care almost entirely of all the main tasks.[67]

The mobility, speed, and accuracy of modern weapons systems are combat multipliers. This factor makes surprise and initiative, especially in the initial period, the most important of all military principles. During the Gulf War, the Soviets defined coalition airpower as devastating. Maj Gen I. Vorobyev, retired Soviet military scientist, underscored the unique role of airpower when he said it played "the decisive role . . . in destroying the enemy. . . . This has never been demonstrated so clearly in any operation in the past."[68] He called for a "prompt and fundamental review of existing [Soviet] ideas and propositions in the field of tactics and doctrine," noting that Iraq's defeat was not caused by "any weakness in weapons or combat equipment, but by the habit, dogmatism, stereotype, and conventionalism in the leadership of the troops. . . . And this is a graphic lesson for everybody. This *includes our armed forces*" (emphasis added).[69] On the operational and tactical levels, the Iraqis made errors forced on them by the loss of initiative and coalition air superiority.[70] The Soviets concluded that any force trying to defend without mobility or without the ability to strike a maneuvering enemy from the air would fail. Maneuvers by large ground forces required air superiority. To a degree, aircraft assumed the primary role as the most maneuverable and long-range means of fighting, despite Iraq's combat advantage in tanks.[71]

The General Staff examined the air operation in the March 1991 issue of *Morskoi sbornik (Naval Anthology)*. It stressed that command of the air made a systematic air campaign possible. In the initial period, the air campaign struck Iraqi command and control (C^2), air defense, and military-industrial targets. Following the initial phase, the campaign shifted to interdiction, seeking to isolate the region of combat operations. Following the air interdiction (AI) phase, the center of gravity for the air operation shifted to direct support of ground forces. Capt First Rank K. Kzheb of the Soviet navy outlined the coalition air operation: "The primary stake in the war was placed in the allies' massive use of their airpower to keep losses on the ground to an absolute minimum. The immediate goal was to disarm, blind, deafen, and decapitate the enemy from the very outset to achieve control of the air. Then, allied airpower was applied at will to systematically destroy the Iraqi strategic infrastructure and 'isolate the area of upcoming combat operations, along with concurrent destruction of Iraq's troops and military equipment.' "[72]

Perhaps the strongest proponent of airpower's role in the Gulf War was General Slipchenko of the General Staff. He noted that the coalition air campaign set the outcome from the opening moments of the Gulf War, even intimating that the war had cast serious doubt on the relevance of the ground forces as traditionally structured. "The Gulf War supports the fact that *air strikes can by themselves form the basis of victory. . . .* Airpower was responsible for the victory, because air superiority altered the complexion of the war from the very outset" (emphasis added).[73]

Force Structure. The principle of strategic posturing had defined how the Soviets generated, positioned, and mobilized forces. It called for forces capable of multidirectional fighting and able to work with Warsaw Pact members; it also required that they deploy in a fully developed TVD. Internal changes within the Soviet Union and the demise of the Warsaw Pact, however, invalidated this concept. With the bulk of the Soviet forces undergoing redeployment, force structuring took on new meaning as regards the concept of strategic security.

From the beginning of the Gulf War, coalition strategic posturing impressed the Soviets. Initially, many Soviet officers thought the coalition mission was impossible, given the multiethnic makeup of the forces and the distances involved. As the war went on, however, this opinion changed. The Soviets cited coalition preparation and cooperation of the forces as crucial to the victory. Further, examination of the coalition heightened their awareness of a professional force. The Soviets saw that coalition professionals performed much better than Iraq's conscript force.[74] Many General Staff officers unanimously concluded that people controlling the technology decided a war's outcome more than the technology itself.[75] Gen N. Kutsenko of the General Staff expressed this sentiment best in his assessment that "more depends on the professional training of the people operating and servicing the equipment than its quality; it is of decisive significance."[76]

With the initial period of war ascending to new importance, the Soviets saw implications for their mobilization planning and force structure. The coalition overcame distances through extensive logistical support. For the Soviets, that placed a premium on developing a rapid-deployment force to project power and protect vital interests. By building a similar capability, they believed they could deter local wars and began reorganizing their forces into a rapid-reaction force.[77] The General Staff argued that a key aspect of the coalition's success lay in its ability to transport people and equipment halfway around the world through the close coordination of air and sea transport.

Technology, Research, and Development. Col-Gen Y. Shaposhnikov, commander in chief of the Soviet air force, noted in an interview that the Gulf War gave the General Staff an opportunity to observe and evaluate American airpower— the first time that circumstances had allowed an assessment under real combat conditions on such an unprecedented scale. Dr. V. Tsygichko, head of Moscow's National Security and Strategic Stability Studies Center, admitted at a lecture at Supreme Headquarters Allied Powers Europe on 5 March 1991, that models run by the General Staff before the Gulf War had grossly overestimated the coalition's losses and failed to predict the outcome. He blamed this failure on not having reliable parameters to assign to the allied weapons, pointing out that their models contained no factors to account for the Iraqis' poor discipline and morale. Finally, he noted that the air campaign lasted considerably longer than most Soviet analysts had predicted.[78]

Of extreme importance, these models contained algorithms based on the Soviets' previous notions of the nature of future war. The failure of the models repudiated the previous doctrinal base for predicting what the nature of future war might hold. Marshal S. Achromeyev supported Tsygichko's views by affirming that the Soviet estimates "were based on classic AirLand Battle doctrine." Increasing the air campaign to 40 days invalidated the projection models. Achromeyev implied that the models had their basis in a Central European scenario by stating, "The conduct of air operations of such duration against an enemy approximately equal in strength would have been impossible."[79]

The General Staff convened another roundtable in mid-March 1991 to evaluate the performance of Soviet air defense equipment in the Gulf War and to determine the effects on research and development (R&D). Senior officers stifled the formal presentations, trying to avoid criticism and contentious issues. Consequently, some junior officers in attendance noted that most of the interesting and compelling comments occurred "in the lobby." Some of the core issues they thought needed attention included the "lamentable condition" of Soviet military science and defense preparations and the failure of their air defense organization (PVO) to provide them with "the most modern systems available." They also commented about the need to replace "obsolete models of weapons that accomplish little, as evidenced by the Gulf War."[80]

Influenced by the coalition's success in the Gulf War, Defense Minister Andrei S. Grachev listed the following seven priority items for continued R&D: highly mobile troops; army aviation; long-range ACMs; command, control, communications, and intelligence (C^3I) systems; space systems; air defense systems; and strategic arms.[81] As a result of the General Staff's analysis of the Gulf War, political and military leaders reached a consensus on maintaining R&D at the expense of procurement, as the Russian defense budget shrinks. The Russians believe they cannot "be second best" in stealth and ACMs,[82] noting that they were seven to 10 years behind in the latter.

After talking to the editorial staff of *Voennaia mysl* in April 1992, Ben Lambeth deduced some broad outlines of the High Command's thinking as regards the meaning of Operation Desert Storm. Four recurrent themes emerged that should affect R&D: (1) the broadened role played by conventional airpower in deciding war's outcome; (2) the criticality of good training and operator proficiency in getting the most out of modern weaponry; (3) the disproportionate leverage offered by high-tech weapons as a force multiplier; and (4) the meaning of these and related findings for future Russian defense planning and policy.[83] According to Lambeth, the Russians concluded that the nature of modern war had changed radically in the last few years, noting that although airpower might not win a war by itself, it had become the decisive force which permitted the attainment of victory, yet kept friendly losses to a minimum. Their assessment contained radical ideas for planners of Russian military doctrine:

- The Soviet concept of redundant, overlapping, and integrated air defenses contained serious flaws.
- Tanks become an endangered species without control of the air.
- Quality beats quantity, but one must have enough of it to matter.
- Coalition warfare works, but it's difficult to conduct.
- Soviet concepts of offensive air operations need revision.
- Top-down centralization remains critical to effective combat operations, but it must have flexibility in execution.
- Hardened shelters no longer shelter.
- Stealth is the wave of the future.
- Ground warfare, as well as air, has undergone a technical revolution.
- The end of the cold war made Gorbachev's defensive doctrine obsolete.[84]

On 8 February 1989, Colonel-General Moiseyev, first deputy defense minister and chief of the USSR Armed Forces General Staff, declared his candidacy as a USSR people's deputy from the Communist Party of the Soviet Union (CPSU). He focused part of his campaign on changing the military doctrinal-review process to give it greater meaning in the General Staff. Additionally, his comments seemed to possess clear foresight in describing the doctrinal review process that followed the Gulf War two years later. His campaign speech noted that "it appears that we should also revise our attitudes toward work on long-term problems. . . . But responsibility for the end results [of the General Staff] has been understated. The situation is different now. . . . Many difficult problems that the troops are encountering today can be traced back, with careful analysis, to our lack of foresight, our shortsightedness. . . . The new nature of the tasks now being resolved requires the development of creative activeness on the part of all directorates and every official; it requires initiative and inquisitiveness in work."[85]

Emerging Russian Post–Gulf War Military Doctrine

The Soviets had to respond to many internal and external political, economic, and social disruptions in the late 1980s and early 1990s, one such response involving a review and revision of their military doctrine. The "crowning blow" may have been their reaction to the Gulf War in light of all the other internal and external changes under way. The Gulf War showed that planning for a counterattack, as Gorbachev's defensive doctrine dictated, required the Soviets to react instead of act. To the Soviets, this was an unacceptable form of action in light of their Gulf War assessment of an era of high-tech weapons.[86]

In May 1992, the Russian High Command released a new draft of military doctrine by publishing it in *Voennaia mysl,* their foremost armed forces theoretical journal.[87] In November 1993, the Russians formalized this effort by releasing the approved doctrine in *Rossiyskiye Vesti (Russian News).*[88] The new doctrine established the prevention of war as the fundamental goal of security policy of the Russian Federation. It also established a system of views regarding the organization of the armed forces, the country's defense preparations, the countermeasures to threats to the state's military security, and the utilization of the armed forces of the Russian Federation. As in prior military doctrines of the former Soviet Union, the effort stated that one carries out the provisions of military doctrine by means of the "coordinated measures of a political, economic, legal, and military nature with the participation of all organs of state power and administration, public organizations, and citizens of the Russia Federation."[89] Military doctrine within the Russian Federation derived its force of law from the agreement and approval of the state's legislative body, the Congress of People's Deputies.

The Threat

The new military doctrine listed several scenarios that future war might take. It placed primary emphasis on meeting threats that endangered Russian sovereignty or territory—either autonomously or as part of the Confederation of Independent States (CIS). It also noted that hostilities might result from economic or political pressure from a major power.[90] In the past, figuring out the character of a threat normally fell to Marxist-Leninist ideology within the sociopolitical dimension of military doctrine.

Although it did not specifically identify potential enemies, the new doctrine listed several factors that could lead to conflict,[91] describing them as possible sources of "military danger."[92] First, the Russians viewed NATO's military power and the American presence in Europe and the Far East as their greatest potential danger.[93] Second, the doctrine examined the anxiety over the rise of global or regional powers, especially Germany, Japan, Iran, and Turkey. Third, the doctrine noted the pressure exerted by the leverage that Western economics might create against the Russian government. Last, it echoed the concern over America's exerting military power beyond its borders to further the aims of foreign policy.[94] The doctrine also described two direct threats to Russia: (1) the introduction of foreign troops into any of its adjacent states—a concept similar to the stereotypical direct threat to *Rodina* [95] and (2) the buildup of air, naval, and ground forces near Russian borders.[96]

View of Future War

According to the new doctrine, local wars represented the most probable type of conflict. Large-scale conventional war could occur when local hostilities directed against the Russian Federation, the CIS, or other states close to Russia's borders escalated into full-fledged coalition war. This evolution to conventional warfare followed a fairly prolonged threat period and general mobilization.[97]

According to this scenario, large-scale intervention by the West against the CIS or Russia could occur with either long or short warning. The hostility probably would occur in two phases. First, the enemy would attack with combined naval and air offensive strikes at important economic and military targets, using PGMs and electronic jamming. These attacks would disable Russian command centers and prevent reserve mobilization and force deployment. The opening attacks would attempt to force an early withdrawal of Russia's allies and least reliable coalition partners from the war. The second phase of the war would include an intense ground campaign conducted under the cover of powerful and decisive air forces. In many ways, the new military doctrine rehashed the factors that won the Great Patriotic War—repulse of a massive conventional invasion requiring full mobilization of all the state's resources.

The Gulf War motivated the Russians to redefine aggression and make adjustments to their fundamental ideas about operational art. The doctrine listed primary tasks to safeguard military security when war threatened or seemed imminent. For the military, such tasks included mobilizing and equipping forces to repulse and defeat an aggressor.[98]

Force Structure and Priorities

The new doctrine contained guidance for the composition and priorities of Russian armed forces. It specified enough forces in permanent readiness to deter and repel local aggression. Further, the doctrine identified mobile reserves capable of rapid response and deployment to repel midlevel aggression when combined with the ready forces. Last, it required strategic reserves to conduct large-scale combat actions. The top priority task for all forces entailed developing and exploiting "the emerging high precision, mobile, highly survivable, long-range, stand-off weapons."[99]

The Russians' second priority was also directly linked to the military-technical aspect of military doctrine. The new doctrine specified "arms, equipment, and C^{3}I systems whose *qualities* allow a reduced *quantity* of arms" and called for reducing serial production while maintaining research, development, and production capabilities that rapidly surge the emerging technologies (emphasis added).[100]

The new doctrine saw the role of the Russian armed forces as defeating missile attacks, protecting strategic targets such

511

as administration and industrial infrastructure, and carrying out retaliatory strikes.[101] Defeating surprise aviation-missile attacks represented a new strategic concept to the Russians. They saw Desert Storm as a new type of combat—the electronic fire operation—consisting of surprise attacks involving massed and prolonged missile, aerospace, electronic, and naval strikes conducted for several days or weeks. Further, the Russians thought that by disrupting the military-economic capability to ensure victory in political and economic arenas, these operations would deny the enemy the ability to continue the war and reconstitute his forces. Unlike massed ground warfare, these attacks did not aim to seize and occupy land.

Differences with Pre–Gulf War Military Doctrine

C. J. Dick points out that the new draft military doctrine was drawn up by a General Staff that had not "undergone a revolution of the mind and who, far from being in tune with Gorbachevian 'new thinking' were still unreconstructed Cold War warriors paying lip service to *perestroika* while trying to preserve the old system as far as they could." This situation divorced the new military doctrine from government policy and reality. In many ways, the new doctrine resembled the old, viewing the world through a distorted prism. It remained hostile to the West—implicitly, if not explicitly. Even after four years of internal political, economic, ideological, and social strife, the new military doctrine persisted in worst-case analysis. According to Dick, the Russian military failed to recognize this approach as a major cause of the collapse of the Soviet economy in the first place.[102]

In a marked departure from the pre–Gulf War Gorbachev era, the new doctrine made no provision for restricting the scale or depth of the Russian army's counteroffensive. Additionally, it made no explicit references to defensive strategy or defensive operations. In many ways, the new military doctrine reminded one of Brezhnev doctrine, albeit a high-tech version. But it differed significantly from that of the Gorbachev era in several other ways. Specifically, the old doctrine had emphasized the prevention of war by repelling aggression, and the new doctrine specified optimized forces for all possible wars and combat missions.[103] The new doctrine's main objective entailed "localiz[ing] a seat of tension and terminat[ing] military operations at the earliest possible stage in the interests of creating preconditions . . . on conditions that accord with the interests of the Russian Federation. . . . The forms, methods and means of conducting combat operations that best accord with the prevailing situation and ensure that the initiative is seized and the aggressor defeated must be chosen."[104]

Under Gorbachev's military doctrine, reasonable sufficiency meant conducting no large-scale conventional operations. Under the new doctrine, however, the conventional-sufficiency provision provided for additional deployments, making large-scale conventional operations possible and clearly rejecting Gorbachev's prohibition against large-scale conventional offensives.[105] Gorbachev's doctrine stressed repulsing an aggressor and forming subsequent defensive actions based on the nature of the enemy's operations. The new military doctrine amplified an old theme—destruction of the enemy.

The new military doctrine viewed nuclear war as an extension of large-scale conventional operations. Thus, it saw conventional "smart" weapon attacks against C^2 facilities, storage depots for chemical and biological weapons, nuclear energy and research facilities, and nuclear forces themselves in the same light as releasing weapons of mass destruction and inviting retaliation in kind. This perspective significantly departed from a major tenet of the Gorbachev doctrine, which held that nuclear war *will* be catastrophic. The new doctrine refined this assumption to *might* be catastrophic. The old doctrine discussed nuclear war as global in nature—attempting to limit it to specific regions would prove almost impossible. In the new doctrine, however, both concepts were missing, insofar as Russia refuted its commitment to no first use of nuclear weapons, seeing limited regional nuclear war as a possibility.[106]

Doctrinal statements clearly reflect the lessons of the Gulf War. Specifically, the new doctrine expects Russian commanders to balance troop training in both defensive and offensive operations, hold the country's vital areas, restore the status quo along its borders, and eventually rout the enemy. Gorbachev's earlier military doctrine espoused more modest terms of cessation to hostilities. The pre–Gulf War doctrine specifically addressed partial victory, enemy withdrawal, and restoration of peace. The new doctrine's resurrected idea of "total victory" incorporates traditional Soviet thinking that prevailed well into the late 1980s.

Most important of all, the new doctrine stressed the decisive importance of the initial period of war.[107] In Desert Storm, the Russians saw the initial period consisting of air strikes aimed at disrupting enemy strategic deployments, disorganizing civilian and military C^3I, and collapsing any enemy coalition. The Russians' new doctrine specifies the destruction of economic and military targets by ACMs simultaneously or preemptively with electronic warfare.[108] Of significance is the Russians' new belief that ACMs could accomplish missions once thought possible only by nuclear weapons. To the Russians, superiority in EW and C^3I are necessary and sufficient to ensure victory in warfare.[109]

Both the Gorbachev doctrine and the new military doctrine stress the need to obtain high-technology weapons and maintain a mass-mobilization capability. Neither doctrine seems to accept the social, economic, and political reality that might stand in the military's way of carrying out that doctrine. C. J. Dick aptly cites the Russian General Staff for living in an "Alice in Wonderland world," reinforced by its assertion that force reductions can take place only when the right military-technical, economic, and social conditions are created.[110]

Analysis and Implications

In the early 1980s, Marshal Ogarkov argued that emerging technologies were generating a new revolution in military affairs.[111] The Russians' response to Desert Storm and their reformed military doctrine seem to confirm Ogarkov's predictions by (1) reverting from a defensive to an offensive preemptive position; (2) reverting from no nuclear first use to a possibility of nuclear escalation; (3) guaranteeing the 25 million ethnic Russians living in former Soviet states protection from any kind of retaliation; (4) emphasizing the importance of military advancement in command, control, communications, computers, and intelligence (C^4I), smart weapons, and increased mobility; and (5) emphasizing strategic nonnuclear deterrent forces.

Several factors contributed to evolving Russian military doctrine: the explosion of nationalism in the face of communism's collapse, the diminished role of the military in developing policy, and Russian loss in controlling the direction of the CIS. Clearly, the new doctrine represents the Russians' response to what they saw in the Gulf War, especially the impact of airpower on its outcome. More than just a response to social, political, and economic changes, the new doctrine represents the reemergence of the Russian military as a policy developer in the new state. The Russians saw the Gulf War as a new form of war, involving the decisive use of surprise and high-tech systems. More importantly, they saw the initial period of war change from a preparatory phase to perhaps its *only* phase, in which airpower's role had become dominant. Because their doctrine proved inadequate for building on the Desert Storm experience, they changed it to address *their* lessons of the Gulf War.

They did so because they saw that deep first strikes with technologically superior weapons could achieve strategic objectives quickly and inexpensively. Thus, the Russians reverted to a revisionist military doctrine, reinforcing their earlier ideas about the preeminence of the offense. The Gulf War cleared their perception and put security threats in a different light: the need to protect their interests following "the breakup of the former Soviet Union, the loss of their former allies, the emergence of new hotbeds of military tensions along their southern borders, and the deterioration of the internal political and social fabric" of their country.[112] Lambeth is correct when he points out that the fate of the Russian military remains "inseparably tied to the political and economic fate of post-Soviet Russia."[113]

During the final days of the Soviet Union, defense outlays fell more than 23 percent—2.3 million rubles—from the 1990 levels. In 1992 the Russians redirected about 70 percent of their defense budget into the social sector. Additionally, Russian politicians programmed almost 70 percent of the remaining defense budget for construction of military family housing to solve critical shortages and fund social programs for badly deprived military personnel. By late 1993 the promised military funding allocations were more than *three trillion rubles in arrears*. To compensate for declining investment in military equipment, the Russian military bartered first-line arms for capital to augment its declining operations and maintenance costs.[114] Jacob Kipp points out that the Russian military was using many of the arms sales and barters to pay for the cost of demobilization.[115] Yet, the defense minister claimed that the Russian army would "eventually have the most advanced weapons,"[116] while at the same time the economic crisis compelled the Russians to cut their military force structure considerably—to as low as 1.5 million.[117] Clearly, it is a long way from bartering for operations and maintenance funds back to military superpower status.

In the new military doctrine, the General Staff all but ignores political instability from within and prepares to fight an air-space war against a major adversary. To many military and civilian leaders, this strategy represents the Russians' clearest chance at maintaining military superpower status. In the near term, they will rely on countering the US air-space domination of air-space technology—namely cruise missiles, space sensors, stealth, and so forth. For the long term, they plan to build the infrastructure capable of producing the advanced technologies they need for the Russian armed forces. Somewhere in between is what Mary FitzGerald calls the "transition period," with its reliance on limited nuclear war to deter and defeat worse-case threats. Given the Russians' analysis from the Gulf War that they lag the United States in weapons technology, their policy of nuclear first use makes sense. The revolution in military technology meant that the Russian Federation would no longer hold its own in a conventional conflict with the United States. What better way to avert military disaster than to convince their adversary that Russia would use nuclear weapons from the very outbreak of war? This tactic provides protection only in the near term and does not solve Russia's other problems with military technology.[118] In short, this threat of a return to massive retaliation may have a healthy component of deception, designed to delay the outbreak of a conflict until Russia masters new advances in warfare.

According to Andrei Kokoshin, civilian deputy defense minister in charge of Russia's military-industrial complex (VPK), the new doctrine focuses R&D efforts to create a "scientific-technical reserve in critical technologies."[119] The new doctrine reduces serial production but maintains R&D and production capacity to rapidly surge new technology when required. This allows the R&D effort to "hover," so that the defense industry can leap over a generation of weapons by focusing on prototypes. Their own analysis of the Gulf War should have taught the Russians that future war will be short and decisive and will have a fairly short notice. Even the five-month buildup and redeployment during Operation Desert Shield proved fairly rapid, given the amount of material and personnel involved. Relying on hovering assumes that Russia will have sufficient strategic warning to change prototypes and hovered technology into weapons for employment. The timing of future war may leave the Russians no time to turn technological potential into weapons reality.[120] It is one thing to possess the R&D but another matter to turn that into weapons production.

One cannot discuss Soviet/Russian military doctrine apart from the political structure from which it is derived. The new doctrine still implies that the political-social means give the military doctrine form; however, it completely ignores political means for preventing war. It never mentions crisis management or war termination. As in the Great Patriotic War, destruction of the enemy and victory become possible only when armed force carries out the will of the state. The force structure needed to station forces forward to protect borders and the capital expenditure for high-tech weapons should cause concern to Russia as it tries to rebuild its economy. To carry out this new military doctrine, Russia will need to spend on the military as it did before, risking the same economic disaster. In the new Russian military lexicon, the idea of "geopolitics" replaces that of the domination of the political-social component of military doctrine. This change amplifies the Russians' primary focus on threats nearer to their own borders, with aggression from former Soviet states and forces within Russian autonomous regions taking on added importance.

Perhaps even more perplexing, the new military doctrine identifies factors beyond those discussed in the former versions. The new doctrine's identification of rights of Russian citizens in foreign states, external political pressure, and economic pressure as an excuse for war is most troubling.[121] Speaking in February 1994, President Yeltsin called Russia the "guarantor of stability" throughout the former Soviet Union, saying that the fate of ethnic Russians living in neighboring states was "our national concern. . . . When it comes to violations of the lawful rights of Russian people, this is not the exclusive internal affair of some country, but also our national affair, an affair of our state."[122] He warned East European countries not to join NATO without Russia. Further, he noted that Russia's foreign policy sought to promote the country's own interests. Surely, Russia's neighbors will worry about these ill-defined rights and the use of military force.

Everywhere one looks in Russia today, the military is implementing ambitious plans to reshape its forces. Clearly, economics and the demise of the Soviet Union forced a good deal of this restructuring on the Russian military. In many cases, the final force structure was determined by what the Russians could afford—not what their new doctrine advocated. The Russian air force is a case in point.[123] The new structure makes the once powerful air defense forces extinct, with their combat elements absorbed by the Russian air force. The surface-to-air units of the defense forces will go to the ground forces. The independent air armies of the Supreme High Command are restructured into territorial commands, in which frontal aviation forces will also reside. This reorganization fractures the Russians' air forces vertically and horizontally at the exact time their new doctrine reinforces what they say they learned about airpower from the Gulf War. With the new doctrine focused on threats from the "near abroad,"[124] army mobile forces have emerged as preeminent.

Thus, the Russians reverted to a military functional structure based on their stereotypical operational art. Although they recognize that Western airpower and space power represent the primary threat to Russian joint combat operations, practical Russian airpower theory plays down its independent role in combat operations, thus emphasizing its support of ground operations. Regardless of emerging aerospace technology, then, Russian airpower will remain fragmented.

Clearly, the new doctrine gives the Russian military exactly the theoretical base it always wanted. By 1991 the Russian military had become institutionally paralyzed. The new thinking under Gorbachev led to radical changes in security policy that proved increasingly untenable. In 1987 the Ministry of Defense began subverting and resisting Gorbachev's changes to a defensive posture. In effect, progressive dissolution of political controls over the military emancipated the General Staff to act, first covertly and then openly, in revising doctrine to its former offensive high. As Communist Party control atrophied, the General Staff increasingly expanded its influence over politicians and elevated its standing with President Yeltsin by putting down the "White House" revolt. Col-Gen Igor Rodionov's opposition to Russia's first doctrinal draft, which refuted the first use of nuclear weapons, eliminated defensive sufficiency, and refined the nature of future war, indicated the rise of the Russian military in political stature and control. The net result is a politicized Russian military. Rather than accept tenets of doctrine passed to it from its political masters, as in the past, the military formed its own doctrinal ideas and passed them to the politicians for approval. More importantly, Rodionov's success in changing the doctrine to a more provocative and revisionist view by carrying it from a defensive to an offensive posture, shows how far the politicization process may already have come. The Russian military is now a developer of doctrine—not just an implementer, as in the past. The emergence of an offensively structured doctrine dramatically displays the commitment that Yeltsin is willing to make to the military.

Today, the pressing demands of military housing and social crisis within its forces preoccupy the Russian military. Force modernization, training, tactics, and other mission-related concerns remain on the back burner. Clearly, the new military doctrine shows that the Russians became excessively impressed and concerned about the technological wizardry unleashed during Desert Storm. Preoccupied with looking outward, they neglected to look inward at the contribution made by the former Soviet military to the collapse of the Soviet Union and the Warsaw Pact.

In essence, Russian military doctrine lacks reality. Any analyst reading the new doctrine must wonder whether the Russians learned any lesson at all from the collapse of the USSR, the Warsaw Pact, and the Russian economy. Even though the populace of the former Soviet Union rejected the military's perception of the requirements for defense, the Russian Federation General Staff seems determined to continue chasing that chimera. At a time when Russians are seeking help from the West to stimulate their economy and social structure, one wonders about the Russian General Staff's grasp of reality—namely, Russia's status in the world, the condition of the CIS, and the domestic situation. A close reading of the Russian Federation's draft military doctrine shows a clear danger of Russian military policy moving divergently from foreign and domestic policies.

Notes

1. Charles Dick, "Russian Views on Future Wars," *Jane's Intelligence Review*, September 1993, 390.

2. M. A. Gareev, "On Military Doctrine and Military Reform in Russia," *Journal of Soviet Military Studies*, December 1992, 540.

3. Doctrine *(voennaia doctrina)*, as defined by the Soviets, has two important framing aspects: sociopolitical and military-technical. The military policy of the Communist Party expressed the sociopolitical aspect, based on a classic Marxist-Leninist view of the world. Its ideas about the political essence of modern war stemmed from the nature of the Soviet state and social system, and from historical principles of military organizational development. It took account of the international correlation of forces and a scientifically based thesis on the psychological and moral-political nature of the people.

The military-technical aspect determines the character of the military threat and the type of armed struggle to be fought. It serves as the basis for determining defense requirements and needs of the armed forces. Further, it establishes the means to conduct armed struggle and prepare the armed forces to accomplish their missions and tasks. See Timothy L. Thomas, "The Soviet Military on 'Desert Storm': Redefining Doctrine?" *Journal of Soviet Military Studies*, December 1991, 594–620; Soviet Studies Research Centre, *The Sustainability of the Soviet Army in Battle* (Sandhurst, United Kingdom: Royal Military Academy, 1986), 4–32; and *The Voroshilov Lectures: Materials from the Soviet General Staff Academy*, ed. Graham H. Turbiville Jr. and comp. Ghulam D. Wardak, vol. 1, *Issues of Soviet Military Strategy* (Washington, D.C.: National Defense University Press, 1989), 380–84.

4. *The Voroshilov Lectures*, vol. 1, 385.

5. Benjamin Lambeth, *How to Think about Soviet Military Doctrine* (Santa Monica, Calif.: RAND, 1978), 4.

6. Charles J. Dick, "Initial Thoughts on Russia's Draft Military Doctrine," *Journal of Soviet Military Studies*, December 1992, 552.

7. Strategy dealt with the preparation, timing, and execution of strategic operations by groups of fronts in separate or adjacent theaters of military operations (TVD); operational art concerned actions of fronts and other operational groupings. TVD is a Russian acronym for *Teatr voenykh deistvii.* In the Soviet context, *front* describes an organization of tactical units into an operational-level force structure. Fronts are created from combined-arms armies, tank armies, and front air armies. In the Soviet lexicon, the term describes force structure, organization, and strategic mission instead of a geographical area. See *The Voroshilov Lectures*, vol. 1, 357–68.

8. Ibid., 55–59.

9. Thomas, 595.

10. John G. Hines and Donald Mahoney, *Defense and Counteroffensive under the New Soviet Military Doctrine* (Santa Monica, Calif.: RAND, 1991), 13.

11. The "initial period of war" occurs when operations are carried out by those forces deployed before the outbreak of war to achieve the initial strategic objectives or to create favorable conditions for the committal of main forces which are mobilizing and deploying during the initial period. Dick, "Initial Thoughts," 555.

12. M. V. Gareyev, "Frunze—Military Theorist," in Hines and Mahoney, 13.

13. Michael MccGwire, "Soviet Military Doctrine: Contingency Planning and the Reality of the World War," *Survival*, May–June 1980, 107, 112.

14. One analyst stated that "lessons learned by the Soviet military leadership during World War II . . . provided the most important impetus to the development of modern Soviet military doctrine." See William Schneider Jr., "Soviet General-Purpose Forces," *Orbis*, Spring 1977, 96.

15. Dr. Jonathan R. Adelman, "The Evolution of Soviet Military Doctrine, 1945–84," *Air University Review*, March–April 1985, 28.

16. V. D. Sokolovskii, *Soviet Military Strategy*, trans. Herbert Dinerstein, Leon Gourè, and Thomas Wolfe (Englewood Cliffs, N.J.: Prentice-Hall, 1963), 83.

17. S. N. Kozlov, *The Officer's Handbook: A Soviet View*, trans. multilingual section, secretary of state, government of Canada (Washington, D.C.: Government Printing Office, 1971), 29.

18. Marshal V. D. Sokolovskii pointed out that "armed conflict in ground theaters would also be different," predicting that missile attacks would become the primary means of defeating an enemy's ground forces, missiles, tanks, and aircraft. He saw nuclear weapons as the primary means of resolving combat in a TVD. Sokolovskii, 299, 306.

19. *The Voroshilov Lectures*, vol. 1, 263–76.

20. S. Biryuzov, "The Lessons of the Beginning Period of the Great Patriotic War," *Soviet Military Review*, no. 8 (1964): 26.

21. M. Povaliy, "Development of Soviet Military Strategy," *Soviet Military Review*, February 1967, 70.

22. *The Voroshilov Lectures*, vol. 1, 382.

23. Hines and Mahoney, 7.

24. B. Samorukov, "Combat Operations Involving Conventional Means of Destruction," *Soviet Military Review*, August 1976, 28–30.

25. Adelman, 33.

26. Quoted in Dr. Robert F. Miller, "Echoes of *Perestroika*," *Pacific Defense Reporter*, December 1989–January 1990, 7.

27. Graham T. Allison Jr., "Testing Gorbachev," *Foreign Affairs*, Fall 1988, 23–26.

28. Andrew C. Goldberg, "The Present Turbulence in Soviet Military Doctrine," *Washington Quarterly*, Summer 1988, 164–67.

29. Raymond L. Garthoff, "New Thinking in Soviet Military Doctrine," *Washington Quarterly*, Summer 1988, 137–41.

30. Dimitriy Yazov, "Interview with General Yazov," *Danas*, 15 November 1989, 54–58, in Joint Publications Research Service (JPRS), JPRS-UMA-89-002-L, 19 January 1989, 8.

31. Hines and Mahoney, 100.

32. Boll uses evidence from Soviet and East German archives to make clear that the Soviets' war plans were clearly offensive at a time when their "official" doctrine was defensive. He implies that at the operational, tactical, and training levels, the Soviet and Warsaw Pact militaries disregarded the defensive doctrine imposed by Gorbachev. See Michael M. Boll, "By Blood, Not Ballots: German Unification, Communist Style," *Parameters*, Spring 1994, 71–75.

33. Lt Col Lester W. Grau, "Continuity and Change: A Soviet General Staff View of Future Theater War," *Military Review*, December 1991, 13–17.

34. Marshal Ogarkov had seen this technological advantage coming for the West as early as 1984:

> Rapid changes in the development of conventional means of destruction and the emergence in developed countries of automated reconnaissance-strike complexes; long-range, highly accurate, terminally guided combat systems; remotely piloted vehicles; and quantitatively new electronic control systems make many types of weapons global and make it possible to increase sharply (by at least an order of magnitude) the destructive potential of conventional weapons bringing them closer in terms of effectiveness to weapons of mass destruction. The sharply increased range of conventional weapons makes it possible to extend combat not just to the border regions, but to the territory of the entire country. This was not possible in past wars. This qualitative leap in the development of conventional means of destruction will inevitably entail a change in the nature of the

---

preparation and conduct of operations, which will in turn predetermine the possibility of conducting military operations using conventional systems in qualitatively new, incomparably more destructive forms than before.

Quoted in I. Rodionov, "Approaches to Russian Military Doctrine," *Koennaya mysl*, special edition, July 1992, in JPRS-UMT-92-012-L.

35. Vitaly Shabanov, "USSR Deputy Defense Minister for Armaments: The Country's Defense—New Approaches," *Krasnaya zvezda*, 18 August 1989, in *Foreign Broadcast Information Service (Soviet Union)* (FBIS-SOV)-89-160, 21 August 1989, 119–22.

36. M. A. Moiseyev, "From Defense Doctrine Positions: Colonel-General M. A. Moiseyev, Candidate USSR People's Deputy Meets Communists from the USSR Armed Forces General Staff," *Krasnaya zvezda*, 10 February 1989, in FBIS-SOV-89-028, February 1989, 77–81.

37. Ibid., 79.

38. John Erickson, "The Soviets: More Isn't Always Better," *Military Logistics Forum*, September–October 1984, 59–60.

39. US Army, *Soviet Armed Forces* (Carlisle, Pa.: War College Press, 1988), 46.

40. John Erickson, Lynn Hansen, and William Schneider, *Soviet Ground Forces: An Operational Assessment* (Boulder, Colo.: Westview Press, 1986), 214–18.

41. I. Krupchenko, "Methods of Exploitation in the Operational Depth with Forces of Tank Armies and Tank and Mechanized Corps," *Soviet Military Historical Journal*, 1981, 70–81.

42. A. I. Radzievskiy, *Army Operations*, ed. and trans. Soviet Studies Research Center (Sandhurst, United Kingdom: Soviet Studies Research Center, 1977), 61.

43. Field Manual (FM) 100-2-1, "The Soviet Army: Operations and Tactics," final draft, 18 June 1990, 11-3 through 11-4, 11-24 through 11-27.

44. Philip A. Peterson and John R. Clark, "Soviet Air and Anti-Air Operations," *Air University Review*, March–April 1985, 42.

45. *The Voroshilov Lectures*, vol. 1, 315–16.

46. Ibid., 312–13.

47. Benjamin Lambeth, *Desert Storm and Its Meaning: The Viewpoint from Moscow* (Santa Monica, Calif.: RAND, 1992), v.

48. In fact, Gen V. Lobov, former chief of staff of the Warsaw Pact, said that the Gulf War would give NATO an "unfair" advantage, pointing out that the Warsaw Pact was in the process of dissolution, but NATO had the opportunity to test weapons in the Gulf: "The fact alone that the Warsaw Pact will soon disappear but NATO will remain means that there is no longer any parity." See Brigitta Richter, "Interview with General V. Lobov, Warsaw Pact Chief of Staff: The War Has Become a Means of Destroying Iraq," *Der Morgen*, 18 February 1991, in FBIS-SOV-91-036, 22 February 1991, 81.

49. Mikhail Moiseyev, "On Occasion of an Anniversary," *Krasnaya zvezda*, 29 February 1991, in FBIS-SOV-91-041, 1 March 1991, 53.

50. David M. Glantz, "Soviet Military Art: Challenges and Change in the 1990s," *Journal of Soviet Military Studies*, December 1991, 558, 565.

51. See Jacob Kipp, "First Lessons of the War," *Foreign Military Studies Office (FMSO) Daily Bulletin*, 22 July 1991; and S. Korolev, "In Too Much of a Hurry with the Bombing," *Rabochaia tribuna*, 29 January 1991, in FBIS-SOV-91-023, 4 February 1991, 17.

52. Oleg Moskovskiy, "Interview with Major General V. Zhurbenko, Chief of the Main Department, USSR Armed Forces General Staff," *Tass*, 26 February 1991, in FBIS-SOV-91-038, 26 February 1991, 11.

53. Mary C. FitzGerald, "The Soviet Military and the New Air War in the Persian Gulf," *Airpower Journal*, Winter 1991, 65–66, 76–77.

54. Mary C. FitzGerald, "Russia's New Military Doctrine," *Military Intelligence*, October–December 1992, 24–26.

55. Thomas, 615.

56. V. Slipchenko, "Soviet Officers' Visit to Army War College," Soviet Army Studies Office Network (SASONET) report (Fort Leavenworth, Kans.: Foreign Military Studies Office, 25 March 1991).

57. Thomas, 602.

58. See Nikolay Buryga, "Interview with General V. Gorbachev . . . Tanks Will Not Save the Day," *Izvestiya*, 21 January 1991, in FBIS-SOV-91-014, 22 January 1991, 18–19.

59. Nikolay Buryga, "Military Experts Examine and Assess War in Gulf," *Izvestiya*, 21 January 1991, in FBIS-SOV-91-014, 18–19.

60. Kipp.

61. Quoted in FitzGerald, "The Soviet Military," 73.

62. Vladimir Chernyshev, "Tass Military Expert Views Military Maneuvers," *Tass*, 17 January 1991, in FBIS-SOV-91-013, 18 January 1991, 8.

63. Ben Lambeth points out that the Soviets identified the wrong airpower theorist, claiming that Desert Storm came closer to supporting Billy Mitchell's ideas: "Whereas Douhet had looked on aircraft other than bombers as ancillary—nice to have, perhaps, but not absolutely necessary—Mitchell could argue the case for all types. The important thing for him was not strategic bombing, but rather the centralized coordination of all air assets under the control of an autonomous air force command, freed from its dependency on the army. If that goal could be achieved, he felt, everything else would fall into its place." See Lambeth, *Desert Storm and Its Meaning*, 50; and David MacIsaac, "Voices from the Central Blue: The Air Power Theorists," in Peter Paret, ed., *Makers of Modern Strategy: From Machiavelli to the Nuclear Age* (Princeton, N.J.: Princeton University Press, 1986), 631.

64. Thomas, 598.

65. Cited in Kipp.

66. Cited in ibid.

67. A. Sidorov, "Interview of Lieutenant General of Aviation Maliukov: The Gulf War: Initial Conclusions—Air Power Predetermined the Outcome," *Krasnaya zvezda*, 14 March 1991, in FBIS-SOV-91-053, 19 March 1991, 50–51. Lt Col Ed Mann, USAF, expanded this idea: "There is nothing wrong with Air-Land Battle so far as it goes. It's fine when ground forces are the primary tool, but it assumes they always will be. While airpower plays an important and integral role in the ground battle . . . that's not all it can do. Sometimes airpower alone, or in a lead role, can be more effective and save lives. Airpower doctrine doesn't deny utility to Air-Land Battle. It goes beyond it to consider additional options." See Lt Col Edward C. Mann, "Operation Desert Storm? It Wasn't Air-Land Battle," *Air Force Times*, 30 September 1991, 27, 61.

68. Quoted in Lambeth, *Desert Storm and Its Meaning*, 67–69.

69. Ibid.

70. Thomas, 600.

71. Buryga, "Interview," 18–19. Asked about Iraq's numerical superiority in tanks, General Gorbachev replied that Iraq did indeed hold a numerical advantage and that the bulk of the Iraqi tanks were the Soviets' newest T-72s. He pointed out, however, that the "400 Apaches are capable of nullifying Hussein's advantage. . . . Having no opposition in the air, the coalition will be able to carry out its task one way or another." Buryga, "Interview," 18–19.

72. Quoted in Lambeth, *Desert Storm and Its Meaning*, 71.

73. V. Slipchenko, "Major General Slipchenko of the Soviet General Staff Academy Answers Questions during a Working Session before the Start of the NDU Conference," SASONET report (Fort Leavenworth, Kans.: Foreign Military Studies Office, 28 March 1991), 12. When asked about the success of the strategic air campaign, Slipchenko said, "First and foremost was your ability to fly so many sorties per day. Never in our wildest calculations did we believe you could sustain so many sorties logistically and overcome pilot fatigue. After winning air superiority . . . the war became . . . a war of technology, something Hussein did not have." Lambeth, *Desert Storm and Its Meaning*, 72–73.

74. Buryga, "Interview," 19.

75. S. Bogdanov, "The General Staff Is Closely Monitoring the Developing Situation," *Krasnaya zvezda*, 31 January 1991, in FBIS-SOV-91-022, 1 February 1991, 6.

76. N. Kutsenko, "Lessons of Combat Operations," *Izvestiya*, 28 February 1991, in FBIS-SOV-91-042, 4 March 1991, 41.

77. Gelyy Batenin, "How to Overcome the 1941 Syndrome," *New Times*, 26 February 1991, 12–14.

78. Shaposhnikov and Tsygichko quoted in Brian J. Collins, "Airpower in the Persian Gulf: Soviet Analysis," SHAPE Defense Studies (Brussels: Supreme Headquarters Allied Powers Europe, 12 February 1992), 12.

79. S. Achromeyev, "Achromeyev Comments on Iraqi Defeat," *Novoye vremya*, no. 10 (March 1991), in JPRS-UMA-91-018, 8 July 1991, 54.

80. A. Ladin, "Prepared Statements from the Podium, Honest Talk in the Lobby," *Krasnaya zvezda,* 22 March 1991, in FBIS-SOV-060, 28 March 1991, 38.

81. Cited in Maj Gen I. Losev and Lt Col A. Yakovlevich, "Desert Storm Revisited: Lessons from the Persian Gulf War," *Vestnik protivovoz dushnoy oborony,* 7 July 1992, JPRS-UMA-92-040, 57–59.

82. Quoted in Maj Gen V. Shevchenko, "Soviet Air Force Col-Gen Shaposhnikov Assesses Air War in Gulf," *Krasnaya zvezda,* 25 January 1991, FBIS-SOV-91-021, 9.

83. Lambeth, *Desert Storm and Its Meaning,* 43–44.

84. Ibid., 69–88. One apocalyptic Soviet correspondent, Pavel Felgengauer of *Nezavisimaya gazeta,* may have expressed a concern on the minds of many of the General Staff when he said, "The indestructible Red Army, made up for the most part of unprofessional officers and semi-trained conscripts, could hardly manage to put up sustained resistance to the professional NATO armies and modern highly accurate superweaponry. The clash of brute force and reason, a bullfight in essence, would end, like all bullfights, with the moment of truth." Quoted by Stanislav Kondrashov in "Political Observer's Notes," *Izvestiya,* 28 January 1991, in FBIS-SOV-91-021, 31 January 1991, 15.

85. Moiseyev, "From Defense Doctrine Positions," 81.

86. Thomas, 594.

87. FitzGerald, "Russia's New Military Doctrine," 6.

88. "Basic Provisions of the Military Doctrine of the Russian Federation: Russia's Military Doctrine," *Rossiyskiye vesti,* 18 November 1992, in FBIS-SOV-92-222-S, 1–11 (hereinafter Russian Draft Military Doctrine).

89. Ibid., 1.

90. Ibid., 2–3.

91. Ibid.

92. The draft doctrine defines "military danger" as an immediate threat of direct aggression against the Russian Federation, describing the danger in terms of social, political, territorial, religious, national-ethnic, and other conflicts. The military danger derives from the desire of a number of states and political forces resolving their problems through armed struggle. It describes armed conflict from aggressive nationalism and religious intolerance as posing "a special danger." A military danger becomes a "military threat" when there is an immediate danger of war. See ibid., 2–3.

93. Moiseyev, "From Defense Doctrine Positions," 78.

94. Natalie Gross, "Reflections on Russia's New Military Doctrine," *Jane's Intelligence Review,* August 1992, 339.

95. *Rodina* (the motherland) is a Russian concept that links preservation of state, cultural pride, and nationalism. It elevates patriotism and self-sacrifice for the motherland to a near-religious level. See Dick, "Russian Views," 362. Marshal Sergei F. Akhromeyev noted as early as March 1991 that "a military threat to the Soviet Union no longer exists, but a military *danger* does" (emphasis added). According to Timothy Thomas, Defense

Minister Yazov later echoed these concerns about military danger instead of military threat. See Thomas, 596.

96. Russian Draft Military Doctrine, 2–3.

97. Ibid., 5–6.

98. Ibid., 5.

99. Ibid., 7–9.

100. FitzGerald, "Russia's New Military Doctrine," 45.

101. Russian Draft Military Doctrine, 5–6.

102. Dick, "Initial Thoughts," 560.

103. Russian Draft Military Doctrine, 6–8.

104. Ibid., 8.

105. FitzGerald, "Russia's New Military Doctrine," 45–46.

106. Russian Draft Military Doctrine, 2.

107. Ibid., 6.

108. Ibid.

109. FitzGerald, "Russia's New Military Doctrine," 46.

110. Dick, "Initial Thoughts," 562.

111. Amidst the domestic stagnation of the Brezhnev years and the resurgence of American strength, Ogarkov evinced deep concern about the Soviets' ability to keep pace with the "truly revolutionary transformation of military affairs now occurring as a result of the development of thermonuclear weapons, the rapid evolution of electronics and weapons based on new physical principles, as well as the wide, qualitative improvements in conventional weaponry." Quoted in Ilana Kass and Fred Clark Boli, "The Soviet Military: Back to the Future?" *Journal of Soviet Military Studies*, September 1990, 392.

112. Aleksandr Stukalin, "Armed Forces Viewed after One Year in Existence," *Kommersant-Daily*, 8 May 1993, in FBIS-SOV-93-088, 10 May 1993, 36–38.

113. Benjamin S. Lambeth, "Red Phoenix Redux: The Fitful Emergence of a New Russian Air Force," draft (Santa Monica, Calif.: RAND, March 1994), x.

114. Ibid., 28–32.

115. An interesting observation by Kipp pertains to the impact of arms sales on the overall Russian economy. Since industrial plant costs were already accrued (sunk costs) and with labor costs also very low, military sales were actually making money and stimulating the economy. Although one central theme of this essay holds that the Russian economy will have a deleterious effect on the Russian military, Kipp's reasoning might at first appear to counter that notion. It might prove interesting to consider how much of the Russian military the politicians are willing to sell for this temporary economic stimulation. I do not believe that the Russians will "mortgage the state" at the expense of the military. Dr. Jacob Kipp, Foreign Military Studies Office, Fort Leavenworth, Kans., interviewed by author, 21 March 1994.

116. Aleksandra Nadzharov, "Defense Minister Grachev Interviewed," *Nezavisimaya gazeta*, in FBIS-SOV-93-109, 9 June 1993, 47.

117. A. Zarayelyan, "Commentator Views Russian Army Anniversary," *Moscow Ostankino Television First Channel*, 7 May 1993, in FBIS-SOV-93-088, 10 May 1993, 37.

118. Mary C. FitzGerald, Hudson Institute, Washington, D.C., interviewed by author, 24 March 1994.

119. Quoted in Mary C. FitzGerald, "Russia's Vision of Air-Space War," *Air Force Magazine*, December 1993, 79.

120. During the mid-1980s, I participated with top US scientists and industrialists in several industrial mobilization forums conducted at the Naval War College during the annual Global Wargame and at National Defense University. The main problem with industrial mobilization and surge was "rampup." For example, changing from peacetime production of one type of US missile to its wartime surge requirements took about 18 months. Certain technologies (computer chips, optics, composite materials, etc.) tend to be the pacing items in the production hierarchy. The problem was not economic. No amount of money could increase the production rate of some of the subcomponents. Certainly, one might build new production facilities and hire additional technicians, but the lead time for capital improvements and training might add four to five years to the production schedule. This surge delay had to do with a weapons system in the US serial production pipeline. If only a prototype or shelved technology were available, going from no production to surge would certainly take considerably longer.

121. Draft Russian Military Doctrine, 2–3.

122. Quoted in Fred Hiatt, "Yeltsin Promises Assertive Russia," *Washington Post*, 25 February 1994, 1.

123. Brian Collins, "Russia Fragments Its Airpower," *Air Force Magazine*, February 1994, 62–65.

124. More and more Russians use the term *near abroad* in reference to the ex-Soviet nations on Russia's rim.

Chapter 14

Ascendant Realms: Characteristics of Airpower and Space Power

Maj Bruce M. DeBlois*

At the onset of World War I, the United States found itself in a position as a major world sea power, arguably second only to Britain. Completion of the Panama Canal provided evidence of its desire to dominate the Western Hemisphere. The Navy maintained several overseas bases, a force structure of more than two dozen battleships, and a variety of other support vessels. A thriving industrial base that focused on overseas trade supported this seafaring nation. Twenty-five years earlier, however, that same nation had no overseas territories, only a few modern battleships, a military dispersed over its own frontier, an economy based on internal commerce, and a population that still viewed itself as an agrarian-based democracy. What happened to dramatically change the national focus over this relatively short period of time? Simply stated, the time was right.

A unique combination of factors contributed to the rise of American naval power during the first decade of the twentieth century. Primary among those factors was the acclaimed sea power vision of Alfred T. Mahan's book *The Impact of Sea Power upon History, 1660–1783*, published in 1890, which provided a clear operational means by which an emerging sea power could attain international status. That vision resonated with an American population in the process of becoming more aware of its international position—and with a dynamic young president, Theodore Roosevelt. As assistant secretary of the Navy, he had recognized the potential of the United States as a world leader, as well as the mechanism to attain it: sea

---

*The author recognizes the significant contributions of Maj Cynthia A. S. McKinley, a strategy and policy analyst for Headquarters Air Force Space Command/XPXS, and Maj Michael A. Rampino, a J6 (Communications Directorate) strategy and policy analyst for the Joint Chiefs of Staff.

power as prescribed by Mahan. If the popular Mahanian theoretical base and presidential endorsement were not enough, technological growth (smokeless guns, turbine engines, and submarines), naval successes in the Spanish-American War (1898), several South American ventures, and a growing threat of German naval power in the Pacific all gave impetus to the production of a very capable Navy. The rise of American sea power pushed the United States onto the international stage.[1] The lesson is clear: if those periods possess (1) the necessary resources, (2) an *unencumbered* economy, (3) an immediate motivation (here, an immediate threat), and (4) a common vision that supports specific technologies, they are temporary and present windows of opportunity.

At the turn of the century, the United States stood poised on the threshold of a great era: the preeminence of sea power. We are again at the turn of a century and again at the threshold of another great era: the preeminence of space power. The question is no longer one of "if" but "when." Is the time right for the US military to follow suit with a Mahanian-type book outlining *The Influence of Space Power upon History?* Are airpower theory and doctrine logical points of departure? The answers to these questions lead directly to key military issues dealt with in this chapter: What impact can current airpower theory have on space power theory? Is a separate Space Force required? If so, when?

To determine the potential impact of airpower theory upon space power theory, one must understand current Air Force thinking, which is offered here as an "aerospace power conjecture"—to wit, one should build space power theory and doctrine upon airpower theory and doctrine. Current Air Force doctrine strongly indicates acceptance of this conjecture. Specifically, Air Force Manual (AFM) 1-1, *Basic Aerospace Doctrine of the United States Air Force,* states that "the aerospace environment can be most fully exploited when considered as an indivisible whole. Although there are physical differences between the atmosphere and space, there is no absolute boundary between them. The same basic military activities can be performed in each, albeit with different platforms and methods."[2] Air Force Space

Command's practice of distinguishing between the two media, however, apparently has had some impact on Air Force doctrine. Air Force Doctrine Document (AFDD) 1, "Basic Air Force Doctrine," the yet-to-be-published replacement for AFM 1-1, recognizes some distinction between air and space forces, although the latest version of that doctrine still reflects the "aerospace power" mentality: "The distinguishing qualities of aerospace power are flight and the ability to rise above the earth's surface and operate in three dimensions through and above the atmosphere."[3]

This essay does not accept the aerospace power conjecture at face value but examines its plausibility by evaluating both airpower and space power against a backdrop of the roles, missions, and characteristics of each. The examination of roles and missions is relatively short because roles and missions have typically not served as the primary justification for establishing separate theories for the application of military power[4] (vested, in turn, in separate services). Differences in land power, sea power, and airpower stem from distinctions in characteristics—that is, the different means by which one prosecutes the roles and missions. Correspondingly, the Army, Navy, and Air Force organize, train, and equip the joint war-fighting command.

If an examination of the characteristics of airpower and space power shows great similarity among them, one can accept the aerospace power conjecture—which would prove extremely useful, since one could build space power theory upon 50 years of airpower theory.[5] One could embed space responsibility in the very strong culture of the Air Force—currently the de facto approach. If, on the other hand, examination of the characteristics of airpower and space power yields significant differences, then one must reject the aerospace power conjecture. Perhaps drawing from the more general principles of airpower, land power, and sea power theory, one would then have to build space power theory from its foundations. The most prudent, unbiased means of accomplishing this would require a distinct Space Force. In the following discussion, the novelty—not the relative importance—of space power warrants the emphasis on space-related issues.

Roles and Missions

A role is a general military objective, while the mission is the means of accomplishing it. Missions are options—not laundry lists of what forces always do—and the role/mission pairing is not exclusive.[6] Current Air Force doctrine emphasizes war-fighting roles and missions[7] but overlooks the operationalization of the strategic aspects of the "global presence" concept. "The foundation of this approach is power projection. Power projection is a means to influence actors or affect situations or events in America's national interests. It has two components: warfighting and presence."[8] The concept of presence used here explicitly connotes the idea of being in the environment (physically or virtually). Further, it implicitly connotes the idea of global watchfulness or vigilance. The following six roles and missions, created from a base of doctrine and literature, facilitate comparison between the air and space realms. They reflect the need to recognize both the peacetime and wartime operational roles that support the strategic concept of global presence. The first two deal specifically with ongoing peacetime operations while the last four deal with conventional war-fighting operations:

1. role: realm presence.

    mission: posturing the full complement of military capability and/or maintaining the recognized capability to access and dominate a particular realm with the intent to deter or compel allies and adversaries in consonance with US national objectives.[9]

2. role: realm vigilance.

    mission: continuous monitoring and analysis of and from the realm in support of global awareness. This includes a subset of information operations (weather, intelligence, surveillance, and reconnaissance).

3. role: realm control.

    mission ("counterrealm"): discriminating application of combat power against enemy forces within the realm or against their infrastructure supporting the realm.[10]

4. role: force application.

   mission: discriminating application of combat power from the realm against critical nodes of an adversary.[11]

5. role: force enhancement.

   mission: enabling military functions in order to multiply combat effectiveness. This includes refueling, special operations, and information operations (electronic combat; weather; intelligence; command, control, communications, and computers [C⁴]; precision navigation; surveillance; and reconnaissance).[12]

6. role: force support.

   mission ("sustenance of assets; defense"): logistical support (lift, deployment of forces, maintaining/replenishing/sustaining deployed forces, and base operability) and defense of assets to support sustained combat operations.[13]

Although the details of prosecuting the missions may vary due to the *characteristics* of the realm, these roles and related missions apply equally to airpower, land power, sea power, and space power. All forms of military power have the peacetime responsibilities of presence and vigilance. Primary wartime objectives of airpower, land power, sea power, and space power include providing force enhancement and force support to facilitate both realm control and the potential of force application. If one can find a distinction between space power and the other forms of military power within the context of general roles and missions, it lies in the role of force application.

Airpower, land power, and sea power are all currently capable of force application and have historical precedents for its use. Furthermore, although aircraft were initially used for surveillance and reconnaissance in a support role, ever since the strategic doctrinal conception of airpower, people have viewed it primarily as an offensive application of force.[14] But the capability of space power force application remains unproven, and no precedent exists for its use. The force application role from space may never be politically palatable because it is "unilaterally forbidden by congressional mandate (e.g. prohibition against deploying an anti-satellite system), and curtailed by international treaties (e.g. the Anti-Ballistic Missile Treaty)."[15] Even as a mental construct, force application from space does not begin with the primacy of the offensive. In fact, current technological pursuits and funding emphasize the use of space weapons in defensive roles—for example, the ongoing discussion about employing space weapons for ballistic missile *defense.*[16]

These roles and missions, though sorted, are complementary in practice. Clearly, realm presence, force enhancement, and force support facilitate realm control and force application. Moreover, the six generic or "joint" roles and missions are not unique to airpower and space power but apply equally to land power and sea power.

Apart from the minor distinction made in the force application role, the *objectives* of the roles and missions of airpower, land power, sea power, and space power are indistinguishable. Whether or not the *means of prosecuting these objectives* are similar or distinctive remains to be seen. Historically, the specific means by which one pursues roles and missions have distinguished airpower, land power, and sea power. These means traditionally appear as rules of employment, tenets of military power, or capability to achieve the immutable principles of war. To avoid debate, one can use the general term *characteristics* of military power to accommodate all of these notions.

One can place various characteristics of military power in a taxonomy of politics, development and employment, realm access, realm environment, and realm-afforded capability.[17] Such characteristics provide the basis for distinguishing among airpower, land power, and sea power. The purpose here is to determine whether these same characteristics distinguish or unify space power and airpower. Before proceeding, however, one would do well to briefly examine US space policy.

Space Policy

Emotional, legal, and rational political considerations directly affect the will to use space power and, as such, influence standing US space policy. Indeed, they have the effect of putting the political will to weaponize space very much in question.

Emotional Factor

Competing schools of thought lie at the root of the debate over space weaponization. In his book *On Space Warfare*,[18] Lt Col David Lupton summarizes four competing schools of thought that surfaced during the 1980s, when the issue of weaponizing space received a great deal of publicity.

The Sanctuary School views space as a realm free of military weapons but allows for military-related systems that provide the functions of treaty verification, intelligence activities, and so forth. Advocates maintain that the only way to ensure the legal overflight aspect of current space treaties is to declare space as a war-free zone or sanctuary. This school calls for virtually no funding of military space programs aimed at weaponizing space. The Sanctuary School of thought has a substantial following in the domestic and international populace, though many people within the military see it as a "head in the sand" approach to national security.

The Survivability School also argues that military forces should deemphasize space access, but for less idealistic reasons. It assumes that space forces are inherently exposed and vulnerable. Survivability adherents assert that the probability of using nuclear weapons in the remoteness of space is higher than in other media. This notion—along with the fact that weapons effects have longer ranges outside an inhibiting atmosphere, as well as the inherent vulnerability of predictable orbit locations—supports the survivability position. Remoteness also allows for plausible deniability of the attacker, which increases the probability of attack. The Survivability School calls for recognizing that space forces are not dependable in crisis situations. Thus, one should limit military space missions to communications, surveillance, reconnaissance, and weather reporting. From this perspective, investment strategies ought to fund those missions, along with redundant space/terrestrial programs and perhaps ground-based antisatellites (ASAT).

The Space Control School recognizes space power as coequal with airpower, land power, and sea power; thus, military space policy must balance investments in airpower, land power, sea power, and space power to meet the anticipated threat. The Department of Defense (DOD) and the Air Force have favored the Space Control School since the 1980s. Current political emphasis on jointness and the mentality that "everybody has a hand in space" prompt a Space Control School approach, as clearly reflected in published and proposed Air Force and joint doctrine.[19]

The High-Ground School advocates space as the high ground—the location from which a nation will win or lose future wars. Using space-based ballistic missile defense (BMD) to convert the current offensive stalemate of mutually assured destruction to mutually assured survival has some appeal. The supporters of this school advocate the militarization of space and the adoption of a corresponding policy. In their view, investments ought to focus on both offensive and defensive space systems at the expense of air, land, and sea systems. Funding would include space-based ASATs, directed-energy weapons (DEW), and BMD with maneuverable, space-to-space, space-to-air, and space-to-ground capability. Air-to-space (airborne laser or kinetic miniature homing vehicle ASATs)[20] and ground-to-space (direct-ascent ASATs) systems would also warrant investment.

Objecting to the weaponization of space on moral grounds (Sanctuary School) or on grounds of space systems' vulnerability (Survivability School) may seem as unrealistic as objecting to maintaining a military at all. Yet, space power advocates must appreciate that objections made from an emotional perspective are a real issue—one that could manifest itself in policy as dictated by the democratic process.

Legal Factor

In addition to the various schools of thought, several important treaties have made a significant impact on military space policy. Of note are the following:

1. The Outer Space Treaty (OST) of 1967 states that international law applies beyond the atmosphere. The

treaty reemphasized standing international laws (e.g., one sovereign state cannot threaten the territorial integrity or political independence of another—United Nations [UN] Charter, 1947) and initiated new space-related laws (e.g., free access to space and celestial bodies for peaceful intent, prohibitions on national appropriations of space or celestial bodies, prohibitions on putting any weapons of mass destruction in space or on celestial bodies).

2. The Antiballistic Missile (ABM) Treaty of 1972 (United States and USSR only) banned the development, testing, and deployment of space-based ABMs.

3. The Convention on Registration (1974) requires parties to maintain a registry of objects launched into space and report orbital parameters and general function of those objects to the UN.

4. The Environmental Modification Convention (1980) prohibits the hostile use of environmental modification.

What is not stated in international law is probably more important than what is; legal interpretation follows the convention that if the law does not explicitly prohibit something, it implicitly allows it.[21] One must also understand that treaties are just mutual agreements between signatories—they hold in peacetime but not necessarily in wartime.[22] Given these considerations, weapons of mass destruction, ABMs, and environmental modification weapons are all prohibited, but many conventional weapons (including ASATs) and tests of those weapons are allowed in space. The appropriation of space or any celestial body is illegal. Military maneuvers, bases, or installations on celestial bodies (the Moon) are also illegal; however, military maneuvers, bases, and installations in space (artificial satellites) constitute legal uses of that realm. Unreported space vehicles are prohibited, but reporting vague functional specifications and changing orbital parameters after launch are not prohibited.

In addition to international law, several domestic laws affect how the military might use space, although they certainly do not inhibit the use of space. They include the

Communications Act of 1934, whereby the president can commandeer private communications assets in times of crisis, and the Commercial Space Launch Act of 1984, which provides commercial customers access to military space-launch facilities (at a price). Taken as a whole, international and domestic law limits but does not preclude the conventional weaponization of space.

Rational Factor

Military space policy, which derives from national security policy, must support national security and international collective security interests and remain consistent with domestic economic and social interests. Any treaty negotiation aimed at bolstering national security would have to consider a variety of factors. To name a few, current military space capabilities along with the corresponding dependencies of the United States, our allies, and our potential adversaries are of primary importance. From a broader perspective, investment in expensive space weapons creates an opportunity cost; trade-offs with more conventional military systems become a significant consideration. The difficult matter of verification, which remains a concern, was a prime motivator behind the US rejection of several Soviet treaty proposals to control space weapons in the early 1980s.[23]

The bureaucratic decision process that combines the emotional, legal, and rational factors into a coherent space policy is complex. Analysis of bureaucratic decision making at the level of national policy is a science (or an art) unto itself.[24] Certainly, personal agendas, timing, and organizational structures all play a role in such decisions. This essay assumes that a rational decision-making authority recognized national security and/or international collective security as primary drivers, understood the emotional perspective and legal limitations, and subsequently produced the current space policy. The unilateral congressional moratorium on the funding of space-based weapons resulted from that rational process, which is not mandated by law but perhaps by better judgment.[25] Emerging from this decision process are the national, DOD, and Air Force policies pertaining to the military use of space. National space policy includes the following points:

1. The United States is committed to the exploration and use of outer space by all nations for peaceful purposes and for the benefit of all mankind. Peaceful purposes allow for activities in pursuit of national security goals.

2. The United States will pursue activities in space in support of its inherent right of self-defense and its defense commitments to its allies.

3. The United States rejects any claims to sovereignty by any nation over outer space or celestial bodies, or any portion thereof, and rejects any limitations on the fundamental right of sovereign nations to acquire data from space.

4. The United States considers any space systems of any nation to be national property with the right of passage through and operations in space without interference.[26]

DOD space policy calls for fulfilling the military space functions of space support, force enhancement, space control, and force application,[27] whereas Air Force space policy offers the following provisions:

1. Space power will be as decisive in future combat as airpower is today.

2. We must be prepared for the evolution of space power from combat support to the full spectrum of military capabilities.

3. The Air Force must integrate and institutionalize space throughout its operations.

4. The Air Force must accomplish four missions.

   a. aerospace control (acquire and operate ASATs [battle management and command, control, and communications (C^3) for space control operations]).

    b. force application (develop, deploy, and operate BMD if the United States decides to pursue it [battle management and C^3 for force application]).

    c. force enhancement (acquire and operate navigation, meteorology, tactical warning and assessment, nuclear detonation detection, and multiuser communications systems).

    d. space support (provide launch support).[28]

The policies do not read congruently; that is, the national space policy reads as if it is of the Sanctuary School (subtly leaving an option to weaponize), while the DOD and Air Force policies read as Space Control School perspectives, anticipating space weaponization. Air Force policy even seems to suggest that current space control doctrine might appropriately shift to a high-ground doctrine in the future.[29] Although the policies are not congruent, they make sense. National policy typically reflects the posture of where the United States would like to see the world community proceed, while DOD and service policies reflect the military's role of anticipating and preparing for aggressive action in defense of US national security interests.

Political Characteristics of Military Power

Three characteristics of military power that directly affect political decisions regarding the use of a particular realm include political access to the realm, sovereignty, and the likelihood of reduced casualties. *Political access* refers to domestic and international attitudes and agreements that have the potential of inhibiting access to a particular realm. *Sovereignty* addresses the issue of national claims in the realm, whereas *likelihood of reduced casualties* concerns the emerging idea that a combination of (1) precision lethality bolstered by technology and (2) the media's access to the battlefield has reduced American and international tolerances of casualties.

Political Access to the Realm

Political access to the realm does not show up in current literature on airpower, land power, and sea power because in times of crisis, people rarely call into question the political will to dominate those realms.[30] Political control—imposing limitations on the application of military power—is a constitutional reality. Limitations placed on the employment of airpower—rules of engagement (ROE)—particular to each situation distinguish airpower from space power. Air campaign planners have the freedom to plan for the full exploitation of the air realm and recognize that ROE may constrain the use of the plan in a given situation. Space campaign planners must recognize fundamental limitations on the exploitation of the space realm, even in the planning phase.

Rational, emotional, and legal factors, discussed above, produce these limitations, which affect current policy as well as transient actions such as the current bans on ASAT production and testing, in place since 1985. Rational and emotional factors currently dominate; that is, the limitations do not affect what we can do but what we have the will to do. The distinction between the access of airpower and space power to the respective realms stems from political limitations placed upon military access and use of space, referred to here as "political access." A political limit to the access of military space has existed since the 1960s and is not likely to disappear in the near future. Airpower does not have such a limitation on access. Therefore, *political access to the realm is a characteristic advantage of airpower.*

Sovereignty

Nations retain sovereignty over their air realm, but by virtue of the Outer Space Treaty of 1967, they can claim no sovereignty of the space realm—sovereignty rests with the spacecraft and not the medium.[31] Although this situation imposes some limitations since no national borders protect space assets, it facilitates most operations. Unrestricted access to and overflight of every nation on Earth exist for space operations but not for air operations, a situation that poses advantages for a nation with superior space power and disadvantages for less capable space powers. International agreements supporting *free rights to the space realm are a characteristic advantage of space power.*

Likelihood of Reduced Casualties

Operation Desert Storm evidenced at least two new facets of warfare: extensive media coverage, which brought the war into people's living rooms, and unprecedented precision-strike capabilities. The combination of witnessing both unjust collateral damage and having a capability to avoid it has placed another political constraint on American involvement in military ventures: reduced casualties.[32] Calls to limit casualties have currently made airpower the military instrument of choice. Precision capability affords limited collateral risk, while stealth and the remoteness of the airborne platform minimize operator risk. Space power, as opposed to airpower, offers a remoteness/precision trade-off. By virtue of being even further removed from the battlefield, space power provides lower operator risk[33] but higher risk of collateral casualties (due to less precision caused by that remoteness). *The concept of requiring reduced casualties distinguishes airpower and space power on two counts:*

1. The remoteness of space affords reduced operator casualties: *limited risk to US personnel is a characteristic advantage of space power.*

2. The proximity of the air affords reliable precision and reduced collateral damage: *limited risk to collateral personnel is a characteristic advantage of airpower.*

Political characteristics of military power are transient; that is, they exist by human convention and are subject to change. Although the similarities or distinctions between airpower and space power suggested by these characteristics remain transient, they are currently real considerations and will probably not change significantly in the near future. Several more characteristics, which owe their existence to human convention, involve the way people have chosen to develop and employ military systems and operations.

Development and Employment
Characteristics of Military Power

After considering the political merits of airpower and space power, one may logically begin analyzing them by examining their technological development and the means by which one uses them (employment). Research, development, operational insertion, and command/control/execution constitute the process by which emerging technologies integrate with and contribute to military power. Basic research and development (R&D) and operational insertion methods are similar for air, land, and sea services, as dictated by the DOD acquisition system. Features of this process that could highlight similarities or distinctions between airpower and space power include relative technology dependence and philosophies of command and control (C^2) and execution.

Technology Dependence

The development of air and space technology is virtually synonymous with high technology. Humans have existed in the land and sea realms for thousands of years. Although technological advance remains crucial to exploiting both realms, people do not need it to access them. In contrast, people have needed high technology to provide air and space access from the outset. Investment in high-technology R&D is essential to the progress of both airpower and space power. More so than on land or at sea, where technology is a force multiplier and numbers are often the determinant, in air and in space, technology is not just the force multiplier but the force itself. In the future, the role of humans will remain essential, but their primary value will lie in the preparation and orchestration of assets before the fight—not in a fight that will occur at speeds beyond human comprehension. Exposure of expensive technological assets may distinguish airpower and space power in terms of environmental characteristics (see below). Insofar as both airpower and space power heavily depend on advanced technology for access and manipulation of air and space, *technology dependence is a characteristic similarity of airpower and space power.*

543

Command and Control

Parceling out ground or sea forces may seem realistic—for example, one cannot immediately move the Pacific Fleet to support an Atlantic crisis. Air and space forces do not have such a constraint on speed of response: they can affect any part of the battle space within much shorter time spans. Experience dictates that optimum use of air forces requires centralized C^2 to orchestrate limited resources. The same ubiquity of capability driving high demand on a limited supply of assets exists for space forces. Additionally, the current space architecture of predominantly unmanned space assets efficiently linked to centralized ground control stations strongly suggests that centralized C^2 is the most prudent option.

Although current Air Force doctrine calls for it,[34] centralized space C^2 simply doesn't exist. Gen Charles A. Horner, USAF, Retired, former commander in chief (CINC) of US Space Command (USSPACECOM), when asked by Sen. Sam Nunn, chairman of the Senate Armed Services Committee, "Are you in charge of space?" felt compelled to reply, "That depends." It depends because CINCSPACE is the one CINC who exercises little control over his or her own command. The National Aeronautics and Space Administration (NASA), Defense Information Systems Agency, Ballistic Missile Defense Office, Central Intelligence Agency, Central Imagery Office, National Reconnaissance Office, National Oceanographic and Atmospheric Administration, Departments of Commerce/ Transportation and Interior, National Science Foundation, and White House Office of Science and Technology Policy all intrude upon CINCSPACE's budget, and many of the same organizations intrude upon his or her launch, on-orbit control, R&D, and acquisition authority.[35]

The ubiquity and responsiveness of air and space assets both require centralized control in order to orchestrate optimum allocation of assets throughout the battle space. In this regard, *centralized C^2 ought to be a characteristic similarity of airpower and space power.* Unfortunately, US government bureaucracy has not permitted this level of control of space assets or operations. *Centralized C^2 is a characteristic advantage of airpower.*

Execution

Air Force doctrine cites "effective spans of control, responsiveness, and tactical flexibility" as justification for the decentralized execution of airpower.[36] This essay does not challenge the historical legacy supporting this air doctrine for manned flight. Suffice it to mention that one may question the value of decentralized execution when (if) centrally controlled unmanned aerial vehicles (UAV) come to dominate the air realm. Ironically, experience in the space realm may provide insights for those airpower theorists considering centralized execution.

Space provides for an ideal adaptation of centralized execution. The tactical flexibility typically provided by decentralized execution is not an efficient option for employing centrally controlled, speed-of-light-responsive, unmanned national space assets with global reach. Space power requires centralized execution in order to orchestrate optimum use of assets throughout the battle space. Tactical effectiveness will rest on speed-of-light requests for support to some central buffer, priority assignment (some automated, some screened), and subsequent centralized execution. An extreme example warranting decentralized execution might involve spaced-based-laser close air support. But even though the requirement is near instantaneous, a priority-one input by the field commander would still have to go through a central control node that would subsequently execute the command. Assigning direct control of a satellite to the local commander would waste the potential use of the asset in other areas of the battle space at other times.

Air Force space doctrine currently under development agrees. For example, in the draft version of AFDD 4, "Space Operations Doctrine," Gen Thomas D. White comments that "a lack of centralized authority would certainly hamper our peaceful use of space and could be disastrous in time of war. Failure to properly coordinate peaceful space activities under common direction could cause confusion. . . . In war, when time is of the essence and quick reaction so necessary, centralized military authority will surely be mandatory." Further, with regard to unity of command, the document observes that "centralized control and decentralized execution are essential to the successful and optimal use of space power. Since space forces are global in nature and include critical national assets, they should be tasked and assigned from a global perspective. In a regional conflict, the theater commander should have control over accurate and timely products from space but should not have actual physical control of the satellite, its control systems, or ground control nodes."[37]

This view marks a significant departure from air doctrine, which calls for the regional commander's complete physical control of assigned air assets. Ironically, Air Force doctrine maintains that this is still decentralized execution—but nowhere does that doctrine explain decentralized execution. This situation clearly results from force-fitting a basic tenet of airpower onto space power. If the regional commander "should not have actual physical control of the satellite, its control systems, or ground control nodes," where does that control lie? The answer is that the centralized control of space assets—and the controlling element for remote space assets—is almost always the executing element.

General White's comment strongly supports "centralized military authority." The span of "military authority" encompasses C^2 and execution. Decentralized execution requires both a clear understanding of the mission and the autonomy to carry it out. The price of optimally applying space assets across the worldwide battle space is a centralized buffer with automated or screened prioritization, which detracts from the autonomy of any one regional commander. Both cost and capability optimization of space assets drive centralized control and centralized execution. Airpower, on the other hand, does not have to make the autonomy/efficiency trade-off. Most airpower assets are not national assets with near-instantaneous global reach. As such, efficient operation warrants assigning air assets to regional commanders, an arrangement that affords both efficient centralized control and offers lower-level commanders/operators the tactical flexibility of decentralized execution. *Decentralized execution is a characteristic advantage of airpower.*

Consideration of the political and development/employment characteristics of military power has revealed several distinctions and similarities between airpower and space power. But these characteristics have resided in human creations—politics, laws, development methods, and employment plans. More fundamental to the comparison is the physical nature of the two realms.

Realm-Access Characteristics of Military Power

Technological advances in aerodynamics, materials, propulsion, guidance, and control all facilitated access to the air realm at the turn of the twentieth century. Similarly, in astrodynamics, ongoing studies of forces and motion in space suggest that proliferated access to the space realm is near at hand. But one should remain cautious about such technological optimism: "Scientists and engineers now know how to build a station in space that would circle the Earth 1,075 miles up. . . . Within the next 10 or 15 years, the Earth will have a new companion in the skies, a man-made satellite that could be either the greatest force for peace ever devised, or one of the most terrible weapons of war—depending on who makes and controls it."[38]

Surprisingly, those comments came from Wernher von Braun, speaking in 1952. Relatively recent experience with understanding the air realm, together with the ability to rapidly overcome air-flight-related technical obstacles, naturally led to the same expectation for spaceflight-related technical obstacles. The experiences of the last 45 years with space research have emphasized a real difference between understanding a theoretical environment and building systems to gain physical access to it. The air access–space access analogy breaks down for several reasons: access to the air realm, at the lowest technological level, is as easy as throwing a rock or glider. But space is not a realm to which we have immediate access or in which we have experience. Prior to specifically addressing the realm-access characteristics of airpower and space power, therefore, one needs some background regarding space-lift efforts, including significant technical hurdles to space lift, technological development designed to negotiate those hurdles, and the means by which the United States nurtures that technological development.

Boost to the space realm requires a large amount of energy that must be generated, harnessed, focused, and stabilized. To illustrate the difference in energy requirements for aircraft-type and spacecraft-type operations, one should consider the thrust required to place an F-16 aircraft into low Earth orbit (LEO). Scaling the thrust-to-(weight-to-orbit) ratio of the space shuttle down—or scaling the Atlas thrust-to-(weight-to-orbit) ratio up—yields roughly 1.15 million pounds of thrust required to get an F-16-sized vehicle with a reasonable payload to LEO.[39] Current air-breathing F-16 engines produce 29,000 pounds of thrust[40]—roughly one-fortieth the amount required by an F-16-sized, space-capable, non-air-breathing, rocket-powered spacecraft. Thus, thrust requirements provide one indication of the drastic differences between aircraft and spacecraft technologies.

Furthermore, to make the space vehicle F-16-like for operations, one would need to reconfigure and pull the external, expendable booster stages inside the craft and drastically reduce the elaborate ground-support infrastructure required by current space operations. Aircraft-type operations for a spacecraft are easy to imagine, but the analogy hides the fact that from an engineering perspective, aircraft operations and spacecraft operations differ not merely in the *degree* of advanced technology required but differ fundamentally in the *kind* required. As a further complication, any means of gaining access to the space realm must work equally well in the very different environment of the air realm, since one must traverse the atmosphere in order to reach space.

The remoteness of space also causes serious maintenance and supportability problems. When aircraft components malfunction, the aircraft lands to be fixed. When aircraft run out of fuel, tankers refuel them in the air, or they land for refueling. Spacecraft currently have neither of these options.[41] Whether the motive is operations or maintenance and support, access to space becomes a matter of getting there—and that requires space lift.

One use of the term *lift* involves moving something from one place to another. Airlift and space lift are similar in this regard. A fundamental difference, however, exists between the two. Physical access to the space realm is the objective of space lift, while the objective of airlift is not one of physical access to the air realm but one of delivering materials to different points on the ground. Two technological methods for gaining space access are afoot: better propulsion and lighter payloads. Each appears to hold promise; indeed, an entire community has dedicated itself to achieving physical access to space. Such access to the air and space realms remains distinct and affects both operations and maintenance/support.

Physical Access to the Realm (Operations)

Intense efforts are under way to overcome the very daunting task of cheap, on-demand access to space—a task that is orders of magnitude more complex and fundamentally different than that which allowed access to the skies. Regardless of technical advances, access to the space realm requires mastery of the air and space realms, which is inherently much more difficult than the mere mastery of the air realm. *Access to the realm (operations) is a characteristic advantage of airpower.*

Physical Access to the Realm (Maintenance and Support)

The maintainability and supportability aspects of airpower depend upon a *ground*-based infrastructure that deals with assets on the *ground*. Maintainability and supportability of space power, at least for the foreseeable future, require a *ground*-based infrastructure to deal with assets orbiting in space. In addition to this complication, space systems are technically more complicated than air systems and will require more sophisticated maintenance and support operations.

The real problem, though, lies in fixing these technologically advanced spaceborne systems when they fail. That task often requires access that is far and away more difficult than returning an aircraft to the maintenance shop.[42] In addition to the cost of access, one requires significant technological improvements in communications, rendezvous docking, and space-robot technology for future resupply activities in space.[43] No matter the state of technological advance, the maintainability and supportability of space systems as compared to that of air systems are destined to be much more technically difficult, as well as much more costly. *Access to the realm (maintenance and support) is a characteristic advantage of airpower.*

Realm-Environment Characteristics of Military Power

Methods of operations within the air and space realms are drastically different. The underlying cause of this difference lies in the unique composition, size, and position of the respective realms—characteristics that have significant impact on the employment of military power.

Composition of the Realm

Space is both a more threatening environment to life and a more difficult environment in which to operate. The fundamental difference between air and space is composition: air is a medium of substance, whereas space is void of substance. Altitude provides the one measure that correlates with the presence of that substance which defines our atmosphere. Air density drops off exponentially with altitude,[44] as does a human's ability to exist and function there (table 1).

If the lack of necessary elements for human survival is not threatening enough, the presence of harmful elements ought to be. Although mass in space is rare, energy is not. The most dangerous effect of solar radiation is its capacity to produce heat. Since a satellite in space is thermally isolated, it has no natural means to vent excess energy absorbed from the sun. Without the screening and natural cooling capability of the atmosphere, an object in space quickly overheats on the sunlit side. Resolution requires a technological means of collecting excess energy and radiating it back into space. Balancing the level of heat in any spaceborne system presents a difficult

Table 1

The Changing Atmospheric Medium

Altitude (km)	Density (d)/Density at Sea Level (d_0)
0	$d_0 = 10^{18}$ particles/cm^3
5	$d = .492 \times d_0$ (one-half of Earth's atmosphere is below this)
10	$d = .242 \times d_0$ (supplemental oxygen required for respiration)
15	$d = .119 \times d_0$ (supplemental pressure and oxygen required for respiration)
24	$d = .033 \times d_0$ (compressing external air is no longer economical; humans require self-contained environments)
32	$d = .011 \times d_0$ (operating limit of turbojet engines)
45	$d = .002 \times d_0$ (operating limit of ramjet engines)
100	$d = 10^{12}$ particles/cm^3 (aerodynamic effects become insignificant)
1,000	$d = 10^5$ particles/cm^3
2,000+	d = one particle/cm^3 (the "hard vacuum" of space)

problem—even more so if that system must meet the very narrow tolerances for sustaining human life.

Aside from heat, surges of electromagnetic energy—often due to solar flares associated with solar or cosmic radiation, radio bursts, proton events, and geomagnetic storms—can also pose a threat. High-energy solar or cosmic radiation can prove lethal to humans, while radio bursts, proton events, and geomagnetic storms can interrupt communications. Another space hazard involves energetically charged particles that often become trapped in magnetic fields associated with planets or stars (such as Earth's Van Allen radiation belts). These particles can pose serious threats to space systems and humans. Due to the amounts of electromagnetic radiation in space, unfiltered by the atmosphere, all space-faring systems require a variety of thermal and radiation shields—but shields may not be enough.

In many cases, shielding will not protect a space vehicle from micrometeoroid impacts. The *Pegasus Explorer* XVI satellite reported 62 penetrations in its seven-month space mission during 1963. Although the impacts did not seriously hamper operations, the sheer number of strikes was surprising. The extremely small size of most space meteors (10^{-5} grams) is offset by their incredible speeds (between 30,000 and 160,000 MPH). Coupled to this naturally occurring problem is the growing amount of man-made space debris. Over seven thousand objects larger than 10 cm and an estimated 30,000 to 70,000 smaller objects between 1 cm and 10 cm have been deposited into Earth orbit. But the real problem may be the 10 billion objects in the .1 mm to 1 cm range that we currently have no means of tracking.[45] For example, a .2 mm paint-chip impact on a side window necessitated a $50,000 shuttle window replacement following shuttle mission STS-7. The high velocity and relative permanence of most spaceborne platforms make them extremely vulnerable to space-faring debris. In addition to thermal and radiation shields, debris shields—as well as continuous long-range monitoring and maneuver capability— reduce the risk of impact damage.

Perhaps the most distinctive feature between the air and space environments is not a matter of the threat that the space medium poses to human life, but a matter of physical operations allowed by the composition of the air realm: aerodynamics and the two fundamental forces afforded by the air medium—drag and lift. In space, there is no cushion of air (i.e., drag) upon which to float and maneuver; further, there is no lift to gain altitude.[46] For example, the terminal velocity of a free-fall parachuter is between 100 and 120 MPH. By contrast, no terminal velocity exists in space. If a person were to free-fall in the Earth's gravitational field[47] without the benefit of an air cushion, his or her velocity after traversing 20,000 feet in 35 seconds would amount to an astonishing 770 MPH.

One cannot overstate the benefit of lift within the atmosphere.[48] Mankind has known of rockets for thousands of years yet forsook the question of flight until the discovery of lift. Aircraft require propulsion for manned flight, but the real test of flight rests with the ability to manipulate that propulsion in a manner that optimizes lift. To illustrate the benefits of lift, one should consider a situation that uses no lift. Fuel consumption rates of a British Aerospace Sea Harrier on a typical combat air patrol (CAP) mission allow a 90-minute flight. The same aircraft can stay airborne in a fixed location (no lift, thrust only) for approximately 23 minutes.[49] Lift quadruples the flight time and adds the benefit of maneuver. Had the same Harrier required thrust capability (without lift) to maneuver in a CAP role at standard aircraft speeds, its flight time would amount to just a few minutes. Obviously, the lift/glide factor in our ability to man the skies remains very significant—a factor not available in space.

Space maneuver requires one of two modes: free fall in orbit or thrust-powered maneuver. Both modes differ drastically from maneuvering through the air. From the reference frame of the satellite, orbits are simply the right combination of lateral velocity and altitude that allow the Earth to move out from beneath the free-falling satellite. Thrust-powered maneuver from a fixed orbit position requires an incredible amount of thrust for altitude changes, as illustrated by the example above and by previous discussions of space lift. Lateral changes are permanent; that is, the atmosphere exerts no damping effects once the satellite is in motion. A lateral move to a fixed distance in space requires thrust in the opposite direction to initiate the move—and an equal amount of thrust in the same direction to halt the move.

The operating medium of space differs dramatically from the air realm. People cannot live in the medium and cannot "fly" in it. If humans are to realize the advantages offered by space, they must continue to develop technological solutions that accommodate them and their systems in that hostile environment. Those solutions, along with the nature of the environment, will dictate the need for unique operations and corresponding doctrine. The composition of the space realm bears absolutely no resemblance to the composition of the air realm. *Composition of the realm is a characteristic advantage of airpower.*

Size of the Realm

One may locate a conservative air-space boundary at an altitude of 100 km, the point beyond which aerodynamic effects become negligible (see table 1). The volume of atmosphere encompassed by this boundary is roughly 5.18 x 10^{10} km^3. Near Earth space, from the 100 km altitude out to geosynchronous earth orbit (GEO), encompasses roughly 3.13 x 10^{14} km^3—more than six thousand times the operating environment of the atmosphere.[50] As technology advances and "near Earth" comes to encompass the Moon, the operating space environment increases a thousandfold beyond GEO. The larger the size of the realm, the more potential for freedom of movement and military operations. *The size of the realm is a characteristic advantage of space power.*

Position of the Realm

The relative position of the realm with respect to other realms is an important environmental characteristic. Because the space environment encloses the air environment, space operations have a tactical advantage over air operations. The space environment also has an energy advantage because it maintains the high ground. If one overlooks the access problem previously addressed, space power enjoys an obvious advantage due to elevation. *The relative position of the realm is a characteristic advantage of space power.*

If the environmental characteristics of the air and space realms are so drastically different, why such a strong effort to merge the two? In order to justify exploitation of the aerospace environment as a unified whole, AFM 1-1 points to the fact that no absolute boundary exists between air and space. The authors erroneously assert that the distinction between land, sea, and aerospace forces is attributable to a clear boundary between each. They further propose that since a clear boundary does not exist between air and space, one can make no such distinction.[51] But the distinction between military realms is based on the nature of the environment—not on the boundaries between them. The flawed logic of AFM 1-1 probably results from creating evidence to support a decision already made—specifically, consumption of space roles and missions by the Air Force. Unsurprisingly, an initial draft of AFDD 1, which clearly separated air and space without ever using the term *aerospace*, was disapproved. But the term dominates the latest draft version of AFDD 1 (14 May 1996), which is now on the verge of acceptance.[52]

The only difference between the air and space environments is altitude and/or level of technology required to operate within the realm. The fundamental flaw in such an argument rests in the very different mediums. The air realm, which varies continuously with altitude, is dense with substance, screened from cosmic radiation, and confined to an area within 100 km of the Earth's surface. The space realm, however, is a constant, void of substance, immersed in radiation, and literally infinite in dimension. If substance density is a valid gauge, the difference between the air and space realm is a factor of 1,018; if size is the criterion, the difference is far greater. Differences in composition and size require significant differences in the technological means of conquering those mediums. The technological requirements that distinguish flying in air from traversing space are more profound than the distinction between motion in water and traversing the atmosphere. Both sea and air travel involve progressing through a medium of substance, whereas space travel involves motion within a void. Scientists and engineers have a more difficult time merging air and space environments as compared to merging air and sea environments, yet one hears nothing of "aerosea" power.

The man-made political, development, and employment characteristics, as well as the inherent realm-environment characteristics of military power significantly distinguish space power from airpower. Correspondingly, these differences drive different capabilities.

Realm-Afforded Capability
Characteristics of Military Power

Autonomy of operation, surveillance and reconnaissance, duration (staying power/presence), range, maneuver, flexibility of response, precision, speed of response, firepower, and stealth are all capability characteristics of military power. As one might expect, differences in political, logistical, and environmental characteristics between the air and space realms dictate differences in the ability to project military power from those realms. In order to make a fair comparison of air and space capability, one must assume the existence of a reasonable number of space-based surveillance and strike-capable assets. Clearly, a capability comparison between an existing developed force (airpower) and an existing but immature force (space power) would not prove very useful. Decisions made today will influence force structure and capabilities 20 years from now. Assuming a more mature space power appropriately levels the playing field upon which those decisions are made.

Autonomy

Evaluation of this characteristic assumes that system dependence on external information is undesirable. Lack of autonomy represents vulnerability. This view does not advocate complete decentralization but simply recognizes the fact that, necessary or not, external dependence further exposes the system. Considering just the communications aspect of any spaceborne system, one notes that large-scale data transmission capacities will require innovations in both data transmission (bandwidth and data-link security) and processing (expert systems for data synthesis and computing power). The advent of remotely piloted airborne vehicles will place the same requirements on many airborne platforms. The critical element in the evaluation of this characteristic is not whether the system is airborne or spaceborne but whether the system is manned or unmanned. Unmanned systems inherently lack autonomy and critically depend on secure, high-transmission data links. Because spaceborne systems are much more difficult to man, *autonomy is a characteristic advantage of airpower.*

Surveillance/Reconnaissance

The idea that space assets provide omniscience/omnipresence is a common one: "24 hours-a-day, 365 days-a-year, continuous multispectral sensor data, instantly fused and synthesized into processed information" represents a typical embellishment of the real situation.[53] Computing power becomes the means to achieve this goal.

But military planners do not realize that although "24 hours-a-day, 365 days-a-year, continuous multispectral sensor data" is within reach, the ability to instantly fuse and synthesize it into processed information is a myth. Military war games continue to overlook the very difficult problem of processing, assuming it to be a simple matter of computing power. Typically, planners summarize the concept as a "data fusion" black box and summarily dismiss it.[54]

A brief examination of the "data fusion myth" requires familiarity with the following terms:

- *data* - raw perception of the environment by any variety of means: sensed, encoded, and communicated.
- *information* - decoded and collected data by a few simple categorizing algorithms or methods.
- *knowledge* - the recall of information as it applies to a specific situation.
- *understanding* - coordination of many groups of *knowledge* as they may apply to a variety of situations.
- *wisdom* - coordinated understanding in the context of a lifetime of experience.
- *vision* - use of wisdom to construct a path to the future.

The data fusion myth blindly assumes the potential of complete automation at all levels, from data acquisition through insightful decision making (e.g., data - information - knowledge - understanding - wisdom ["genius"] - vision). Automation of these functions diminishes as the process proceeds from data to vision. Wisdom and vision simply are not programmable. Computers do not make decisions; they can only follow the algorithms—programmed paths that lead to decisions. The data fusion accomplished by any computer will be only as good as the decision paths previously coded into it by the programmer, who is removed in time, space, and responsibility from the very decision being made (i.e., he or she has no particular situational awareness). One cannot synthesize massive amounts of data in a variety of forms, from a variety of platforms, in order to tailor the results for a particular application, by massive computation alone. Advances in computing power have facilitated the potential for processing, but computing power does not equate to processing. Inflated expectations of data fusion provide more of a problem for space power simply because experience has tempered airpower expectations.

In spite of this weakness, one must not understate the impact of space surveillance and reconnaissance capabilities— highlighted by the Gulf War. A host of US and foreign communications, navigation, surveillance, early warning, and meteorological satellites contributed to the coalition war effort.[55] In the future, such support will proliferate,[56] one-meter resolution will become available commercially by 1997,[57] and one can only imagine the real limit of resolution capability. Very fine resolution and wide-area coverage, multiplying current levels of data flow, only complicate the problem of data fusion. If planners continue to dismiss data fusion simply as a computing-power problem, massive amounts of data flow will leave the analyst or operator drowning in data but starving for knowledge. Data obtained from airborne platforms bears the same burden; space-based systems simply afford a wider range of data opportunities. The persistence and position afforded by space platforms present the opportunity to collect huge quantities of surface data; the difficulty lies in deciding what data to collect, how to process it, and what to do with the processed information. Given the benefit of position, *surveillance and reconnaissance capability provides a characteristic advantage of space power.*

Duration

Geosynchronous satellites provide a persistent and continuous presence. One can also arrange satellites in LEO to provide a similar presence.[58] Aircraft presence is transient, and even though long-loiter UAVs may extend aerial presence significantly, aircraft presence requires sortie generation and support—satellites do not. *Duration is a characteristic advantage of space power.*

Range

Airpower and space power both have global range. Either medium provides access to any surface target. The range of space power extends beyond the near-Earth environment, currently out to GEO. Although airpower assets such as airborne lasers or kinetic miniature homing vehicle ASATs may soon offer regular access to LEO, they will not have access to deep-space locations. Considerable time may pass before the range extension of space power exceeds that of airpower, particularly in a strike capacity. Inherently, though, *range is a characteristic advantage of space power.*

Maneuver

A satellite in LEO (200 km) travels at roughly 7,790 meters per second (17,425 MPH).[59] A small satellite (100 kg) traveling at this speed has the kinetic energy roughly equivalent to an F-16 traveling at Mach 2 (sea level).[60] Unlike the F-16, however, the satellite has no air on which to maneuver or slow down, and because it is so expensive to lift fuel to space, satellites typically have very little energy available to provide on-orbit thrust, which in turn equates to maneuverability. The cross-range capability of satellites is so low, in fact, that the most maneuverable, powered, space concepts—the current reusable launch vehicle (RLV) designs—allow only for eleven hundred miles of lateral maneuver capability.[61] This essay has already mentioned the incredible costs incurred by lifting mass (fuel) to orbit for such maneuvers. These are daunting obstacles; as such, the virtual immobility of spaceborne assets from fixed orbit stands as their biggest drawback. *Maneuver is a characteristic advantage of airpower.*

Flexibility

System flexibility equates to options. Spacecraft options as compared to aircraft options are severely limited on several counts:

1. As discussed, the energy cost of *maneuvering* space assets reduces the number of target options.

2. The energy cost of *access* to space inhibits satellite reconfiguration, resulting in a lack of reconnaissance and strike options. One can reconfigure aircraft prior to launch in order to meet particular situational needs. In the event of a crisis, most of the space power available is already present; satellite strike and reconnaissance capabilities are not reconfigurable without high-cost space lift and/or on-orbit maneuver.

3. The *absence of autonomy* (unmanned) requires spacecraft to rely on data-linked decisions regarding available options. The time delay or data-link vulnerabilities could limit options.

The flexibility that characterizes military power is not merely a summation of maneuver, access, and autonomy characteristics. Maneuverable, autonomous systems with easy realm access could conceivably lack flexibility. The combination of extreme limitations on autonomy, maneuver, and access characteristics of space power severely constrains flexibility. *Flexibility is a characteristic advantage of airpower.*

Precision

Automated terminal guidance and control are equally applicable from the air and space. Remote, data-linked terminal guidance provides its own inherent limitations, however. Because data-link vulnerability is always an issue, as are weather restrictions, the Air Force continues to retain manned aircraft with ballistic bombing capability. Typically, in the absence of terminal guidance, the precision of ballistic weapons is directly related to release range—and release range from terrestrial targets is less for air assets as compared to the further-removed space assets. The proximity of the air realm provides *precision as a characteristic advantage of airpower.*

Speed of Response

If one removes the three previously considered limitations of space power (maneuver, flexibility, and precision) from the calculation,[62] space-based response time can become almost instantaneous. Airpower response time can occur as quickly as putting F-117s on target anywhere in the world within 24 hours of notification; however, providing sustained airpower (limitation of duration) requires extensive mobilization—witness the huge buildup prior to the onset of Desert Storm.[63] The potential for immediate response of space-based platforms makes *speed of response a characteristic advantage of space power.*

Firepower

An Mk 84 two-thousand-pound all-purpose bomb without any explosive charge, released at 30,000 feet and 530 knots, carries the energy equivalent to roughly 145 pounds of TNT. The same Mk 84 dumb bomb in LEO carries one hundred times the energy—the explosive power of seven tons of TNT.[64] This may seem like a great deal, but several mitigating factors come into play:

1. If that energy is employed, most is lost due to drag effects upon reentry.

2. The explosive power of modern conventional weapons comes from their explosive filling rather than their kinetic energy: the explosive charge of an Mk 84—428 kg of Tritonal[65]—is equivalent to roughly nine hundred pounds of TNT. Other conventional explosives marginally exceed Tritonal capacity.[66]

3. Many lofted weapons (e.g., cluster bombs) require specific velocities for employment, completely negating the space-stationed energy advantage.

4. The cost of putting "dumb" energy in orbit is prohibitive (at $10,000/pound, putting a "dumb" Mk 84 in orbit would cost an astronomical $20 million).[67]

As far as mass is concerned, firepower from space has significant limitations. Directed energy weapons provide another option. Currently, concerted efforts are under way to produce high-powered lasers with very significant atmospheric range. The Phillips Laboratory's airborne laser program has

561

pushed laser state of the art to new levels: megawatt power, submicroradian beam control (one-foot "wiggles" at 200 km), and lethal ranges extending out to hundreds of kilometers.[68] Beaming energy to a spaceborne platform, storing it, and reradiating it from a satellite DEW becomes at least plausible. Of course, whatever one can do from the remoteness of space, one can also accomplish from the air, without the need to radiate the energy to the platform—exactly the approach of the airborne laser. Although space strike may prove more responsive, firepower capability from space has significant limitations. Assuming a surface target, the proximity of the air realm provides *firepower as a characteristic advantage of airpower.*

Stealth

Because of their close proximity to the surface, aircraft are exposed to low-technology, surface-based threats such as antiaircraft artillery and surface-to-air missiles. Their exposure, however, is transient and limited by various unpredictable factors: timing, flight path, velocity, maneuverability, stealth technology, and weather.

The high speed and remote aspects of spacecraft clearly provide certain security advantages. A spacecraft in near-circular LEO with an apogee and perigee of approximately 2,128 miles travels a set path at a known velocity of roughly 17,420 MPH, while a satellite in a near-circular GEO (22,241 miles) requires a velocity of 6,880 MPH to remain stationary, relative to the Earth's surface.[69] But as technical access to space proliferates, the advantages of remote speed give way to the disadvantages of predictable locations and paths. Physical cluster areas at LEO, GEO, and Lagrange points[70] also add to the exposure of space assets. Additionally, the absence of an inhibiting atmosphere greatly extends space-based sensing capability and weapons effects, further complicating the space-security issue. Historically, space support based in the continental United States has remained more centralized than air-support infrastructure, thus increasing its vulnerability. After defining stealth as a military term referring to the difficulty of acquiring, locking, and killing a potential target, and after comparing the transient, maneuverable, low-level capabilities of airpower with the predictable, continuous exposure of space assets, one concludes that *stealth is a characteristic advantage of airpower.*

Summation and Integration of Characteristics

To support military decisions regarding the employment of airpower and/or space power, one must integrate capability characteristics in the context of the current situation. An inherent limitation of examining each of these characteristics independently is that, in reality, one must consider them in total. One makes trade-offs between positive and negative attributes in order to determine the correct response, depending on the situation. For example, a skirmish halfway around the world may require immediate response time, light firepower, and extreme precision. A directed-energy, space-to-surface, strike-capable satellite may provide the appropriate speed of response, but due to its remoteness and weather limitations, the satellite may not provide the required precision. In terms of the assessment of characteristics, this circumstance is reflected by both space power's advantage in speed of response and airpower's advantage in precision. The decision maker must trade off these advantages required by the given situation and choose the best approach. As discussed above, planners often overstate the concept of data fusion, which will not supplant a continued requirement for military genius.[71]

Conclusion

Clearly, the characteristics of airpower and space power are quite different, as indicated by highlighting their relative advantages (table 2). Only the characteristic of technological dependence shows a significant similarity between airpower and space power. One should note, however, that technological advances will mitigate some of the differences in characteristics. Unfavorable characteristics of airpower may change significantly with the advent of long-loiter UAVs, while

---

Table 2

Characteristic Advantages of Airpower and Space Power

	Airpower	*Space Power*
Politics	Political access to the realm	Sovereignty Likelihood of reduced casualties
Development/ Employment	Centralized C^2 Decentralized execution	
Realm Access	Access to the realm (operations) Access to the realm (maintenance/support)	
Realm Environment	Composition of the realm	Size of the realm Position of the realm
Realm-Afforded Capability	Autonomy Maneuver Flexibility Precision Firepower Stealth	Surveillance and reconnaissance Duration Range Speed of response

---

unfavorable characteristics of space power may change with the advent of transatmospheric vehicles (TAV). Determining whether or not a given characteristic is advantageous to airpower as opposed to space power—or vice versa—is debatable and not critical to the argument. The significant differences between airpower and space power discussed within the context of each characteristic, however, are critical to the argument. In spite of the potential for some technological mitigation of the vast differences in the characteristics of airpower and space power, one must conclude that *the aerospace power conjecture is false.*

That is, one cannot build space power theory and doctrine in general upon airpower theory and doctrine. Theories and doctrines of airpower, land power, and sea power may contribute significantly to the development of the theory and doctrine of space power, but space power clearly requires fundamental, bottom-up, theoretical and doctrinal development. The most conducive environment for such development remains a separate space corps or service.

Before completely dismissing the aerospace power conjecture, one might articulate a consistent argument that favors it: the merging of airpower and space power as aerospace power is based upon their functional equivalence (employing military power from the third dimension). No distinct boundary exists between the two, and they both afford the same elevated perspective of the battlefield. Technology will eventually overcome the significant environmental distinctions between the air and space media. The technological pursuit of space planes provides evidence that once technology overcomes the space medium, military function will blur any environmental distinction.

This argument is compelling and has its merits. The counterargument, however, is at least as compelling: the merging of land and sea power as "surface power" is based upon their functional equivalence (employing military power from the two-dimensional surface). The boundary between the two is not so distinct, and they both afford the same surface perspective of the battlefield. Environmental distinctions between land and sea media are significant, but technology has overcome them. So why is there no surface power following? The answer is that five hundred years of Western experience have demonstrated that the argument, though consistent, is wrong. Despite the existence of a functional equivalence between two forms of military power (accepted as the roles-and-missions equivalence at the outset of this essay) and the existence of the technical means to accomplish those functions, the fact remains that the environment and the technological means that posture us in those environments remain different. This is true of land and sea power; the examination of characteristics indicates that it is also true of airpower and space power.

The additional argument posed by advocates of the space plane is beside the point. Should a space plane actually come to exist, it would merely reflect the capabilities of both airpower and space power. Historically, though, dual-environment vehicles have proved more expensive and less capable than separate vehicles designed especially for each environment—witness the failure of the national aerospace plane (NASP). (One should note that there are few, if any, sea-capable tanks.) Such experience should at least call into question the wisdom of pursuing a space plane in the first place. Thus, doctrinal unification of aerospace power is no more justifiable than doctrinal unification of surface power.

In spite of compelling evidence that airpower and space power remain distinct, one can argue credibly that the Air Force, in practice, ought to manage both. The current, battle-proven emphasis on jointness runs counter to splitting off another component of the joint force and thereby providing one more seam in the battlefield. Fiscally, a separate space organization would require more overhead—a distinct bureaucracy, independent R&D, test and evaluation programs, and another acquisition stovepipe. The counterargument concedes that any new capability necessarily entails a cost. Because the United States could not exploit the new strategic capabilities offered by airpower in the confines of Army culture and doctrine, it paid the cost of producing a separate Air Force. Likewise, we cannot exploit the new capabilities offered by space power in the confines of Air Force culture and doctrine. We need only decide whether that capability justifies the cost.

Roles, missions, and basic tenets have always served as unifying themes across the services. Joint doctrine reflects common roles, missions, and tenets. Land, sea, and space power, as well as airpower, are functionally equivalent, based upon these common roles and missions. Furthermore, airpower and space power are closely tied by their mutual strategic function of effecting the use of military power from the third dimension. But airpower, land power, and sea power part company in the pursuit of those common roles, missions, and tenets. Realm-unique characteristics have justified the segregation of the air, land, and sea services. Comparing and contrasting the characteristics of airpower and space power serves to highlight the fact that space power is also a unique form of military power. Space power—as much as airpower, land power, and sea power—warrants separate development of theory and doctrine, as well as a separate service to organize, train, and equip forces to support that doctrine. It's a good news/bad news situation for the Air Force.

First, the bad news (and the answer to both questions put forward at the outset): *once technological development allows us to pursue the full spectrum of roles and missions from space, and the domestic will recognizes that the capability justifies the cost, the Air Force will have to cut its child loose in the form of a new Space Force.*[72] Ironically, this essay has repeatedly cited Joint Doctrine Tactics, Techniques, and Procedures (JDTTP) 3-14, *Space Operations,* to support many statements made herein, even though the essay's conclusion is diametrically opposed to Rear Adm Richard Macke's opening statement in that publication:

> Space cannot be considered a separate warfare arena. It crosses all warfare areas and all warfare services. Just as space surrounds and encompasses the entire globe, it surrounds, encompasses, and supports all warriors. To say space is the battleground of any unique warfighting group is paramount to disaster. All warfighters, regardless of the device on their chest or color of their uniform, must embrace space, understand space, and use space or be destined not to enjoy the tremendous advantage space can give.[73]

This is simply wrong. If one subtracts 50 years and replaces *space* with *air,* the same old flawed argument presents itself. It became apparent then, as it does now, that the characteristics of the new realm differed so dramatically from those of the current realms, that one needed a new service to organize, train, and equip forces in order to employ the tenets and satisfy the roles and missions assigned to joint military forces.

The statement in JDTTP 3-14 indicates an attitude of responsibility sharing that has forced the military away from a basic tenet of space power—centralized control. An elite Air Force Association (AFA) advisory group made the statement, "Who's in charge of the space program is *the* fundamental problem" (emphasis in original). That is on target. However, the group erred in concluding that "the solution lies in vesting R&D and acquisition functions for military space requirements of *all services* in the Air Force" (emphasis in original).[74] The distinctions between airpower and space power, as well as the service infighting that would result, suggest that such a solution is simply unworkable. A more palatable solution lies in the creation of a Space Force. The entire argument made in the AFA report supports such a move and eliminates many of the drawbacks mentioned. In any event, given the major differences in airpower and space power, such a Space Force is clearly on the horizon. The question is no longer *if* but *when* and *how.*

When

As mentioned above, we should create a separate Space Force when the technological development and domestic will allow pursuit of the full spectrum of roles and missions from space (i.e., not yet). Apparently, a compelling immediate motivation is missing. We find ourselves in a period that possesses (1) the necessary resources, (2) an unencumbered economy,[75] (3) a weak immediate motivation (here, the threat of proliferated space access), and (4) a common vision that supports specific technologies. It may be temporary, but it presents a window of opportunity.

The lack of centralized control—which results in service infighting, inefficiency, and duplication—may warrant a move now. A reasonable compromise would entail creation of a Space Force whose roles and missions statements do not include force application but whose theoretical and doctrinal development ought to include the potential for force application from space. Aspects of each service culture should contribute to that theoretical and doctrinal development: we must plan to fight while living and operating in a hostile environment (Navy), from a fixed, possibly fortified position/orbit (Army), and achieve the objective by force application from the third dimension (Air Force). The dominant nature of the last element, together with the fact that one must traverse the air in order to reach space, currently gives the Air Force a lead role in developing space systems.[76] The Air Force is clearly the primary player in military space, having an estimated budget of $2.6 billion for fiscal year 1996, as compared to projected Army spending of $110 million and Navy spending of $120 million.[77]

An often overlooked spin-off of the notion of a separate Space Force, however, carries good news for the Air Force. As noted, space power has some attributes that airpower cannot match, but the opposite is also true. *The danger of the Air Force's holding on to responsibility for space is that it will lose sight of the very necessary and unique capabilities that airpower, apart from space power, provides.* In addition to losing focus on airpower organization and doctrine, the Air Force will inevitably shortchange airpower if it tries to hold on to space in terms of organizing, training, and equipping space forces, despite limited funding.[78] Segregating airpower and space power is a good move for both, leaving experts in each to decide how best to develop theory and doctrine and subsequently invest in supporting organization, training, and equipment.

How

Because the standard military acquisitions approach for investment in space power may be premature, the following suggestion may have some merit: *Given the enormity of the physical problems discussed and the opportunity afforded by the collapse of a major threat, perhaps the United States ought to spend more of its current space budget on space-related education, training, and R&D, as opposed to operations and procurement.* If technological difficulties are enormous now and if theoretical technical advances continue at the current pace, it makes sense that access to space will become much cheaper in the future. Rather than producing next-generation dinosaurs, it is better to put money into R&D that will benefit the United States 25 years from now.

Objections to the effect that this would mean abandoning the defense technological and industrial base (DTIB) are unfounded. All fiscal decisions affect the DTIB. The question is not one of supporting the DTIB but of deciding what part of the DTIB to support: near-term manufacturing/production lines and operations or education, science, and R&D leading to long-term capabilities. The idea of a flawed approach that leads to the misallocation of limited military resources (i.e., trying to do too much too soon) is not new. The Third Reich made enormous investments in rocket technology—to the benefit of technology and to the detriment of Germany: "The technical fascination of being able to break through traditional limits . . . had overwhelmed any rigorous analysis of its likely impact. The most fundamental flaw in their thinking lay in the lack of any well-thought-out strategic concept of how the missile could actually affect the course of the war. It was the product of a narrow technological vision that obscured the strategic bankruptcy of the concept."[79]

At many military "futures and technology" conferences, the space technology of choice always assumes space weaponization in the form of various systems, such as TAVs. Why? The international community seems strongly opposed to the weaponization of space. Might an investment now to produce military space systems in the near term be a narrow technological vision that obscures the strategic bankruptcy of the concept? Some of the futures studies directed by the Air Force chief of staff are seriously considering the possibility of moving funds away from systems and toward basic research.[80]

We are on the threshold of a new era—the preeminence of space power. One should note that the preeminence of sea power did not immediately follow the ability to access the seas but required prolific, developed access to the realm, as well as domestic will, economic capability, and an accommodating international environment. The convergence of these factors for space has not occurred but seems close at hand. Any examination of the characteristics of airpower and space power shows that the two are not identical. The time is right to establish an organizational structure that can plan for our future in space but not inhibit the unique and necessary development of airpower. When the worldwide technological, economic, and political environment does converge—and space power becomes preeminent—will the United States be an economically burned-out nation that boosted the world into space 20 years early, or will it lead the world into space when the forces converge naturally?

Unity of command and unity of effort are basic military and managerial concepts that date from antiquity. For a brief period in the 1960s, President John F. Kennedy provided that unity, and it propelled us to the Moon. Such unity in the space community is sorely lacking today. The Air Force is the wrong place to focus that unity. To do so constitutes an attempt to force the merger of two unique realms. That is bad for space power and bad for airpower. The Air Force ought to be a major player—but not the only player. A unifying, independent space organization—drawing on the experience of NASA, the three armed services, and industry—has the best chance of making the right investment choices today that will put the United States at the forefront of space power tomorrow.

Notes

1. E. B. Potter, ed., *Sea Power: A Naval History* (Annapolis: Naval Institute Press, 1981), chap. 18. The notion of motivating discussion by alluding to the emergence of sea power at the turn of the century comes from a paper by Lt Col R. Pelligrini, prepared for a course in Science, Philosophy, Military Theory, and Technological Investment Strategy, School of Advanced Airpower Studies, Maxwell AFB, Ala., April 1995.

2. AFM 1-1, *Basic Aerospace Doctrine of the United States Air Force*, vol. 1, March 1992, 5.

3. AFDD 1, "Basic Air Force Doctrine," draft, 14 May 1996, 1.

4. As used here, military power is synonymous with land, sea, and space power, as well as airpower. The four realms recognized here are air, land, sea, and space; the prospect that information constitutes a fifth realm is yet to be confirmed and is not assumed.

5. One should note, however, that despite the publication of a variety of airpower theories, there is no comprehensive theory of airpower on par with the land power theory of Clausewitz or the sea power theory of Mahan. See H. Winton, "Air Power Theory: A Black Hole in the Wild Blue Yonder," *Air Power History* 39 (Winter 1992): 32.

6. As noted in AFM 1-1, a strategic attack (e.g., bombing an aircraft factory) can be a vital part of the realm-control mission, even if people typically see it as a force application mission.

7. AFDD 1 states that global reach/global power is supported by five war-fighting pillars: air superiority, space superiority, precision employment, information dominance, and global mobility (page 11). AFDD 4, "Space Operations Doctrine," 22 May 1996, states that Space Force operations should gain space superiority, which is further broken down into the conventional roles of control, force application, force enhancement, and force support (pages 6–10).

8. Department of the Air Force, *Global Presence* (Washington, D.C.: Department of the Air Force, 1995).

9. For example, air presence includes forward basing of airpower assets, the recognized projection capability of US airpower, involvement of airpower in humanitarian efforts, and the strategic role of the Air Force's intercontinental ballistic missile (ICBM) force.

10. The definition provided here is consistent with Air Force and joint doctrine on the subject of air and space forces: "Aerospace Control," role no. 1 in AFM 1-1, vol. 1, 7; "Counterair, Counterspace, and Counter-information" in AFDD 1, 42; "Space Control" (assure friendly use while denying use to the enemy) in AFDD 4, 4; "Space Control" in Joint Doctrine Tactics, Techniques, and Procedures (JDTTP) 3-14, *Space Operations*, April 1992; and "combat against enemy forces in space and their infrastructure" in the latest draft of JP 3-14, 13 March 1996. As used here, the term *discriminate* emphasizes US tendencies to avoid the use of indiscriminate weapons (weapons of mass destruction, various "nonlethal" weapons, etc.).

11. Subtle but important differences exist between Air Force and joint doctrine regarding force application. While joint doctrine focuses only on attack against enemy *forces*, Air Force doctrine allows for the possibility of attacking enemy critical nodes or key *targets*, including both enemy forces (interdiction, close air support, and C^2 attack) and strategic critical nodes (strategic attack) that are not necessarily part of the enemy force.

12. The definition provided here is consistent with Air Force and joint doctrine on the subject of air and space forces. The one internal discrepancy involves lift. AFM 1-1 includes lift in force enhancement, while JDTTP 3-14 puts it under force support. This essay assumes that lift falls under support, not enhancement, as does AFDD 4 (see page 9). As noted earlier, though, the role and mission matchups are not exclusive. Further, although one typically assumes that space assets will support terrestrial military functions, force enhancement could eventually cut both ways—that is, terrestrial assets may support space warfare.

13. The definition provided here is consistent with Air Force and joint doctrine on the subject of air and space forces.

14. See Giulio Douhet, *The Command of the Air,* trans. Dino Ferrari (1942; new imprint, Washington, D.C.: Office of Air Force History, 1983); and Phillip S. Meilinger, *Ten Propositions Regarding Air Power* (Washington, D.C.: Air Force History and Museums Program, 1995), 14–19.

15. AFDD 4, "Space Operations Doctrine," draft, August 1995, 5.

16. "Defining Missile Defense: What Missile, Which Defense?" *Military Space* 13 (8 January 1996): 1–5. Current budget debates focus on the level of Department of Defense (DOD) ballistic missile defense (BMD) spending. This is not a question of whether or not to pursue BMD but one of how much and how soon. President William Clinton recently vetoed the $3 billion proposed by Congress, which exceeded his request of $2.44 billion.

17. The outdated AFM 2-25, *Air Force Operational Doctrine—Space Operations,* March 1991, sorted Space Force characteristics into environ-mentally, logistically, and politically influenced characteristics. The taxonomy used in this essay renames these as realm environment, realm access, and political characteristics, and adds the categories of development/employment and realm-afforded capability.

18. Lt Col David Lupton, *On Space Warfare: A Space Power Doctrine* (Maxwell AFB, Ala.: Air University Press, 1988), 33–46.

19. AFM 1-1; AFDD l; AFDD 4 (1995); JDTTP 3-14; FM 100-5, *Operations*, 14 June 1993, 2-16 through 2-18; JP 3-14 ("purpose: to present a framework for thinking about future space control operations"). One should note that although capabilities-based planning has merit, threat-based and objective-based planning are other options worth consideration.

20. Paul Stares, *The Militarization of Space: US Policy, 1945–1984* (New York: Cornell University Press, 1985), 206–7. As early as 1978, miniature homing vehicles were successfully launched from F-15 platforms, using first-stage boost via a modified Boeing short-range attack missile (SRAM) and second-stage boost via a Vought Altair III.

21. Maj Ronald M. Reed, USAF judge advocate, Maxwell AFB, Ala., interviewed by author, January 1996. Additionally, "as with all other branches of international law, space law is based on the premise that conduct is presumed to be lawful in the absence of prohibitions." C. Christol, *The Modern International Law of Outer Space* (New York: Pergamon Press, 1982), 59–60.

22. "Legal writers differ greatly in their views of the effect that the outbreak of war between parties to a treaty has on that instrument. A general statement on the subject would have to mention that certain treaties, such as those regulating the conduct of hostilities, actually come into full effect at the outbreak of war; that treaties of friendship or alliance, as well as all other agreements classifiable as political in nature, concluded between opposing belligerents prior to a war, come to an end at the beginning of the conflict; that nonpolitical agreements are suspended for the duration of the conflict; and that a certain few types of treaties involving matters such as private property rights and possibly also boundary agreements not related to frontiers involved in the conduct of hostilities remain in force during the war. Similarly, agreements that by their very nature were final in character would not be affected at all by the outbreak of war." Gerhard von Glahn, *Law among Nations: An Introduction to Public International Law* (New York: Collier-Macmillan, 1981), 623–24.

23. Air University (AU)-18, *Space Handbook: A Warfighter's Guide to Space*, vol. 1, December 1993, 41.

24. Several well-known texts include G. Allison's *Essence of Decision* (New York: HarperCollins, 1971); and J. March's *A Primer on Decision Making* (New York: Free Press, 1994).

25. Not published as official US space policy, the unilateral move not to fund the production of ASAT weapons and their testing in space occurred in the late 1980s in response to a similar move by the Soviets. Current US funding decisions do not favor the weaponization of space.

26. *National Space Policy*, National Security Directive 30 (Washington, D.C.: Office of the White House Press Secretary, 2 November 1989).

27. *Department of Defense Space Policy* (Washington, D.C.: Government Printing Office, March 1987).

28. Findings of the Air Force Blue Ribbon Panel on the Future of the Air Force in Space, as reported in AU-18, vol. 1, 73.

29. See C. McKinley, "Air Force Space Command's High Ground Strategy," draft, AFSPACECOM/XPX, 23 February 1996.

30. P. Calvocoressi and G. Wint, *Total War: The Story of World War II* (New York: Pantheon Books, 1972), 522. One should note that the political will to dominate a particular realm has historically been a "touchy" issue when humanity is on the threshold of gaining significant access to a new environment. The Hague Convention of 1899 prohibited the bombardment of cities from aerial balloons at the outset of mankind's accession to the air. This prohibition, however, was not renewed in 1907.

31. The Navy means of satisfying its role of forward presence (demonstrating national commitment) differs somewhat from the air or land means. Freedom of the seas does not require negotiated forward basing of air and land assets on sovereign territory. By virtue of the Outer Space Treaty of 1967, the means of satisfying forward presence in space is much more akin to the means of doing so on the sea.

32. One can argue that this is simply the result of recent US fighting for matters of less than "vital" interests. It does not detract from the significance of the characteristic, because American military involvement in foreign ventures that require fighting for less than vital interests will no doubt continue.

33. Space operators are typically "remote"—data-linked to the space asset but physically isolated from the battlefield by virtue of being based in the continental United States.

34. AFDD 4, 22 May 1996, 3.

35. See Air Force Association Special Report, *Facing Up to the Space Problem*, 1 November 1994.

36. AFM 1-1, 8.

37. AFDD 4 (1995), 3.

38. Wernher von Braun, "Man Will Conquer Space Soon," *Collier's*, 22 March 1952, 1. One should note that, at the time, the Van Allen radiation belts had yet to be discovered. Von Braun did not realize that an orbit at an altitude of 1,075 miles would be a dangerous place to put a space colony. This raises another caution regarding our lack of experience in space: what else don't we know?

39. The shuttle carries its empty weight of 105,000 kg and a maximum payload of 21,140 kg to LEO (204 km, 28.45°) and uses a total launch thrust of 7,781,400 pounds (6,600,000 pounds in the first two minutes contributed by the solid-rocket expendables, and 1,181,400 pounds over the first eight minutes and 50 seconds by the orbiter main engines). An Atlas II can place 6,000 kg in a similar orbit with its 485,000 pounds of launch thrust. *Jane's Space Directory* (Alexandria, Va.: Jane's Information Group Ltd., 1995), 274.

Placing an empty F-16 (11,300 kg) and a reasonable payload (3,700 kg) in the same location via a shuttle-type approach requires 15/105 the thrust of the shuttle—roughly 1.1 million pounds. Placing an empty F-16 and reasonable payload in the same location using an Atlas-type approach requires 15/6 the thrust of the Atlas—roughly 1.2 million pounds.

40. The 29,000 pounds of thrust of the F-16's General Electric F110-GE-129 engine is at sea level; thrust declines slowly with increasing altitude, and the mass density of air above 20 miles will cause the engine to flame out.

41. The space shuttle does have a capability to service and/or retrieve spacecraft, but it is neither efficient nor responsive.

42. One can make a good argument that if spacecraft are small and cheap and if launch is fast and cheap, satellites ought to be replaced—not recovered and repaired. The counterargument is (1) those are big *ifs* and (2) one would eventually have to deal with an abundance of throwaway space systems because they would clutter LEO.

43. Theo Pirard, "Space Ambitions in a Changing World," *Spaceflight,* January 1996, 2.

44. Density = exp(−mgz/kT), where z is altitude, m is the molecular weight in kg of air, g is the local acceleration of gravity, k is Boltzmann's constant, and T is temperature (degrees Kelvin).

45. R. McNutt, "Orbiting Space Debris: Dangers, Measurement and Mitigation" (Hanscom AFB, Mass.: Phillips Laboratory Directorate of Geophysics, 1992).

46. Although the "air" has one-millionth the density at LEO as opposed to sea level, the net accumulation of drag effects at LEO can become significant over the extended duration of satellite lifetimes.

47. Integrating acceleration of 32 ft/s² with respect to time (t), velocity = 32t ft/s, and integrating this again with respect to t, distance = 16t² ft. Note: 88 ft/s = 60 MPH.

48. The propulsion benefit of lift in the atmosphere does come at the cost of drag. The example demonstrates that the benefit clearly outweighs the cost.

49. Harrier in CAP: 1.5 hrs. Stationary Harrier, with the same fuel load as the CAP Harrier (2 x 228 gal external tanks + 757 gal internal) = 1,213 gal, at ~ 6 lb/gal ⇒ ~7,300 lb of fuel. The Harrier's Pegasus 11-61 engine takeoff performance rating is 23,800 lb of thrust, while an optimistic estimate of its specific fuel consumption is .8 lb/hr for every pound of thrust. The burn rate for a stationary Harrier is about .8 x 23,800 = 19,040 lb per hour. With 7,300 lb of fuel, the Harrier could stay in such a position for roughly 23 minutes. *Jane's Atlas of the World's Aircraft* (Alexandria, Va.: International Thomson Publishing Company, 1995).

50. The volume of a sphere of radius r is $V_r = (4/3)7\pi r^3$. Using the radius of the Earth $r_e = 6,371$ km, the volume of the atmosphere below 100 km is $V_{100} = V_{6,471} - V_{6,371} = 5.18 \times 10^{10}$ km³, and the volume of space out to GEO is $V_{GEO} = V_{42,157} - V_{6,471} = 3.13 \times 10^{14}$ km³.

51. AFM 1-1, vol. 2, 63–70.

52. See AFDD 1, draft, 15 August 1995 and 14 May 1996.

53. J. Hyatt et al., *Space Power 2010* (Maxwell AFB, Ala.: Air University, May 1995), 32.

54. The aerospace control war game, held at the Air University Wargaming Center, Maxwell AFB, Ala., August 1995, and the Navy's technology initiatives game (TIG)-95, National Maritime Intelligence Center, Suitland, Md. (attended by this author).

55. P. Anson and D. Cummings, "The First Space War: The Contribution of Satellites to the Gulf War," in Alan D. Campen, ed., *The First Information War: The Story of Communications, Computers, and Intelligence Systems in the Persian Gulf War* (Fairfax, Va.: AFCEA International Press, 1992), 130.

56. N. Hudson, "Air Force Researching Ground-Based Lasers," *Air Force Times*, 30 May 1993. Air Force Space Command estimates that 30 countries will have satellite reconnaissance capability by the year 2000.

57. For information about the USA Eyeglass Satellite, see Berner, Lanphier, and Associates, "Many Nations Feed Commercial Imagery Market," *Space News*, 6 March 1995.

58. That is, in coordinated orbital paths and networks.

59. Circular Keplarian Orbital Velocity: $V_c = (m_e G/r_s)^{1/2}$ where Earth mass: $m_e = 5.974 \times 10^{24}$ kg,

Earth radius: $r_e = 6{,}371$ km,

Satellite orbital radius: $r_s = r_e + $ altitude, and

Newton's gravitational constant $G = 6.673 \times 10^{-11}$ Nm^2/(kg^2)

Orbital Velocity LEO (200 km): 7,789 m/s ~ 17,425 MPH

60. Kinetic energy, or work done against inertia, is the appropriate measure since the inertia of the satellite must be maneuvered.

Mach 2 at low altitude ~ 1,440 MPH or ~ 645 m/s

Kinetic energy $KE = (1/2)mv^2$:

$KE_{sat} = (1/2) \times 100$ kg $\times (7{,}800$ m/s$)^2$ ~ 3×10^9 Nm

$KE_{F-16} = (1/2) \times 14{,}625$ kg $\times (645$ m/s$)^2$ ~ 3×10^9 Nm

61. M. Rampino, Maxwell AFB, Ala., interviewed by author, January 1996. The figure mentioned is *not* an eleven-hundred-mile lateral movement in orbit capability. It refers to lift-and-drag-aided RLV maneuverability within the atmosphere, minimizing the more expensive proposition of spending fuel to change orbit.

62. This assumes that the right satellites are in the right orbit (limitation of maneuver) with the right capability (limitation of flexibility) and that those satellites can precisely acquire the right target (limitation of precision).

63. Thomas A. Keaney and Eliot A. Cohen, *Gulf War Air Power Survey*, vol. 3, *Logistics and Support* (Washington, D.C.: Department of the Air Force, 1993), chap. 3.

64. Total Energy = Kinetic + Potential Energy

$KE_{sat} = (1/2) \times 908$ kg $\times (7{,}800$ m/s$)^2$ ~ 2.762×10^{10} Nm

$PE_{sat} = 908$ kg $\times (9.807$ N/kg$) \times 200{,}000$ m ~ 1.781×10^9 Nm

$TE_{sat} = 2.94 \times 10^{10}$ Nm

A one ton (2,000 lb) TNT explosion equates to 4.184×10^9 Nm.

530 knots ~ 608 MPH ~ 272 m/s

$KE_{30K} = (1/2)$ x 908 kg x $(272 \text{ m/s})^2$ ~ 3.359 x 10^7 Nm

$PE_{30K} = 908$ kg x (9.807 N/kg) x 30,000 m ~ 2.671 x 10^8 Nm

$TE_{30K} = 3.007$ x 10^8 Nm

65. Duncan Lennox and Arthur Rees, eds., *Jane's Air Launched Weapons*, no. 19, *Low Drag General Purpose Bombs* (Alexandria, Va.: Jane's Information Group Ltd., 1992).

66. Lt J. Wesson, Air Force Wright Labs, Eglin AFB, Fla., telephone interview by author, February 1996. Tritonal has 120–125 percent of the explosive power of TNT, while state-of-the-art conventional explosives—including experimental APET-257 and PWX MOD19—have demonstrated explosive capability on the order of 140 percent of TNT. Surprisingly, few if any new explosive materials have presented themselves since World War II. Current research efforts basically address evolutionary improvements to TNT derivatives.

67. Joseph Anselmo, "NASA Issues Wake-Up Call to Industry," *Aviation Week & Space Technology*, 19 February 1996.

68. Lt Col Stephen A. Coulombe, "The Airborne Laser: Pie in the Sky or Vision of Future Theater Missile Defense?" *Airpower Journal* 8, no. 3 (Fall 1994): 62.

69. Circular Keplarian Orbital Velocity calculation yields

Orbital Velocity GEO (35,786 km): 3,075 m/s ~ 6,880 MPH

Orbital Velocity LEO (204 km): 7,787 m/s ~ 17,420 MPH

70. Lagrange points are gravity wells in space—equilibrium points that remain stationary with respect to the rotating coordinate frame. Five naturally occur in the near-Earth/Moon environment.

71. As defined by Carl von Clausewitz, genius affords human decision making based on wisdom and requires intellect, experience, and bold moral character. *On War*, ed. Michael Howard and Peter Paret (Princeton, N.J.: Princeton University Press, 1976).

72. One could also make a good argument that functional commands could take on the responsibility of organizing, training, and equipping all forces (i.e., provide the money). This would be a dramatic shift, since the services would be relegated to operational corps status. As such, the new Space Force already exists in the form of US Space Command. This essay, however, does not address this level of the organizational argument.

73. JDTTP 3-14, 1.

74. Gen Russell E. Dougherty et al., *Facing Up to the Space Problem*, Air Force Association Special Report, 1 November 1994, 12.

75. The present economy is at least as "unencumbered" as that of the late nineteenth century. The lack of an immediate threat actually affords the luxury of redirecting funds toward new environment exploits.

76. Dougherty, 14.

77. "Military Space $ on Rise in FY96," *Military Space*, 20 February 1995, 1.

78. From the space power perspective, space systems will also find it difficult to compete with air systems in an Air Force environment.

79. Michael Neufeld, *The Rocket and the Reich: Peenemünde and the Coming of the Ballistic Missile Era* (New York: Free Press, 1995), 52.

80. Revolutionary planning efforts include *New World Vistas: Air and Space Power for the 21st Century* (Washington, D.C.: USAF Scientific Advisory Board, 1995–1996), which seriously considers basic research as a funding priority; and *2025* (Maxwell AFB, Ala.: Air University Press, 1996), consisting of three monographs and four volumes of white papers.

Chapter 15

Reflections on the Search for Airpower Theory

Dr. I. B. Holley Jr.

Technology advances—novel weapons as well as ancillary equipment—are devised, but until suitable doctrines are formulated to optimize their potential, they remain under-exploited. In short, there is an intellectual dimension to every significant advance in weaponry. *The Paths of Heaven* is about that intellectual dimension, beliefs, and the manner in which military people and scholars have conceptualized the way they would exploit the air weapon as it has evolved in the twentieth century.

Some people have been rigorously disciplined in their thinking; others have not, clearly reflecting the limitations of their thought processes and, by implication, their deficiencies in education. When one attempts to grapple with the problem of how these thinkers, especially officers in the different services at various times, have tried to integrate technological innovations effectively in their organizations, the crucial importance of professional military education becomes clear. A service that does not develop rigorous thinkers among its leaders and decision makers is inviting friction, folly, and failure.

In an attempt to embrace all these varied individuals, this book's subtitle promises that *The Paths of Heaven* is an account of "the evolution of airpower theory"—a survey of some of the leading thinkers. In studying the foregoing chapters, this author was struck by the unsystematic, undisciplined thinking that all too often characterized the writings of the "theorists" described. Establishing a baseline against which to measure the thinkers in question may be useful.

One can classify ideas by the way they are authenticated.[1] The following array of terms gives us a useful spectrum against which to set our airpower thinkers:

- *Theories* are ideas that are systematically prepared for authentication.
- *Visions* are ideas *not* systematically prepared for authentication.
- *Illusions* are ideas that could not survive systematic preparation for authentication.
- *Myths* are ideas that exempt themselves from any systematic authentication.
- *Facts* are ideas that have already passed the authentication process.
- *Falsehoods* are ideas certain to fail the authentication process.

Clearly, Gen Giulio Douhet was a *visionary*. With only the scantiest empirical evidence to go on, he visualized the concept of strategic air war. By sheer imagination, he also recognized the necessity of air supremacy or what he called "command of the air"—all this before Italy had even entered the war in 1915. Not surprisingly, these profound visions of what the future would bring were, when it came to details, seriously flawed. Douhet failed to anticipate the character of air-to-air combat, vastly overestimated the impact of conventional bombing, and misunderstood the importance of aircraft other than bombers. In these and many other respects, Douhet's vision was decidedly flawed. But the evidence of experience would overcome these details. The significance of visionaries lies not in the details but in the stream of thought they set in train.

Although Douhet's works were not widely used by military schools in other countries, his vision of strategic airpower undoubtedly was a significant inspiration to Edgar Gorrell and Gen Billy Mitchell, who carried his ideas to the United States and ran with them in their own way. We may conclude, then, that Douhet had a grand *vision* of airpower, but—lacking the factual evidence of experience—his vision was not systematically prepared for authentication. It would remain elusive and difficult to assess.

The British thinkers about airpower, Hugh Trenchard and Jack Slessor, had an advantage over Douhet in that they had more extensive experience in the application of the air weapon. Given the fragile condition of British ground forces, Trenchard early defined the offensive character of airpower, concentrating on air superiority and interdiction. But he also visualized the importance of strategic bombing and late in the war had the opportunity to organize an independent air force to that end. In contrast to Douhet, he specified appropriate industrial targets big enough to be identified from the air—evidence of practical realism born of experience.

Thus far, Trenchard would seem to rank as a theorist, resting his ideas on factual evidence, but like so many airpower thinkers, he indulged in visions or even illusions. When he claimed that the psychological effects of bombing outweighed the material as 20 to one, he was speculating—with no whit of factual evidence to support his contention. If this had been an ill-judged remark casually tossed off, one would attach no great significance to it, but his belief that airpower could break the morale of enemy populations—which in turn would force the hostile government to sue for peace—became one of his basic tenets. This view of "war [as] largely a psychological effort" (p. 54)[2] found its way into Royal Air Force (RAF) manuals throughout the interwar period—an example of an unsupported belief or supposition becoming the basis of service doctrine.

The idea that war was largely a psychological effort reached even more deeply into British thinking. Given the vulnerability of London, so accessible by air from the Continent, and given the British propensity to be repelled by the thought of indiscriminate bombing of cities (read "women and children"), responsible RAF officers were at pains to insist that their targets would be legitimate industrial sites supporting the enemy war effort. Even from the vantage point of hindsight, it is easy to see how completely this line of thinking under-estimated the scope of population control in an authoritarian state.

Although RAF thinking about airpower contained flaws, there was also a good deal of sound thinking based on the experience of World War I—as revealed by Jack Slessor's writings. His perceptions on the need for close cooperation with ground forces and the utility of collocating air and ground headquarters were fully certified by World War II. Nonetheless, one is left aghast at the extent to which unchallenged assumptions permeated RAF official thinking, given that the very survival of the nation almost certainly hinged on the soundness of its airpower.

Was Billy Mitchell, "the messiah of American airpower" (p. 80), any more rigorous in his thinking than his RAF contemporaries? The present-day United States Air Force has made an icon of Mitchell, but a close reading of his writing shows how shallow his analysis actually was. Moreover, his most spectacular accomplishment, sinking the battleship *Ostfriesland,* involved—as his naval critics charged, not to put too fine a point on it—cheating.

The whole story of the battleship trials is more complex than the popular image of Mitchell's triumph. To begin with, the Navy offered as a target the obsolete battleship *Iowa,* unmanned and radio-controlled, steaming off the Virginia Capes. Mitchell, well aware of how difficult it would be to *find* a moving ship, let alone *hit* it, declined the offer. He preferred a sitting duck.

By the agreed-upon terms of the *Ostfriesland* trial, Air Service bombers were to make a series of attacks with different weights of bombs, allowing for inspection between bombings. Attacks were to be carried out at a prescribed altitude, above the probable volume of antiaircraft fire if the vessel actually had been manned and defended. Mitchell ignored these terms, especially the altitude stipulations, and dropped his bombs from an unrealistically low level to ensure fatal hits. He got what he wanted—those wonderful photographs of the *Ostfriesland,* keel up and about to plunge to the bottom.

In short, were Mitchell's claims to have replaced the Navy mere *illusions* (ideas that could not survive systematic preparation for authentication) rather than sound theories? Should we knock him off his pedestal with the righteous indignation of iconoclasts? Perhaps so on the facts of the matter. But there's another perspective. Like Douhet, Mitchell was more *visionary* than *theorist.* He was a careless and unsystematic thinker, but he inspired men with his *vision*. Hap Arnold, Carl Spaatz, and Ira Eaker—to name only the obvious individuals—were among his votaries, carrying the torch for strategic airpower and an independent air force through the difficult interwar years. Sometimes visions and even myths are more powerful than the most meticulously and rationally supported theories.

Mitchell brought trouble on himself needlessly. In calling for a single air arm that would include the air components of the Navy, he aroused the implacable opposition of the sailors. Had he given even superficial thought to British experience—the failure that followed the absorption of naval air assets by the RAF—he could have avoided the opposition on the part of the Navy that has persisted in some quarters even to the present.

Ironically, Mitchell may have been the unwitting agent in creating the carrier Navy. Although all battleship admirals were by no means as reactionary and opposed to aviation as sometimes pictured, the *Ostfriesland* sinking clearly played directly into the hands of the small coterie of naval aviation pioneers. Even the most obdurate mossback admirals could scarcely reject the naval pilots' contention that the Navy would be far better off developing its own air arm than allowing the task to slip into the hands of Mitchell and his congressional allies, who were calling for an independent air service with a monopoly of all military aviation.

The Navy's success in developing aviation appears to hinge on two fortuitous events. The first was the decision to put William Moffett, a "safe" and experienced battleship admiral, in charge of aviation. The second was the unintended consequence of the naval disarmament treaty of 1922. Forced to discontinue construction on two unfinished battle cruisers, the Navy, at the instigation of Moffett, converted these hulls into the carriers *Lexington* and *Saratoga*. Is it too much to suggest that the doctrinal development and training of naval aviators provided by these two carriers in the interwar years were crucial to the Navy's role in winning the war in the Pacific in World War II? By the end of that war, carrier admirals were governing the Navy in much the same way bomber generals would govern the Air Force a few years later. In this respect, one might say that naval aviators were somewhat more successful than their Air Force colleagues in bringing their organization and airpower theory together.

French aviation fared badly in World War II. Several factors contributed to this; the political upheavals of the Popular Front and the labor unrest that followed, as well as the nationalization of the aircraft industry, all took their toll. The root cause, however, lay in the prevailing perception of airpower. Senior army leaders saw support of the army as the primary mission of aviation. Moreover, the high command was defense oriented, so even after the air arm became a separate service in the 1930s, even modest attempts to foster a strategic role were blunted.

Some airmen, inspired by Douhet's vision, articulated the notion that strategic bombardment might have a major role in bringing victory. But in the prevailing climate, which frowned on dissent from established doctrine, scant support existed for any radical shift to offensive strategic aviation. This chill on free discussion is all the more curious in light of the superb educational infrastructure the French military possessed in the *École Superior*. Was it actually as good as people perceived it to be? Whatever the shortcoming of French theory and practice with regard to aviation, no evidence shows that it had significant impact one way or another on airpower theory in the United States during the interwar years.

Although Douhet's vision of strategic bombardment had both direct and indirect impacts on US thought, this was not true for most other Italian theory and practice during the interwar years. In a cynical display of early "political correctness," Air Marshal Italo Balbo paid lip service to Douhet, who was a favorite of Mussolini, but put into practice the concepts of Gen Amedeo Mecozzi, which favored army support over an independent, strategic role for aviation. The Italian air force performed effectively in its army-support role in Spain, thus seeming to confirm the validity of Mecozzi's theories.

A massive strategic bombardment of Barcelona, ordered by Mussolini, not only failed to break the will of the Catalonians but stiffened their resistance. This may have persuaded Mecozzi that he was on the right track in downplaying Douhet's ideas, but from the vantage point of the present it is of particular interest, for it was a lesson that seems to have had no impact whatever on the British belief that strategic bombing would result in the collapse of civilian morale. This British failure to derive much benefit from the air operations of the Spanish Civil War, a neglect roughly paralleled by the United States, raises questions about the character and effectiveness of the attaché and observer systems then in place—not to mention the whole question of military intelligence.

Soviet influence on US airpower theory in the interwar years was virtually nonexistent. This is scarcely surprising, given the language barrier, the long delay in establishing formal diplomatic recognition, and the country's general remoteness. Because of the backwardness of Soviet industry, one doubts whether the USSR could have fielded an effective strategic bomber force, even if Stalin's paranoia had not liquidated such promising theorists of strategic air war as Mikhail Tukhachevsky and A. N. Lapchinsky.

Of all the European powers, Germany was in the best position to perfect airpower theory. Even though denied an air force by the terms of the Versailles Treaty, the country had already established a firm tradition on which to mount an independent air arm. During World War I, it acquired a centralized air command and a separate air general staff. During the Weimar years, the Germans kept these alive with a shadow staff and their curious eight-year expatriate operation in Russia. With the Luftwaffe's strong tradition of objective after-action reporting and thorough analysis of foreign airpower theories, its officers in the 1930s came up with a remarkably broad-gauge doctrine that stressed the primacy of strategic bombardment but did not neglect the importance of tactical support of the armies.

Thus by 1936, Luftwaffe doctrine called for a bomber-heavy force. Several circumstances were to warp this orientation substantially. Because the Luftwaffe lacked an adequate bombsight in quantity production, its experience with high-level bombing proved disappointing. Further, thinking largely in Continental terms, especially of France and Poland as enemies, the Germans designed their bombers for relatively short-range flights. And just at this juncture, Gen Ernst Udet witnessed the effectiveness of US Navy dive-bombers and returned home to insist on converting the Luftwaffe to a dive-bomber force. The success of Condor Legion dive-bombers against Republican ground forces in Spain exercised a subtle but powerful reorientation of Luftwaffe thought toward support of the army.

What then was the message that all the Continental powers displayed on the eve of World War II to any potential inquirer? All gave lip service to the possibility of a strategic strike force, but they configured their air arms and oriented their doctrine largely in terms of support for ground arms. Little in the surviving record suggests that US officers of the interwar years engaged in any serious inquiry into European air theory. It seems clear, however, that with the exception of the RAF, the air arms of the great nations of Europe offered substantial affirmation to the prevailing notion of the US Army General Staff that the principal function of aviation was to support ground forces.

In the United States, the air arm was still a part of the Army. The experience of World War I had convinced Army leaders that aviation remained a vital component—absolutely necessary to survival. For that reason, they clung tenaciously to retaining control of air assets. They were not totally blind to the concept of strategic bombing, but their views of what this constituted tended to be more restricted to Army concerns than were the views of airmen.

If Army leaders seemed less than enthusiastic about strategic air, one must admit that they had some good reasons for their stand. During the war, strategic bombing had failed to measure up to the brash claims and expectations of Billy Mitchell and others. In one notable incident, a flight of American Expeditionary Force (AEF) bombers into Germany had become disoriented and mistakenly landed on a German airfield. The Germans, with an uncharacteristic sense of humor, sent a message across Allied lines saying, "Thanks for the airplanes, but what should we do with the flight commander?" The nub of the difficulty, of course, lay in the fact that the claims of strategic bombing visionaries far outstripped the technical capabilities of equipment then available. The situation persisted almost down to the beginning of World War II, when long-range, high-altitude bombers such as the B-17 became available.

With the Army clinging to the air arm as essential to its operations, votaries of Mitchell's vision came to believe that only by creating a separate service would aviation ever be able to prove that it could provide a more efficient route to victory than that offered by conventional surface forces. A rational approach to this goal would seem to call for a campaign to convince the Army that aviation could accomplish the strategic mission without jeopardizing the support function.

Unfortunately, Mitchell's followers were, for the most part, zealots who sponsored bills in Congress to establish a separate air force with its promise of a strategic raison d'être. This only hardened Army determination to hang on to its air arm. The very word *strategic* became anathema, making it increasingly difficult for airmen to secure funds for ever-heavier, long-range, high-altitude bombers rather than aircraft more suited to Army support roles. With some justice, the Army could complain that airmen were ungrateful. After all, the War Department spent an increasing percentage of its funds on the air arm—more than a quarter of its annual outlay by the eve of World War II. From the perspective of the infantry, artillery, and all the supporting services, the Air Corps seemed to be getting more than its fair share— especially in proportion to the small number of air officers involved.

Why were the airmen so blind? Why did they fail to see that the situation called for subtle tactics and a better understanding of Army sensibilities? The answer appears to lie in the institutional arrangements established to develop Air Corps leaders. In its final configuration, the nearest thing airmen had to a think tank was the Air Corps Tactical School (ACTS)—supposedly their premier educational institution—at Maxwell Field, Alabama. Sadly, ACTS was more oriented to training than to true education, as revealed by the doctrines devised there.

The faculty of ACTS were, for the most part, hardworking officers, brave men, and able pilots. They were not, on the whole, broadly educated. They turned out doctrines that pursued the Mitchell vision but largely lacked the necessary authentication. In many respects, their doctrinal pro-mulgations were *illusions* (ideas that could not survive systematic preparation for authentication). The meandering positions taken by both sides in the debate over the issue of escort fighters for strategic bombers, described in an earlier chapter, are but one example that illustrates the lack of rigor in the thinking of airmen. They confused supposition with fact, and they left unexplored and unanswered assumptions floating in midair. To be sure, some perceptive individuals— students as well as faculty—did on occasion raise skeptical challenges, but these seldom seem to have led to any significant reworking of the official line. In sum, although official and unofficial historians laud ACTS, a close study of the thinking done there in the interwar years can often be an embarrassment to the present-day Air Force.

Isn't it ironic that one finds the portrait of Muir "Santy" Fairchild, the man who had the vision to establish Air University after World War II, in an obscure position at the back entrance to the magnificent Air University Library. By contrast, Claire Chennault, whose shoddy thinking and self-serving retrospective distortions muddied the doctrinal picture so badly, is memorialized with a prominently placed granite monument. One can only hope that the monument reflects his World War II leadership of the Flying Tigers—not the quality of his thinking at ACTS as an airpower theorist.

In sum, the officers who advanced airpower theory at the interwar Air Corps Tactical School were undoubtedly on the right path when they defined the primary objective of the air arm as strategic. But their thinking on how best to implement that faith was seriously flawed. Their assumptions about bomber defense were unrealistic, as were their assumptions about the accuracy of precision bombing, which largely ignored considerations of weather and the difficulties of navigation and target identification. For all their talk about the "industrial web," when the war came, their target folders, for the most part, were empty. Given the paucity of funds for experimentation, one could forgive them for many shortfalls if the record showed that they were asking searching questions on these topics, even if they lacked the resources to answer them. But they were *not* asking such questions, and *that* is the lesson that should goad future generations of Air Force officers.

Among all the notable airpower thinkers, Alexander de Seversky is one of the most interesting. He is the outsider. Although he had a spectacular career as an air officer in the Russian service in World War I, his advocacy for airpower came many years later, when he was a civilian and successful aircraft designer. So he came to his role from a rather different context than did virtually all the other advocates of strategic air. In point of fact, de Seversky was not really an original thinker and contributor to theory but a publicist, propagandist, and purveyor of the ideas of others.

De Seversky is, however, well worth consideration, for his career sheds a good bit of light on the very shortcomings that this chapter addresses. He was a brilliantly creative engineer and aircraft designer whose P-35 fighter represented a great stride forward in its day; it proved especially noteworthy for its influence on the mighty "Jug"—the P-47 of World War II. But de Seversky's brilliance extended beyond designing aircraft. He was certainly on the right track when he patented a scheme for air-to-air refueling and formulated big plans for internal tankage to extend the range of fighter aircraft. To be sure, a patent on air-to-air refueling is not the same thing as a fully perfected system in actual use after much trial and error. Of interest here is the brush-off he received from Air Corps officials when he proffered these ideas.

Airpower theory is not just a matter of defining the various roles and missions of air weapons. Such theory requires the conceptualization of ways to implement it. De Seversky saw the need for bomber escorts to accompany strategic bombers, which would require long-range capabilities. He turned to increased internal tankage and the notion of air-to-air refueling. At the time, neither possibility may have been an entirely satisfactory solution to the problem, but he was thinking toward a solution, whereas Air Corps leaders were not.

The ultimate solution to the escort fighter was, of course, the drop tank. Here, too, Air Corps leaders were so narrowly committed to the mission of fighters in their fighter-versus-fighter role that they refused to visualize them functioning as escorts. Long after the need to extend fighter range was manifest, no less an individual than Carl Spaatz recommended against the adoption of drop tanks. Curious about the seeming blindness on the part of an unquestionably able officer, this writer sought out the staff correspondence on this issue. Sure enough, Spaatz signed the document, but it was drafted by one of his subordinates—Hoyt Vandenberg. Is it not ironic that the two men who later became the first and second chief of staff, respectively, of the newly established US Air Force both displayed so little imagination in grappling with this critical problem?

De Seversky was a brilliant designer but a mediocre businessman, so nudging him out of control of his company so that it could achieve a high level of production was probably a prudent move. But did Hap Arnold handle the transition as tactfully as he should have? The depth of Arnold's involvement remains unclear, but given the assault on de Seversky's self-esteem, not only ousting him from his position but also wounding his pride by changing the name of his company to Republic Aircraft was probably a mistake. Surely, Arnold might have expended greater effort in assuaging de Seversky's damaged ego. This too was an aspect of airpower thinking. Arnold's failure would cost him—and the air arm—dearly.

Was de Seversky a good publicist and propagandist? He was certainly indefatigable, and undoubtedly he had a profound impact upon public opinion in the United States. Nonetheless, he too was a flawed thinker. His petty vindictiveness toward Arnold was counterproductive, and his public criticism of the Air Force would have been more productive if done privately. Even more serious was his unexplained but implacable criticism of the Navy, which was rapidly turning into an effective carrier service, even as he lambasted battleship dogma.

Did the atomic bomb substantiate Douhet's and Mitchell's claims about strategic bombing? Well, yes and no. On the one hand, the atom bomb certainly made it possible to destroy a nation. On the other hand, nations soon learned that the balance of terror—usually presented as the doctrine of mutually assured destruction (MAD)—gave political and military leaders reason to peer over the abyss and draw back. This was *deterrence*, an aspect of airpower theory not envisioned by the early military theorists. Curiously enough, theory in the nuclear world has remained largely the product of academic scholars rather than military officers and has involved a subtlety of reasoning far more sophisticated than that of the early airpower thinkers.

The scholars seemed to turn the equation upside down. Intercontinental missiles for destroying enemy weapons destabilize because they offer a first-strike threat, but their launching facilities are vulnerable. By contrast, submarine-launched missiles, though less accurate, pose a real threat to civilian populations. Thus, they become a stabilizing force because their relative invulnerability makes them available for a second strike. As Karl Mueller observes, this amounts to saying that "being able to kill weapons is bad, while being able to kill people is good" (p. 303). After coming to the obvious conclusion that antiballistic missile (ABM) defenses are destabilizing, we enter treaties to curb their use. This is not a characteristic posture for military men who have generally favored more weapons rather than fewer.

But wait. As George Orwell might have put it, some weapons—at least in the eyes of airmen—seem to be more equal than others. Despite the success of the German V-2, the Air Force was slow to enter the missile field. Just before stepping down at the end of World War II, Hap Arnold was willing to leave missile development to the Army and the Ordnance Department, saving for the Air Force only those aircraft that depended upon wings for sustentation. This was but a flagrant example of what Carl Builder later called the "Icarus Syndrome"—the Air Force's love affair with the airplane.[3] The story of the Air Force's reluctance to fund missile research, even up to the appearance of the capable Minuteman in the 1960s, underscores this failing. The Soviet success with *Sputnik I* in 1957 jarred Air Force thinkers into a reappraisal of intercontinental missiles. Perhaps even more significant in changing Air Force thought was the Navy's success in developing submarine-launched inter-continental missiles.

A cynic might be inclined to suggest that interservice rivalry may be a more powerful incentive to realistic thinking about airpower than the traditional goad of hostile threat. By the same sort of reasoning, the intense desire to hang on to the airplane has led to some wonderfully imaginative innovations:

stealth, standoff weapons, and a whole range of electronic devices to suppress enemy measures, which have certainly gone far in prolonging the useful life of manned aircraft.

When low intensity conflicts (LIC) became especially acute in the 1960s, some casting about occurred in the Air Force to define the role of airpower in relation to such threats. Not surprisingly, however, given their preoccupation with strategic air war à outrance, especially against the Soviet Union, Air Force officers showed remarkably little interest in devising doctrines appropriate for LIC. No significant airpower thinker emerged with a particular interest in this area. At best, the Air Force seemed to see its tasks primarily in a supporting role, although the gunship perfected during operations in Vietnam showed promise for the future. The shallowness of the air arm's interest in its LIC role may well have stemmed from the fact that the preeminent air weapon for LIC operations is the helicopter. Since Army helicopters satisfied that need, air officers seemed to lose interest.

If Air Force officers showed little interest in the air aspects of LICs, this did not in any case signal declining interest in airpower theory. With the Vietnam quagmire behind it, the nation welcomed two significant airpower theorists—Col John Boyd and Col John Warden. Both were far more sophisticated in their reasoning than most of their predecessors. Along with the officer corps as a whole, both were also better educated than those who had gone before them.

Taking his cue from Basil H. Liddell Hart ("think in terms of paralyzing") and J. F. C. Fuller ("brain warfare, a shot through the head"), Boyd conceived of proper strategy as one that disrupted or incapacitated the enemy's ability to cope by forcing him to operate at a tempo beyond his ability to respond effectively. Success favors the side that can observe, orient, decide, and act (OODA) sooner than the enemy. Which is to say, one must get inside his "OODA loop" or decision-making cycle. In sharp contrast to the fatally flawed "methodical battle" of the French, with its carefully planned time-phased actions, Boyd's thinking required the exercise of initiative at low echelons—opportunistic, fast-breaking, imaginative leadership. He saw any single doctrinal path to victory as predictable and therefore vulnerable. For Boyd, the issue was not a matter of doctrine, but of doctrines—a whole quiver full of options to be applied in rapid, staccato thrusts. His approach to strategic paralysis did not entail battering the enemy's economy but his leadership and its control over the country.

In a similar vein, John Warden's conceptualization of the air campaign was more political than economic.[4] His scheme for translating national political objectives and strategic goals into theater air campaigns involved identifying the enemy's center of gravity—the point where he is most vulnerable to air attack. Although Warden visualized five concentric rings—targets in descending order of priority—he leaves no doubt that leadership at the national center, and in each successive ring or target, is always the preferred objective.

The beauty of Warden's work for the strategic planner is the way he relates *ends* (political objectives), *ways* (strategies to attain those ends), and *means* (identifying specific targets to execute the chosen strategy). Because his well-trained team carried out this process in planning air operations for Operation Desert Storm, we have a helpful degree of authentication for Warden's airpower theories. Taken together, the work of Boyd and Warden offers an impressive index of the remarkable advance in airpower thinking beyond the crudities of Douhet and Mitchell. However, that both Boyd and Warden retired as colonels strongly suggests the marginal status of airpower theorists in the contemporary Air Force.

The increasing sophistication of airpower thought represented by the work of Boyd and Warden had parallels in many respects elsewhere in the Air Force. One sees a notable instance of this in the greater willingness of airmen to work constructively with the Army to resolve the long-standing problem of hammering out an effective air-ground relationship. Many factors contributed to this "partnership"; indeed, the very use of the term seemed to signal a new set of attitudes in both parties. In part, the shift in attitude may have reflected the rise of the "fighter mafia," replacing the "bomber mafia" in Air Force command circles. The net result was a mutual recognition that the Army and the Air Force depended upon one another. The Army knew that it could not operate without air cover, and the Air Force understood that it depended heavily upon ground forces to screen its air bases.

The Army and Air Force achieved much of the rapprochement between 1946 and 1986, culminating in major doctrinal promulgations by both services. These specified the roles of each service in the new partnership called "AirLand Battle," even though in actual fact the devised doctrines extended beyond any given "battle" to the campaign as a whole. Confidence in the viability of the concept of AirLand Battle increased as a result of the authentication it acquired from repeated testing of its features in Red Flag force-on-force air combat trials and Blue Flag air-ground command post exercises.

Although the services achieved heartening advances in harmonizing air-ground cooperation by tactical units, agreement proved harder to obtain at the operational level of command. Airmen have long insisted that, for optimum effect, the character of airpower demands centralized control and decentralized execution. But should this leave every decision on the allocation of sorties—for interdiction, by way of example—entirely to the judgment of the air component commander? Understandably, Army corps commanders, under heavy pressure from the enemy, objected to being left to the mercy of a decision by a distant air component commander—especially since the intelligence for making such decisions would have to come from ground sources. Experience from World War II had shown that collocation of higher command headquarters could resolve many of these tensions, but the manpower-saving decision to eliminate Army headquarters threatened this promising solution—at least temporarily.

If the Army–Air Force turf battle had remained merely a debate over theoretical control procedures to be defined in doctrinal manuals, the issue might have continued endlessly. But the issue was not theoretical. The two services operated in an active theater, in NATO, with a realistic cold war enemy across the border. Further, living within the political realities of multinational NATO made the Air Force acutely aware of Clausewitz's definition of war as an extension of politics. This may not have induced Air Force officers to give up their convictions or rewrite their doctrinal manuals, but it certainly did force them to accommodate, at least within NATO, an approved doctrine on interdiction.

The old saw "he who is persuaded against his will is of the opinion still" may be pertinent here. The Air Force made concessions in the NATO context but probably did not significantly alter its theory of airpower in so doing. Characteristically, bureaucratic fiefdoms—when confronted with intractable differences—defer rather than resolve them.

Were the procedural adjustments—the agreements hammered out between the Army and the Air Force and among the constituent member nations of NATO—an expression of airpower theory? Or were they merely an incremental accommodation arrived at by the labors of a multitude of staff officers—conferring, bargaining, and adjusting—with all sides making good-faith efforts to find acceptable common ground, only occasionally digging in their heels when they sensed some vital interest to their service was at stake. Does this mean that airmen become recalcitrant only when some fundamental tenet of their perception of airpower theory is threatened?

In such negotiations, no individuals stand out as preeminent theorists. Staff assignments rotate; generals come and go. Procedures to ensure control, coordination, and synchronization are contrived. One may consider these adjustments advances in airpower theory only insofar as one extends the definition of that theory to include means as well as ways and ends.

Although the Soviet threat that originally mobilized NATO has diminished—for the moment at least—studying how the Soviets and their successors think about airpower remains worthwhile. Any such study should begin with a caveat. The Soviet Union was never really an integral part of Europe. One should expect differences from a nation that failed to standardize the gauge of its railroads in conformity with the nations of Western Europe. In the USSR the term *doctrine,* for example, was not at all the same as what it meant in Western culture. Doctrine for the Soviets was mandatory and carried the sanctions of law. What the Soviets called military art comes closer to what the West called doctrine.

During World War II, the Soviet air arm was essentially a ground-support force, an orientation continued until the death of Stalin in 1953. Under his successor, Nikita Khrushchev, Soviet airpower theory changed drastically. He pushed for greater emphasis on strategic air war, with aircraft capable of delivering nuclear weapons. More importantly, he downgraded conventional ground forces and moved the major share of the defense budget to strategic rocket forces, with an eye toward preemptive strikes. But the realization that NATO nuclear forces were at least a generation ahead of the Soviets' led to a gradual shift from offensive thinking to defensive.

The war in the Gulf had a chilling impact on Soviet thinking. The miserable performance of Soviet arms in Iraqi hands proved profoundly disturbing. The tank-heavy Soviet army found it especially disconcerting that tanks had become "an endangered species without control of the air" (p. 508). Although senior Soviet officers, in characteristic authoritarian fashion, tended to stifle criticisms arising from elaborate analysis of the Gulf War experience, younger officers managed to come up with a realistic assessment of the future character of air war that parallels US airpower theory in many respects. Notably, the pendulum of theory once again swung back from Mikhail Gorbachev's "defensive doctrine" to an appreciation for the primacy of the offensive. The collapse of the Soviet Union leaves the significance of this shift very much in doubt—especially insofar as it relates to investments in research and development for space.

The final substantive chapter in this volume attempts to provide a rigorous analysis of the comparative characteristics of airpower and space power. The analysis is indeed illuminating, dealing as it does with the radically different characteristics of the air and space realms. However, in contrast to the earlier chapters of this book, which treat their subjects historically and descriptively, this chapter sets up what its author calls a space power conjecture, positing that space power is merely an extension of airpower. Major DeBlois then sets out to demonstrate that the conjecture is false. The Air Force, he concludes, will eventually have to cut loose its child and create a separate Space Force.

Whether one accepts or rejects the author's thesis depends upon one's willingness to recognize his conjecture as the operative question. Certainly, the characteristics of the air and space realms pose drastic differences that will undoubtedly produce acute tensions in contests for funding between the two realms. But does it inexorably follow that such differences must lead to separate institutions? The continued existence of the Marine Corps within the Navy shows just how malleable the armed services can be in the face of logic to the contrary. As the Air Force moves increasingly toward unmanned vehicles and as the Icarus Syndrome weakens, will not the thrust for institutional survival virtually dictate a drive to retain space as an appropriate responsibility?

What, then, do the foregoing chapters tell us about airpower theory? Much of what has been written on the subject is not, strictly speaking, airpower theory at all but descriptions of varied efforts to implement the then-current conception of such theory. Across the decades from the Wright brothers' first powered flight, theorists have generally promised more than they can deliver. The frictions and uncertainties of war, described so well by Clausewitz, persist in emphasizing the distance between theory on the one hand and actual execution in war on the other. Even the advent of nuclear weapons, for all their destructive potential, has not brought complete fulfillment to theorists' claims. This has resulted not from any limitation on the awesome power of the weapons but from the fear of comparable retaliation.

What insights emerge from this survey of airpower thinkers? First and foremost is the troubled and erratic development of the concept of the air weapon as primarily a support for ground arms. This is understandable in light of the centuries-long history of surface warfare, with its deeply embedded traditions, slowly evolved doctrines, and elaborate systems of officer education and training. Moreover, the fact that early visionaries such as Douhet and Mitchell made sweeping claims for airpower that reached far beyond the then-available technology tended to induce skepticism in traditionally conservative military circles. As the capabilities of the air weapon improved, surface forces became increasingly anxious to control this new weapon. The more persistent their grasp, the more insistent the airpower advocates became in claiming that aviation was primarily an offensive strategic weapon with an independent role in war. This unfortunate tension, which still lingers in some measure, became muted with the post-Vietnam air-ground "partnership"—a coming together significantly hastened by the necessity of cooperating in a NATO context.

The airpower advocates themselves caused some of the difficulty encountered in winning acceptance of their strategic vision when they disagreed over the nature of their targets. Those who visualized civilian morale as the primary target differed from those who saw the industrial web—the economic infrastructure—as the main objective. Both views suffered from lack of evidence. Those who favored morale as the target did so as an act of faith; those who favored economic targets displayed a surprising lack of effort in defining and refining their target folders. This, in turn, suggests the generally flawed character of air-arm intelligence efforts.

Yet another common thread that runs through the history of airpower theory is the Icarus Syndrome, mentioned earlier. The enthusiasm of pilots for flying, although understandable in itself, has led to a persistent downgrading and neglect of many supporting aspects of the air weapon. The stunting of bomber self-defense during the interwar years offers a classic illustration, as does the treatment of logisticians and other groundlings in the same period. But the most striking instance of the Icarus Syndrome is the Air Force's long delay in putting major resources into missiles. One may well ask whether the resistance of so many people to the acceptance of space weapons as a logical extension of the Air Force sphere of operations is yet another manifestation of the lack of rigor in the service's professional education system.

Finally, can any survey of airpower be truly comprehensive if it neglects to consider the role of carrier aviation and submarine-launched strategic missiles? Interservice rivalry is a valuable goad to progress. True, it can be wastefully duplicative, but one should never overlook the value of competition.

The airplane has been around for nearly one hundred years, but, given its remarkable potential, surely one is surprised by the dearth of really comprehensive thinkers and theorists on airpower. Science and technology have made enormous strides—putting people on the Moon and precision-guided weapons into the third window to the left in the designated target—but has our professional military education system kept pace?

The more than nine decades of air-arm thought depicted in this volume lead to one rather obvious conclusion: airpower theory, aerospace power theory, is forever unfinished. The challenge to a rising generation of air officers is manifest. Will they develop the rigorously authenticated theories required by successive advances in technology, or will they be satisfied with ill-supported visions or even suffer illusions?

Notes

1. Thomas Sowell, *Knowledge and Decisions* (New York: Basic Books, 1980), 4–5.

2. Parenthetical page references in the text are to *The Paths of Heaven.*

3. See Carl H. Builder, *The Icarus Syndrome: The Role of Air Power Theory in the Evolution and Fate of the U.S. Air Force* (New Brunswick, N.J.: Transaction Publishers, 1994).

4. See John A. Warden III, *The Air Campaign: Planning for Combat* (Washington, D.C.: National Defense University Press, 1988).

Contributors

Lt Col Mark A. Clodfelter was a professor of airpower history at the School of Advanced Airpower Studies (SAAS) from 1991 to 1994. He received his BS from the US Air Force Academy in 1977, MA from the University of Nebraska, and PhD from the University of North Carolina. He is the author of the critically acclaimed *The Limits of Air Power: The American Bombing of North Vietnam* (Free Press, 1989), as well as numerous articles dealing with military and airpower history. A weapons controller with a tour in South Korea, he is currently professor of aerospace studies at the University of North Carolina at Chapel Hill. His latest project is a history of American strategic bombing, to be published by Free Press.

Dr. James S. Corum has been a professor of comparative military studies at SAAS since 1991. After completing his undergraduate education at Gonzaga University, he received an MA from Brown University, an MLitt from Oxford University, and a PhD from Queen's University in Canada. A major in the US Army Reserve, he has served as an intelligence officer in Germany and Honduras. His award-winning book *The Roots of Blitzkrieg: Hans von Seeckt and German Military Reform* (University Press of Kansas, 1992) was a History Book Club selection. He has also written numerous articles on the Luftwaffe, military history, and the role of airpower in peacekeeping operations. His forthcoming book on the Luftwaffe will soon be published by the University Press of Kansas.

Maj Bruce M. DeBlois has been a professor of air and space technology at SAAS since 1994. After receiving a BS and an MS in mathematics from Union College, he attended Oxford University, where he received his doctorate in computational fluid mechanics in 1991. He has served as a research analyst at Nellis Air Force Base (AFB), Nevada, and as a research astrophysicist in Sunnyvale, California. He is the author of several articles on scientific and engineering subjects, as well as "Dropping the Electric Grid," the top research project at Air Command and Staff College in 1994. He is currently editing a book on space theory and doctrine.

Prof. Dennis M. Drew was the dean of SAAS in 1991–92 and has been the assistant dean of SAAS since his retirement from the Air Force in 1992. He completed his undergraduate work at Williamette University and earned graduate degrees at both the University of Wyoming and the University of Alabama. During his 28-year career in the Air Force, he served as a personnel officer, missile crew commander, staff officer at Headquarters Strategic Air Command, and director of the Airpower Research Institute at Maxwell AFB, Alabama. One of the world's leading authorities on airpower doctrine, he is the author of three books, dozens of articles, and a biweekly column in *Air Force Times*. In addition, he was the primary author of the 1992 edition of AFM 1-1, *Basic Aerospace Doctrine of the United States Air Force*.

Lt Col Peter R. Faber served as a professor of airpower history at SAAS from 1992 to 1994. After completing his undergraduate work at UCLA in 1976, he went on to receive graduate degrees from the University of Arkansas and the University of Alabama, and is completing his PhD at Yale University, under the guidance of Sir Michael Howard and Paul Kennedy. He is the author of numerous articles on airpower history and theory, and in 1989 was chosen as the outstanding instructor in the History Department at the US Air Force Academy. He has served as a missile crew commander and is currently a student at the US Naval War College.

Lt Col David S. Fadok graduated from SAAS in 1994. He was a distinguished graduate of the US Air Force Academy in 1982. Selected as a Rhodes Scholar, he graduated from Oxford University in 1984 with a master's degree in psychology, philosophy, and physiology. He has flown as an aircraft commander and instructor pilot in both EC-130s and C-5s, and has served in the Plans Division on the staff at Headquarters Air Mobility Command, Scott AFB, Illinois. At the present time, he is the commander of the 2d Air Refueling Squadron at McGuire AFB, New Jersey.

Lt Col Edward J. Felker graduated from SAAS in 1994. He has an undergraduate degree from the University of Maine and graduate degrees from Ball State University and the US Army's Command and General Staff College at Fort Leavenworth, Kansas. He has served as a logistics officer in Turkey and Germany, as an analyst in the Checkmate Division on the Air Staff in the Pentagon, and as a maintenance squadron commander. He is currently assigned to the Doctrine Division in the Joint Warfighting Center at Fort Monroe, Virginia.

Dr. I. B. Holley Jr. was one of the founding fathers of SAAS, recognizing early on the importance of airpower education within the Air Force. The dean of American military airpower historians, he is professor emeritus at Duke University and has also taught at West Point and National Defense University. During his prestigious academic career, he has published three books, including the seminal *Ideas and Weapons: Exploitation of the Aerial Weapon by the United States during World War I* (Yale University Press, 1953—now in its third edition) and dozens of articles on military and airpower history, theory, and doctrine. After receiving his PhD from Yale University, he enjoyed a long and distinguished career in the Air Force Reserve, retiring in 1981 as a major general.

Col Maris "Buster" McCrabb was professor of economic warfare at SAAS from 1994 to 1996. After completing his undergraduate work at Bowling Green State University, he received an MS and MPA from Troy State University and then completed his DPA at the University of Alabama. A fighter pilot and Fighter Weapons School graduate, he has flown F-4s and F-16s in the Philippines, Germany, and Korea, as well as in combat during the Persian Gulf War. He is one of the Air Force's leading experts on air campaign planning, has published extensively on the subject, and is currently chief of the Command and Control Integration Division at Headquarters Air Combat Command, Langley AFB, Virginia.

Col Phillip S. Meilinger was the dean of SAAS from 1992 to 1996. He graduated from the Air Force Academy in 1970 and the University of Colorado in 1975. He received his PhD from the University of Michigan in 1985. A command pilot, he has flown C-130s and HC-130s in both Europe and the Pacific, while also serving a tour on the Air Staff in the Pentagon from 1989 to 1991. He is the author of *Hoyt S. Vandenberg: The Life of a General* (Indiana University Press, 1989), as well as over 20 articles on airpower theory, history, and employment. At present, he is a professor in the Strategy and Policy Department at the US Naval War College in Newport, Rhode Island.

Dr. David R. Mets has been a tenured professor of technology and innovation at SAAS since 1990. After graduating from the Naval Academy in 1953, he transferred to the Air Force, where he spent 27 years, including a tour as commander of an AC-130 gunship squadron during the Vietnam War. He received his master's degree from Columbia University and his PhD from the University of Denver. Between 1976 and 1979, he was editor of the *Air University Review* at Maxwell AFB, Alabama. He has written three books, including a biography of Gen Carl Spaatz—*Master of Air Power: General Carl A. Spaatz* (Presidio Press, 1988)—and dozens of articles and reviews dealing with airpower history. He is currently completing histories of air-delivered munitions and of Air Force–Navy rivalry over aviation issues.

Dr. Karl P. Mueller has been a professor of comparative military studies at SAAS since 1994. After finishing his undergraduate work in political science at the University of Chicago, he received his MA and PhD in politics from Princeton University. Before coming to SAAS, he taught political science at Kalamazoo College and the University of Michigan. He has authored several articles on alliance and deterrence theory, and his book on that subject will soon be published by Cornell University Press.

Dr. Harold R. Winton has been a tenured professor of military history and theory at SAAS since 1990. He graduated from West Point in 1964 and served a distinguished career in the Army, including three tours in Vietnam as a Green Beret and as deputy director of the Army's School of Advanced Military Studies. He received his MA and PhD from Stanford University in 1977, studying under Peter Paret. He is the author of *To Change an Army: General Sir John Burnett-Stuart and British Armored Doctrine, 1927–1938* (University Press of Kansas, 1988) as well as numerous articles on military history and theory. He is currently completing a manuscript on the Battle of the Bulge that will be published by the University Press of Kansas.

Index

Air Ministry, 48, 66, 68
Air Ministry (French), 153–54, 157
Air Ministry (Italian), 161, 176
airpower
   American, 79–80, 83, 88
   as artillery, 26, 64, 186
   atomic, 346–47
   attributes of, 9, 15, 23, 26, 254, 371, 418
   British, 72
   carrier, 126–27
   conventional, 288, 294, 307–8
   counterguerrilla, 329
   decisiveness of, 19–20, 79, 269
   defensive, 26
   effectiveness of, 256, 268
   French, 328
   global, 263–64, 267
   land based, 126, 129, 184, 197
   limits of, 28
   long range, 197
   missions, 157
   nonnuclear, 280
   offensive, 70, 86
   operational, 279
   peaceful applications of, 265
   peacetime roles of, 187
   as propaganda, 257, 265
   psychological effects of, 51
   Russian, 166, 519
   strategic, 12–14, 18, 41, 44, 51–52, 65, 72, 164, 171, 202, 206, 214, 250, 252, 255, 261, 269, 279, 290–93, 306–7, 331, 334, 357, 385, 580, 583, 586, 589
   tactical, 12–13, 30, 65, 171, 255, 328, 334, 426
Air Service, 33, 80, 85–91, 96, 99, 101–2, 104–5, 107, 119–20, 124, 184–92, 196–97, 204–10, 212–14, 242–43, 383, 582
Air Service Field Officers' School (ASFOS), 186, 211, 213–14, 216
Air Service Information Office, 188
Air Service Tactical School (ASTS), 33, 187, 198, 211, 213–14, 216
Air Service Technical Section, 85, 383
Air Service Training and Operations Group, 213–14
airships, 43, 93–94, 103, 119, 122
air-space boundary, 530, 554, 565

airspace control, 455–56, 466
airspace control authority (ACA), 455, 465–66
airspace control system (ACS), 466
Air Transport Command, 217
Air University, 329, 331, 335, 337, 588
Air War College, 336, 344
Air War Plans Division, Plan 1 (AWPD-1), 187, 224–25
Algeria, 335–36
Alksnis, Ya. I., 167
Allen, Lew, 423
Allied Air Forces Central Europe (AAFCE), 422–24, 457, 460
allied
   armies, 170
   tactical air force (ATAF), 455, 457, 459–60
   tactical operations center (ATOC), 454–55, 459–60
Allied Command Europe, Mobile Force (AMF), 463
Allied Forces Central Europe (AFCENT), 422–24, 451, 455
American Expeditionary Force (AEF), 85, 87, 184–85, 197, 213, 586
amphibious operations, 135–36
Andrews, Frank, 108, 207
annihilation, 4, 23, 215, 299, 308, 361
Anthis, Rollen H., 336
antiaircraft artillery (AAA), 168, 218, 220, 288, 562
Antiballistic Missile (ABM) Treaty, 534, 537
antisatellites (ASAT), 535–37, 539, 541, 559
antisubmarine warfare (ASW), 119, 135, 263
apportionment, 454, 467
Arab-Israeli War, 406
armistice, 7, 17, 35, 48, 74, 87, 91, 127, 184–85
Armor Center, 415
arms
   control, 131, 287, 303–4
   race, 290, 450, 500
Army Air Corps, 199
Army Air Forces (AAF), 83, 201, 203, 212, 225, 247, 251–52, 256, 258, 263
Army Air Service, 216
Army Command and General Staff College, 211
Army League of the United States, 195
Army War College, 199, 205, 210
Arnold, Henry H. "Hap,"47, 83, 104, 106–8, 186–90, 198, 200–201, 203, 207, 217, 224–25, 245–47, 251, 256, 258, 266, 583, 590–91

Canada, 464
capital ships, 100, 120, 128–29, 136, 242, 250
Caproni, Gianni, 3, 6, 98, 184
carrier task force, 129, 136
Carter, Jimmy, 408
Catalonia, Spain, 162
Center for Low Intensity Conflict, 344
centers of gravity (COG), 57, 64, 66, 195, 198, 216, 325–26, 339, 343, 365, 371–74, 376–78, 386–88, 466, 471, 496, 504, 593
Central Army Group (CENTAG), 422–23
Central Imagery Office, 544
Central Intelligence Agency (CIA), 410, 544
centralized
    control, 283, 338, 421–22, 454, 457, 466, 544–46, 567–68, 594
    execution, 545–46
    military authority, 546
Central Powers, 83
Chain, John T., 420
Chassin, G. J. M., 328
Checkmate Division, 370, 373
Chennault, Claire, 52, 188, 244, 588
Chernyshev, Vladimir, 503
Chess Air, 188
Chief of Naval Operations (CNO), 118, 123, 131, 134
China, 81, 92, 369
China-Burma-India theater, 324
Churchill, Winston, 48–49, 258, 298
civil
    aviation, 16–17
    defense, 289–90, 303–4
civilian
    casualties, 25, 469
    morale, 20–21, 30, 585
Clausewitz, Carl von, 96, 34, 116–17, 220, 268, 360, 364–65, 372, 374, 377–81, 388, 416, 443, 594, 597
close air support (CAS), 152, 158–61, 171–75, 338, 342–43, 400, 405, 407–10, 414, 421–26, 429, 448, 456–57, 459–60, 465, 472, 545
coalition forces, 1, 25, 197, 385, 433, 463, 502, 504–8, 510–11, 558
Coastal Command, 258
coastal defense, 120, 199, 202
Coffman, Robert D., 467

El Salvador, 340, 347
encounter battle, 163
Environmental Modification Convention, 537
Estes, Howell, 205
Ethiopia, 161, 204
Eurocorps, 462
Europe, 33, 62, 66, 70, 81, 83, 85, 119, 151, 159, 184, 213, 224,
   245, 249, 251, 269, 305, 327–28, 339, 347, 400, 405–7, 409,
   413–15, 430, 433, 443, 446–47, 451, 461–62, 464, 467–68, 470,
   489, 494, 510, 586, 595
European Command, 470

Fairchild, Muir, 216–17, 219, 588
Falk, C. E., 190
Fall, Bernard, 335
Far East, 510
Far East Air Forces (FEAF), 331
Farley, James A., 192
Fascist Party, 8, 160
fast transient maneuvers, 363–64
Fechet, James E., 108
Federal Aeronautics Administration, 108
Federal Republic of Germany, 445
Felmy, Helmuth, 170, 172
Ferrying Command, 217
Fiebig, Martin, 165
Field Officer's School, 194
5th Bomber Command, 217
V Corps, 415
Fifth Fleet, 131
Fighter Command, 52, 67, 125
fighter mafia, 593
Fighter Weapons Center, 410, 412
firebombing, 281
fire support coordination line (FSCL), 427, 457
1st Aero Squadron, 89
I Air Corps (French), 155
First Army, 86, 89
1st Brigade, 86
I Corps, 86
1st Infantry Division, 87
FitzGerald, Mary C., 499–500, 516

621

Frunze, Mikhail, 163
Fullam, William, 120
Fuller, J. F. C., 171, 358–59, 361, 371, 592
future war, 321, 382, 385, 387, 401, 407, 430–31, 485, 487–89, 496, 498–502, 506, 510, 517, 519, 536

Gabriel, Charles A., 420, 430, 432
Gallery, Dan, 134–35
Gamelin, Maurice-Gustave, 153, 157–59, 176
Gareyev, M. V., 488
gas warfare, 25, 57
Gaulle, Charles de, 157, 446
General Board of the Navy, 121, 125
General Headquarters (GHQ)
    Air Force, 105–6, 108, 201–4, 209–11, 222–23
    Brigade, 84
    Reserve, 88
General Staff Academy (Soviet), 165
Geneva Disarmament Conference, 57, 204
Geneva Protocols, 25
geopolitics, 517
George, Harold Lee, 107–8, 194, 216–18, 224
geosynchronous earth orbit (GEO), 554, 559, 562
Germany, 7, 11–12, 20, 22, 24, 30, 42–44, 46–47, 69, 71, 85, 87–88, 121, 135, 151, 168–69, 171, 176, 185, 221, 224, 249–50, 257, 260, 288, 307, 384, 449, 510, 570, 585–86
    air force, 161, 165, 168–69, 173–76
    air service, 168–69
    army, 46, 82, 84–85, 165, 168–71, 173–74
    military, 168–69, 171
    navy, 119, 168, 175, 240
    rearmament of, 204
Gilkeson, A. H., 223
Glantz, David M., 498–99
global
    awareness, 532
    presence, 532
    reach, 545–46
    war, 328
Goldwater-Nichols Department of Defense Reorganization Act, 432, 444, 467, 470
Golovine, Nicholas N., 22

Goodpaster, Andrew, 451, 460
Gorbachev, Mikhail, 491, 494, 508–9, 512–14, 519, 596
Göring, Hermann, 175
Gorrell, Edgar "Nap," 6–7, 80, 85–86, 88, 183, 186, 383, 580
Gothlin, Oliver P., Jr., 223
Grachev, Andrei S., 507
Grau, Lester, 494
Great Britain, 7, 20, 30, 32, 41–43, 46, 48, 50–51, 57, 61–62,
    67–71, 84, 94, 119, 123, 125, 172, 175, 249, 251, 261, 281, 284,
    306, 336–37, 382, 451, 529
    air force, 50, 121
    army, 45–47, 49, 61, 63–64, 70, 250
    navy, 49, 63, 119–20, 125, 250
Great Patriotic War, 302, 511, 517
Greely, Adolphus, 81
Green, John, 342
ground
    attack, 154
    battle, 90, 157, 160
    campaign, 153, 511
    commander, 65, 82, 84, 422–23, 427, 429, 457–58, 460
    defenses, 183
    forces, 12–13, 20, 47, 55, 65, 94, 107–8, 152, 158, 164–65, 166,
        170, 184, 202, 206, 212–13, 250, 265, 372, 402, 408, 414,
        418–19, 427, 448, 456, 468–70, 488, 490–91, 497, 502,
        504–5, 518, 581–82, 586, 594
    operations, 62, 429, 519
    support, 421
    warfare, 96, 265, 489, 508, 512
Guadalajara, Spain, 166
Guatemala, 340, 347
guerrillas, 324, 333, 335–36, 340–42
    operations, 336
    tactics, 324, 329, 331, 341
    warfare, 322, 402
Gulf War. See Persian Gulf War
Gullion, Allen, 103–4

Haig, Douglas, 45, 47
Halsey, William, 130–31
Hammes, Thomas, 340
Hammond, Grant, 341, 382

Hannibal, 19

Hanoi, North Vietnam, 335

Hansell, Haywood, 206, 210, 216–17, 224

Harbord, James G., 85

Hardie, Robert L., 336

Harmon, Millard F., 198, 223

Harris, Arthur, 70–71

Hay, James, 83

Henderson, David, 43–44

high-altitude precision daylight bombardment (HAPDB), 186, 192, 211–12, 216–17, 219–22, 224

Hines, John, 493

Hirohito, 258

Hiroshima, Japan, 259, 281

Hitler, Adolph, 33, 70, 133, 249

HMS
  Prince of Wales, 129, 250
  Repulse, 129, 250

Ho Chi Minh, 331

Horner, Charles A., 544

House Military Affairs Committee, 101

Howard, Michael, 400

Howell Commission, 184, 210

Hukbalahaps (Huks), 322, 326, 328, 330

Hurlburt Field, Florida, 419

Hussein, Saddam, 433, 499, 502

hyperwar, 378

Ia Drang Valley, 402

Icarus Syndrome, 591, 597–98

Iceland, 463

immediate-reaction forces, 464

incendiary attacks, 87

independent air force (IAF), 14, 23, 49, 79–80, 86, 88–91, 94–95, 99, 102–8, 125, 128, 133–34, 136, 151, 153, 169, 176, 186–87, 208–10, 225, 256, 267, 291, 322, 333, 346, 581, 583, 587

Independent Force, 44, 46–47, 52

India, 48–49, 61, 81, 92

Indochina, 326, 328, 405

Indonesia, 330

industrial
  revolution, 4

war, 108, 263, 269, 322, 328, 331–32, 340
Lindbergh, Charles, 190, 250
lines of communications (LOC), 130, 156, 199, 202, 336, 343, 345–46, 383, 468
Lipetsk, USSR, 165
Lloyd George, David, 47
logistics, 324–25, 329
London, England, 43, 50, 57, 60, 71, 121, 581
Lovell, George E., Jr., 223
low earth orbit (LEO), 548, 558–59, 561–62
low intensity conflict (LIC), 269, 321–23, 331, 340, 342–44, 592
Luce, Stephen B., 117
Ludendorff, Erich, 174, 176
Ludlow-Hewitt, Edgar, 56, 59–60
Luftwaffe, 24, 33, 59, 67, 70, 154, 159, 172, 174–75, 221, 249–50, 585–86. *See also* Germany
Lupton, David, 535
Luxembourg, Belgium, 463

MacArthur, Douglas, 129, 198, 262
MacArthur-Pratt Agreement, 199–200, 203
Macke, Richard, 567
Macmillan, Harold, 291
Maginot Line, 153, 250
Mahaffey, Fred K., 420
Mahan, Alfred Thayer, 34, 101, 116–17, 119, 123–24, 130, 261, 529–30
Mahoney, Donald, 493
major subordinate commander (MSC), 455, 471
Malaya, 326, 328, 335–36, 342
Malayan Emergency, 337, 342
Malayan People's Anti-Japanese Army, 326
Maliukov, A. E., 502–3
Manchuria, 204
maneuver
  battle, 361
  forces, 471, 493
  war, 166, 170, 364
Manhattan Project, 281, 292
Manila, 326
Mao Tse-tung, 323, 369–70
March, Peyton, 87

Moris, Maurizio, 2, 4
Morocco, 153
Morrow Board, 90, 103–5, 204, 209
Morrow, Dwight, 103
Moscow Academy for Air Commanders, 165
Moscow, USSR, 461, 489, 506
mujahideen, 340, 342
multiple independently targeted reentry vehicle (MIRV), 284, 287, 303
multiple launch rocket system (MLRS), 427
Mussolini, Benito, 8, 18, 162, 584
Mustin, Henry, 118–19, 124
mutual assured destruction (MAD), 10, 292, 295–98, 300–302, 304–7, 536

Nagasaki, Japan, 259, 281
Naisbitt, John, 387
Napoléon, 8, 133, 378
National Aeronautics and Space Administration (NASA), 544, 571
national
    aerospace plane (NASP), 566
    defense, 193, 197–200, 210, 249, 430
    objectives, 119, 265, 532
    policy, 407, 540
    security, 79, 115, 118, 124, 136, 306, 405, 535, 538–39
National Defense Act of 1916, 83
nationalism, 193
National Oceanographic and Atmospheric Administration, 544
National Reconnaissance Office, 544
National Science Foundation, 544
National Security League, 197
National Security and Strategic Stability Studies Center, 506
National War College, 371
nation building, 333, 338
naval
    blockade, 116, 128, 130, 132–33, 135, 294
    commander, 467
    forces, 36, 103, 107, 123, 184, 197, 202, 250, 408
    operations, 197, 305
    thinking, 136
    warfare, 41, 115, 119, 151
Naval Academy, 117–18

632

Naval Aircraft Factory, 125
Naval On-Call Force Mediterranean, 463
Naval War College, 116–17, 120, 124, 126–27, 131, 335
Nazi
  Germany, 66, 69
  ideology, 174
Nellis AFB, Nevada, 410, 412, 419
Netherwood, Douglas B., 200
Newport Agreement/Conference, 133–34
Nicaragua, 340
Nimitz, Chester, 131, 133
XIX Tactical Air Command, 412
Nivelle, Robert, 83
Nixon, Richard M., 334, 403
Nolan, Kimberly, 455, 472
North Africa, 71
North American Aerospace Defense Command (NORAD), 217
North Atlantic Council, 463
North Atlantic Treaty Organization (NATO), 327, 405, 408, 410,
  413, 415, 421, 430, 443–56, 458–73, 490, 492–94, 498–99, 510,
  518, 594–96, 598
  Central Region, 424, 445, 448, 456–57, 467
  Northern Region, 445, 456
  Southern Region, 445, 456, 462
  Tactical Air Working Group, 424
Northern Army Group (NORTHAG), 422, 457
Northrop Corporation, 285
North Sea, 42
North Vietnam, 334
North Vietnamese Army (NVA), 402
Norway, 250–51, 456
nuclear
  age, 294
  arms control, 280
  attack, 282, 286, 289, 308, 447
  decapitation, 307
  deterrence, 299
  employment, 451
  energy, 513
  escalation, 300–301, 304, 491–92, 514
  first strike, 289–90, 295–97, 300–301, 303–7, 591
  fission, 281

fleet, 197, 544
theater, 217
war, 123, 127, 131, 135–36, 583
Palestine, 49
Panama, 20, 499
Panama Canal, 123, 194, 197, 529
Pape, Robert, 368
parallel
attack, 307, 375–76, 382, 388
operations, 15–16, 63
warfare, 365, 374
paralysis, 15, 52, 60, 65, 217–18, 264, 358–63, 365–66, 368–69,
373, 375–76, 379, 382–84, 387–89. *See also* strategic
paratroop force, 173, 175
Paret, Peter, 330
Paris, France, 83, 446
parochialism, 196
Parsons, David, 343
Partnership for Peace (PFP), 462, 464–65
Partridge, Earl "Pat," 188
Paschall, Rod, 340
Patrick, Mason, 89, 91–92, 107–8, 185–86, 191, 198, 204, 242
Patton, George, 412
peacekeeping, 322, 464
peacemaking, 322
peacetime contingency operations, 322
Pearl Harbor, 120, 122–23, 127, 129, 131, 248
Pentagon, 301, 370, 372, 402
Pentland, Pat, 377
People's Anti-Japanese Army, 326
People's Liberation Army, 326
Perera, Guido, 208, 210
perestroika, 491, 500, 512
Perry, Robert, 455, 472
Pershing, John J., 85–89, 184, 186, 209
Persian Gulf War, 1, 13, 20, 24, 30–31, 285, 306, 321, 344, 374,
385, 414, 444, 461, 463, 467, 471, 485–86, 496, 498–509,
511–18, 558, 596
Peru, 340, 347
Petain, Philippe, 153, 176
Philippines, 81–82, 92, 126, 322, 326, 328, 337, 340
Phillips Laboratory, 561

preemptive attack, 287, 289, 301, 304–5

Preparedness Movement, 195

Primary Flying School, 188, 190

principal subordinate commander (PSC), 455, 467, 471

Pritchard, Gilbert L., 332–33

professional military education, 579, 598–99

Progressivism, 186, 220

Project Control, 265

propaganda campaigns, 174

protracted revolutionary war, 325–27, 329–31, 334–40, 343–47, 369–70

psychological operations (PSYOP), 330, 338, 343

Pujo, Bertrand, 152

Pustay, John, 335

Rabaul, New Britain, 217

RAF Staff College, 32, 42, 72

Ramstein Air Base, West Germany, 460

RAND, 286, 292, 301, 386, 409–10, 486

Randolph Field, Texas, 190

rapid-deployment force, 506

rapid-reaction force, 464, 506

rapid response, 511

Reagan, Ronald, 290, 305

reconnaissance, 3, 14, 23, 82–83, 121, 127, 129, 152–54, 157, 170–71, 186, 196, 332, 341–43, 407–8, 418, 427, 453, 493, 502, 532–33, 555

Red Flag, 419, 594

reentry vehicle (RV), 284, 289

Reichswehr, 171

Reid, Frank, 103

remotely piloted vehicles (RPV), 108, 410, 556

Republic Aircraft, 246, 590

research and development (R&D), 16, 192, 507, 517, 543–44, 566–67, 569, 596

reserve forces, 464

Return of Forces to Germany (REFORGER), 411

reusable launch vehicle (RLV), 559

revolution
    airpower, 294, 307
    aviation, 281
    industrial, 384

Special Air Warfare Center, 331–33
special operations, 331, 339, 342, 344, 408, 418, 453, 533
special operations forces, 421
Sperrle, Hugo, 170, 172
Spruance, Raymond, 130–31
Sputnik I, 283, 591
Stalingrad, USSR, 489
Stalin, Joseph, 163, 165, 167, 302, 489–90, 585, 596
standoff munitions, 410
Starry, Donn A., 415–16, 419, 423, 430
stealth, 374, 507–8, 516, 542, 556, 562–63, 592
Stein, David, 452, 454–55, 472
Stirling, Yates, Jr., 123
Strait of Dover, 119
Strategic Air Command (SAC), 292, 328, 332, 336
strategic
    air force, 47
    air war, 580, 585
    attack, 325, 334, 374, 403, 407, 465–67, 471
    aviation, 85
    decapitation, 297
    defense, 302–5
    paralysis, 307, 357–63, 368, 370, 376–77, 382–84, 386, 388–89,
        593. *See also* paralysis
    posturing, 505
    strikes, 47
    superiority, 332
    thinking, 120
    triad, 135
Strategic Arms Limitation Treaty (SALT), 289
Strategic Bombing Survey, 217
Strategic Defense Initiative (SDI), 290
strategists
    airpower, 373–74, 376–77, 388
    civilian, 286
    military, 381
    NATO, 469
    nuclear, 286, 292, 328
strategy
    airpower, 185, 268, 444
    annihilation, 360, 375
    attrition, 360

Trenchard, Hugh, 28, 41–53, 56–58, 61, 63, 65, 70–72, 79–80, 84–85, 95, 125, 130, 171, 266, 362–63, 382–83, 581

trench warfare, 83, 90

Truman Doctrine, 446

Truman, Harry S, 133, 262, 265

Tsygichko, V., 506

Tukhachevski, Mikhail, 163–64, 166–67, 585

Turkey, 3, 463, 472, 510

Twentieth Air Force, 132

21st Bomber Command, 217

Twining, Nathan C., 124, 205

U-boats, 119, 125

Udet, Ernst, 175, 585

Udorn AFB, Thailand, 423

Unification Act of 1947, 133

United Kingdom, 444–45, 452, 454, 457, 471

United Nations (UN), 131, 462, 499, 537

United States, 6, 14, 25, 30, 33, 70, 79, 81, 83, 87, 89–90, 92, 97–101, 104–5, 108, 115–17, 125, 133–35, 183, 185, 187, 189–90, 192–99, 204, 212, 239, 242–43, 249, 251–52, 254, 257, 260–64, 267–69, 283–84, 286–90, 295, 297, 299–300, 302, 306, 327, 332–33, 337, 347, 370, 382–83, 399–400, 403, 407, 443–46, 450–52, 454, 457, 462, 464, 467, 471, 490–91, 498–99, 503, 510, 516, 529–30, 532, 537–40, 548, 562, 566, 569–71, 580, 584–86, 590

United States Air Force, 79–80, 109, 124, 134–35, 209, 212, 224, 258, 263–64, 286, 321–22, 330–34, 338–40, 342, 344–46, 357, 370, 399–405, 407–16, 418–33, 444, 450–53, 455–58, 465, 468–70, 531, 536, 538–40, 555, 560, 566–71, 582–84, 588, 590–98

United States Air Service, 6–7

United States Army, 81–82, 85–90, 94–96, 99–100, 102–4, 106–7, 117, 119–20, 124–26, 131, 184–87, 191–92, 194, 198–99, 201, 203–11, 213–15, 219, 258, 263–64, 327, 344, 371, 399–433, 451–52, 458, 531, 566, 568–69, 586–87, 591–95

United States Army Air Service, 185

United States fleet, 134

United States Marine Corps, 117–18, 124, 134, 330, 419, 452, 597

United States Naval Institute, 117

United States Navy, 82, 90, 93–94, 99–103, 106–7, 115–20, 122, 124–29, 131–36, 184, 186, 188, 191–201, 203–4, 206–9, 222,

247–48, 256, 258, 263–64, 419, 452–53, 529–31, 568–69, 582–83, 585, 590–91, 597
United States Senate, 262
United States Space Command (USSPACECOM), 544
United States Strategic Bombing Survey, 132, 136
unity
    of command, 88, 206, 208, 545, 570
    of effort, 570
unmanned aerial vehicles (UAV), 545, 558, 564
USS
    Chicago, 116
    Langley, 93, 126
    Lexington, 93–94, 115, 122, 126–27, 583
    Ranger, 127
    Saratoga, 93–94, 115, 122, 126–27, 583
Utz, Curtis, 127

Vandenberg, Hoyt, 590
Vauthier, P., 33, 157
Versailles Conference/Treaty, 169, 585
Vessey, John W., Jr., 423
Victory through Air Power, 251, 254–56, 265
Vietcong, 25
Vietminh, 327–29
Vietnam, 25, 269, 327, 329–30, 332–33, 335–37, 347, 399, 402–3, 405, 407, 409–11, 413–14, 431–32, 455, 592, 598
Vietnam War, 31, 243, 333, 339, 346, 399, 403, 405, 409, 412–14, 423, 429–30, 458
vital centers, 1, 11–14, 17, 28, 53–54, 59, 62–63, 95–96, 98–99, 101, 128, 186, 198, 215–17, 221, 252, 255, 259, 268, 334, 362, 371, 383
Vorobyev, I., 504
Voroshilov Lectures, 486
Vuillemin, Joseph, 155

Walker, Kenneth, 107–8, 193, 212, 216–18, 224
war
    of attrition, 8–9
    fighting, 66
    games, 123, 132, 165, 171–72, 176, 212, 417, 557
Warden, John M., III, 343, 357–58, 363, 370–79, 381–82, 384–89, 425, 428–29, 592–93

☆U.S. GOVERNMENT PRINTING OFFICE:1998-638-202/